SAP ERP Financial Accounting and Controlling

Configuration and Use Management

Andrew Okungbowa

Apress®

SAP ERP Financial Accounting and Controlling: Configuration and Use Management

ISBN-13 (pbk): 978-1-4842-0717-8

ISBN-13 (electronic): 978-1-4842-0716-1

Trademarked names, logos, and images may appear in this book. Rather than use a trademark symbol with every occurrence of a trademarked name, logo, or image we use the names, logos, and images only in an editorial fashion and to the benefit of the trademark owner, with no intention of infringement of the trademark.

The use in this publication of trade names, trademarks, service marks, and similar terms, even if they are not identified as such, is not to be taken as an expression of opinion as to whether or not they are subject to proprietary rights.

While the advice and information in this book are believed to be true and accurate at the date of publication, neither the authors nor the editors nor the publisher can accept any legal responsibility for any errors or omissions that may be made. The publisher makes no warranty, express or implied, with respect to the material contained herein.

Managing Director: Welmoed Spahr
Acquisitions Editor: Susan McDermott
Developmental Editor: Anne Marie Walker
Editorial Board: Steve Anglin, Mark Beckner, Gary Cornell, Louise Corrigan, James DeWolf, Jonathan Gennick, Robert Hutchinson, Michelle Lowman, James Markham, Susan McDermott, Matthew Moodie, Jeffrey Pepper, Douglas Pundick, Ben Renow-Clarke, Gwenan Spearing, Matt Wade, Steve Weiss
Coordinating Editor: Rita Fernando
Copy Editor: Kezia Endsley
Compositor: SPi Global
Indexer: SPi Global

Distributed to the book trade worldwide by Springer Science+Business Media New York, 233 Spring Street, 6th Floor, New York, NY 10013. Phone 1-800-SPRINGER, fax (201) 348-4505, e-mail orders-ny@springer-sbm.com, or visit www.springeronline.com. Apress Media, LLC is a California LLC and the sole member (owner) is Springer Science + Business Media Finance Inc (SSBM Finance Inc). SSBM Finance Inc is a Delaware corporation.

For information on translations, please e-mail rights@apress.com, or visit www.apress.com.

Apress and friends of ED books may be purchased in bulk for academic, corporate, or promotional use. eBook versions and licenses are also available for most titles. For more information, reference our Special Bulk Sales–eBook Licensing web page at www.apress.com/bulk-sales.

Any source code or other supplementary materials referenced by the author in this text is available to readers at www.apress.com. For detailed information about how to locate your book's source code, go to www.apress.com/source-code/.

*This book is dedicated to God Almighty for His Greatness
and for seeing me through the difficulties encountered when writing this book.*

Contents at a Glance

About the Author xxi

Acknowledgments xxiii

Introduction xxv

▉Chapter 1: Customizing Organizational Structure in SAP ERP 1

▉Chapter 2: Defining the Chart of Accounts 27

▉Chapter 3: Document Control 41

▉Chapter 4: Defining Tolerance Groups for G/L Accounts and Employees.............. 55

▉Chapter 5: Creating a General Ledger (G/L) 65

▉Chapter 6: Clearing Open Items.. 81

▉Chapter 7: Maintaining Currency Types and Currency Pairs 101

▉Chapter 8: Defining Adjustment Accounts for GR/IR Clearing........................... 111

▉Chapter 9: Defining the House Bank.. 117

▉Chapter 10: Defining Tax on Sales and Purchases 151

▉Chapter 11: Customizing a Cash Journal 163

▉Chapter 12: Financial Statement Versions (FSV)... 173

▉Chapter 13: Integration of FI with Other SAP ERP Modules 189

▉Chapter 14: Defining FI Accounts Receivable and Accounts Payable................. 203

▉Chapter 15: Defining the Dunning Procedure and Correspondence 263

▉Chapter 16: Customizing Special G/L Transactions.. 281

▉Chapter 17: End User - Accounting Document Posting 297

■**Chapter 18: Customizing the Controlling Module**.. **359**

■**Chapter 19: Customizing New General Ledger Accounting** **421**

■**Appendix A: Useful General Ledger Accounts** **469**

■**Appendix B: Some Useful Transaction Codes** **547**

Index **555**

Contents

About the Author ....**xxi**

Acknowledgments ....**xxiii**

Introduction ....**xxv**

■**Chapter 1: Customizing Organizational Structure in SAP ERP** 1

Organizational Structure 1

The Client..2

Company Code..2

Let's Start Customizing 3

Define a Company 5

Define a Company Code 9

Assign Company Code to Company 12

Business Area.. 14

Define a Business Area..14

Segment 15

Define a Segment 15

Fiscal Year Variant 16

Year Independent...17

Year Specific or Year Dependent 18

Maintain Fiscal Year Variant 18

Assign the Fiscal Year Variant to the Company Code 21

Opening and Closing Posting Periods...21

    Define Variants for Open Posting Periods 22

    Assign Variants to Company Code 23

    Specify Open and Closing Periods...24

Summary...26

■Chapter 2: Defining the Chart of Accounts 27

The Chart of Accounts 27

Create the Chart of Accounts...29

Assign Company Code to Chart of Accounts 31

Define Account Group...32

Define Retained Earnings Account...37

Summary...39

■Chapter 3: Document Control 41

Document Control...41

    Document Type 42

    Posting Key 43

Defining Number Ranges 44

    How to Display Number Intervals 47

    How to Delete Number Range Intervals...47

    How to Copy Document Number Ranges...48

Understand and Manage Field Status Variants 49

    Define Field Status Variants...50

    Display Field Status Variants 52

    Assign Company Code to Field Status Variants 52

Summary...53

■**Chapter 4: Defining Tolerance Groups for G/L Accounts and Employees............ 55**

Tolerance Groups... 55

Define Tolerance Groups for G/L Accounts 56

Define Tolerance Groups for Employees.. 60

Define Default Tolerance Groups for Employees.. 60

Define Tolerance Groups for Employees with a Group Key.. 62

Assign Users to Tolerance Groups 63

Summary... 64

■**Chapter 5: Creating a General Ledger (G/L) 65**

General Ledger 65

What Is a Master Record? 66

Creating G/L Account Master Records... 67

Create a G/L Account: Office Supplies 68

Create a G/L Account (Called Office Expenses) Using a Template 76

Display G/L Accounts.. 78

Summary... 79

■**Chapter 6: Clearing Open Items... 81**

Clearing Open Items... 81

Manual Clearing Overview... 82

Prepare Automatic Clearing.. 83

Create Accounts for Clearing Differences 84

Define a Maximum Exchange Rate Difference 86

Checking the Company Code Settings 89

Foreign Currency Valuation 91

Exchange Rate Types.. 91

Define Valuation Methods.. 92

Prepare Automatic Postings for Foreign Currency Valuation 94

    Exchange Rate Difference Using the Exchange Rate Key (KDB) 95

    Exchange Rate Differences for Open Items/GL Accounts 96

    Exchange Rate Difference for Open Items–Account Payable 99

Summary 100

■**Chapter 7: Maintaining Currency Types and Currency Pairs** **101**

Currencies 101

Exchange Rate Types 102

Define a Standard Quotation for Exchange Rates 103

Enter Prefixes for Direct/Indirect Quotation Exchange Rates 104

Define Translation Ratios for Currency Translation 106

Enter Exchange Rates 108

Summary 110

■**Chapter 8: Defining Adjustment Accounts for GR/IR Clearing** **111**

GR/IR Clearing 111

Invoiced But Not Yet Delivered 113

Delivered But Not Yet Invoiced 115

Summary 116

■**Chapter 9: Defining the House Bank** **117**

House Bank 117

Define House Banks 119

Define Bank Accounts for Your House Banks 121

Bank Statements 123

    Electronic Bank Statement 124

    Make Global Settings for Electronic Bank Statements 125

    Configure a Manual Bank Statement 136

Check Deposits...142

    Define Posting Keys and Posting Rules for Check Deposits 143

    Create and Assign Business Transactions 148

    Define Variants for Check Deposits 148

Summary..150

Chapter 10: Defining Tax on Sales and Purchases 151

Sales and Purchases Tax...151

Basic Settings 153

Define Tax Codes for Sales 154

Define Tax Accounts for Sales 156

Define Tax Codes for Purchases 158

Define Tax Accounts for Purchases 160

Assign Taxable Codes to Non-Taxable Transactions..161

Summary..162

Chapter 11: Customizing a Cash Journal 163

Cash Journal 163

Create G/L Accounts for a Cash Journal..164

Specify the Amount Limit for a Cash Journal 164

Define Number Range Intervals for Cash Journal Documents 165

Set Up the Cash Journal...167

Create, Change, and Delete Business Transactions...168

Set Up Print Parameters for the Cash Journal 170

Summary..171

Chapter 12: Financial Statement Versions (FSV)...................................173

Financial Statement Versions 173

Define Financial Statement Versions...174

    Step 1: Create Items 176

    Step 2: Reassign Items as Subordinates 177

Step 3: Assign FSV Nodes to G/L Accounts 182

Step 4: Define the Credit/Debit Shift.. 183

Check Assigned G/L Accounts to FSV... 185

Summary... 187

■Chapter 13: Integration of FI with Other SAP ERP Modules 189

Integrate FI with Other SAP Modules 189

Material Management (MM) 191

Configure Automatic Postings 192

Sales & Distribution (SD) 197

Prepare Revenue Account Determination.. 198

Summary... 201

■Chapter 14: Defining FI Accounts Receivable and Accounts Payable............... 203

Accounts Payable and Accounts Receivable 203

What Is a Customer Account Group?... 204

Define Account Groups with Screen Layout (Customer).. 205

Maintain the Field Status Group for the General Data of the Customer Account Group 206

Enter Accounting Clerk Identification Code for Customers... 208

Create Number Ranges for Customer Account Groups... 209

Assign Number Ranges to Customer Account Groups.. 211

What Is a Vendor Account Group? 211

Define Account Groups with Screen Layout (Vendors) 212

Maintain the Field Status Group for General Data for the Vendor Account Group 213

Enter a Accounting Clerk Identification Code for Your Vendors 214

Create Number Ranges for Vendor Accounts.. 215

Assign Number Ranges to Vendor Account Groups 217

Terms of Payment 217

Installment Plan.. 221

Defining a Cash Discount Base for Incoming Invoices 224

Incoming Invoices/Credit Memos Enjoy Transactions 224

    Defining Document Types for Enjoy Transactions 225

    Defining Tax Code per Transaction 226

Defining Accounts for Net Procedures 227

Defining Accounts for Cash Discounts 228

    Defining Cash Discounts Granted 228

    Defining Account for Cash Discount Taken 228

    Defining an Account for a Lost Cash Discount 229

    Defining Account for Overpayments/Underpayments 229

Manual Outgoing Payments 232

    Define Tolerances for Vendors 232

    Define Reason Codes for Manual Outgoing Payments 234

    Define Accounts for Payment Differences (Manual Outgoing Payments) 237

Automatic Outgoing Payments 238

    All Company Codes 238

    Paying Company Codes 240

    Payment Methods in Country 243

    Payment Methods in Company Codes 243

    Bank Determination for Payment Transactions 247

    Bank Accounts 248

Sort Methods and Adjustment Accounts for Regrouping Receivables/Payables 251

    Define Sort Methods 252

    Define Adjustment Accounts for Receivables/Payables by Maturity 254

Adjustment Posting/Reversal 258

    Permit Negative Postings 259

    Define Reasons for Reversal 259

Summary 260

■Chapter 15: Defining the Dunning Procedure and Correspondence 263

Dunning 263

Define the Dunning Area 263

Define the Dunning Procedures 264

Correspondence 272

Define Correspondence Types 273

Assign Programs to the Correspondence Types 274

Define Sender Details for a Correspondence Form 275

Determine Call-Up Functions 277

Define Reply Addresses for Balance Confirmation 277

Summary 279

■Chapter 16: Customizing Special G/L Transactions 281

Special G/L Transactions 281

Technical Factors 282

Down Payments 283

Down Payment Received 284

Down Payment Requests (Customer) 286

Define Account for Tax Clearing (Customer Down Payments) 287

Down Payment Made 289

Down Payment Requests for Vendors 290

Define Account for Tax Clearing (Vendor Down Payments) 291

Guarantees 292

Define Alternative Reconciliation Accounts for Customers (Guarantees) 292

Define Alternative Reconciliation Accounts for Vendors (Guarantees) 293

Define Accounts for Automatic Offsetting Entry 293

Summary 295

■**Chapter 17: End User - Accounting Document Posting** **297**

Customer/Vendor Master Record 297

  Create Customer Master Record 298

  Create Vendor Master Record 300

Accounts Receivable—Document Entry 302

  Customer Invoice Posting 302

  Posting a Credit Memo 306

Holding and Parking Documents 308

  Holding Documents 308

  Calling Up a Held Document 309

  Parking Documents 310

  Parking/Editing a Document 311

Incoming Payments 311

  Posting a Standard Incoming Payment 312

  Posting a Partial Payment 315

  Posting Residual Items 317

Customer Down Payments 318

  Posting a Customer Down Payment Request 318

  Posting Customer Down Payments 319

  Clearing Customer Down Payments 321

Display Account Balances 323

  Display Customer Account Balances 323

Display Line Items 326

  Display/Change Customer Line Items 326

Correspondence 327

  Request Correspondence 327

  Print Correspondence 328

Execute Dunning 331

  Display Dunning Details 334

  Print Dunning 335

Accounts Payable—Document Entry 335

    Vendor Invoice Posting 336

Manual Outgoing Payment 338

    Outgoing Payment 338

Automatic Payments 340

    Check Lots 340

    Automatic Payment Program 342

Use the Cash Journal 353

    Cash Receipts 354

    Cash Payments 355

Summary 357

■Chapter 18: Customizing the Controlling Module 359

The Controlling Module 359

    General Controlling 360

    Organizational Controlling 360

Cost Element Accounting 370

    Make Default Settings for Automatic Creation of Primary and Secondary Cost Elements 370

    Create Batch Input Session 372

    Execute a Batch Input Session 374

    Primary Cost Element 376

    Secondary Cost Elements 378

Cost Center Accounting 379

    Define the Standard Hierarchy 379

    Create Cost Center Group 386

    Use Statistical Key Figures 391

    Change Activity Output/Prices Planning 393

    Compare Cost Centers: Actual/Plan/Variance 394

Profit Center Accounting 395

Basic Settings.. 396

Maintain Controlling Area Settings 396

Create Dummy Profit Center... 398

Set Control Parameters for Actual Data... 399

Maintain Plan Versions 400

Define Standard Hierarchy for Profit Centers 401

Define Profit Center 404

Define Number Ranges for Local Documents.. 406

Assign Profit Centers to Cost Centers.. 407

Posting Controlling Documents 409

Display Line Items 410

Profit Center: Interactive Reporting 412

Distribution 413

G/L Account Posting... 417

Display Actual Cost Line Items for Cost Centers.. 418

Summary.. 419

■Chapter 19: Customizing New General Ledger Accounting 421

New General Ledger.. 421

Leading Ledger.. 422

Non-Leading Ledger 422

Define Ledgers for General Ledger Accounting 423

Define Currencies of Leading Ledger 424

Define and Activate Non-Leading Ledgers 427

What Is a Scenario in General Ledger Accounting?... 429

Assign Scenarios and Customer Fields to Ledgers for Leading Ledger 430

Define Ledger Group.. 435

Accounting Principles... 435

Real-Time Integration of Controlling with Financial Accounting 437

Assign Variants for Real-Time Integration to Company Codes 439

Account Determination for Real-Time Integration 440

Document Types 441

    Define Document Types for Entry View in a Ledger 442

    Define Document Types for General Ledger View 443

Document Splitting 444

    Classify G/L Accounts for Document Splitting 445

    Classify Document Types for Document Splitting 449

    Zero-Balance Clearing Account 449

Posting General Ledger Accounting Documents 450

    Enter G/L Account Documents 451

    Enter G/L Account Document for Ledger Group 451

Reverse Document 453

Document Display 456

Closing 458

    Foreign Currency Valuation 459

    Balance Carry Forward 461

Summary 468

■Appendix A: Useful General Ledger Accounts 469

Chapter 5 469

    General Ledger 469

Chapter 6 476

    Automatic Clearing Differences 476

    Foreign Currency valuation 478

Chapter 8 486

    GR/IR Clearing 486

Chapter 9 492

    House Bank 492

    Bank Statement 494

Chapter 10 504

    Tax on Sales/Purchases 504

Chapter 11 506

Cash Journal 506

Chapter 13 511

Integration of FI with Other Modules 511

Chapter 14 517

Terms of Payment 517

Define Sort Method and Adjustment Accts to Regrouping 522

Chapter 16 533

Special G/L Transaction 533

Down Payments 538

Chapter 19 544

New General Ledger 544

■Appendix B: Some Useful Transaction Codes 547

FI 547

End User: Accounting Document Posting 551

Controlling 553

Index 555

About the Author

Andrew Okungbowa is an accountant, an expert in SAP Financial, and a trainer. He is currently the CEO of Wonderful Consulting, a company offering FI/CO, Business Analysis, and Project Management consulting services to medium and large corporations. He holds a Master's Degree in Investment and Finance.

Acknowledgments

It is obvious that without the contribution of other people, this book would not have been possible. Hence, I want to offer my thanks to some wonderful people who have contributed immensely to the success of this book by way of their talented insights, critical reviews, and support.

First, I thank Rita Fernando, our Coordinating Editor, for the effective coordination of the book project from start to finish.

I particularly want to acknowledge Anne Marie Walker, our Developmental Editor, for painstakingly editing the initial draft and the final draft of the manuscript. My thanks goes to Kezia Endsley, our Copy Editor, who spotted every typographical error and pointed them out in good time. I also want to thank Susan McDermott, our Acquisitions Editor, for her invaluable contribution and SPi Global for converting the manuscript into this book.

My thanks goes to my dear wife Hephzibah and my beautiful daughter Zoe-Chelsea for their encouragement and support. I love you guys.

I also want to acknowledge the following people for their contribution to the success of this book. Jeff Olson who started the journey of this book with me. To my pastors, Pastor Olukayode and Iwalola Owolabi, for their prayers and encouragement. To my brothers, Osasu, Frank, and Ben Soko, for their support.

I will not forget to say thank you to my friend John Adjara, who sparked the idea to write this book by advising me to convert my lecture notes into a book.

Finally, I also want to thank all those who have contributed one way or another to the success of this book but whose names are not mentioned.

Introduction

In this introduction, I explain the meaning of the acronym SAP, the origin of SAP, and the concept of SAP implementation. We will go further to look at Enterprise Resource Planning (ERP) as it relates to SAP, the importance of SAP, and the steps involved in implementing SAP ERP.

What Is SAP?

SAP (Systems, Applications, and Products) in data processing is the leading ERP (Enterprise Resource Planning) business application software in the market today. The software provides a unified platform that allows business processes integration. SAP is developed by SAP AG, a German software company founded in 1972 by five ex-IBM employees. With its headquarters in Germany, SAP has regional offices around the world.

SAP is used by many Fortune 500 companies worldwide as a business solution for processing operational data and for generating reports in real-time, which helps all levels of management make better decisions and enables them to manage business processes effectively and efficiently.

ERP (Enterprise Resource Planning)

ERP is accomplished through business software packages like SAP that are made up of application modules that companies use to store data and manage business processes as a whole. Modules involve accounting, human resources, security, supply chain management, and more. These modules are used to manage the "8Ms," (Man, Material, Machine, Money, Method, Minutes, Management, and Marketing). The idea is to improve efficient management enterprise resources.

Besides SAP, ERP packages are produced by Oracle (PeopleSoft), BAAN, JD Edwards, and Siebel, among others.

The Importance of SAP ERP

Since its inception in 1972, SAP has gained international acceptance across the world by large organizations as the most preferred business solution package. SAP ERP is structured in three-tier layers, which makes it a robust ERP software solution. Apart from being the most widely used application software in the world today, the following benefits are derived from the use of SAPERP.

Real-Time Three-Tier Architecture

SAP supports a real-time three-tier (R/3) architecture made up of these three layers:

- *Presentation Layer*: This is the first layer in a typical three-tier architecture and it serves as the input device that controls the SAP system. It is user-friendly Graphical User Interface (GUI) that's used by the end-user to input data into the system. It also serves as a data-output device. The presentation layer communicates with the application layer.

- *Application Layer*: This layer serves as the middleman in a SAP system. It's where the all processing is done. The application layer can be referred to as the central processing unit (CPU). It collects data from the database, processes it, and passes it to the presentation layer.

- *Database*: Allows the data to be stored, called up, and modified.

The real-time three-tier architecture allows separate business processes to function under a single, integrated business management information system.

Customizable Solution

SAP ERP 6.0 is scalable and suited for medium and large organizations, since it provides a customizable solution using the structured programming language, ABAP/4. This flexibility allows companies to customize the system to meet their specific needs. In order to enable customers and partners to customize the SAP application to meet their specific-business requirements, SAP comes with the Easy Access menu and the Implementation Guide (IMG) menus.

Easy Access

The Easy Access menu is a user-specific point of entry into the SAP system. It is the first screen that comes up when you logon to SAP. It is designed in a tree structure containing a list several key items that provide the options that allow you to navigate the system and perform tasks and business processes. For example, you can perform transactions and generate reports and access web addresses (where you can access documents from a remote internet server).

IMG (Implementation Guide)

The IMG is a generic tool that you can use to customize business processes and requirements to meet specific needs of a company. You are presented with three implementation variants in SAP:

- *SAP Reference IMG*. This is a standard structured hierarchical tool in R/3 system (real-time three-tier architecture) that contains the procedures for customizing various country settings and application modules in the SAP system.

- *Project IMG*. Configuration process can be very daunting. To help manage the complexity involved when using the reference IMG, you can create each implementation project based on specific functions needed for business processes and requirements. For example, you could use it to reduce the project scope to specific objects such as countries.

- *Project View IMG*. You choose certain properties by specific criteria in order to generate views to organize your project activities. For example, a project view could hold each activity required in a project IMG.

Matchcode

Matchcode is a user-friendly search function designed to help you lookup or retrieve data records stored in the system. It's an efficient way of looking for records stored in the system when you do not remember their keys.

Supports Other Operating Systems

SAPERP 6.0 EHP7 is very versatile and supports various operating systems, such as:

- Microsoft Windows 2000 professional, Microsoft XP professional, and Microsoft Server 2003
- HP UX 11.11 and HP UX 11.23
- Novell SUSE SLES9
- Sun Solaris 9 and Sun Solaris 1
- IBM AIX 5.2 and IBM AIX 5.3

Unified Platform

SAP provides the platform where all business processes are executed in a single system and share common information.

Incorporating Multiple Languages and Currencies

SAP ERP is ideal for multinational organizations because of the flexibility incorporated, which allows the system to run on multiple currencies and use different languages. These features make SAP a global software solution.

Integrated ERP Solutions

SAPERP is an integrated ERP package that incorporates other modules. These include Financial (FI), Controlling (CO), Material Management (MM), Sales and Distribution (SD), Production Planning (PP), Human Resources (HR), Financial Supply Chain Management (FSCM), Customer Relationship Management (CRM), and others.

Reduced Implementation Cost

The cost and time needed to implement SAP can be reduced by applying rapid-implementation techniques using global and industry-specific templates during customization.

Global Presence

As the market leader in ERP, the SAPERP solution is currently used in over 28 industry sectors and has a strong global presence in more than 120 countries worldwide. This number is predicted to rise.

SAP FICO

FICO stands for Financial (FI) and Controlling (CO). These are the two core modules in SAP and are tightly integrated to help management maintain and generate financial reports for efficient decision-making and strategic planning.

Financial (FI)

The FI module is a business process designed specifically for organizations to maintain their financial records efficiently on a daily basis, for management to be able to ascertain their financial position, and for those who need to generate financial statutory reports for external purposes to meet the needs of various stakeholders in real-time.

The FI module consists of other sub modules, including: General Ledger (G/L), Accounts Receivable (AR), Accounts Payable (AP), Bank Accounting, Asset Accounting, Special Purpose Ledger, Travel Management, and so on.

FI is integrated into other modules like Sales and Distribution (SD) and Material Management (MM). Postings made in these modules with financial implications are posted real-time to FI.

Controlling (CO)

The Controlling module is designed specifically to provide operational information to management to aid better decision-making, and for formulating strategic and operational planning. In SAP ERP, the Controlling module is composed of the following sub modules: Cost Element, Cost Center, Internal Order, Activity-Based Costing, Product Costing, Profitability Analysis, and Profit Center.

Why This Book?

This book arose out of my sincere desire to simplify the complexity involved in SAP FICO configuration. It is also an attempt to make SAP FICO configuration an interesting career path for those so inclined.

As a SAP trainer at the corporate and individual level, I've learned that the best way to teach is to design a systematic approach that guides beginners step by step through using all learning resources available. This can make learning fun and interesting. That is what I have done in this book.

You'll find that *SAP ERP Financial Accounting and Controlling: Configuration and Use Management* is one of the most illustrative SAP FI books on the market. It includes numerous screenshots and practical examples. Even those without prior configuration knowledge or skills of any sort will be able to follow each step with ease, which is what makes this book unique.

To promote a better understanding of the complexities and concepts of the activities throughout the book, I followed a problem-based approach that tries to replicate real-world situations. As you work through each problem, you will gain the practical experience needed to become an expert in the world of SAP. Every problem used in the book is geared to meet business processes and requirements unique to each customizing step, but the overall objective is to equip you as a functional SAP consultant on the completion of this book.

The book covers the financial (FI) module, the controlling (CO) module, the new general ledger (G/L) accounting modules, and some aspects of end-user postings.

This book is unlike others in that it incorporates IMG (Implementation Guide) and accounting. The IMG side of the system is where SAP configurations are performed and the accounting side of the system is where end-users input data into the system. It is also unique in giving readers a great opportunity to learn the rudiments of FI, CO, new G/L implementation, and accounting for end-users simultaneously. The benefit of combining the SAP implementation and Easy Access is that you have an opportunity to explore both sides of the system to gain an in-depth understanding of how data flows in the system. Additionally, trainers will find the book excellent material for those charged with showing others how to configure and use SAP FICO.

A Quick Overview of the Book's Contents

Each chapter provides a sequence to be followed in customizing SAP FICO from start to finish. The sequence has been arranged to give you the opportunity to work through a complete FICO customizing lifecycle progressively. Each chapter includes all the configuration concepts or activities necessary for your customizing or draws on a previous chapter.

Chapter 1 sets the scene by looking at organizational structure and explains how to create various objects in SAPR/3. This includes how to create company codes, business areas, segments, country-specific settings, and so forth.

Chapter 2 explains and defines the Master Record, including how to edit the Chart of Accounts and how to assign a company code to the Chart of Accounts. It further explores how to define the Account Group and Retained Earnings account.

Chapter 3 looks at the purpose of document control and various forms of document types in the SAP R/3 system. It also looks at the steps involved in defining number ranges and setting field status variants. It emphasizes the various principles along with the importance of posting keys, normal and special posting periods, and how to create variants for posting periods.

Chapter 4 explores posting authorizations by discussing the purpose of posting authorization, defining tolerance groups for G/L accounts and employees, assigning users to defined tolerance groups, and creating accounts for clearing differences.

Chapter 5 takes a look at the general ledger and its sub ledgers. It covers when to use line items and open item management, how to create G/L accounts, and how to set other objects settings to consider when creating G/L accounts.

Chapter 6 discusses clearing open Items and various types of open-item clearing issues. It covers configuring automatic open item clearing, maximum exchange rate difference settings, the importance of foreign currency valuation, foreign currency balance sheet accounts, and G/L account balances managed on an open-item basis. It also looks at types of exchange rates and how open items are valued in foreign currency.

Chapter 7 explains how to define local and foreign currencies for company codes, maintain the relationship between currencies per currency type, and the purpose of exchange rates. It also explores how to maintain the various exchange rate types and how to define translation ratios for currency transactions.

Chapter 8 explores how to define GR/IR (Goods Receipt/Invoice Receipt) and how to configure GR/IR settings in the SAP R/3 system.

Chapter 9 deals with the House Bank and how master records are created in it. It explains using the House Bank ID and account ID, bank statements supported by SAP, creating global settings for electronic bank statements, configuring manual bank statements, defining posting keys and posting rules for check deposit, and defining variants for check deposit.

Chapter 10 looks at taxes on sales and purchases, including VAT. It covers how to create sale and purchase taxes in SAP R/3, how to specify the tax category in the G/L accounts to which taxes are posted, how to assign the basic tax code for sales and purchases, how to specify the accounts to which different tax types are posted, and how to assign tax codes for non-taxable transactions.

Chapter 11 covers the cash journal by explaining what it is and explaining which items are defined when setting up a new cash journal. It identifies the document types for cash journal items, explains how to create G/L accounts for cash journals, and how to set up the cash journal.

Chapter 12 explains the Financial Statement Versions (FSV). The chapter looks at how to create an FSV from scratch, covers the specifications to be conducted when defining FSV, how to call up FSV hierarchy nodes, and how to assign appropriate G/L accounts.

Chapter 13 explores the Integration of FI with other modules in SAP R/3. This includes automatic postings of material to FI, using the valuation class of material as the key to which the G/L account materials are posted, the settings for automatic posting configuration, how to create inventory accounts using the BSX transaction key, how to create corresponding credit accounts for GR/IR clearing account using the WRX transaction key, how integration of FI and SD works, how to prepare revenue account determination, and how to define accounts for overhead cost controlling.

Chapter 14 deals with Accounts Receivable and Accounts Payable, including the steps involved in creating a payables/receivables, the function of the account group, how to create IDs for accounting clerks, how to create vendor/customer details, how to resolve number range overlaps, and more. It also covers payment terms in SAP, the purpose of defining payment terms in SAP R/3, and how to create installment plans. The chapter also defines the sort method and adjustment accounts for regrouping receivables/payables, and adjustment accounts for receivables/payables by maturity. Finally, the chapter shows you how to adjust or post document reversals using the negative posting method, and how to define reasons for reversal.

Chapter 15 covers correspondence and dunning, including how to define correspondence types, sender details, the various levels involved in defining dunning. It explains how to determine special G/L transactions so the system can dun them.

Chapter 16 looks at why it is important to disclose special G/L transactions separately by using alternative reconciliation accounts. It provides an explanation of special G/L transactions, including guarantees, down payments, and bills of exchange. It also covers down payments in depth.

Chapter 17 looks at how to create and change vendor/customer master records in Easy Access, how to post invoices in the system, how to treat credit memos, how to hold and park documents, how to manage incoming and outgoing payments, how to process partial payments and residual items, how to generate dunning, and how to manage cash journal postings.

Chapter 18 explores some of the Controlling modules, starting with the overall organizational structure. It then looks at cost element accounting, cost center accounting, and profit centers.

Chapter 19 looks at the new general ledger and its benefits, the leading/non-leading ledgers, how to define ledgers and currencies, what scenarios are and how to assign them to ledgers. It also briefly explains accounting principles and how to assign them to ledger groups. Finally, it covers real-time integration of controlling (CO) with FI, how to define documents for entry view in a ledger, the classification of G/L accounts for document splitting, zero-balance clearing, and more.

Appendix A covers all the appropriate G/L accounts needed for your configuration.

Appendix B provides some useful transaction codes that allow you to access tasks easily rather than going through the menu path, which may be time-consuming.

■ ■ ■

CHAPTER 1

Customizing Organizational Structure in SAP ERP

In this chapter, you learn how to customize the key organizational units in Financial Accounting (FI). At the end of this chapter, you will be able to:

- Define a company
- Define a company code
- Assign a company to a company code
- Define a business area
- Define a segment
- Define and assign fiscal year variants to a company code
- Define open and closing periods variants and assign variants to a company code

Organizational Structure

Organizational structure is a formal line of command structured systematically to highlight the order of authority, relationships, position, communication, duties, responsibilities, and reporting procedure in an organization. The primary objective of an organization is to utilize its resources effectively to maximize return to the shareholders. To do this, an organization needs a formal organizational chart (organogram) spelling out how tasks and activities are allocated, coordinated, and supervised. In addition, it shows how information flows between various management levels.

SAP tends to mimic the conventional organizational structure in the representation and distribution of tasks in the system based on functions and departments. In SAP, the structure is made up of organizational units just like the conventional organizational structure in a business.

The organizational units in FI in SAP ERP are specifically geared toward meeting business functions and generating reports (financial statements) for external purposes while meeting legal regulations. Creating an organizational unit is a minimum requirement in SAP FI.

Organizational structure in FI is company code-specific. As part of organizational structure customization in a SAP system, it is therefore mandatory to define appropriate organizational units in the system for the system to be able to perform your business processes effectively.

Figure 1-1 depicts the organizational units in Financial Accounting and the sub-modules within Financial Accounting in SAP ERP using an organizational chart. The sub-modules in Financial Accounting include Accounts Payable, Accounts Receivable, General Ledger, Asset Accounting, and so on. Data entered at this level is valid for all company codes and organizational units in the client.

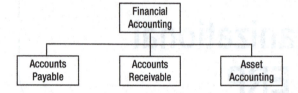

Figure 1-1. *Example of organizational units of Financial Accounting in SAP*

The Client

The *client* is an independent unit in the SAP ERP with its own master records and sets of tables. Data entered at this level is valid for all company codes (defined in the next section) and organizational units in the client. In other words, all the company codes in the client will have access to data created at this level. For that reason, the client is said to be the highest level in a SAP system hierarchy. The benefit of the client is that data is entered only once, thus eliminating duplication, reducing redundancies, and saving resources like storage space. As all company codes in the client can have access to the same data created at this level, the need to create individual data for each company code is eliminated.

Each client has its own unique log-on key, which must be entered by the user in order to access the client and perform business processes.

In a client, you can define one or more company codes. Likewise, one or more business areas can be assigned to one or multiple company codes, as depicted in Figure 1-2.

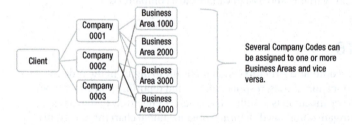

Figure 1-2. *Many-to-many relationships between company codes and business areas*

Company Code

A company code is a separate independent and legal entity that allows you to model and remodel your business organization based on financial reporting requirements (such as the profit and loss statements and balance sheets). Every company code in SAP ERP is represented with a unique four-character code. The code allows you to identify a company in a client. This is the case in an environment where you have more than one company code in a client.

In practice, global corporations have operations in several countries across the globe and it is often mandatory for global corporates by law to meet legal reporting and disclosure requirements in each country of their operation. Every country has its own accounting regulations with which companies operating within their border must comply. SAP ERP is beneficial in this aspect, because it allows organizational units in the same corporate organization functioning in various countries to function independently for reporting purposes. This enables you to meet specific tax and other legal reporting requirements by allowing you to use a separate unique company code for a company in each country.

In the SAP ERP when customizing company code, you define the following items:

- Company name

- Country

- Language key

- Currency

In addition, a company code must be assigned at least one operational or primary chart of accounts needed for business processes in the company code. Occasionally, a group chart of accounts may be needed for controlling purposes and a country-specific chart of accounts may be needed to meet country-specific reporting requirements. A group chart of accounts is optional. You will learn about chart of accounts in detail in Chapter 2.

Let's Start Customizing

When you log on to SAP ERP, the SAP Easy Access screen is displayed (Figure 1-3).

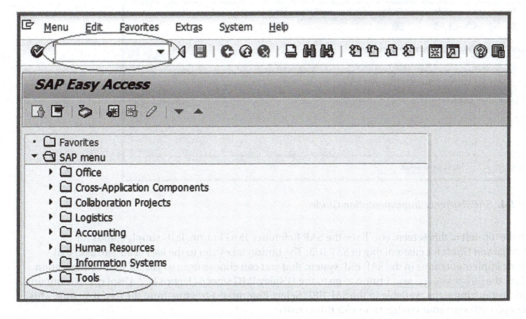

Figure 1-3. *Select Tools to commence customizing*

The Easy Access screen contains a list of functions to choose from. It is the initial point of entry into the SAP ERP. In order to call up the Customizing: Execute Project screen where you will commence your customzing, follow the menu path: SAP Easy Access ➤ Tools ➤ Customizing ➤ IMG ➤ Execute Project (SPRO) ➤ SAP Reference IMG.

A quicker way to access the same screen is by using transaction codes. Transaction codes are used to navigate a task in a single step, by bypassing the standard menu path that involves several time-consuming steps. You use a transaction code (TC) to access the task you want to execute by typing it into the Command Field, which is the blank field circled in red on the top-left side of the screen in Figure 1-3. Transaction codes are standard sets of alphabets and figures recognized by a SAP system that allow you to access specific tasks in SAP. The benefit of using transaction codes is that it is faster to access tasks or enter a customizing workspace that you want to execute in SAP.

The SAP Project Reference Object (SPRO) is a standard transaction code that allows you to access the Customizing: Execute Project screen without using the menu path. SAP ERP comes with a set of tables containing transaction codes. This table can be assessed by typing **SE38** into the Command Field to go to the ABAP Editor: Initial, where you will look for the transaction code you want to use. The ABAP Editor: Initial is beyond the scope of this book. However, you can also access transaction codes on the Easy Access screen by choosing Extras ➤ Settings on the menu bar at the top of the screen or simply by pressing Shift+F9 on your keyboard. The Settings screen pops up with several options to choose from. Select Display Technical Names, which is the last item of the displayed list of available options by making sure that the checkbox is activated. Then press Enter. This action allows the system to display technical names before every function. A list of useful transaction codes appears in Appendix 2, which you can use as a reference.

To call up the Customizing: Execute Project screen, type **SPRO** into the Command Field now. Figure 1-4 will appear. This screen allows you to go to IMG Display screen, where you can select from the list of displayed tasks to commence your customizing.

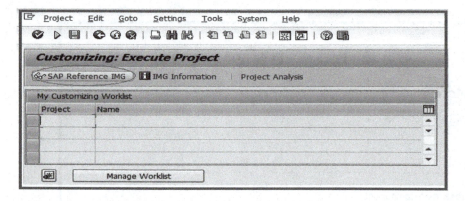

Figure 1-4. *SAP Reference Implementation Guide*

In the top-left of this screen, you'll see the SAP Reference IMG button. IMG simply stands for *Implementation Guide* for customizing in SAP R/3. The button takes you to the lists of all the tasks that constitute implementations in the SAP ERP system that you can choose from as part of your configuration.

Click the SAP Reference IMG button to go to the Display IMG screen (Figure 1-5). Display IMG contains a list of customizing steps available in the SAP ERP. Select Enterprise Structure from the tree structure. This is where you will start your configuration for this activity.

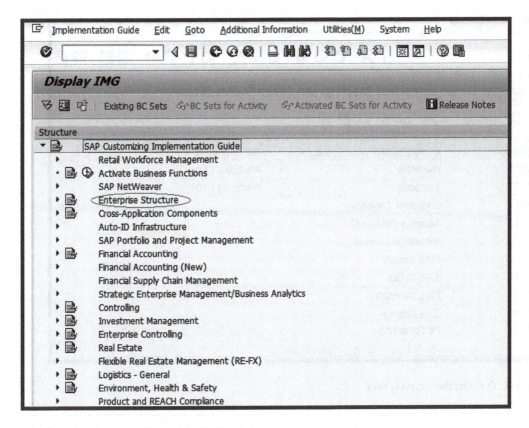

Figure 1-5. *Customizing the Display IMG screen*

In the Enterprise Structure under Financial Accounting, you will define your company, Company Code, Business Area, and Segment and assign a company code to your company.

Define a Company

In SAP, a *company* is an organizational unit treated as a legal entity from which a financial statement is generated in line with legal requirements. It is mandatory that a company be defined at least as part of financial accounting component to which one or more company codes are assigned in the SAP ERP system. You will define a company at this initial stage and then later in this chapter you will also define a company code and assign the company to the company code.

There are two ways to access the screen where company is defined in SAP R/3. You can follow this menu path: IMG ➤ Enterprise Structure ➤ Definition ➤ Financial Accounting ➤ Define Company or you can use the transaction code OX15. This is a standard transaction code for creating your . When you use either the menu path or the TC, the Change View "Internal Trading Partners": Overview screen appears (Figure 1-6). This is where you define the parameters for your new company. This screen displays the list of company codes in the system as an overview before you define your own company code.

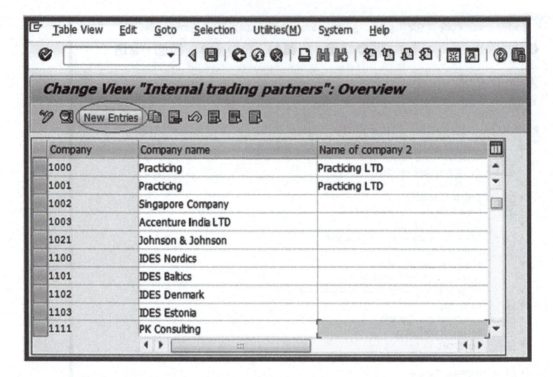

Figure 1-6. Defining the company code

■ **Note**　Notice in Figure 1-6 that a list of company codes is displayed on the screen. This is normal, as other company codes may already exist in the system.

Click the New Entries button to go to the next screen, which is called New Entries: Details of Added Entries (Figure 1-7). You will define your company code using four characters and your company details.

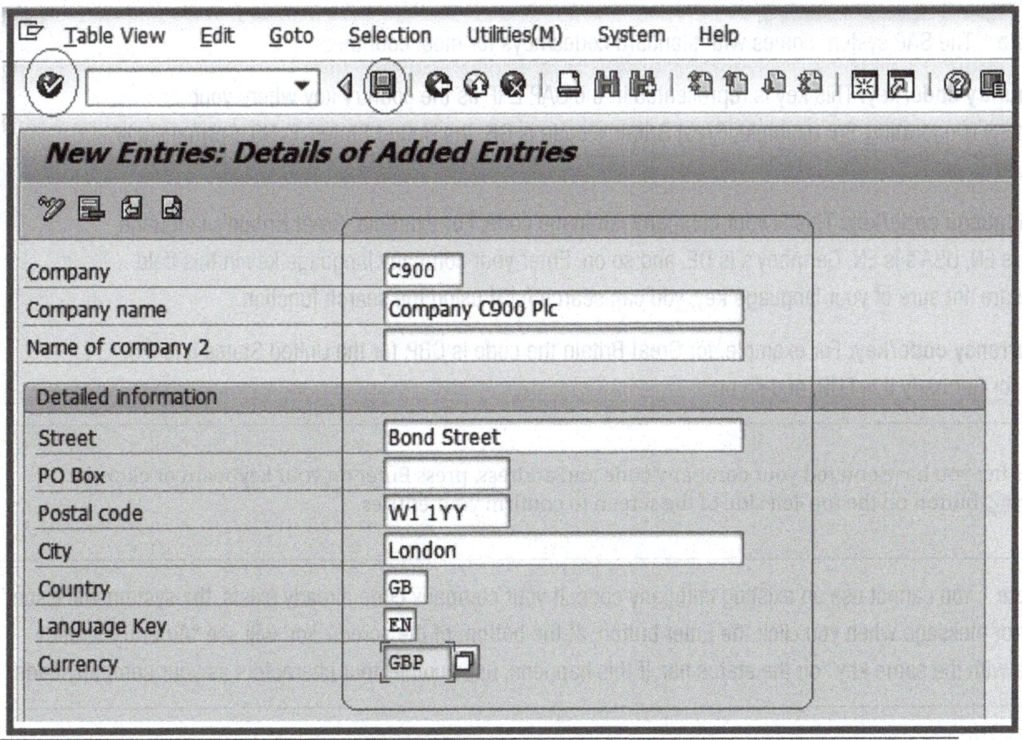

Figure 1-7. *New Entries screen to enter your company's details*

The New Entries: Details of Added Entries screen is divided into two sections. The first section contains fields where you will enter your company code and company name. You have the option of entering a second company in the section if you have more than one company name. The second section is the detailed information section and it contains the field that will enable you to enter the company's address, language key, and your company currency. Update the following fields using this information:

> **Company:** Enter four alphanumeric characters as your company code in this field. This code will serve as your company identifier in an environment where multiple company codes exist in the system. You can use up to four characters of your choice as you deem fit.

> **Company Name:** Enter your company name in this field. For example, the company name we use in this activity is Company C900 Plc. This field allows up to 25 characters.

> **Detail Information:** This section allows you to enter information about your company. Details entered here can include a correspondence address and the currency used when generating company code financial statements. Enter your company's address, post code, city, country code, language key, and currency code in the appropriate fields.

■ **Note** The SAP system comes with standard codes/keys for most countries:

—**Country code/key:** This key is represented in the SAP ERP as the country key where your company is operating. For example, Great Britain's code is GB, the United States' is US, Germany's is DE, and so on.

—**Language code/key:** This is your company language code. For example, Great Britain's language code is EN, USA's is EN, Germany's is DE, and so on. Enter your company language key in this field. If you are not sure of your language key, you can search for it using the search function.

—**Currency code/key:** For example, for Great Britain the code is GBP, for the United States it is USD, for Germany it is EUR, and so on.

After you have entered your company code and address, press Enter on your keyboard or click the Enter ✅ button on the top-left side of the screen to confirm your entries.

■ **Note** You cannot use an existing company code. If your company code already exists, the system will issue an error message when you click the Enter button, at the bottom of the screen. You will see "An entry already exists with the same key" on the status bar. If this happens, use another four characters as your company code.

Finally, click Save 💾. The system will notify you that ☑ Data was saved on the status bar at the bottom of the screen.

Since this is your first configuration exercise, when you try to save a newly created item the Prompt for Customizing Request screen will pop up. Customizing request allows the system to store your entries for transportation to other SAP systems. This happens only once, when you save your configuration the first time. If this screen pops up, follow these steps to create your request:

1. Click the Create Request 🗐 icon on the Prompt Customizing Request pop-up screen. This allows you to create your unique change request. You can create your own request number or choose from existing request numbers.

2. The Create Request screen is displayed. This screen allows you to enter a short description as a request description. Enter any description of your choice in the Short Description field and click the Save 💾 button.

3. The Prompt for Customizing Request dialog box is displayed again. Click the Enter ✅ button to save your configuration so far. Once the system has saved your settings, the system will notify you that ☑ Data was saved on the status bar.

The next step in your configuration process is to return to the IMG Structure to perform another customizing task. Click the Back 🔙 button on top-right side of the screen twice to return to the IMG Structure Implementation Guide. The implementation guide contains lists of all actions requiring implementation in SAP R/3.

Define a Company Code

In this exercise, you define your company code. You can define more than one company code if required. In the SAP ERP, the company code is an organizational unit used in FI to structure a business process for financial reporting purposes. SAP FI gives you the option to edit (create from scratch) your company code or copy the parameters of an existing company code and modify them to meet your requirements.

In this activity you will create your company code from scratch instead of copying existing company code parameters. Choose Edit Company Code Data from the displayed list in Figure 1-8. Follow the menu path: IMG ➤ Enterprise Structure ➤ Definition ➤ Financial Accounting ➤ Edit, Copy, Delete, Check Company Code or use the transaction code OX02 to go to the Choose Activity screen.

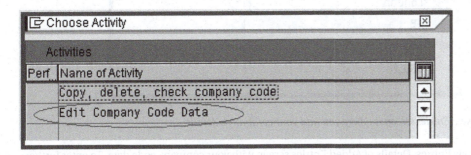

Figure 1-8. Editing the company code data

■ **Note** If you choose to copy an existing company's data from the list of displayed company codes in the system instead of creating a new company code from scratch, use the activity Copy, Delete, Check Company Code in Figure 1-8. This allows you to copy an existing company's code data that comes standard in the SAP system. Examples of standard company codes in SAP are 0001, 1000, 2000, and so on. The company code you have copied will retain most of the properties of the copied company code. Not all the properties are retained, so make sure you go through each step involved in customizing and update all the inherited properties of the copied company code to your own company code as appropriate.

■ **Tip** It is advisable to create your company code from scratch, as this will give you the opportunity to cover every step involved in customizing your company code.

When you choose Edit Company Code Data, the New Entries: Details of Added Entries screen is displayed (Figure 1-9). This screen allows you to enter your company code details in the appropriate fields. The company code details you enter in this screen will be treated by the system as your company data. The screen is divided into two sections. The first section contains the fields for your company code and name. The second section, which is the Additional Data section, contains your company's city, country, currency, and language.

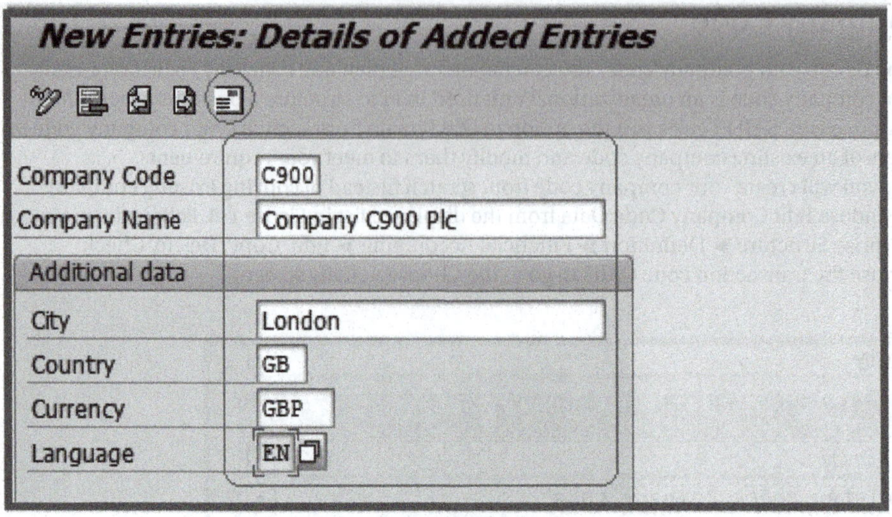

New Entries: Details of Added Entries

Company Code	C900
Company Name	Company C900 Plc
Additional data	
City	London
Country	GB
Currency	GBP
Language	EN

Figure 1-9. *The New Entries screen is where you add your company's details*

Update the New Entries: Details of Added Entries screen with your company code data. To enter further address details, click the Address (Shift+F5) ▣ button at the top of the screen. This action will call up the Edit Address screen (Figure 1-10). This screen enables you to update your company code master record with the relevant information.

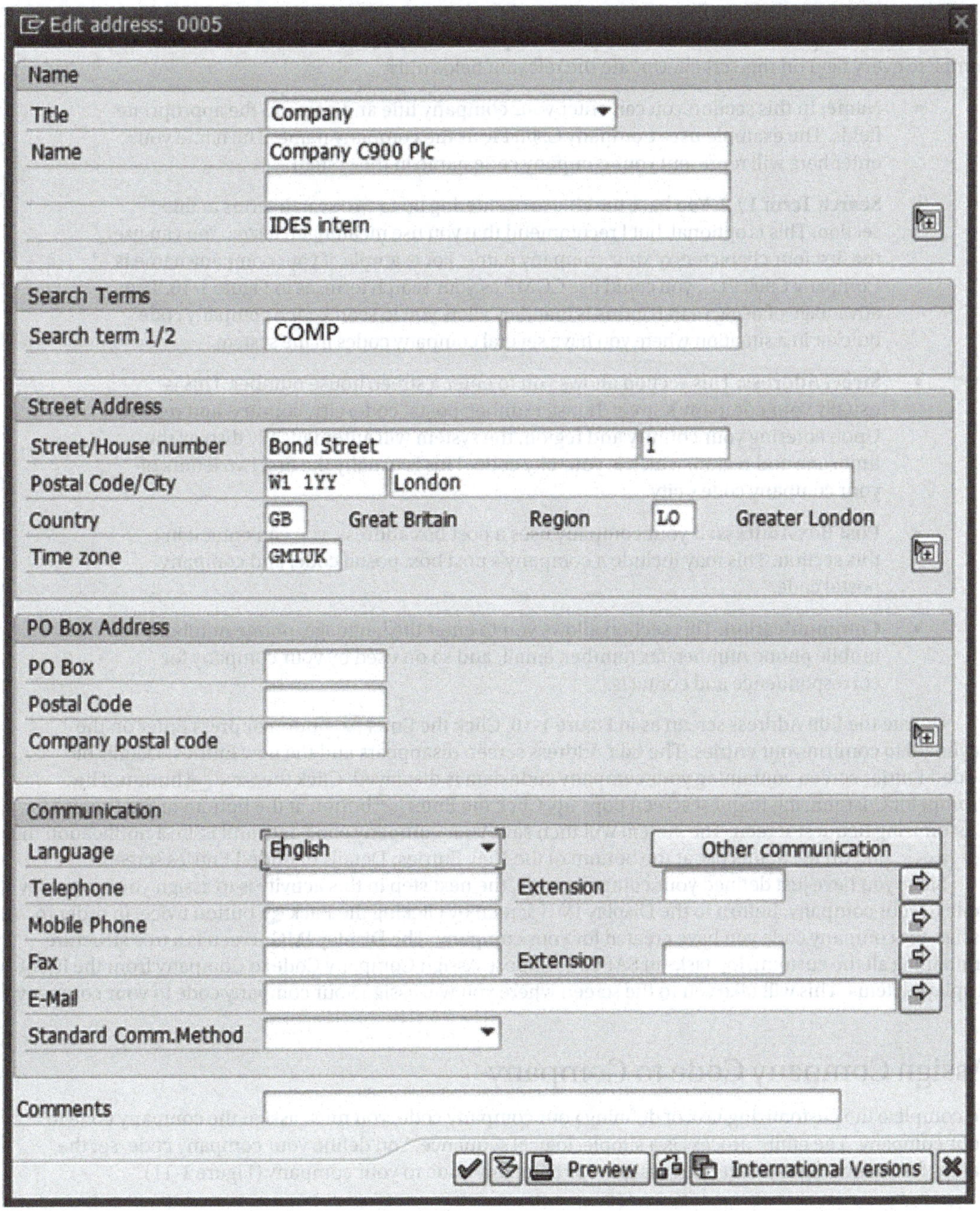

Figure 1-10. *The screen to enter your company's address and contact details*

This screen is divided into five sections: Name, Search Terms, Street Address, PO Box Address, and Communication. Update each section with your company code information. It is not mandatory that you complete every field on this screen. Update the relevant fields only:

- **Name:** In this section you can enter your company title and name in the appropriate fields. The example uses Company C900 Plc as the company name. The name you enter here will represent your company code name in the system.

- **Search Term 1 / 2:** You have the choice of entering up to two search terms in this section. This is optional, but I recommend that you use meaningful terms. You can use the first four characters of your company name. For example, if your company name is Company C900 PLC, you could use COMP as your search term, as in Figure 1-10. The advantage of using search terms is that they allow you to search for a company code quicker in a situation where you have several company codes in the system.

- **Street Address:** This section allows you to enter a street/house number. This is usually your company's street/house number, postal code/city, country, and region. Upon entering your country and region, the system will automatically display the timezone and region, which is your city code. This is usually the first two letters of your company code's city.

- **Post Box Address:** If your company uses a post box address, you can enter it in this section. This may include a company's post box, postal code, and company postal code.

- **Communication:** This section allows you to enter the language, phone number, mobile phone number, fax number, email, and so on used by your company for correspondence and contacts.

Update the Edit Address screen as in Figure 1-10. Click the Enter ✔ button or press Enter on the keyboard to confirm your entries. The Edit Address screen disappears and the new Entries: Details of Added Entries screen containing your company code data is displayed. Click the Save 🖫 button. The Prompt for Customizing Request screen pops up. Click the Enter ✔ button at the bottom of the Prompt for Customizing Request screen. The system will then save your company code data and issue a notification that ✔ Data was saved on the Status bar at the bottom of the New Entries: Details of Added Entries screen.

Since you have just defined your company code, the next step in this activity is to assign your company code to your company. Return to the Display IMG screen by clicking the Back ⬅ button twice, in order to assign the company code you have created for your company. The Display IMG screen is a tree structure containing all the customizing tasks in SAP R/3. Choose Assign Company Code to Company from the list of displayed items. This will take you to the screen where you will assign your company code to your company.

Assign Company Code to Company

To complete the customizing task of defining your company code, you must assign the company code to your company. The entire process is a simple, logical sequence. You define your company code, set the values for your company code, and assign your company code to your company (Figure 1-11).

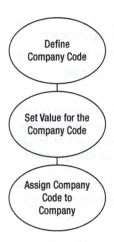

Figure 1-11. *Steps involved in defining and assigning a company code to a company*

You assign your company code to your company from the Change View "Assign Company Code -> Company": Overview screen (Figure 1-12). To access this screen, use the menu path: Enterprise Structure ➤ Assignment ➤ Financial Accounting ➤ Assign Company Code to Company or use the transaction code OX16.

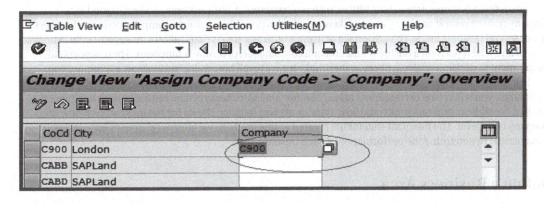

Figure 1-12. *Assignment of your company to its company code*

The Change View "Assign Company Code -> Company" Overview screen contains a list of company codes in the system. You may have a large number of companies in the system. Instead of having to scroll to search for your company among the company codes in the system, you can simply click the ▣ Position... button at the bottom of the Change View "Assign Company Code -> Company": Overview screen. The Another Entry screen pops up. Enter four identifier characters that make up your company code into the company code field and click the Enter ☑ button. Your company code will automatically be displayed on top of the company code list on the Change View "Assign Company Code -> Company" Overview screen.

■ **Note** In SAP ERP R/3, you can create more than one company code depending on your client's needs. If you chose to define another company code, repeat the previous steps by defining a company and a company code using another company code and name, and then assigning that company code to the company.

You will notice that your company code is displayed on top of all the company codes in the system. Your company code and city are displayed and the company field is blank. Simply type your company code into the company field. If you cannot remember your company code, use the Search function or Matchcode button next to the company field to search for your company code, as depicted Figure 1-12. After you enter your company code, save your company code settings.

Now that you have assigned your company code to your company, let's look at how to define a business area, which will serve as an organizational unit for a specific segment of your business operations. You can use this for internal reporting purposes.

Business Area

A *business area* is an organizational unit that represents a specific business segment in SAP that defines a functional area of operation, a plant, or an area of responsibility. For example, business areas can be a product the company sells, a geographical location, and so on. Business area is optional and is intended purely for internal financial reporting. They can be used across company codes for reporting. They are also viewed as balancing entities that can produce their own set of financial statements.

You define a business area in SAP ERP using four characters. A business area can be assigned to a company code or several company codes. Likewise, it is also possible to assign a company code to a business area or several business areas. The advantage of using a business area is that it allows management to generate internal financial reports on a business function or a combination of business functions. These reports aid management in decision-making, because they make it easy to tell how well a business area is performing.

You can create more than one business area, depending on your client's requirements. In the exercise that follows, you will create two business areas: *London and Manchester*. Once business areas are created, it is then possible to generate profit-and-loss statements and balance sheets for business areas below the company code level. The financial statements created at this level are for internal purposes only and help management to determine the performance of each business area.

Define a Business Area

> **Problem**: *Your client wants to be able to access the performance of their business divisions by generating internal performance reports consisting of P&Ls and balance sheets for two business areas. You have been asked to define two business areas for your company code for Manchester and London to satisfy this requirement.*

Defining a business area enables you to complete the settings that will allow your company to maintain financial statements by function, sales area, plant, or geographical location. Let's define the business areas for Manchester and London. Follow the menu path: IMG ➤ Enterprise Structure ➤ Definition ➤ Financial or use transaction code OX03.

The Change View "Business areas": Overview screen is displayed. This is a table containing the list of business areas in the system. Click the New Entries button at the top-right side of the screen to access the screen where you will define your business area. The New Entries: Overview of Added Entries screen is displayed. This is a blank table of several rows and two columns that allows you to specify your business area code and add a description of your business area (Figure 1-13).

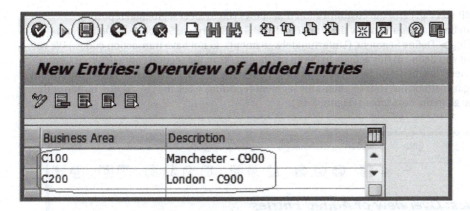

Figure 1-13. *The main screen for defining business areas*

Update the following fields:

- **Business Area:** Enter four characters for the business area. This code will enable you to identify your business areas. Figure 1-13 shows that we have created two business area codes: C100 for London and C200 for Manchester.

- **Description:** This field will enable you to enter the names or short descriptions of your business areas.

When you're satisfied with your settings, in order to ensure that the system accepts your entries, click Enter ✔ to confirm your entries. Then save 📄 your business areas.

Segment

A *segment* is used to highlight items disclosed in financial reporting by segment. This is opposed to a business area, which forms part of an organizational unit for which a financial statement is drawn for internal purposes. Accounting principles and standards (U.S. GAAP, IFRS, IAS, and so on) mandate that companies produce segmental reporting in certain situations for external purposes. A segment may be a department, product, or geographic location. Segmental reporting is purely for transparency purposes when reporting the profit and risk situations of segments within an enterprise. The underlying reason behind this requirement is to assist users of the financial information to make better judgments about an entity's involvement in different activities. Segment accounting allows a company to report the performance of their segment's activities individually. The importance of segment reporting is that it places more emphasis on segment performance.

Define a Segment

Problem: *Company C900 wants to be able to produce segmental reporting for two divisions of their operations. Your task is to define the two segments for Company C900 thus:*

1. Television and video systems as SEG-A

2. Refrigerators and coolers as SEG-B

In the SAP ERP, you can carry out customization that allows you to meet segmental reporting requirements. To define a segment, follow this menu path: IMG ➤ Enterprise Structure ➤ Definition ➤ Financial Accounting ➤ Define Segment. (Unfortunately, segments do not have transaction codes.) We will look at the segment you define in this activity in depth in Chapter 20, in the section entitled "Profit Center."

The Change View "Segments for Segment Reporting": Overview screen is displayed. This is the screen where you will begin customizing your segments for segment reporting. Click the New Entries button at the top of the screen to go to the next screen (Figure 1-14).

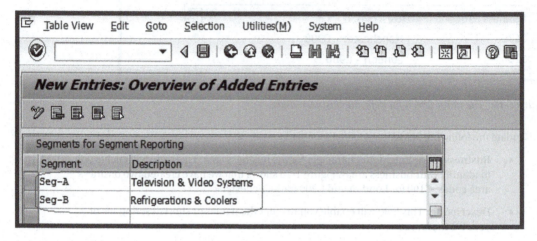

Figure 1-14. *The main screen for defining segments*

You will enter your segments in the system by updating the following fields:

- **Segment:** Enter a segment key in this field. This key will enable you to identify the segment in the system. We used segment key SEG-A for Television & Video Systems and SEG-B for Refrigerators & Coolers in this activity.

- **Description:** Enter your segment name or description in this field.

When you have updated the segments for segment reporting, click the Enter ✅ button at the top of the screen to confirm your entries and save 🖫 your segment configuration.

The next step in this customizing activity is to create a fiscal year variant for your company code.

Fiscal Year Variant

The *fiscal year* represents the accounting year or annual accounting period. A *fiscal year variant* defines your company's accounting posting periods. A proper business accounting transaction normally covers a 12-month period. The normal rule is that business transactions are assigned to the period during which the transaction took place. The fiscal year variant is customized to match your company's fiscal year, which does not necessarily have to be the same as the normal calendar year (that is, January to December). SAP ERP is dynamic enough to fit into your company's calendar or fiscal year.

Fiscal year variant is defined with posting periods. *Posting periods* are technical terms used to refer to months. In SAP ERP, the fiscal year is made up of 12 posting periods. Besides the normal 12 posting periods, you can define up to four special posting periods, which are used for posting year-end adjustments to closed periods. For example, if the normal fiscal period is closed, adjustments can still be posted in one of the four special periods.

■ **Note** In SAP ERP you cannot exceed a maximum of 16 periods at any given time.

In SAP ERP, posting periods are identified by posting dates. As you can see in Figure 1-15, a fiscal year variant can be defined either as:

- Year independent
- Year specific (dependent)

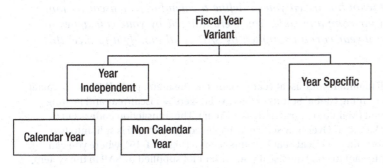

Figure 1-15. *Types of fiscal year variants*

Year Independent

With *year independent,* the accounting periods of a company remain the same each year (that is, the financial reporting year is constant). For example, an enterprise fiscal year is January to December of each year. There are two types of year independent fiscal year variants in SAP:

- **Calendar year:** The posting period is the same as the calendar year, usually 12 months. The posting period runs 12 months each year. For example, the U.S. financial year starts in January and ends in December.

- **Non-calendar year:** These are time periods that start and end any month of the year, except January and December. In the UK, for example, the fiscal year starts in April and ends in March. Since the non-calendar year did not start in January 1st, you use indicator -1 or +1 for the period of the year that belongs to the former or latter fiscal year.

■ **Note** February is counted as 29 days irrespective of actual number of days in February in order for the system to take leap year into consideration.

The SAP system comes with standard fiscal year variants. We recommend that you use the standard fiscal year variants supplied by the system. As examples, the fiscal year variant for the United States (January to December) is K4 and the fiscal year variant for the UK (April to March) is V3.

You can copy and modify the standard fiscal year variant.

If you decide to define your own fiscal year variant, use a two-digit alphanumeric identifier of your choice as your variant and maintain your fiscal year variant as appropriate.

Year Specific or Year Dependent

Year specific is used when the fiscal year/posting periods vary from year to year. This is uncommon in practice.

An example of a situation when this will arise is when posting periods are either greater than 12 months (extended fiscal year) or are less than 12 months (shortened fiscal year). The reason for a shortened fiscal year could be as a result of a company winding up or any other special reasons.

Maintain Fiscal Year Variant

> **Problem:** *The accounting team has asked you to define a calendar year fiscal variant (January–December) for your company code. You were advised by your colleagues to copy K4—the standard fiscal year variant supplied by SAP—and modify it to meet this requirement.*

To access the screen where you will maintain your fiscal year variant, use the menu path: IMG ➤ Financial Accounting (New) ➤ Financial Accounting Global Settings (New) ➤ Ledgers ➤ Fiscal Year and Posting Period ➤ Maintain Fiscal Year Variant (Maintain Shortened Fiscal Year). The transaction code is OB29.

The Change View "Fiscal Year Variants" Overview screen is displayed. This screen is split into two sections, the Dialog Structure section and the Fiscal Year Variants section (Figure 1-16), where you can customize your fiscal year. Since you want to copy the fiscal year variant K4 supplied by SAP in the system, you should use the [Position...] button at the bottom to search for the fiscal year variant you want to use (in this case, it's K4).

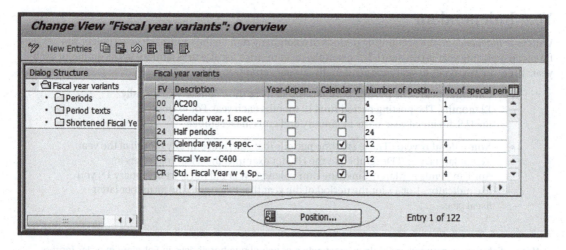

Figure 1-16. *Searching for the fiscal year variant you want to copy*

When you click the Position button, a dialog box called Another Entry (Figure 1-17) pops up. This dialog box enables you to search for the fiscal year variant supplied by the system (K4) that you want to adapt to your fiscal year variant.

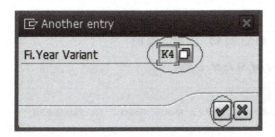

Figure 1-17. *Entering the fiscal year variant*

Enter **K4** in the FI. Year Variant field to call up K4 from the list of variants in the system.

Select K4 from the variant list and click the Enter button ✅. The Change View "Fiscal Year Variants": Overview screen is displayed (Figure 1-18). This screen allows you to copy an existing fiscal year supplied by the system or create your own fiscal year variant from scratch (see the following tip to create your own). To copy a fiscal year variant, select it and click the Copy icon 📑 on the top of the screen. When you copy a fiscal year variant, you are also copying its dependent settings defined by SAP.

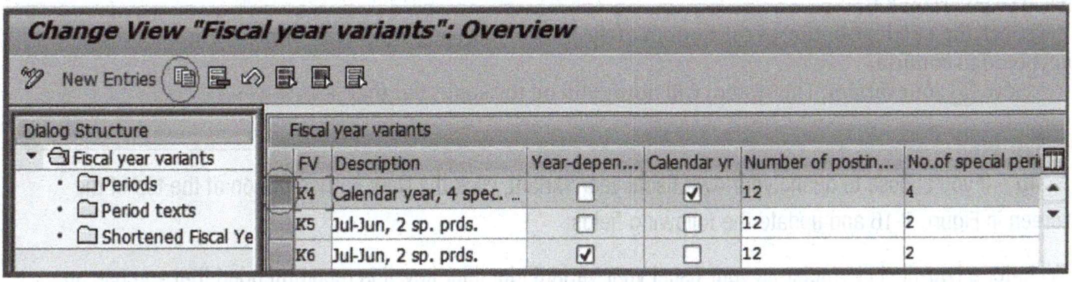

Change View "Fiscal year variants": Overview						
✎ New Entries 📑 📑 ⇗ 📑 📑 📑						

Dialog Structure	Fiscal year variants					
▼ 📁 Fiscal year variants	FV	Description	Year-depen...	Calendar yr	Number of postin...	No.of special peri
• 🗀 Periods	K4	Calendar year, 4 spec. ...	☐	☑	12	4
• 🗀 Period texts	K5	Jul-Jun, 2 sp. prds.	☐	☐	12	2
• 🗀 Shortened Fiscal Ye	K6	Jul-Jun, 2 sp. prds.	☑	☐	12	2

Figure 1-18. *Copying the fiscal year variant*

■ **Note**   When you copy a fiscal year variant, you have to change the fiscal year variant key to your own. Otherwise, you will not be able to save the fiscal year variant you have copied, because the system does not allow duplicate fiscal year keys. Once you have copied K4, change the fiscal year variant from K4 to any variant of your choice.

If possible, avoid using the letters K or V as part of your fiscal year variant key, because many of the standard fiscal year variant keys supplied by the system start with either K or V.

To match the example we're using in Figure 1-19, change the content of FV to C4 and change the Description field to Fiscal Year Variant – C900.

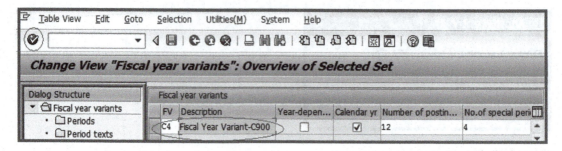

Figure 1-19. *Updating the fiscal year variant*

When you click the Enter ✅ button or press Enter on your keyboard, the Specify Object to be Copied screen pops up. This screen allows you to copy just the dependent entries or all of the dependent entries of the fiscal year variant you have marked for copying.

Since you want to copy all of the dependent entries of the fiscal year variant K4, click the ⬜ copy all ⬜ command button.

The Information dialog pops up, telling you the number of dependent entries you have copied from fiscal year variant K4.

Click the Enter ✅ button at the bottom of the information pop-up screen or press Enter on your keyboard to confirm.

Save 🖫 your variant. The system will notify you on the status bar that ✅ Number of entries copied: 1 .

■ **Tip** If you choose to define your own fiscal year variant, click the New Entries button at the top of the screen in Figure 1-16 and update the following fields:

FV: Enter a two-digit character as your fiscal year variant identifier key. It is recommended that you use an alphanumeric identifier. In the example in this section, the standard fiscal year variant supplied by SAP in the system, K4 (calendar year), was copied and modified to meet our desired requirement.

Description: This field allows you to describe or name your fiscal year variant. In the example in this section, the fiscal year variant C900 was used.

Year Dependent: If the fiscal year/posting periods vary each year, check the Year-Dependent checkbox. This is not very common in practice.

Calendar Yr: If the fiscal year is the same as the normal calendar year each year, check the Calendar Year checkbox.

Number of Posting Periods: Here you specify the number of posting periods. This will normally be a 12-month period.

No. of Special Posting Periods: SAP R/3 system allows up to four special periods for making postings outside the normal accounting periods.

Assign the Fiscal Year Variant to the Company Code

It is mandatory that you assign a fiscal year to a company code in SAP. Since you have defined or copied your fiscal year variant, the next step is to assign it to your company code. It is also possible to assign the standard fiscal year variant supplied by SAP in the system directly to your company code without having to define your own fiscal year variant. Follow this menu path: IMG ➤ Financial Accounting (New) ➤ Financial Accounting Global Settings (New) ➤ Ledgers ➤ Fiscal Year and Posting Period ➤ Assign Company Code to a Fiscal Year Variant or use the transaction code OB37. You will then access the screen where you will assign the fiscal year you have defined to your company code (Figure 1-20).

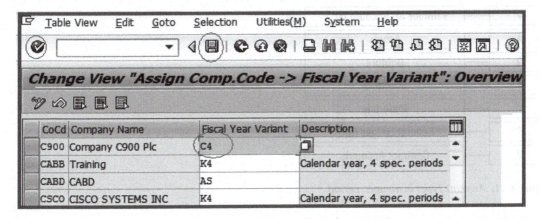

Figure 1-20. *Assigning the company code to the fiscal year variant*

The Change View "Assign Comp.Code -> Fiscal Year Variant": Overview screen is displayed. To assign your company code to your fiscal year variant, search for your company code by using the Position button

⊞ Position... or using the scroll down arrow ▲▼ and assigning your fiscal year variant as appropriate.

Enter **C4** in the Fiscal Year Variant column or use the Search function 🔲 to search for your fiscal year variant (in this case, C4). Make sure that your fiscal year is entered into the Fiscal Year Variant column.

Click the Save 🖫 button to save your fiscal year variant assignment.

■ **Note**   The system may issue a warning message that says, 'No postings are possible without fiscal year,' and the Save button is suppressed. This normally happens when some company codes are not assigned a fiscal year variant. If this happens, click the Enter button or press the Enter key on your keyboard several times until the Save button is activated. Then save your work. The system will notify you on the status bar that your data was saved.

Opening and Closing Posting Periods

As mentioned previously, accounting transactions are usually assigned to periods. Posting periods are defined in fiscal year variants. The benefit of defining variants to open periods is to avoid the problem of posting accounting transactions to the wrong period. This is achieved by opening current periods and closing all other periods. At the end of the current period, the period is closed and the next period is opened.

It is compulsory that at least two posting period intervals be open at any given time. On the other hand, you can open several posting periods at the same time (that is, more than two posting periods).

Posting periods are independent of the fiscal year; that is, they are not dependent on nor controlled by the fiscal year. Posting periods are defined at the global level in SAP ERP. This makes them accessible to several company codes in the system.

In SAP ERP, opening and closing periods are differentiated by account types. This allows you to determine which accounts are posted to a specific posting period. For example, posting can be permitted for accounts payable but not to accounts receivable. You can specify several account types simultaneously as part of your customizing open periods. Figure 1-21 lists the basic account types in SAP R/3.

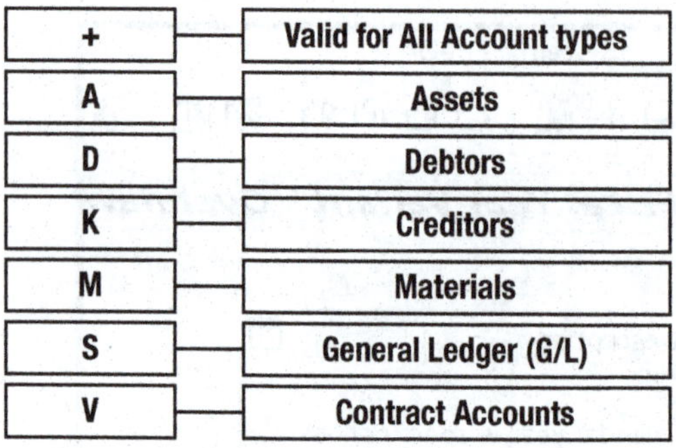

+	Valid for All Account types
A	Assets
D	Debtors
K	Creditors
M	Materials
S	General Ledger (G/L)
V	Contract Accounts

Figure 1-21. Account Types in an open period

In SAP ERP, it is mandatory that for each posting period, you specify the minimum account type '+' for each open period. This account type is valid for all account types. The benefit of applying account types to an open period is that the system can determine whether a posting period specified in the posting period variant you defined can be posted to using the posting date entered in the document header.

As part of customizing opening and closing periods, the following items are defined:

- Define variants for open posting periods

- Assign variants to company codes

- Specify open and close posting periods

Let's look at each in turn.

Define Variants for Open Posting Periods

Problem: You need to define the variants for posting periods for company C900 and assign the variant you have defined to the company code.

To define variants for open posting periods, follow the menu path: IMG: Financial Accounting (New) ➤ Financial Accounting Global Settings (New) ➤ Ledgers ➤ Fiscal Year and posting Periods ➤ Posting Periods ➤ Define Variants for Open Posting Periods or use the transaction code OBBO.

■ **Note** Every company code must be assigned its own variant for open posting periods.

The Change View Posting Periods: Define Variants: Overview screen is displayed. This is the screen where you define variants for opening posting periods. Click the ⌷New Entries⌷ button on top of the screen.

The New Entries: Overview of Added Entries screen is displayed (Figure 1-22). This screen allows you to specify your company code variant code and the name of your variant. In practice, the posting period variant key is defined using your company code and your company name as the posting variant name.

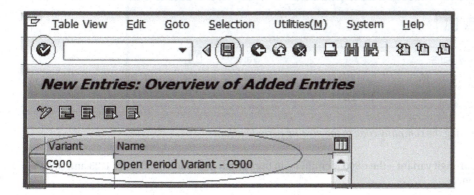

Figure 1-22. *Overview of the added entries*

Update the following fields:

- **Variant:** Enter four characters as the posting variant key in the variant field. It's best to make it your company code. The code you enter here will be used when assigning posting variants later to your company code.

- **Name:** Enter the description or a variant name that best describes your variant in this field. In our example, we used Open Period Variant – C900 as our variant name.

Click the Enter button to confirm the variant you entered into the system. If the variant already exists in the system, the system will notify you on the status bar that "An entry already exists with the same key." SAP R/3 does not allow duplicate variant keys. All you have to do when faced with this problem is use another variant key that the system will accept. Otherwise, the Save icon will be inactive and you will not be able to save your variant. Once the system accepts your variant, the Save button is activated and you can save your work. Save 🖫 your posting variant.

The next step is to assign the posting period variant to the company code.

Assign Variants to Company Code

The assignment of posting period variants is a part of customizing variants for opening periods. Every company code in SAP R/3 must be assigned a posting period variant. To access the screen where you can assign your company code to a posting period variant, use this menu path: IMG: Financial Accounting (New) ➤ Financial Accounting Global Settings (New) ➤ Ledgers ➤ Fiscal Year and Posting Periods ➤ Posting Periods ➤ Assign Variants to Company Code. Or use the transaction code OBBP.

The Change View "Assign Comp.Code -> Posting Period Variants": Overview screen is displayed. Using the Position button at the bottom of the screen, search for your company code and update the variant fields by entering the variant for open posting periods that you defined (Figure 1-23).

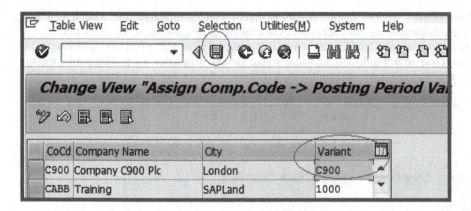

Figure 1-23. *Assigning the company code to the posting period variant*

Enter your four-digit variant—the C900 identifier—in the variant field shown in Figure 1-23 and save your customization.

Specify Open and Closing Periods

Problem: You can define your posting periods from scratch or you can copy existing posting periods and modify them to meet your requirement. To simplify your configuration, your colleagues have asked you to copy posting periods from company code 1000 and modify them to meet the client's requirements.

As mentioned, posting periods are opened in fiscal year variants. You can open and close several posting periods simultaneously in SAP R//3. The advantage of opening and closing periods is that it helps prevent you from posting transactions to the wrong period in the sense that only valid periods are open. Any periods not relevant for posting are closed. To go to the screen where you can open and close posting periods, follow this menu path: IMG: Financial Accounting (New) ➤ Financial Accounting Global Settings (New) ➤ Ledgers ➤ Fiscal Year and Posting Periods ➤ Posting Periods ➤ Open and Close Posting Periods or use the transaction code OB52.

The Change View "Posting Periods: Specify Time Intervals": Overview screen is displayed (Figure 1-24).

Select all the accounts (+ A D K M S) belonging to company code 1000 that you want to copy from the list of displayed variants.

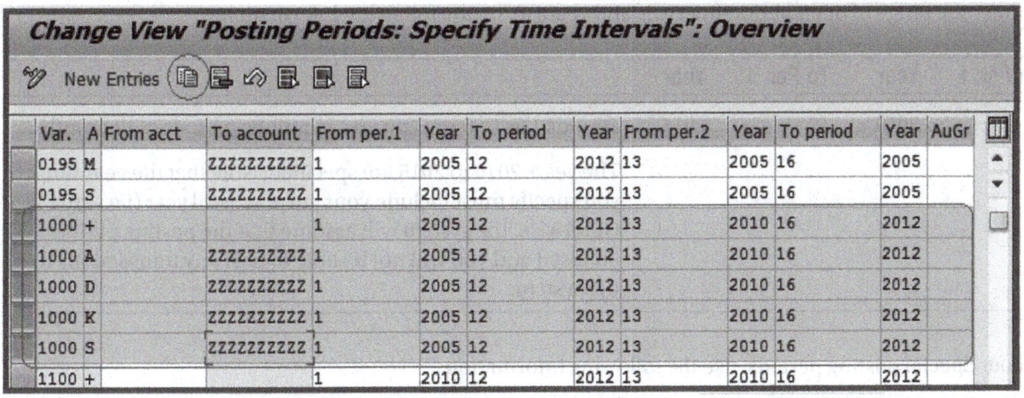

Change View "Posting Periods: Specify Time Intervals": Overview

New Entries

Var.	A	From acct	To account	From per.1	Year	To period	Year	From per.2	Year	To period	Year	AuGr
0195	M		ZZZZZZZZZZ	1	2005	12	2012	13	2005	16	2005	
0195	S		ZZZZZZZZZZ	1	2005	12	2012	13	2005	16	2005	
1000	+			1	2005	12	2012	13	2010	16	2012	
1000	A		ZZZZZZZZZZ	1	2005	12	2012	13	2010	16	2012	
1000	D		ZZZZZZZZZZ	1	2005	12	2012	13	2010	16	2012	
1000	K		ZZZZZZZZZZ	1	2005	12	2012	13	2010	16	2012	
1000	S		ZZZZZZZZZZ	1	2005	12	2012	13	2010	16	2012	
1100	+			1	2010	12	2012	13	2010	16	2012	

Figure 1-24. Copying the posting period intervals

Click the Copy button at the top-left side of the screen or choose Edit ➤ Copy As from the menu bar to copy the selected posting periods in Figure 1-24. The system will paste the variants you copied from company code 1000 to a new Change View "Posting: Specify Time Intervals"; Overview screen.

Update the variant identifiers 1000 by replacing them with your own C900 variants, as shown on the screen in Figure 1-25.

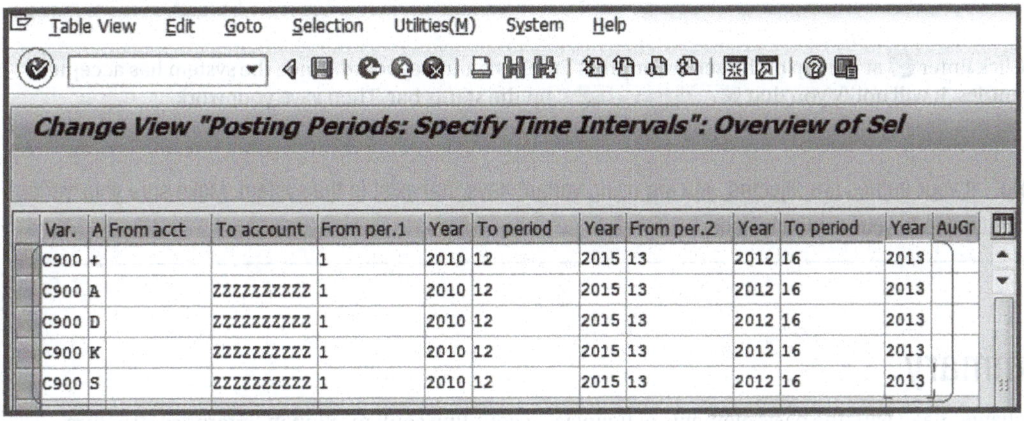

Table View   Edit   Goto   Selection   Utilities(M)   System   Help

Change View "Posting Periods: Specify Time Intervals": Overview of Sel

Var.	A	From acct	To account	From per.1	Year	To period	Year	From per.2	Year	To period	Year	AuGr
C900	+			1	2010	12	2015	13	2012	16	2013	
C900	A		ZZZZZZZZZZ	1	2010	12	2015	13	2012	16	2013	
C900	D		ZZZZZZZZZZ	1	2010	12	2015	13	2012	16	2013	
C900	K		ZZZZZZZZZZ	1	2010	12	2015	13	2012	16	2013	
C900	S		ZZZZZZZZZZ	1	2010	12	2015	13	2012	16	2013	

Figure 1-25. Update Posting Period Intervals

■ **Tip** SAP has 12 normal posting periods and up to 4 special periods.

Enter the range of open period intervals and years using the following information:

From Per. 1	Year	To Per. 1	Year	
1	2010	12	2015	Periods 1 to 12 represent an accounting periods of 12 months.
				The years 2010 to 2015 are specified. Note that the year range you specify must include your current fiscal year (i.e., 2012). Otherwise, the system will assume that the posting period is closed and you will not be able to post any transactions to the system.

Four Special posting periods, use the following information:

From Per. 1	Year	To Per. 1	Year	
13	2012	16	2013	Periods 13 to 16 represent the special periods of four months for posting year-end adjustments to a closed fiscal year.
				The years 2012 to 2013 are specified. The current fiscal year is January to December 2012. Since you want to allow four months after the normal posting period to allow for adjustment posting at the end of the year, you should specify any year beyond 2012 to allow for the special period.

Click Enter ✅ at the top of the screen or press Enter on your keyboard. Once the system has accepted your entries, it will notify you that ☑ Number of entries copied: 5 on the status bar. Then save your work.

■ **Note**   If your entries are rejected, you are using variant keys that exist in the system. Make sure your variant keys are unique to your company code.

Summary

This chapter dealt with the basic elements of financial accounting configuration in Enterprise structure, which is fundamental to the configuration of the remaining chapters in this book. As part of the activities covered in this chapter, you learned what organizational structure is and how to customize organizational units in SAP ERP. As part of your customizing process, the chapter taught you how to define a company code and a fiscal year variant and how to assign a fiscal year to a company code. Other topics that were covered in this chapter include how to define posting periods and how to apply account types to open periods.

In the next chapter, you will learn how to customize master data, a chart of accounts, and retained earnings.

CHAPTER 2

■ ■ ■

Defining the Chart of Accounts

In this chapter, you learn how to define the chart of accounts, create general ledgers, and assign the chart of accounts to company codes.

At the end of this chapter, you will be able to:

- Demonstrate an understanding of the various charts of accounts represented in SAP ERP.

- Create a chart of accounts.

- Assign a company code to a chart of accounts.

- Define an account group to the chart of accounts.

- Define a retained earnings account.

The Chart of Accounts

A chart of accounts is a fundamental financial tool in SAP ERP. It contains the list of general ledger (G/L) accounts used by a company code or several company codes for posting daily financial activities and for reporting financial performance to the financial statement and balance sheet. Transactions are classified by transaction type in the chart of accounts. It holds basic information about the structure of general ledger accounts in the SAP ERP system, such as account numbers and names, as well as other control parameters that determine how G/L accounts are created and function in SAP ERP.

The benefits of the chart of accounts are that it:

- Defines the basic structure for creating G/L accounts.

- Gives you the flexibility to use the same chart of accounts for several company codes.

You can assign an additional two charts—country-specific and group—to the minimum required operational chart of accounts in a company code. Add country-specific chart of accounts when you want to be able to generate reports to meet country-specific reporting requirements and add group chart of accounts for consolidation purposes.

Three steps are involved in configuring the chart of accounts in SAP R/3 (Figure 2-1).

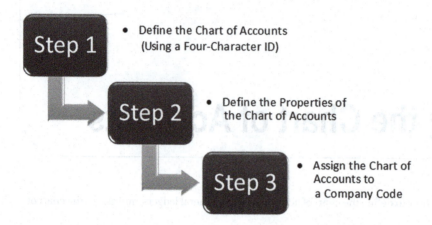

Figure 2-1. *Steps involved in the customizing a chart of accounts*

To create a general ledger and assign it to a company code, you must assign an operational chart of accounts to each company code in SAP ERP. One operational chart of accounts can be assigned to several company codes if those company codes have identical general ledger structures.

There are three charts of accounts in SAP ERP. Figure 2-2 shows the three charts of accounts and their purposes in SAP R/3.

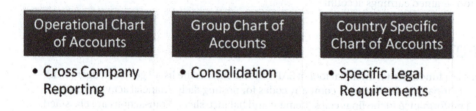

Figure 2-2. *Available charts of accounts in SAP R/3*

The functions of the three charts of accounts in SAP ERP are explained here:

- *Operational chart of accounts*: This is also referred to in the industry as a *common* chart of accounts. It is used to post the daily financial accounting and cost accounting transactions. Each company code must be assigned an operational chart of accounts.

- *Group chart of accounts*: Contains the corporate G/L accounts applicable to all company codes in the group. It's purely for consolidation reporting for the group.

- *Country-specific chart of accounts*: This optional chart of accounts is important when a company in a corporate group is required by law to produce a financial report specifically to meet a country's reporting requirements.

Since you now know what a chart of accounts is and understand the various chart of accounts available in SAP ERP, you're ready to learn how to create a chart of accounts. The sample principle is applicable to the three chart of accounts when customizing. The only difference is that they are used to meet different reporting requirements.

Create the Chart of Accounts

Problem: *Your task as an SAP FI consultant is to create a chart of accounts for company C900 Plc and assign it to your company code.*

The chart of accounts you create will contain a list of G/L accounts used by your company code for reporting and posting activities. The chart of accounts is configured as a global setting. This means that the chart of accounts is available to all company codes in the client rather than just one. The following menu path will take you to the screen where you can customize your chart of accounts: IMG: Financial Accounting (New) ➤ General Ledger Accounting (New) ➤ Master Data ➤ G/L Accounts ➤ Preparations ➤ Edit Chart of Accounts List. You can also use the transaction code OB13.

■ **Note**   You can create your own chart of accounts or you can copy the standard ones supplied by SAP.

The Change View "List of All Charts of Accounts": Overview screen is displayed (Figure 2-3). This screen contains a list of all the charts of accounts that exist in the system. You can assign any of these charts to your company code or create your own chart of accounts. This is matter of choice or your requirements. This is where you create your chart of accounts.

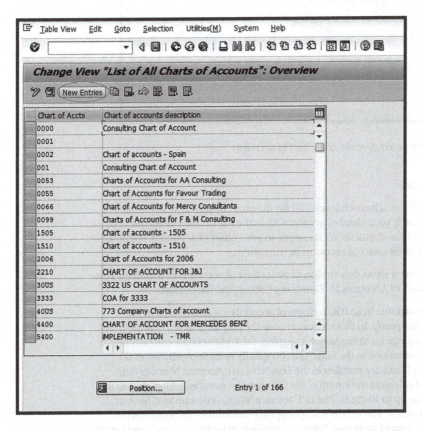

Figure 2-3. The initial screen where you start defining your chart of accounts for your company code

Click the (New Entries) button on the top-left side of the screen to go to the New Entries: Details of Added Entries screen (Figure 2-4), where you will enter the information for the new chart of accounts.

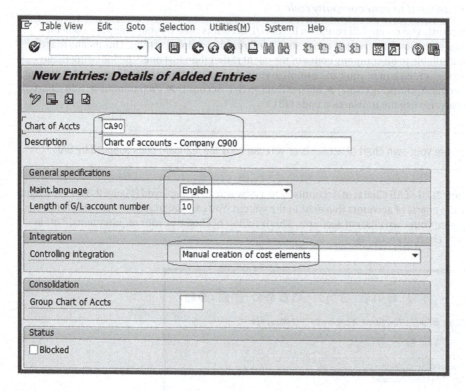

Figure 2-4. *The screen where you define the new chart of accounts*

Update the following fields:

> **Chart of Accts:** Enter a four-character ID for the chart of accounts key. This will allow you to identify your chart of accounts from the list of chart of accounts in the system. This four-character ID is unique to your chart of accounts. It cannot be used for any other chart of accounts in the system.

> **Description:** Enter a short description of your chart of accounts in this field. This activity uses Chart of Accounts for Company C900 as the description.

> **General Specifications:** In SAP R/3, charts of accounts are maintained in the language that you specify. In this section, choose the language that you want to use from the language list in the Maint. Language field. Master data can only be displayed and maintained in the language you specify here. Secondly, enter the length of your G/L account number in the Length of G/L Account Number field. There is no hard rule as to the length of the G/L account number. SAP gives you the flexibility of using up to 10 digits. The G/L account length is determined by your company's preference. The length you specify here determines the length of G/L number of your chart of accounts. This example uses 10 for the G/L accounts length.

Integration: As mentioned, you must assign your company code to a chart of accounts. You can also assign a country chart of accounts and/or group chart of accounts to meet certain reporting requirements. Country-specific charts are assigned to a chart of accounts using alternative account numbers. In SAP ERP all accounts, both internal and external, are managed technically by an integrated accounting system. The Controlling area uses the corresponding company code charts of accounts to manage cost elements. Assigning the controlling area to a company code is referred to as *integration*.

In the Integration section, you can choose whether you want the controlling integration to maintain cost elements manually or automatically. Although the system defaults to manual creation of cost elements, you can change this to automatic if necessary. I recommend that you use the manual creation of cost elements, which you will see in Chapter 18. Here's what each option permits going forward:

- *Manual creation of cost element*: The system will not automatically create primary cost elements when you create your G/L accounts. Instead, you have to manually do this.

- *Automatic creation of cost element*: When a new G/L account is saved, the related cost elements are automatically created.

    Consolidation: Enter the group chart of accounts used by your corporate group. The group chart of accounts you enter here will be required when creating corporate G/L accounts that are used for consolidating financial statements reporting for the corporate group.

    Status: This section of the screen allows you to activate the blocked checkbox. This function blocks postings to the G/L account unless this checkbox is deactivated. For example, you can block your chart of accounts from being posted to until you have completed your configuration. We recommend that you not activate this function, unless your company or client requires this.

After updating the New Entries: Detail of Added Entries screen, click the Enter ✅ button at the top of the screen to confirm your entries and save 💾 your chart of accounts.

The next step is to assign your company code to the chart of accounts you just created. To do this, you have to return to the Display IMG screen. Click the Back 🔙 button at the top of the screen twice to return to the Display IMG screen. You will select the next task from the list of displayed IMG tasks in the next exercise.

Assign Company Code to Chart of Accounts

Several company codes can be assigned to one chart of accounts, but only one operational chart of accounts is assigned to a company code (a group chart of accounts for consolidation reporting and a country-specific chart of accounts for meeting specific country reporting requirements can also be assignment to a company code). In most cases, there are several predefined charts of accounts in the system, which you can assign to your company code. To assign your company code to a chart of accounts, follow this menu path: IMG: Financial Accounting (New) ➤ General Ledger Accounting (New) ➤ Master Data ➤ G/L Accounts ➤ Preparations ➤ Assign Company Code to Chart of Accounts. Or you can use the transaction code OB62.

The Change View "Assign Company Code -> Chart of Accounts Overview screen is displayed. Click the [🔲 Position...] button at the bottom of the screen and then search for your company code. You will notice that the Chrt/Accts field in Figure 2-5 is blank. Search for the chart of accounts you have defined by clicking the Search function button next to the Chrt/Accts field or by typing your chart of accounts in the Chrt/Accts field.

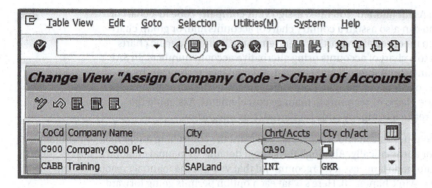

Figure 2-5. *Assigning a chart of accounts to a company code*

■ **Tip** You have the option of assigning additional charts of accounts to your company code based on specific reporting needs. For example, if you want to provide a consolidated corporate report, assign a group chart of accounts to your company code with the operational chart of accounts. Likewise, if your goal is to provide country-specific reporting needs, you can assign a country chart of accounts to your company code.

Enter your chart of accounts in the Chrt/Accts field and then click the Enter ✅ button on the top-left side of the screen to confirm your entries. Finally, click the Save button 🖫 to save your chart of accounts.

The next step is to define the account groups for the chart of accounts you just created. Account groups allow you to classify the G/L accounts that you will be creating in Chapter 5 into the right categories and assign the appropriate number ranges.

Define Account Group

A chart of accounts holds a large number of account types, and they determine how G/L accounts are created in SAP ERP. For proper management, accounts are systematically classified into appropriate account groups by grouping accounts with similar tasks together in the same general ledger. For example, all G/L accounts related to revenue are grouped together and assigned the same number range (array of numbers assigned to an object). G/L accounts belonging to account groups such as Liabilities, Expenditure, and Assets are also grouped together in the appropriate group and number ranges.

Figure 2-6 illustrates how account types are classified into account groups. For example, the number range 1–1000 is assigned to the Asset account group, and related account types like Land & Building, Furniture & Fittings, and Motor Vehicles are treated as assets in accounting. Likewise, the number range 1001–2000 is assigned to the account group Revenue, and it contains related account types like Sales, Interest Received, and Other Income. Finally, the number range 2001–3000 is assigned to the account group Expenditure, and it contains account types like Salaries, Office Supplies, and so forth.

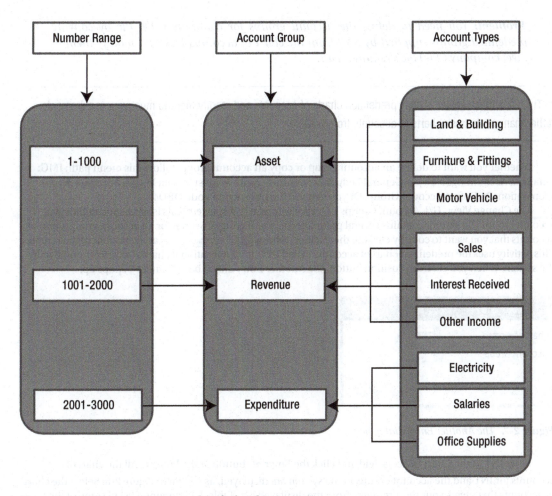

Figure 2-6. *How account types are classified within account groups*

Why are account groups important? There are two main reasons:

- They determine the number ranges assigned to an account when creating a G/L account.

- They determine the screen layout for creating G/L accounts in the company code area.

In this activity, instead of creating your own account groups, you will copy some of the predefined account groups from the INT chart of accounts supplied by the system. INT stands for *international* chart of accounts. These are universal charts of accounts supplied by SAP. They are not company code-specific; you can use them across company codes.

■ **Note**   You can create your own account groups or copy the account groups that meet your requirements from the predefined list and then modify them to meet your needs.

Problem: *You need to define the account groups for company C900 Plc by copying predefined groups supplied by SAP from the chart of accounts INT and modify them to meet company C900 Plc's requirements.*

■ **Tip** It is much easier to copy predefined charts of accounts and modify them to meet your requirements, rather than create fresh charts of accounts from scratch.

Whether you want to define an account group or copy an account group, follow this menu path: IMG: Financial Accounting (New) ➤ General Ledger Accounting (New) ➤ Master Data ➤ G/L Accounts ➤ Preparations ➤ Define Account Group. Or you can use the transaction code OBD4.

The Change View "G/L Account Groups": Overview screen is displayed. This is where you define your account group. The system contains several predefined account groups. Search for an account group/chart of accounts that you want to copy by clicking the Position button [🔳 Position...] at the bottom of the screen. This activity uses the predefined chart of accounts called INT (the international chart of account) supplied by the system. When you click the Position button, the Another Entry dialog box (Figure 2-7) pops up.

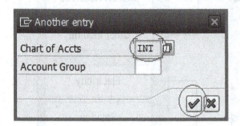

Figure 2-7. The Another Entry dialog box

Enter **INT** in the Chart of Accts field and click the Enter [✔] button at the bottom. All the chart of accounts for INT and the account groups in the system are displayed, as shown in Figure 2-8. Select the chart of accounts that meets your requirements from the displayed list. Table 2-1 contains a list of some of the charts of accounts that you can use and customize.

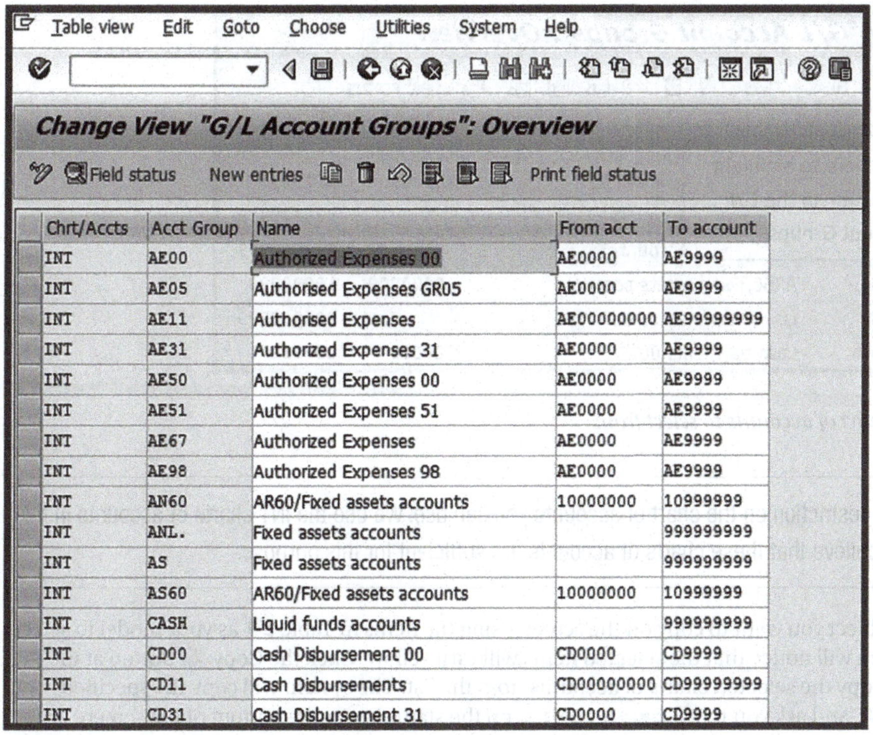

Figure 2-8. *Lists of charts of accounts and account groups*

Using the data in Table 2-1, highlight the listed charts of accounts and account groups shown in Figure 2-9.

Table 2-1. *A list of values you can use for your chart of accounts*

Chrt/Accts	Acct Group	Name	From Acct	To Acct
INT	AS	Fixed assets accounts		999999999
INT	CASH	Liquid funds accounts		999999999
INT	G/L	General ledger G/L accounts		999999999
INT	MAT	Material management accounts		999999999
INT	PL	P&L accounts		999999999
INT	RECN	Recon. Account ready for input		999999999

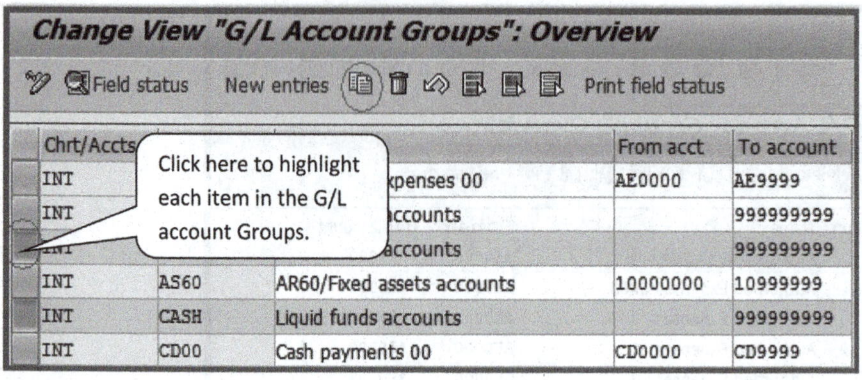

Change View "G/L Account Groups": Overview

⟍⟋ Field status   New entries 📄 🗑 ⬧ 🗐 🗐 🗐   Print field status

Chrt/Accts			From acct	To account
INT		xpenses 00	AE0000	AE9999
INT		ccounts		999999999
INT		ccounts		999999999
INT	AS60	AR60/Fixed assets accounts	10000000	10999999
INT	CASH	Liquid funds accounts		999999999
INT	CD00	Cash payments 00	CD0000	CD9999

[Callout: Click here to highlight each item in the G/L account Groups.]

Figure 2-9. *List of chart of accounts to select from*

■ **Note**   There is no restriction on the chart of accounts you can use. We use the INT charts of accounts in this activity, because we believe that these charts of accounts are sufficient for this purpose.

Click on each object you want to copy on the screen using the items in Table 2-1 as your model to select or highlight them. You will notice that the selected items will turn yellow. Click the Copy 📄 button at the top of the screen to copy the selected charts of accounts from the list. The system will copy the specified charts of accounts INT and ask you to ☑ Specify target entries on the status bar at the bottom of the screen. Modify the copied chart of accounts by changing the content of Chrt/Accts fields from INT to your own chart of accounts that you defined earlier. This activity uses the CA90 chart of accounts, as shown in Figure 2-10.

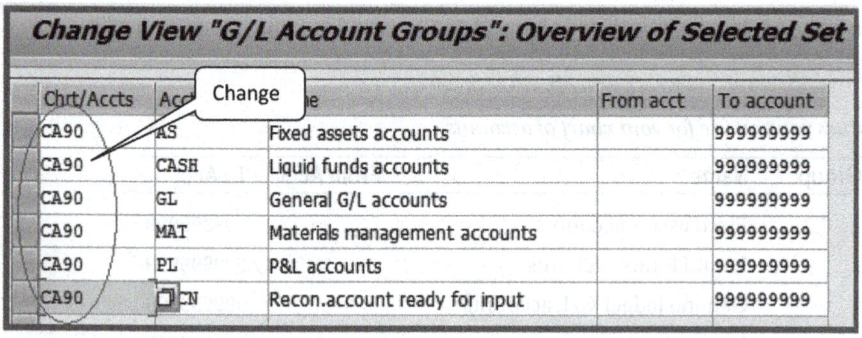

Change View "G/L Account Groups": Overview of Selected Set

Chrt/Accts	Acc	ie	From acct	To account
CA90	AS	Fixed assets accounts		999999999
CA90	CASH	Liquid funds accounts		999999999
CA90	GL	General G/L accounts		999999999
CA90	MAT	Materials management accounts		999999999
CA90	PL	P&L accounts		999999999
CA90	☐CN	Recon.account ready for input		999999999

[Callout: Change]

Figure 2-10. *Updated chart of accounts list*

Once you have changed the chart of accounts in Chrt/Accts from INT to your chart of accounts, click Enter ✅ at the top of the screen to confirm your entries and save 🖫 your work.

The final step in this activity is to define the retained earnings account. It will allow the system to transfer the net profit or loss in the P&L account at the end of the year to the balance sheet. Considering that the P&L account group is defined in the chart of accounts, it is important to also define a retained earnings account separately in order to allow profit or loss at the end of the year to be carried forward to the balance sheet as retained earnings or loss. Click the Back ⬅ button on the top-left side of the screen to return to the tree structure. From there, you will choose the next task in your configuration (Define Retained Earnings Account). You can also use the menu path described in the following section.

Define Retained Earnings Account

In accounting, a portion of the profits is held back at the end of a fiscal year as retained earnings (net profit) after distributing dividends to the shareholders in proportion to their investment in a corporation. Normally, the net profit or net loss figure is carried forward to retained earnings on the balance sheet. For example, Figure 2-11 shows that the retained earnings of $300 on the income statement is carried forward to the balance sheet.

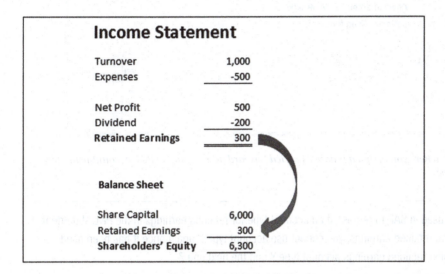

Income Statement

Turnover	1,000
Expenses	-500
Net Profit	500
Dividend	-200
Retained Earnings	300
Balance Sheet	
Share Capital	6,000
Retained Earnings	300
Shareholders' Equity	6,300

Figure 2-11. *Illustration of retained earnings on the income statement and balance sheet*

The amount carried forward is either added to the shareholders' equity, if profit is realized, or deducted from the shareholders' equity, if a loss is incurred. This indicates the profit position of a corporation.

When you're customizing, retained earnings are assigned to the profit and loss (P&L) statement account type defined in the chart of accounts area of the P&L account. At the end of the year the system will automatically carry forward the balance of the P&L account to the retained earnings account. To define retained earnings in SAP R/3, follow this menu path: IMG: Financial Accounting (New) ➤ General Ledger Accounting (New) ➤ Master Data ➤ G/L Accounts ➤ Preparations ➤ Define Retained Earnings Account. Or you can use the transaction code OB53.

The Enter Chart of Accounts dialog box pops up. Enter your chart of accounts code in the Chart of Accounts field. Then click the Enter ☑ button to call up the Maintain FI Configuration: Automatic Posting – Accounts screen (Figure 2-12), where you assign the account type for retained earnings to the G/L account in your chart of accounts. This account assignment will allow the system to use the automatic function to carry forward retained earnings to the balance sheet. A typical account type commonly used in SAP R/3 is X. If you have more than one retained earnings to enter in the chart of accounts in the P&L Statement fields in your chart of accounts, you can use account types Y and Z to add additional retained earnings in your chart of accounts. This activity uses X for the P&L account type and CA90 for the chart of accounts, since we are only looking at one retained earnings.

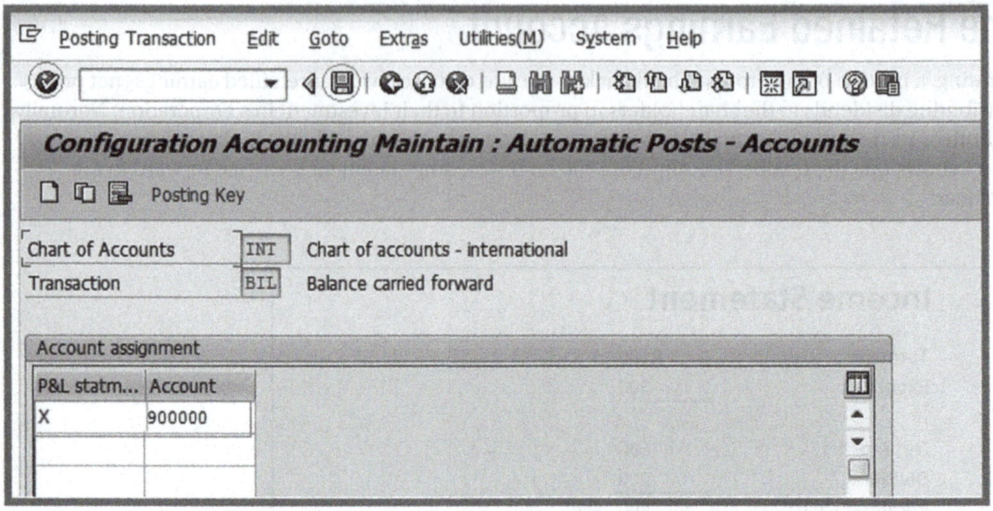

Figure 2-12. *The screen where you assign a balance carried forward account to the P&L account using the appropriate account type*

■ **Note** X is a symbol used in SAP to represent an account type for retained earnings in the P&L statement. If you have more than one retained earnings, you cannot use account type X again once it has been used. You have to assign the next retained earnings account type Y and the next one Z.

Enter the account type in the P&L statement field and the appropriate G/L account in the Account field. This example uses X as the account type and 900000 as the G/L account. Click Enter ✅ at the top of the screen to accept your entries.

■ **Note** Since you have not created a G/L account for retained earnings, the system will issue a warning message on the status bar that says ⚠ Account 900000 not created in chart of accounts CA90. Click the Enter button twice or press the Enter button on your keyboard twice. The system will accept your G/L account temporarily to allow you to continue customizing. In Chapter 5, you will learn how to create G/L accounts.

Finally, save 💾 your retained earnings. The system will notify you that ☑ Changes have been made on the status bar at the bottom of the screen.

Summary

This chapter explained what a chart of accounts is and how you define one. You also learned how to create a chart of accounts, which will serve as the structure for G/L accounts that you create in Chapter 5. You learned how to assign the chart of accounts you created to company codes. In order to complete this activity, you copied account groups for the INT (international) chart of accounts, which you then modified to meet your needs. Finally, you learned how to define a retained earnings account and an accounts type, which you assigned to your P&L accounts. This enables the system to automatically transfer the net profit or net loss after the distribution of dividends to the balance sheet as retained earnings.

The next chapter looks at the importance of document control in SAP ERP and explains how it affects the documents posted in the system.

CHAPTER 3

■ ■ ■

Document Control

In this chapter, you will be looking at the purpose of document control, the application of important document types, and the importance of posting keys in SAP ERP.

At the end of this chapter, you will be able to:

- Explain what document control is

- Define number ranges

- Define field status variants

Document Control

Hundreds of documents are created by companies as a result of transactions arising from business operations. To manage documents posted in the SAP system, it is important that they are categorized and stored sequentially for easy retrieval. Once a transaction is posted, the system generates a document, assigns a document number to the generated document, and saves the generated document in the system.

Every posting in the SAP system generates a document, and the document remains open until it is cleared and archived. For example, when an invoice is posted in the system, the system generates a document and assigns a document number. The invoice remains in the system as an open item. When payment is received for the invoice, the amount received is entered into the system and cleared with the outstanding invoice.

As mentioned earlier, hundreds of transactions are posted in the ERP system and identifying a document among hundreds of documents may become difficult. SAP uses a document-control technique that allows the system to structure document storage in a systematic manner using the document number, company code, and fiscal year.

The document number assigned to a document is obtained from the number range intervals that you will define later in this activity for your company code and your company fiscal year. Hence a document can only be identified in SAP ERP using the following items:

- **Document number**: This is a unique number that is assigned to a document automatically by the system during document posting or manually by the user during data input.

- **Company code**: This is your company's identification code.

- **Fiscal year**: This is your company's accounting year code. This is usually a 12-month period.

During document entry the user must specify the appropriate control keys for each document posted in the system. Every document in SAP ERP is controlled by two important keys:

- Document type

- Posting key

Document Type

Document type plays a very important role in SAP ERP and is defined by two-character values. This two-character key distinguishes the business transaction to be posted, such as vendor invoice, customer invoice, vendor invoice payment, and so on. It also determines document storage and the account to be posted. For example, the document type DR indicates a customer invoice posted to a customer account. Figure 3-1 lists some of the important document types. The importance of the document type is that it determines documents to be posted, the document storage type, and the account type to be posted.

Document Types	
KR	Vendor Invoice
KZ	Vendor Invoice Payment
KG	Vendor Credit Memo
DR	Customer Invoice
DZ	Customer Invoice Payment
DG	Customer Credit Memo
AB	Accounting Document
SA	G/L Account Document

Figure 3-1. *Important document types in SAP R/3*

Document types are defined at the global level, which makes them available to all company codes within the client. Document types are used to control different business transactions in SAP ERP. Document type controls the following:

- Which business transactions are to be posted. The importance of this is that it is easier to display line items based on the type of business transactions involved.

- Posting to account types when you assign appropriate document types to business transactions. For example, the document type DR will post to a customer account; KR will post to a vendor account; and so on. During document posting, you enter the document type in the document header field. This enables the system to differentiate between accounts to be posted.

- The number ranges for document numbers. The system assigns a number range to a document during posting, using the number range you created. The number range allows the system to store documents in the system based on similar number ranges. Number ranges therefore control document storage in the system.

> ■ **Note** SAP comes with standard document types, which you can use as your document types. Some of the standard document types delivered by SAP are listed in Figure 3-1. You can also create your own document types, but it's better to copy the standard document types supplied by SAP instead of creating your own document types from scratch. The reason is that when you create your own document types, you also need to make modifications to the standard table supplied by SAP, which can be time consuming.

You have two options when defining a document number range in SAP ERP:

> *Up to a future fiscal year*: You define a large number range that the system assigns to documents systematically as a document number over one fiscal year. The system chooses the number from the number range that comes up next until the number range is finished. This method has the drawback of running out of numbers once the entire number range is used.

> *Each fiscal year*: You define a number range for each year. You can define number ranges for future years in advance. So at the beginning of next year, the system starts from the first number in the number range you defined for that year. The advantage of this method is that the number range is always sufficient.

Posting Key

Posting keys are defined by a two-digit number. They control the structure of line item entries in SAP ERP. Posting keys are defined at the client level, which makes them accessible to all company codes in the system. (Put another way, all company codes in the system within the same client can use the same posting keys simultaneously.) The importance of the posting key is that it determines the account type (that is,, if the account type is debit or credit) and the screen layout in SAP ERP. In order for the system to determine how an item is posted in the system, a posting key is entered during data entry. The posting key controls the following:

- The account to be posted
- Whether the line item should be posted as a debit or a credit
- How data you entered in the system is updated

SAP comes with predefined posting keys. Some important posting keys with their default posting key values are listed in Figure 3-2.

	Debit	Credit
GL Transaction	40	50
Customer Invoice	01	50
Vendor Invoice	40	31

Figure 3-2. *Important posting keys*

Defining Number Ranges

Problem: *You are to demonstrate to FI junior consultants how to define and copy number ranges for document postings.*

A document in SAP ERP is assigned a unique number from a predefined number range. You define a number range in a sequential order and assign it to a two-character document type during document-range customizing. You can define number ranges in two ways in SAP ERP: by creating your own number ranges or by copying the standard number ranges supplied in the system.

▩ **Note**   A document type can be represented by numbers or characters, or it can be alphanumeric.

The number ranges you define in this activity will be assigned automatically to documents by the system during document posting. To get to the screen where you define number ranges, use this menu path: IMG: Financial Accounting (New) ➤ Financial Accounting Global Settings (New) ➤ Document ➤ Document Number Ranges ➤ Documents in Entry View ➤ Define Document Number Ranges for Entry View. Or you can use transaction code FBN1.

The Number Ranges for Accounting Documents screen is displayed (Figure 3-3). This screen is where you create the number ranges for your company code. Enter your company's four-digit company code in the company code field on the screen, shown circled in red. In this activity, the company code is C900.

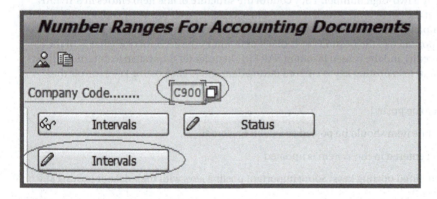

Figure 3-3. *Number ranges for an accounting document*

To maintain number ranges for your company code, click the ⌇ Intervals button circled in red on the screen in Figure 3-3. This will display the Maintain Number Range Intervals screen, where you will create your number ranges. Notice that the input fields on the Maintain Number Range Intervals screen are inactive. Click the ▨ Interval button at the top-left side of the screen to activate the screen input fields for number intervals insertion. Now update the following fields on the Insert Interval screen to match those in Figure 3-4.

No: This is the field where you enter your number range identifier. For example, you can start with 01, 02, and so on. These numbers allow you to define your number ranges in a systematic manner.

Year: The year you enter determines the validity of your number range. It is important that you include the current year in your number range. This enables the system to assign a number range from the lower limit upward for each fiscal year automatically. The advantage of this method is that the number range is always sufficient. On the other hand, if you want the system to use a number range up to a future fiscal year, enter **9999** in the year field. The system will always use the next available number from the predefined number range.

From number: This is the lower limit for your number range intervals (that is, the starting point of your number range). You can enter up to 10 numbers in this field. For example, 010000000.

To number: This is the upper limit for your number range intervals (that is, where your number range ends). You can enter up to 10 numbers in this field. For example, 01999999999.

Current number: No entry is needed in this field. This field shows the current number range that has been assigned by the system. During configuration, this figure always defaults to 0.

Ext: When this checkbox indicator is selected, the system will allow the users to assign external numbers to documents during posting. If the checkbox is blank, the system will assign numbers to documents automatically from the number range intervals you specify here.

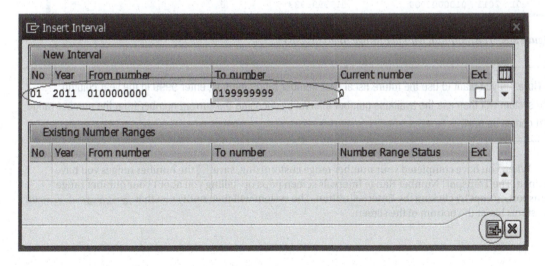

Figure 3-4. *Specification of number range intervals*

Click the Insert 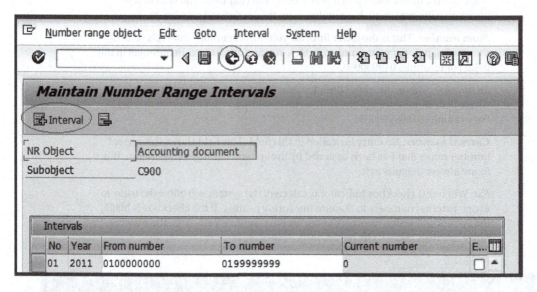 button circled in red on the bottom-right side of the screen in Figure 3-4 or press Enter on your keyboard. The system will accept your number range specification. The number range intervals you specified here will be assigned to documents during document posting by the user. In the example in Figure 3-4, we used 01 as the number range identifier, 2011 as the year, and 0100000000–0199999999 as the number range interval.

As part of this exercise, continue to specify number range intervals for the years 2012, 2013, 2014, 2015, 2016, 2017, and 2018. To do this, click Interval at the top-left side of the screen to specify the number range for each year individually (Figure 3-5).

Figure 3-5. *The Maintain Number Range Intervals page*

■ **Note**   If you want to use the future fiscal year number range method, enter **9999** in the year column. The system will then use the available number interval by choosing the current number from the number range that comes up next.

When you have completed your number range customizing, save 🖫 the number ranges you have defined. The Transport Number Range Intervals screen pops up, telling you about your number range transport. Accept by clicking the Enter ✔ button. The system will then notify you that ☑ The changes were saved on the status bar at the bottom of the screen.

How to Display Number Intervals

To display the number range intervals you have created—to see what you have done—click the Back 🌐 button at the top-left side of the screen to return to the previous screen (Number Ranges for Accounting Documents). Click the [𝒮 Intervals] button on the screen. Your number ranges will be displayed, as shown in Figure 3-6.

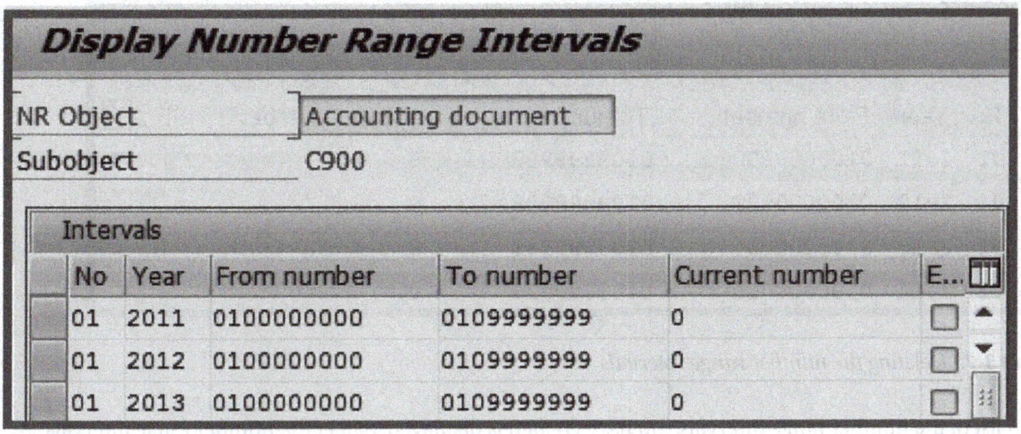

Display Number Range Intervals

NR Object	Accounting document
Subobject	C900

Intervals

	No	Year	From number	To number	Current number	E...
	01	2011	0100000000	0109999999	0	☐
	01	2012	0100000000	0109999999	0	☐
	01	2013	0100000000	0109999999	0	☐

Figure 3-6. *The Display Number Range Intervals page*

How to Delete Number Range Intervals

Before you can look at how to copy predefined number ranges provided by SAP in the system, you have to first delete the number ranges you just created. That's because the system will not allow you to create an existing number range in the system. So delete the number ranges you created for the years 2011, 2012, 2013, 2014, 2015, 2016, 2017, and 2018.

On the Display Number Range Interval screen in Figure 3-6, click the Back 🌐 button at the top-right side of the screen to return to the Number Ranges for Accounting Documents screen.

The system will automatically default to your company code in the Company Code field. Otherwise, enter the company code you desire in the company code field manually and click the [✎ Intervals] button to call up the number intervals you created earlier. The Maintain Number Range Intervals screen is displayed (Figure 3-7).

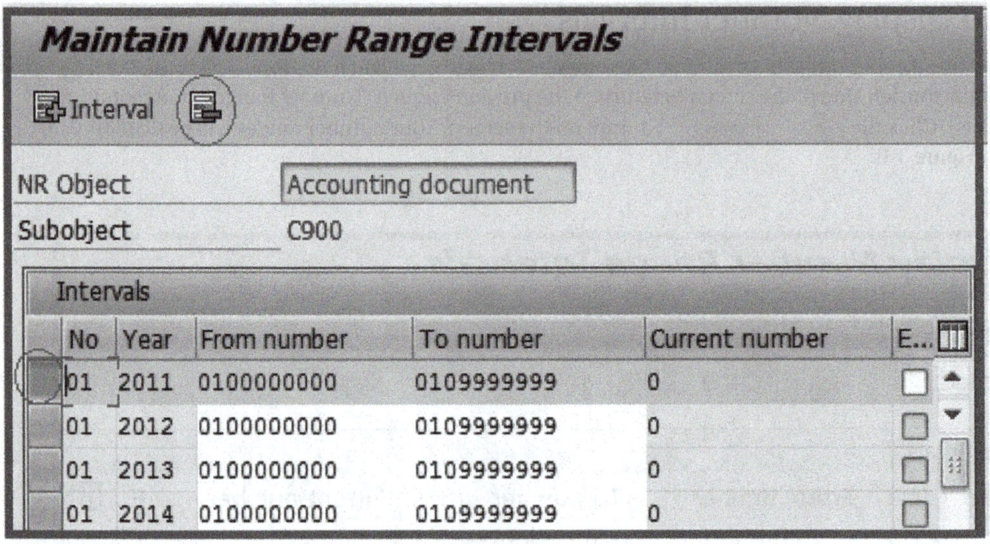

Maintain Number Range Intervals

Figure 3-7. Deleting the number range intervals

A list of the number range intervals you have created is displayed. Select the number range intervals that you want to delete. For this activity, select all the displayed number range intervals—2011, 2012, 2013, 2014, 2015, 2016, 2017, and 2018. Click the Delete 🗑 button at the top of the screen to delete them.

After deleting all the displayed number range intervals, notice that the Maintain Number Range Intervals screen becomes blank and the fields on the screen become inactive, which indicates you cannot enter values into these fields. Click the Save 💾 button to complete the task.

How to Copy Document Number Ranges

> *Problem: You need to copy the standard number range intervals from the company code 1000 and modify them to meet your number range intervals requirement.*

Now let's take a look at how to copy standard number range intervals from a predefined company code and then modify them to meet your requirements. In this case, we'll use 1000, which is supplied by SAP in the system. This step is optional, but we'll go through it so you know how to copy predefined number ranges.

Copied number range intervals work exactly the same way as number range intervals that you create. The advantage of copying number range intervals is that it is easier and quicker to copy multiple number ranges simultaneously, instead of having to create each individual fiscal year number ranges. To go to the screen where you define document number range intervals, follow this menu path: IMG: Financial Accounting (New) ➤ Financial Accounting Global Settings (New) ➤ Document ➤ Document Number Ranges ➤ Documents in Entry View ➤ Define Document Number Ranges for Entry View. Or, you can use the transaction code FBN1.

The Number Ranges for Accounting Documents screen is displayed (see Figure 3-3 earlier in the chapter). This is where you copy the predefined number range intervals from another company. Enter the company code for which you want to copy number ranges in the company code field, and click the Copy 📋 button at the top right of the screen. The Copy: Company Code dialog box pops up (Figure 3-8). As you can see, in this activity we copied company code 1000 containing predefined number ranges. It is not necessary that you copy company code 1000 number ranges. This is purely a matter of choice. But we recommend that you copy one of the following company codes: 0001, 1000, 2000, or 3000. These are some of the standard company codes with predefined number ranges supplied by SAP. On the Copy: Company Code screen, you specify both the company code from which you want to copy the number ranges and your company code.

Figure 3-8. *The copy company code number range intervals*

The system will default to the source company code in the From field. Enter your company code in the To field. Since you are copying company code 1000's number range intervals to your company code C900, click the Copy 📑 button circled in red at the bottom of the Copy: Company screen. The system will copy the number range intervals from company code 1000 to company code C900 and issue a notification on the status bar as follows: ☑ CoCode 1000 was copied to C900 .

You can display the number ranges you have just copied by clicking the &r Intervals button

Understand and Manage Field Status Variants

Field status variants are variants that hold the *Field Status Groups* in SAP R/3. A Field Status Group defines the screen layout for a general ledger account entry and controls document creation within a company code. Based on your specification, the Field Status Groups determine which fields accept input during document entry, as well as whether a field should be inactive, be required, or be optional.

In SAP R/3, field statuses are defined as global settings and are assigned Field Status Groups. Field status variants are independent of company codes (that is, they are available to all company codes in the client), because they are created at the client level. A Field Status Group is entered in the company code section of the GL accounts in the G/L account master records during the creation of a G/L account.

The Field Status Group you define controls the appearance of certain data entry fields in the data screen for G/L accounts.

■ **Note** It best to simply copy the standard field status variants supplied by SAP.

Define Field Status Variants

Problem: Copy the predefined field status variants for company code 1000 supplied by the system and modify them to meet your requirements.

In SAP R/3, several company codes can use the same field status groups. As part of customizing field status variants, you can specify field status variants and assign your company code to the field status variant you have defined. To proceed to the screen where you define field status variants, follow the menu path: Financial Accounting (New) ➤ Financial Accounting Global Settings (New) ➤ Ledgers ➤ Fields ➤ Define Field Status Variants. You can use the transaction code OBC4 instead, if you want.

The Change View "Field Status Variants": Overview screen is displayed (Figure 3-9). This screen is where you maintain your field status variant and assign field status groups to it.

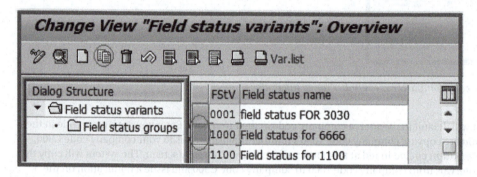

Figure 3-9. Copying the field status variants

Search for field status variant 1000, which is the one we'll use to copy. Then select it and copy it. When you copy the field status variants supplied by the system, you also copy any associated tables and parameters.

■ **Note**   Field status variant 1000 is simply the one we are using for this activity, but you can copy any field status variant from the list of variants supplied by SAP, because trying to create your own field status variant can be very difficult and time consuming. For example, you can copy field status variant 0001, 2000, and so on and get the same result.

Click the Copy ▦ icon circled in red at the top of the screen. The Change View "Field Status Variants": Overview of Selected Set screen is displayed (Figure 3-10) showing the field status variants you have copied.

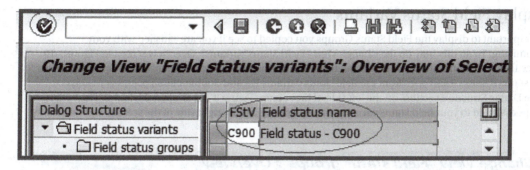

Figure 3-10. Editing the field status variants

Change the content of the following fields:

> *FStV*: Enter your field status variant key into this field. You can enter up to four characters as your key. Since you have copied the field status variant from company code 1000, change the field status variant 1000 to your own field status variant identifier of C900.

> *Field status name*: This field allows you to provide a short description or a name for your field status variant. Replace the content of this field with your own field status variant description, for example **Field Status Variant – C900**.

■ **Tip**   It is advisable to use your company code as your field status variant.

Click the Enter ⊘ button at the top of the screen or press Enter on your keyboard for the system to accept your entries. A dialog box—Specify Object to Be Copied—pops up, telling you the number of entries and dependent entries that you are about to copy. You can either copy the entry with dependent entries (that is, the field status variant with the field status groups it holds) or copy just the entry itself without dependent entries. (If you take the latter approach, you will have to define the dependent entries for your field status variants; otherwise, your field status variant may not work properly.) If you want to copy the field status variants with dependent entries, click the Copy All button on the screen. If you don't want to copy dependent entries with the field status variants, click the Only Copy Entry button on the screen. In this activity, the object we are copying includes dependent entries. Click the [copy all] button to copy the object with all its dependent entries. The system will issue an Information screen telling you the number of dependent entries copied. Click the Enter ✔ button at the bottom of the Information screen or press Enter on your keyboard to confirm that you are satisfied with the copied entries. Then click the Save 💾 button to save your field status variant.

Display Field Status Variants

It is important to display the Field Status Groups you copied to see if you are satisfied with your customizing. To do this, stay on the Change View "Field Status Variants": Overview screen in Figure 3-10. Notice that your field status variant is at the top of the list displayed on the screen. Select or highlight your field status C900 Field status - C900 from the field status variants list and double-click ☐ Field status groups in the Dialog Structure section, on the left side of the screen (Figure 3-11) to open the folder. The field status groups assigned to your field status variant will be displayed on the right side of the screen.

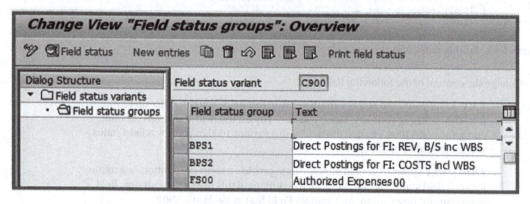

Figure 3-11. *The Field Status Groups you copied are displayed*

Assign Company Code to Field Status Variants

As mentioned earlier, field status variants are company code-independent since they are created at the global level. The field variant you just defined—C900—can be assigned to more than one company code. The next step in this activity is to assign the field status variant to your company code. The field status variant assigned to your company code will control the appearance of the data entry field in the data screen. To go to the screen where you can assign a field status variant to your company code, follow the menu path: IMG: Financial Accounting (New) ➤ Financial Accounting Global Settings (New) ➤ Ledgers ➤ Fields ➤ Assign Company Code to Field Status Variants. You can use the transaction code OBC5 if you prefer.

The Change View "Assign Company Code ➤ Field Status Variant" Overview screen is displayed (Figure 3-12) with list of company codes. Search for your company code by clicking the 🖩 Position... button at the bottom of the screen.

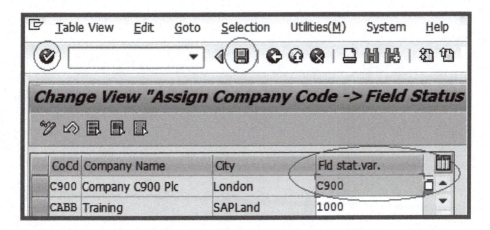

Figure 3-12. *Assigning a company code to a field status variant*

Assign your field status variant to your company code. In this activity, we used C900. Save ⊞ your company code assignment. The system will notify you that ☑ Data was saved at the bottom of the screen on the status bar.

Summary

This chapter explained document control by looking at document type and posting keys and their functions in SAP ERP. As part of the customizing exercise, you learned how to create number ranges, how to display the number ranges you created, and how to delete a number range. You also learned how to copy predefined number ranges provided by SAP in the system. You also learned the importance of field status variants. Finally, you learned how to create your own field status variants by copying predefined field status variants provided by SAP and learned how to assign field status variants you created to your company code.

Chapter 4 looks at how to define tolerance groups for GL accounts and define employee tolerance groups. Chapter 4 also walks through the various steps involved in customizing tolerance groups by first defining them and then assigning users to them to create accounts for clearing differences.

CHAPTER 4

■ ■ ■

Defining Tolerance Groups for G/L Accounts and Employees

In this chapter, you will learn the purpose of tolerance groups and how to define them in SAP R/3. At the end of this chapter, you will be able to:

- Define tolerance groups for G/L accounts
- Define tolerance groups for employees
- Define tolerance groups for employees with a group key
- Assign users to tolerance groups

Tolerance Groups

Tolerance groups determine limits upon which acceptable payment differences are based. During document posting, the system will check for any difference and match it against the defined limits to determine if the difference is within the specified limits and automatically post the differences to a predefined account. If the difference is outside the set limit, the system will automatically reject the posting.

It is a normal business practice for payment differences to occur in a business transaction. The bottom line here is, what is the business willing to accept as an acceptable payment difference for a given business transaction? This occurs when an invoice amount entered in the system is different from the actual amount received to clear the outstanding invoice. For example, an outstanding invoice amount is $1,000 and the amount paid to clear the outstanding invoice is $950, leaving you with a difference of $50. If the acceptable limit for your tolerance groups is $45, the system will reject your posting because the difference is above the acceptable limit. On the other hand, if the payment difference is $45 or less, the system will accept your posting and post the difference to a specified predefined account, because the difference is within the defined acceptable limit.

There are several reasons why differences occur. A typical example is as a result of goods damaged on transit that reduce the value of the goods delivered. This brings up the concept of *materiality*, which is what a business considers to be material or significant differences that cannot be overlooked or ignored. To enable the system to perform limit checks, your company must define an acceptable payment difference.

Tolerances are necessary mainly for control purposes. In SAP ERP, maximum amounts deemed acceptable by a business are defined in tolerances in a company code and assigned to a tolerance group. Tolerances dictate payment difference authorizations (that is, tolerances are company code specific and determine the amount accounting clerks are permitted to post to the system per transaction for invoice clearing). Tolerances also allow you to specify settings that control the discounts that accounting clerks can grant per invoice as well as any tolerances over payment.

The advantage of using tolerances is that during posting, the system will automatically determine if payment differences are within the acceptable limits you defined. If a payment difference is within the payment difference limit, the system will accept the posting. If a payment difference posting exceeds the specified limit, the system will reject the posting. Tolerances reduce potential posting errors made by accounting clerks during document entry.

Three tolerances are represented in SAP ERP; we will look at each in turn:

- Tolerance groups for G/L accounts
- Tolerance groups for employees
- Tolerances for customers/vendors (discussed in Chapter 14)

The three levels of tolerance represented in SAP R/3 are depicted in Figure 4-1.

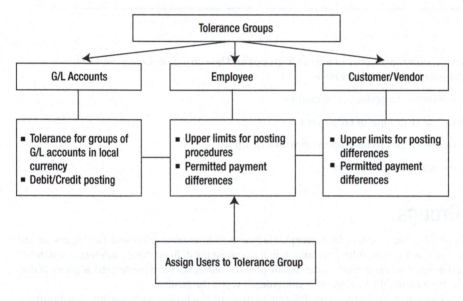

Figure 4-1. *The three levels of tolerance groups*

Define Tolerance Groups for G/L Accounts

Tolerance groups for G/L accounts define the limits within which credit and debit differences in local currencies are considered acceptable. The accounts' differences are posted automatically during G/L account clearing. The tolerance groups defined for G/L accounts in this activity are eventually assigned to the general ledger account's master record. During the account-clearing process, the system checks the tolerance groups to ascertain if the differences are within acceptable limits, as specified by your settings, and automatically posts the differences, if any, to the predefined accounts.

> **Problem:** *The accounts team at company C900 plc wants you to define acceptable payment differences, which will then be posted automatically to appropriate predefined accounts during document posting.*

In this activity, you will be looking at the two steps involved in customizing tolerance groups for G/L accounts. You will learn how to customize default tolerance groups for G/L accounts and how to assign a group to the tolerance groups you defined for your G/L accounts.

The two tolerance groups defined in the configuration of tolerance for groups are as follows:

- **Default Tolerance Group.** This is a G/L tolerance *without* a tolerance group. You define this by leaving the Tolgroup blank (this is a default tolerance group and it is valid for all G/L tolerance groups in the system).

- **Tolerance Group.** As opposed to default tolerance groups, this is a G/L tolerance *with* a tolerance group. Here, you assign a specific tolerance group to the G/L tolerance. Unlike the G/L tolerance *without* a tolerance group, this tolerance group is valid only for the specified G/L tolerance groups. For example, if accounting clerks in group A are assigned to certain G/L tolerances, the system will not allow accounting clerks in group B to post to these G/L accounts during document entry.

Go to the screen where you will first define the default tolerance group by following this menu path: IMG: Financial Accounting (New) ➤ General Ledger Accounting (New) ➤ Business Transactions ➤ Open Item Clearing ➤ Clearing Differences ➤ Define Tolerance Groups for G/L Accounts. You can also use the transaction code OBA0.

The Change View "Tolerances for Groups of G/L Accounts in Local Currency": Overview screen appears (Figure 4-2).

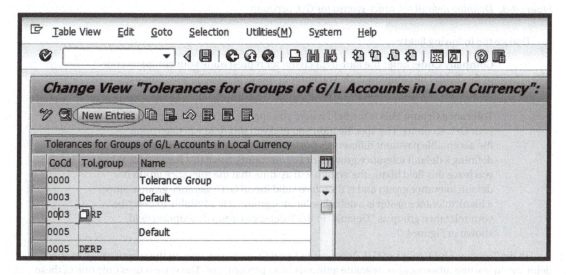

Figure 4-2. *Here is where you define tolerance groups for G/L accounts*

A list of existing tolerance groups is displayed on the screen. To create a default tolerance group, click New Entries on the top-left side of the screen. The New Entries: Details of Added Entries screen is displayed (Figure 4-3). This screen is where you specify tolerances for groups of G/L accounts.

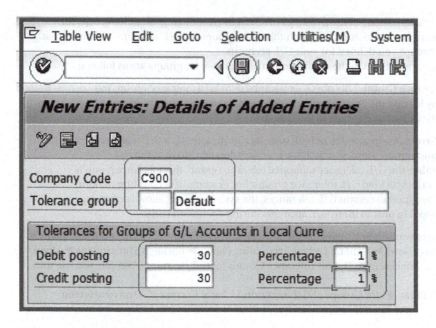

Figure 4-3. Defining default tolerance groups for G/L accounts

Update the following fields:

Company Code: Enter the four-digit character representing your company code in this field. The company code you enter in this field must be your company code or the company code you want to assign to your tolerance group.

Tolerance Group: This is the field where you specify the tolerance group for your G/L accounts. The specification you make in this field will determine the acceptable payment differences posted to the G/L accounts. Since you are defining a default tolerance groups for G/L accounts, leave this field blank. When you leave this field blank, the system will assume that the tolerance group is a default tolerance group and is therefore valid for *all* G/L tolerance groups. Since a blank tolerance group is a default tolerance group, it is advisable to describe your tolerance group as "Default" in the Tolerance Group description field shown in Figure 4-3.

In the Tolerance for Groups of G/L Accounts in Local Currency section on the screen, you can specify debit/credit posting differences as absolute amounts or as percentages. The system uses only one of these specifications, either amount or percentage. During document posting, the system will check the amount and the percentage you specify and automatically use whichever is lower.

After updating the screen in Figure 4-3, click the Enter ✅ button at the top-left corner of the screen to confirm your entries and save 🖫 your tolerance for groups for G/L accounts.

The second step in this activity is to define the G/L tolerances *with* a tolerance group. This is when you assign a group to the G/L tolerance. Only the assigned group can post differences within the acceptable limit in the system. To go to the screen where you will carry out this configuration, click the Back ⬅ button at the top-left of the screen to return to the previous screen (Change View "Tolerances for Groups of G/L Accounts in Local Currency"), shown in Figure 4-2. You will define your tolerance there.

On the Change View "Tolerances for Groups of G/L Accounts in Local Currency:" Overview screen, click the [New Entries] button at the top of the screen. The New Entries: Details of Added Entries screen (Figure 4-3) is displayed. Update the following fields to match those in Figure 4-4:

Company Code: Enter the four-digit company code that you want to apply to your tolerance group in this field.

Tolerance Group: Enter a four-digit character of your choice as the tolerance group key in this field. You can create as many tolerance groups as required by your company. The tolerance group key you define here will be assigned to a username. A username could be referred to as the user logon ID assigned to the user. In this activity, we used CLK1 as the tolerance group (Figure 4-4).

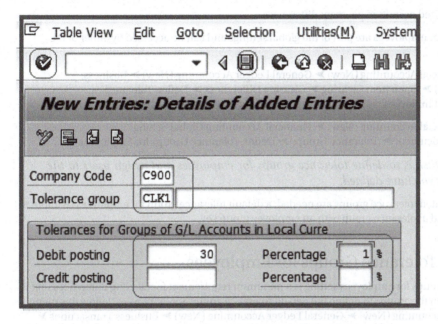

Figure 4-4. *Defining tolerance groups for G/L accounts with tolerence group*

■ **Note**   The relationship of the user ID and the tolerance group is a many-to-one relationship. That means that several user logon IDs can be assigned to the same tolerance group, but a user logon ID can be assigned to only one tolerance group.

In the Tolerance for Groups of G/L Accounts in Local Currency section of the screen, specify the debit/credit postings (in amounts and in percentages) in the appropriate fields.

Click the Save button 🖫 to save your tolerance group for G/L accounts.

The next step is to define tolerance groups for employees. In this activity, you will define the limits that the system uses to determine the amount per document (invoice amount) and per open items (outstanding balance) that a user is permitted to post to the system.

Define Tolerance Groups for Employees

Tolerance groups set for employees define what an employee is permitted to post to the system. In order for the system to automatically determine the amount an employee can post to the system per document and per open items, you need to specify the following settings:

- The maximum amount per document the employee is permitted to post

- The maximum amount the employee can enter in the system per open item in customer/vendor account item

- The maximum cash discount per line item that the employee is permitted to grant to a customer or vendor

- The authorized permitted payment differences

Tolerance groups for employees are part of the global settings and can be accessed by either of the following menu paths:

- IMG: Financial Accounting (New) ➤ General Ledger Accounting (New) ➤ Business Transaction ➤ Open Item Clearing ➤ Clearing Differences ➤ Define Tolerance Groups for Employees

- IMG: Financial Accounting (New) ➤ Financial Accounting Global Settings (New) ➤ Document ➤ Tolerance Groups ➤ Define Tolerance Groups for Employees

Problem: *Your task is to define tolerance groups for employees and assign users to the tolerance groups you have defined.*

Two employee-related tolerance groups are needed: a default tolerance group for employees (without a tolerance group key) and a tolerance group with an employee group key.

Define Default Tolerance Groups for Employees

The default tolerance groups for employees setting is a minimum requirement for clearing differences that is valid for *all* employees in the group. To define the default tolerance groups for employees, follow this menu path: IMG: Financial Accounting (New) ➤ General Ledger Accounting (New) ➤ Business Transactions ➤ Open Item Clearing ➤ Clearing Differences ➤ Define Tolerance Groups for Employees. Or use the transaction code OBA4.

The Change View "FI Tolerance Groups For Users": Overview screen is displayed. On the top-left side of the screen, click the `New Entries` button. You will then go to the screen where you will create default tolerance groups for employees.

In the New Entries: Details of Added Entries screen (Figure 4-5), update the following fields:

>**Group:** Leave this field blank. Leaving it blank tells the system to treat this entry as the default tolerance group. A default tolerance group is a minimum requirement for all employee groups in the system. This is applicable when employees are not assigned to any specific tolerance group.

>**Company Code:** Enter your company code in this field. The company code you enter will serve as the company code for your tolerance groups for employees.

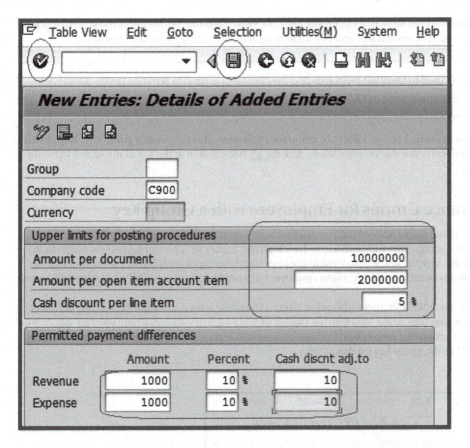

Figure 4-5. *The Group item is blank, which sets it as the default tolerance groups for employees*

In the Upper Limits for Posting Procedures section of this screen, enter the maximum amount an employee can post to the system per document. Fill in the following fields:

- **Amount per Document:** This is the maximum amount per document an employee is authorized to post. It is important to note that an employee will not be able to exceed the amount entered here during document posting.

- **Amount per Open Item Account Item:** This is the maximum amount per open item that the employee can enter in the line item in a vendor/customer account. An employee can post only an amount up to the specified amount made here per open item. The system will reject anything exceeding the specified amount.

- **Cash Discount per Line Item:** This is the maximum cash percentage discount per line item that the employee can grant. When an employee grants a discount during document posting, the system will check to make sure that the discount granted is within acceptable levels, per the line item you define here.

In the Permitted Payment Differences section of this screen, specify the Amount, Percentage, and Cash Discount Adjustment in the Revenue/Expenses fields as the permitted payment differences. During payment difference posting, the system will check the amount against the percentage and automatically use whichever is less.

After updating the screen shown in Figure 4-5, click the Enter ✅ button at the top of the screen or press Enter on your keyboard. The system will accept your settings. Finally, save 💾 your configuration.

■ **Note**   The dot (.) is used to separate thousands and the comma (,) is used to separate pence/cents. For example, 190,222.22 is represented in SAP as 190.222,22.

The next step is to create another tolerance group for employees, this time with a group key. To go to the screen where you will carry out this configuration, click the 🌐 Back button at the top of the screen to return to the previous screen.

Define Tolerance Groups for Employees with a Group Key

The group key you define in this activity will be assigned to one or more usernames (logon IDs) in the system for a tolerance group. This will be discussed in detail in Chapter 19. The employees you assign to the tolerance group in this activity will be restricted to the payment differences specified in the tolerance group. In other words, during document posting, these employees will not be able to exceed the permitted payment differences you specify.

On the Change View "FI Tolerance Groups For Users": Overview screen, click the ⎡ New Entries ⎤ button at the top of the screen. You'll go to the New Entries: Details of Added Entries screen, where you can specify the settings for tolerance groups for employees. Update the screen in Figure 4-6. Enter a group key in the Group field. We used CLK1 as the group key for this activity.

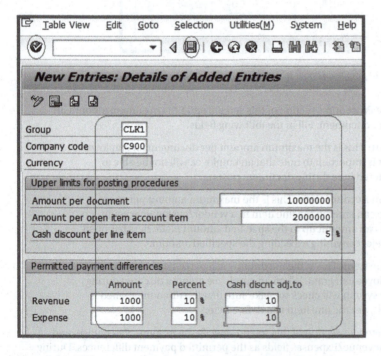

Figure 4-6. *Tolerance groups for employees with a group key*

Click the Enter ✅ button at the top-left side of the screen or press Enter on your keyboard to have the system accept your specifications. Then save 🖫 your configuration.

After you've completed the configuration of tolerance groups for employees, the next step is to assign user IDs to the tolerance groups you just defined.

Assign Users to Tolerance Groups

In this activity, you will assign an employee to a special tolerance group for posting and clearing payment differences. To go to the screen where you will assign employees to a tolerance group, follow this menu path: IMG: Financial Accounting (New) ➤ General Ledger Accounting (New) ➤ Business Transactions ➤ Open Item Clearing ➤ Clearing Differences ➤ Assign Users to Tolerance Groups. Or you can use the transaction code OB57.

The Change View "Assign Users ➤ Tolerance Group": Overview screen is displayed. This screen will display a list of usernames assigned to tolerance groups. To assign a username to a tolerance group, click the New Entries button at the top of the screen. The screen in Figure 4-7 is then displayed.

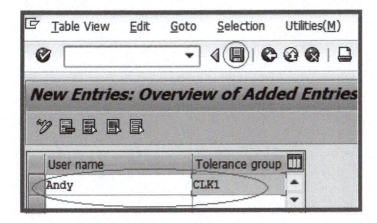

Figure 4-7. Assign users to tolerance groups

Update the following fields on the screen:

> **User Name:** Enter the user ID you want to assign to a tolerance group in this field. The username you enter here is the user's logon ID. This will allow the user to post an amount in the system up to the defined tolerance limit specified in the tolerance group you have assigned to that user.
>
> **Tolerance Group:** Enter the tolerance group key you defined in Figure 4-6. This will allow the user assigned to this tolerance group to post an amount within the tolerance limit defined for this tolerance group.

■ **Note** The username should be your logon user ID. For example, Student1, Student2, Student3, User1, and so on.

After you have assigned a user ID to the tolerance group, click the ⊘ Enter button at the top-right side of the screen or press Enter on your keyboard and save 🖫 your configuration.

Summary

This chapter explained how tolerances serve as control mechanisms in SAP ERP. You looked at the steps involved when creating tolerances. You also looked at how the system controls payment differences through the tolerances you set during the customization process.

We took you through all the customization processes involved in creating tolerance groups for G/L accounts. This included defining the limits within which credit and debit differences in local currencies are considered by the system during posting. You also learned how to customize settings for tolerance groups for employees. You learned how to define default tolerance groups for employees and tolerance groups for employees with a group key.

Finally, as part of the customizing exercise, you learned how to assign users to tolerance groups that you defined.

In the next chapter, you learn what a G/L master record is and how to create G/L accounts in SAP ERP.

CHAPTER 5

■ ■ ■

Creating a General Ledger (G/L)

In this chapter, you learn how to create G/L accounts, use line items, and open item management in G/L accounts.

At the end of this chapter, you will be able to:

- Explain what a general ledger is

- Describe what a master record is

- Create G/L account master records

- Use a template to copy a G/L account

General Ledger

Business transactions are sorted and stored in G/L accounts that apply the double entry principle—dual control (debit and credit). Transactions posted to G/L accounts are classified into assets, liabilities, income, and expenditures, from which financial statements are drawn.

All financial transactions with business partners are posted to sub-ledgers in SAP ERP. Financial transactions are treated in accounting as debit or credit transactions. Several sub-ledgers are created in SAP R/3 to store financial accounting transactions in the system. The summary, or balance of sub-ledgers, is automatically posted in real-time to the reconciliation (general ledger) accounts as debit balance or credit balance by the system. For example, in Figure 5-1, the amounts of 1,500 and 2,000 were posted to Motor Vehicle and the amount of 5,000 was posted to Furniture & Fittings in the sub-ledger accounts. The system automatically posted the balances of both sub-ledgers to the G/L account in real-time.

Sub-ledgers are a subset of the general ledger used for recording individual items and transactions in accounting. Sub-ledgers include individual accounts payable, accounts receivable, assets, and bank account information. They hold accounts payable details such as the vendor's name, number of transactions, dates, discounts, and payment terms Transactions are posted in the system as they arise in the sub-ledger. The summary or balance of sub-ledgers is posted to reconciliation accounts. In other words, balances in the sub-ledger are posted to the reconciliation accounts. The reconciliation accounts hold the balances of sub-ledgers from which a financial statement is drawn. The advantage of a reconciliation account is that it gives you a snapshot of the sub-ledger.

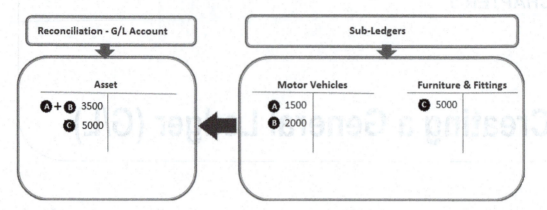

Figure 5-1. *Automatic posting of sub-ledger balances to a reconciliation account*

■ **Note** Reconciliation accounts are G/L accounts that hold sub-ledger balances. Reconciliation accounts could be referred to as G/L accounts containing sub-ledger totals. The system automatically posts all postings to sub-ledgers to G/L reconciliation accounts. Therefore, reconciliation accounts are G/L account summaries of sub-ledgers in SAP R/3. Reconciliation accounts are assigned to business partners in the business partners' master records.

Users don't manually post to reconciliation accounts. The system automatically posts to the reconciliation accounts in real-time.

Next, you need to know what a general ledger master record is and how it controls accounting transactions in the general ledger accounts.

What Is a Master Record?

A *master record* contains vital information held in a business system database that remains relatively unchanged over a long period of time. This is the case when sets of data are commonly accessed, used, and shared by different individuals for different purposes across an organization in order to fulfill business processes in real-time. For example, a vendor's details held in the system may be used by various departments. The sales team needs the vendors' details in order to send them sales offers; the marketing department needs this information to send out marketing promotions; the accounting department needs the information for invoices and other accounting purposes; and so on.

Information that aids efficient business processes and tends not to change frequently (such as a customer/vendor name and address) is held in the system database. The idea behind maintaining a master record is to avoid having to re-enter the same information multiple times, thereby saving input time and avoiding unnecessary waste of system resources and redundancies (to free storage space and improve system speed). It's better to not have to enter or store the same data in the system database several places.

Some typical examples of master data in a SAP R/3 database include customer data, vendor data, bank data, G/L accounts, material data, and so on.

- **Transaction Data:** Data triggered as a result of events arising from day-to-day business transactions. A typical transaction data is time-driven with a numerical value and often refers to one or more objects in the system. Examples of transaction data in SAP R/3 include invoices, payments, credit memos, and goods receipts.

- **Table Data:** Sets of tables containing data about objects, such as payment terms, tolerances, pricing conditions, and so on.

Now that you know what a master record is, let's look at how to create G/L account master records in SAP ERP. A G/L master record contains data relating to a G/L account that remains in the system relatively for a while. The data held in the G/L master record controls the general ledger account behavior. The G/L master record also governs the treatment and posting of accounting transactions to the G/L accounts in the system.

Creating G/L Account Master Records

Various options are available when creating G/L master records in SAP ERP:

- *Create G/L accounts with reference*: This allows you to copy existing G/L accounts from another company code to yours. The company code you are copying the G/L accounts from is referred to as the "source" company code and your company code is the "target" company code. SAP comes with a standard chart of accounts and company codes in the system, along with sets of G/L account master records that can be copied when creating your G/L account master records. The benefit of copying existing G/L account master records is that your G/L account master records will inherit their properties, which saves time.

- *Data transfer workbench*: This is when you transfer G/L account master records from a legacy system. This function is ideal when you want to transfer G/L accounts from another system into SAP.

- *By copying*: The system allows you to copy G/L account master records already in the system. This is possible only when you have an existing chart of accounts that meets your requirements. For example, a chart of accounts that has a structure that matchs your G/L account master record could be copied in this manner.

- *By creating manually*: This is when you have to physically create G/L account master records individually. The drawback to this method is that it is time consuming, especially when you have to create large numbers of G/L accounts.

Let's look at how to create G/L accounts in SAP ERP. In this activity, you will create your G/L accounts manually. This will give you the fundamental understanding of how to create G/L accounts step-by-step. You will also be looking at how to copy G/L accounts using existing G/L accounts as a template.

■ **Note**   All transactions in SAP FI work with G/L accounts. In the remaining chapters in this book, you will be creating G/L accounts, which you will assign to objects in your subsequent configurations.

Problem: *You've been asked to create G/L accounts for the following items:*

- *Office supplies*
- *Misc. office expenses*
- *Sales revenue*
- *Share capital*

Create a G/L Account: Office Supplies

Let's start by creating a G/L account for office supplies. To create your G/L accounts, follow this menu path:
SAP Easy Access: Accounting ➤ Financial Accounting ➤ General Ledger ➤ Master Records ➤ G/L Accounts ➤
Individual Processing ➤ Centrally. Or use the transaction code FS00.

The Edit G/L Account Centrally screen is displayed (Figure 5-2). The G/L accounts you create here are
available to all company codes in the system. This means that all the company codes in the system with the
same operational chart of accounts and same G/L structure can use the same G/L account (that is, several
company codes can use one G/L account).

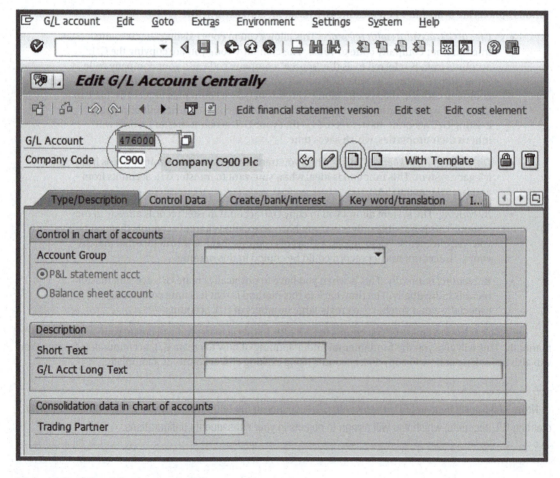

Figure 5-2. Edit a G/L account centrally

Update the following fields:

> **G/L Account:** Every G/L account in SAP ERP must be assigned a number, which serves as the G/L account number. Enter your G/L account number in the G/L Account field. The G/L account number that you enter here is restricted to the length of the G/L account number you specified when customizing the "Create Chart of Accounts" section in Chapter 2. The G/L account number is used to reference the G/L account. See the following note.

> **Company Code:** Every company represented in SAP ERP must be assigned a company code. Company codes are assigned to G/L accounts in the system. Enter your company code in the Company Code field. The company code you enter in this field will allow you to assign a G/L account to your company.

■ **Note**   The number you enter in the G/L Account field must be within the number range intervals you defined for your account group in Chapter 2.

Notice that only the company code and general ledger fields are open for data entry on this screen, while the remaining fields (circled in red) on the screen are inactive. This means the fields are not ready for data input.

■ **Note**   The Edit G/L Accounts Centrally screen has four important buttons that will help you create and navigate your G/L account:

Display 🖉. This button is used to display a G/L account in the system.

Change 🖉. This button is used to change or edit G/L account details.

Create 🗋. This button is used to create a new G/L account.

🗋 With Template   This button allows you to copy an existing G/L account in the system using a template. This can be very handy if you are copying similar G/L accounts, because it allows the system to classify similar G/L accounts into the same account group and number range intervals.

The next step is to update the Control in the Chart of Accounts section of the screen (Figure 5-3). To activate the fields for data input, click the Create 🗋 button on the right side of the screen.

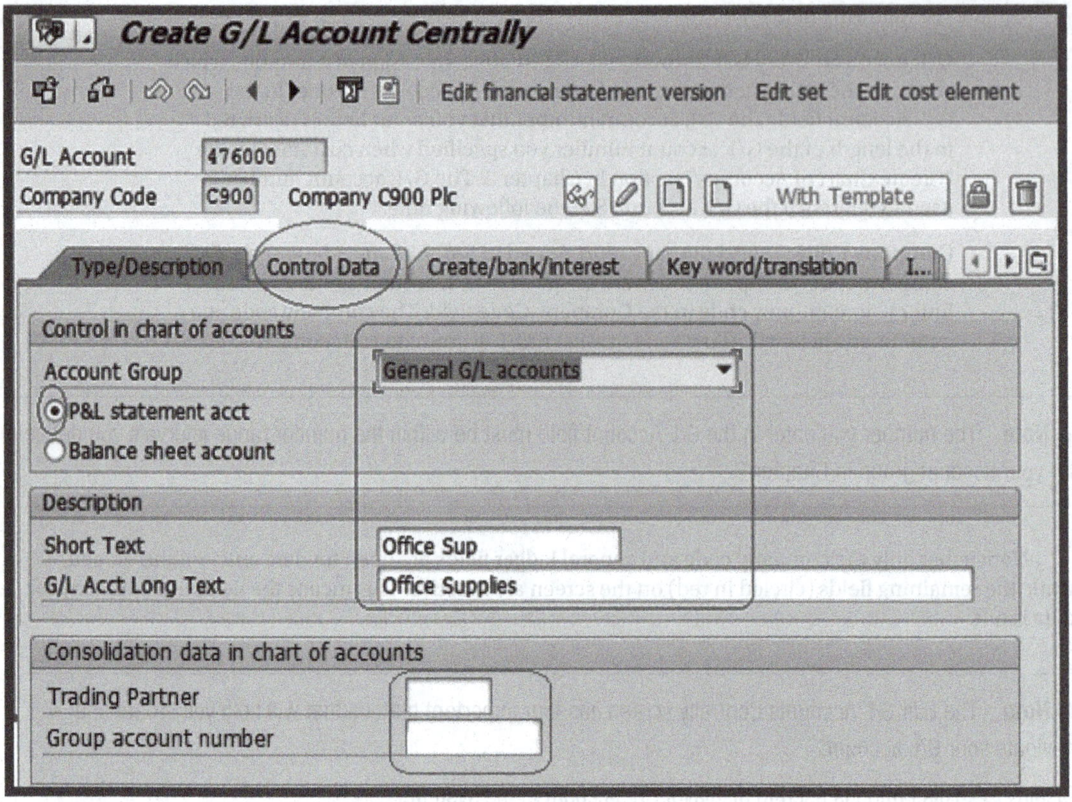

Figure 5-3. *Create G/L account centrally—the Type/Description tab*

Update the following fields:

> **Account Group:** As explained in Chapter 2, the account group is a tool in the SAP ERP that determines how master records are created. The importance of the account group is that it classifies G/L transactions into the same account groups you specified in Define Chart of Account in Chapter 2. When you click the drop-down arrow next to the Account Group field on the Control in the Chart of Accounts section, a list of the account groups you defined earlier is displayed. Select the account group appropriate for your G/L account. For example, if your G/L account is for posting transactions relating to assets, select Fixed Assets Accounts from the Account Group list displayed. All postings relating to assets will be classified as such, and the system will automatically assign a number to the item from the number range interval belonging to this account group. For this activity, we used General G/L Accounts as the Account Group.

P&L Statement Account: This has a radio button. When activated, transactions posted to this G/L account will allow the system to treat the G/L items as P&L statement account items when generating financial statement reports. In this activity, we are creating a G/L account for office supplies. In accounting, office supplies are an expense so they are treated as a P&L item. Hence, you should select P&L Statement Acct.

Balance Sheet Account: Likewise, if the radio button for Balance Sheet account is clicked, items posted to the G/L account are treated as balance sheet account items during financial statement reporting.

Short Text: When creating a G/L account, you need to give a descriptive name to your G/L account. This will allow you to identify individual G/L accounts in the system. Since we are creating a G/L account for office supplies, we'll use Office Sup as our short text description.

G/L Account Long Text: Likewise, the G/L account long text field will allow you to use more detailed, descriptive text as your G/L account description or name. For example, general office supplies.

■ **Note**   In the Consolidation Data in the Chart of Accounts section in Figure 5-3, you can enter a trading partner and group account number for your G/L account. This is necessary if your company prepares consolidated financial statements for its corporate group. In that case, you should enter the company code responsible for the preparation of the consolidation account for the corporate group in the Trading Partner's field and enter the consolidated G/L account number in in the Group Account Number field. The consolidated G/L account allows you to prepare consolidated financial statements for your corporate group in SAP ERP.

The next step is to update the field in the Control Data section of the screen. This section of the screen contains the account control in the company code. Click the Control Data tab circled in red in Figure 5-3. The Control Data section will come to the forefront (Figure 5-4).

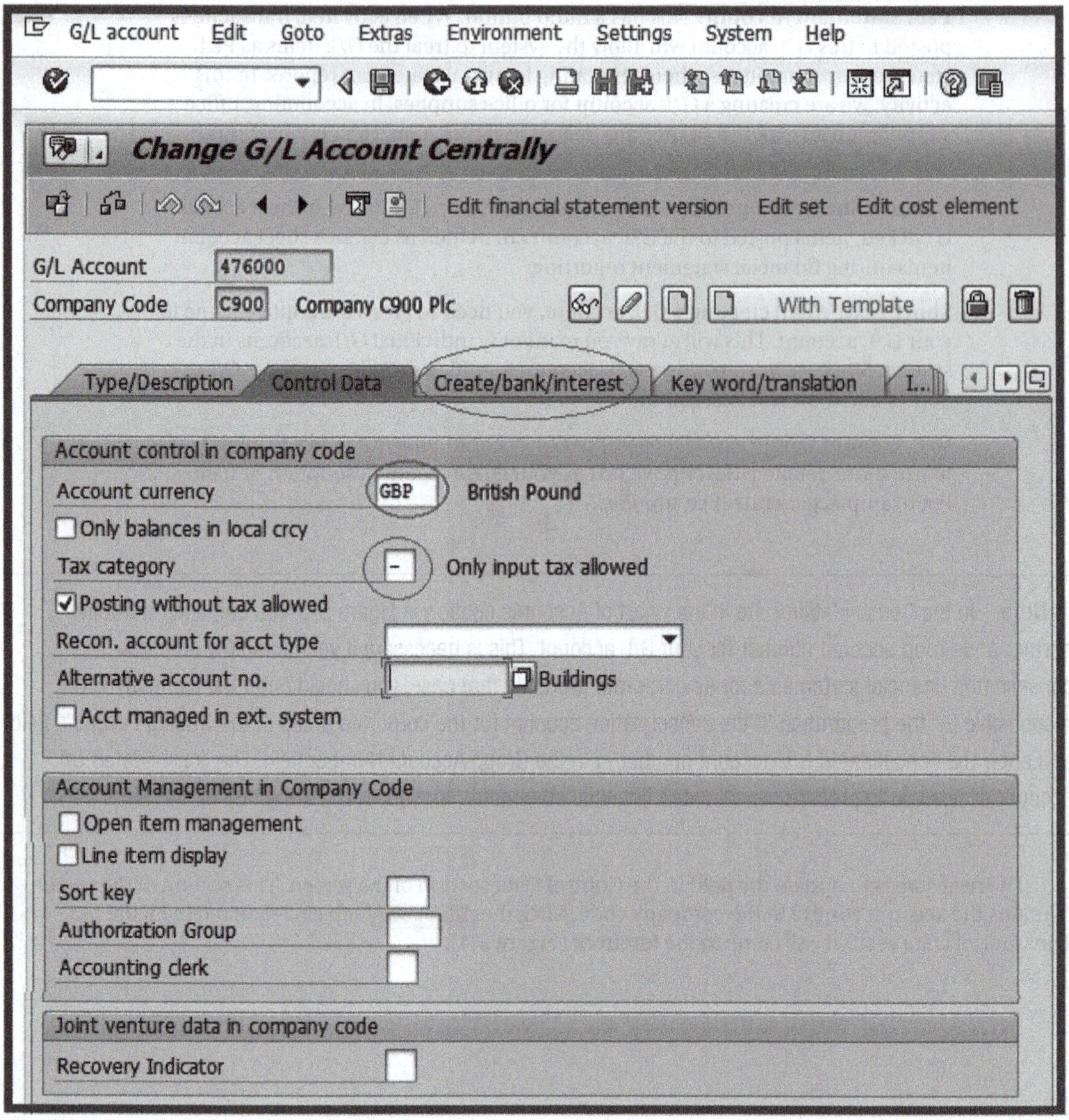

Figure 5-4. *Create G/L account centrally—the Control Data tab*

Update the following fields on the Control Data tab:

Account Currency: This is the Company Code section of the G/L account master record data where you specify the currency of your G/L accounts. It is important to use the local currency for your G/L accounts for each company code. The advantage of using local currency is that it allows postings to be made to the G/L account in any currency and then converted. Postings made in foreign currency are translated into local currency. However, you can also choose to specify foreign currency as your G/L account currency. The drawback to this approach is that posting to the G/L account can only be made in this currency. The system automatically defaults to the local currency of your company code when creating a G/L account. This project examines a UK-based company, so the company code currency is GBP (Great Britain Pounds).

Only Balances In Local Currency: Click the Only Balances In Local Currency checkbox if the transactions posted to this account must be maintained in local currency only. When you click this checkbox, the system will display and manage all currencies in the G/L master record in local currency (that is, the company code currency). This is important when you do not want the system to post any exchange rate differences that may occur, but you want to clear several currencies arising from transactions with your company code currency (local currency). It is important to note that you do not click the Only Balances In Local Currency checkbox for Accounts Payable (AP) and Accounts Receivable (AR) reconciliation accounts, because most transactions posted in AP & AR are in various currencies. Only Balances In Local Currency is clicked for balance sheet accounts without open item management, cash discount account clearing, or Goods Received (GR)/Invoice Receipts (IR) clearing accounts.

Tax Category: This field allows you to specify if the G/L account is tax relevant. Using the Search Function button next to the Tax Category field, select the appropriate tax symbol that you want to use in your G/L account from the displayed tax list. The Tax Category could either be input tax or output tax. For example, if input tax is selected, every posting to this G/L account must contain input tax. In this activity, we used input tax "-" as the tax category.

Posting Without Tax Allowed: This allows postings without tax to be posted in the G/L account, even though the tax category indicator is set.

Reconciliation Account for Account Type: In the G/L master record, you use the Reconciliation Account For Account Type drop-down to specify that the G/L account is a reconciliation account. This function allows you to select from a list of reconciliation account types, for example, Assets, Customers, Vendors, and so on. Once this option is set, the G/L account will be considered a reconciliation account by the system. It is advisable that you maintain at least one reconciliation account in the general ledger. Every posting in the sub-ledger in SAP ERP is automatically posted to a corresponding reconciliation account. The reconciliation accounts are updated with sub-ledger balances as soon as transactions are posted in sub-ledgers. This procedure allows you to generate financial statements at any time from the general ledger.

Open Item Management: By clicking this checkbox in the G/L master record, when you display line items in an account, the system will display all line items in the account marked as open or cleared. This option is ideal if you want to see items not cleared, or outstanding balances at any given point in time in an account. This makes it possible for you to determine if a posting exists in the G/L account that needs offsetting against a particular business transaction (that is, clearing an open item with payment).

Use open item management for the following accounts:

- Bank accounts

- GR/IR accounts

- Salary accounts

Line Item Display: This selection allows you to display or view business transactions posted to the account line-by-line.

Line item can lead to data redundancy (this is where same the data is stored twice or more in the system) and takes additional system resources. Therefore, line items should not be activated for the following items:

- Reconciliation accounts—If you need further breakdown of these accounts, you can view them in the respective sub-ledgers.

- Sale or Turnover accounts—You can view further details of these accounts in Sales Order Management.

- Material accounts—Further details on these accounts can be obtained from Material Management.

- Tax accounts—Detailed tax information can be obtained from related tax documents.

Sort Key: When this indicator is set in the G/L account master record, it allows you to set the sort key according to the sort key number you assigned. SAP comes with a list of standard sort keys you can choose from. The most commonly used sort keys are the first nine.

Sort Key	Description
001	Posting date
002	Doc. no, fiscal year
003	Document date
004	Branch account
005	Local currency amt
006	Doc. currency amount
007	Bill/exch. due date
008	Cost center
009	External document no.

The system automatically fills the assignment field in the line item based on the sort key you assigned to your general ledger master (this is done in the company code segment of your company code). When you assign a document number as your sort key and then display line items, the system will automatically sort your line items based on your selection criteria according to the document number. You can access the sort item list by using the search function on the Sort Key field.

The final step in creating the G/L account master record is to update the field in the Control of Document Creation in the Company Code section of the screen. Click the Create/bank/interest tab (Figure 5-5). You then need to update the Field Status Group field.

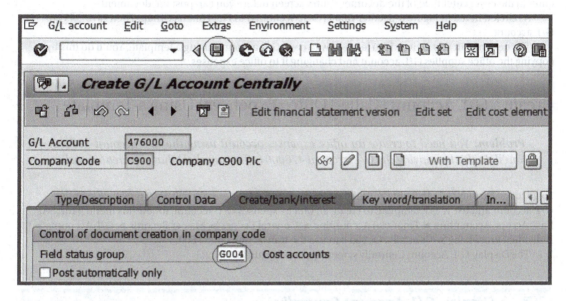

Figure 5-5. *Create G/L account centrally—the Create/Bank/Interest tab*

The Field Status Group field determines whether a field should be suppressed, required, or optional during document entry. If a field is set to suppressed, users will not be able to enter data into it during document entry. If the field is set to required entry, users are required to enter data into the field during document entry. If optional entry is set for a field, users can either input data in the field or leave it blank. Field status groups are entered in the Field Status field of the general ledger master record in the company code-specific area of each G/L account.

A field status variant contains a field status group, and a field status group is assigned to a company code in SAP ERP. SAP comes with a predefined field status group, which you can use for your field status variant. It is also possible to create your own field status groups, but we recommend that you use the predefined field status group provided by SAP in the system. When you create your own field status group, you also have to define the associated tables. This is beyond the scope of SAP FI.

Figure 5-6 shows some of the predefined field status groups in SAP ERP. You can access the list by clicking the Search Function key by the Field Status group.

Field status group	Text
G001	General (with text, allocation)
G003	Material consumption accounts
G004	Cost accounts
G005	Bank accounts (obligatory value date)
G006	Material accounts
G007	Asset accts (w/o accumulated depreciatn)
G008	Assets area clearing accounts
G009	Bank accounts (obligatory due date)

Figure 5-6. *Some of the standard SAP-supplied field status groups*

In the example in Figure 5-5, the G004-Cost Accounts field status group is assigned to the G/L master record. The reason we chose G004-Cost Accounts is because office supplies is an expense, and when you post entries in the G/L accounts, the system will automatically ask for the cost center, which you have to enter in the cost center field of the document entry screen before you can post the document.

As circled in red in Figure 5-5, enter **G004** (Cost Accounts) in Field Status Group. Then save 🖫 your G/L account.

The next step in this activity is to learn how to copy G/L accounts using a template. You'll do this by copying the office supplies G/L account and changing it to office expenses.

Create a G/L Account (Called Office Expenses) Using a Template

> **Problem:** *You need to create an office expenses account using the G/L account 477000. You'll do this by copying the G/L account 476000 (office supplies) that you created earlier.*

To go to the Display G/L Account Centrally screen (Figure 5-6), where you will copy the office supplies G/L account and use it as a template to create an office expenses G/L account, follow this menu path: SAP Easy Access: Accounting ➤ Financial Accounting ➤ General Ledger ➤ Master Records ➤ G/L Accounts ➤ Individual Processing ➤ Centrally. Or you can use the transaction code FS00.

The Display G/L Account Centrally screen appears (Figure 5-7).

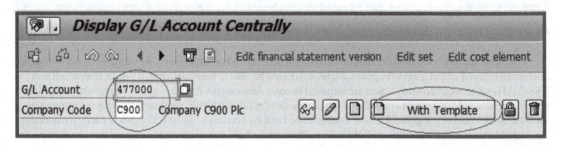

Figure 5-7. *Create a G/L account with a template*

In the G/L Account field, enter your proposed G/L account number for expenses. This number must be within the range you defined for your account group in Chapter 2. In this activity, we used 477000. Also, enter your company code in the Company Code field. Then click the 🗋 With Template button on the top-right side of the screen, circled in red in Figure 5-7. The Reference Account dialog box pops up, as shown in Figure 5-8. Enter the G/L account number that you want to copy (office supplies) in the G/L Account field and update the Company Code field as well.

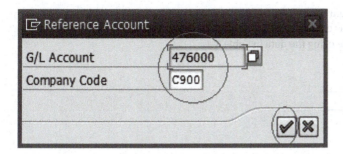

Figure 5-8. *Reference Account dialog box*

Enter the reference G/L account you want to copy in the G/L Account field, and the reference Company Code you are copying in the Company Code field. Click the Enter ✔ button to confirm your action. The system will then paste details of the G/L account you have copied into your new G/L account.

Change the contents of the Short Text field to a short G/L account name, and change the G/L Acct Long Text field to Office Expenses, as shown in Figure 5-9. Save 🖫 your G/L account.

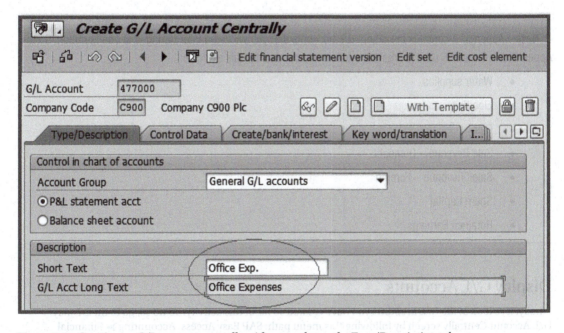

Figure 5-9. *Creating an G/L account centrally with a template—the Type/Description tab*

G/L accounts are a fundamental configuration in SAP ERP, so you will be creating several G/L accounts during the course of this book. As part of this exercise, follow the steps in the preceding section to create an account for Administration Cost Accounting using the data in Table 5-1.

Table 5-1. *Administration Cost Accounting*

Field	Input
G/L Account	472000
Company Code	C900
Account Group	General G/L accounts
P&L Statement Acct	◉
Short Text	Admin Cost a/c
G/L Acct Long Text	Administration Cost Account
Tax Category	___
Field Status Group	G004 Cost accounts

■ **Note**   Appendix A contains the others G/L accounts that you will need later during your configuration. Go to Appendix A – Chapter 5 now to create the following accounts for this exercise:

- Water supplies
- Electricity
- Gas
- Sale Revenue – Domestic
- Sales Revenue – Foreign
- Share Capital
- Retained Earnings

Display G/L Accounts

Finally, let's look at the G/L accounts you have created so far in this activity. To do so, go to the Display G/L Account Centrally screen by following this menu path: SAP Easy Access: Accounting ➤ Financial Accounting ➤ General Ledger ➤ Master Records ➤ G/L Accounts ➤ Individual Processing ➤ Centrally. Or you can use the transaction code FS00.

Leave the G/L Account field blank and enter your company code in the Company Code field. Click the Search 🔲 button next to the G/L Account field. It's circled in red in Figure 5-10.

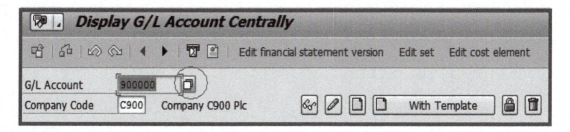

Figure 5-10. *Displaying the G/L account*

The G/L Account Number screen pops up. Notice that your Company Code and Chart of Accounts is entered by default. If they are not inserted for any reason, you should enter them yourself and click the Enter ✔ button at the bottom of the screen to confirm your action. The G/L accounts that you have created so far will be displayed (Figure 5-11).

G/L Ac	CoCd	Long Text
1000	C900	Share Capital
472000	C900	Administration Cost Account
473000	C900	Water Supplies Account
474000	C900	Electricity Account
475000	C900	Gas Account
476000	C900	Office Supplies
477000	C900	Office Expenses
800000	C900	Sales Revenue (Domestic)
810000	C900	Sales Revenue (Foreign)
900000	C900	Retained Earnings

Figure 5-11. *List of G/L accounts*

Summary

This chapter explained what a general ledger is and also described what a master record is. You went through the configuration steps involved in creating a G/L account master record and learned how to copy a G/L account using an existing G/L account as a template. You also looked at the relationship among G/L accounts, sub-ledgers, and reconciliation accounts.

In the next chapter, you will learn how to set automatic open item clearing and how to define the exchange rate and foreign exchange rate valuations.

■■■

CHAPTER 6

Clearing Open Items

In this chapter, you learn how to prepare automatic clearing for open items, define a maximum exchange rate difference, and perform foreign currency valuation.

At the end of this chapter, you will be able to:

- Prepare automatic clearing

- Create accounts for clearing differences

- Define a maximum exchange rate difference

- Check company code settings

- Define valuation methods

- Prepare automatic postings for foreign currency valuations

Clearing Open Items

In SAP R/3, posted transactions with business partners are said to be open or partially complete until full payments are made and the related accounts are cleared. For example, a business partner sends in an invoice; the invoice is posted in the system. At this point, the transaction remains an open item in the account until payment of an equivalent amount of the invoice is made and the account is cleared.

Once payment is made and cleared with the associated open item, the system generates a document number. Only then is the transaction complete. Figure 6-1 illustrates how open item clearing is treated in SAP ERP.

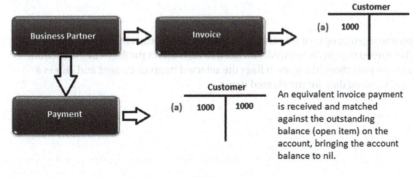

Figure 6-1. Open item clearing in SAP R/3

Assume that on January 1, 20XX, a customer ordered 1,000 items, the accompanying invoice was generated, and the invoice was entered into the system immediately.

The amount of 1,000 remains in the account as an open item. At this point the transaction is unfinished, because payment has not been received.

On February 1, 20XX, payment of $1,000 is received. The incoming payment is matched with the open item of 1,000 and cleared. The net effect of this transaction will be a nil balance. At this point, the transaction is complete.

Account clearing can be carried out for an individual item or for collective items in the system. The SAP ERP system documents clearing can be carried out manually or automatically using automatic payment programs. Clearing open items manually means that the user performs the clearing process, whereas the system performs automatic clearing. For the system to perform automatic clearing of open items, you have to specify certain settings during customizing.

In this chapter, you will complete an exercise on how to set up *automatic* clearing. Later, in Chapter 19, you will look at how to perform manual clearing of open items in detail. But before I walk through an automatic clearing configuration, I'll briefly describe the two options in manual clearing.

Manual Clearing Overview

There are two ways to clear open items in the system manually: posting with clearing and account clearing.

Posting with Clearing

Posting with clearing occurs when an open item on an account is matched against payment and cleared to bring the account balance to nil. It is also possible to group open items, match them with payments, and clear them simultaneously. The system will mark them as cleared items, assign a clearing document number, and enter the date that the items are cleared in the system.

In SAP ERP, posting with clearing can be performed on an individual open item or on a group of open items (that is, several open items in the system are cleared with a payment simultaneously). Posting with clearing can also be performed on an account type and several currencies at the same time by assigning payment to open items. When you're using the posting with clearing option, the net effect should be that the business transactions end up with a zero balance. Open items and payment included in the clearing must be equal. For example, the balance on an account of £1000 must be equal to a payment receipt of £1000.

On the contrary, if the open items and payment are not equal, it is still possible to post the difference in the system. The system will treat the posting as a payment on the account and not as a cleared item. Payment on account is when the item remains in the system as an open item.

Account Clearing

G/L accounts and sub-ledgers managed in open items are cleared using an account clearing procedure. With account clearing, you don't need to post an item. All you need to do is select the items in the account that balance out to zero. When you post them, the system flags the selected items as cleared and enters a clearing document number and clearing date for the cleared items.

Prepare Automatic Clearing

***Problem:** The accounting staff wants to clear open items using the Automatic Clearing function. Your task is to maintain settings that will allow the system to clear open items using the Automatic Clearing function.*

In SAP ERP, you define account types for customers, vendors, and general ledger accounts, and set the criteria for the assignment number (used in relation to the sort key, which enables the automatic clearing process in FI), business area, and trading partners (used to control vendor/customer payment/transaction) for grouping an account with open items for automatic clearing. Once these settings are made, the system-clearing program will look for open items in local and foreign currency that equal a zero balance, group them together, and clear them simultaneously. The system then generates a clearing number and date and enters them into the cleared document.

In order for the system to perform automatic clearing, you need to customize certain specifications. As part of your customization, you specify several criteria, including account type and number. You can also define up to five additional criteria.

To customize automatic clearing programs, follow this menu path: IMG: Financial Accounting (New) ➤ General Ledger Accounting (New) ➤ Business Transactions ➤ Open Item Clearing ➤ Prepare Automatic Clearing. Or you can use the transaction code OB74.

The Change View "Additional Rules For Automatic Clearing": Overview screen appears and displays the list of existing automatic clearing criteria in the system. To create your own automatic criteria, click the New Entries button at the top-left of the screen. The New Entries: Overview of Added Entries screen appears (Figure 6-2).

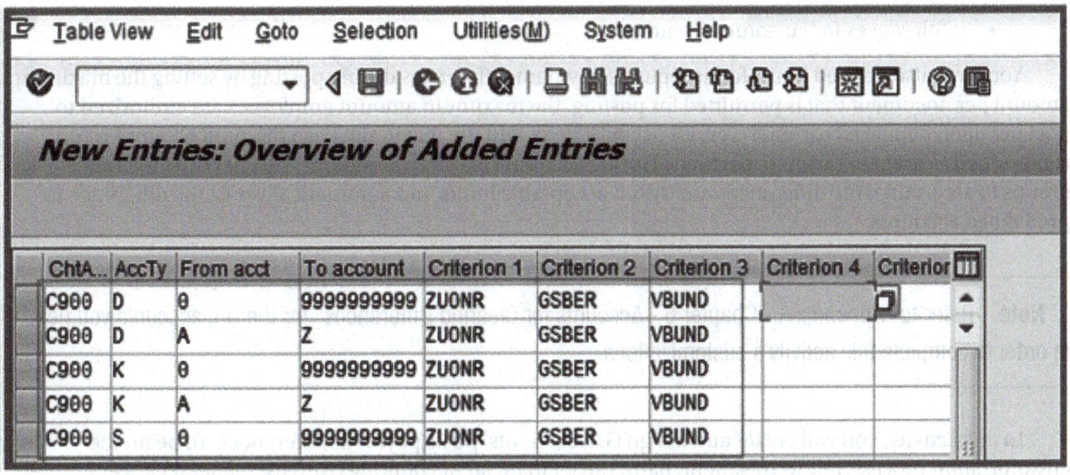
Table View
Edit
Goto
Selection
Utilities(M)
System
Help
New Entries: Overview of Added Entries
ChtA... AccTy From acct To account Criterion 1 Criterion 2 Criterion 3 Criterion 4 Criterior
C900 D 0 9999999999 ZUONR GSBER VBUND
C900 D A Z ZUONR GSBER VBUND
C900 K 0 9999999999 ZUONR GSBER VBUND
C900 K A Z ZUONR GSBER VBUND
C900 S 0 9999999999 ZUONR GSBER VBUND

***Figure 6-2.** Defining additional rules for automatic clearing*

Update the following fields:

Chart of Accounts: Enter your Chart of Account in this field. This is the four-digit character you defined in Chapter 2.

Account Type: Enter the account type in this field. In SAP ERP, account types are represented by letters, such as D (customer), V (Vendor), and S (General Ledger).

From Account/To Account: Specify the account range for each activity type for internal and external number range assignments. For internal number assignments, use the range 0 to 99999999999. For external number range assignments, use the range A to Z.

Criterion 1-3: Define the criteria for open item clearing in the Criterion 1, Criterion 2, and Criterion 3 fields.

■ **Note**   Criterion 1 is the technical field ZUONR for an assignment number. Criterion 2 is the technical field GSBER for a business area. Criterion 3 is the technical field VBUND for a trading partner.

Click the Enter ✅ button at the top-left of the screen or press Enter on your keyboard to confirm that the system accepts your entries. Then click save 💾 to save your customizations.

In the next activity, you will look at how to assign G/L accounts for automatic clearing. This is an important aspect of the customization process, as it gives you the opportunity to see how the G/L accounts you have created are assigned in the system to automatic posting.

Create Accounts for Clearing Differences

Chapter 4 looked at the three levels of tolerance represented in SAP ERP, namely:

- Tolerance groups for G/L accounts
- Tolerance groups for employees
- Tolerances for customers/vendors

You have also defined limits for acceptable payment differences during posting by setting the maximum amount per document that is permitted for posting, the maximum amount employees are authorized to post per open item in a customer/vendor account item, and the maximum cash discount an employee is permitted to grant to business partners. During account clearing, the system will check the tolerance groups to ascertain if the differences are within acceptable limits and automatically post the difference to predefined accounts.

■ **Note**   Refer to "Appendix A - Chapter 6 - Accounts for Clearing Differences" for the G/L accounts you need in order to complete this activity's customizations.

In this activity, you will create and assign G/L accounts' posts payment differences. To begin the customization process, follow this menu path: IMG: Financial Accounting (New) ➤ General Ledger Accounting (New) ➤ Business Transactions ➤ Open Item Clearing ➤ Clearing Differences ➤ Create Accounts for Clearing Differences. You can also use the transaction code OBXZ.

The Enter Chart of Accounts dialog box pops-up. Enter *your* chart of account key in the Chart of Accounts field and click Enter ✅ at the bottom of the screen or press Enter on your keyboard. The Configuration Accounting Maintain: Automatic Posts – Rules screen is displayed (Figure 6-3). This is where you set the automatic posting rules to determine if accounts are posted as debits or credits and also where you include tax codes with your account assignment.

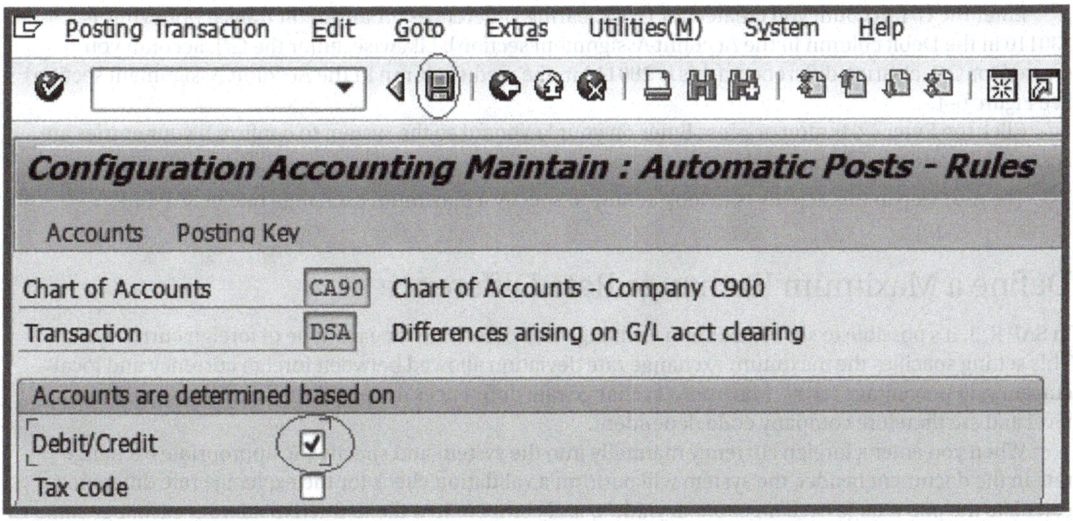

Figure 6-3. *Specifying debits/credits for account determination*

Click the Debit/Credit checkbox circled red in the Accounts Are Determined Based On section. This function allows you to assign G/L accounts for both debits and credits to automatic posting. If you click the Tax Code field, you will also need to specify your tax code. The tax code you specify will be applied to the G/L account. The Tax Code checkbox is blank in this example. This means that all tax codes can be posted in the G/L accounts you assign in this activity for payment differences. Click the Save 🖫 button. The Maintain FI Configuration: Automatic Posting – Accounts screen appears (Figure 6-4). This is where you assign the predefined G/L accounts for posting payment differences for automatic posting.

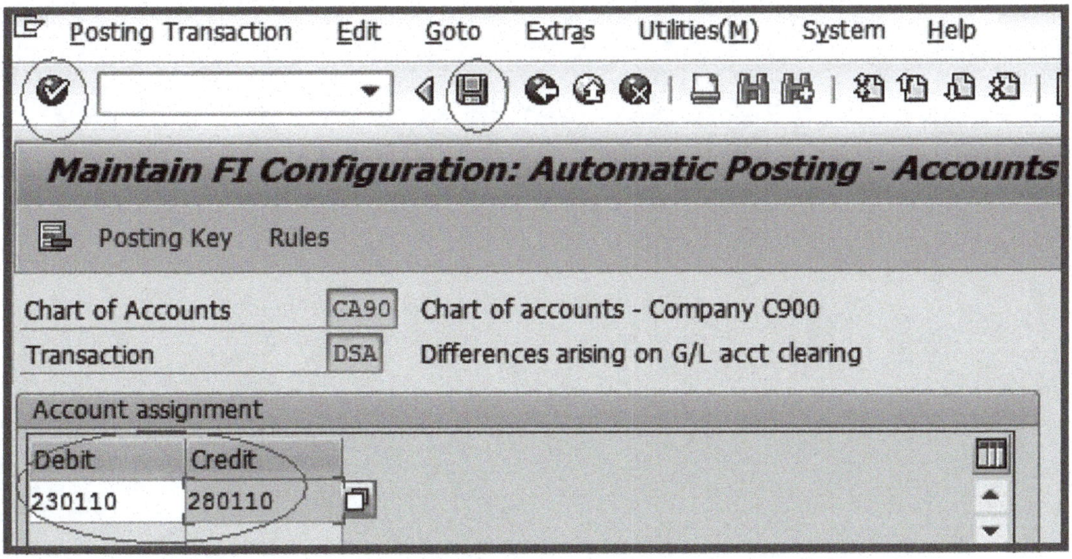

Figure 6-4. *Account determination for automatic posting*

Enter the G/L account you created for G/L Clearing Differences for any debit transactions (this is 230110 in the Debit column in the Account Assignment section). Likewise, enter the G/L account you created for G/L clearing differences (this is 280110 in the credit column in the Account Assignment section) See Figure 6-4.

Click the Enter ✅ button or press Enter on your keyboard so the system to confirm if your entries are accepted. Then save 💾 your work.

The next step in this activity is to look at how to specify a maximum exchange rate in SAP ERP.

Define a Maximum Exchange Rate Difference

In SAP R/3, it's possible to set a maximum exchange rate difference for each type of foreign currency. This setting specifies the maximum exchange rate deviation allowed between foreign currency and local currency, in percentage terms. Maximum exchange rate differences are performed at the company code level and are therefore company code dependent.

When you enter a foreign currency manually into the system and specify the appropriate exchange rate in the document header, the system will perform a validation check for the exchange rate difference, calculate the percentage exchange rate deviation, and compare it to the defined maximum exchange rate difference. If the exchange rate difference exceeds the maximum exchange rate difference you defined, the system will issue a warning. This measure ensures that any errors are identified and rectified early.

For example, if 10% is specified as the maximum exchange rate difference, when the exchange rate exceeds this specified rate, the system will automatically identify this problem and issue a warning message. Figure 6-5 illustrates how the system performs checks in SAP ERP using a flowchart.

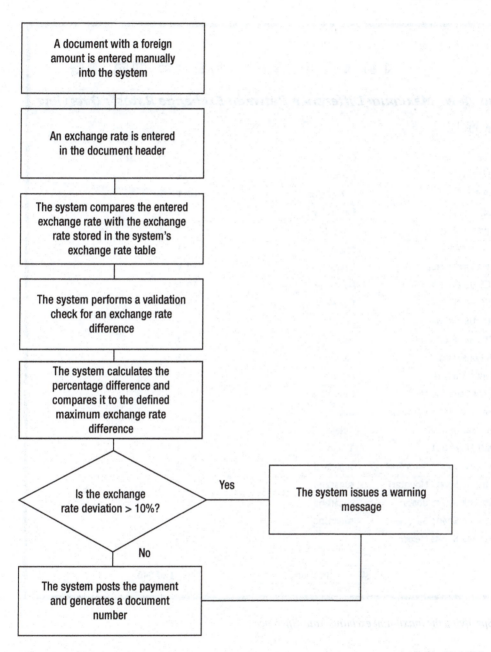

Figure 6-5. *A flowchart diagram depicting how maximum exchange rate is processed in SAP R/3*

Now let's set the maximum exchange rate difference in SAP ERP. To define the maximum exchange rate difference, follow this path: IMG: Financial Accounting (New) ➤ Financial Accounting Global Settings (New) ➤ Global Parameters for Company Code ➤ Currencies ➤ Maximum Exchange Rate Difference ➤ Define Maximum Exchange Rate Difference per Company Code. You can also use the transaction code OB64.

The Change View "Maximum Differences Between Exchange Rates": Overview screen appears (Figure 6-6). This screen contains the list of company codes defined previously in the system.

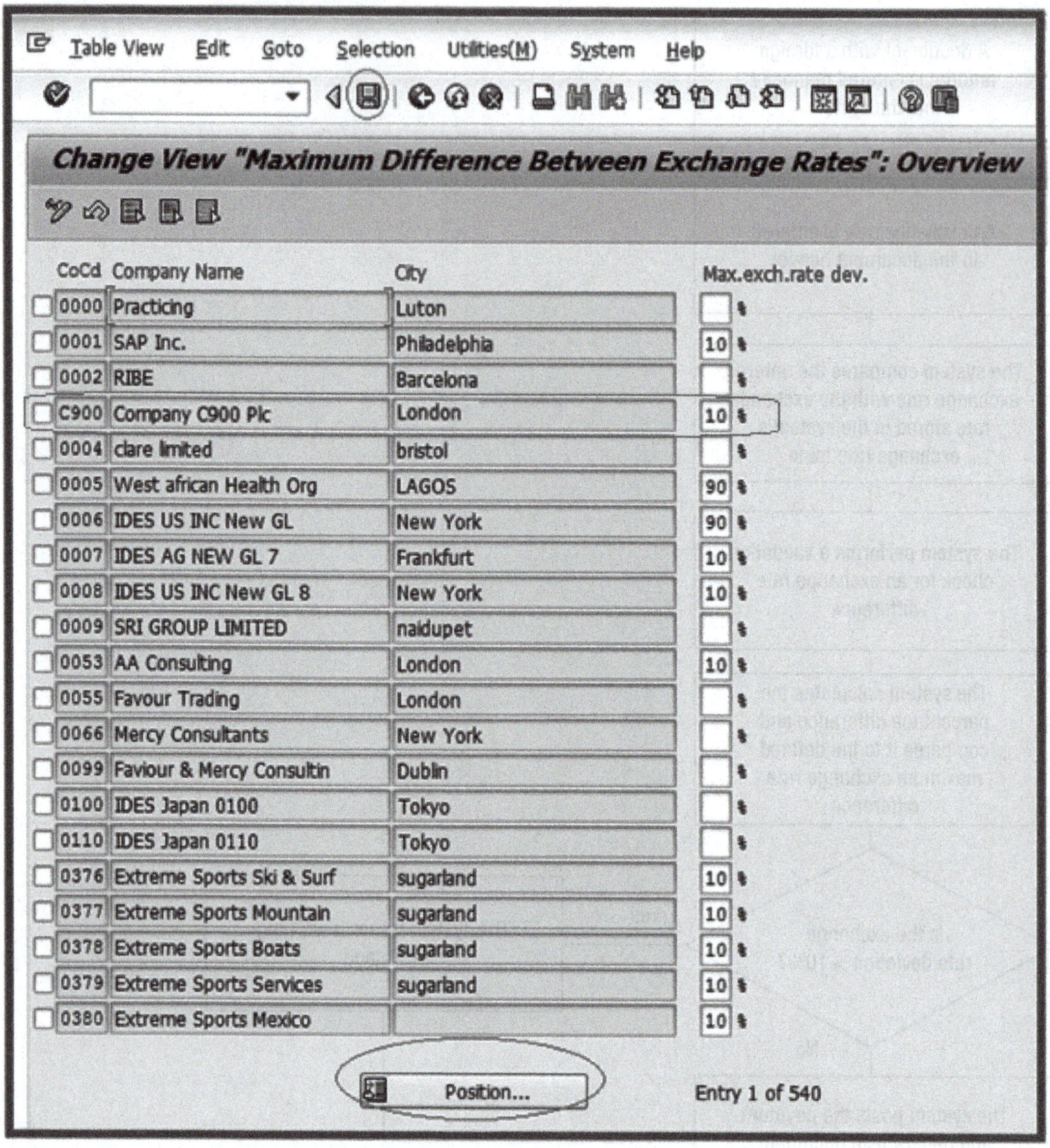

	CoCd	Company Name	City	Max.exch.rate dev.
☐	0000	Practicing	Luton	☐ %
☐	0001	SAP Inc.	Philadelphia	10 %
☐	0002	RIBE	Barcelona	☐ %
☐	C900	Company C900 Plc	London	10 %
☐	0004	clare limited	bristol	☐ %
☐	0005	West african Health Org	LAGOS	90 %
☐	0006	IDES US INC New GL	New York	90 %
☐	0007	IDES AG NEW GL 7	Frankfurt	10 %
☐	0008	IDES US INC New GL 8	New York	10 %
☐	0009	SRI GROUP LIMITED	naidupet	☐ %
☐	0053	AA Consulting	London	10 %
☐	0055	Favour Trading	London	☐ %
☐	0066	Mercy Consultants	New York	☐ %
☐	0099	Faviour & Mercy Consultin	Dublin	☐ %
☐	0100	IDES Japan 0100	Tokyo	☐ %
☐	0110	IDES Japan 0110	Tokyo	☐ %
☐	0376	Extreme Sports Ski & Surf	sugarland	10 %
☐	0377	Extreme Sports Mountain	sugarland	10 %
☐	0378	Extreme Sports Boats	sugarland	10 %
☐	0379	Extreme Sports Services	sugarland	10 %
☐	0380	Extreme Sports Mexico		10 %

Position...   Entry 1 of 540

Figure 6-6. *Specifying the maximum exchange rate difference*

Click the [Position...] button at the bottom of the screen to search for your company code from the list of company codes displayed. Assign a maximum exchange rate difference to your company code by entering the percentage rate in the Max.exch.rate.dev box. In this activity, we used 10 (10%) as the maximum exchange rate.

Save 🖫 your settings.

Checking the Company Code Settings

Although it is *not* mandatory, it is recommended that you check your company code settings to see the customizations you have made so far. You can check your company code settings in the global parameters by following this menu path: IMG: Financial Accounting (New) ➤ Financial Accounting Global Settings (New) ➤ Global Parameters Company Code ➤ Enter Global Parameters. Or you can use the transaction code OBY6.

The Change View "Company Code Global Data:" Overview screen is displayed (Figure 6-7). From the list of displayed company codes, search for your company code. Select your company code from the list of company codes by clicking on it.

Figure 6-7. The Company Code Global Data Overview screen

Click the Details ⊗ button at the top-left side of the screen (circled in red in Figure 6-7). The Change View "Company Code Global Data": Details screen is displayed (Figure 6-8). This screen displays all the global settings in your company code. You can specify other important settings here.

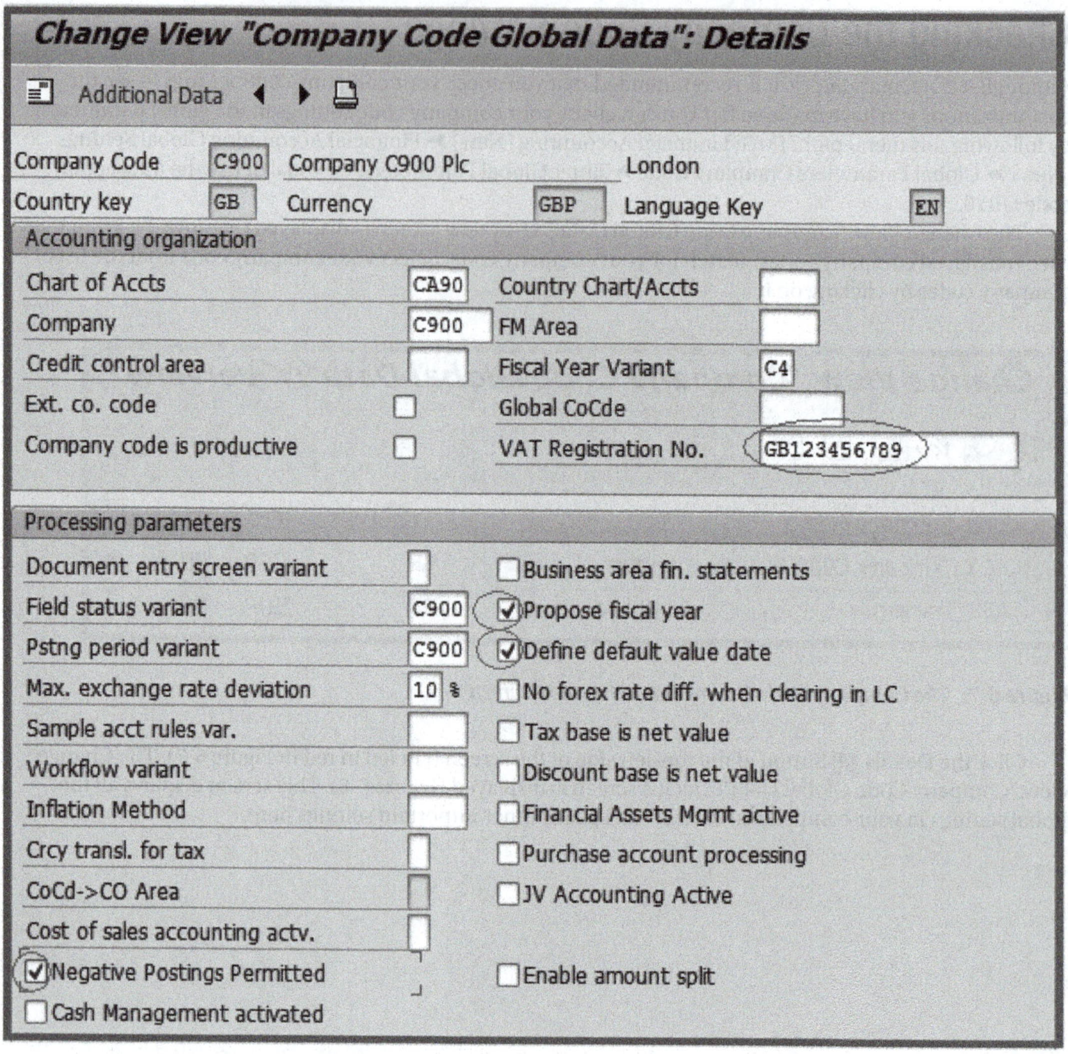

Change View "Company Code Global Data": Details

▤ Additional Data ◀ ▶ 🖨

Company Code	C900	Company C900 Plc		London	
Country key	GB	Currency	GBP	Language Key	EN

Accounting organization

Chart of Accts	CA90	Country Chart/Accts	
Company	C900	FM Area	
Credit control area		Fiscal Year Variant	C4
Ext. co. code	☐	Global CoCde	
Company code is productive	☐	VAT Registration No.	GB123456789

Processing parameters

Document entry screen variant		☐ Business area fin. statements
Field status variant	C900	☑ Propose fiscal year
Pstng period variant	C900	☑ Define default value date
Max. exchange rate deviation	10 %	☐ No forex rate diff. when clearing in LC
Sample acct rules var.		☐ Tax base is net value
Workflow variant		☐ Discount base is net value
Inflation Method		☐ Financial Assets Mgmt active
Crcy transl. for tax		☐ Purchase account processing
CoCd->CO Area		☐ JV Accounting Active
Cost of sales accounting actv.		
☑ Negative Postings Permitted		☐ Enable amount split
☐ Cash Management activated		

Figure 6-8. The Company Code Global Data Details screen

Update the following items:

> **VAT Registration No.:** Entering data in this field is optional. Do this only if your company requires it. When you enter your company's VAT registration number, the system will automatically use this number for VAT correspondence.

> **Propose Fiscal Year:** This field is optional. When you click this checkbox, the system will automatically propose a fiscal year during document entry.

Define Default Value Date: This setting is also optional. When you select it during document entry, the system will automatically propose a current date when entering a document into the system.

Negative Postings Permitted: When this checkbox is clicked, this will allow you to reverse transactions in the system without posting the reversed document and the associated reversal document. In other words, the original transaction figures in the system will stay the same as before.

When you have updated the Change View "Company Code Global Data": Details screen as shown in Figure 6-8, click the Enter ✅ button at the top-left side of the screen and then save 💾 your work.

The next step in this configuration exercise is to customize foreign currency valuation in SAP ERP. As part of this customization process, you will also define valuation methods and learn how to specify the automatic posting settings for foreign exchange valuation.

Foreign Currency Valuation

Problem: *The accounting staff wants to be able to maintain foreign currency and valuate open items in foreign currencies. Your task is to explain to the accounting staff what exchange rate type is, to define the valuation methods, and to perform other settings that will allow the accounting staff to achieve their objectives.*

In order to create financial statements at a key date in SAP ERP, you need to define foreign currency valuation. The importance of defining foreign currency valuation is that foreign currency balance sheets and open items are valuated using it.

Once you have defined your foreign currency valuation and specified the appropriate accounts, the system will consider the following accounts and items during foreign currency valuation:

- G/L accounts in foreign currency related to foreign currency balance sheet accounts

- Open items posted in foreign currencies

In SAP ERP you have the option of performing currency valuation in group currency (that is, parallel currency) or in company code currency. You'll look at how to define foreign exchange valuation methods in SAP ERP. But before defining these valuation methods, let's take a quick look at exchange rate types in SAP ERP.

Exchange Rate Types

The different exchange rates for each currency pair are defined in the system and are differentiated by exchange rate type. The following exchange rate types are represented in SAP ERP using the following symbols:

- Bank selling rate – B (bank selling rate between currency pair)

- Bank buying rate – G (bank buying rate between currency pair)

- Average rate – M (average between selling rate and buying rate). You can obtain selling rate or buying rate using average rate and the spread. This is done by adding or deducting the spread from the average rate.

Exchange rate types are discussed further in Chapter 7.

Define Valuation Methods

Valuation methods determine the method used to perform foreign currency valuation, which constitutes part of the closing procedures in SAP ERP. During customizing, you can define valuation methods for open items such as bank balance, customer, and vendor. With valuation methods, you can perform specifications for balances and for individual valuation. You have a list of valuation procedures to choose from. For example, the lowest value principle, the strict lowest value, and so on.

Let's explore how to create foreign currency valuation methods for open items related to customers/vendors maintained in foreign currency. To do this, follow this menu path: IMG: Financial Accounting (New) ➤ General Ledger Accounting (New) ➤ Periodic Processing ➤ Valuate ➤ Define Valuation Methods. Or you can use the transaction code OB59.

The Change View "Foreign Currency Valuation Methods": Overview screen is displayed. Click the New Entries button at the top of the screen. The New Entries: Details of Added Entries screen will appear (Figure 6-9).

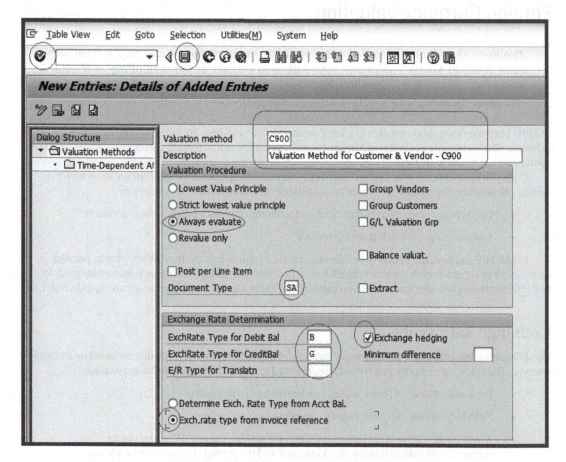

Figure 6-9. *Foreign currency valuation methods for a customer/vendor*

As part of customizing the valuation method, you need to update the following fields on the screen:

Valuation Method: Enter a four-digit code as the key for your valuation method. This identifies your valuation method.

Description: Enter a short text description that best describes your valuation method.

Lowest Value Principle: The valuation calculation is carried out per item total. When this valuation procedure is set, the valuation is displayed only if exchange loss occurs (when the difference between local currency amount and the valued amount is negative).

Strict Lowest Value Principle: Valuation calculation is carried out per item total. The valuation is displayed only if the new valuation has a greater devaluation and/or revaluation for credit entries than the previous valuation.

Always Evaluate: Allows revaluation to be taken into consideration.

Revalue Only: With this procedure, revaluation is considered when there is exchange loss.

Document Type: Enter an appropriate document type in this field. This is the key that distinguishes business transactions in SAP ERP. For example, SA is the G/L document type.

ExchRate Type for Debit Bal: Enter B (the standard transaction at bank selling rate) in this field. This exchange rate type takes into consideration the valuation of foreign currency items having a positive balance.

Exch.Rate Type for Credit Bal: Enter G (the standard transaction at bank buying rate) in this field. Unlike the standard transaction at bank selling rate, this exchange rate type takes into consideration the valuation of foreign currency items having a negative balance.

Exchange Hedging: By clicking this checkbox, it means that you want the system to value your foreign exchange items at a hedged exchange rate. Hedging is a procedure employed to eliminating risk that may arise from business transactions in foreign currencies.

Exch.Rate Type from Invoice Reference: When you click this radio button, currency valuations are conducted based on currency valuation based on balance with reference to invoice reference.

When you have updated the screen, click the Enter 🗸 button on the top-left corner of the screen to confirm your entries. Then save 🖫 your specification.

This next step in customizing foreign currency valuation is to create another foreign currency valuation method for the bank balance maintained in foreign currency. Use this menu path: IMG: Financial Accounting (New) ➤ General Ledger Accounting (New) ➤ Periodic Processing ➤ Valuate ➤ Define Valuation Methods. Or use the transaction code OB59. You will be returned to the Change View "Foreign Currency Valuation Methods": Overview screen. Click the New Entries button on the top-left side of the screen. Update the screen as shown in Figure 6-10.

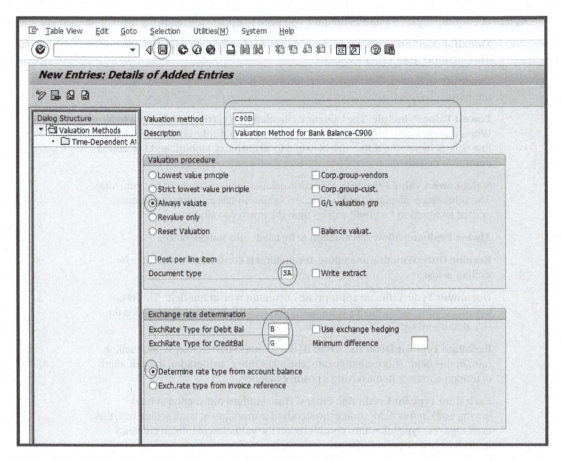

Figure 6-10. *Foreign currency valuation methods for a bank balance*

Click the Enter ✔ button on the top-left side of the screen to confirm your entries; then click Save 💾.

Prepare Automatic Postings for Foreign Currency Valuation

Exchange rate differences normally arise when you're valuating open items in foreign currency. The settings you carry out here will allow the system to automatically post exchange rate differences arising from open items valuation and foreign currency balances to the accounts you specify.

Preparing automatic postings for foreign currency valuation is nothing other than simply assigning accounts to G/L accounts where you want the exchange rate differences to be posted.

■ **Note** Before you proceed with this activity, refer to "Appendix A- Chapter 6, Prepare Automatic Postings for Foreign Currency Valuation" to create the G/L accounts you will need for your configuration.

To customize automatic postings for foreign currency valuation, follow this menu path: IMG: Financial Accounting (New) ➤ General Ledger Accounting (New) ➤ Periodic Processing➤ Valuate ➤ Foreign Currency Valuation ➤ Prepare Automatic Postings for Foreign Currency Valuation. Or you can use the transaction code OBA1.

The Configuration Accounting Maintain: Automatic Posts – Procedures screen is displayed (Figure 6-11). This screen contains a list of exchange rate procedures and transaction keys that you assign to accounts.

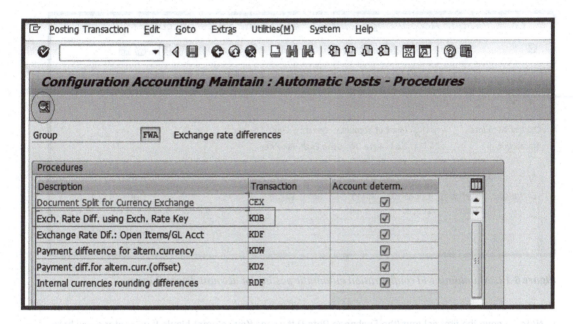

Figure 6-11. *Maintaining an automatic posting for an exchange difference using an exchange rate key*

In this activity, you will assign accounts to the following automatic procedures:

- Exchange rate difference using the exchange rate key (KDB)

- Exchange rate difference for open items—accounts receivable

- Exchange rate difference for open items—accounts payable

Exchange Rate Difference Using the Exchange Rate Key (KDB)

When valuating open items, such as business transactions, foreign exchange rate differences can be losses or gains. Exchange rate difference loss is an expense and is posted to the Foreign Exchange Loss account. Likewise, foreign exchange differences realized are posted to the Foreign Exchange Gain account and to a Balance Sheet Adjustment account.

The Exchange Rate Difference Using Exchange Rate Key (KDB) process allows you to assign exchange rate loss and gain accounts to your valuation method. It also allows the system to automatically post losses or gains arising from exchange rate differences during open item valuation to the accounts you specify when you customize the exchange rate difference for open items in the G/L account later. Let's look at how to do this. Select Exch.Rate Diff. Using Exch.Rate Key – KDB from the list of exchange rate procedures in Figure 6-11 and click the Details ⬚ button at the top-left side of the screen.

The Enter Chart of Accounts dialog box will appear. Enter your chart of accounts ID (*CA90*) in the Chart of Accounts field. Click the Enter ✅ button to confirm your entry. The Configuration Accounting Maintain: Automatic Posts – Accounts screen is displayed (Figure 6-12). This is where you assign automatic posting procedures to the appropriate G/L accounts. Enter the appropriate G/L account for exchange rate difference losses in the Expense Account field and the exchange rate difference gains (E/R gains) in the E/R Gains Account field.

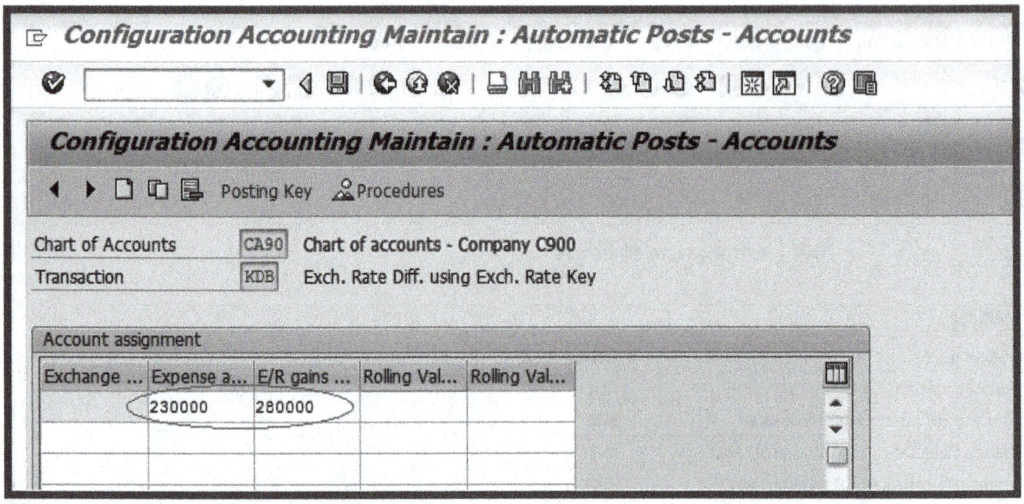

Figure 6-12. *Maintaining FI configuration automatic posting for account determination*

■ **Note** Leave the first column (the Exchange Rate Difference Key column) blank. If you enter a key here, you have to specify this in the related G/L account master record; otherwise, your foreign currency valuation account will not work.

Click the Enter 📀 button or press Enter on your keyboard. The system will confirm your entries. Save 💾 your work.

The next step is to assign the accounts to the exchange rate difference for open items (G/L account). To return to the Configuration Accounting Maintain: Automatic Posts – Procedure screen (shown in Figure 6-11), click the Back 📀 button at the top-left of the screen.

Exchange Rate Differences for Open Items/GL Accounts

In this and the next activity, you will define exchange rate differences for open items for one Accounts Receivable and one Accounts Payable account. You can define several accounts for exchange rate differences for several open items in the system, but we are restricting our definition of exchange rate difference for open items to only two items in this exercise. This will give you a feel of how to customize exchange rate differences for open items. In your spare time, you can define more accounts.

First, let's look at how to define an exchange rate difference for accounts receivable open items. The settings you configure will allow the system to automatically post exchange rate differences to the assigned G/L accounts when valuating open items and foreign currency balances for accounts receivable.

You define the exchange rate difference for open items for account receivable using foreign trade debtor as the example. Select Exch.Rate Dif. Open Items/G/L Acct–KDF from the list of exchange rate procedures in Figure 6-13 and click the Details 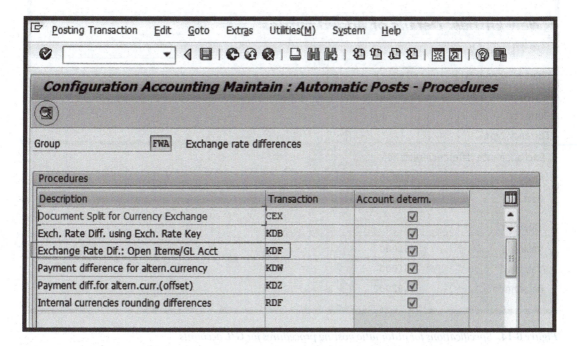 button on the top-left corner of the screen.

Figure 6-13. *Maintaining an automatic posting procedure for an exchange rate difference: Open Items/G/L Accounts*

The Change View "Acct Determination for OI Exch. Rate Differences": Overview screen is displayed. This is where you customize automatic posting procedures for the appropriate G/L accounts, assign the G/L accounts for exchange rate differences realized for losses and gains, and assign the G/L accounts for losses and gains arising from the exchange rate valuations. To input data, click the `New Entries` button at the top of the screen. The New Entries: Details of Added Entries screen is displayed (Figure 6-14).

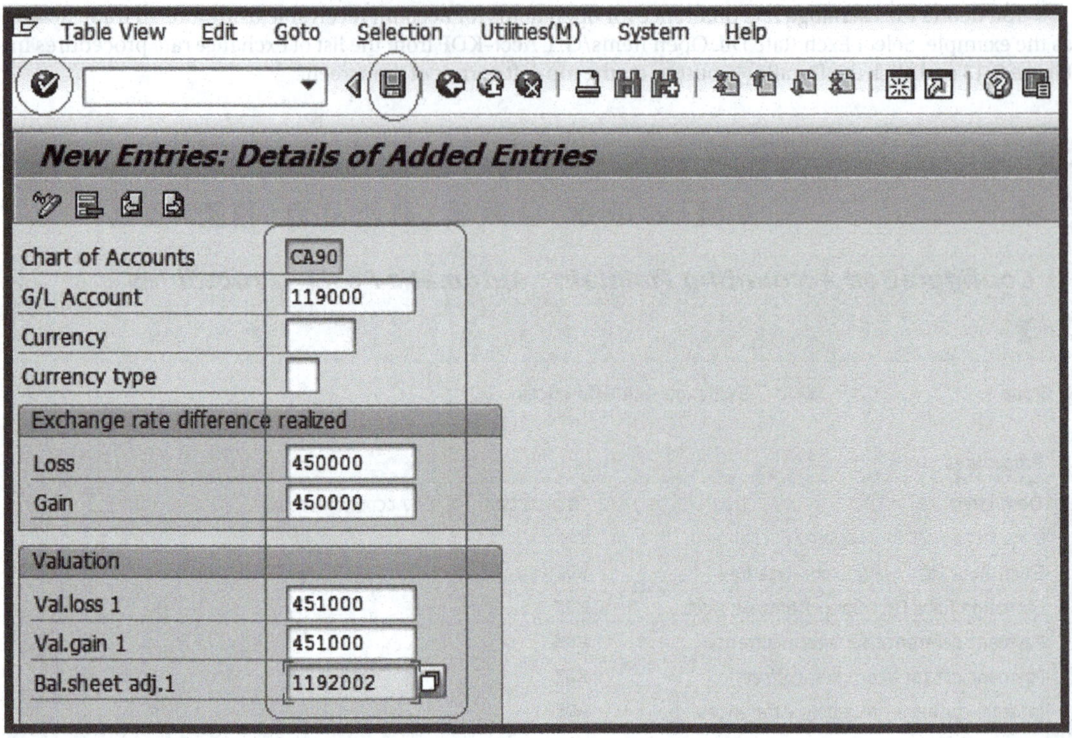

Figure 6-14. Specifications for automatic posting procedures for G/L accounts

Update the following fields:

> **Chart of Accounts:** The chart of accounts you enter in this field will allow you to assign the G/L accounts created in this chart of accounts to the appropriate fields (G/L account, Loss, Gain Val.loss1, Val.gain1 and Bal.sheet adj.1) and allow the system to carry out automatic postings to the specified G/L accounts.

> **G/L Account:** Enter a G/L account for account receivable. This is the G/L account to be updated. In this activity, we used a G/L account for Trade Debtor (Foreign).

> **Loss:** Assign the G/L account where losses arising from exchange rate differences are realized and posted.

> **Gain:** Assign the G/L account where gains arising from exchange rate differences are realized and posted.

> **Val.loss 1:** Assign the G/L account where you want losses arising from foreign currency valuation to be posted.

> **Val.gain 1:** Assign the G/L account where you want gains arising from foreign currency valuation to be posted.

> **Bal.sheet adj.1:** Open items valuation of foreign currency adjustments of receivables and payables are posted in the G/L account you enter in this field.

Table 6-1 lists the G/L accounts used in this activity.

Table 6-1. *List of G/L Accounts for Automatic Posting Procedures—Account Receivable*

Field	Value	Description
Chart of Accounts	CA90	This is defaulted by the system. You can overwrite the content of this field manually.
G/L Account	119000	G/L account for Trade Debtor (Foreign)
Exchange Rate Difference Realized		
Loss	450000	Foreign exchange valuation G/L account
Gain	450000	Foreign exchange valuation G/L account
Valuation		
Val.loss 1	451000	Foreign exchange valuation G/L account
Val.gain 2	451000	Foreign exchange valuation G/L account
Bal.sheet adj.1	119002	G/L account for Bal. Sheet Adj. (trade debtors)

After updating the screen, click the Enter 🗹 button at the top-left corner of the screen or press Enter on your keyboard. The system will accept your entries. Save 🖫 your configuration.

Next, you will assign accounts to an exchange rate difference for open items–account payable. You need to return to the Configuration Accounting Maintain: Automatic Posts - Procedure screen in Figure 6-13, where you will continue customizing. To do so, click the Back 🔙 button on the top-left corner of the screen.

Exchange Rate Difference for Open Items–Account Payable

Settings you configure here allow the system to automatically post exchange rate differences to the assigned G/L accounts when valuating open items and foreign currency balances for accounts payable.

On the Configuration Accounting Maintain: Automatic Posts - Procedure screen shown earlier in Figure 6-13, select Exch.Rate Dif. Open Items/G/L Acct–KDF again from the list of exchange rate procedures and click the Details 🖧 button at the top-left corner of the screen. The Change View "Acct Determination for OI Exch. Rate Differences": Overview screen is displayed. To input data, click the New Entries button at the top of the screen; the New Entries: Details of Added Entries screen is displayed. Using the data in Table 6-2, update the screen.

Table 6-2. *List of G/L Accounts for Automatic Posting Procedures—Account Payable*

Field	Value	Description
Chart of Accounts	CA90	This is the default; otherwise, enter it manually.
G/L Account	213000	G/L account for exchange rate expense
Exchange Rate Difference Realized		
Loss	450000	Foreign exchange valuation G/L account
Gain	450000	Foreign exchange valuation G/L account
Valuation		
Val.loss 1	451000	Foreign exchange valuation G/L account
Val.gain 2	451000	Foreign exchange valuation G/L account
Bal.sheet adj.1	219003	G/L account for Bal. Sheet Adj. (trade creditors)

Click the Enter ✅ button or press Enter on your keyboard. The system will accept your entries. Then save 💾 your configuration.

Summary

This chapter explained how to clear open items in SAP ERP. As part of the discussion, you learned how business transactions are generated and posted in the system as open items, and how open items are cleared with payments. You learned about various ways of clearing open items in SAP ERP.

These included posting with clearing (when payments are matched with open items in the system to achieve a nil balance) and account clearing (by selecting group of items and matching them against a payment results in nil balance). We went on to show you how to customize settings for automatic clearing. As part of the automatic clearing configuration, you learned how to define account types for customers, vendors, and G/L accounts and set criteria for assignment, business areas, and trading partners for grouping an account with open items for automatic clearing. You also looked at maximum exchange rate difference settings per foreign currency in a company code. You saw how the maximum exchange rate differences you specify are executed in the system.

You also learned how to check your company code settings in the global parameters to ensure that you did not omit important settings. The process you used was the Negative Posting Permitted checkbox. It allows you to reverse transactions in the system without altering the original transaction figures.

Before creating a financial statement, it is important that you define foreign currency valuation, so that the foreign currency balance sheet and open items in foreign currencies are valuated as part of foreign currency valuation. You also learned how to define foreign currency valuation and specify the appropriate accounts the system will use during that valuation.

Finally, you looked at how to prepare automatic postings for foreign exchange valuation that will allow the system to post exchange rate differences to appropriate G/L accounts automatically.

The next chapter looks at how to maintain an exchange rate in SAP ERP that will allow you to translate amounts into the appropriate currency. In the process, you will maintain the relationship between a currency pair using appropriate ratios.

■ ■ ■

CHAPTER 7

Maintaining Currency Types and Currency Pairs

In this chapter, you learn how to customize local and foreign currencies for company codes.
At the end of this chapter, you will be able to:

- Maintain exchange rate types

- Define a standard quotation for exchange rates

- Enter prefixes for direct/indirect quotation exchange rates

- Define translation ratios for currency translation

Currencies

In SAP ERP accounting, transactions are measured in monetary terms. Therefore, it is necessary to specify a currency for each transaction you enter in the system. In order for the system to manage the currency ledgers, you must specify a standard currency code during data entry. The International Organization Standardization (ISO) sets these currency codes, such as GBP for British Pound sterling, USD for the U.S. Dollar, and so on. The company code currency is usually referred to in SAP R/3 as the local currency; other currencies are called foreign currencies.

SAP R/3 is very dynamic in that it allows you to simultaneously maintain ledgers in parallel currencies in conjunction with the company code currency (local currency), for example, in group currency or hard currency.

As part of your customizing exercise, you will define the following items:

- Standard quotation for exchange rates

- Prefixes for direct/indirect quotation exchange rate

- Translation ratios for currency translation

SAP ERP uses two major currency quotations for currency translation: direct and indirect quotations.
In addition to translating amounts into appropriate currencies, exchange rates can also be used for valuation, conversion, transactions, and planning.

Exchange Rate Types

In SAP R/3 several exchange rates are defined and stored for each currency pair. Several exchange rates are held in the system, so it's important that the rates be adequately differentiated. An exchange rate type serves as the mechanism by which exchange rates are differentiated (Figure 7-1).

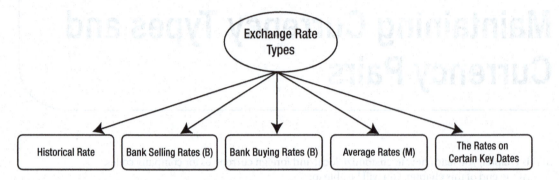

Figure 7-1. Available exchange rate types

When you are maintaining an exchange rate, you can use one of the following tools:

- *Inversion*: Used to calculate an opposite rate from a given exchange rate. The drawback with inversion is that the calculation based on an opposite rate is inadequate. Therefore, it is recommended that you not use it for the average rates (M) exchange rate type.

- *Base currency*: The currency type (for example, USD) that you use in a currency pair for foreign currency translation for a given exchange rate type. This is ideal when you have to translate between several currencies. By using a base currency, you can simplify the problems involved in maintaining several exchange rates.

- *Exchange rate spread*: The constant difference between exchange rate types. For example, the difference between the average rate and bank selling rate or bank buying rate.

In SAP you can use direct or indirect quotations as standard quotations for exchange rates. A *standard quotation* is the universal quotation used for managing exchange rates in foreign currency. You have the choice of defining direct or indirect quotations for each currency pair in an exchange rate. You will look at this in detail in the next section.

Define a Standard Quotation for Exchange Rates

Problem: *Your client wants to be able to maintain exchange rates in a SAP R/3 system. To meet this requirement, you have been asked to define direct and indirect quotations for each GBP/USD currency pair.*

In SAP ERP, exchange rates are quoted as direct or indirect. In this activity you will maintain a direct quotation and an indirect quotation for each currency pair that you want to use as the standard quotations for your exchange rate:

- *Direct quotation*: When one unit of foreign currency is expressed as one unit of your company code currency. For example, one unit of the foreign currency USD 1.00 is displayed in the local currency as GBP 0.56120.

- *Indirect quotation*: When one unit of local currency (your company code) is quoted for one unit of foreign currency. For example, one unit of the local currency GBP 1.00 is quoted as the foreign currency USD 1.63120.

You can define a direct or indirect quotation in the exchange rate table, which becomes available to the users during data input. The exchange rate table contains a list of all exchange rates between various currencies for a range of dates in the system. To display the exchange rate table, use this menu path: Accounting ➤ Financial Accounting ➤ Account Payable ➤ Environment ➤ Current Settings ➤ Enter Exchange Rate.

Let's look at how to define a standard quotation for exchange rates. To go to the screen where you will do this, follow this menu path: IMG: SAP NetWeaver ➤ General Settings ➤ Currencies ➤ Define Standard Quotation for Exchange Rates. You can also just use the transaction code ONOT.

The Change View "Maintenance View TCURN": Overview screen is displayed. To begin customizing your currency quotation, click the [New Entries] button. The New Entries: Overview of Added Entries screen is displayed (Figure 7-2). This is where you define the settings for your currency quotations.

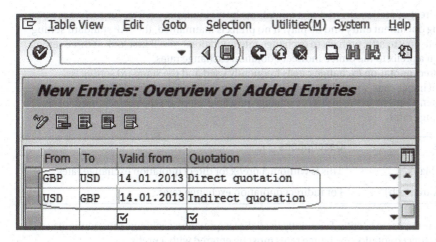

Figure 7-2. Quotation for exchange rates

■ **Note** This activity uses GBP/USD as the currency pair. You can use any currency pair of your choice. The choice of currency pair you ultimately use will be based on your client's requirements.

Update the following input fields:

Valid From: Enter the date you want your exchange rate quotation to start. The system will consider the date you entered in this field as the start date for your exchange rate quotation.

Quotation: Enter the quotation type your company is using as an exchange rate quotation (whether you want your currency pair to be direct or indirect quotation).

■ **Tip** Use today's date in the Valid From field as the start date for your exchange rate quotation.

Click the Enter ⊘ button on the top-left side of the screen to confirm your entries and then save 🖫 your exchange rate quotation.

During exchange rate quotation, it is possible for users to enter a direct quotation as an indirect quotation mistakenly, and vice versa. To avoid this from happening, prefixes are used to differentiate between direct and indirect quotations. In the next activity, you will assign prefixes to exchange rate quotations.

Enter Prefixes for Direct / Indirect Quotation Exchange Rates

You can differentiate indirect quotations from direct quotations by maintaining prefixes for exchange rates, which you can use during document entry and display. If no prefix is maintained, the SAP standard setting is applied. To demonstrate how to affix prefixes to exchange rate quotations, you'll first look at three setting scenarios and then assign a prefix to the direct/indirect quotation exchange rates.

In scenario 1, the direct quotation exchange rate is frequently used and the standard setting is frequently used as the exchange rate. To set this up, leave the exchange rate setting for the direct exchange rates field blank and append a prefix to the indirect exchange rate field. Here are the prefixes used for indirect quotation exchange rates:

Fields	Values	Descriptions
D (Direct)	Leave blank	This is without a prefix for direct quotation exchange rates.
I (Indirect)	/ (forward slash)	For indirect quotation exchange rates.

This setting will allow the users to enter frequently used direct quotation exchange rates without a prefix. The rarely used indirect quotation exchange rates must be entered with a prefix.

In scenario 2, indirect quotation exchange rates are frequently used and direct quotation exchange rates are rarely used. In this case, you can leave the exchange rate setting for indirect quotation for exchange rates blank and assign a prefix to the rarely used direct quotation exchange rates. Here are the prefixes used for direct exchange rate quotations:

Fields	Values	Descriptions
I (Indirect)	Leave blank	This is without prefix for indirect quotation exchange rates.
D (Direct)	* sign	For direct quotation exchange rates.

This setting will allow the users to enter indirect quotation exchange rates without a prefix.

In scenario 3, indirect and direct quotation exchange rates are used equally, so you need to assign a prefix to both individually. Here are the prefixes to use for both the direct and indirect quotations exchange rates.

Fields	Values	Descriptions
D (Direct)	* sign	For direct quotation exchange rates.
I (Indirect)	/ (forward slash)	For indirect quotation exchange rates.

This way, the system will always request that the users enter a prefix when a quotation for exchange rates is entered. The prefix the user enters allows the system to determine whether to use a direct or indirect quotation exchange rate.

> **Problem:** *Your client uses direct quotation exchange rates frequently and seldomly uses indirect quotation exchange rates. You have been asked by your team to define indirect quotation exchange rates with a prefix. (This will help users enter the correct quotation rate.)*

This activity assumes that indirect quotation is rarely used and that direct quotation exchange rates are frequently used. To assign a prefix to direct/indirect quotation exchange rates, follow this menu path: IMG: SAP NetWeaver ➤ General Settings ➤ Currencies ➤ Enter Prefixes for Direct/Indirect Quotation Exchange Rate. Or you can use the transaction code OPRF.

The Change "Direct/Indirect Quotation Prefixes for Exchange Rates" Overview screen is displayed. To assign a prefix, click the `New Entries` button on the top-left side of the screen. The New Entries: Overview of Added Entries screen is displayed. Since this scenario uses the direct exchange rate frequently and rarely uses indirect exchange rate, you leave the D (Direct) field blank and enter / into the I (Indirect) field (Figure 7-3). Click Save 📘.

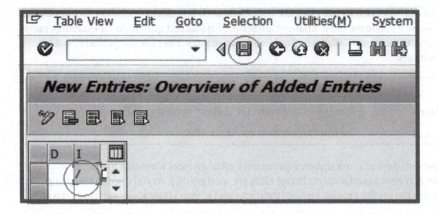

Figure 7-3. *Assigning a prefix for an indirect exchange rate quotation*

Because SAP ERP translates currency by using ratios for each currency type and currency pair, the next step is to define the ratios that will be used for currency translation.

Define Translation Ratios for Currency Translation

You specify the ratios for each currency pair and for each exchange rate type. For example, you specify that on 14/04/2013 the exchange rate for GBP to USD is calculated as a 1:1 ratio. This translation ratio will apply during currency translation and will be displayed during exchange rate translation. Go to the screen to define your translation ratios for currency translation by using this menu path: IMG: SAP NetWeaver ➤ General Settings ➤ Currencies ➤ Define Translation Ratios for Currency Transaction. Or you can use the transaction code OBBS.

A Warning screen pops up with a message that changes made may cause inconsistencies (Figure 7-4).

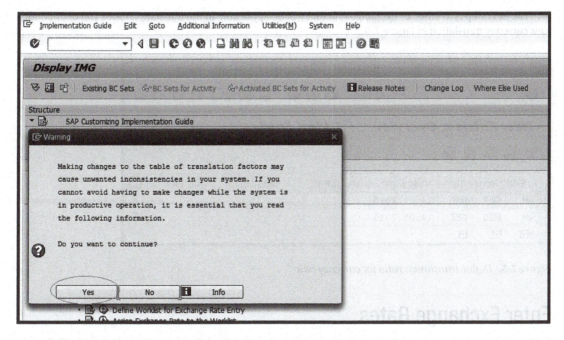

Figure 7-4. *Warning that changes may cause inconsistenies in the system*

Click the [Yes] button at the bottom-left side of the pop-up screen to confirm your action. The Change View: "Currencies: Translation Ratios": Overview screen is displayed. This is where you define the translation ratios. To enter data in the system, click the [New Entries] button on the top-left side of the screen. The New Entries: Overview of Added Entries screen appears (Figure 7-5). This is where you specify the settings for the translation ratio.

Update the following fields:

> **ExRt:** This field allows you to specify an exchange rate for your currency pair. For example, M is the standard translation at average rate. Enter the exchange rate that you want to use in this field. This activity uses M (average). When you use exchange rate type M, you can easily determine the bank selling or bank buying exchange rate by adding or subtracting the exchange rate for the average rate.
>
> There is no hard rule about the exchange rate type you use here. You can use any of the three exchange rate types (G-bank buying rate, B-bank selling rate, and M-average rate), but we advise that you stick to your company's standard.
>
> **From/To:** Enter your currency pair. This activity uses GBP/USD as the currency pair.
>
> **Valid From:** This is the date you want your exchange rate translation to be valid from. It is recommended that you use the current date.
>
> **Ratio (From):** Enter the ratio you want to use for your currency translation. This example uses a ratio of 1:1.

Click the Enter ✅ button on the top-left side of the screen to confirm your entries and then click Save 🖫.

The next step is to enter an exchange rate that will be applicable to the translation ratios you defined for your currency translation in Figure 7-5.

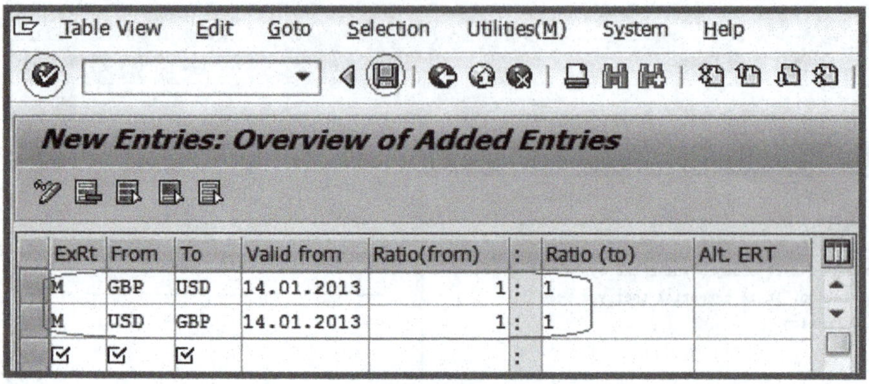

Figure 7-5. *Define translation ratio for currency pair*

Enter Exchange Rates

Exchange rates are used to translate one currency to another and are defined on a period basis (the Valid From field). The rates play an important role during posting and clearing because they are used to translate foreign amounts posted and cleared to your company code's currency (the local currency). Secondly, exchange rates determine the gain or loss arising from exchange rate differences and valuate open items and balance sheet accounts in foreign currency during the closing process.

The exchange rate setting is applicable to all company codes. Exchange rate types are supplied by SAP. We recommend that you use the M exchange rate type for your foreign currency translation during document posting or clearing in exchange rate field (ExRt). An exchange rate type must exist in the system, and the M type exchange rate is applicable to all company codes.

You will specify the following conversion objects for:

- Exchange rate type

- Valid from

- Currency key

To enter your exchange rate, use this menu path: IMG: SAP NetWeaver ➤ General Settings ➤ Currencies ➤ Enter Exchange Rates. Or use the transaction code OB08.

The Change View "Currency Exchange Rates": Overview screen is displayed. This is where you enter your exchange rate. To enter your exchange rate in the system, click the New Entries button on the top-left side of the screen. The New Entries: Overview of Added Entries screen appears (Figure 7-6).

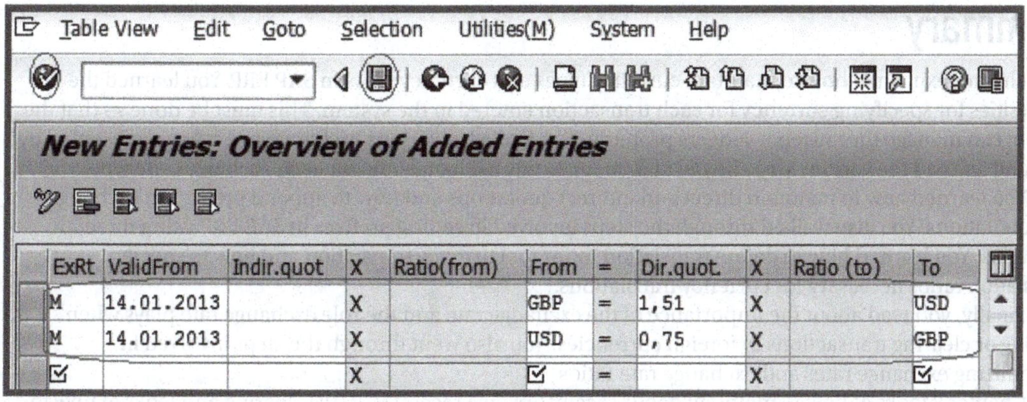

Figure 7-6. *General settings for the exchange rate*

Update the following fields:

> **ExRt:** Enter the exchange rate that you want to use in this field. We recommend that you use M (average rate) as your exchange rate type.
>
> **Valid From:** This is the date you want your exchange rate to be valid from. We recommend that you use current date (today's date).
>
> **From/To:** Enter your currency pair. This activity uses GBP/USD as the currency pair.
>
> **Dir.quot.:** Since you are using direct quotation for your exchange rate, enter the exchange rates for GBP and USD in this field.

Once you have updated the screen, click the Enter 🗸 button on the top-left side of the screen and save 🖫 your settings. Upon saving, note that the exchange rate ratio you specified is displayed in the ratio fields (Figure 7-7).

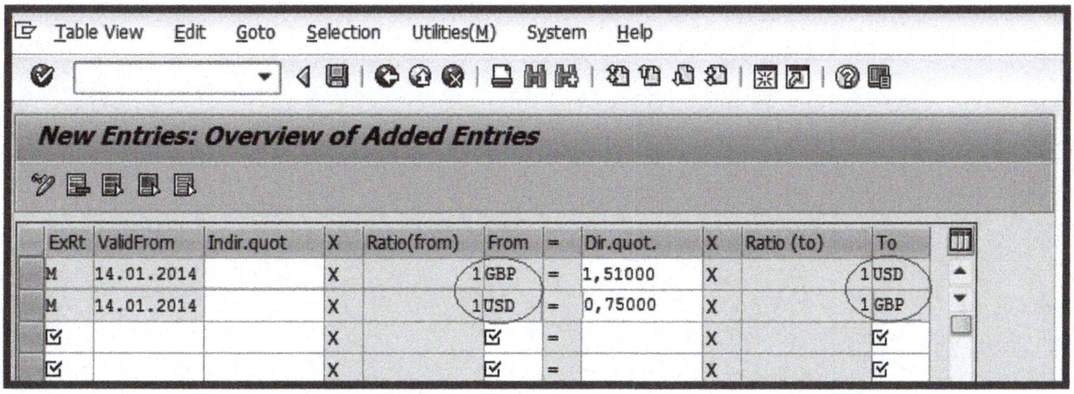

Figure 7-7. *The completion of the general settings for exchange rate*

Summary

This chapter explained how to maintain currency types and currency pairs in SAP ERP. You learned the necessities for specifying currency for each transaction entered in the system. This must be done so that the system can manage the currency ledgers properly. You looked at various exchange rate types represented by SAP and learned the various steps involved in maintaining exchange rate for each exchange rate type.

You learned how to maintain direct and indirect quotations and how to append prefixes to exchange rate quotations. You also walked through the steps involved in setting prefixes in SAP ERP using three scenarios. You learned how to define translation ratios for currency translation and how to specify translation ratios necessary for currency translations.

Finally, you read about the importance of the exchange rate and the role exchange rate plays when posting or clearing transactions in foreign currencies. You also went through the steps involved in customizing exchange rates and exchange rate ratios.

Chapter 8 looks at how to maintain goods receipt/invoice receipt (GR/IR) clearing and looks at how to maintain accounts for automatic postings during GR/IR clearing.

■ ■ ■

Defining Adjustment Accounts for GR/IR Clearing

In this chapter, you learn about the Goods Receipt/Invoice Receipt (GR/IR) and learn how to define adjustment accounts for GR/IR.

At the end of this chapter, you will be able to:

- Understand how GR/IR clearing accounts are posted in the system using a double entry procedure.

- Customize GR/IR settings for good that have been invoiced but not yet delivered.

- Customize GR/IR settings for goods that have been delivered but not yet invoiced.

- Customize GR/IR settings for posting offsets to a GR/IR clearing account.

GR/IR Clearing

It's normal in some business settings for goods to be delivered before the associated invoice arrives and is paid. This type of transaction is referred to in SAP ERP as *delivered but not yet invoiced*. Likewise, it is possible for an invoice to arrive before the goods do. This is referred to in SAP ERP as *invoiced but not yet delivered*.

To account for the movement of invoices and goods in the system, *provisional accounts* (clearing accounts) are used. They offset any timing differences between invoice receipt and goods delivery. To account for these differences, you define *adjustment accounts* (clearing accounts for goods that have been received but not yet invoiced) and *target accounts* (clearing accounts for invoices received when goods have not been delivered). This is used for automatic posting of GR/IR to offset postings (this is an account that writes off the balance of another account). So that the system can reflect these temporary discrepancies, transfer postings are made on the balance sheet date. The system analyzes the transactions in the GR/IR clearing accounts. It then posts the outstanding balances to adjustment accounts and subsequently posts any differences to offsetting accounts.

Differences in quantity between goods delivered and the invoice receipt result in a debit balance in the GR/IR clearing account. When you receive an invoice for part of a delivery, the invoice amount is posted to the inventory account and to the GR/IR clearing account based on your settings on the balance sheet date. Transfer postings are performed to identify the part of goods delivered but not yet invoiced to the relevant adjustment account. The program then posts an offsetting entry to the goods delivered but not yet invoiced adjustment account (the target account). After the financial statement has been generated at a given key date, these postings are reversed.

Figure 8-1 illustrates how GR/IR clearing accounts are posted in the system using a double entry procedure. For example, goods worth $1500 were delivered to you, but you got an invoice for $1000.

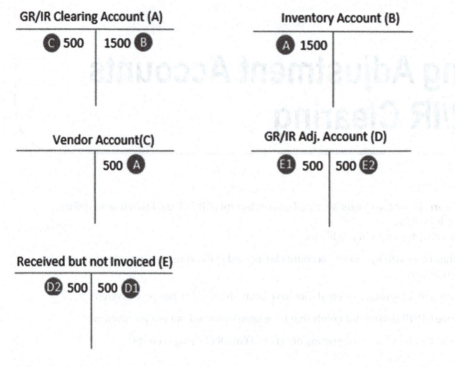

Figure 8-1. *Accounting transaction showing differences between goods delivered and the invoice receipt*

The $1500 Ⓐ of goods is posted as a debit item in the Inventory Account (B) and the corresponding credit posting of $1500 Ⓑ is carried out by the system to the GR/IR Clearing Account (A). The balance of $500 Ⓒ (the $1500 goods delivered less the partial delivery invoice of $500) is posted to the credit side of the Vendor Account (C). A corresponding debit balance of $500 Ⓐ is posted to the GR/IR Clearing Account (A). The system will then post the $500 Ⓓ1 and Ⓔ1 difference between goods delivered and invoice receipt to the GR/IR Adjustment Account (D), and post an offsetting entry to the Received but not Invoiced Account (E). Upon the creation of financial statements, the Ⓓ2 and Ⓔ2 postings are reversed at a balance sheet date.

___

■ **Note**   Before you proceed with the settings in this activity, go to "Appendix A, Chapter 8, GR/IR Clearing" to create the GL accounts for your configuration.

___

The next section looks at the steps involved in customizing the GR/IR clearing accounts when an invoice is received but goods have not yet been delivered.

Invoiced But Not Yet Delivered

Problem: You have been asked to define clearing accounts for offsetting goods that have been invoiced but not yet delivered. This is when an invoice has been received but the goods have not been delivered. When the invoice is posted in the system, the inventory account is credited and the GR/IR clearing account is debited.

You will define the clearing account for offsetting a posting in the system. Go to the screen where you will perform the setting for GR/IR clearing account in the system by following this menu path: IMG: Financial Accounting (New) ➤ General Ledger Accounting (New) ➤ Periodic Processing ➤ Reclassify ➤ Define Adjustment Accounts for GR/IR Clearing. Or you can use the transaction code OBYP.

The Configuration Accounting Maintain: Automatic Posts – Procedure screen is displayed (Figure 8-2). This is where you define adjustment accounts for GR/IR clearing.

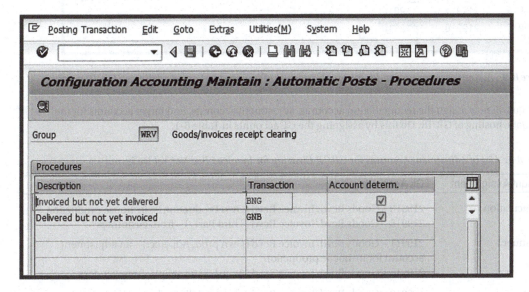

Figure 8-2. *Defining automatic postings for GR/IR clearing*

Select the Invoiced But Not Yet Delivered option from the displayed list of items in Figure 8-2 and click the Details button on the top-left side of the screen to go to the next screen where you will enter your settings. The Enter Chart of Accounts dialog box pops up. Enter your chart of accounts in the Chart of Accounts field and click the Enter button or press Enter on your keyboard. The Configuration Accounting Maintain: Automatic Posts – Accounts screen is displayed (Figure 8-3), where you will assign accounts for your GR/IR clearing.

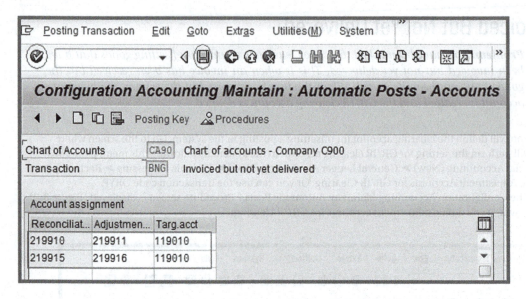

Figure 8-3. *Account determination for automatic posting of invoiced but not yet delivered GR/IR accounts*

You will now assign the reconciliation accounts, adjustment accounts, and target accounts for the automatic posting of GR/IR. Do this by assigning the GL accounts in Table 8-1.

Table 8-1. *List of Adjustment Accounts for GR/IR Clearing for Invoiced But Not Yet Delivered*

Account Assignment	GL Accounts
Reconciliation	219910 – Goods Rcvd/Invoice Rcvd (Own Production)—in-house production 219915 – Goods Rcvd/Invoice Rcvd (Third Party)—from customers
Adjustment	219911 – Goods Rcvd/Invoice Rcvd (Own prod. Adj. Acc.)—an adjustment account for in-house production 219916 – Goods Rcvd/Invoice Rcvd (Acqrd. Externally)—from vendors
Target	119010 – Goods Rcvd/Invoice Rcvd—not yet delivered 119010 – Goods Rcvd/Invoice Rcvd—not yet delivered

After updating the screen, click the Enter ✅ button on the top-left side of the screen or press Enter on your keyboard. The system will accept your entries. Save 🖫 your account assignment.

It is a common business practice for customers to receive goods they ordered and then be invoiced for the goods at a later date. The next step in this activity is to look at how to assign accounts for automatic posting when goods are delivered to the customers but have not yet been invoiced.

Delivered But Not Yet Invoiced

Problem: You have been asked to define clearing accounts for offsetting postings for goods delivered but not yet invoiced.

When goods are received but not yet invoiced, the inventory account is debited and the GR/IR clearing account is credited.

In order for the system to carry out automatic postings to various accounts that are affected by this transaction, you must assign appropriate accounts to your GR/IR clearing. You need to go to the screen where you will carry out account assignment for GR/IR clearing for offsetting postings. Follow this menu path: IMG: Financial Accounting (New) ➤ General Ledger Accounting (New) ➤ Periodic Processing ➤ Reclassify ➤ Define Adjustment Accounts for GR/IR Clearing. Or you can use the transaction code OBYP.

The Configuration Accounting Maintain: Automatic Posts – Procedure screen appears (Figure 8-2). To define goods delivered but invoice not received adjustment accounts, select Delivered But Not Yet Invoiced from the list of items displayed on the screen and click the Details 🔍 button on the top-left side of the screen. The Chart of Accounts screen pops up. This screen will take you to your chart of accounts. Enter your chart of accounts in the Chart of Accounts field and click the Enter ✔ button on the bottom-right side of the screen. The Configuration Accounting Maintain: Automatic Posts – Accounts screen is displayed. Here, you specify the accounts for automatic posting for your GR/IR clearing for goods delivered but not yet invoiced. Assign the accounts using the information in Table 8-2 (Figure 8-4).

Table 8-2. *List of Adjustment Accounts for GR/IR Clearing for Goods Delivered But Not Yet Invoiced*

Account Assignments	GL Accounts
Reconciliation	219910 – Goods Rcvd/Invoice Rcvd—(Own Production)
	219915 – Goods Rcvd/Invoice Rcvd—(Third Party)
Adjustment	219911 – Goods Rcvd/Invoice Rcvd—(Own Prod. Adj. Acc.)
	219916 – Goods Rcvd/Invoice Rcvd—(Acqrd. Externally)
Target	119015 – Goods Rcvd/Invoice Rcvd—not yet delivered
	119015 – Goods Rcvd/Invoice Rcvd—not yet delivered

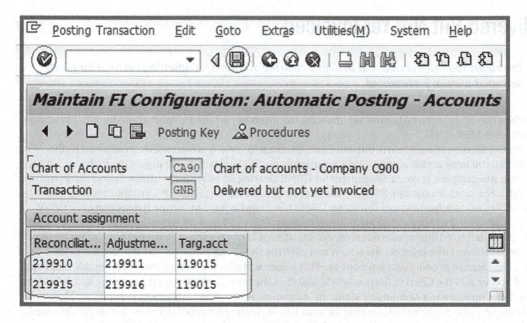

Figure 8-4. Account determination for automatic posting for GR/IR for delivered but not invoiced

The accounts you assign here will allow the system to perform automatic postings to these accounts. After updating the screen, click the Enter ✅ button at the top-left side of the screen or press Enter on your keyboard to confirm your entries. Then save 🖬 your account assignment.

Summary

When accounting for invoices and movement of goods in the system, you must define provisional accounts (clearing accounts) that offset postings when goods and invoices aren't simultaneously delivered and paid. This chapter illustrated how GR/IR clearings are posted in the system using the double entry procedure. You then learned how to define adjustment accounts, reconciliation accounts, and target accounts for automatic posting for GR/IR clearing in SAP ERP.

You also learned how to assign various accounts to GR/IR clearing and learned how this works in SAP ERP during posting of transactions whereby goods are received and not yet delivered and whereby an invoice is received and the goods are not yet delivered.

Chapter 9 defines a house bank and explains how it's configured in SAP ERP. You will also be looking how SAP ERP supports bank statements. As part of that chapter, you will learn how to define posting keys and posting rules for bank statements and check deposits, respectively.

■ ■ ■

Defining the House Bank

In this chapter, you learn how to customize the house bank in financial (FI).
At the end of this chapter, you will be able to:

- Describe what a house bank is

- Identify the components of a master record in a house bank

- Define a house bank

- Use a house bank ID and an account ID

- Identify bank statements supported by SAP

- Assign global settings for an electronic bank statement

- Configure a manual bank statement

- Define posting keys and posting rules for check deposits

- Define variants for check deposits

House Bank

The banks that hold your company code bank account are referred to as *house banks* in SAP ERP (for example City Bank, Bank of America, etc.). A company code can have more than one house bank assigned to it. Figure 9-1 shows how house banks are structured in SAP ERP.

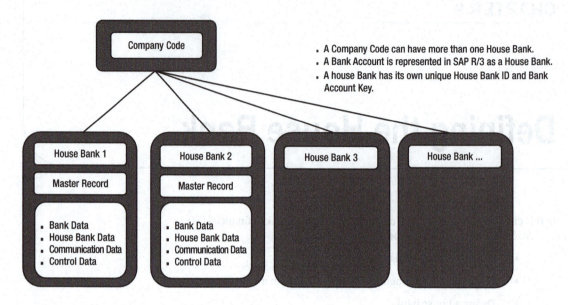

Figure 9-1. *The structure of a house bank in SAP R/3*

Each house bank has its own master record that's stored centrally in the bank directory. The master data that's stored in the bank directory is made up of the following sections:

- *Bank Account Data section*: This section contains your company code bank account number, which is a unique account number issued by your bank to you. Your company code IBAN (International Bank Account Number) is an internationally recognized account number used for international transaction payments. Your company code local currency is the currency used by your company code. A G/L account number is assigned to your bank's G/L account.

- *House Bank Data section*: Contains bank currency, which is the currency used by your bank. A *bank key*, which is sometime referred to as your bank sort code, is a unique identification code for your bank.

- *Communication Data section*: Contains telephone and contact persons at your bank.

- *Address section*: Contains your bank address details, including your bank name, region, street, and city.

- *Control Data section*: Contains a Bank Account Number, SWIFT (Society for World-Wide Interbank Financial Telecommunication) code, and so on. The SWIFT code is used for identifying banks in international payment transactions. The first four characters contain the bank code (alphabetical characters only). The next two characters contain the ISO (in numeric digits) and two alpha digits for the country code.

- *EDI section*: EDI stands for Electronic Data Interchange and is used to process electronic business transactions between different applications.

- *Data Medium Exchange (DME) section*: Enter general data for data medium exchange in this section. These are predefined file formats that meet the requirements of your financial institution. DME allows the system to send and receive data in DME format.

A combination of the house bank ID and the account ID makes up the bank account in the SAP R/3 system. You enter the house bank ID and the account ID in the G/L account so that the system can recognize the appropriate G/L account during bank transactions. The bank group is used for classifying banks. The concept of an account group is helpful when you use the same bank as your business partners. For example, all the business partners might belong to the HSBC bank group. The aim of the classification is to group banks together in such a way that payment transactions within a group can be carried out as fast as possible (this is referred to as *payment optimization*).

■ **Note**   When a business partner (customer/vendor) has more than one bank account for payment, the bank type in the customer master record is used to distinguish between different banks. During invoice processing, the SAP ERP user can decide which bank to use by choosing a matchcode in the partner bank field in the partner's master data. The matchcode is a user-friendly tool in SAP that assists you in searching for data stored in the system. Matchcode maintenance is outside the scope of this book, as it requires technical knowledge of the ABAP4 (the programmers).

Before proceeding with your house bank configuration, go to "Appendix A, Chapter 9, House Bank" to create the appropriate G/L accounts needed for your house bank configuration.

The next section explains how to define house banks for your bank accounts in SAP ERP.

Define House Banks

As mentioned, banks used by company codes in the SAP ERP system are called *house banks*. A combination of the house bank ID and the account ID makes up the bank account in SAP R/3 system. The house bank ID and the account ID you define are used by the payment program to determine the banks to use during invoice payment.

■ **Note**   The SAP ERP system comes with examples of standard house banks. If you are not confident in configuring a house bank, take a look at them as a guide.

> **Problem:** *Company C900 Plc has two bank accounts (Barclays Bank and HSBC Bank). You need to define the house banks for both bank accounts.*

To define house banks, use the menu path: IMG: Financial Accounting (New) ➤ Financial Accounting Global IMG: Financial Accounting (New) ➤ Bank Accounting ➤ Bank Accounts ➤ Define House Bank. Or you can use the transaction code F112.

The Determine Work Area: Entry screen pops up and requests your company code. When you enter your company code in the Company Code field, the system will automatically determine your company code house bank work area. Enter your company code in the Company Code field on the screen and click the Enter ☑ button at the bottom of the screen or press Enter on your keyboard. The Change View "House Banks" Overview screen, where you start the customizing your house bank, is displayed (Figure 9-2).

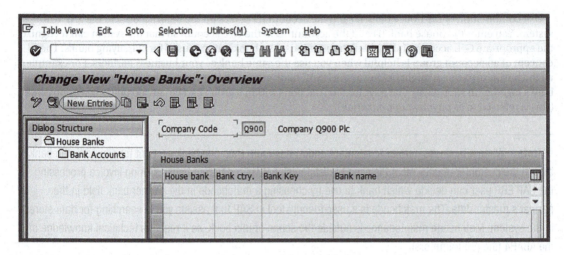

Figure 9-2. *The initial screen where you start customizing your house bank*

Click the New Entries button on the top-left side of the screen (circled red in Figure 9-2). This will take you to the screen in Figure 9-3, where you will define the house bank for your company code.

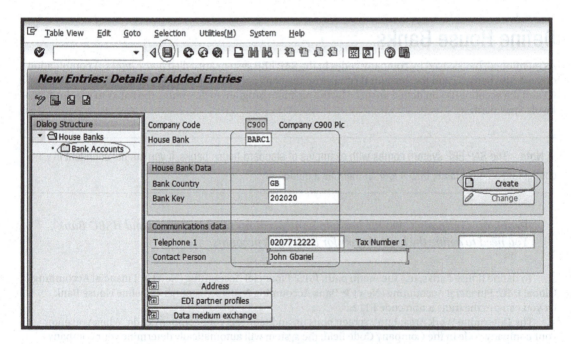

Figure 9-3. *The screen where you create the house bank for your company code*

Update the following fields:

Company Code: Since you have entered it when you determined work area for your company code earlier, the system will enter your company code as the default.

House Bank: Enter your house bank ID in this field. You can enter up to five digits as your house bank ID. This ID will enable you to identify this bank account, especially when you have multiple house banks. The house bank ID is also entered in the bank account G/L account master data and customer/vendor master record for the automatic payment program.

Bank Country: Enter your country ID (for example, for Great Britain, you would enter **GB)**. This is a predefined key supplied by SAP in the system. The importance of the bank country ID is that it allows you to identfy your house bank country. The country ID also forms part of the IBAN and SWIFT numbers for international payments.

Bank Key: Enter your bank sort code. This helps identify your bank and the branch. This key is very important as it forms part of the IBAN and SWIFT numbers used for international payments.

Telephone: Enter the bank's telephone number.

Contact Person: Enter your account manager or other bank staff member who is designated by the bank to your account.

After updating the preceding fields, click the ⬜ Create button on the right side of the screen. This will call up the Bank Data screen, where you can enter more information about your house bank. For example, you can enter your bank address, region, and so on. Once you have added your entries, click Continue ✔ on the bottom-right side of the screen to confirm your entries and save 💾 your house bank.

The next step in this activity is to define your bank account. This is found in the on the left side of the screen in Figure 9-3, circled in red.

Define Bank Accounts for Your House Banks

Since you want to define the bank account for your house bank, double-click the (• ☐ Bank Accounts) folder on the left side of the New Entries: Details of Added Entries screen (see Figure 9-.3). The Change View "Bank Accounts": Overview screen is displayed; this is the initial screen where you will select the house bank you want to define a bank account for. If this is the first house bank you have created, the screen will be blank.

Click the New Entries button on the top-left side of the screen. The New Entries: Details of Added Entries screen is displayed (Figure 9-4). This is where you specify your bank account data.

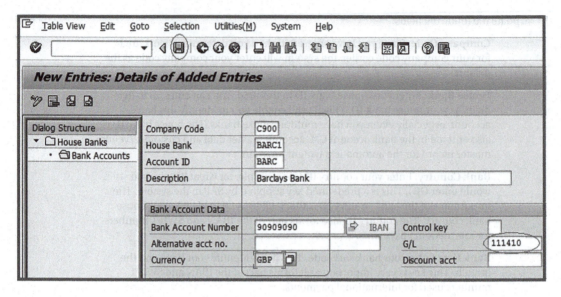

Figure 9-4. *The bank details entry screen*

Update the following fields using your company's bank data, or you can use the data on the screen for this activity:

> **Company Code** and **House Bank:** The system automatically uses the data you entered when you defined your house bank earlier.

> **Account ID:** This is a unique account ID that you enter in your G/L account for your bank account. You can enter up to five digits as your account ID.

> **Description:** Enter a short text describing your bank account. This is usually the name of your bank.

> **Currency:** Usually, companies use different bank accounts for different currencies. Enter the currency that your company uses for this bank account.

> **G/L:** Enter the G/L account for your bank account in this field. This is the G/L account you created for your bank account in "Appendix A, Chapter 9, House Bank" before you started your configuration.

■ **Note** When you want to enable e-banking, click the EDI partner profiles (see Figure 9-3) to attach the EDI partner to your house bank. EDI provides standard formats that allow business partners to exchange data electronically.

You have just created your house bank. You can now save it by clicking the Save 💾 button.

Following the steps in Define Bank Accounts for your House Banks section earlier and using the information in Table 9-1, define another bank account and house bank for the HSBC bank.

Table 9-1. *Data to Define the HSBC Bank Account and House Bank*

Field Name	Bank Data
Company Code	Enter your company code in this field.
House Bank	HSBC1
Bank Country	Enter your country code in this field. For example, for Britain use GB or for Germany, use DE.
Bank Key	Enter your bank unique sort code in this field.
Address Section	Enter your bank address.
Account ID	HSBC
Description	HSBC Bank
Bank Account Number	Enter your bank account in this field.
Currency	Enter your country currency code in this field. For example, the currency code for United States is USD and for Germany, it's EUR.
G/L	Enter the G/L account you want to post your bank transactions in this field.

Bank Statements

A *bank statement* is a summary of financial transactions, such as incoming and outgoing payments that took place during a given period on an account. This is the state of your cash position. SAP ERP supports two types of bank statements: electronic bank statements and manual bank statements.

Before you create your electronic and manual bank statements, it is recommended that you first create the following clearing accounts (refer to "Appendix A, Chapter 9, House Bank"), which your bank transactions will be posted to:

Main Bank Account: As the name suggests, this is the general bank account entered in the house bank master data. This account serves as a reconciliation account that holds the bank account balance.

Checks Received: The checks you received for invoice amounts from your customers or business partners for supplying them goods or for providing services are posted to this account.

Other Interim Posting: Reconciliation items are posted to this account.

Check Issued out: Check payments made by your company to its creditors or business partners for goods/services received are posted to this account.

Outgoing Wire Transfer: This is an electronic method of funds transfer from your company to a business partner to mitigate due invoice(s). This is a very fast way of transferring money from one person to another or from one company to another.

Incoming Cash: Cash received by your company from business partners for a business transaction are posted to this account.

Outgoing Cash: Cash payments made by your company relating to business transactions to business partners are posted to this account.

■ **Note**   We have provided information in "Appendix A, Chapter 9 Bank Statement" that will enable you to create the G/L account that you will need to customize your bank statement. We recommend that you first create the necessary G/L account before creating your bank statement.

The next section defines an electronic bank statement and explains how to set up an electronic bank statement (EBS) framework. Later in this chapter, you will define manual bank statements.

Electronic Bank Statement

An *electronic bank statement* is simply a bank statement generated by your bank in an electronic format. It provides detailed information about the movement of funds in your bank account created at the house bank during any given period. With SAP R/3 it is possible to retrieve bank statements electronically using bank communication management. Bank communication management manages multiple bank communication interfaces that allow you to connect to your bank using a defined standard protocol. When a bank statement is uploaded to SAP ERP, it can serve the following purposes:

- Clears all bank clearing accounts in the system to the bank main account (this is the general bank account entered in the house bank master data).

- Uses the bank statement to perform automatic bank reconciliations in the system.

SAP R/3 supports various electronic bank statement formats, including Multicash, SWIFT, BAI, BAI2, and others:

- *Multicash*: Invented by Omikron a German Company, Multicash is an electronic bank statement format that allows the SAP ERP system to communicate with the bank system. The format is split into two file formats. AUSZUG.TXT holds the bank statement header information and UMSATZ.TXT contains the bank account transactions information.

- *SWIFT (Society for World-Wide Interbank Financial Telecommunication)*: This is a computer-based switching system used by banks for making payments related to international transactions.

- *BAI (Bank Administration Institute)*: This is a standardized electronic file format used for cash management between the bank and the account holder. The bank transmits BAI file formats to the account holder who in turns downloads or inputs the file into the system, generates a bank statement, and performs bank reconciliation.

- *BAI2*: This is the latest release of a cash management balance report. It is very similar to BAI in functionality. The only difference is that BAI2 contains more detailed information.

Make Global Settings for Electronic Bank Statements

In this activity, you will configure seven global settings for your electronic bank statement. The list of these settings is displayed on the left side of the Change View "Create Account Symbols": Overview screen.

Four of the settings that you will be customizing are also applicable to manual bank statements, so you don't need to define them again during the manual bank statement configuration:

Create Account Symbols: The accounts symbols that you create as part of your electronic bank customizing will specify the G/L accounts and subledgers that the bank statement transactions are posted to.

Assign Accounts to Account Symbols: This allows you to assign or map account symbols to appropriate G/L accounts and subledgers.

Create Keys for Posting Rules: Posting keys determine the posting rules applicable to the general ledger and subledgers.

Define Posting Rules: Posting rules represent how business transactions in the bank statement use appropriate posting keys, document types, and posting types. For example, incoming checks, checks out, bank transfers, bank charges, and so on.

Problem: The accounting team at company C900 Plc wants to upload their bank statements electronically using the defined bank communication standard. SAP supports various electronic bank statement formats, including Multicash, BAI, BAI2, SWIFT, and so on. It is your responsibility to define the appropriate settings needed to allow the accounting team to upload bank statements electronically so they can clear several bank clearing accounts and carry out automatic bank reconciliation.

To go to the screen where you will customize the electronic bank statement, follow this menu path: IMG: Financial Accounting (New) ➤ Bank Accounting ➤ Business Transactions ➤ Payment Transactions ➤ Electronic Bank Statement ➤ Make Global Settings for Electronic Bank Statement. Or you can use transaction code OT83.

The Determine Work Area: Entry dialog box pops up. Enter your company code in the Company Code field on the screen and click the Enter ☑ button at the bottom of the screen or press enter on your keyboard. The Change View "Create Account Symbols:" Overview screen is displayed (Figure 9-5). This is the initial screen for customizing electronic bank statements. The left pane of this screen shows all the nodes you will need to customize.

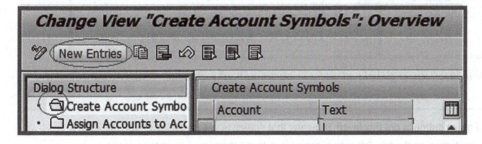

Figure 9-5. *The initial screen for global settings for an electronic bank statement—Create Account Symbols*

■ **Tip**   To ensure that your configuration is complete, work through the folders on the left side of the screen systematically from the top down.

Step 1: Create Account Symbols

The first step in this activity is to create account symbols for these accounts. Notice that the Create Account Symbol folder on the left pane of the screen is open. This is the first item on the list.

■ **Note**   An open folder indicates that this is the current item you want to customize; all other folders remain closed. If the folder you want to work on is not open, double-click it.

Click the New Entries button. The New Entries: Overview of Added Entries screen is displayed (Figure 9-6). This screen will allow you to create your own account symbols for your electronic bank statement. Update the New Entries screen with your account symbol.

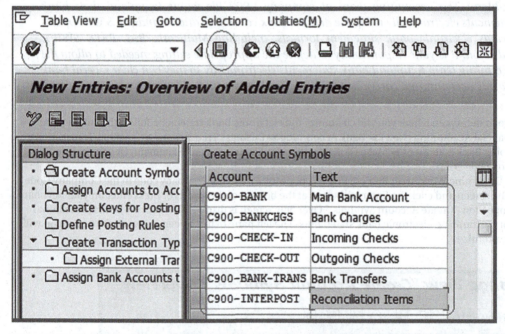

Figure 9-6. *The input screen for global settings for an electronic bank statement—Create Account Symbols*

■ **Tip**   If New Entries button is not displayed, it means that screen is set to display mode. Click the Display/Change 🖉 button on the top-left side of the screen to set the screen to change mode.

There is no hard rule for creating account symbols. You don't necessarily have to use the account symbols used here. You can formulate your own. If you are using your own account symbols, make sure that you use meaningful descriptions. The account symbols you create in this activity will be assigned to the subledgers and the general ledger you created in your house bank in Step 2.

■ **Note** Once someone else has used an account symbol, the system will not allow you to use that same symbol, so you might have to get creative.

Once you have updated the screen in Figure 9-6 with your account symbols, click the Enter ✅ button on the top-left side of the screen to ensure that the system accepted your entries. Save 💾 your account symbols.

The next step is to assign the G/L accounts to the accounts symbols you just created.

Step 2: Assign Accounts to Account Symbols

By assigning accounts to the account symbols, the system will automatically map the subledgers and the G/L account that transactions are posted to when users retrieve bank statements electronically. For example, checks received are posted to the Incoming Checks account, charges are posted to the Bank Charges account, and so on.

To go the next screen where you will assign accounts to account sysmbols, double-click the `☐ Assign Accounts to Account Symbol` folder on the left side of the screen. The Change View "Assign Accounts to Account Symbol": Overview screen is displayed. This is where you will assign accounts to account symbols.

Click the `New Entries` button on the top-left side of the screen to display the New Entries: Overview of Added Entries screen. This is where you assign the account symbols to your system account.

Enter each of your account symbols in the Acct. Symbol fields. If you cannot remember your account symbols, you can look for them using the Search function 🔍 button. The Bank Statement: Account Symbol screen contains lists of all the account symbols in the system, including the ones you created for your electronic bank statement (Figure 9-7).

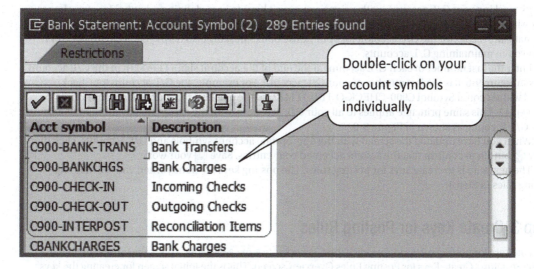

Figure 9-7. Global settings for an electronic bank statement—the list of account symbols

Click the Scroll ⬆⬇ button to search for your account symbols and assign them to the system account symbols appropriately on the New Entries: Overview of Added Entries screen (Figure 9-8).

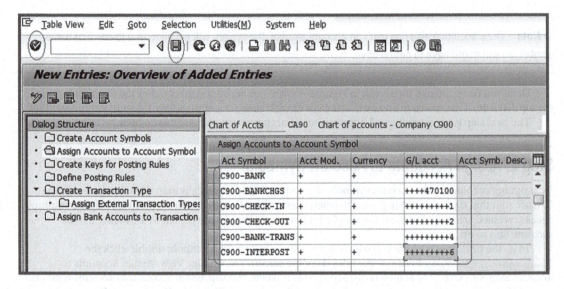

Figure 9-8. *Global settings for an electronic bank statement—Assign External Transaction Types*

In order to avoid defining separate account symbols for each house bank account, enter a plus sign (+) in the Account Modification and Currency fields. Also, if you want to avoid having to define separate account symbols and different G/L accounts for every house bank in the system, we advise that you mask the G/L account field.

By masking your G/L accounts with + signs, you won't have to keep defining a symbol for every house bank when a new G/L is defined. When you mask your G/L accounts with ++++++++++, the system will automatically recognize the G/L account for your house bank. Masking also helps you avoid input errors when you're maintaining G/L accounts.

Enter the last number of each G/L account at the end of the account sign ++++++++n in the G/L account fields in Figure 9-8. n is the last number of your G/L account. For example, the G/L account for Check Issued with Account Symbol C900-CHECK-OUT is 111412, so the masking for your G/L account would be ++++++++++2. This same principle applies to all your G/L accounts, with the exception of your main house bank G/L account, as shown in Figure 9-8.

When you have updated the screen with the appropriate account symbols and G/L accounts, click the Enter 🟢 button to confirm that the system accepted your entries. Save 💾 your work.

The next step is to create keys for posting rules. The posting keys are handy when you are defining posting rules in Step 4.

Step 3: Create Keys for Posting Rules

To create keys for posting rules, double-click the ☐ Create Keys for Posting Rules folder. This is the third item on the Dialog Structure. Create Keys for Posting Rules Overview screen. This is the initial screen for creating the keys for posting rules. To proceed to the New Entries: Overview of Added Entries screen (Figure 9-9), where you will define the keys for posting rules, click the New Entries button on the top-left side of the screen.

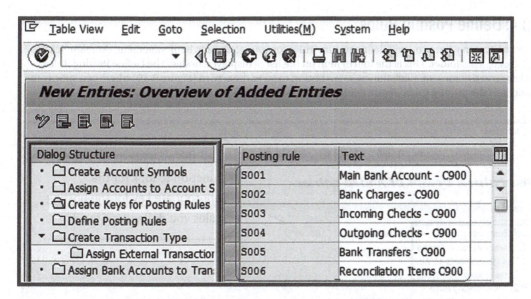

Figure 9-9. *Global settings for an electronic bank statement—Create Keys for Posting Rules*

■ **Note**   You can use the posting keys supplied by SAP or you can create your own posting keys from scratch. In this activity, we recommend that you create your own posting keys so you'll know how to do so.

Using the data on the New Entries: Overview of Added Entries screen, create posting rules for each of your account symbols. In this activity, we created six keys for posting rules and described the keys for posting rules in the Text section (see Figure 9-9).

■ **Tip**   The system allows a maximum of six digits for a posting rule key.

Update the screen as shown in Figure 9-9. Click the Enter ⊘ button on the top-left side of the screen to confirm your entries and save 🖫 your keys for posting rules.

■ **Note**   The posting keys for posting rules used in this activity are for illustration only. You can use any keys and any descriptions of your choice.

In Step 4, you will define the posting rules that are assigned to related external transactions.

Step 4: Define Posting Rules

To go to the screen where you will define posting rules for your electronic bank statement, double-click the ☐Define Posting Rules folder. This is the fourth item on the list of displayed nodes. The Define Posting Rules Overview screen comes up. Click the New Entries button to go to the screen (Figure 9-10) where you specify the definitions of the posting rules. Figure 9-10 defines posting rules for incoming checks.

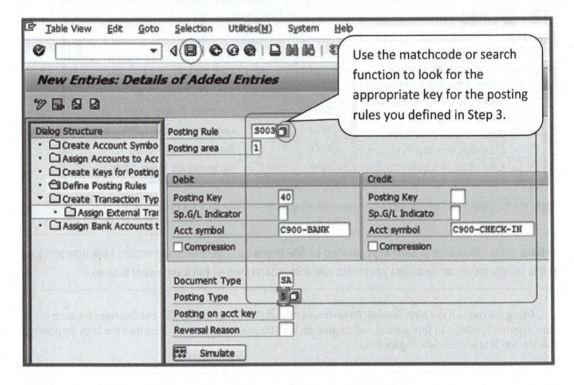

Figure 9-10. Global settings for an electronic bank statement—Define Posting Rules for Check-In

Update the following fields:

Posting Rule: Enter the keys for posting rules that you defined in Step 3 in the Posting Rule fields. Posting rules are used by the system to determine which G/L accounts and subledgers to post transactions to. For example, the key S003 was created for incoming checks.

Posting Area: The SAP ERP system comes with two standard values for the posting area (1-Bank Accounting and 2–Subledger Accounting). The posting area allows the system to post to either of the specified areas based on your specification.

Posting Key: Enter the appropriate posting key in this field. Posting key allows the system to determine whether a line item should be treated as debit or credit and the account type to post transactions to. It also controls the field status for document entry.

Acct Symbol: You have already defined a number of accounts symbols. Enter the appropriate account symbol in this field. The account symbol you enter here will allow the system to determine which account the related transaction is posted to when users retrieve bank statements electronically.

Document Type: Allows you to differentiate between transactions and allows the system to determine which business transaction to be posted to.

Posting Type: It is mandatory that you enter one posting type in the Posting Type field. The posting type is used during account clearing. For example, Posting Type 5-clears the credit G/L account. This can be found by using the Search icon next to the posting type field (see Figure 9-10).

■ **Note**   This configuration is for incoming checks. The accounting entries for check receipt is to debit your bank account using the Debit Posting key 40, since money is coming in. Likewise, it will credit a corresponding incoming check clearing account.

Similarly, the configuration for outgoing checks is the reverse. They credit your bank account using posting key 50 and debit the corresponding outgoing check clearing account.

After updating the screen in Figure 9-10, click the Enter 🗹 button to confirm your entries. Save 🖫 your work.

Next, you need to define the posting rules for the remaining business transactions (S004-Check in, S005-Wire Transfer-out, S002-Bank Charges, and S006-Other Interim Post).

Click the Back 🔄 button to return to the previous screen, called Change View "Define Posting Rules": Overview, where you will define more posting rules.

Follow Step 4 to define posting rules for the remaining business transactions for your electronic bank statement, but this time use the information in Tables 9-2 through 9-5.

Table 9-2. Define Posting Rules for Issued Checks

Field Name		Data to Enter
Posting Rule		Enter the key for the posting rule you defined for checks (S004).
Posting Area		Enter the bank accounting (1).
Acct Symbol	Debit	Enter the account symbol you defined for checks issued (C900-CHECK-OUT).
Posting Key	Credit	Enter the posting key (50) for credit posting.
Acct Symbol		Enter the account symbol you defined for your main bank account (C900-BANK).
Document Type		Enter the bank statement document type (SA) for the G/L account posting.
Posting Type		Enter the bank statement posting type (4) for the debt clearing G/L account.

Table 9-3. *Wire Transfer Out*

Field Name		Data to Enter
Posting Rule		Enter the key for the posting rule you defined for the wire transfer-out (S005).
Posting Area		Enter the bank accounting (1).
Acct Symbol	Debit	Enter the account symbol you defined for the wire transfer-out (C900-BANK TRANS).
Posting Key	Credit	Enter the posting key (50) for credit posting.
Acct Symbol		Enter the account symbol you defined for your main bank account (C900-BANK).
Document Type		Enter the bank statement document type (SA) for G/L account posting.
Posting Type		Enter the bank statement posting type (4) for the debt clearing G/L account.

Table 9-4. *Bank Charges*

Field Name		Data to Enter
Posting Rule		Enter the key for posting rule you defined for bank charges (S002).
Posting Area		Enter the bank accounting (1).
Acct Symbol	Debit	Enter the account symbol you defined for bank charges (C900- BANKCHGS).
Posting Key	Credit	Enter the posting key (50) for credit posting.
Acct Symbol		Enter the account symbol you defined for your main bank account (C900-BANK).
Document Type		Enter the bank statement document type (SA) for the G/L account posting.
Posting Type		Enter the bank statement posting type (1) for post to the G/L account.

Table 9-5. *Other Interim Posts*

Field Name		Data to Enter
Posting Rule		Enter the key for the posting rule you defined for INTERPOST (S006).
Posting Area		Enter the bank accounting (1).
Acct Symbol	Debit	Enter the account symbol you defined for Other INTERPOST (C900- BANKCHGS).
Posting Key	Credit	Enter the posting key (50) for credit posting.
Acct Symbol		Enter the account symbol you defined for your main bank account (C900-BANK).
Document Type		Enter the bank statement document type (SA) for the G/L account posting.
Posting Type		Enter the bank statement posting type (1) for posting to the G/L account.

The next step is to create transaction types to customize your electronic bank statements. This transaction type will be assigned to the external posting rules in Step 6.

You'll create the names and descriptions of the various transaction types you require. House banks that use identical lists of business transaction codes (external transactions) can be assigned to the same transaction type in Step 6.

Step 5: Create Transaction Type

When creating transaction types, you define the transaction type key and provide a name that describes your transaction types. The transaction types you create are assigned to external transactions. The benefit of a transaction type is that it will allow you to group house banks with the same lists of external transaction keys and assign them to the same business transaction. The idea behind this concept is that you assign external transaction codes of house banks once per transaction type rather than doing this individually per house bank.

Before assigning external transaction types to posting rules, you must first create the transaction type. Double-click on the ☐ Create Transaction Type button to call up the Define Posting Rules Overview screen, where you will create your transaction type. Then click the New Entries button on the top-left side of the screen to create a transaction type. Update the following fields (Figure 9-11):

> **Trans. Type:** Enter a code of your choice in this field as your transaction type. This field can accept up to eight digits. In this activity, we used the company code C900 to make it easy for us to identify the code.
>
> **Name:** Enter a short description for your transaction type.

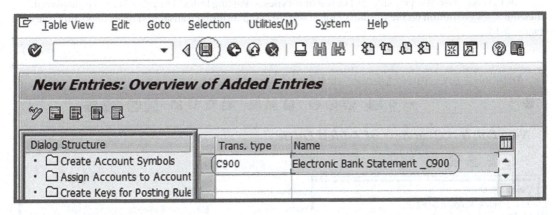

***Figure 9-11.** Global settings for an electronic bank statement—Create Transaction Type*

After updating the screen, click the Enter ✅ button to confirm your entries and save 💾 your configuration.

In the next step, you assign external business transaction codes to the internal posting rules you created in Step 4.

Step 6: Assign External Transaction Types to Posting Rules

You assign external business transaction codes to internal posting rules so you can use the same specifications you configured for different business transaction codes in house banks.

To go to the screen where you will assign business transactions to posting rules, select the transaction type (Electronic Bank Statement) you created (Figure 9-12) and double-click the ☐ Assign External Transaction Types to Posting Rules folder.

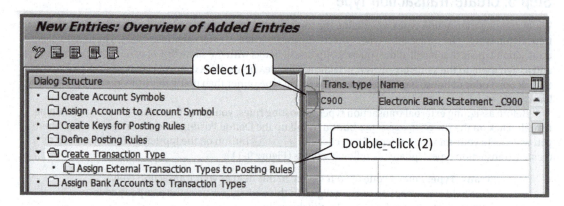

Figure 9-12. Assigning external transaction types to posting rules initial screen

The Change View "Assign External Transaction Types to Posting Rules" Overview screen is displayed. Click the New Entries button on the top-left of the screen to assign external transaction types to posting rules (Figure 9-13).

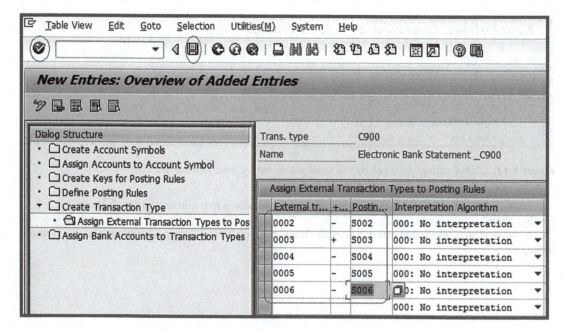

Figure 9-13. Assigned external transaction types to posting rules

Update the following fields:

> **External Transaction:** Enter your external transaction codes in this field. This can be up to four digits for each transaction type using the system-posting rule. Use meaningful transaction codes, preferably in sequence to avoid ambiguity, such as 0002, 0003, 0004, 0005, and 0006.

> **+/- Sign:** Use these signs to further differentiate external transactions. The plus (+) sign in the front of external transaction code indicates receipt and the minus (-) sign indicates payment.

> **Posting Rule:** Enter the posting rules you defined in Step 4.

Click the Enter ✅ on the top-left side of the screen to confirm that the system accepted your entries and save 💾 your work.

Finally, you'll assign the transaction types you just created to the bank account you defined for your house bank.

Step 7: Assign Bank Accounts to Transaction Types

It is not uncommon when you have multiple house banks to use individual transaction types to differentiate business types. In this case, each house bank must be assigned its own transaction type. In this activity only one transaction type was created (C900 in Step 5). You can define more than one transaction type on your own. The number of transaction types you create depends on your client's requirements.

On the left side of the screen, double-click the Assign Bank Account to Transaction Types folder to call up the Assign Bank Account to Transaction Types Overview screen. This is where you assign bank accounts to transaction types. Click the `New Entries` button on the top-left side of the screen to assign bank accounts to transaction types (Figure 9-14).

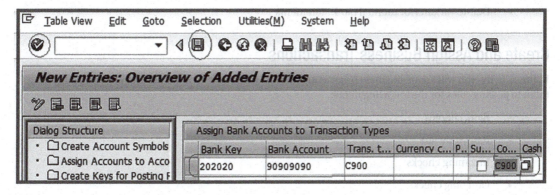

Figure 9-14. *Assigning bank accounts to transaction types*

Update the following fields:

>**Bank Key:** Enter your bank key in this field. This is your bank key or sort code that you created when you customized your house bank.

>**Bank Account:** Enter your bank account number in this field. This is your house bank account number and your company's real bank account number.

>**Transaction Type:** Enter the transaction type you created in Step 5.

■ **Note** Although you created two house banks—Barclays Bank and HSBC Bank—in this activity, you will be assigning only one house bank (Barclays Bank) to your transaction type. However, there is no restriction to the number of banks you can assign to a transaction type.

The bank key and the bank account used here are obtained from the house bank you created earlier.

Click the Enter 🗹 button to confirm your specifications and save 🖫 your work.

You have now customized an electronic bank statement. Next, you'll configure a manual bank statement.

Configure a Manual Bank Statement

Most of the settings you configured as part of your electronic bank statement are applicable to a manual bank statement, so you will not be creating them again. Hence you will customize only the following nodes:

- Create and assign business transactions
- Define variants for manual bank statements

Create and Assign Business Transactions

In this activity, you will create business transactions, assign them to individual posting keys, and allocating them to posting rules for the following items:

- Bank charges
- Bank transfers
- Incoming checks
- Outgoing checks
- Reconciliation items

■ **Note** You don't need to create new posting rules for the manual bank statement; you can use the posting rules you created for the electronic bank statement.

Follow this menu path to customize your manual bank statement: IMG: Financial Accounting (New) ➤ Bank Accounting ➤ Business Transaction ➤ Payment Transactions ➤ Manual Bank Statement ➤ Create and Assign Business Transaction. Or use transaction code OT52.

The initial screen where you will specify the manual bank statement, called Change View: Manual Bank Statement Transactions": Overview, appears. Click the New Entries button on the top-left side of the screen. The New Entries: Overview of Added Entries screen is displayed (Figure 9-15). This is where you create new business transactions for your manual bank statement and assign them to the posting rules you defined previously.

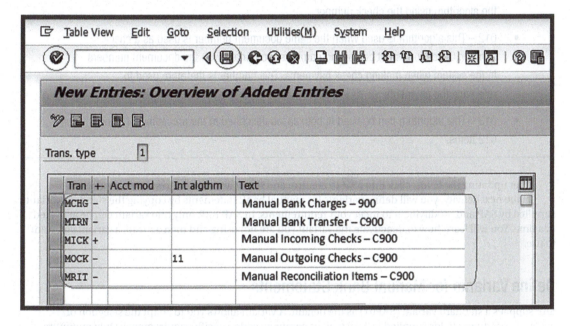

Figure 9-15. *Creating and assigning business transactions*

Update the following items:

> **Transaction:** Enter the transaction codes that you want to use for your manual bank statement. You can enter a maximum of four digits for each transaction type for the system-posting rule. For example, in this activity we used MCHG for Manual Bank Charges, MTRN (Manual Transfer for Bank Transfer), MICK (Manual Incoming Checks for Incoming Checks), MOCK (Manual Out Going Checks) for outgoing checks, and MRIT (Manual Reconciliation Items) for reconciliation Items.

■ **Note** You can use any transaction code as long as it makes sense to you.

> **+/- Sign:** This field allows you to further differentiate your business transactions. The plus (+) sign in front of a business transaction code indicates receipt and the minus sign (-)indicates payment.
>
> **Int algthm:** Enter 011 in the outgoing check field only.
>
> **Text:** Enter short texts that describes each item transaction here.

■ **Note** The algorithm you can use for outgoing checks are listed here:

- 011 – This algorithm is used for outgoing checks when the check number is different from the payment document number. This is the case when the bank uses prenumbered checks. The check numbers are therefore obtained from the bank statement in the house bank, and the appropriate document numbers are identified by the algorithm using the check number.

- 012 – This algorithm is used when the same document number is used as a check number. Check forms not containing numbers are printed with the document numbers in the system when making check payments. This number is therefore used to reference the payments.

- 013 – This algorithm can be used in both cases described in the preceding 011 and 012 items.

After updating the fields, click Enter ✅ to confirm and then click save 💾 to save your work.

In the next activity, you will define variants for manual bank statements by copying the standard variant supplied by SAP and modifying it to meet your requirements. In SAP ERP, only one variant can be activated at a time. You will learn how to deactivate the variant you are not using and then activate a variant you want to use.

Define Variants for Manual Bank Statements

SAP supplies a standard variant (SAP01) as the default. A variant allows you to adapt the selection of account assignment fields supplied by SAP to your company code-specific requirements. Only minimum modification is allowed for this standard variant, but you can use it for your manual bank statement. You can copy the standard variant (SAP01) and modify it to meet your company's specific requirements. To customize these variants, follow this menu path: Financial Accounting (New) ➤ Bank Accounting ➤ Business Transaction ➤ Payment Transactions ➤ Manual Bank Statement ➤ Define Variants for Manual Bank Statement. Or you can use transaction code OT43.

■ **Note** If you choose not to use the standard variant supplied by SAP, but instead decide to create your own, you must deactivate the standard variant SAP01 and then activate your own variant. You will learn how to activate and deactivate variants later in this chapter.

The Maintain Screen Variant: List screen is displayed. This is where you define variants for manual bank statement. Since you are copying the standard variant supplied by SAP in the system, click the Copy 🗔 button at the top of the screen. The Copy Variant screen pops up (Figure 9-16). Enter the variant you want to copy (SAP01) in the From Variant field and enter your own variant identifier key in the To Variant field. Then click the Enter ☑ button to confirm your request. This action will allow you to copy the properties of the standard variant (SAP01) to your variant (C900).

Figure 9-16. *The Copy Variant dialog box*

An information screen with a warning ("Field FEBMKA-MEHRW is Missing on Reference Screen") pops up. Ignore this warning and confirm the copy by clicking the Enter ✔ button. Once the copy is confirmed, the system will automatically copy the standard variant's properties to your variant code. The Maintain Screen Variant Fields screen is displayed (Figure 9-17) showing the inherited properties of the standard variant that you copied. Modify the items on this screen to meet your requirements by deleting the items that you do not need.

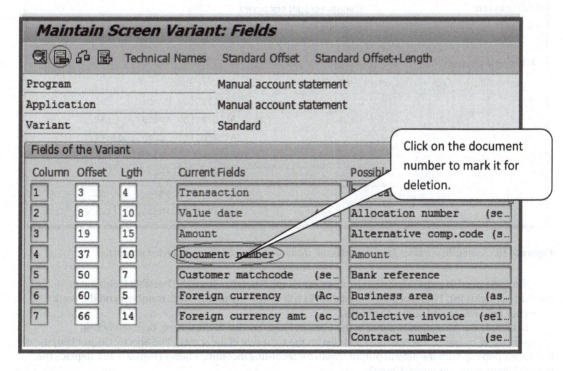

Figure 9-17. *Maintain variants for manual bank statement with all properties copied*

As part of the customizing process in this activity, delete the following items not needed in your manual bank statement:

- Document number

- Customer matchcode

- Foreign currency

- Foreign currency amt

Click on the item you want to delete from the list—for example, select Document Number to mark it for deletion—and click the Delete ▣ button on the top-left side of the screen (circled in red in Figure 9-17).

After clicking on Delete button, the document number disappears from the list of items on the screen. Repeat the same steps to delete the other items (that is, Customer Matchcode, Foreign Currency, and Foreign Currency Amt). Your variant will then look like the one shown in Figure 9-18.

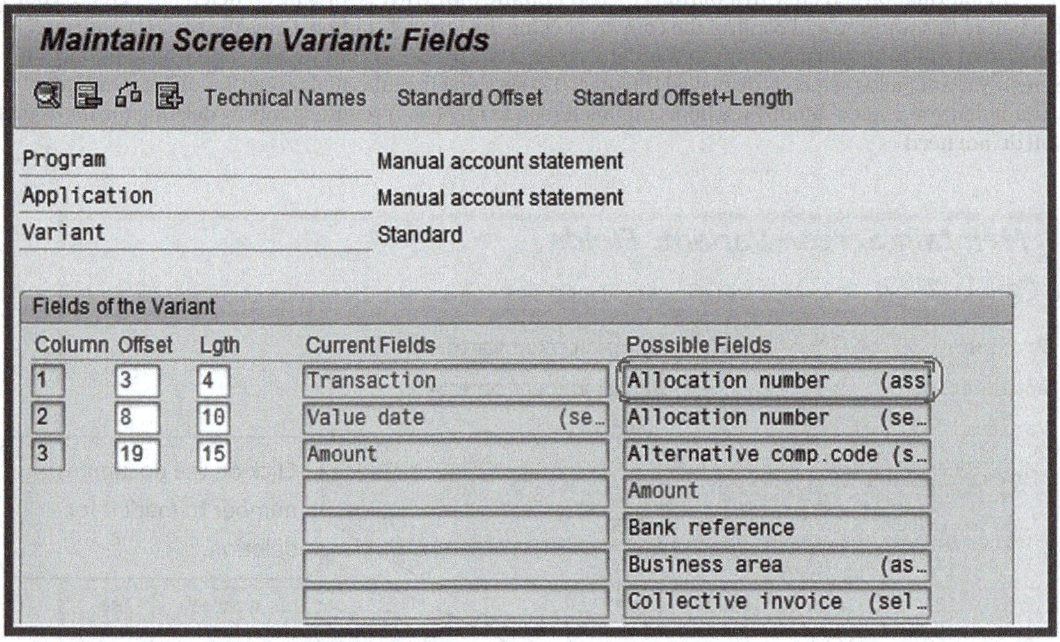

Maintain Screen Variant: Fields

🔍 ▣ 🔎 ▣   Technical Names   Standard Offset   Standard Offset+Length

Program	Manual account statement
Application	Manual account statement
Variant	Standard

Fields of the Variant

Column	Offset	Lgth	Current Fields	Possible Fields
1	3	4	Transaction	Allocation number (ass
2	8	10	Value date (se..	Allocation number (se..
3	19	15	Amount	Alternative comp.code (s..
				Amount
				Bank reference
				Business area (as..
				Collective invoice (sel..

Figure 9-18. *Maintain variants for manual bank statement after deleting unneeded properties*

Next, you need to move Allocation Number and Bank Reference from the Possible Fields list to the Current Fields list. The Allocation Number field will record incoming check numbers and the Bank Reference field will record outgoing checks.

To include the Allocation Number in the Current Fields section of the screen, double-click on `Allocation number` (ass) in the Possible Fields list on the right side of the screen. The Specify Output Length dialog box pops up with the default output length for recording incoming checks (Figure 9-19). Replace the default length with your desired length.

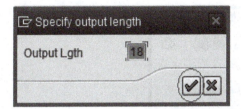

Figure 9-19. *Output length for allocation number*

Click the Continue ✔ button to confirm your output length specification. The Allocation Number (Ass) will now appear in the Current Fields list under Amount (Figure 9-20).

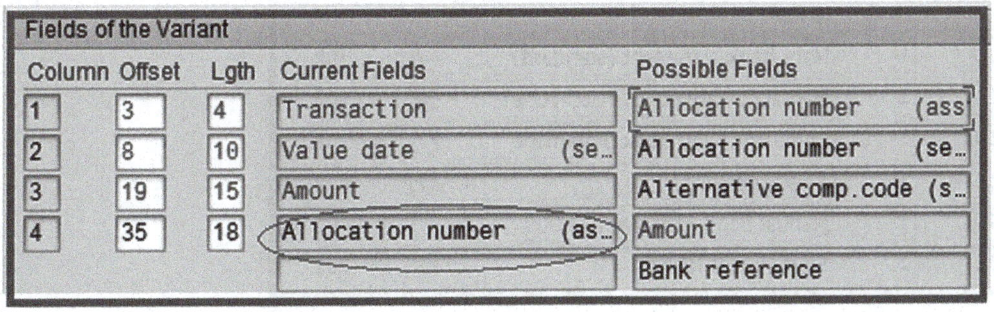

Fields of the Variant				
Column	Offset	Lgth	Current Fields	Possible Fields
1	3	4	Transaction	Allocation number (ass
2	8	10	Value date (se…	Allocation number (se…
3	19	15	Amount	Alternative comp.code (s…
4	35	18	Allocation number (as…	Amount
				Bank reference

Figure 9-20. *Maintaining variant for manual bank statements— recording incoming checks*

Next, include the Bank Reference in your Current Fields list. Double-click Bank Reference in the Possible Fields list. The Specify Output Length dialog box pops up with a default length. Enter the desired length in the Output Length field and click the Enter button to confirm your changes. Your variant screen will now look like the screen in Figure 9-21.

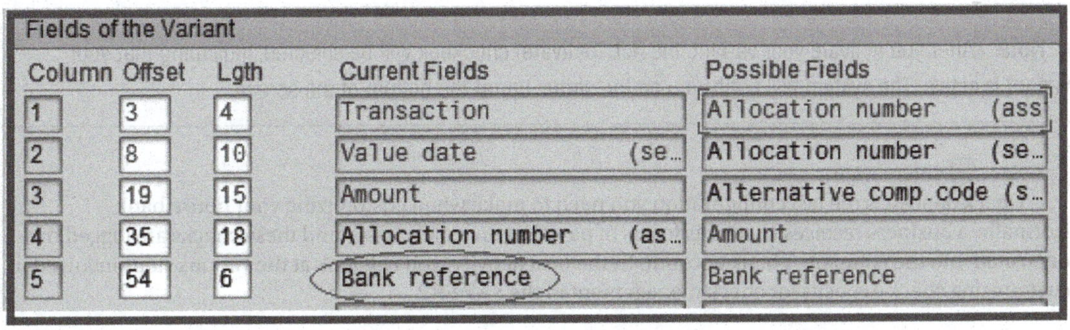

Fields of the Variant				
Column	Offset	Lgth	Current Fields	Possible Fields
1	3	4	Transaction	Allocation number (ass
2	8	10	Value date (se…	Allocation number (se…
3	19	15	Amount	Alternative comp.code (s…
4	35	18	Allocation number (as…	Amount
5	54	6	Bank reference	Bank reference

Figure 9-21. *Maintaining variants for manual bank statements—recording outgoing checks*

Save 💾 your work. The next step is to change the variant name to your own. Click the Back ⟲ button to return to the Maintain Screen Variant List screen (Figure 9-22). Search for your variant (C900) among the displayed variant names and change the copied variant name to your own. In this activity, we used Manual Bank Statement – C900 as our variant name.

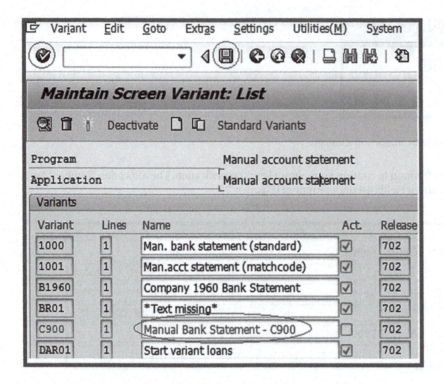

Figure 9-22. *Changing the copied variant name to your own variant name*

Click the Enter ⟲ button to confirm your changes and save 🖫 your variant.

Now you need to activate the variant for your manual bank statement for it to work effectively. Make sure that your variant is selected. You will notice that your variant name turns red. Click the Activate 🗓 icon on the top-left corner of the screen to activate your variant.

■ **Note**   After you activate your variant, the Act. (activate) checkbox will be selected, indicating that your variant is active. The system will notify you on the status bar at the bottom of the screen.

Save 🖫 your variant.

Check deposit is the last configuration you need to make when customizing your house bank. Normally, a business receives checks as forms of payment on a daily basis, and these checks are logged or deposited into the company's bank account. In the next activity, you will look at the various steps involved in customizing check deposits for check management in the SAP ERP.

Check Deposits

Check deposit customization is useful in an environment where large volumes of checks are deposited and processed simultaneously in the system. The settings carried out here will allow checks received by your company to be entered and processed in the SAP ERP system.

When customizing check deposits, the following steps are involved:

1. Define posting keys and posting rules for check deposits.

2. Create and assign business transactions.

3. Define variants for check deposits.

■ **Note** The reason you define posting keys and posting rules for check deposits before you create and assign business transactions to posting rules is that the accounting symbols needed to specify business transactions are defined in posting keys and posting rules for check deposit customizing.

Define Posting Keys and Posting Rules for Check Deposits

You will go through the following four steps as part of this activity:

1. Create account symbols.

2. Assign accounts to an account symbol.

3. Create keys for posting rules.

4. Define posting rules.

To customize these options, follow this menu path: IMG: Financial Accounting (New) ➤ Bank Accounting ➤ Business Transactions ➤ Check Deposit ➤ Define Posting Keys and Posting Rules for Check Deposit.

The Determine Work Area Entry dialog box is displayed. Enter your chart of accounts in the Chart of Accounts field and click the Enter ☑ button. The Change View: "Create Account Symbols": Overview screen is displayed. This is where you will customize the settings. You will work through the displayed nodes on the left side of the screen using a top-down approach from Steps 1 to 4 to avoid missing anything.

Create Account Symbols

Account symbols are useful for grouping similar business transactions such as check receipts/deposits together and they determine which accounts transactions are posted based on the criteria you specify in your house bank.

On the Change View: "Create Account Symbols" Overview screen, notice that a list of nodes is displayed on the left side of the screen and that the Create Account Symbols yellow folder is open. This indicates the item you want to customize.

■ **Tip** Make sure that the folder of the item you are customizing is open. If that folder is not open, double-click on it to open it.

Click the New Entries button to go to the screen where you will create account symbols for your check deposits (Figure 9-23). Update the following fields:

Account: Enter your account symbol identifier key in the account field and enter a description of your account symbol in the text field. There is no hard rule about the account symbol/description to use. It's best to use meaningful account symbols and descriptions here.

Text: Enter a short text description that best describes your account symbol.

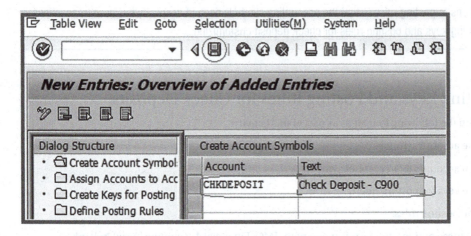

Figure 9-23. *Creating an account symbol for check deposits*

Click the Enter ✓ button to confirm your entries and save 🔲 your account symbols.

Assign Accounts to an Account Symbol

To assign G/L accounts to the account symbol, select the account deposit symbol that you just created from the list of account symbols displayed and then double-click on the Assign Accounts to Account Symbol folder (Figure 9-24).

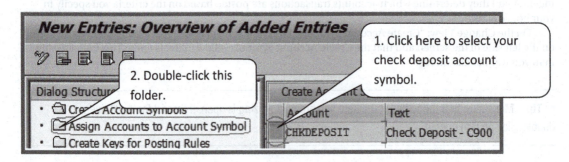

Figure 9-24. *The inital screen for assigning accounts to an account symbol*

You don't need to create another account symbol. You have already done this when customizing your electronic bank statement. When you double-click Assign Accounts to Account Symbol on the left side of the screen in Figure 9-25, the system will automatically display the accounts and the account symbols you created for your check deposits.

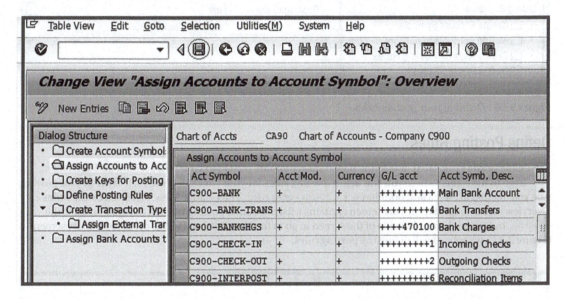

Figure 9-25. *Assigned accounts to an account symbol for check deposits*

Save 🖫 your work.

■ **Tip** If the system did not assign your accounts to the account symbols, you have to assign them manually.

Create Keys for Posting Rules

Posting rules are representations of business transactions related to check deposits. This includes check receipts to clear accounts, check clearing for customers, and so on. The key you define here will automatically determine the posting rule applicable to the general ledger and subledgers.

On the Change View "Assign Accounts to Account Symbol": Overview screen, double-click the ⬚ Create Keys for Posting Rules folder. The Create Keys for Posting Rules Overview screen appears.

Click the New Entries button on the top-left side of the screen to go to the New Entries: Overview of Added Entries screen (Figure 9-26) to create posting keys for posting rules. Enter a new key of your choice in the Posting Rule field and enter a short text in the Text field that best describes the posting rule for your check deposits.

After updating the screen, click Save 🖫 to save the key for posting rules.

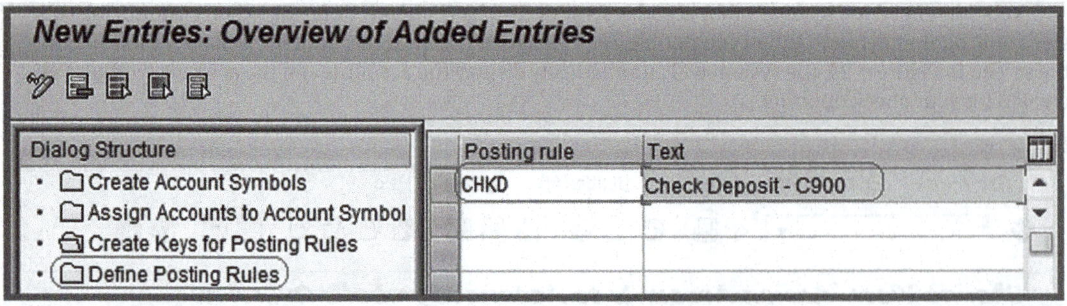

Figure 9-26. *Defining your posting rules*

Define Posting Rules

You define posting rules that determine how transactions are posted to your G/L account and subledger.

To go to the screen where you will define posting rules for your check deposits, select the key for posting rule you defined in Step 3 and double-click 🗀 Define Posting Rules. The Change View: "Define Posting Rules": Overview screen is displayed. This screen contains a list of defined posting rules in the system. Click the New Entries button on the top-left side of the screen to go to the New Entries: Details of Added Entries screen (Figure 9-27), where you will define the posting rules.

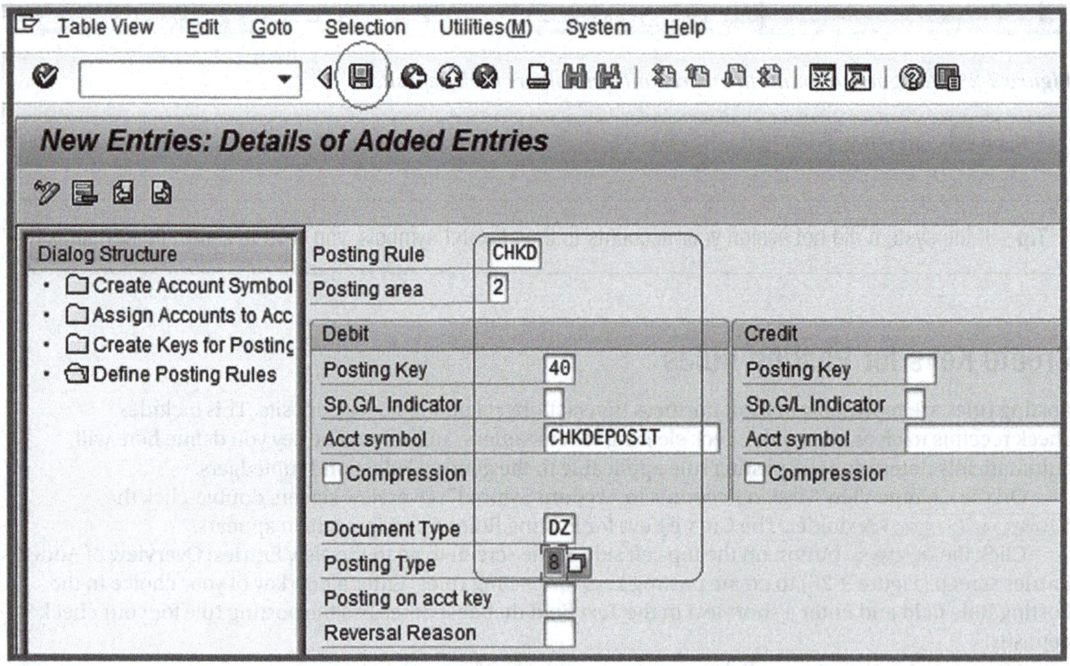

Figure 9-27. *Specifying the settings for the posting rules*

Update the following fields:

Posting Rule: Enter the posting rule for your check deposits that you defined in Step 3.

Posting Area: Specify the posting area for your check deposits. For example, 1 - Bank accounting for posting transactions that affect the general ledger only or 2 - Subledger Accounting for posting transactions to the subledger.

Posting Key: The standard posting keys in SAP ERP are 40 – Debit Posting and 50 – Credit Posting. The posting key you specify here will determine whether, for example, incoming checks are posted to the debit or credit side of the general ledger account or subledgers.

Account Symbol: Enter your check deposit account symbol. The specification made here groups together similar business transactions.

Document Type: Determines document storage in the system and the account types to be posted. For example, document type DZ is for customer payments. A document type can be found using the Search function in the document type field.

Posting Type: Allows you to specify how postings should be treated by the system. For example, when you click the Search icon in the Posting Type field, the standard list of posting type is displayed, as shown in Figure 9-28.

1	Posting to g/L accounts
2	Post Subledger Account - Debit
3	Post Subledger Account - Credit
4	Creditors Clear bebit G/L account
5	Clear credit G/L account
7	Clear debit subledger account
8	Clear credit G/L subledger account
9	Reset & rev, clear

Figure 9-28. *A list of standard posting types supplied by SAP*

■ **Note** SAP comes with predefined standard posting rules that you can copy and modify. You can also create your own posting rules from scratch. Standard posting rules can be found on the Change View: "Define Posting Rules": Overview screen.

After updating the New Entries: Details of Added Entries screen, click the Enter 🗸 button on the top-left side of the screen to confirm. Save 🖫 your posting rules.

Now you can create and assign business transactions, which will assign your account symbol for check deposits.

Create and Assign Business Transactions

In this activity, you will create and assign business transactions by specifying indicators for your check deposits and allocating the indicators to the defined posting rules. To go to the Change View "Check Deposit Transactions": Overview screen, follow the menu path: IMG: Financial Accounting (New) ➤ Bank Accounting ➤ Business Transactions ➤ Check Deposit ➤ Create and Assign Business Transactions. Or you can use the transaction code OT53.

The Change View "Check Deposit Transactions": Overview screen is displayed. Click the New Entries button to go to the New Entries: Overview of Added Entries screen (Figure 9-29). To specify the account symbol and business transaction for your check deposits, update the following fields:

> **Transaction Indicator:** In this field you specify a transaction indicator for check deposits and allocate it to a posting rule. You can use a maximum of four characters as your transaction indicator.

> **+/-:** Specify whether your business transaction is a positive (+) value or a negative (-) value using the plus and minus signs (the + sign indicates an incoming payment and the - sign indicates an outgoing payment).

> **Post. Rule:** Assign your predefined posting rule to the transaction indicator you defined earlier in the "Define Posting Rules" section.

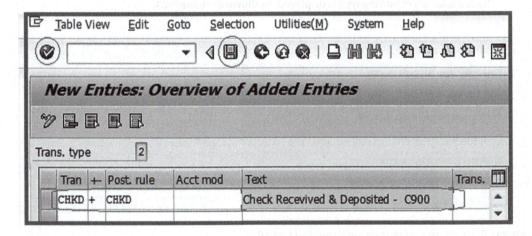

Figure 9-29. *Check deposit transactions*

Click the Enter ✓ button and save 🔚 your check deposit transactions.

Finally, as part of customizing the check deposits, you will define variants for check deposits.

Define Variants for Check Deposits

SAP comes with standard variants so you don't have to define another variant. On the other hand, you can create your own variant if you choose not to use the standard variant supplied by SAP.

In this activity, you will use the standard variant supplied by SAP for check deposits, which you will modify to determine the input fields for check deposits during data entry.

You will define variants for check deposits by copying the standard variant (SAP01), because it is easier to copy a standard variant and modify it to meet your requirements. This will save you the time of having to create your variant afresh. To go to the screen where you will define variants for check deposits, follow this menu path: IMG: Financial Accounting (New) ➤ Bank Accounting ➤ Business Transactions → Check Deposit ➤ Define Variants for Check Deposit. Or use the transaction code OT45.

The Maintain Screen Variant: List screen is displayed. This screen contains a list of exisitng variants. Since you are copying the standard variant, click the Copy 🔲 icon at the top of the screen. The Copy Variant dialog box pops up. Enter the variant you want to copy (SAP01) in the From Variant field and the key you want to use for your variant in To Variant field. We advise that you use your company code as your variant key or code. Click the Enter ✅ button to confirm that you want to copy the variant. An information dialog box with a warning (Field FEBMKA-MEHRW is Missing on Reference Screen) pops up. Ignore the warning and click the Enter ✅ button to copy. The system will automatically copy the standard variant to your variant code.

Next, the Maintain Screen Variant Fields screen for the variant you copied is displayed. Modify the content of this screen to meet your company's requirement. Delete the items you do not need and include the items you want to include in your variant.

The items in the Current Field section of the screen are active and the items in the Possible Field section are items you can include in your variant as input fields.

Delete the following items, as you don't need them in your check deposit variant. You do this by selecting the item you want to delete in the Current Field section and clicking the Delete 🖳 button on the top of the screen.

- Three-digit check number

- Eight-digit bank key

- Bank account number

- Document number

As part of this process, you should include the 10-digit check number in the Possible Field section as an input field for the check deposits. Double-click on that item to move it from the Possible Field section to the Current Field section (Figure 9-30).

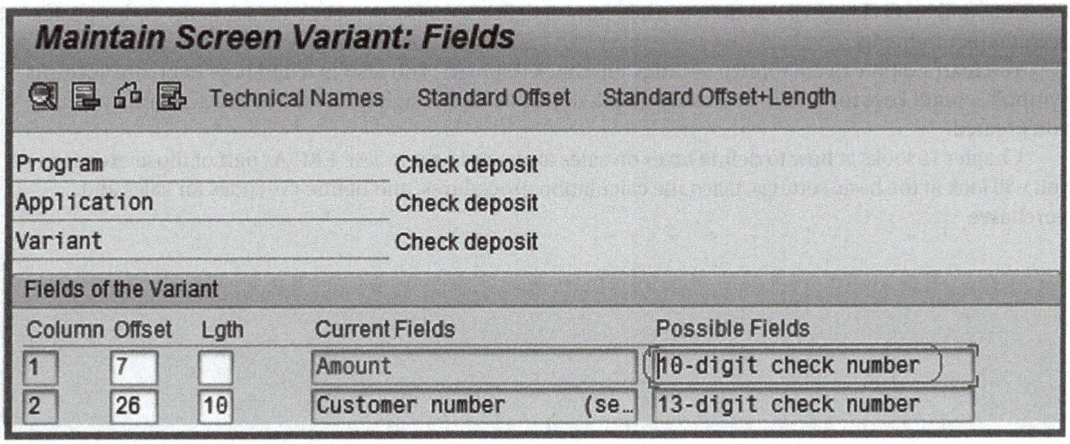

Figure 9-30. *Maintaining variants for check deposits*

The Specify Output Length dialog box pops up with a default output length. Enter 10 in the Output Length field and click the Enter ☑ button to confirm the changes. The 10-digit check number will appear in the Current Fields List under Customer Number. Save 🖫 your variant. Click the Back ↻ button on the top-center of the screen to return to the Maintain Screen Variant: List screen. Search for the variant you copied among the displayed variants. Change the default variant name (Check Deposit) to your own variant name. We used Check Deposit-C900.

The final step is to activate your check deposit variant. To do this, click the Activation 🛈 icon on the top-left side of the screen.

The final aspect of the house bank customization is the cash journal, which is covered in Chapter 11.

■ **Note**   Cash journal configuration is deliberately covered in Chapter 11 so that you can first complete the configuration for tax on sales/purchases in Chapter 10. You will need the sales and purchases tax code in order to customize the cash journal.

Summary

This chapter explained what a house bank is and demonstrated how house banks are maintained in SAP ERP. You learned about each specification when configuring your house bank and learned what each does. As part of customizing the house bank, you defined a bank ID and an account ID, which are the key aspects of your house bank configuration, and learned how to apply them to the G/L account where your bank account transactions are posted.

You went on to learn about various house banks represented in SAP ERP. You defined the accounts that bank statement transactions are posted to and learned how to customize electronic and manual bank statements. You went through the stages involved in customizing global settings for electronic and manual bank statements. In doing so, you created account symbols that the system uses to determine the G/L accounts and created subledgers, where the bank statement transactions are posted. You then looked at how to assign accounts to account symbols and how to create keys for posting rules. You learned how to define posting rules that are assigned to appropriated transactions (for example, for checks in, checks out, bank transfers, and bank charges). You then learned how to define variants to meet your company code-specific account requirements.

You learned how to customize settings for check deposits. You also learned how to create account symbols, create keys for posting rules for check deposits, and assign accounts to the account symbols you created.

Chapter 10 looks at how to define taxes on sales and purchases in SAP ERP. As part of those exercises, you will look at the basic settings, learn the calculation procedures, and define tax codes for sales and purchases.

■ ■ ■

Defining Tax on Sales and Purchases

In this chapter, you learn various forms of taxes as they are represented in SAP ERP and learn how to define taxes on sales and purchases.

At the end of this chapter, you will be able to:

- Describe what a tax on sales/purchases is

- Create a sales/purchases tax code

- Specify a tax category in the G/L accounts to which taxes will be posted

- Identify basic tax codes for sales and purchases

- Specify the accounts to which different tax types are posted

- Assign tax codes to non-taxable transactions

Sales and Purchases Tax

SAP supports various tax codes for different countries. This chapter covers only sales and purchases taxes. Sales/purchases taxes are referred to VATs (value added taxes) in most countries. These are taxes are levied on invoiced goods and services payable by the consumer and are held on behalf of the tax authority. There are two major VATs—input taxes and output taxes. Input taxes are levied on purchases of goods and services received from vendors. Output taxes are charged on the sale of goods and services provided to customers. For example, Company A buys goods from Company B and charges a 20% VAT on the invoice price of the goods. Company A sells goods to company Y and charges Company Y a 20% VAT. Company A reconciles its VAT account and the difference is sent to the tax authority. Figure 10-1 illustrates this scenario.

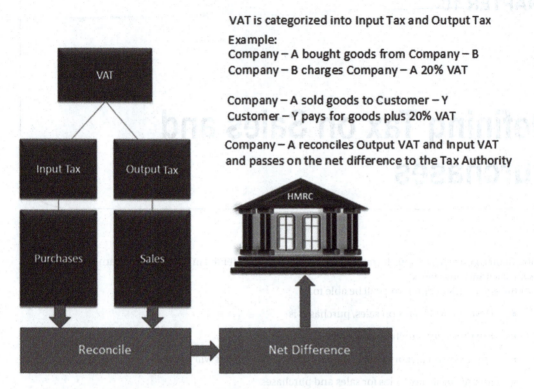

VAT is categorized into Input Tax and Output Tax

Example:
Company – A bought goods from Company – B
Company – B charges Company – A 20% VAT

Company – A sold goods to Customer – Y
Customer – Y pays for goods plus 20% VAT

Company – A reconciles Output VAT and Input VAT
and passes on the net difference to the Tax Authority

Figure 10-1. *How taxes on sales/ purchases (VATs) work*

VAT is split into input and output taxes. A tax category is specified in the G/L accounts so the system can determine and post the correct tax to the appropriate account. SAP ERP comes with the following tax categories:

- < is the input tax

- > is the output tax

The tax category specification is very important, because it allows the system to determine whether the tax posted is an input tax or output tax and make postings to the appropriate accounts. If you do not want to post your taxes manually (you want the system to automatically post the taxes during document posting), you must select Post Automatically Only in the appropriate general ledger where the taxes are posted.

All other G/L accounts can have one of the entries in Table 10-1 in the Tax Category field.

Table 10-1. *A List of Tax Categories in SAP ERP*

Value	Description
Blank	Non-tax relevant postings (bank postings)
-	Postings that require an input tax code (reconciliation accounts payables from goods and services)
+	Postings that require an output tax code (reconciliation accounts receivables from goods and services)
*	Postings that require any tax code
XX	Postings with the predefined tax code

Several steps are involved in customizing sales and purchase taxes in SAP ERP. Now that you know what sales and purchase taxes are, let's look at the steps involved in customizing them.

Basic Settings

SAP R/3 comes with standard settings for sales and purchase taxes for most countries. It is recommended that you stick with the standard settings, because they are up to date and typically adequate for most tax requirements. The only time you should define the basic settings is when your taxes are not included in the standard settings. In this activity, you do not need to configure any settings, but it's a good idea to look at the basic settings to make sure that they meet your needs. As part of this exercise, check your company's calculation procedure to make sure that it is covered in the system and make sure that your country is assigned to the appropriate calculation procedure.

The standard Calculation Procedures setting comes with the basic specifications for sales/purchases taxes and contains the calculation and account postings for various countries. To check the condition types and procedures for every tax procedure group and the applicable calculation rules, follow this menu path: IMG: Financial Accounting (New) ➤ Financial Accounting Global Settings (New) ➤ Tax on Sales/Purchases ➤ Basic Settings ➤ Check Calculation Procedure. Or you can use transaction code OBYZ.

Once you have checked your country calculation procedure, the next step is to assign your country to the calculation procedure. Follow this menu path to check your country: IMG: Financial Accounting (New) ➤ Financial Accounting Global Settings (New) ➤ Tax on Sales/Purchases ➤ Basic Settings ➤ Basic Settings ➤ Assign Country to Calculation Procedure. Or you can use transaction code OBBG.

Make sure your country tax procedure is assigned to the appropriate calculation procedure (Figure 10-2). If your country code is not assigned to your country's calculation procedure, you have to assign it manually.

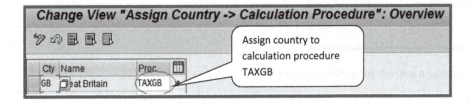

Figure 10-2. *Assigning a country to a calculation procedure*

In this example, the target country is Great Britain. Therefore, you should make sure that the country tax code (Great Britain's is TAXGB) is assigned to the tax procedure, which is circled in red in Figure 10-2. You can click the Search button to call up the list of all the country tax procedures. Search for your country tax procedure and assign it. Save 💾 your tax procedure.

■ **Note** Before you move to the next step, go to "Appendix A, Chapter 10, Tax on Sales/Purchases" to create the G/L accounts for input tax and output tax, which you will need when configuring the tax postings.

You need to define separate tax codes for sales and purchases. In the next activity, you will define the tax code for sales specific to your company based on your country's requirements.

Define Tax Codes for Sales

A tax code contains one or more tax rates that are applicable to different tax types represented in SAP ERP. It is recommended that you define different tax codes for different tax types and rates. If your company has operations in more than one country, you should define separate sales/purchase tax codes for each country. Secondly, in some countries, you must report tax-exempt or non-taxable items to the tax-governing bodies. Hence, you should define a 0 value tax code to report tax-exempt or non-taxable sales.

> **Problem:** *In the UK, the output sales tax (VAT) is 20%. Company C900 Plc wants you to define a 20% sales tax code, which users will apply to sales during document entry, and to specify the G/L account that output sales tax will be posted to.*

To define tax code for sales, follow this menu path: IMG: Financial Accounting (New) ➤ Financial Accounting Global Settings (New) ➤ Tax on Sales/Purchases ➤ Calculation ➤ Define Tax Codes for Sales and Purchases. Or you can use transaction code FTXP.

The Country dialog box pops up. This screen allows you to determine the country-specific settings that you want to use for your tax code. Enter your country code in the Country field. In this activity, for example, we used the GB (Great Britain) country code. Click the Enter ✅ button at the bottom of the screen to go to the initial screen, called Maintain Tax Code: Initial Screen, where you define your tax code (Figure 10-3).

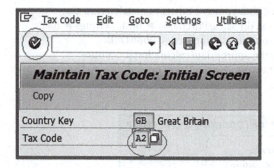

Figure 10-3. *Maintaining a tax code for output/sales tax*

■ **Tip**   You can define more than one tax code, such as 5%, 10%, 20%, and so on. There is no restriction to the number of tax codes you can create.

To define a tax code for output/sales for your company's country code, simply enter two digits as your tax code into the Tax Code field. Click the Enter 🗸 button or press Enter on your keyboard. The Properties screen (Figure 10-4) pops up. This screen allows you to specify the properties for your tax code.

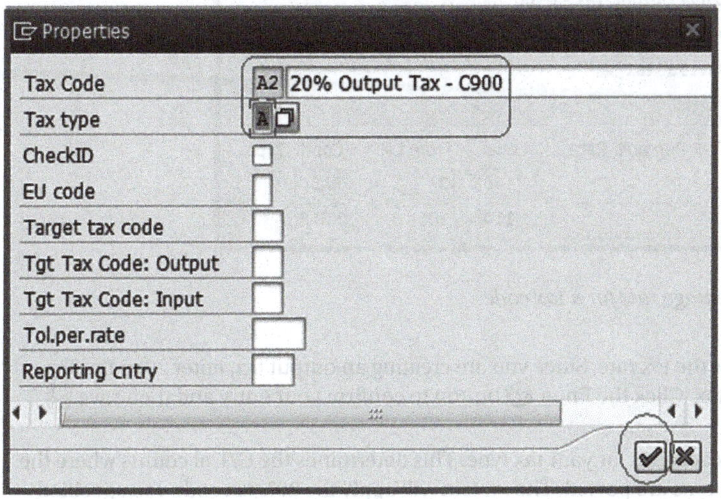

Figure 10-4. Specifying the tax code properties

Update the following fields:

> **Tax Code:** Enter the tax code you want to use for your sales or output tax in this field and also provide a short description.

> **Tax Type:** SAP ERP comes with two tax types—A is for output tax and V is for input tax. Since you are defining the tax code for an output tax, enter tax type A in this field.

■ **Note**   You cannot use the same tax code twice when defining another tax code with different tax rate. Since you have already used A2 for a 20% tax code, you cannot use it again for another tax rate. You have to choose another tax code. For example, for a tax rate of 5%, use A5 as your tax code, A10 for 10%, and so on. Once you have entered the appropriate data in the Properties screen, click Enter 🗸 to confirm your entries. The Maintain Tax Code: Tax Rates screen is displayed (Figure 10-5). This screen allows you to enter the tax percentage for the output tax.

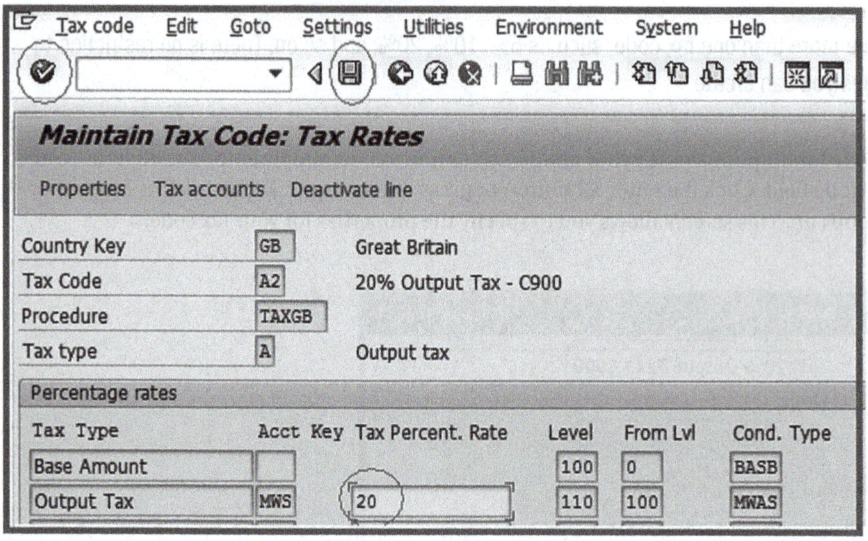

Figure 10-5. *Specifying the tax percentage rate for a tax code*

This activity assumes that 20% is the tax rate. Since you are creating an output tax, enter 20 in the Tax Percentage Rate field for the output tax. Click the Enter ✔ button to confirm your entry and then save 🖫 your configuration.

The next step is to define the tax account for your tax type. This determines the G/L accounts where the tax amounts arising from tax calculations are posted. The system will apply the 20% tax code you specified to the total invoice and calculate the tax amount for the output tax. It will then post this amount to the G/L account you assigned.

Define Tax Accounts for Sales

In this section, you'll specify the G/L account for tax types that output taxes are posted to. The system will automatically determine the G/L account that your tax types are posted to based on your specifications. The system will calculate the tax amount based on the percentage rate entered in your tax code and the specified tax type and automatically post the tax amount to the account you assign to your tax code. Follow this menu path to go to the screen where you will assign the account for your tax code: IMG: Financial Accounting (New) ➤ Financial Accounting Global Settings (New) ➤ Tax on Sales/Purchases ➤ Posting ➤ Define Tax Accounts. Or you can use transaction code OB40. The Configuration Accounting Maintain: Automatic Posts - Procedures screen is displayed. At this level, you will specify the account that you want your account type to post your taxes to. Since you need to define the account you want output sales tax to be posted to, click the scroll 🔼🔽 buttons on the left side of the screen to search for Output Tax – MWS in the Procedures section (Figure 10-6).

Configuration Accounting Maintain : Automatic Posts - Procedures

Group	%TX	Taxes on sales/purchases

Procedures

Description	Transaction	Account determ.	
Sales tax 4	MW4	☑	
MWH < missing >	MWH	☑	
Output tax	MWS	☑	
A/R PST	MWZ	☑	

Figure 10-6. *Automatic posting procedure screen for output tax*

To go to the screen where you will assign the account that output taxes are posted to, select
Output tax   MWS from the Procedures section and click the Detail 🔍 button on the top-left side of the
screen. The Enter Chart of Accounts dialog box pops up. Enter your chart of accounts in the Chart of
Accounts field and click the Enter ☑ button at the bottom of the screen to confirm your entry. The
Configuration Accounting Maintain: Automatic Posts Rules screen is displayed. On this screen, you can
specify posting rules for automatic posting. When you click the Save 💾 button at the top of the screen, the
Configuration Accounting Maintain: Automatic Post- Accounts screen is displayed (Figure 10-7). This is
where you assign the account for your output or sales tax code. The system calculates the tax amount based
on the percentage you assigned to your tax code and the account type and automatically posts it to the
account you assign in this activity.

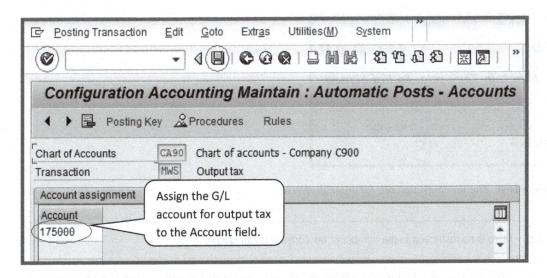

Figure 10-7. *Assigning the G/L account to a tax code for automatic posting*

To assign the account you want the tax amount for output taxes to be posted to, enter the account in the Account field. Click the Enter ✅ button and save 💾 your account assignment.

The same steps you used to define output tax are applicable to input tax, with slight modifications to the tax type and to the account to post the tax amount. For example, the tax type for output tax is A, whereas, the tax type for input tax is V. In the next activity, you will define tax codes for inputs or purchase taxes in SAP ERP.

Define Tax Codes for Purchases

Just like when you're customizing the tax code for sales, you have to define the tax code for purchases using a different tax code, tax type, and G/L account. It is important to create different tax codes for purchases in different countries (if your company operates in more than one country), because each country's tax requirements and specifications differ. Now let's define a tax code for purchases.

> **Problem:** *Company C900 Plc's accounting team wants you to define a 20% purchase tax code that users can apply to purchases during document entry and specify the G/L account purchase taxes are posted to.*

To define a tax code for purchases, follow this menu path: IMG: Financial Accounting (New) ➤ Financial Accounting Global Settings (New) ➤ Tax on Sales/Purchases ➤ Calculation ➤ Define Tax codes for Sales and Purchases. Or you can use transaction code FTXP.

The Country dialog box pops up. This screen allows you to assign your country tax specification to your tax code. Enter your country code in the Country field. We used GB (Great Britain) in this activity

Click the Continue ☑ button at the bottom of the dialog box to go to the next screen, called Maintain Tax Code: Initial Screen, where you will customize your tax code (Figure 10-8).

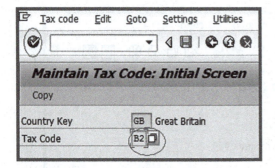

Figure 10-8. *Maintaining a tax code for input/purchases*

■ **Tip** There is no restriction to the number of tax codes you can create.

You define the tax code for input/purchase taxes for your company's country code by simply typing a two-digit tax code in the Tax Code field. There is no hard rule on the tax code that you must use here. It is purely a matter of choice.

Click the Enter ✅ button or press Enter on your keyboard. The Properties screen pops up. This screen allows you to specify your tax code and add a description of it. Update the following fields on the Properties screen:

Tax Code: Enter your tax code and short description of your tax code.

Tax Type: Enter the tax type **V** for input tax. The tax type you define here allows the system to determine whether the tax is an input or output tax.

■ **Note** You cannot use the same tax code twice when defining another tax code with a different tax rate. Since you have already used B2 for a tax code of 20%, you cannot use it again for another tax rate. You have to choose another tax code. For example, for a tax rate of 5%, use B5 as your tax code, B10 for 10%, and so on.

After updating the Properties screen, click the Continue ✅ button at the bottom of the screen. The Maintain Tax Code: Tax Rates screen is displayed (Figure 10-9). On this screen, you specify the percentage rate for your tax code.

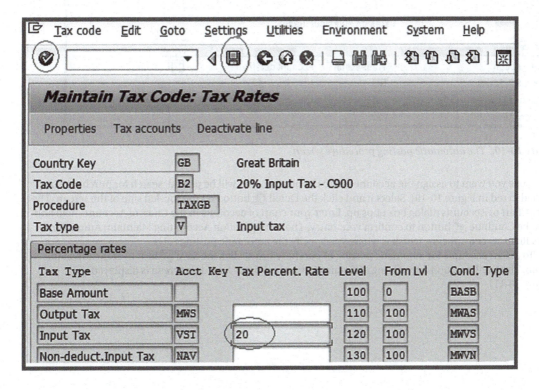

Figure 10-9. *Maintaining a percentage tax rate for the tax code*

This activity assumes a 20% tax rate. Since you are creating an input tax, enter **20** in the tax percentage rate field for input tax. Click the Enter 🗸 button on the top-left side of the screen and save 🖫 your tax code.

The next step is to assign an account to your tax code. In the next activity, you will do just that. Account assignment allows the system to automatically post the input tax to the account you assign.

Define Tax Accounts for Purchases

In this activity, you specify the G/L account for posting taxes. The system will automatically determine the G/L account that your tax types are posted to based on your specifications. Follow this menu path to assign accounts to your tax code: IMG: Financial Accounting (New) ➤ Financial Accounting Global Settings (New) ➤ Tax on Sales/Purchases ➤ Posting ➤ Define Tax Accounts. Or you can use transaction code OB40.

The Configuration Accounting Maintain: Automatic Posts - Procedures screen is displayed. It contains a list of tax types you can choose from (Figure 10-10).

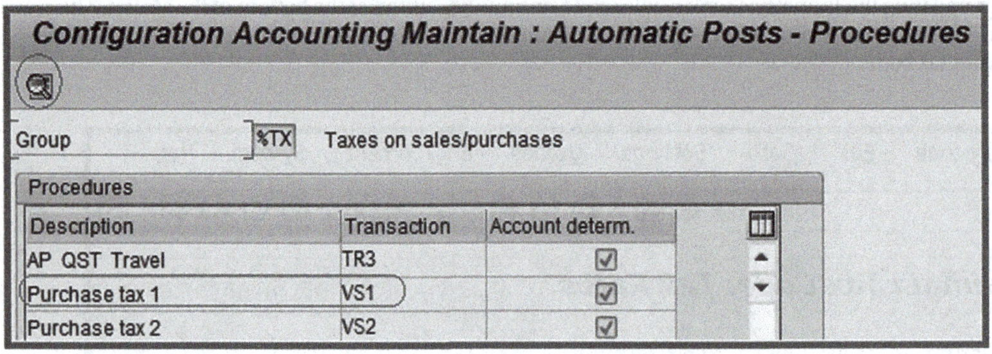

Configuration Accounting Maintain : Automatic Posts - Procedures

Group %TX Taxes on sales/purchases

Procedures

Description	Transaction	Account determ.	
AP QST Travel	TR3	☑	
Purchase tax 1	VS1	☑	
Purchase tax 2	VS2	☑	

Figure 10-10. The automatic posting procedure screen

Since you want to assign the account where the purchase tax will be posted, search for purchase tax (circled in red in Figure 10-10). Select it and click the Detail 🔍 button on the top-left side of the screen. The Enter Chart of Accounts dialog box pops up. Enter your chart of accounts in the Chart of Accounts field and click the Continue ✅ button to confirm your entry. The Configuration Accounting Maintain: Automatic Posts Rules screen appears, which is where you specify the automatic posting rules.

To assign accounts for automatic posting of purchase taxes, click the Save 🖫 button at the top of the screen. The Configuration Accounting Maintain: Automate Posts - Accounts screen is displayed (Figure 10-11).

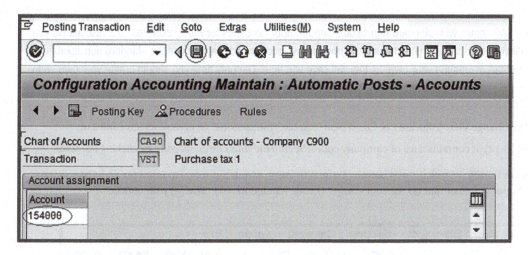

Figure 10-11. *Assigning a G/L account to a tax code for automatic posting*

The next step is to assign the G/L account for automatic postings of purchase taxes. Enter the account for output tax in the Account field (circled in red in Figure 10-11) and save 💾 your account assignment.

To complete the customization process for your tax code, you should define another code for a non-deductible input tax. This is handy when you're posting non-deductible input tax items, such as down payment requests. You can use the non-deductible tax NAV option and the information in Table 10-2 to complete this customization process.

Table 10-2. *Specifications for a Non-Deductible Tax Code*

Field	Value	Description
Country	GB	Use your country code
Tax Code	B3	Non-deductible input tax
Tax Type	V	Tax type for input tax
Non-Deduct. Input Tax – NAV	20	Tax rate in percentage
G/L Account	154000	The account to be posted tax

The next activity, which rounds up this exercise, explains how to assign taxable codes for non-taxable transactions in SAP ERP. In some countries, you must report tax-exempt or non-taxable items to the tax-governing bodies. To do this, you have to assign tax codes to non-taxable transactions.

Assign Taxable Codes to Non-Taxable Transactions

When you have to report tax-exempt or non-tax sales/purchases to a tax authority, it's best to define a 0 value tax code to track these types of transactions.

In this activity, you specify tax codes for input and output taxes, which are used to post non-taxable transactions to the relevant G/L accounts. To assign taxable codes for non-taxable transactions, follow this menu path: IMG: Financial Accounting (New) ➤ Financial Accounting Global Settings (New) ➤ Tax on Sales/Purchases ➤ Posting ➤ Assign Tax Codes for Non-Taxable Transactions. Or you can use transaction code OBCL.

■ **Tip** SAP comes with standard non-taxable input/output tax codes for most countries. SAP also allows you to create your own codes if you choose to. However, we recommend that you use the standard non-taxable codes instead of creating your own, as this will save you time. The only time you should create your own codes is when the standard codes provided by SAP do not meet your requirements.

The Change View "Allocate Co. Cd. -> Non-Taxable Transactions" Overview screen comes up (Figure 10-12). It contains a list of company codes. Search for your company code by clicking the scroll buttons or the [Position...] button. Assign V0 (exempt from input tax) to input tax and A0 (exempt from Output tax) to output tax for your company code (circled in red). Save your efforts.

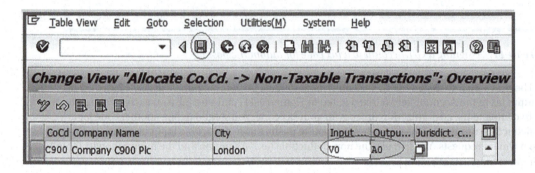

Figure 10-12. *Assigning tax codes to non-taxable transactions*

Summary

This chapter explained sales and purchase taxes and gave examples of sales and purchase taxes in practice. You looked at how sales and purchase taxes are reconciled and how the differences are passed on to the tax authority. You also looked at the various tax categories in SAP and learned how they are applied in the system. Thereafter, you looked at the basic settings involved in customizing taxes and learned about their relationship to country-specific settings. You learned how to assign a country to the calculation procedures.

You created two tax codes for sales and purchases taxes using two-digit codes. You went on to look at how to define tax accounts so that the system will automatically post them where you specify.

Finally, you learned how to assign taxable codes to non-taxable transactions using the standard non-taxable codes.

In Chapter 11, you will look at the final aspect of bank customizing—the cash journal. You will learn how to set up a new cash journal, define a company code for the cash journal, and assign G/L accounts where cash transactions are posted.

■ ■ ■

CHAPTER 11

Customizing a Cash Journal

In this chapter, you learn what a cash journal is and how to customize the required settings for one. At the end of the chapter, you will be able to:

- Set up a cash journal

- Create G/L accounts for your cash journal

- Specify the amount limit for your cash journal

- Define number range intervals for your cash journal

- Create, change, and delete business transactions

- Set up print parameters for your cash journal

Cash Journal

Cash receipts and cash payment transactions are managed in SAP ERP using a cash journal. A *cash journal* is a sub-module in bank accounting that serves as a cash-management tool for companies using SAP to manage their cash transactions. The importance of using the SAP cash journal tool is that it displays opening and closing balances, calculates total cash receipts and total cash payments, and reconciles the cash balance at any time. You can maintain separate cash journals for each company code and for each currency and make postings to customers, vendors, and G/L accounts in FI.

When you're setting up a new cash journal, the following items must be defined:

- The company code that will use the cash journal

- Identification key (usually a four-digit code) that identifies your cash journal

- The name of the cash journal (short text describing your cash journal)

- The general ledger accounts where the cash transactions are posted

- The currency used in your cash journal

- The document type for the following items:

  - General ledger postings

  - Outgoing payments to vendors

  - Incoming payments from vendors

  - Outgoing payments to customers

  - Incoming payments from customers

The first step is to create the G/L accounts that you will assign to the cash journal and to which all cash transactions will be posted.

■ **Tip**   We recommend that you create different cash journals for each currency and each company code you use.

Create G/L Accounts for a Cash Journal

Cash transactions are posted to the G/L accounts assigned to the cash journal. You will learn how to assign G/L accounts to your cash journal later in the "Set Up the Cash Journal" and "Create, Change, and Delete Business Transactions" sections.

> *Problem: Company C900 Plc has large cash transactions and wants you to set up a cash journal for them that will post to the following accounts in FI:*

- *Petty cash*

- *Cash transfers from the bank*

- *Cash transfers to the bank*

- *Cash purchases*

- *Cash sales*

To create the G/L accounts for your cash journal, follow this menu path: IMG: Financial Accounting (New) ➤ Bank Accounts ➤ Business Transaction ➤ Cash Journal ➤ Create G/L Account for Cash Journal. Or you can use transaction code FS00.

Because you learned how to create G/L accounts in Chapter 5, refer back to that chapter for a refresher. We specify how to create the five G/L accounts you need for this exercise in Appendix A. Go to "Appendix, A, Chapter 11, (Cash Journal)" to create the G/L accounts. The G/L accounts you create are assigned to the cash journal in the sections "Set Up Cash Journal" and "Create, Change, and Delete Business Transactions" later in this chapter.

Next, you need to specify the amount limit for your cash journal. This limit will restrict the amount you can post in a single transaction.

Specify the Amount Limit for a Cash Journal

The function of the amount limit is to set a cash limit for your cash Journal in FI. The limit you set for your cash journal serves as a control mechanism, because it allows the system to determine the maximum amount that can be posted per transaction to the cash journal. You'll define the company code, the currency, and the amount limit. The currency is automatically set to your company code's currency. When limits exceed the system settings, you'll get an error message. To set the amount limit for your cash journal, use this menu path: IMG: Financial Accounting (New) ➤ Bank Accounts ➤ Business Transaction ➤ Cash Journal ➤ Amount Limit.

The Change View: "Cash Journal: Amount Limit ": Overview screen is displayed. This screen contains the amount limits already defined in the system. Click the New Entries button on the top-left side of the screen to go to the New Entries: Overview of Added Entries screen, which is where you specify the amount limit for your cash journal (Figure 11-1).

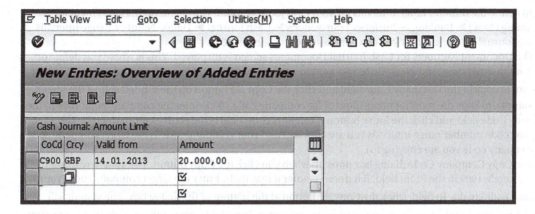

Figure 11-1. *Cash Journal: Amount Limit entry field*

Update the following fields:

CoCd: Enter the company code you are using for your cash journal.

Crcy: Enter the currency key that you want to use for the amount limit. If this field is blank, there will be no restriction to the amount you can post to the system.

Valid From: This is the date you want your amount limit to be valid from.

Amount: This is the maximum amount that can be posted per transaction in the cash journal.

After updating the screen, click the Enter ✅ button on the top-left side of the screen or press Enter on your keyboard to confirm that the system accepted your entries. Save 🖫 your efforts.

■ **Tip** Specifying the amount limit on the cash journal is optional. Do this only when your company wants to set a limit that users can post to the cash journal per transaction.

In the next activity, you will define number range intervals for your cash journal. The system will automatically assign a unique number from the defined number range interval to each document posted to the cash journal.

Define Number Range Intervals for Cash Journal Documents

When a cash journal transaction is posted, a cash journal document is generated and assigned a unique document number from the number range intervals that you define. The document number assigned to the posted cash journal transaction coupled with your company code will allow you to identify the given document within a fiscal year.

Problem: To save time and to ensure that number range intervals for the cash journal are accurate, you have been asked to define a cash journal number range by copying the number range intervals of company code 1000 supplied by SAP and modifying them to meet your requirements.

To define the number range intervals for your cash journal, follow this menu path: IMG: Financial Accounting (New) ➤ Banking ➤ Business Transactions ➤ Cash Journal ➤ Define Number Range Intervals for Cash Journal Documents. Or you can use transaction code FBCJC1.

The Document Numbers for Cash Journal Documents screen is displayed. This is where you define or copy your number range intervals. Since you want to copy an existing interval, enter the company code that you want to copy in the Company Code field and click the Copy 🖺 button on the top-left side of the screen. For example, to copy the number range interval for company code 1000, enter the company code 1000 in the Company Code field and click the Enter button. Company code 1000 is the source company code (the company code number range intervals you are copying) and your company code is the target company code (the company code you are copying to).

The Copy Company Code dialog box pops up when you click the Copy button. The system will enter company code 1000 in the From field. If it doesn't, enter it manually. Enter the target company code (your company code) in the To field. Click the Copy 🖺 button at the bottom of the dialog box. The system will copy the number range intervals from the source company code to the target company code (your company code).

The Transport number range intervals screen pops up with a message. Ignore the message by clicking the Enter ✅ button at the bottom of the screen. The document number range for the Cash Journal screen appears with a notification on the status bar at the bottom of the screen that ☑ CoCode 1000 was copied to C900 . This means that you have successfully copied the number range intervals. The advantage of copying intervals defined by the system is that it's adequate and meets your requirements. This saves you time because you can copy it and make any necessary changes as compared to defining your own number range interval.

It is recommended that you verify the number range you defined. To display the number range you copied from company code 1000 to your target company code, follow these steps.

On the Document Numbers for Cash Journal Documents screen, make sure your company code is entered in the Company Code field. Click the 🔍 Intervals button immediately below the company code field. The number range you copied will be displayed (Figure 11-2).

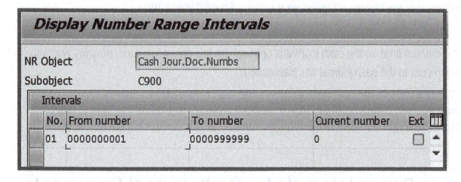

Figure 11-2. Displaying the number range interval

The next step is setting up the cash journal.

Set Up the Cash Journal

In this section, you will specify the settings for your cash journal. This includes the company name that you want to use for your cash journal, the number that will identify the cash journal, the G/L accounts where the cash journal transactions are posted, and so on. To set up the cash journal, follow this menu path: IMG: Financial Accounting (New) ➤ Banking ➤ Business Transactions ➤ Cash Journal ➤ Set Up Cash Journal. Or you can use transaction code FBCJC0.

The Change View "Maintain View for Cash Journals": Overview screen appears. This is where you establish settings for your cash journal. Click the New Entries button on the top of the screen to go the Change View "Maintain View for Cash Journals": Overview screen (Figure 11-3), where you'll configure the appropriate settings.

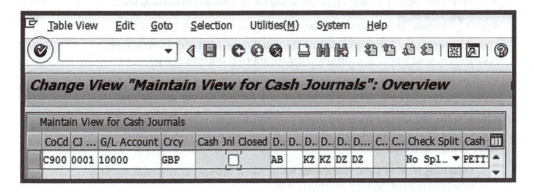

Figure 11-3. Setting up the cash journal

Update the following fields:

CoCd: Enter your company code. This is the company code that you want to use for the cash journal you defined in this activity. It is important to define individual cash journals for each company code. You can define a cash journal per transaction or per currency.

CJ Number: You can enter a maximum of four digits of your choice in this field. If you are creating more than one cash journal, make sure that the numbers you use are logical and sequential (for example, 0001, 0002, 0003, and so on). This number will identify your cash journal. This is important when you have more than one cash journal in the system.

G/L Account: Enter the G/L account number 10000 (for petty cash) you created earlier. When cash journal transactions are entered in the system, they are automatically posed to the G/L account you assign for your cash journal.

Crcy: Enter the currency you want to use in your cash journal. This is usually the company code's currency. On the contrary, if you choose to run your cash journal in a different currency, you must make sure that the option Only Balances in Local Crcy in your cash journal G/L account master data is not checked.

Cash Jnl Closed: Leave this checkbox blank. Leaving the checkbox blank indicates that your cash journal is active. If you click this checkbox, the cash journal will be closed. Click this checkbox only when you want to close your cash journal.

DT: Specify the document types for your cash journal postings. Document type determines the business transaction and account to post your cash journal transaction to. SAP comes with several document types to choose from. For example:

AB – G/L account

KZ – Outgoing payment to vendor

KZ – Incoming payment from vendor

DZ – Incoming payment from customer

DZ – Outgoing payment to customer

You can access these document types by using the matchcode or clicking the

Search 🔍 button. This button is displayed when you click on the input field of your document type. When you click on the matchcode, a list of document types is displayed, from which you can select the appropriate document type.

Cash Payment/Cash Receipt: Leave these fields blank. Leaving these fields blank enables you to post both cash payments and cash receipts to your cash journal.

Check Split: The specification you make here will determine whether the line items of the total posting are split when processing check deposits. You have three options to choose from:

- **Offsetting Item of Total Document Split:** When you specify this item, only the offsetting item of the total posting is split.

- **All Items of Total Document Split:** When this item is specified, the checks posted to the cash journal and the offsetting totals are split.

- **No Split of Line Items of Total Document:** No splitting is performed.

For this activity, select No Split of Line Items of Total Document. This will allow the user to carry out the split manually.

Cash Journal Name: Enter a name that best describes your cash journal. For instance, Petty Cash.

Click the Enter ✅ button to confirm your entries and save 💾 your cash journal.

In the next activity, you will specify the company code, the transaction number, the business transaction, the G/L accounts, the tax code, and the cash journal business transactions for your cash journal.

Create, Change, and Delete Business Transactions

The Create, Change, and Delete Business Transactions function enables you to specify the business transactions for your cash journal. You can create your own business transactions or copy the standard settings provided by the system and modify them to meet your requirements.

So that you gain a thorough understanding of how to customize business transactions in the cash journal, this exercise takes you through the detailed steps, rather than having you simply copy the predefined business transactions supplied by SAP. To maintain your business transactions, follow this menu path: IMG: Financial Accounting (New) ➤ Banking ➤ Business Transactions ➤ Cash Journal ➤ Create, Change, Delete Business Transactions. Or you can use transaction code FBCJC2.

The Change View "Maintain View for Cash Journal Transaction Names": Overview screen is displayed. This screen contains the list of existing business transactions in the system. (If you chose to copy the standard business transactions supplied by SAP, you can do so by selecting the business transactions for company code 1000, for instance, and clicking the Copy button on the top-left side of the screen. You can then modify them to meet your requirements.) Click the ⌷New Entries button to go to the New Entries: Overview of Added Entries screen (Figure 11-4), where you will specify your cash journal business transactions.

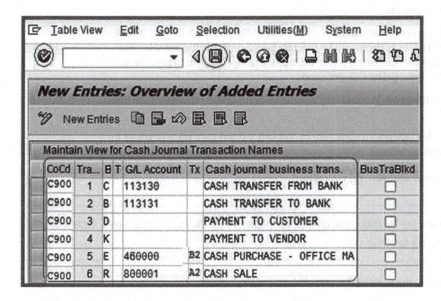

Figure 11-4. *The maintain view for cash journal transaction names*

Update the following fields:

> **CoCd:** Enter the company code that you are using for your cash journal transactions.
>
> **Tran.no:** The transaction number is determined by the system. It usually starts at 1, 2, 3, and so on.
>
> **Bus.Tran.Type:** Enter the business transaction type. SAP comes with predefined business transaction types:
>
> C – Receipt from bank account
>
> B – Payment to bank account
>
> R – Revenue
>
> E – Expense
>
> D – Customer posting
>
> K – Vendor posting

You can access these transaction types by using the matchcode or by clicking the Search 🔍 button.

G/L Account: Enter the G/L accounts that you want to post your cash journal transactions to. The G/L accounts entered here will allow cash transactions to be posted to the appropriate G/L accounts during document posting. For example:

- Cash transfers from the bank

- Cash transfers to the bank

- Expense accounts

Tx: Enter the tax codes for expenses and revenues for your cash journal business transactions. These tax codes will be used by the system to calculate sales and purchases taxes for your cash journal business transactions and to post the tax amount to the appropriate G/L accounts.

Cash Journal Business Trans: Enter a business transaction description for your cash journal.

BusTraBlkd: Set business transaction to blocked if you do not want postings to be made into transactions.

Click the Enter ✔ button and save 💾 your efforts.

■ **Note**   Make sure you use the tax codes you created in Chapter 10 for the input/output taxes. Otherwise, the system will not accept your tax code.

The final step is to set up the print parameters for your cash journal.

Set Up Print Parameters for the Cash Journal

To be able to print the cash journal transactions, you need to set up the print parameters for your cash journal for each company code represented in the system. To set up print parameters for your cash journal, follow this menu path: IMG: Financial Accounting (New) ➤ Banking ➤ Business Transactions ➤ Cash Journal ➤ Set Up Print ➤ Parameters for Cash Journal. Or you can use transaction code FBCJC3.

The Change View "Maintain Print Parameter View for Cash Journal" screen is displayed (Figure 11-5). You can copy the print program from the list of displayed standard print parameters or you can simply use one of the existing print programs if one meets your requirements.

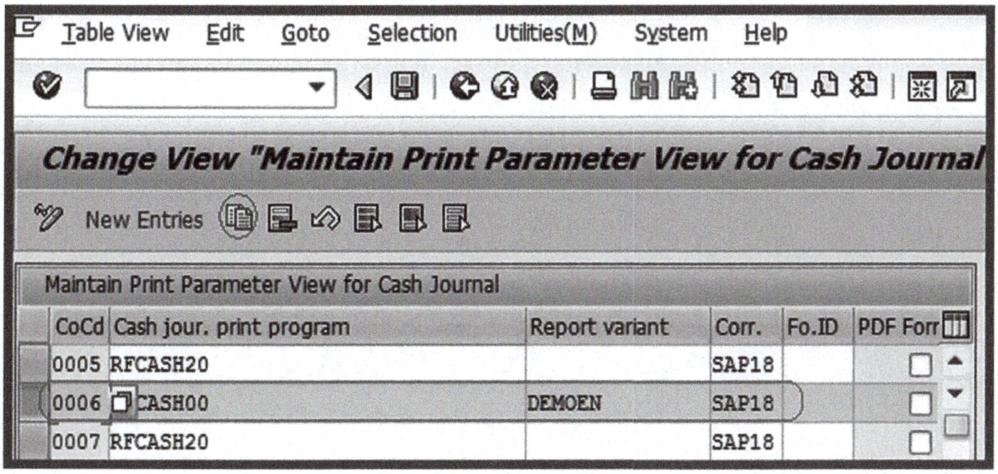

Figure 11-5. *Copying the print parameters for your cash journal*

In this exercise, you will copy the standard print program for company code 0006 supplied by SAP and adapt it to meet your requirements. To copy that print program, select the company code 0006 from the list of cash journal print programs and then click the Copy 📑 button on the top-left side of the screen. This action will specifically copy the company code print parameter you select. Change the company code 0006 to your target company code. Change the Cash Jour. Print Program description to your own. The Report Variant option is a way to output a report that is unique to you. Finally, choose correspondence type SAP18 (this is a print program to print cash doucments) for cash documents.

■ **Note** SAP comes with predefined print parameters that you can copy. It is advisable to copy a standard print parameter and modify it to meet your requirements. However, you can use any print parameter with correspondence type SAP18.

Click the Enter 📀 button on the top-left side of the screen and save 💾 the print parameters.

Summary

This chapter explained how cash receipts and payments transactions are managed using the cash journal and discussed the importance of using cash journals as cash-management tools. You went on to look at various settings that you need to customize your cash journals.

As part of customizing the cash journal, you specified the menu path for creating G/L cash accounts. You then learned how to set an amount limit, which determines the maximum amount that can be posted per transaction to the cash journal. You also learned how to define number range intervals for the cash journal by copying and modifying standard number range intervals in the system. You learned how to set up a cash journal and how to create, change, and delete business transactions. You also learned how to assign documents to your cash journal that will determine how transactions are posted. Finally, you set up the print parameters for your cash journals.

The next chapter explains what a financial statement is and describes the steps involved in defining financial statement versions. You'll learn how to map financial statement versions and assign appropriate G/L accounts from which financial statements are drawn.

CHAPTER 12

■■■

Financial Statement Versions (FSV)

In this chapter, you learn what a financial statement version (FSV) is and go through the basic settings involved in defining financial statement versions.

At the end of this chapter, you will be able to:

- Explain and define financial statement versions (FSV)

- Define an FSV using the appropriate specifications

- Assign FSV hierarchy nodes to the appropriate G/L accounts

Financial Statement Versions

A Financial Statement Version (FSV) forms the basis for drawing up financial statements in SAP ERP. The primary objective of a publically-owned business is to maximize returns on investors' equity. Therefore, the management needs to be able to ascertain the performance of the business in form reports at a given interval to help aid operational and strategic decision-making geared toward improving performance. In SAP ERP, hundreds of business transactions are posted to the general ledger in a fiscal year. But it's not possible to know how well a business is performing from the G/L accounts that transactions are posted to. Hence, the need for FSV.

FSV is part of the closing procedure in SAP ERP. It is a tool designed specifically for generating financial statements (such as profit and loss statements and balance sheets) to meet specific legal disclosure requirements related to certain items (such as assets, liabilities, income, expenses, and so on) in financial reports.

SAP ERP comes with standard, predefined FSV that you can use as a template and adjust to meet your requirements. You can also define your own FSV afresh if you choose not to use the standard FSV supplied by SAP. Interestingly, you can define more than one FSV if you need to meet individual financial statement reporting needs of various stakeholders, such as the tax authority, investors, and internal management reporting.

To define FSV in SAP ERP, you must specify the following items:

- The items to be included in your FSV and the order and the hierarchical structure of each item

- The text describing each financial statement item

- The chart of accounts

- Totals to be displayed in your report

FSV is a combination of G/L accounts structured in hierarchical levels that are defined in the financial statement version's directory and assigned to appropriate accounts. You can define more than one FSV to a specific chart of account or to a group of chart of accounts. Basically, FSV allows you to assign groups of accounts to items in the hierarchy.

Let's look at how to define a basic FSV in SAP.

Define Financial Statement Versions

In this exercise, you go through the various steps involved in customizing FSV. You can define your own FSV from scratch or copy a predefined FSV supplied by SAP and modify it.

> **Problem:** *The accounting team is not sure of the benefits and function of an FSV. You have been asked by company C900 Plc to advise the accounting team on the benefits of using an FSV and then to create an FSV in SAP ERP.*

To define an FSV, follow one of these menu paths:

- IMG: Financial Accounting (New) ➤ General Ledger Accounting (New) ➤ Periodic Processing ➤ Document ➤ Define Financial Statement Versions.

- IMG: Financial Accounting (New) ➤ General Ledger Accounting (New) ➤ Master Data ➤ G/L Accounts ➤ Define Financial Statement Versions.

You can also use transaction code OB58.

The Change View Financial Statement Version Overview screen is displayed. Click the New entries button at the top of the screen to go to the New Entries: Details of Added Entries screen, where you will specify the key for your financial statement version and describe the FSV's general specifications (Figure 12-1).

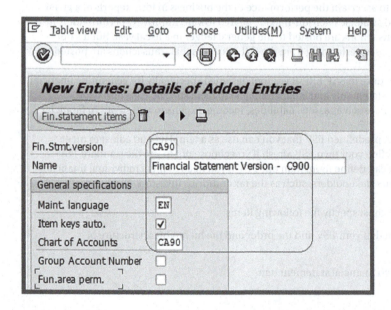

Figure 12-1. Initial entry screen where you start your customizing

Update the following fields:

Fin.Stmt.Version: Enter your proposed FSV in this field. You can enter up to four digits in this field. This will serve as an identification key for your FSV. We recommend that you use your chart of accounts key here. This is ideal for FSV identification for your company code, especially when you have several FSV and company codes in the system.

Name: Enter the text that best describes your FSV.

General Specifications: Specify the following items:

Maint.language: The language code is the language you want the system to use when maintaining FSV. For example, in this exercise we used EN (English).

Chart of Accounts: In this field, you enter your company code's chart of account that you defined in Chapter 2.

Click the Enter 🛡️ button at the top of the screen to confirm your entries and save 💾 your work.

The next step is to create the items for the FSV you just defined. You will create the nodes for the balance sheet, profit and loss statement, and unassigned accounts, which will then be enhanced in subsequent steps. To create the items for your FSV, click the `Fin.statement items` button. The Change Financial Statement Version screen is displayed (Figure 12-2), where you will define the FSV hierarchy nodes for your FSV. The items for the FSV are defined in SAP ERP in a hierarchical structure.

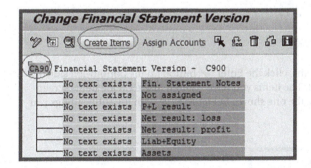

Figure 12-2. *The standard hierarchical structure where you start creating your FSV items*

To simplify the customization process, we will break it into four steps:

1. Create items.

2. Reassign items as subordinates.

3. Assign FSV nodes to G/L accounts.

4. Define the credit/debit shift.

■ **Note**   In practice, before you start creating the hierarchical structure of your FSV, it is advisable that you create a paper sketch of your FSV structure. This will serve as a guide when defining your FSV.

Step 1: Create Items

Notice in Figure 12-2 that the FSV you defined earlier is displayed as the heading in the hierarchy structure. Select the FSV circled in red by clicking on it. We used CA90 as the FSV.

Click the ⎡ Create Items ⎤ button. The Create Items screen will come up. On this screen, the FSV is displayed and the fields below your FSV are blank. You need to update this screen with the subheadings for your FSV items by typing them in (for example, Balance Sheet, Profit & Loss Account, and Unassigned Accounts), as shown in Figure 12-3.

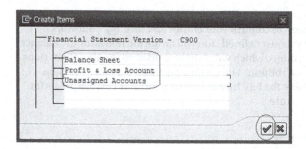

Figure 12-3. *The screen where you create your FSV items*

After typing in the subheading for your FSV items, click the Enter ✔ button on the bottom-left side of the pop-up screen or press Enter on your keyboard. The items you have entered in the Create Items screen will be copied into your FSV. Your FSV will look like the one shown in Figure 12-4, with the subheadings you entered below your FSV.

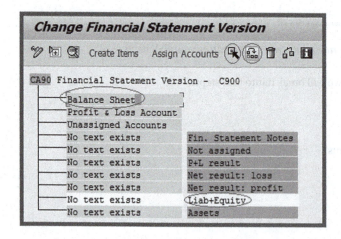

Figure 12-4. *FSV hierarchy structure showing how items are reassigned*

The next step is to reassign items supplied by SAP in Figure 12-4 (for example, P+L result, Net Result: Loss, Net Result: Profit, Liab+Equity, Assets, and so on) to your FSV as subordinates to the subheading you created in the FSV hierarchy. Subordinates will appear in the hierarchy under the subheadings you defined.

Step 2: Reassign Items as Subordinates

Let's start by assigning subordinates to the balance sheet. To reassign Liab+Equity as a subordinate to the balance sheet in your FSV hierarchy, select the Liab+Equity item from the list of FSV items supplied by SAP (see Figure 12-4). Click the Select ▣ button on the top-right side of the screen to select it. Notice that the row containing Liab+Equity turns yellow, indicating that the item has been selected. Then select an item you want to reassign it to from the list of items in the FSV hierarchy. In this case, select Balance Sheet by clicking on it. Click the Reassign ▣ button on the top-right side of the screen to reassign Liab+Equity to Balance Sheet. The Reassign Node dialog box pops up (Figure 12-5).

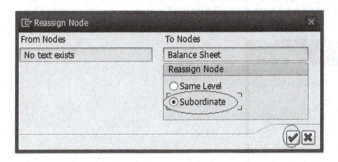

Figure 12-5. *The screen where you reassign an item to the same level or as a subordinate to an existing node in the FSV hierarchy structure*

On the Reassign Node screen, the nodes you are reassigning are specified by the system. On this screen, you can choose to reassign a node to another node at the same level or as a subordinate. In this activity, you are reassigning Liab+Equity as a subordinate to Balance Sheet, so click the Subordinate button. Click the Enter ✔ button at the bottom-right side of the Reassign Node screen to confirm your action.

■ **Note**   Choose Same Level from the Reassign Node screen if you want the item you are reassigning to be on the same level as the item you are assigning it to.

The next step is to add text to the items you have reassigned and determine which totals to output. During FSV review, the texts and totals will be displayed in the balance sheets and profit and loss statements.

Change Item Text

Notice in Figure 12-6 that the node for Assets and Liab+Equity states that No Text Exists. You need to add text to display in the financial statement.

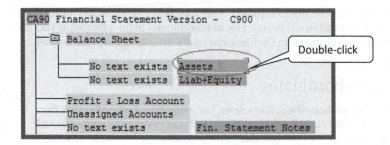

Figure 12-6. Double-click on item to call up the change text screen

To add text to the items in your FSV, double-click on the item you want to add text to. The Item: Change Texts screen will be displayed for that item. For example, if you double-click Assets, the screen that pops up will allow you to add text and activate display totals for Assets only (Figure 12-7).

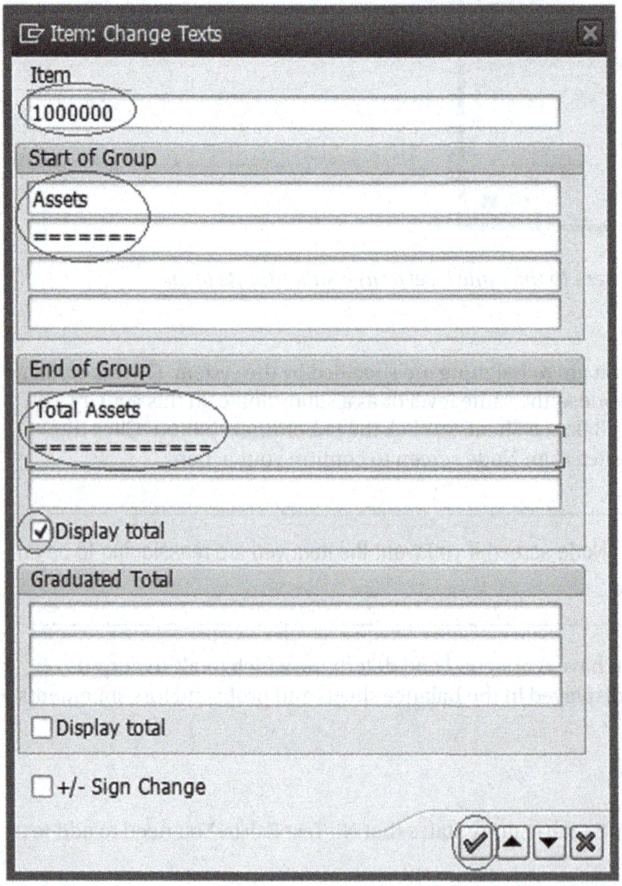

Figure 12-7. Item change text screen

> ■ **Note** When you're defining items in FSV, special codes are assigned to each item to maintain the classification of similar items under the same code and heading. These codes are designed in a systematic manner to form a logical sequence, often referred to as *code classification*. For example, the code for Asset is 200000, and the next items under Asset will be 200100, 200200, 200300, and so on. We will not be covering this topic further, as it is outside the scope of this book.

On the Item: Change Text screen, update the following fields:

> **Item:** Enter the item code and required text and select the totals to be output. We used 1000000 (see Figure 12-7).

> **Start of Group:** Enter the heading name for the specific group of items. The name you enter in this field will be displayed as the heading for the group in the report. If a G/L account is posted, this text is displayed before the item's sub-items during the period.

> **End of Group:** The text you enter here will end the group. For example, Total Assets will be displayed as the last item in the group. If you enter text and select the Display Total option in this section, the total balance for assigned G/L accounts is output during the selected period.

The system should default to the Display Total checkbox being selected; if not, you have to click it. This will display the total amount for the group in the report.

Click the Enter ✅ button on the bottom-right side of the Item: Change Text screen or press Enter on your keyboard. The system will then assign the item classification code to your FSV group. Save 💾 your FSV.

Following the process you just completed for Assets, assign a classification code and text to Liab+Equity using this information:

- Item: 2000000
- Group Start: Liabilities
- Display Total: Activate

Create Items for Liab+Equity

Next, you need to create more items as subordinates for 2000000 Liab+Equity using the Create Items button on the top-left side of the screen. To do this, select 2000000 – Liab+Equity and click the Create button. The Create Items screen is displayed (Figure 12-8). In the Balance Sheet section of your FSV, update the fields under 2000000 with the appropriate items.

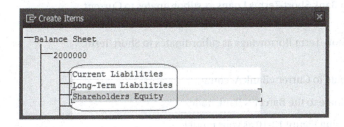

Figure 12-8. *Creating more items in FSV*

To enter your updates in your FSV, click the Enter ☑ button on the bottom-right side of the screen. Your FSV screen will look like the one in Figure 12-9.

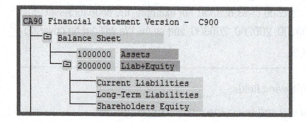

Figure 12-9. *FSV hierarchy structure showing the items created*

Save 🖫 your FSV.

Complete the Nodes for FSV

Follow Steps 1 and 2 (create items and reassign items as subordinates) to create the nodes in your FSV for the following items:

1. Create Intangible Assets, Fixed Assets, and Current Assets as subordinates to Assets.

2. Reassign the P+L Result node to Income Statement and change the name to P+L Result.

3. Assign the Net Result Loss & Net Result Gain nodes to Shareholders Equity.

4. Reassign Net Result: Loss to Shareholders Equity as a subordinate.

5. Reassign Net Result: Profit to Shareholders Equity as a subordinate.

6. Change the name of Net Result: Loss to Retained Earnings.

7. Change Net Result: Gain to Retained Earnings.

8. Reassign the node not assigned to Unassigned Accounts.

9. Click the ⌷ Create Items ⌷ button at the top of the screen and create the following nodes under current assets:

    - Petty Cash and Current Bank Account as subordinates to Cash & Cash Equivalent.

    - Short-Term Borrowings and Bank Short-Terms Loans as subordinates to Current Liabilities.

    - Bank Overdraft and Bank Short-Term Borrowings as subordinates to Short-Term Borrowings.

    - Barclays Bank as a subordinate to Current Bank Account.

    - Bank Overdraft as a subordinate to the Barclays Bank node.

Now complete the nodes for your FSV using Figure 12-10 as your model.

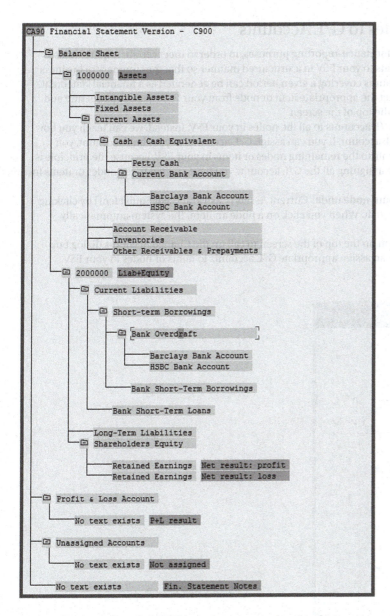

Figure 12-10. *An extended FSV hierarchy structure showing the items you created*

After you have reassigned these items and changed the appropriate text, save 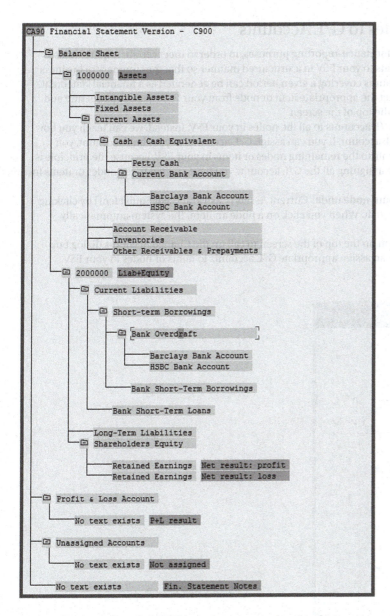 your work.
The next step is to assign your FSV nodes to the appropriate G/L accounts.

Step 3: Assign FSV Nodes to G/L Accounts

FSV is designed specifically for performance-reporting purposes, in order to meet certain requirements. It is important to assign G/L accounts to your FSV in a structured manner so that the summary of business transactions posted to the G/L accounts covering a given period can be generated as a financial statement. To assign G/L accounts to FSV, select the appropriate item or node from your FSV hierarchy structure and click the Assign Account button at the top of the screen.

You will not be able to assign G/L accounts to all the nodes in your FSV. Instead, we can teach you how to assign G/L accounts to your bank account. If you can assign G/L accounts to your bank account, you should be able to assign G/L accounts to the remaining nodes or items in your FSV, because the principle is the same. We advise that you trying assigning all the G/L accounts you have created to the nodes or items in your FSV.

Select the Barclays Bank Account node under Current Assets (Cash and Cash Equivalent) by clicking on it. You will assign a G/L account to it. When you click on a node an item, the system automatically selects the item.

Click the ⌈Assign Accounts⌉ button on the top of the screen to call up the Change Accounts dialog box (Figure 12-11). On this screen you can assign appropriate G/L accounts to items or nodes in your FSV hierarchy structure.

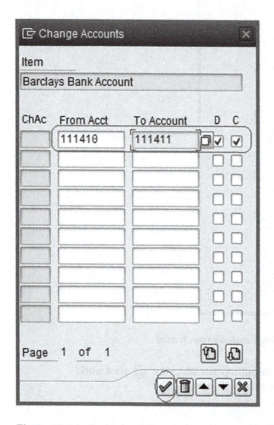

Figure 12-11. *Assigning G/L accounts to an item in FSV*

Update the following fields by entering the G/L account range you want to assign to your FSV node. You also must specify whether your G/L accounts are debit or credit:

> **From Acct:** Enter the starting G/L account number range of the G/L account you want to enter. In this exercise, we used 111410.

> **To Account:** Enter the ending G/L account number range in this field. In this exercise, we used 111431.

■ **Note** The benefits of using a number range is that when you have multiple G/L account numbers, you only need to enter the start and end G/L accounts, and the system will assign the entire range.

> **D:** Stands for debit. When this field is activated or selected, the system will include all the debit G/L accounts in your bank account in the FSV. Select this checkbox.

> **C:** Stands for credit. When this field is activated or selected, the system will include all the credit G/L accounts in your bank account in the FSV. Select this checkbox.

Then click the Enter ☑ button or press Enter on your keyboard. This action will then assign your chart of accounts and G/L account number range to your FSV and indicate if the assigned G/L accounts are debit and/or credit by marking an X.

Notice that the range of G/L accounts that you have assigned will appear under the Barclays Bank Account node in the FSV Hierarchy structure (Figure 12-12).

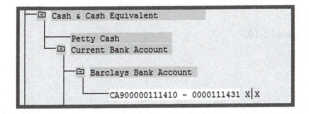

Figure 12-12. *How the G/L accounts assigned to an item are displayed in FSV*

Step 4: Define the Credit/Debit Shift

When your bank has a debit balance, it is considered an asset. This means that you have surplus cash in your bank account. On the other hand, if your bank has a credit balance, it is considered a liability. This means that you owe the bank, and it is referred to as overdraft (short-term borrowing). Cash balance surplus and deficits are disclosed separately in financial statements under different headings. For example, a debit bank balance is treated as an asset and a credit bank balance is treated as an overdraft under liability. So that the system can identify these transactions and disclose them separately in the financial statement (to meet accounting disclosure requirements), you have to specify these settings in your FSV.

Let's look at how this is done using the Barclays Bank Account node in your FSV hierarchy structure as an example.

Select the Barclays Bank Account under Current Assets by clicking on it. Then click the Select ⬛ button at the top of the screen. The item you have selected will turn yellow.

Select the Barclay Bank Account node under Overdraft in the Liability section by clicking on it. On the menu bar, choose Edit ➤ Debit/Credit ➤ Define. The Define Debit/Credit Shift dialog box is displayed. The system will automatically select the first radio button for Debit Item (Barclays Bank Account) and Credit Item (Barclays Bank Account), as shown in Figure 12-13. Click the Enter ✅ button on the bottom-right side of the dialog box to confirm your bank account debit/credit shift assignment.

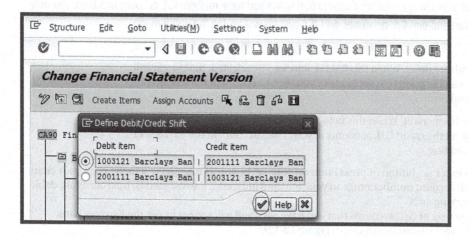

Figure 12-13. *The screen where you confirm the debit and credit item defaulted by the system for your bank account*

Your FSV will now look like the one shown in Figure 12-14.

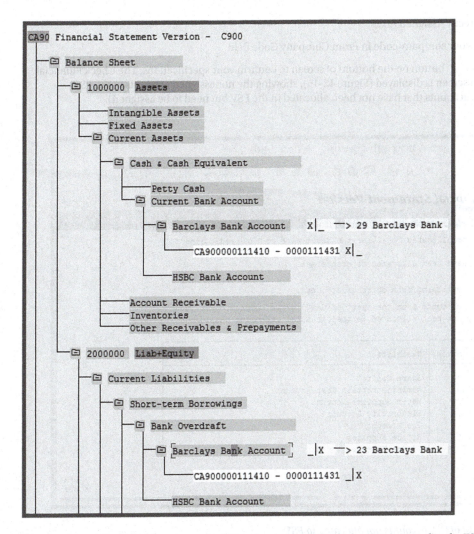

Figure 12-14. *Hierarchical structure depicting the nodes and G/L accounts assigned to the FSV*

Save 💾 your FSV.

The final step in this activity is to check the G/L accounts assigned to the FSV. When you perform a check, the system will tell you the items that have not been allocated to FSV, which will need to be assigned.

Check Assigned G/L Accounts to FSV

After assigning G/L accounts to your FSV nodes, it is important to carry out checks to find out if any of the items (G/L accounts) are not allocated to the FSV in your company code.

To do this, click the Check 🔓 button on the top-right side of the screen. The Carry Out Check dialog is displayed. Make sure the following checkboxes are selected:

- Accts Assigned to 1 Side Only

- Nonassigned Accounts

- Incorrectly Assigned Accts

- Enter your company code in From Company Code field

Click the Enter ✔ button on the bottom of screen to confirm your specifications. The Check Financial Statement Version screen is displayed (Figure 12-15), showing the nonassigned accounts in the FSV (these are the G/L accounts that have not been allocated in the FSV but need to be assigned).

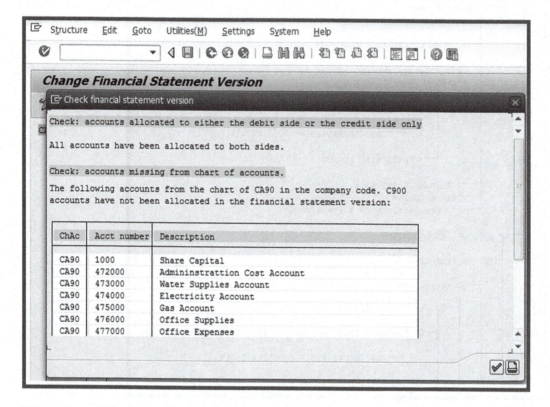

Figure 12-15. *A list of G/L accounts not allocated to FSV*

Go back and assign the displayed G/L accounts on the screen to the appropriate items (nodes) in the FSV. (You learned how to assign accounts to FSV items in Step 3.) Save 🖫 your FSV.

Summary

This chapter showed you how to configure Financial Statement Versions (FSV). In doing this, you learned how to define your own FSV from scratch. This included how to create FSV items using the Create button. As part of this exercise, you created the following items:

- Balance sheet

- Profit and loss account

- Unassigned accounts

You went on to create other nodes and items as subordinates for your FSV. You assigned codes to the items you created and assigned G/L accounts to items in the FSV. Finally, you learned how to check the items assigned to the FSV.

In the next chapter, you will look at how to integrate FI into the other modules, including Material Management (MM) and Sales and Distribution (SD). In Material Management, you will look at the various steps that allow the system to carry out automatic posting from MM to FI.

Finally, you will learn how to assign G/L accounts to SD. In doing this, you will determine the sequence to be used to achieve this objective.

CHAPTER 13

■ ■ ■

Integration of FI with Other SAP ERP Modules

In this chapter, you learn how to integrate FI with other SAP modules as well as how to customize and integrate the Material Management (MM) and Sales & Distribution (SD) modules.

At the end of this chapter, you will be able to:

- Integrate the FI module with other SAP modules

- Explain the Material Management (MM) module

- Configure automatic postings

- Explain the Sales & Distribution (SD) module

- Prepare revenue account determination

Integrate FI with Other SAP Modules

Most, if not all, transactions that take place in other modules in the SAP system trigger postings to the FI module. The idea behind assigning other modules to the FI module is to allow the system to automatically post financial transactions from other modules to FI. This process is referred to as *integration* in SAP ERP. The modules in Figure 13-1 are available for integration within FI.

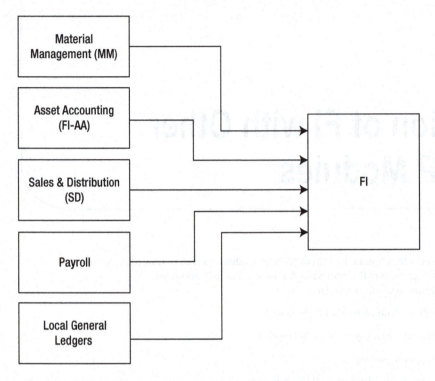

Figure 13-1. *Integrating other SAP modules into FI*

As a result, you need to perform some assignments between these modules in order to allow the system to perform automatic postings between them. For example, when you integrate the Payroll module into the FI module, postings made in the Payroll module are automatically posted to G/L accounts in real-time based on defined criteria.

In Figure 13-1, the Material Management (MM), Asset Accounting (FI-AA), Sales & Distribution (SD), Payroll, and Local General Ledger modules are integrated into FI. Therefore, postings to these modules are automatically posted to FI based on the integration procedures you define.

In this chapter, you learn how to integrate the Material Management (MM) and Sales & Distribution (SD) modules only. In Chapter 18 you integrate the Asset Accounting (FI-AA) module into FI.

■ **Note** Before you begin integrating other modules into FI, you should create the appropriate G/L accounts that you will need. Go to "Appendix A, Chapter 13" (Integration of FI with other modules) to create the appropriate G/L accounts for this exercise.

Material Management (MM)

Moving materials (such as goods issued and received) from one stage to another takes place in the MM module and those actions need to be posted to the FI. To represent the movement of these items in FI, they have to be assigned to G/L accounts in the FI module in the Valuation class. The Valuation class integrates the MM actions to FI and determines the G/L accounts where material movements (such as raw materials, semi-finished products, and finished products) are posted (Figure 13-2). In order for the system to automatically post MM transactions, you need to set its specifications in the Valuation class.

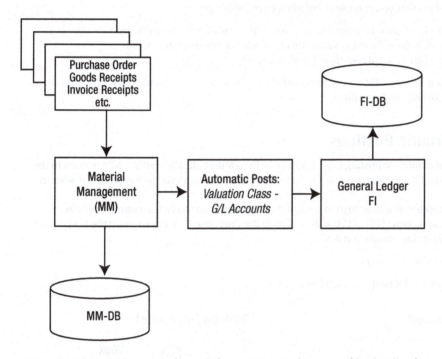

Figure 13-2. *How movement of material in MM is posted in FI-DB (the database)*

To properly classify your materials, you have to define the Valuation class for every material in the Valuation class' fields. SAP supplies standard Valuation classes for this purpose.

You need to configure three settings in order to perform automatic postings from the MM module to FI:

- *Valuation class*: The Valuation class determines the G/L account group materials with the same account characteristics even when they are posted at different stages during material movement. For example, it allows goods receipt of raw materials to be posted to one G/L account and finished products to another. This is achieved by assigning different Valuation classes to materials at different stages. For example, the Valuation class number for Raw Materials is 3000, for Semi-Finished Products is 7900, and for Finished Products it's 7920.

  When creating a material, you must specify a Valuation class in the accounting data for the material. A material is entered in the accounting data view of the material master data. As part of your configuration you must also assign a material type to the Valuation class. This will allow the system to determine

191

whether the Valuation class you defined can be used for the material type. A Valuation class can be assigned to one or more material types. Likewise, a material type can be assigned to one or more Valuation classes. The link between Valuation classes and material types is maintained by the account category reference. A combination of Valuation classes is often referred to as an account category reference.

- *Transaction key or code*:Transaction codes differentiate between transactions and determine the G/L account where the transaction is posted. SAP includes standard transaction keys that you can use to customize your settings.

- *Accounts*:This is where you assign the G/L accounts. You assign G/L accounts to posting transactions for every valuation class, and the postings in MM will automatically generate corresponding postings in FI.

In order for the system to post MM transactions automatically to the G/L accounts in FI, you need to perform the automatic posting configurations.

Configure Automatic Postings

When you customize the automatic postings, the system can then automatically post the MM actions to the appropriate G/L accounts. That means you don't have to manually input material movements; the system will do it for you.

Let's look at an example to see how customizing MM integration into the G/L accounts works in principle. Assume a goods receipt (GR) of £200K is posted to the Purchase Order account in the MM module. The double entry record for this transaction is to:

1. Debit the inventory account.

2. Credit the GR/IR clearing account (Figure 13-3).

Figure 13-3. *Accounting double entry of goods receipt (GR)*

There are two ways to access the screen where you customize these types of automatic postings:

- IMG: Financial Accounting (New) ➤ General Ledger Accounting (New) ➤ Periodic Processing ➤ Integration ➤ Material Management ➤ Define Accounts for Material Management

- IMG: Material Management ➤ Valuation and Account Assignment ➤ Account ➤ Determination ➤ Account Determination Without Wizard ➤ Configure Automatic Postings

The Configuration Accounting Maintain: Automatic Posts - Procedures screen is displayed. This screen contains a list of procedures you can choose from. Choose Inventory Posting BSX from the Procedures list by clicking on it. Then click the Details [ ] button on the top-left side of the screen. The Enter Chart of Accounts dialog box pops up. Enter your chart of accounts code in the Chart of Accounts field. Click the Enter ✅ button at the bottom of the dialog box or press Enter on your keyboard. The Configuration Accounting Maintain: Automatic Posts – Rules screen is displayed. Notice that the system has automatically entered your chart of accounts CA90 and the transaction code BSX for inventory posting. This is where you determine the valuation class for your account assignment.

In the Accounts Are Determined Based On section of the screen, specify the basis on which you want your material valuation accounts to be determined. You do this by setting the posting rules for the Valuation modification, Valuation class, and G/L accounts. Select the Valuation Modif and Valuation Class checkboxes. Click Save 🖫 at the top of the screen for the system to accept your valuation class specification. The Configuration Accounting Maintain: Automatic Posts - Accounts screen is displayed (Figure 13-4). This is where you specify the settings for automatic postings of MM transactions to FI.

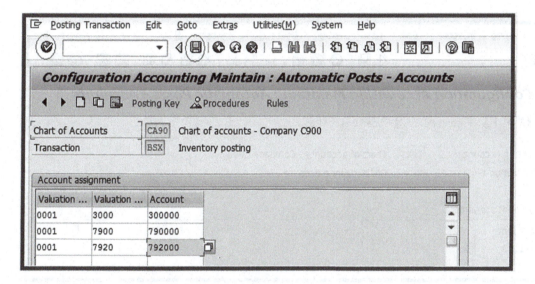

***Figure 13-4.** Maintaining the automatic posting of inventory*

Update the following fields:

> **Valuation Modification:** Enter **0001** in this field for each material (Raw Material, Semi-Finished Products, and Finished Products). This determines accounts posted based on the valuation area or plant (if your valuation area is based on plants). A plant is an organizational unit that distinguishes activities based on business operations. For example, production units.

> **Valuation Class:** Select the appropriate valuation class from the ones supplied by SAP by clicking the Search button. In this instance, select the Validation Class for Raw Material 3000, Semi-Finished Products 7900, and Finished Products 7920.

> **Account:** Enter the G/L Account for Raw Material 300000, Semi-Finished Products 790000, and Finished Products 792000 in the Account field.

Click the Enter ✅ button to confirm your entries and save 🖫 your efforts.

In the double entry example earlier in Figure 13-3, you had two accounts: Inventory and GR/IR. Since you have created an inventory account using the BSX transaction key, the next step is to create a corresponding credit account for the GR/IR clearing account. To do this, you should use the GR/IR clearing account WRX transaction key from the list of procedures on the Configuration Accounting Maintain: Automatic Posts - Procedures screen (see Figure 13-4).

Click the Back ⟲ button on the top of the screen to return to the previous screen (Configuration Accounting Maintain: Automatic Posts - Procedures). Search for GR/IR clearing account WRX from the Procedures list by clicking the scroll ⬍ buttons. Click the Details ⬛ button at the top of the screen to go to the Configuration Accounting Maintain: Automatic Posts – Accounts screen, where you will assign an account to the GR/IR clearing account. Notice that the system will automatically use your chart of accounts CA90 and the transaction code WRX GR/IR clearing account (Figure 13-5).

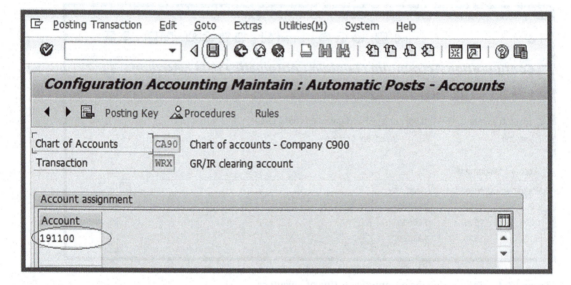

Figure 13-5. *Maintaining the automatic posting for the GR/IR clearing account*

Enter the GR/IR clearing account G/L account 191100 in the Account field and save 💾 your account assignment.

In an automatic posting procedure, there are several transactions and transaction keys that are not covered in this book that you may want to explore on your own. The following transaction keys are important:

- GBB: Offsetting entry for inventory posting

- PRD: Cost (price) differences

- KON: Consignment payables

In this activity you will only be looking at the offsetting entry for inventory posting (GBB), which is a predefined transaction code. Basically, the procedure for assigning a transaction key is the same. GBB has several account groupings that you can choose from based on the relevant movement types. The following list contains the accounting groupings for materials or goods movement types in GBB:

- AUF – Goods receipt for production orders with account assignment

- BSA – Initial entries of stock balances

- INV – Expenses/revenue for inventory differences

- VAX – Goods issues for sales orders without account assignment

- VAY – Goods issues for sales orders with account assignment

- VBO – Consumption for stock of material provided to vendor

- VBR – Internal goods issues to production/cost center

- VKA – Consumptions for sales order SD

- VNG – Scrapping/destruction

- VQP – Sampling

- ZOB – Goods receipt without purchase orders

- ZOP – Goods receipt without production orders

In this activity, you will only be updating general modification VBR (a predefined transaction key supplied by SAP for internal inventory posting to G/L accounts) with the Material Consumption account. After you configure the GBB-offsetting entry for inventory posting, the system will automatically post materials or goods issued to production or cost center to offsetting accounts in FI by debiting the Material Consumption account and crediting the Inventory account for materials.

Let's configure the offsetting entry for inventory GBB now. Follow this menu path: IMG: Financial Accounting (New) ➤ General Ledger Accounting (New) ➤ Periodic Processing ➤ Integration ➤ Material Management ➤ Define Accounts for Material Management. The Configuration Accounting Maintain: Automatic Posts - Procedures screen is displayed. Click the scroll ⬍ buttons to find the Offsetting entry for Inventory GBB in the procedure list. Select it and click the Details 🔍 button at the top of the screen. The Enter Chart of Accounts dialog pops up. Enter your chart of accounts CA90 into the Chart of Accounts field.

Click the Enter ✅ button at the bottom of the pop-up screen to confirm your entry. You will be presented with the Configuration Accounting Maintain: Automatic Posts – Rules screen (Figure 13-6).

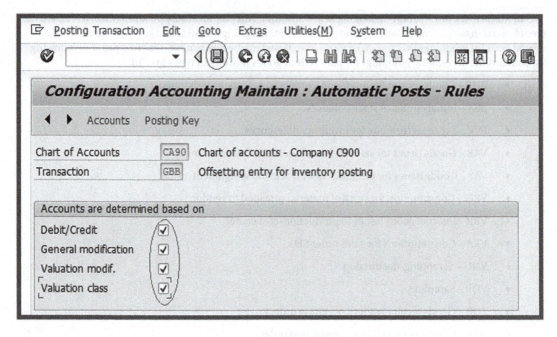

Figure 13-6. *Maintaining the posting rules for automatic posting*

In the Accounts Are Determined Based On section, check the following checkboxes:

- Debit/Credit

- General Modification

- Valuation Modification

- Valuation Class

These items are then made available for input on the next screen. Click Save ▣. The Configuration Accounting Maintain: Automatic Posts – Accounts screen appears (Figure 13-7). Update the screen using the information in Table 13-1.

Table 13-1. *Information Needed to Customize the Automatic Offsetting Entry for Inventory Posting*

Field	Value	Description
Valuation Modif.	0001	Determines accounts posted based on valuation area or plant (if your valuation area is based on plants).
General Modification	VBR	Transaction type used to differentiate account determination. VBR represents internal goods issues to production/cost center.
Valuation Class	3000	An important key that determines the G/L account material that should be posted to at different stages.
Debit	400000	G/L account debit items are posted.
Credit	400000	G/L account credit items are posted.

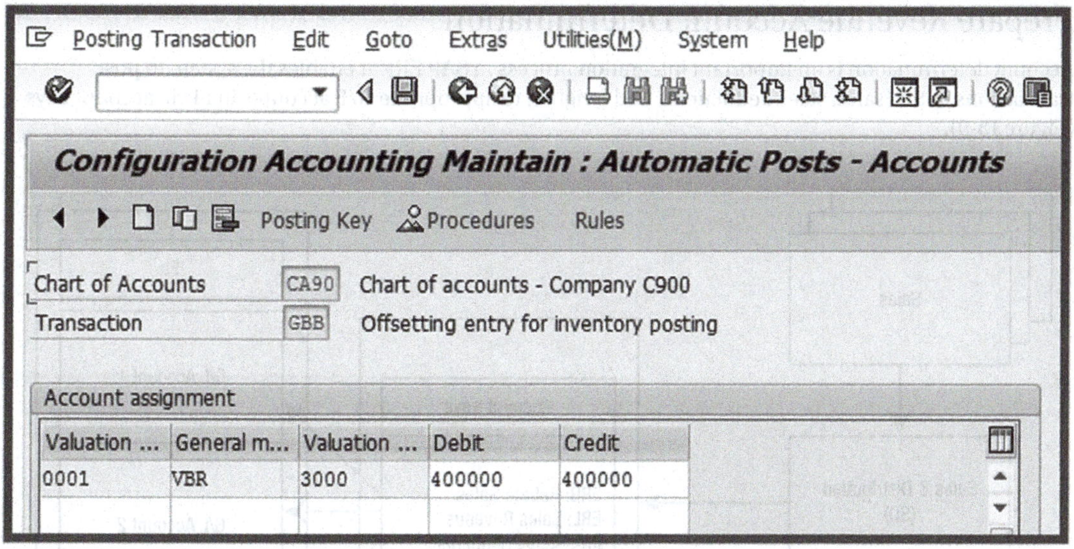

Posting Transaction   Edit   Goto   Extras   Utilities(M)   System   Help

Configuration Accounting Maintain : Automatic Posts - Accounts

◄ ► 🗋 🗇 🖳   Posting Key   🧍Procedures   Rules

| Chart of Accounts | CA90 | Chart of accounts - Company C900 |
| Transaction | GBB | Offsetting entry for inventory posting |

Account assignment

Valuation ...	General m...	Valuation ...	Debit	Credit
0001	VBR	3000	400000	400000

Figure 13-7. Maintaining automatic posting for the offsetting entry for inventory posting

Click the Enter 🗸 button at the top of the screen to confirm your entries and save 🖫 your efforts.

The next step is to integrate FI to Sales & Distribution (SD) to allow the system to automatically post transactions in SD to FI.

Sales & Distribution (SD)

Sales & Distribution (SD) is part of the SAP module and handles business processes from the sales order to the delivery. This module manages customer sales orders, shipping, billing of products, services, and risk management, and more. Billing is a part of the SD function, and all billing transactions that take place in the SD module also form part of the FI transactions, which result in postings in the FI - general ledger.

This section uses the double entry principle to illustrate how an SD billing transaction is recorded in accounting. Assume that a bill is raised in SD for £200K. This will look like the double entry accounting transaction in Figure 13-8.

Figure 13-8. Accounting double entry when an SD document is posted to FI

The next section explains the customizing steps involved in integrating FI G/L accounts to SD in SAP ERP.

Prepare Revenue Account Determination

Account determination is an important integration process in SAP ERP. It enables the system to post transactions in SD (sales, sales deductions, and freights) to appropriate G/L accounts in FI via account keys (Figure 13-9).

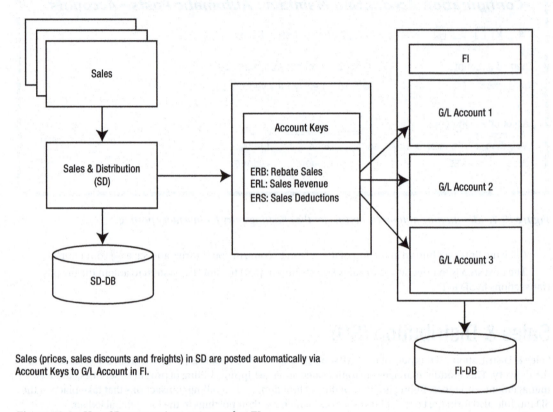

Sales (prices, sales discounts and freights) in SD are posted automatically via Account Keys to G/L Account in FI.

Figure 13-9. *How SD transactions are posted to FI*

SAP comes with standard account keys that you can use to integrate FI and SD. The following list contains the available account keys that you can use when customizing:

- ERB – Rebate Sales

- ERL – Sales Revenue

- ERS – Sales Deductions

- ERU – Rebate Accruals

- EVV – Cash Clearing

When integrating G/L accounts in FI to SD, you first need to specify the items in Table 13-2.

Table 13-2. *Items Needing Specification When Integrating SD to G/L Accounts in FI*

Field	Description
Application	This is where you specify the key for the Sales & Distribution application. The standard application key for SD is V. You can access this key using the matchcode next to the application field.
Condition Type for Account Determination	SAP comes with standard condition types KOFI and KOFK. If your company code is making SD (Sales & Distribution) transactions posting to FI and not to (CO) controlling, use condition type KOFI for the account determination. On the other hand, if you want the system to post SD transactions to FI and CO, you use condition type KOFK.
Chart of Accounts	Here you specify the chart of accounts for your G/L account structure. In this activity, the chart of accounts key is CA90.
Sales Organization	Here you specify the sales organization you want to apply to your account determination. For example, sales organization 0001, 0002, and so on. Sales organizations are distinguished with an identification number in SAP ERP.
Account Key	The account key you specify here will determine the appropriate G/L account transactions relating to sales that are posted. For example, ERL for Sales Revenue, ERS for Sales Deduction, and so on.
G/L Account	The G/L account in FI that transactions from SD are posted to for accounting purposes.

When assigning G/L accounts to SD, you must also determine the sequence to use. In SAP you have five access sequences:

- Cust. Grp/Material Grp/Acct Key

- Cust. Grp/ Acct Key

- Material Grp/Acct Key

- General

- Account Key

Access sequences allow you to specify different G/L accounts for different sales organizations. Based on your settings, the system will go through your settings to determine if a G/L account is assigned to an account key. The system will check the first item in the access sequence, for example, the Cust. GrpMaterialGrpAccKey. If a G/L account is assigned, the system will use the G/L account for revenue posting. If a G/L account is not assigned, the system will go to the next item in the sequence and so on, until the system finds an account key that a G/L account is assigned to. It will use it for posting SD transactions to G/L accounts in FI.

■ **Note**　You should determine the access sequence that you want to maintain for your G/L account.

Let's integrate G/L accounts in FI to SD now. This activity illustrates the steps involved in configuring revenue account determination.

Problem: *Using an account key (Acct Key), assign a G/L account to the Sales Revenue (ERL) and Sales Deductions (ERS) modules.*

You can access the menu path for revenue account determination either in FI or SD:

- IMG: Financial Accounting (New) ➤ General Ledger Accounting (New) ➤ Periodic Processing ➤ Integration ➤ Sales & Distribution ➤ Prepare Revenue Account Determination

- IMG: Sales & Distribution ➤ Basic Functions ➤ Account Assignment/Costing ➤ Revenue Account Determination ➤ Assign G/L Accounts

The Assign G/L Accounts screen is displayed. It contains a list of five access sequences to choose from. Choose Account Key (this is the last item on the list) and then click Details 🔍 at the top of the screen to go to the Change View Acct Key Overview screen. This is the initial screen where you will prepare revenue account determination for the integration of G/L accounts in FI to SD. Click the New Entries button on the top-left side of the screen to go to the New Entries: Overview screen (Figure 13-10).

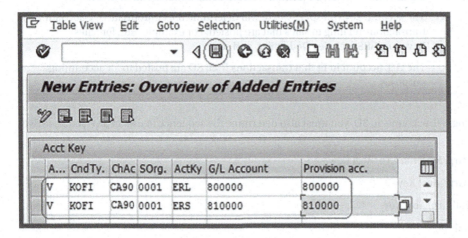

Figure 13-10. *Assigning G/L accounts to an account key*

Update the following fields:

Application: Enter application key V. This is the standard key for SD.

CndTy.: Enter condition type KOFI. This condition type is used for account determination without posting CO (controlling). If you want to be able to post to FI and CO, use the condition type KOFK.

ChAc: Enter the chart of accounts you defined in Chapter 2. This will allow you to use the G/L accounts in your chart of accounts.

SOrg: Enter sales organization 0001. We used 0001 for illustration purposes.

ActKy: Enter account key ERL (sales revenue) and ERS (sales deductions). The account key will allow the system to distinguish between transactions.

G/L Account: Enter the G/L account you want sales revenue to be posted in the G/L account in FI. This activity uses 800000 as the G/L account for illustration purposes.

Provision Acc.: Enter the G/L account you want to post sales deductions to in this field.

Click the Enter button on the top-left side of the screen and save 🖫 your work to complete your configuration.

Summary

This chapter explained the processes involved in integrating FI with other modules in SAP ERP. It briefly discussed material movements that take place in the Material Management (MM) module that need to be posted to FI. This included material issues and receipts. It went on to explore the steps involved in customizing the integration of MM with FI. In customizing MM, we defined the Valuation class for Raw Material, Semi-Finished Products, and Finished Products using the standard valuation keys supplied by SAP and assigning them to appropriate G/L accounts. You also looked at the relationship between Sales & Distribution (SD) and FI. You learned about this through a flow diagram, which explained the concepts involved in configuring SD with FI.

Finally, you also learned how to customize SD in order for the system to determine the appropriate G/L accounts that SD transactions are posted to. In doing so, you specified various condition types and assigned them to G/L accounts. This is necessary so that the system can determine the G/L accounts that SD transactions are posted to.

The next chapter explains how to customize the Accounts Payable (AP) and Accounts Receivable (AR) modules. It explains how to create number ranges for customers/vendors and covers the problems associated with creating number ranges. It defines account groups with screen layouts, explains the use of payment terms and various installment plans, and covers how to configure manual and automatic outgoing payments in SAP ERP. It also looks at how to define adjustment accounts for receivables and payables by maturity, and adjustment posting/reversal of documents using negative postings methods.

CHAPTER 14

■■■

Defining FI Accounts Receivable and Accounts Payable

This chapter explains what accounts receivable and accounts payable are, and also looks at the steps involved in customizing accounts receivable and accounts payable.

At the end of this chapter, you will be able to:

- Understand what accounts payable/receivable is
- Describe an account group and understand its importance
- Maintain the Field Status group for general data about customer account groups
- Define account groups with screen layout
- Define payment terms in SAP
- Maintain terms of payment for an installment plan
- Define document types for enjoy transactions
- Maintain settings for manual outgoing payments
- Define automatic outgoing payments
- Maintain tolerance groups for employees, customers/vendors, and G/L accounts
- Define sort methods and adjustment accounts for regrouping receivables/payables
- Specify adjustment accounts for receivables/payables by maturity
- Define adjustment posting/reversal using negative posting methods
- Understand reasons for reversal

Accounts Payable and Accounts Receivable

Accounts Payable and Accounts Receivable simply represent Customer and Vendor Accounts, respectively. A customer is usually referred to as a debtor and a vendor is called a creditor. A customer is a business partner from whom receivables are due. These business partners owe you money for goods delivered or services rendered. A customer falls under the category of sales. In SAP ERP, a customer must have a master record. A customer master record contains information about a customer account held in the database that's applied to accounting transactions in the system. A vendor is a business partner to whom payables are due. You owe money to vendors for goods and services received. Like a customer, a vendor falls under the category of purchases and has a master record in the SAP system. Likewise, a vendor master record contains information about a vendor account held in the database, which is applied to the accounting transactions.

Configuring accounts receivable and accounts payable entails several steps and can be confusing if you're not careful. We will be going through these steps systematically. First, we will take you through configuring accounts receivable, and then you will learn how to configure accounts payable.

■ **Note** There is no rule as to which account to configure first. Our decision to start with account receivables is purely a matter of choice.

What Is a Customer Account Group?

Customer account groups allow you to classify customers into business partner functions that best fit the nature of the business transaction. Customer account groups control the customer hierarchy containing the customer master record. When a customer account is created, it is assigned to an account group. Normally, an account group serves as a control mechanism that determines the relevant screens and fields to be displayed for input during document entry. This is based on the individual customer's business functions and is maintained in the implementation guide (IMG).

The account group determines the fields displayed for input. You determine whether a field is Required, Optional, or Displayed. When you specify that a field is required for input, the system will make it compulsory to enter data into the field during document entry. For example, you can specify that the customer number, name, and bank data must not be omitted during document entry. Mark information that is not compulsory but may be needed as optional, and if you don't want certain information to be entered during document entry but you want to display the field, mark those fields as displayed or suppressed. You can also hide the fields that you do not want to show by specifying their field status in the general data area.

Another benefit of customer account groups is that they assign a number range systematically for the customer/vendor based on the business partner function. You will look at number range in depth later in this chapter.

SAP provides a list of predefined account groups you can choose from instead of creating your own account groups. The following list includes some of these important account group numbers and names:

- 0001 – Sold to party
- 0002 – Ship to party
- 0003 – Payer
- 0004 – Bill to third party

It's best to use the standard account groups supplied by SAP instead of creating your own account group. You should create an account group only if your company wants you to, in order to meet specific requirements. This exercise teaches you how to create your own account groups from scratch.

■ **Note** You can also define the screen layout for an account group per company code and per activity. We don't cover this process, as it's beyond the scope of this chapter. We believe that the standard setting supplied by SAP is sufficient.

Define Account Groups with Screen Layout (Customer)

Problem: *Company C900 Plc classifies customer account groups into three partner business functions:*

- *Domestic customer*

- *Foreign customer*

- *One-time customer*

Your task is to maintain an account group that will reflect these partners' functions.

In this exercise you will define an account group with the appropriate partner business functions and maintain the field status group for its general data. To customize the account groups for your customer based on partner business functions, follow this menu path: IMG: Financial Accounting (New) ➤ Accounts Receivable and Accounts Payable ➤ Customer Accounts ➤ Master Data ➤ Preparations for Creating Customer Master Data ➤ Define Accounts Groups with Screen Layout (Customers). Or you can use transaction code OBD2. The Change View Customer Account Groups Overview screen is displayed. This is where you define the account groups for your customers. To specify your account group, click the New entries button on the top-left side of the screen (Figure 14-1). You can create as many account groups as you need, such as Foreign Customer, Domestic Customer, One-Time Customer, and so on.

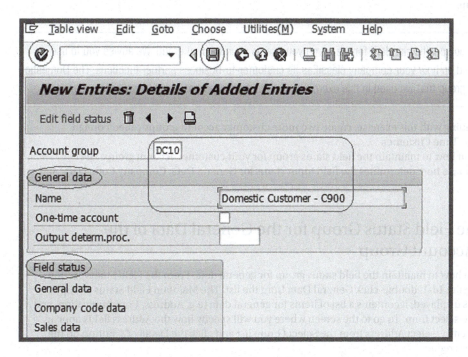

Figure 14-1. *Initial screen for account groups with screen layout (customer)*

The customer account group screen is divided into two sections:

> **General Data:** Contains the account group name field, where you name your customer account group and the area where you specify if the account group is for a one-time customer.

> **Field Status:** Contains general, company code, and sales data. You can specify the field input status for each of these items (whether you want a field to be suppressed, required, or optional) during document entry.

■ **Tip**   If you are creating a one-time customer account group, remember to select the One-Time Account checkbox in the General Data section of the Account Group Entries screen.

Update the following fields:

> **Account Group:** Enter four characters for the account group key. This key will serve as your account group identifier.

> **Name:** Enter a short description that best describes your account group. For example, Domestic Customer, Foreign Customer, One-Time Customer, and so on.

Click the Enter 📝 button on the top-left side of the screen to confirm your entries and then save 💾 your account group.

■ **Note**   There is no specific standard for the name you use as your account group. We advise you to use an account name based on how your company classifies its customer-to-business partner functions. The Domestic Customer Account group that we used in this exercise is for illustration purposes only and is not a standard.

Before continuing with this exercise, create two more customer account groups called Foreign Customer and One-Time Customer.

Next, you learn how to maintain the field status group for your customer account group. The specification you make here determines the field input status for General Data, Company Code Data, and Sales Data.

Maintain the Field Status Group for the General Data of the Customer Account Group

First you will learn how to maintain the field status group for general data. From the Field Status section of the screen in Figure 14-1, double-click General Data from the list. The Maintain Field Status Group: Overview screen is displayed; it contains a list of items for general data (e.g. Address, Communication, and so on) that you can select from. To go to the screen where you will specify how the Address fields appear during document entry, select Address from the Select Group list and click the Details 🔍 button on the top-left side of the screen.

The Maintain Field Status Group: Address screen is displayed (Figure 14-2). This is where you maintain the Field Status for Address. The specifications you input here determine whether a given field is suppressed, required, or optional. Base your settings on your client's requirements. In this exercise, we set the address fields to optional, because we consider the address field less important than items like reconciliation account and sort key.

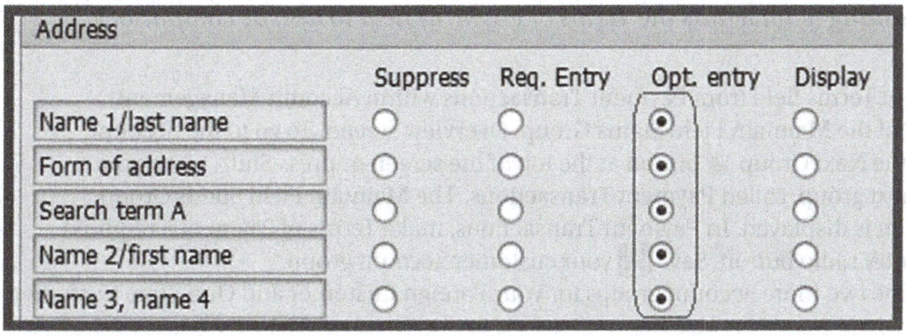

Figure 14-2. The Maintain Field Status Group – Address screen

Set all items in the address field to optional (make sure that all the Optional Entry radio buttons are clicked) and then save 💾 your settings.

> **Problem:** *To ensure that users enter important information during document entry, the accounting team has asked you to make the Reconciliation Account and Sort Key compulsory input fields.*

You modify the Reconciliation Account and Sort Key fields from the Company Code Data in the Field Status section of the Change View "Customer Account Group": Details screen (see Figure 14-1). To carry out your specifications, double-click Company Code in the Field Status section of the screen. The Maintain Field Status Group: Overview screen comes up. This is where you maintain the field status for your input field. Select Account Management from the Select Group list and then click the Choose 🔍 button on the top-left side of the screen or press F2 on your keyboard to go to the next screen, which is called Maintain Field Status Group: Account Management (Figure 14-3). From this screen, you specify the settings for the Reconciliation Account and Sort Key. Set the Reconciliation and Sort Key fields to required and all the other items on the screen to optional. This means that during the data-entry process, the system will require a Reconciliation Account and Sort Key be entered.

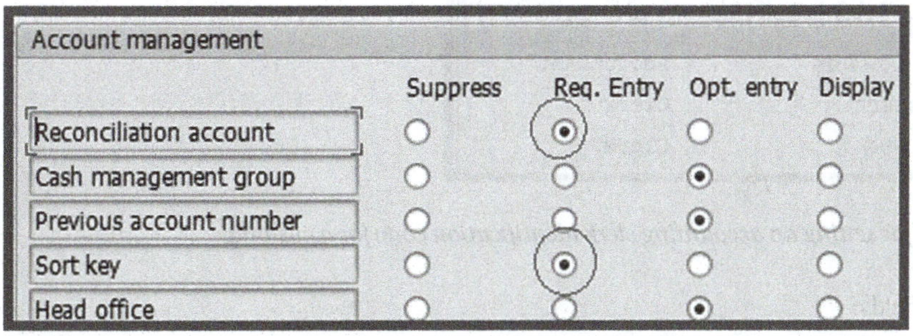

Figure 14-3. The Maintain Field Status Group – Account Management screen

---

■ **Tip** Do not save your work yet, because you next learn how to use the Next Page button.

Problem: *The accounting team wants the Terms of Payment field to also be compulsory.*

You specify the Payment Terms field from Payment Transactions within Account Management in the Select Group section of the Maintain Field Status Group: Overview screen. To go to the Account Management screen, click the Next Group ➧ button at the top of the screen or press Shift+F6 on your keyboard. You'll go to the next group, called Payment Transactions. The Maintain Field Status Group: Payment Transactions screen is displayed. In Payment Transactions, make Terms of Payment a required entry by clicking the Req.Entry radio button. Save 💾 your customer account group.

Before moving on, define two more account groups for your Foreign Customer and One-Time Customer groups.

Enter Accounting Clerk Identification Code for Customers

You need to define the name of the accounting clerks and set their identification codes in this exercise. The ID you define will be entered in the customer master record, which the accounting clerk is responsible for. The system will automatically print the name of the accounting clerk on all correspondence. This code can also be used to sort dunning and payment proposal lists. Follow this menu path to go to the initial screen to define your accounting clerk identification code for customers: Financial Accounting (New) ➤ Accounts Receivable and Accounts Payable ➤ Customer Accounts ➤ Master Data ➤ Preparations for Creating Customer Master Data ➤ Enter Accounting Clerk Identification Code for Customer. The Change View "Accounting Clerks" Overview screen is displayed. Click the New entries button on the top-left side of the screen to go where you will define your accounting clerk's name and ID (Figure 14-4).

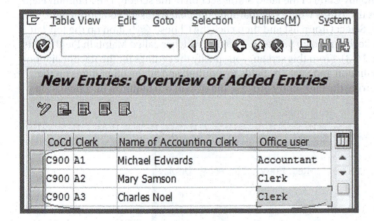

Figure 14-4. Initial screen for setting an accounting clerk identification code for a customer

Update the following fields:

> **CoCd:** Enter your four-digit company code. This will allow you to assign an accounting clerk name and identification code to your company code.

> **Clerk:** These two characters will serve as your accounting clerk identification code in this field, based on company code. This code appears in the customer master records for which the clerk is responsible.

Name of Accounting Clerk: Enter the name of your accounting clerk. This is the name of your accounting clerk assigned to supervise your customer.

Office User: Enter the official position of your accounting clerk assigned to supervise your customer in this field. For example, Account Assistant.

After you have updated the New Entries: Overview of Added Entries screen, click the Enter ✅ button to confirm your entries and save 💾 your work.

The next step is to create number ranges that you will assign to customer account groups. The system can assign a number from a number range to a customer account internally or can allow you to assign a number to a customer account externally, based on your specifications.

Create Number Ranges for Customer Account Groups

We covered number ranges in Chapter 3 in depth, so we will only be looking at how to customize the steps involved in creating number ranges for customer accounts in this exercise. Number ranges for customer accounts are created using a two-character key. When creating number ranges, you must determine the following:

- Which number range intervals the system will use to assign numbers to customer accounts

- Whether numbers are assigned to customer accounts by the system internally or by the user externally during customer account creation

The system will automatically carry out internal number assignment based on the number ranges you assigned to the customer account groups. If you want the users to externally assign numbers to customer accounts, you must click the External Number Range checkbox.

■ **Note**   If the number range intervals you enter already exist (i.e., they have already been used), you may not be able to continue. The system will notify you via the status bar at the bottom of the screen that this interval is already available. This is the complex part of number range configuration. What you have to do in this instance is display the current number range intervals in order to identify the number range intervals that have not been used. Alternatively, you can try several number range intervals randomly until you find an interval that hasn't been used.

To go to the Customer Number Ranges screen where you can create number ranges for your customer accounts you created earlier, follow this menu path: IMG: Financial Accounting (New) ➤ Accounts Receivable and Accounts Payable ➤ Customer Accounts ➤ Master Data ➤ Preparations for Creating Customer Master Data ➤ Create Number Ranges for Customer Accounts. Or you can use transaction code XDN1.

The displayed Customer Number Ranges screen contains three buttons. Click the [🖉 Intervals] button below the company code field. This will display the Maintain Number Range Interval screen, where you can maintain your customer number ranges.

■ **Note**   The Intervals [🔁 Intervals] and Status [🖉 Status] buttons allow you to check existing number ranges and determine the current number intervals of existing number ranges.

For more detailed information on creating number ranges, refer to Chapter 3.

On the Maintain Number Range Intervals screen, click the [Interval] button on the top-left side. The Insert Interval screen pops up (Figure 14-5). This is where you maintain the number range intervals for your customer account groups.

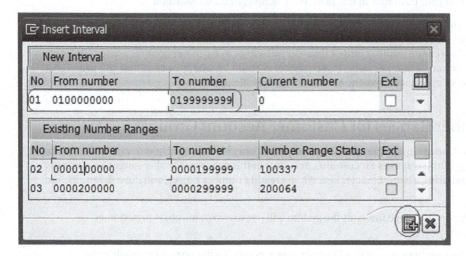

Figure 14-5. *The screen where you define number ranges for your customer accounts*

Enter the number range intervals you are using for your customer accounts in the New Interval section of the screen. Then click the Insert 🛃 button on the bottom-right side of the Insert Interval screen and insert your number ranges in the Existing Number Ranges section.

■ **Tip**   If you are having problems maintaining your number range intervals because of number range overlap, skip this section and go to the next section, entitled "Assign Number Ranges to Customer Account Groups." There, you can assign any existing number range to your customer account groups. This action will allow you to carry on with your configuration.

Save 💾 your number range intervals.

The Transport number range interval screen pops up with a message. Ignore the message and click the Insert ✅ button on the bottom-right side of the screen to confirm your number range intervals.

Using the following data, create another number range:

> **No:** Enter a number such as 02. It defines your number range sequence in this field.

> **From Number:** Enter a number such as 02000000000. It starts the number range in this field.

> **To Number:** Enter a number such as 02999999999. This ends the number range defined in this field.

■ **Note**   You can create as many number range intervals as desired. The number range interval you define depends on your company's requirements.

Next, you'll assign the number ranges you just created to your customer account group.

Assign Number Ranges to Customer Account Groups

The system will automatically use the number range interval you assign to the customer account group when you create a customer account. It does so systematically by selecting the next available number from the number range. To assign number ranges to a customer account group, follow this menu path: IMG Financial Accounting (New) ➤ Accounts Receivable and Accounts Payable ➤ Customer Accounts ➤ Master Data ➤ Preparations for Creating Customer Master Data ➤ Assign Number Ranges to Customer Account Groups. Or use transaction code OBAR.

The Change View "Assign Customer Acct Groups >> Number Range:" Overview screen is displayed. Search for the customer account group for your foreign customer by using the Scroll ⬓ button on the right side of the screen or by clicking the [⬚ Position…] button at the bottom of the screen.

Assign a number range—in this case, 01—to the foreign customer account group (Figure 14-6). Also assign number ranges to the domestic customer account group and the one-time customer account group, such as 02 and 03, respectively.

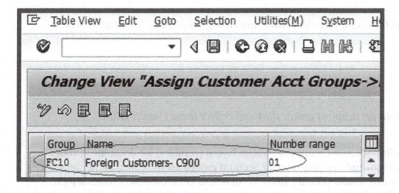

Figure 14-6. *Assigning number range intervals to customer account groups*

After assigning number ranges to your customer account groups, save ⬛ your number range assignment.

You have completed customizing your customer accounts. Let's now proceed to customizing vendor accounts. Customizing vendor accounts is similar to customizing customer accounts.

What Is a Vendor Account Group?

The vendor account group, like the customer account group, allows you to classify vendors within a partner business function that best fits the nature of business transaction involved. Business partners from other countries are classified under the foreign vendor account group; the vendors within your company's country are classified as domestic vendors; and vendors that may likely not repeat business with you in the future are classified as one-time vendors. The vendor account groups control the vendor hierarchy containing the vendor master record. When a vendor account is created, you must assign it to an account group. The account group is a control mechanism that determines which screens and fields are displayed for input.

This is based on the individual vendor's business functions. The account group is maintained in the IMG. The IMG details the steps required for implementing the SAP system and supports you in controlling and documenting the implementation in SAP.

Two important purposes of the vendor account group include:

- It controls whether the input fields in the vendor master record are required, optional, displayed, and so on.

- It also controls the number range assignment when you create vendor accounts.

SAP comes with a predefined account group with a screen layout so you don't have to create your own vendor account groups. We advise that you stick to the standard account group unless your specific company needs dictate the use of special vendor account groups. The next sections explain how to create your own vendor account groups with screen layout.

■ **Note**   As with the customer account groups, you can also define a screen layout for each vendor account group per company code (vendor) or per activity (vendor).

Next, you will define vendor account groups with screen layout for domestic, foreign, and one-time vendors.

Define Account Groups with Screen Layout (Vendors)

Problem: Company C900 Plc classifies its vendor account groups into three categories:

- *Domestic vendor*
- *Foreign vendor*
- *One-time vendor*

You are asked to maintain an account group that will reflect these classifications.

In this exercise, you will define account groups with screen layout (vendors) for domestic vendors. We advise that you define the foreign and one-time vendor account groups on your own, as the steps are pretty much the same. To customize vendor account groups with screen layout, follow this menu path: IMG: Financial Accounting (New) ➤ Accounts Receivable and Accounts Payable ➤ Vendor Accounts ➤ Master Data ➤ Preparations for Creating Vendor Master Data ➤ Define Account Groups with Screen Layout (Vendors). The Change View Vendor Account Groups Overview screen is displayed. Click the New Entries button to create your vendor account group. You can create as many account groups as required.

Update the following fields in Figure 14-7:

> **Account Group:** Enter four characters, such as DV10 (domestic vendors), for your vendor account group. The account group used here is for illustration purposes. We advise that you apply the standard used by your company in classifying its account groups.

> **Name:** Enter the name of your vendor account group in this field, in the General Data section. For example, Domestic Vendor C900.

> **Field Status:** This section contains the general data, company code data, and sales data. You can specify the field input status for each of these items—whether you want a field to be suppressed, required, or optional during document entry.

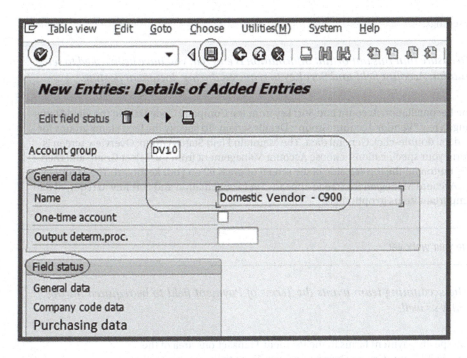

Figure 14-7. *Initial screen for account groups with screen layout (vendor)*

■ **Tip** If you are creating a one-time customer group, remember to click the One-Time Account checkbox in the General Data Section of the Account Group screen.

Click the Enter 🖉 button to confirm the entries you have made and save 🖫 your work.

As part of this exercise and using your discretion following the previous steps, create customer account groups for foreign and one-time vendors.

The next step is to maintain the field status group for your vendor account group. This setting will determine the field input status for general data, company code data, and purchasing data.

Maintain the Field Status Group for General Data for the Vendor Account Group

To specify the field status group, double-click General Data in the Field Status section of the New Entries: Details of Added Entries screen (see Figure 14-7). This will display the Sub-Group list for General Data. Select the item you want to define the field status for from the Select Group list (address, communication, and so on). Select Address from the Select Group list and click the Choose 🗨 button on the top-left side of the screen. The Maintain Field Status Group: Address screen is displayed. This is where you maintain the field status for the address. These settings determine whether a given field should be suppressed, required, or optional, and should be based on your client's requirements. For this exercise, set the Address fields to optional, as they are of minor importance.

■ **Tip** Make sure all the items in the Address field are set to optional.

Save 💾 your settings.

Problem: *To ensure that this important information is entered, you have been asked to set the Reconciliation Account field and Sort Key to required during document posting.*

You modify the Reconciliation Account and Sort key from the Company Code Data in the Field Status section of the Change View "Vendor Account Group": Details screen. To specify the field status groups for the company code data, double-click General data. The Maintain Field Status Group: Overview screen is displayed. To perform your specifications, choose Account Management from the Select Group and then click the Choose 🔍 button on the top-left side of the screen or press F2 on your keyboard. The Maintain Field Status Group: Account Management screen appears. Set Reconciliation and Sort Key to required and set the other less important items to optional.

■ **Tip**   Do not save your work yet.

Problem: *The accounting team wants the Terms of Payment field to be required during document entry as well.*

You can specify payment terms in the Payment Transactions area of the Maintain Field Status Group: Overview screen. To go to the next group below Account Management, click the Next Group 📄 button on the top of the screen or press Shift+F6 on your keyboard. The Maintain Field Status Group: Payment Transactions screen is displayed. Under Payment Transactions, make the terms of payment a required entry by clicking the Req.Entry radio button. Save 💾 your vendor account group.

Repeat this process to specify the field status for your foreign vendor account group.

Next, you will enter the accounting clerk name under an identification key for the accounting clerk responsible for the vendor.

Enter a Accounting Clerk Identification Code for Your Vendors

The accounting clerk's name and Identification code (ID) can be entered in the vendor/master record, which determines what the clerk is responsible for. The system will automatically print the name of the accounting clerk on all correspondence and this code can also be used to sort dunning and payment proposal lists. Follow this menu path: IMG: Financial Accounting (New) ➤ Accounts Receivable and Accounts Payable ➤ Vendor Accounts ➤ Master Data ➤ Preparations for Creating Vendor Master Data ➤ Define Accounting Clerks. The Change View "Accounting Clerks" Overview screen, which is the initial screen for maintaining accounting clerks for vendors, is displayed. Click the New entries button on the top-left side of the screen to go to the actual screen (Figure 14-8) where you will customize the accounting clerk's ID.

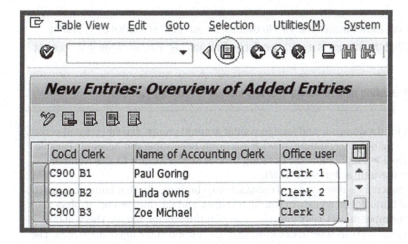

Figure 14-8. Accounting clerk identification code for vendors

Update the following fields:

> **CoCd:** Enter the four-character company code. This will allow you to assign the accounting clerk's name and identification code to your company code.

> **Clerk:** Enter two characters. This becomes the accounting clerk's identification code.

> **Name of Accounting Clerk:** Enter the name of the accounting clerk assigned to supervise this vendor.

> **Office User:** Enter the official position of the accounting clerk in this field. For example, Account Assistant.

Click the Enter 🗸 button to confirm your entries and save 🖫.

To complete this process, it is important to create number ranges and assign them to vendor account groups. These number range intervals will be assigned systematically to vendors when you create new vendor accounts.

Create Number Ranges for Vendor Accounts

Vendor account number ranges are created with two-digit keys. It's important that you specify the following when creating number ranges for vendor accounts:

- The number intervals that will be used as the account number for your vendor accounts

- Whether the number assignment is internal or external

When you create a vendor account, the system will automatically assign a number to a vendor account from the number ranges you assigned to the customer's account group. If you want users to assign numbers to vendor accounts, select the External Number Range checkbox.

■ **Note** The SAP system does not allow number intervals to overlap. If your number interval does overlap, the system will issue a warning that the interval is already available. Find another number range that does not overlap.

It is also possible to choose from existing number range intervals instead of creating your own.

To create a number ranges for the domestic and foreign vendor account groups that you created earlier, following this menu path: IMG: Financial Accounting (new) ➤ Accounts Receivable and Accounts Payable ➤ Vendor Accounts ➤ Master Data ➤ Preparations for Creating Vendor Master Data ➤ Create Number Ranges for Vendor Accounts. Or use transaction code XKN1.

The Vendor Number Ranges screen is displayed and contains three buttons. The first button creates new number ranges, the second button displays existing number ranges, and the third button displays your number range status. To create number ranges, click the [🖉   Intervals] button on the screen. This will take you to the Maintain Number Range Intervals screen. Click the [🖳 Interval] button at the top of the screen. The Insert Interval screen pops up. This is where you create the number ranges for your vendor account groups. Using the following information, specify your vendor account group number range intervals.

Using the following data, create another number range:

> **No:** Enter a number, such as 03, that defines your number range sequence.

> **From Number:** Enter a number, such as 03000000000, that you want to use to start a number range.

> **To Number:** Enter the number, such as 03999999999, that you want to end the number range you have defined.

After specifying your number ranges, click the Insert 🖳 button on the bottom-right side of the Insert Interval screen. This will move your number range to the Existing Number Range section onscreen.

■ **Tip** If you are having problems specifying your number range intervals because of overlap issues, skip this section and go to the next section, entitled "Assign Number Ranges to Vendor Account Groups," to assign an existing number range to your vendor account groups. This action will allow you to carry on with your configuration.

Save 🖬 your number range intervals. The Transport Number Range Intervals screen pops up with a message. Ignore the message and click the Insert ☑ button on the bottom-right side of the screen to confirm your number range intervals.

As part of this exercise, repeat the steps in the section entitled "Create Number Ranges for Vendor Accounts" to create another number range interval using the following information:

> **No:** Enter a number, such as 04, that defines your number range sequence.

> **From Number:** Enter a number, such as 04000000000, that you want to use to start a number range.

> **To Number:** Enter a number, such as 04999999999, that you want to end the number range you defined.

■ **Note** You can create as many number range intervals as desired. The amount of number ranges you define depends on your company's requirements.

Assign Number Ranges to Vendor Account Groups

To complete the vendor account groups' setup, you have to assign number ranges to them. Follow this menu path: IMG: Financial Accounting (New) ➤ Accounts Receivable and Accounts Payable ➤ Vendor Accounts ➤ Master Data ➤ Preparations for Creating Vendor Master Data ➤ Assign Number Ranges to Vendor Account Groups. Or use transaction code OBAS. The *Cha*nge View Assign Vendor Account Groups – Number Range Overview screen, containing a list of existing number ranges, is displayed. Search for the vendor account group called dv10-domestic vendor by using the Scroll button or by clicking the [🔲 Position...] button at the bottom of the screen. Assign the number range 03 to the domestic vendor account group account.

Likewise, search for your foreign vendor account group and assign the number range 04 to the foreign vendor account group. Save 💾 your number range assignments.

Terms of Payment

It is a normal business practice for business partners to enter into some form of payment agreement that governs their business relationship regarding invoice payment and cash discounts awards. This type of agreement is referred to as the terms of payment. Terms of payment refer to conditions with business partners for goods sold or services offered in relation to how payments are made. The terms of payment define invoice due dates and cash discounts offered within a specified period. For example, your company might agree to offer a discount of 5% to business partners A and B if they pay an outstanding invoiced amount within five days, a 2% discount when paid within 10 days, and so on, as depicted in Figure 14-9.

Business partners agree to payment terms on invoice payment.
If agreed-upon conditions are fulfilled, a discount is awarded

Figure 14-9. *Terms of payment flow.*

The terms of payment you define during configuration are assigned to the business partner's master record. When you assign the terms of payment key (this is a freely definable four-character field that holds the terms of payment that the system uses to calculate discounts) to a business partner's master record, the system will automatically default to the terms of payment during document entry. Otherwise, the user has to enter the terms of payment key manually when entering the document in the system. SAP also comes with a pre-defined standard terms of payment. You can perform the following specifications:

> **Payment Terms:** This is a four-digit character key that determines how a discount is granted. Payment terms are expressed as a percentage rate that determines the cash discount granted or received. Payment terms are defined for both customers and vendors and they become valid during document entry. We recommend that you define separate payment terms for customers and vendors because changes in customer payment terms may not apply to vendors.

Day Limit: The day limit is optional and is used to specify the date by which terms of payment are valid. It defines the terms of payment that are date dependent. One term of payment key can have two terms of payment, but with different day limits. This allows you to specify a given day of the month to which you may want the payment terms to apply.

Account Type: Determines whether payment terms relate to customers or vendors and posts business transactions to appropriate accounts in the system.

Baseline Date: The date to which the terms of payment apply. This is the date the system uses to determine the invoice due date. If you want the system to default to a baseline date for payment, you should specify the date to be used.

If you want the system to default to a baseline date during document entry, set the appropriate option from a choice of three default dates:

- Document date
- Document posting date
- Document entry date

If you do not want the system to default to a baseline date, but rather want to enter a date manually during document entry, use the No Default option.

The Payment Terms section of the screen is where you set the actual payment terms and conditions for your payment terms key. This includes installment payment, percentage rates for your payment terms, and the days they apply to.

■ **Note**   It is advisable to use separate terms of payment for vendors and customers. Changes may occur in customer payment terms that aren't relevant to your payment agreements with vendors.

Maintaining Terms of Payment (Customer)

Problem: *Company C900 Plc offers discounts to a customer using the following terms of payment:*

- *5% for immediate payment*
- *2% for payment made within 15 days*
- *No discount for payment in 30 days*

As an FI consultant, you need to these terms of payment in the system.

To maintain terms of payment for customer, follow this menu path: IMG: Financial Accounting (New) ➤ Account Receivable and Accounts Payable ➤ Business Transaction ➤ Outgoing Invoices/Credit Memos ➤ Maintain Terms of Payment. Or use the transaction code OBB8. The Change View "Terms of Payment": Overview screen appears. Click the New entries button at the top of the screen. The New Entries: Details of Added Entries screen appears, which is where you customize your terms of payment settings (Figure 14-10).

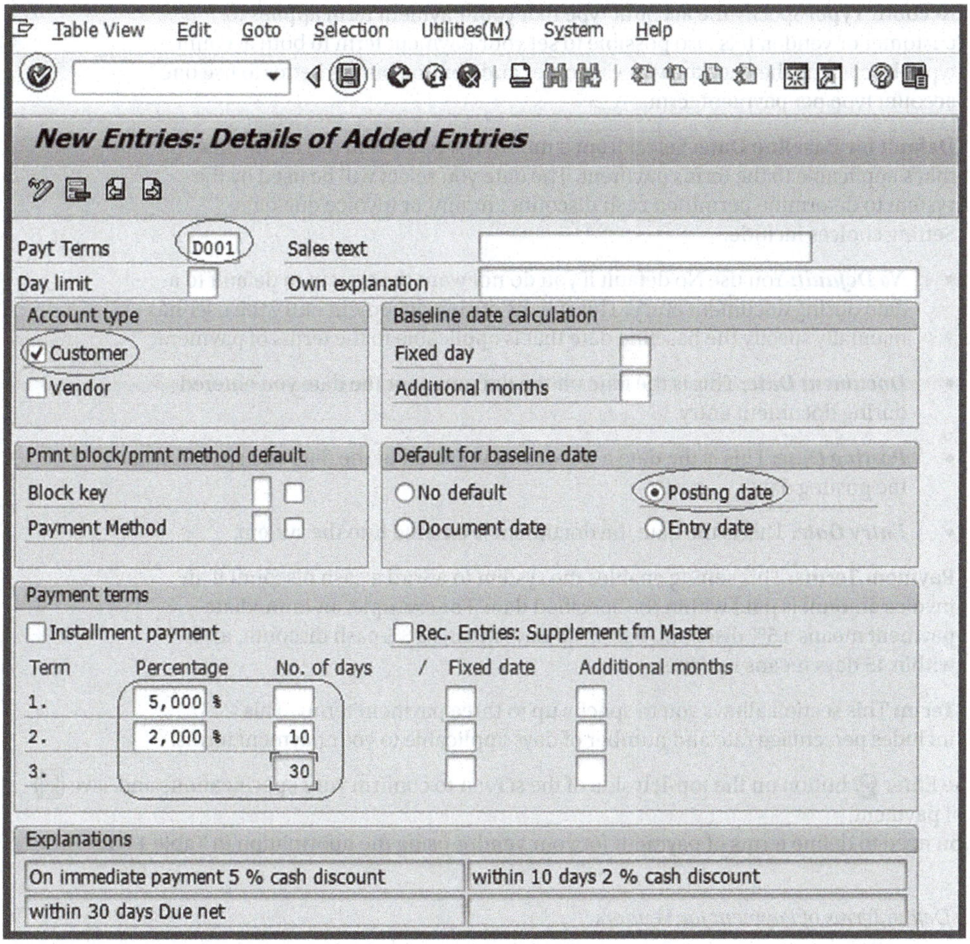

Figure 14-10. *Screen where terms of payment are maintained*

Update the following fields:

> **Payment Terms:** Contains the defined conditions for granting or receiving a cash discount. Payment terms are defined by entering four characters in this field as your term of payment key. This key will serve as your payment term, which is entered in the master record of the customer/vendor.

> **Day Limit:** Specify a given date of the month that you want the payment terms to apply, in relation to a corresponding payment.

> **Own Explanation:** Specify your own special description relating to your payment terms. The description you specify here will replace the system-generated explanation.

Account Type: Specify the account type that your payment term applies to, customer or vendor. It is also possible to set your payment term to both account types by clicking the checkbox for Customer and Vendor, but it's better to use one account type per payment term.

Default for Baseline Date: Select from a number of options to use as the date that's applicable to the terms payment. The date you select will be used by the system to determine permitted cash discount amount or invoice due date. Setting choices include:

- *No Default:* You use No default if you do not want the system to default to a date during document entry. This means during document entry the user has to manually specify the baseline date that is applicable to the terms of payment.

- *Document Date:* This is the date on the document or the date you entered during document entry.

- *Posting Date:* This is the date a document is posted or the date you specified as the posting date.

- *Entry Date:* This is the date the document is entered into the system.

Payment Terms: This setting enables the system to award a cash discount if an invoice amount is paid within the specified date. For example, an immediate payment means a 5% discount, within 15 days means a 3% cash discount, and within 45 days means net due.

Term: This section allows you to specify up to three payment terms. This includes percentage rate and number of days applicable to your payment terms.

Click the Enter ✅ button on the top-left side of the screen to confirm your specifications and save 💾 your terms of payment.

Next, you need to define terms of payment for your vendor using the information in Table 14-1.

Table 14-1. *Define Terms of Payment for Vendors*

Field Name or Data Type	Values	
Payment Terms	V001	
Account Type		
Vendor	Select	
Default to Baseline Date		
Posting Date	Select	
Payment Terms		
Term	**Percentage**	**No. of days**
1.	5%	Blank
2.	3%	15
3.		45

Installment Plan

Another important aspect of payment terms is the installment plan. Business partners sometimes enter into some form of agreement that enables them make payment systematically over a specified period. Your company might give its customers the opportunity to pay what they owe over several months until the full invoice amount is paid. Let's walk through the steps involved in maintaining an installment plan.

The total invoice amount is divided into partial amounts and paid at different dates until the invoice amount is cleared or paid in full. For example, your company agrees with a customer to pay 20% of an invoice amount of $400 USD monthly over a five-month period. Thus, the installment plan will allow your company to receive $80 USD monthly over the agreed five-month period until the amount is paid in full.

When customizing an installment payment plan, you specify the following items:

- Number of installments for your payment terms. This is the number of payments needed to pay off the outstanding amount.

- The percentage rate that will be applied to clear the outstanding invoice amount (the percentage rate specified must be equal to 100%).

- Define terms of payments for individual installments for each percentage rate applicable to your installment plan.

The system will automatically split the installments once the payment is defined and assign the payments to the business partner's master record. The system will also create a line item for each installment.

> *Problem: You have been asked to create a terms of payment for an installment plan, where 10% of the invoice amount is paid immediately, 40% is paid within 60 days, and the balance is paid within 90 days.*

Maintaining Terms of Payment for an Installment Plan

You maintain the terms of payment for each percentage rate you are using. In this exercise, you will use 10%, 40%, and 50%. You have to maintain terms of payments for each of these percentage rates. Let's customize the terms of payment for your installment plan, maintain one term of payment to a percentage rate, and then apply the same steps to the remaining percentage rates. To maintain terms of payment, follow this menu path: IMG: Financial Accounting (New) ➤ Account Receivable and Accounts Payable ➤ Business Transaction ➤ Incoming Invoices/Credit Memos ➤ Maintain Terms of Payment. Or use transaction code OBB8.

The Change View "Rem of Payment": Overview screen is displayed. This is an overview screen containing the existing terms of payments. Click the `New entries` button at the top of the screen to go to the New Entries: Detail of Added Entries screen, which is where you customize your terms of payment settings. Update the following fields:

> **Payment Terms:** Enter four characters. This key allows you to store payment conditions in your terms of payment and identify your terms of payment when you have more than one term of payment in the system. In this exercise, we used DO10 ((discount offered-10) as our terms of payment (this is a freely defined key). The terms of payment you define here is applicable to all payment terms. We will be looking at this in depth in the next exercise when defining payment terms.

> **Own Explanation:** Describe the payment terms for your installment plan. Enter this description in this field: *10% Payable immediately, 40% in 60 days & 50%.*

Account Type: Specify the account type you want to apply to your payment terms. Since you are maintaining payment terms for your customers, click the Customer checkbox.

Default to Baseline Date: The date you select here will determine the default baseline date. In this exercise, we used the posting date. Click the Posting Date checkbox.

Terms: Specify the terms, percentage rates, and number of days for your payment terms. For this exercise, leave this section blank.

When you have updated the New Entries: Detail of Added Entries screen, click the Enter 🗸 button on the top-left side of the screen to confirm your specifications. Then save 🖫 your payment terms.

The next step is to define payment terms for the percentage rates you are applying to your installment plan. We will define payment terms for each of these percentage rates: 10%, 40%, and 50%.

Maintaining Payment Terms for an Installment Plan

You also have to maintain payment terms for each percentage rate in the installment plan quite differently from the one you defined for cash discount, because each payment term holds different conditions. First let's set up the percentage rate of 10% for your payment terms for immediate payment and then do the remaining percentage rates. To go to the screen where you will define the payment terms for your percentage rates, follow this menu path: IMG: Financial Accounting (New) ➤ Account Receivable and Accounts Payable ➤ Business Transaction ➤ Incoming Invoices/Credit Memos ➤ Maintain Terms of Payment. Or use transaction code OBB8.

The Change View "Terms of Payment": Overview screen is displayed. This is where you customize your payment terms. Click the ⌷New entries⌷ button at the top of the screen. This will take you to the New Entries: Detail of Added Entries screen. Update the following fields:

Payment Terms: Enter a four-digit character that key you want to use as payment terms for 10% (percentage rate) in this field. We used P010 in this exercise.

Own Explanation: Enter a short description of your payment terms in this field. We used 10% payable immediately for this exercise.

Account Type: Select customer as your account type since this payment terms relates to installment plans with customers. Click the Customer checkbox.

Default to Baseline Date: Select the posting date as your baseline date.

Terms: Leave this section blank since 10% payment is due immediately. You do not need to set up any payment terms.

When you have updated the screen, click the Enter 🗸 button on the top-left side of the screen to confirm and then save 🖫 your terms of payment. The system will take you back to the previous screen, called Change View "Terms of Payment": Overview. The next step is to define the payment terms for 40% to 60 days. To return to the next screen where you will specify your payment terms, click the Next Entry 🗒 button on the top-right side of the screen or press F8 on your keyboard to go to the New Entries: Details of Added Entries screen. Update the screen as follows:

Payment Terms: P040 (payment terms for 40%)

Account Type: Select Customer

Default to Baseline Date: Select Posting Date

Terms: Enter **60** in the No. of Days field

Click the Enter ✅ button on the top-left side of the screen to confirm. Then save 💾your terms of payment.

Finally, the last step in this exercise, you have to define payment terms of 50% for 90 days. Click the Next Entry 🗐 button on the top-right side of the Change View "Terms of Payment": Overview screen or press F8 on your keyboard to go to the New Entries: Details of Added Entries screen. Update the appropriate fields on the screen with the following information:

> **Payment Terms:** P050 (payment terms for 50%)
>
> **Account Type:** Select Customer
>
> **Default to Baseline Date:** Select Posting Date
>
> **Terms:** Enter 90 in the No. of Days field

Click the Enter ✅ button on the top-left side of the screen to confirm. Then save 💾your terms of payment.

The final aspect of customizing the installment plan is to specify the terms of payment, the installment number, the percentage rate, and the payment terms for the installment payments.

Defining the Payment Terms for Installment Payments

To define the payment terms for installment payments, follow this menu path: IMG: Financial Accounting (New) ➤ Account Receivable and Accounts Payable ➤ Business Transaction ➤ Incoming Invoices/Credit Memos ➤ Define Terms of Payment for Installment Payments. Or use transaction code OBB9.

The Change View Terms of Payment for Holdback/Retainage Overview screen is displayed. Click the New entries button on the top-left side of the screen to go to the New Entries: Overview of Added Entries screen. This is where you set your terms of payment for installment payments. Using the Search 🗗 button, display the Terms of Payment list. Search for the installment plan and terms of payment you created earlier and use them to update the fields in New Entries: Overview of Added Entries screen (Figure 14-11).

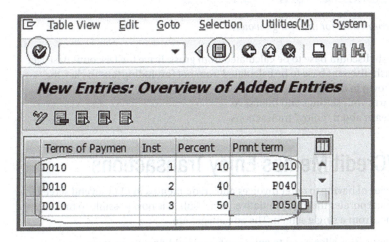

Figure 14-11. Setting up payment terms for installment payments

Click the Enter ✅ button on the top-left side of the screen to confirm your specifications and save 💾 your terms of payment.

In the next exercise, you will learn how to define a cash discount base for incoming invoices, which will determine whether the cash discount base should be calculated as a net or gross value.

Defining a Cash Discount Base for Incoming Invoices

A cash discount base is calculated either as a net or gross value, depending on your country's regulations.

The settings you make in this exercise per company code determine whether the taxed amount is considered in the base amount calculation. To go to the Change View "Cash Discount Base": Overview screen to define a cash discount base for incoming invoices, follow this menu path: IMG: Financial Accounting (New) ➤ Account Receivable and Accounts Payable ➤ Business Transaction ➤ Incoming Invoices/Credit Memos ➤ Define Cash Discount Base for Incoming Invoices. The Change View "Cash Discount Base": Overview screen is displayed (Figure 14-12). Search for your company code by clicking the [Position...] button at the bottom of the screen.

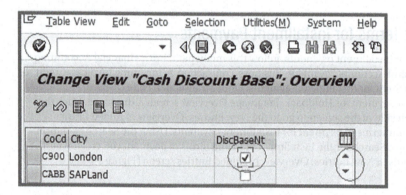

Figure 14-12. *Setting the cash discount base for incoming invoices*

If your company wants the cash discount base to be calculated from gross, leave the Discount Base Net checkbox blank. If you want the cash discount base to be calculated from net (excluding taxes), click the Discount Base Net checkbox, as shown in the figure.

Click the Enter button to confirm your settings and then save.

In the next exercise, you will learn about "enjoy" transactions.

Incoming Invoices/Credit Memos Enjoy Transactions

SAP has eliminated the redundancies of having to enter invoices and credit memos in FI in several screens. You now use a single screen that incorporates the enjoy initiative. As a result, it is now possible to make document entries and credit memos from a single screen. The advantages are

- Single screen transactions (this allows you to enter, park, and hold documents on a single screen without losing context)

- User-friendly interfaces

Let's go through the steps involved in defining document types for enjoy documents and defining tax codes per transaction.

Defining Document Types for Enjoy Transactions

When you define document types for enjoy transactions, the system will automatically default to a document type during document entry (incoming invoices and credit memos). If the enjoy transaction document type is not defined, the system will automatically propose the document type from the previous document entry. You can overwrite the proposed document type. To define document types for enjoy transactions, follow this menu path: IMG: Financial Accounting (New) ➤ Account Receivable and Accounts Payable ➤ Business Transaction ➤ Incoming Invoices/Credit Memos ➤ Incoming Invoices/Credit Memos ➤ Enjoy ➤ Define Document Types for Enjoy Transaction. Or use transaction code OBZO.

The Change View Document Types for Enjoy Transaction Overview screen is displayed. To specify the document types for enjoy transactions, click the ⌈New entries⌋ button on the top-left side of the screen. The New Entries: Overview of Added Entries screen is displayed (Figure 14-13).

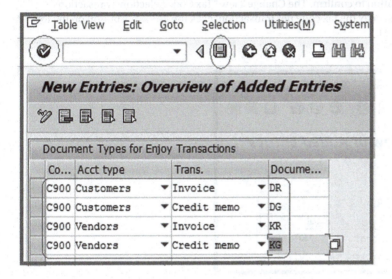

Figure 14-13. *Defining document types for enjoy transactions*

Update the following fields:

> **Company:** Enter your company code (C900) in his field. This will apply the settings to your company code.
>
> **Acct Type:** Enter the account type you want the system to use as the default during document entry. For example, Customers/Vendors.
>
> **Trans.:** Using the pull-down arrow next to the field to display the predefined transactions list supplied by SAP, enter the transaction description that fits the account type you want to apply the default setting to.
>
> **Document:** Enter the document type to use as the default. For example:
>
>> DR – Invoice (Customers)
>>
>> DG – Credit Memo (Customers)
>>
>> KR – Invoice (Vendors)
>>
>> KG – Credit Memo (Vendors)

These settings allow the system to automatically propose the document type during document entry. Click the Enter ✅ button on the top-left side of the screen and save 💾 your work.

Defining Tax Code per Transaction

The settings in the Define Tax Code per Transaction section allow you to select a subset from the tax codes. As part of this definition, you specify tax code per transaction and per country key and then you can select a subset from defined tax codes in the system during document entry. To define a tax code per transaction, follow this menu path: IMG: Financial Accounting (New) ➤ Account Receivable and Accounts Payable ➤ Business Transaction ➤ Incoming Invoices/Credit Memos ➤ Incoming Invoices/Credit Memos ➤ Enjoy ➤ Define Tax Code per Transaction. Or use transaction code OBZT.

The Country Entry dialog box pops up. Enter your Country key (GB in this exercise) in the Country Key field and click the Enter ☑ button to confirm. The Change View "Tax Code Selection Transactions" Overview screen is displayed. To specify the tax code per transaction, click the ⌑New entries⌑ button on the top-left side of the screen (Figure 14-14).

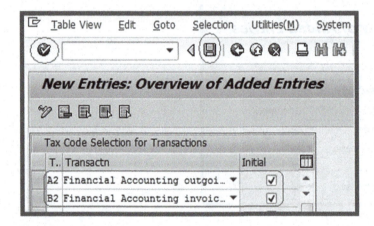

Figure 14-14. *Specifying a tax code per transaction*

Update the following fields:

> **Tax Code:** Enter your output tax code in the first field and your input tax code in the next field.

> **Transaction:** Enter the appropriate transaction for your tax codes. For example, for Output Tax, select Financial Accounting Invoice Receipt and for Input Tax, select Financial Accounting Outgoing Invoice.

Click the Enter ✅ button on the top-left side of the screen and then save 💾 your work.

■ **Note** A2 is the tax code for output tax (Financial Accounting for outgoing invoice) and B2 is the tax code for input tax (Financial Accounting for Incoming Receipt).

In the next exercise, you will define accounts for a net procedure for cash discount clearing.

Defining Accounts for Net Procedures

A net procedure setting defines how a cash discount is treated against invoices when a vendor invoice is posted with a document type for net procedure. Once the net procedure is defined, discounts posted to an expense or balance sheet accounts are automatically reduced by the cash discount. Also, during invoice posting, a similar discount amount is posted to a cash discount clearing account.

■ **Note** Before you define an account for a net procedure, you need to create the G/L account that you will assign to the net procedure. See "Appendix A – Chapter 14" to create the G/L accounts needed to complete this exercise before continuing your customizing.

To define accounts for a net procedure, follow this menu path: IMG: Financial Accounting (New) ➤ Account Receivable and Accounts Payable ➤ Business Transaction ➤ Incoming Invoices/Credit Memos ➤ Define Account for Net Procedure. Or use transaction code OBX.

The Enter Chart of Accounts dialog box pops up. Enter your chart of account ID (CA90) in the Chart of Accounts field. Click the Enter ☑ button at the bottom of the dialog box. The Configuration Accounting Maintain: Automatic Posts - Rules screen is displayed. You don't need to specify any rules for the account for net procedure. Click Save 🖫. The Configuration Accounting Maintain: Automatic Posts - Accounts screen is displayed (Figure 14-15). Update the account field by assigning the G/L account for clearing supplier discounts (net method) 193000 (circled in red in Figure 14-15).

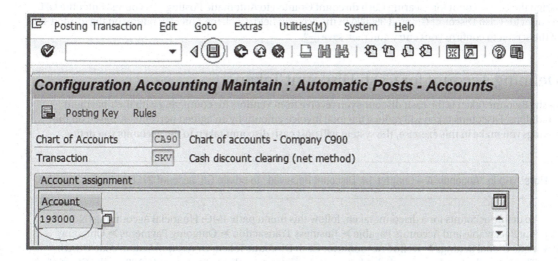

Figure 14-15. *Account determination for automatic posting – net procedure*

Click the Enter 🅥 button on the top-left side of the screen to confirm your entry and save 🖫 your account assignment.

In the next exercise, you will define the accounts that cash discount granted, cash discount taken, lost cash discounts, and overpayments/underpayments are posted to. Then you will define your payment block reasons.

Defining Accounts for Cash Discounts

In this activity you specify accounts that you want to post cash discounts granted to, cash discounts taken, and lost cash discounts.

Defining Cash Discounts Granted

Cash Discount Granted is the cash discount you give to a customer for complying with the agreed terms of payment. The discount granted reduces the total invoice amount by an agreed percentage. Based on the settings you make in this exercise, the system will post cash discounts granted to the accounts you define.

■ **Note**   Go to "Appendix A – Chapter 14, Cash Discount Granted," to create G/L account 8800000 for this exercise.

To define accounts for discount granted, follow this menu path: IMG: Financial Accounting (New) ➤ Account Receivable and Accounts Payable ➤ Business Transaction ➤ Incoming Payments – Incoming Payments Global Settings ➤ Define Accounts for Cash Discount Granted. Or use transaction code OBXI.

The Enter Chart of Accounts dialog box pops up. Enter your chart of accounts (CA90) in the Chart of Accounts field and click the Enter ☑ button at the bottom of the dialog box. The Configuration Accounting Maintain: Automatic Posts - Rules screen is displayed. Click Save 💾 at the top of the screen. The Configuration Accounting Maintain: Automatic Posts - Accounts screen is displayed, which is where you assign the G/L account for Clearing Cash discount Granted to Automatic Posting – Accounts. Enter the G/L account for Cash Discount Granted 880000 in the account field. Click the Enter ☑ button on the top-left side of the screen to confirm your entry and then save 💾.

Defining Account for Cash Discount Taken

Cash Discount Taken is the cash discount you receive from vendors for complying with their payment conditions. Discounts taken will reduce the total invoice amount by an agreed percentage. Based on the settings you make in this exercise, the system will post cash discount taken to the accounts you define.

■ **Note**   Go to "Appendix A – Chapter 14, Discount Received" to create G/L account 276000 for this exercise.

To define accounts for a discount taken, follow this menu path: IMG: Financial Accounting (New) ➤ Account Receivable and Accounts Payable ➤ Business Transaction ➤ Outgoing Payments ➤ Outgoing Payments Global Settings ➤ Define Accounts for Cash Discount Taken. Or use transaction code OBXU.

The Enter Chart of Accounts dialog box pops up. Enter your chart of accounts (CA90) in the Chart of Accounts field and click the Enter ☑ button at the bottom of the dialog box. The Configuration Accounting Maintain: Automatic Posts - Rules screen is displayed. Click Save 💾 at the top of the screen. The Configuration Accounting Maintain: Automatic Posts - Accounts screen is displayed, which is where you assign the G/L account for Clearing Cash discount taken to Automatic Posting – Accounts. Enter the G/L account for Cash Discount taken 276000 in the account field. Click the Enter ☑ button on the top-left side of the screen to confirm your entry and then click Save 💾.

Defining an Account for a Lost Cash Discount

Discount lost normally arises as a result of failing to comply with payment terms (failure to pay an invoice amount within a specified period). To define an account for a lost cash discount, it is advisable to first create a G/L account for discount loss, because you will need to assign the account for lost cash discount to a G/L account.

■ **Note** Go to "Appendix A – Chapter 14, Discount Lost" to create G/L account 880010 for this exercise.

To define accounts for lost cash discounts, follow this menu path: IMG: Financial Accounting (New) ➤ Account Receivable and Accounts Payable ➤ Business Transaction ➤ Outgoing Payments ➤ Outgoing Payments Global Settings ➤ Define Accounts for Lost Cash Discount. Or use transaction code OBXV.

The Enter Chart of Accounts dialog box pops up. Enter your chart of accounts (CA90) in the Chart of Accounts field on dialog box and click the Enter ☑ button at the bottom of the dialog box. The Configuration Accounting Maintain: Automatic Posts - Rules screen is displayed. Click Save 🖫 at the top of the screen. The Configuration Accounting Maintain: Automatic Posts - Accounts screen is displayed, which is where you assign the G/L account for clearing lost cash discount to Automatic Posting – Accounts. Enter the G/L account for lost Cash Discount taken 880010 in the Account field. Click the Enter ⊘ button on the top-left side of the screen to confirm your entry and then click Save 🖫.

Defining Account for Overpayments/Underpayments

Customizing an account for overpayments/underpayments allows the system to make postings to revenue and expense accounts if the following conditions are present:

- Payment difference arises as a result of overpayment or underpayment.

- It is not possible to post differences through cash discount adjustments.

- When the difference falls within tolerance limits for an automatic adjustment posting.

■ **Note** Go to "Appendix A – Chapter 14, Overpayments/Underpayments," to create G/L account 881000 for this exercise.

To define accounts for overpayments/underpayments, follow this menu path: IMG: Financial Accounting (New) ➤ Account Receivable and Accounts Payable ➤ Business Transaction ➤ Outgoing Payments ➤ Outgoing Payments Global Settings ➤ Define Accounts for Overpayments/Underpayments. Or use transaction code OBXL.

The Enter Chart of Accounts dialog box pops up. Enter your chart of accounts (CA90) in the Chart of Accounts field on dialog box and click the Enter ☑ button at the bottom of the dialog box. The Configuration Accounting Maintain: Automatic Posts - Rules screen is displayed. Click save 🖫 at the top of the screen. The Configuration Accounting Maintain: Automatic Posts - Accounts screen is displayed, which is where you assign the G/L clearing account for unauthorized customer discounts to Automatic Posting – Accounts. Enter the G/L account for unauthorized customer discounts 881000 in the account field. Click the Enter ⊘ button on the top-left side of the screen to confirm your entry and then click Save 🖫.

Defining Accounts for Bank Charges (Vendor)

Bank Charges (Vendor) are incidental expenses arising from a business transaction with business partners and are posted to an expense account in FI. In this exercise you will define an account for your bank charges and assign it to an expense account. This will allow the system to automatically post these expenses to a bank charges account, which is an expense account.

■ **Note** You created a bank charges account in Chapter 9, so you don't need to create another one here. You can use the bank charges account you created previously to do automatic posting in this exercise.

To define accounts for bank charges (vendor), follow this menu path: IMG: Financial Accounting (New) ➤ Account Receivable and Accounts Payable ➤ Business Transaction ➤ Outgoing Payments ➤ Outgoing Payments Global Settings ➤ Define Accounts for Bank Charges (Vendor). Or use transaction code OBXK.

The Configuration Accounting Maintain: Automatic Posts - Procedures screen is displayed. This screen contains a list of procedures including bank charges you can choose from. Double-click Bank Charges from the list of the displayed procedures (Figure 14-16).

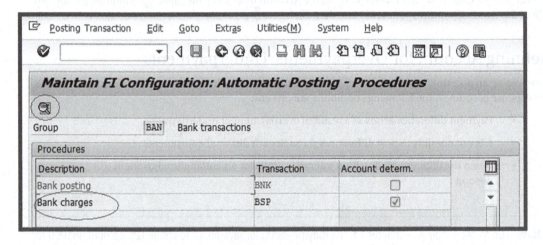

Figure 14-16. *The initial screen for specifying bank posting and bank charges*

The Enter Chart of Accounts dialog box pops up. Enter your chart of accounts (CA90) in the Chart of Accounts field and click the Enter ☑ button on the bottom-right side of the screen. The Configuration Accounting Maintain: Automatic Posts - Rules screen is displayed, which is where you specify the rules for your bank charges account. You are not specifying any rules for your bank charges, therefore, click the Save 🔲 button at the top of the screen to go to Configuration Accounting Maintain: Automatic Posts - Accounts screen. This is where you assign an account to the bank charges for automatic posting. Enter the G/L Account – Bank Charges 470100 (created in Chapter 9) in the Account field and click the Enter ✅ button on the top-left side of the screen to confirm. Save 🔲 your efforts.

In the next exercise, you will define payment block reasons, which are used to specify the reason for blocking an invoice from being paid. Normally, the system will request the reason why you want to block an invoice from payment. There are several reasons for blocking invoices from being paid in practice, but we will be looking only at some and then define payment block reasons in the system.

Defining Payment Block Reasons

When defining reasons for blocking payments, there are a few specifications you need to consider. You can specify whether payment blocks can be changed in payment proposals or during manual payment. You can also specify whether documents defined with block keys can be cleared during manual payment processing or if changes are not allowed.

The reasons you define in this exercise allow you to differentiate why invoices are not to be paid. Standard block reasons are supplied by SAP, which you can use if you do not want to define your own.

Payment block reasons are valid for all company codes. This means all company codes within the client or in the system can use the payment block reasons in the system without having to define payment block reasons that are company code specific. When customizing payment block reasons, you need to update the following fields:

> **Block Ind.:** This is a block indicator key that is defined with a one-digit character key. This key contains reasons for blocking payments. It's entered in a document to block an invoice from being paid for a specified reason.

> **Description:** Enter a short description stating why this payment is being blocked.

> **Block Indicators:** Allows you to specify how you want the payment block reason you defined to function. You have three options to choose from:

>> **Change in Payment Proposal:** When you want changes to be carried out during the payment proposal. It is possible to remove a payment block when processing the payment proposal, but when you set this proposal, changes cannot be made during payment proposal processing.

>> **Manual Payment Block:** If you do not want documents assigned with a block key to be cleared during manual payment clearing, then choose this option.

>> **Not Changeable:** Changes cannot be made during payment proposal processing or during manual payment.

To define the payment block reasons, follow this menu path: IMG: Financial Accounting (New) ➤ Account Receivable and Accounts Payable ➤ Business Transaction ➤ Outgoing Payments ➤ Outgoing Payments Global Settings ➤ Payment Block Reasons ➤ Define Payment Block Reasons. Or you can use transaction code OB27.

The Change View Payment Block Reasons Overview screen appears containing the list of previously defined payment block reasons. To define your own payment block reasons, click the New entries button on the top-left side of the screen to go to the New Entries: Overview of Added Entries screen (Figure 14-17), where you define your block reasons.

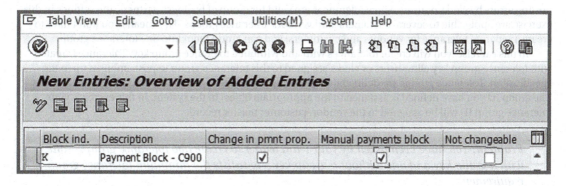

Figure 14-17. Defining payment block reasons

Update the following fields:

>**Block Ind.:** Enter your payment block reason key in this field. This is usually defined using a single-digit character. In this exercise, we used K as our payment block reason key for illustration purposes. This key is a freely definable payment block reason key. You can use any key of your choice.

>**Description:** Enter a meaningful short statement describing your payment block reason. As an example, we used Payment Block C900 as our payment block reason. You can use any meaningful description of your choice.

>**Change in Pmnt Prop.:** When you select the change in payment proposal checkbox, the payment block cannot be removed during an automatic payment program run.

>**Manual Payments Block**: Documents defined with a payment block key cannot be cleared during manual payment processing.

Save 💾 your work.

Manual Outgoing Payments

Manual Outgoing Payments allow users to manually post vendor's payments and clear open items on the vendor's account against payments made. You will be looking at manual payments in depth in Chapter 17. In order for users to be able to perform manual outgoing payments, you must:

- Define tolerances for vendors
- Define reason codes for manual outgoing payments
- Define accounts for payment differences

Define Tolerances for Vendors

Three tolerance groups are maintained in SAP FI. We covered the employee tolerance group and the G/L account tolerance group in Chapter 4. This section covers the Customer/Vendor tolerance group. For more information on tolerance groups, refer to Chapter 4.

As mentioned, tolerances are simply control mechanisms that are designed to limit the amount input clerks are permitted to post to the system. It also serves as a control measure that determines the discounts a clerk is authorized to grant, the payment differences they are permitted to post in the system, and tolerances for payment advice. The advantage of setting tolerances is that they impose restrictions and help avoid major posting errors by clerks or users. Since tolerances are valid for group of business partners, the settings in this exercise are applicable to several customers' and vendors' tolerance groups. This means you don't have to create a separate tolerance for vendors and customers; you can group them into one tolerance group.

In this exercise, you will create tolerances with and without a tolerance group key. Tolerances created with tolerance group key allow users or clerks assigned to this tolerance group to post amounts up to the specification. Tolerance groups are defined using four-digit characters, which serves as the group ID or key. The group ID you have defined is assigned to the appropriate object in the system. In this exercise, your tolerance group ID will be assigned to the vendor/customer master record.

>***Problem:*** *You have been asked by your team leader to create two tolerance groups—one with a group key and one without a group key—to satisfy the minimum tolerance group requirement.*

To define tolerances, follow this menu path: IMG: Financial Accounting (New) ➤ Account Receivable and Accounts Payable ➤ Business Transaction ➤ Outgoing Payments ➤ Manual Outgoing Payments ➤ Define Tolerances (vendors). Or you can use transaction code OBA3. The Change View Customer/Vendor Tolerances Overview screen is displayed. This screen contains a list of existing tolerances. To define your own tolerances, click the [New entries] button on the top-left side of the screen to go to New Entries: Details of Added Entries screen (Figure 14-18).

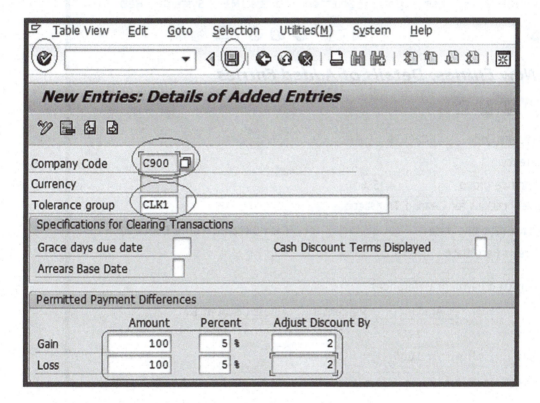

Figure 14-18. *Defining tolerance groups*

Update the following fields:

> **Company Code:** Enter the four digits of your company code in this field to assign your company code to your tolerance group.

> **Currency:** Enter the local currency in this field. The currency you enter in this field will be the default during document entry.

> **Tolerance Group:** Enter a four-digit ID as your tolerance group in this field. This ID will be assigned to your tolerance group relating to vendors.

In the Permitted Payment Differences section of the screen, update the following fields:

> **Gain/Loss:** Enter the permitted payment differences that users are permitted to post in amount and in percentage. When posting a document, the system will check the amount and the percentage of the document amount posted and use whichever is lower.

> **Adjust Discount By:** Specify the discount adjustment allowed.

Since you will also create another tolerance group without a group key, don't save your work yet. Click the Next Entry ⬚ button on the top-left side of the screen or press F8 on your keyboard to call up the New Entries: Details of Added Entries screen. Update the screen shown in Figure 14-19. Make sure that the Tolerance Group field is blank.

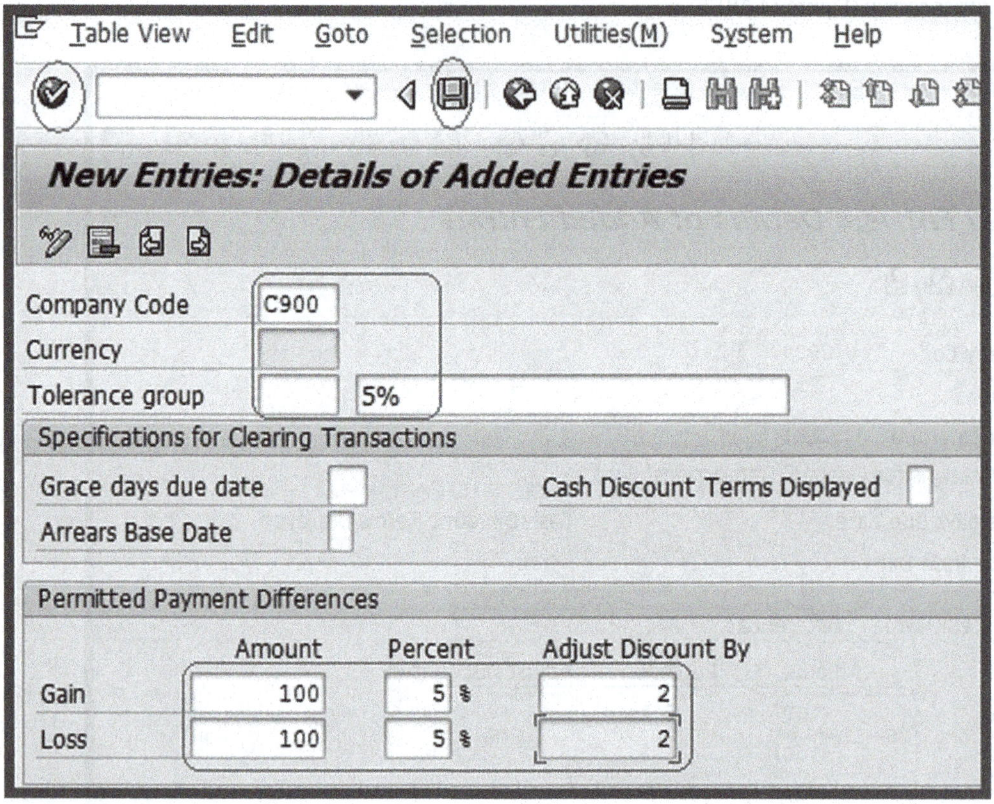

Figure 14-19. *Setting up the standard tolerance group (without a group key)*

Now save 💾 your work.

Define Reason Codes for Manual Outgoing Payments

Payment differences normally arise when clearing open items against payments. The difference is compared to the tolerance limit allocated to the employee making the posting. If the difference is deemed to be immaterial, the payment is done automatically and the system will adjust the cash discount up to the amount specified, or the system can write it off to a special account. Otherwise, the payment has to be processed manually.

If payment difference is outside the tolerance limit, the payment has to be processed manually in one of the following ways:

Partial Payment: You enter the partial payment against the open item in the system and assign a reason code. When a partial payment is posted, all documents remain in the account as open items.

Residual Item: When you assign the residual item and assign a reason code, the system will clear the original net amount and the payment, while the residual item remains in the account as an open item.

Payment on Account: All items remain open.

There are several reasons for payment differences. It is important to specify reasons for payment differences when posting partial payments or residual items. SAP has the flexibility that will allow you to assign more than one reason codes to a payment difference. You can do this by clicking the Distribute Difference button on the top-right side of the payment screen. We will be looking at this in detail in Chapter 17.

Reason code is part of overpayment/underpayment. It is defined per company code. You specify a correspondence type, which is assigned to the following items when posting payment and clearing open items manually. For example Partial Payments, Residual Posting, or Posting on Account. By setting further indicators during configuration, you can include the following optional functions with your reason code:

Charge Off Difference: When this checkbox is set for a reason code, the payment difference will be posted to a separate G/L account automatically.

Disputed Item: This allows disputed items to be excluded from credit checks.

Do Not Copy Text: When this checkbox is clicked, you have to enter reason code text into the segment text field of the residual item or the partial payment manually. If the indicator is not set, the system will automatically copy the reason code text you defined in your configuration into the segment text.

Let's go to the screen where you will configure reason codes for your manual outgoing payments. Follow this menu path: IMG: Financial Accounting (New) ➤ Account Receivable and Accounts Payable ➤ Business Transaction ➤ Outgoing Payments ➤ Manual Outgoing Payments ➤ Overpayment/Underpayment ➤ Define Reason Codes (Manual Outgoing Payments). Or use transaction code OBBE.

The Determine Work Area: Entry dialog box pops up. This screen allows you to assign your company code to the reason code you defined. Enter your company code (C900) in the Work Area field and click the Enter ✓ button on the bottom-right side of the screen to confirm your entries. The Change View Classification of Payment Differences Overview screen is displayed. Click the New entries button to call up the New Entries: Overview of Added Entries screen (Figure 14-20).

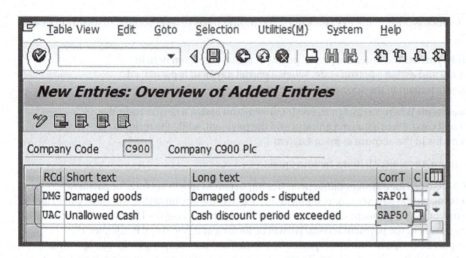

Figure 14-20. Assigning reason codes to manual outgoing payments

Update the following fields:

> **RCd:** Enter a three-digit character code in this field. It represents your reason code. This code will allow you to store text and the correspondence type for your reason code.

> **Short Text:** Enter a short description of your reason code in this field. For example, in this exercise, we used Damaged Goods.

> **Long Text:** Enter a full description of your reason code in this field. For example, we used Damaged Goods - Disputed.

> **CorrT:** Specify the correspondence type for your reason code in this field. SAP comes with standard predefined correspondence types you can choose from. Click the pull-down arrow next to the Correspondence Type field to display the list of correspondence types supplied by SAP. Select the correspondence type that best meets your requirement. For example, the code for payment notice with line items is SAP01 and the code for difference 050 payment notice is SAP50.

Confirm your entries by clicking the Enter button on the top-left side of the screen and then save 🖫 your work.

■ **Note**   You can create as many reason codes as you want. We advise that you take a look at the reason codes for company code 1000 (a standard company supplied by SAP as a guide) before defining your own reason codes.

The next step is to define accounts for payment differences. The settings you make will allow the system to automatically post payment differences to the accounts you specify.

Define Accounts for Payment Differences (Manual Outgoing Payments)

Payment differences are posted to a special account in SAP ERP. In this exercise, you assign payment differences by reason to your G/L account so that the system can automatically post payment differences to that G/L account. To assign your account follow this menu path: IMG: Financial Accounting (New) ➤ Account Receivable and Accounts Payable ➤ Business Transaction ➤ Outgoing Payments ➤ Manual Outgoing Payments ➤ Overpayment/Underpayment ➤ Define Accounts for Payment Differences (Manual Outgoing Payment). Or use transaction code OBXL.

■ **Note** You have already created the G/L account (Unallowed Customer Discounts 881000) required for this configuration in a previous exercise. So you don't need to define it again; all you need to do is simply assign it to the payment differences.

The Enter Chart of Accounts dialog box pops up. Enter your chart of account code (CA90) in the Chart of Accounts field and click the Enter ✅ button on the bottom-right side of the dialog box. The Configuration Accounting Maintain: Automatic Posts - Accounts screen is displayed. Enter the appropriate G/L account for payment differences in the Account field (Figure 14-21).

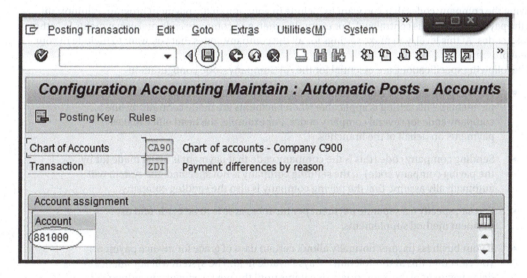

Figure 14-21. *Account determination for automatic posting*

Save 💾 your work.

Finally, in the accounts receivable and accounts payable configuration, you will customize automatic outgoing payments, which consists of several steps. You will go through these steps using a top-down approach, starting with the top item and working to the bottom.

Automatic Outgoing Payments

The Automatic Outgoing Payments program is a SAP payment-management tool that manages payments of multiple open invoices, posts payment documents, and prints payment media using EDI (Electronic Data Interchange) or DME (Date Medium Exchange) simultaneously. The payment program can be accessed from the user side (easy access) and the IMG (implementation guide) side. If you are a consultant, we recommend that you perform your configuration in the IMG side of the system and advise that you work from top down ensure that your payment program settings are complete. Several levels and steps are involved when customizing a payment program in SAP ERP:

1. All company codes

2. Paying company codes

3. Payment methods in country

4. Payment methods in company codes

5. Bank determination for payment transactions

6. House banks

All Company Codes

Specifying the company codes that you want to include in your automatic payment program is important when the payment process is centralized. For example, when one company code makes payments for other company codes. At this level, you make settings for all the company codes that you want to include in your payment program.

The following specifications are essential for the All Company Code configuration:

- Paying company code (this is the company code responsible for processing outgoing payments). This setting is applicable when payments are made centrally by one company code for several company codes. For example, the head office makes payments on behalf of the branches.

- Sending company code (this is the company code that payment is being made for by the paying company code). If the sending company is not specified, the system will automatically assume that the paying company is also the sending company.

- You can specify if a separate payment per business area is to be made and use payment method supplements.

- If your business partner normally allows certain days of grace for invoice payment, you can enter this in the Tolerance Days Payable field. The system will automatically delay payment of the appropriate due items until the next payment run as long as it is within the grace period.

- You can also specify special G/L transactions for vendors' and customers' settlements using the following special G/L indicators list supplied by SAP: 7 is a down payment for current assets, 9 is a down payment request, A is a down payment on current assets, and so on. You can access this list using the matchcode by the Special G/L Transaction to be paid field in Figure 14-22.

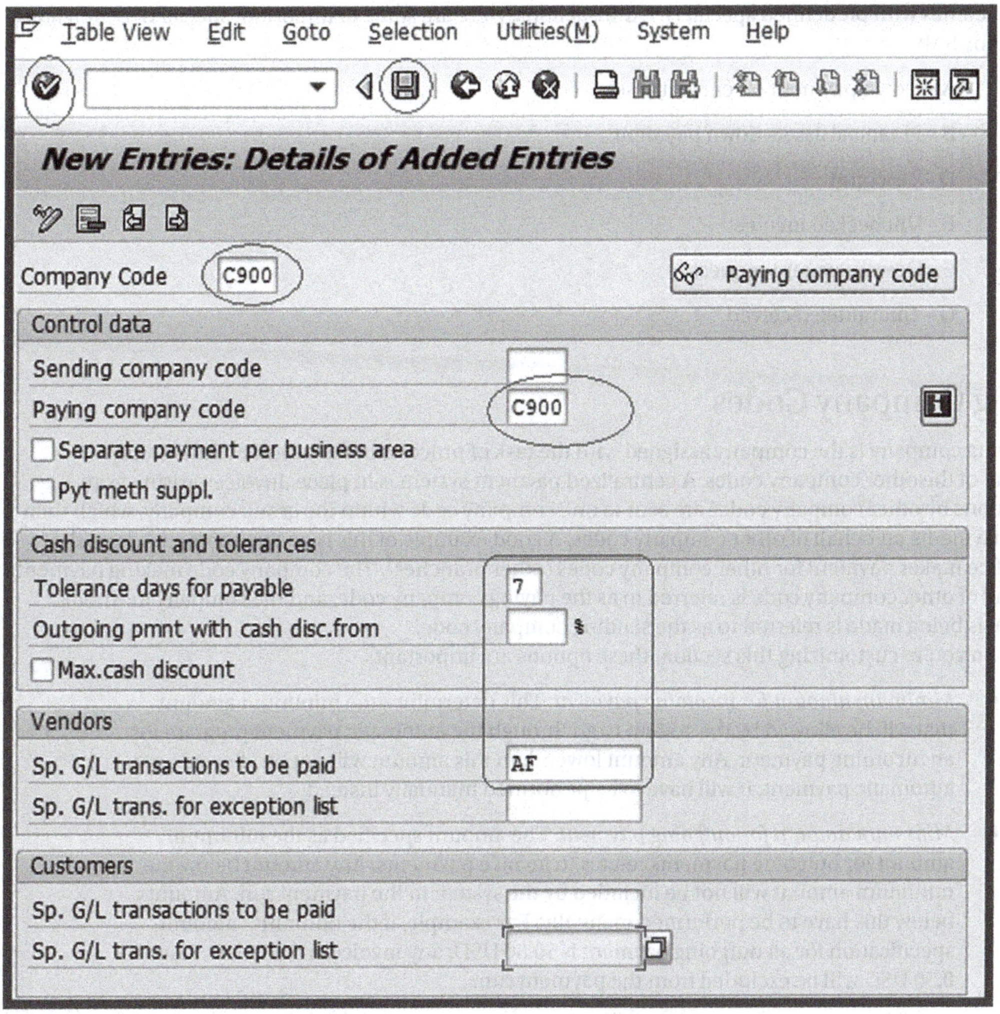

Figure 14-22. Setting up all company codes for payment transactions

To set up all company codes for payment transactions, follow this menu path: IMG: Financial Accounting (New) ➤ Account Receivable and Accounts Payable ➤ Business Transaction ➤ Outgoing Payments ➤ Automatic Outgoing Payments ➤ Payment Method/Bank Selection for Payment Program ➤ Set Up All Company Codes for Payment Transactions. Or use transaction code FBZP. The Change View "Company Code" Overview screen is displayed to customize payment transactions. Click the New entries button on the top-left side of the screen and update your settings using Figure 14-22 as a guide.

Confirm your entries by clicking the Enter 🗸 button on the top-left side of the screen. Then save 🖫 your work.

SAP comes with predefined special G/L transactions. Here are some of important special G/L indicators supplied by SAP:

A – Down payment on current assets

B – Financial assets down payment

D – Discount

E – Unchecked invoice

F – Down payment request

G – Guarantee received

Paying Company Codes

The paying company is the company assigned with the task of processing the payment transactions on behalf of the other company codes. A centralized payment system is in place. Invoices arising from transactions by other company codes are sent to one company code within the group company, which then makes payments on behalf of other company codes. A good example of this is an environment where the head office makes payment for other company codes (other branches). The company code making payment on behalf of other company code is referred to as the paying company code, and the company to whom payment is being made is referred to as the sending company code.

When you're customizing this section, these options are important:

- *Minimum amount for incoming payment*: This determines the minimum amount that will be allowed by the system to go through the automatic payment program for an incoming payment. Any amount lower than this amount will not be allowed as an automatic payment, it will have to be performed manually instead.

- *Minimum amount for outgoing payment*: The amount specified as the minimum amount for outgoing payments relates to invoice payments. Any amount below the minimum amount will not be included by the system in the payment run. Amounts below this have to be performed manually. For example, if the minimum amount specification for an outgoing payment is $0.50 USD, any invoice amount less than 0.50 USD will be excluded from the payment run.

- *Forms*: SAP comes with standard payment program forms in SAPScript. SAPScript defines the form layout that meets certain country specific and international payment methods. You can choose from several standard forms when defining your paying company code. The benefit of using the standard forms defined in SAPScript is that it saves you from having to use the wrong print program. There are two types of forms in this exercise—forms for printing a payment advice and the EDI accompanying sheet form. You will be looking an example of printed payment advice and EDI accompany sheet in Chapter 17 when you look at running payment program.

- *Sender details*: Specify the texts you want to use for your letter header, letter footer, and your company code sending address.

Let's customize the paying company code by following this menu path: MG: Financial Accounting ➤ Account Receivable and Accounts Payable ➤ Business Transaction ➤ Outgoing Payments ➤ Automatic Outgoing Payments ➤ Payment Method/Bank Selection for Payment Program ➤ Set Up Paying Company Codes for Payment Transactions.

The Change View Company Cods Overview screen is displayed. Click the New entries button on the top-left side of the screen to bring up the New Entries: Details of Added Entries screen (Figure 14-23). On this screen, you specify the minimum amount for an incoming payment and the minimum amount for an outgoing payment in the appropriate fields.

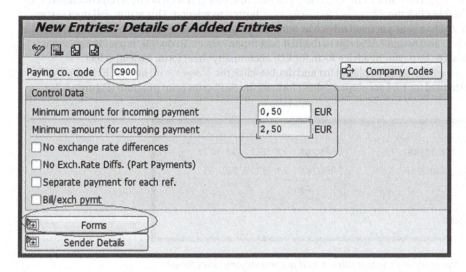

Figure 14-23. Setting the minimum amount for outgoing/incoming payments

The next step is to assign SAPScripts, which are country specific, to the paying company code (the form for the payment advice and EDI accompany sheet form). To do this, click the Forms button at the bottom-left side of the screen to expand the screen to the Form section (Figure 14-24), where you specify the SAPScript you want to use as your form layout.

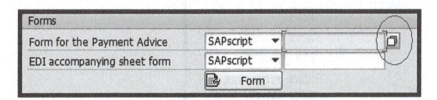

Figure 14-24. Specifying the form for payment advice/EDI accompanying sheet form using the Search function

---

■ **Note** SAP comes with several standard payment forms you can use as your payment advice and EDI accompany sheet. The exercise uses the International SAPScript form called F110_IN_AVIS for payment advice and the script form called F110_EDI_01 for the EDI accompanying sheet form. You can use any other form of your choice. In practice, you should use your country-specific SAPScript or what your company recommends.

To assign a form for the payment advice, click the Search button `SAPscript ▼` ⌖ circled to display SAP script Form Tree (Display Mode). On this displayed SAPScript Form Tree (Display Mode) Structure List of Countries represented in the system, under Payment Medium, choose (▸ International). A list of forms stored under international is displayed. Select the form you deem appropriate. For this exercise, click 🗐 ✇ Payment Advice Note (International). The Form F110_IN_AVIS (Avis (international)) screen is displayed containing the list of languages. Double-click the (🔛 Language EN Translate, Saved) button to select it. This action will then assign SAPScript F110_IN_AVIS to your payment advice as the print program.

The next step is to also assign SAPScript to the EDI accompany sheet. To do this, repeat the previous steps you used to assign the payment advice form for EDI accompany sheet form. Instead select 🗐 ✇ EDI Accompanying Sheet) from the displayed list and double-click the 🔛 Language EN Activ button. F110_EDI_01 is entered into the form field for EDI accompany sheet form as the SAPScript print program (Figure 14-25).

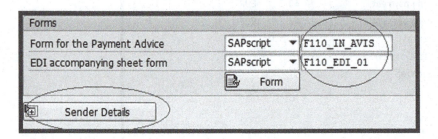

Figure 14-25. *Specifying the of payment advice/EDI accompanying sheet forms*

The final step of this exercise is to assign senders details to the paying company code. The values you enter will determine how the sender details are displayed in correspondence. Click the 🖭 Sender Details button at the bottom-left side of the screen to expand the sender details for SAPScript forms. Using the information in Figure 14-26, update the Sender Details for SAPScript Forms fields.

Sender Details for SAPscript Forms	
Text ID	ADRS
Letter header	ADRS_HEADER
Footer	ADRS_FOOTER
Signature text	ADRS_SIGNATURE
Sender	ADRS_SENDER

Figure 14-26. *Specifying the Sender details*

Click the Enter 🗸 button on the top-left side of the screen to confirm your entries and save 🖫 the settings for the paying company code.

Payment Methods in Country

The Payment Methods in Country option is a list of standard payment methods procedures per country you can choose from. Payment methods, although similar, vary from country to country. It is important that your company uses its country payment methods when making payments to business partners, but it is not compulsory that your company code use the all payment methods applied to your country in the payment program (automatic outgoing payments). You can select the specific payment methods that best meet your company's requirements from the list. Most countries have more than one payment method. For example, checks, wire transfers, bills of exchange, and so on.

Only minimum settings are required when customizing payment methods, because SAP comes with standard payment methods for most countries. Although you can also create your own payment methods, we advise that you stick to the standard payment methods, as they are typically sufficient for any configuration. You will not be making any settings in this exercise, but we recommend that you take a look at the payment methods supplied by SAP to make sure your country payment method is included. If your company's country payment is not provided, you have to create one by following this menu path: IMG: Financial Accounting (New) ➤ Account Receivable and Accounts Payable – Business Transaction ➤ Outgoing Payments ➤ Automatic Outgoing Payments ➤ Payment Method/Bank Selection for Payment Program ➤ Set Up Payment Methods per Country for Payment Transactions.

Payment Methods in Company Codes

The Payment Methods in Company Codes option contains the payment methods your company chooses to use in the payment program as a means of making outgoing payments to business partners. Payment Methods per Company Codes are obtained from country payment keys defined in payment methods per country. A company code does not necessarily have to use the system's payment methods per country. It's possible code to use some or all of the available payment methods, depending on your requirements. The specifications you make here determine the payment methods the system will use when making automatic payments to your business partners.

When customizing the payment methods per company codes, you need to specify the following:

- The paying company's code (this is the company responsible for processing and making outgoing payments).

- The payment method that your company code is using, such as check or bank transfer.

- Amount limits. These apply to your payment methods. You specify the minimum and maximum amount that the system will not exceed when making payments. Any payment below the minimum or above the maximum will be excluded from the payment run in the payment program.

- Other specifications include:

  Foreign Payments/Foreign Currency Payments For Foreign Currency Transactions: The payment method will allow the system to process foreign currency payments and receipts. Make payments to/from business partner's bank abroad.

243

Bank Selection Control: This allows the use of optimization either by bank group or by postal order. When you want the payment program to make payment from bank within the same clearing house, click the Optimize By Bank Group radio button .Funds are transferred more quickly and easily from your house bank in the shortest possible time to the business partner's bank account. This is possible only if you assign your bank in the master record to the bank group that you have defined. On the other hand, if you optimize by postal code, the house bank that's closer to the business partner bank postal code is used.

Let's set up payment methods per company code by following this menu path: IMG: Financial Accounting (New) ➤ Account Receivable and Accounts Payable ➤ Business Transaction ➤ Outgoing Payments ➤ Automatic Outgoing Payments ➤ Payment Method/Bank Selection for Payment Program ➤ Set Up Payment Methods per Company Code for Payment Transactions.

The Change View Maintenance of Company Code Data for a Payment Method screen is displayed. On the top-left side of the screen, click the New entries button to specify the paying company code data for a payment method (Figure 14-27).

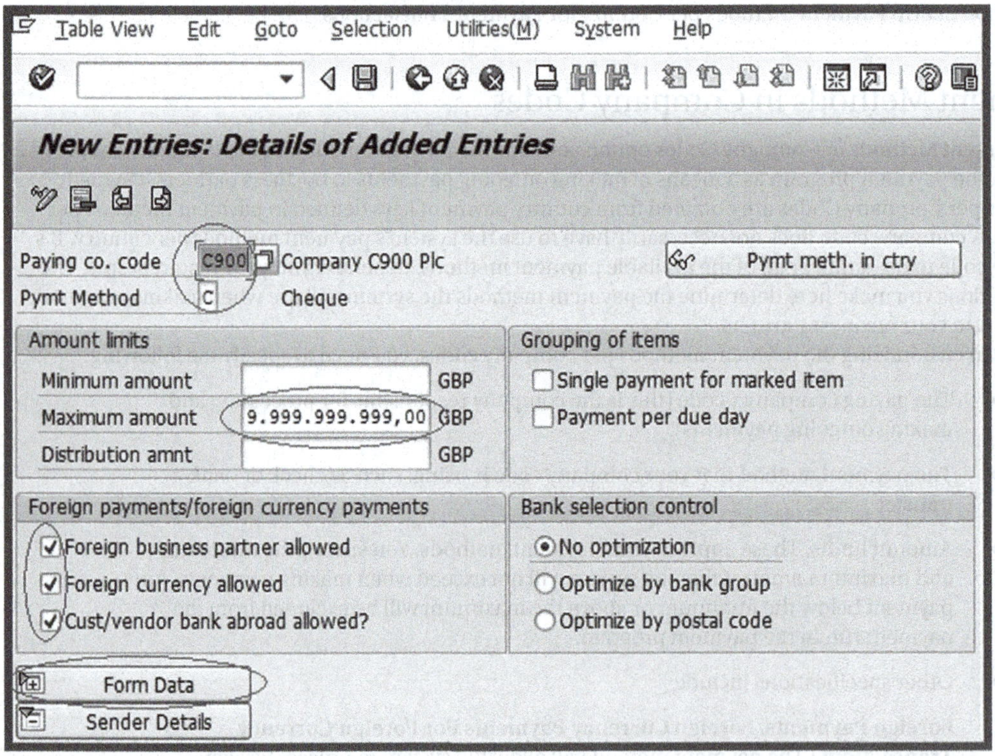

Figure 14-27. *Maintaining paying company code data for a payment method*

Update the following fields:

> **Paying Co. Code:** Enter the company code that you want to use for transaction payments.
>
> **Payment Method:** Specify the payment method key you are using in your payment program. (For example: Check, C). This specification is based on your company's preferred method of payment.
>
> **Minimum Amount:** Enter the amount limit in this field. Any payment below the minimum amount will be omitted from the payment run. If the field is blank, there will be no minimum amount limit. In this exercise, we left the field blank.
>
> **Maximum Amount:** Enter the maximum amount limit in this field. Any payment in excess of the maximum amount will be automatically excluded from the payment run.
>
> **Foreign Business Partner Allowed:** When this option is selected, the system will include foreign business partners in the payment run.
>
> **Foreign Currency Allowed:** When this option is selected, specified foreign currencies are allowed in the payment run.
>
> **Cust/Vendor Bank Abroad Allowed:** When this option is selected, the system will allow payments to/from bank accounts abroad to be included in the payment run.

The next step is to assign a standard payment form in SAPScript to your company code payment method using the international version and check (with check management) to print checks. Click the [Forms] button on the bottom-left side of the screen to expand it. Update the Forms section of the screen using the following information:

- Form for the Payment Medium: F110_PRENUM_CHCK

- Next Form: Leave blank

The final step is to specify the sender's details, which will be printed on the checks. Click the [Sender Details] button at the bottom-left side to expand the Drawer on the Form section. Update the screen as shown in Figure 14-28.

Forms

Form for the Payment Medium	SAPscript ▼ F110_PRENUM_CHCK
Next form	SAPscript ▼
	📄 Form

Drawer on the form

Company C900 Plc

London

UK

Sorting of the

Correspondence	K2
Line items	E2

⊞ Pyt adv.ctrl

Figure 14-28. Specifying the form for payment medium

■ **Note** Pyt Adv.Ctrl is the section of the screen where you add an advice note to the payee. For example, if you want to print a payment note every time a payment is generated, you choose Always Payment Advice. The only difference with the check payment method is the form section. (You don't need to print anything on a bank transfer payment, since these payments are made via the bank.) Therefore, in the Payment Advice Note Control section, click the None radio button and leave the SAPScript for Form for the Payment Medium blank.

Click the Enter 📀 button on the top-left side of the screen to confirm your entries and then save 💾.

To see your company code payment method, click the Back 🔙 button on the top of the screen to return to the Change View Maintenance of Company Code Data for a Payment Method screen. The payment methods you defined in this exercise are displayed (Figure 14-29).

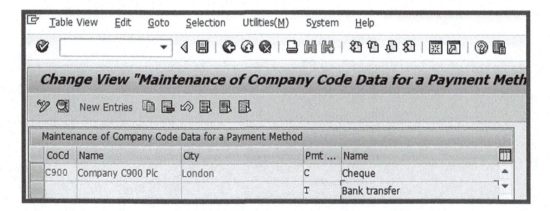

Figure 14-29. Company code data for a payment method

Bank Determination for Payment Transactions

Normally, companies have more than one bank account from which payments are made. The specifications you make in the Bank Determination for Payment Transactions section allow you to prioritize which bank accounts should be used when making payments. If there aren't sufficient funds to make a payment in the first bank account, the system will use the second bank account you specify, and so on. First, you have to specify the ranking order for the bank accounts. Secondly, you have to specify the house banks that payments are made from and the subaccounts that those payments are posted to. Third, you have to specify the available funds in each of the bank accounts. Finally, you may want to specify the value date, which defines the maximum number of days between the payment run and the bank value date within which payment should be made, as well as expenses/charges (includes fees/charges). This last step is not covered in this exercise, because value date is used by default and expenses/charges are rarely used in payment program.

■ **Note** Before you start customizing bank determination for payment transactions, make sure that the house banks you are applying to your payment transaction have been defined. You can see how to define a house bank in Chapter 9.

Follow this menu path: IMG: Financial Accounting (New) ➤ Account Receivable and Accounts Payable ➤ Business Transaction ➤ Outgoing Payments ➤ Automatic Outgoing Payments ➤ Payment Method/Bank Selection for Payment Program ➤ Set Up Bank Determination for Payment Transactions. The Display View "Bank Selection": Overview screen comes up. Make sure the Bank Selection folder on the left side of the screen is open. Work through each folder displayed under the Bank selection folder (Figure 14-30) from top down to ensure that you don't miss anything.

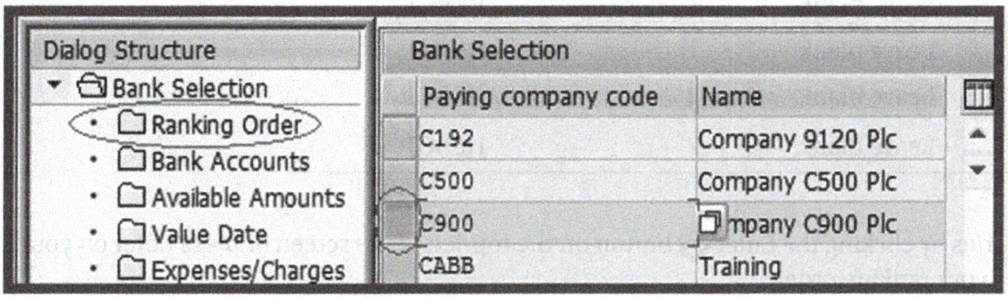

Figure 14-30. *House bank payment ranking order*

The first step is to specify the bank ranking order for payment purposes.

Ranking Order

Payments are made in order of ranking from your house bank by the payment program. The system will check the bank account with the highest priority for sufficient funds. If there are enough funds, payment will be made from the first house bank in order of ranking. If there are insufficient funds in the first house bank, the system will check the second house bank for sufficient funds and make payment from the house bank if it has sufficient funds.

To customize the ranking order for your payment program, click the Position button at the bottom of the screen. Select your company from the Bank Selection list on the left side of the screen and double-click the ⬚Ranking Order folder embedded in Bank Selection. The Change View Ranking Order Overview screen is displayed. Click the ⬚New entries⬚ button to specify the bank ranking for house banks. Update the following fields:

> **Payment Method:** Enter the payment method you want to use in your payment transaction in the appropriate order. (For example, if you want payment to be made by check or bank transfer, enter C for check payment and T for bank transfer in the payment method field.) During the payment run, the system will automatically apply the payment method that you entered in the payment method to your payment transaction.

> **Currency:** Enter the currency key that you want to apply to payment transaction. If this field is blank, the payment program carries out the payment in any currency. Only the currency that you specified will be used by the payment program.

> **Ranking Order:** Enter the ranking order that you want the system to make payment from your house bank. For example ranking order 1, 2 and so on.

> **House Bank:** Enter the house banks you want to use for your payment transaction in the ranking order of payment in this field.

Use the information in Table 14-2 to specify the ranking order.

Table 14-2. *Specification of Ranking Order for Your Payment Program*

Payment Method (PM)	Currency (Crcy)	Bank Ranking	House Bank
C	Leave blank	1	BARC1
T	Leave blank	1	BARC1
C	Leave blank	2	HSBC1
T	Leave blank	2	HSBC1

Confirm your entries by clicking the Enter 🗹 button on the top-left of the screen or press Enter on your keyboard and save 🖫 your ranking order.

The next step is to specify the bank accounts your payment program will make payments from and to determine which subaccounts payments your payment program will posted to.

Bank Accounts

Bank accounts allow you to specify which house banks the payment program can make payments from and where outgoing payments are posted during a payment run. Payments are posted to subaccounts based on payment method. For example, an outgoing payment made with a check is posted to the subaccount for checks. Likewise, payments made with bank transfer are posted to the subaccount for bank transfers.

■ **Note** You have already created the bank accounts needed for this configuration in Chapter 9 in the House Bank section. However, make sure that you have created the appropriate G/L account for your bank account.

Double-click the ⌑Bank Accounts folder on the left side of the screen (see Figure 14-30). The Change View Bank Accounts Overview screen appears. Click the New entries button on the top-left side of the screen. The New Entries: Overview of Added Entries screen is displayed, where you will determine the settings for your payment program. Update the following fields:

> **House Bank:** Enter the house banks you want to use for your bank account in this field in payment ranking order. (For example, you want payment to be made first from your Barclays Bank Account. On the contrary if there are no sufficient funds in Barclays Bank Account, then use HSBC Bank Account, and so on.)

> **Payment Method:** Enter the payment method you want to use in your payment transaction and in the appropriate order. (For example, if you want payment to be made by check or bank transfer, enter C for check payment or T for bank transfer in the payment method field.) During the payment run, the system will systematically apply the payment method that you entered in the payment method to the subaccounts.

> **Currency:** Enter the currency key that you want to apply to the payment transaction. If this field is blank, the payment program will carry out the payment in any currency. Only the currency that you specified will be applicable to the subaccount in your payment program.

> **Account ID:** Enter your bank account's ID in this field. You created this account ID in Chapter 9.

> **Bank Subaccount:** Enter the G/L account that you created in for the check account and the bank transfer account in Chapter 9.

Using the information in Table 14-3, specify the banking accounts for your payment program.

Table 14-3. *Specifications of Banking Accounts for Your Payment Program*

House Bank	Payment Method (PM)	Currency (Crcy)	Account ID	Bank Subaccount
BARC1	C	Leave blank	BARC	111412
BARC1	T	Leave blank	BARC	111414
HSBC1	C	Leave blank	HSBC	113155
HSBC1	T	Leave blank	HSBC	113158

Confirm your entries by clicking the Enter ✅ button on the top-left side of the screen or pressing Enter on your keyboard. Then save 💾 your work.

■ **Note**   Subaccounts the payment methods are posted to:

G/L account 111412: Barclays Bank Check issued out (the account check payments posted for Barclays Bank).

G/L account 111414: Barclays Bank Outgoing transfer (payments made by bank transfer are posted in this account for Barclays Bank).

G/L account 113155: HSBC Bank Check issued out (this is the account check payments are posted for HSBC).

G/L account 113158: HSBC Bank Outgoing transfer (payments made by bank transfer are posted in this account for HSBC).

The final step is to specify the available amount in each bank account used by your payment program.

Available Amounts

The Available Amounts field holds the funds available in your selected bank accounts. You specify the amount available for incoming and outgoing payments. During the payment run, the payment program will check the selected bank accounts to find the bank account with sufficient funds, based on your ranking order. If the funds are insufficient in the first bank account, the payment program will automatically check the second bank account, and then the third bank account, until it finds a bank account with sufficient funds for payment.

The payment program does not conduct amount splits, but the system can check your bank account based on ranking order to find out which bank account has sufficient funds for payment. If none of the bank accounts assigned to the payment have sufficient funds, payment will not be carried out. Before running the payment program, ensure that you have available funds.

Double-click the ☐ Available Amounts folder on the left side of the screen (see Figure 14-30) and the Change View "Amount Available": Overview screen is displayed. Click the New entries button at the top of the screen and the New Entries: Overview of Added Entries screen comes up. Update the following fields:

> **House Bank:** Enter the House Bank key you defined in your house bank customizing in Chapter 9. This will allow you to specify available funds in the bank account with this house bank key in your payment program.
>
> **Account ID:** Again, enter the Bank Account ID you defined in the house bank section of Chapter 9. In conjunction with the house bank key, you specify the available funds for each of the selected bank accounts in your payment program.
>
> **Days:** This field is important when you want to post payments before their due date. If you are not posting payment of bill exchange due date, enter 999 in this field. This indicates the maximum number of days you can include in your payment.

Using the information in Table 14-4, specify the banking accounts for the paying company code (Figure 14-31).

Table 14-4. *Specifications of Amount Available for Outgoing Payment*

House Bank	Account ID	Days	Currency	Amount Available for Outgoing Payment
BARC1	BARC	999	GBP	9.999.999.999.999.00
BARC1	BARC	999	GBP	9.999.999.999.999.00

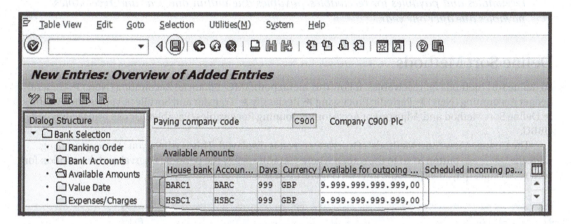

Figure 14-31. *Specifying the available amounts*

■ **Note** Use dots (.) to separate amounts in units of hundreds and commas (,) to separate amounts in units of tens. For example, 1000 is represented in the system as 1.000,00.

Confirm your entries by clicking the Enter ✅ button on the top-left side of the screen and save 💾 your configuration.

Sort Methods and Adjustment Accounts for Regrouping Receivables/Payables

Accounting standards define how companies classify and disclose receivables and payables according to their remaining life. SAP provides the facilities to perform this function in the sort methods and adjustment accounts for regrouping receivables/payable. The remaining life of AR and AP is defined in the sort method. For example, AR remaining life is classified as less than one year or more than one year. Payables' remaining life is classified as less than one year, 1-5 years, and more than five years.

The settings you define here allow you to classify receivables and payables into periods or years. For example, receivables/payables due within a year are classified as receivables/payables due within one year. Likewise, the receivables/payables due after one year, but within five years, are classified as receivables/payables due between one to five years. Other items due outside these periods are classified as receivables/payables due after five years. It is important to classify transactions arising from receivables and payables in the G/L account based on periods to allow proper disclosure in the financial report.

In this exercise, you will define settings that allow you to sort receivables and payables items into periods.

> *Problem: Company C900's accounting staff wants to be able to classify receivables and payables in the G/L accounts in periods for proper disclosure in the financial statement. Your task as FI consultant is to define sort method and adjustment accounts for regrouping receivables and payables for receivables/payables due within one year and receivables/payables due after one year.*

Define Sort Methods

To define sort methods for receivables, follow this menu path: IMG: Financial Accounting (New) ➤ General Ledger Accounting (New) ➤ Periodic Processing ➤ Reclassify ➤ Transfer and Sort Receivables and Payables ➤ Define Sort Method and Adjustment Accts for Regrouping Receivables/Payables. Or use transaction code OBBU.

The Change View "Sort Methods": Overview screen is displayed. This is where you start customizing. Click the New entries button to go to the screen where you will specify the periodic interval and description for your receivables/payables periodic interval (Figure 14-32).

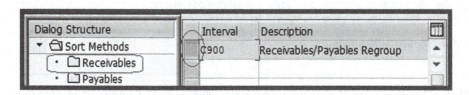

Figure 14-32. *The initial periodic interval screen*

Double-click the Receivables folder. In the Interval field, enter **C900**, and in the Description field, enter **Receivables/Payables Regroup**.

■ **Note** We recommend that you use company code as the sort methods interval in this exercise, because this will enable you to trace your sort method to your company code. This is important, especially when you have more than one company code.

Save your configuration.

Period Intervals for Receivables

The next step is to create the periodic intervals for receivables due within one year and receivables due after one year. To create the periodic intervals for receivables, select the periodic interval (C900) that you defined earlier. Since you are sorting receivables in this exercise, double-click the ☐ Receivables folder from left pane of the screen. The Change View "Receivables": Overview screen is displayed. Click the New entries button to go to the New Entries: Overview of Added Entries screen to create the periodi intervals for receivables (Figure 14-33).

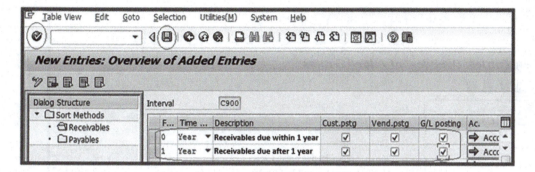

Figure 14-33. *Creating periodic intervals for receivables*

Update the following fields:

> **From:** Enter **0** for receivables due within one year and **1** for receivables due after one year.

> **Time Unit:** You have three options to choose from: Day, Month, and Year. Using the drop-down arrow, select Year for each field. This will classify the receivables on a yearly basis.

> **Description:** Enter the descriptions for each interval: "Receivables due within 1 year" and "Receivables due after 1 year".

> **Cust.Pstg:** When you click the Customer Posting checkbox, the system will classify receivables based on your interval specifications.

> **Vend.Pstg:** When you click the Vendor Posting checkbox, the system will classify payables based on your interval specifications.

> **G/L Posting:** When you click the G/L posting checkbox, the system will classify postings to the G/L account based on your interval specifications.

Click the Enter ⊘ button on the top-left side of the screen to confirm your entires and save 🖫 your work.

Periodic Intervals for Payables

Next, you need to define the periodic intervals for payables due within one year, payables due between one and five years, and payables due after five years. To create the periodic intervals for payables, select the periodic interval (C900) you defined earlier in Figure 14-32 and double-click the ⬚Payables folder on the left pane of the screen. The Change View "Payables": Overview screen is displayed. Click the New entries button to go to the New Entries: Overview of Added Entries screen, where you'll create the periodic interval specifications for payables. Update the screen using the data shown in Figure 14-34.

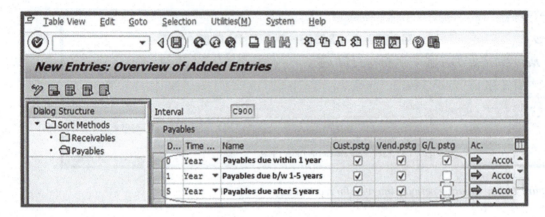

Figure 14-34. *Creating periodic intervals for payables*

Click the Enter ✅ button or press Enter on your keyboard to confirm the entries and then save 💾 the periodic intervals you have defined.

Define Adjustment Accounts for Receivables/Payables by Maturity

In this exercise, you define adjustment accounts for receivable and payables by maturity. The system will automatically post to the accounts you assigned for each period interval based on your specifications.

■ **Note**   Before defining adjustment accounts for receivable/payables by maturity, you must first create the G/L accounts you will need for your configuration. Go to "Appendix – A, Chapter 14" (Define Adjustment Accounts for Receivables/Payables by Maturity) to create the G/L accounts.

This exercise only defines adjustment accounts for receivables/payables by maturity for foreign receivables/payables. The same procedure is applicable when you create domestic and one-time receivables/payables. We advise that you create accounts for domestic and one-time payables/receivables on your own.

Receivables Due Within One Year

To maintain automatic posting procedures for adjustment accounts for receivables/payables by maturity, follow this menu path: IMG: Financial Accounting (New) ➤ General Ledger Accounting ➤ Periodic Processing ➤ Reclassify ➤ Transfer and Sort Receivables and Payables ➤ Adjustment Accounts for Receivables/Payables by Maturity. Or use transaction code OBBV.

The Maintain FI Configuration: Automatic Posting – Procedures screen is displayed. Click Receivables within 1 year from the displayed procedures list and then click the Choose 🔍 button on the top-left side of the screen. The Enter Chart of Accounts dialog box pops up. Enter your chart of accounts (CA90) in the Chart of Accounts field and click the Enter ✅ button at the bottom of the screen. The Maintain FI Configuration: Automatic Posting – Accounts screen appears (Figure 14-35), which is where you perform the specifications for adjustment accounts for receivables due in one year. Using the information in Table 14-5, update the screen.

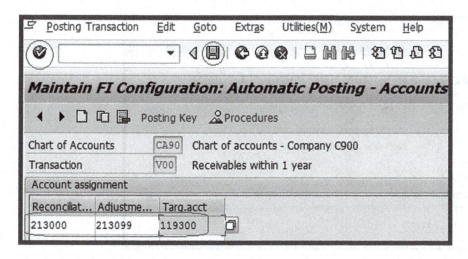

Figure 14-35. *Assigning G/L accounts to periodic intervals for automatic posting of payables due within one year*

Table 14-5. *The Accounts for Posting Receivables Due Within One Year*

Reconciliation	Adjustment	Trag. Acct.
213000 – Trade creditors, foreign	*213099 – Trade payable, foreign, adjustment*	*119300 – Vendor with a debit balance*

Click the Enter ⊘ button on the top-left side of the screen to confirm your entires and save 🖫 your account assignment.

Receivables Due After One Year

On the Maintain FI Configuration: Automatic Posting – Procedures screen, select `Receivables due after 1 year` from the displayed procedures list and click the Choose 🔍 button on the top-left side of the screen. Enter your chart of accounts (CA90) in the Chart of Accounts field of the Chart of Accounts screen and click the Enter ☑ button at the bottom of the screen to proceed to the Maintain FI Configuration: Automatic Posting – Accounts screen. Update the screen in Figure 14-36 using the information in Table 14-6.

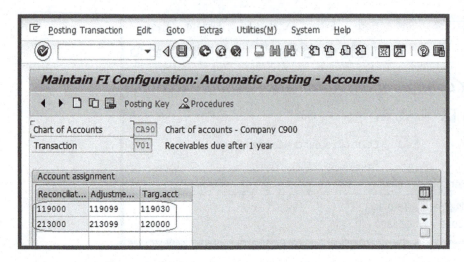

Figure 14-36. *Assigning G/L accounts to periodic intervals for automatic posting of receivables due after one year*

Table 14-6. *The Accounts for Posting Receivables Due After One Year*

Reconciliation	Adjustment	Trag. Acct.
119000 – Trade debtors, foreign	*119099 – Trade receivables, foreign, adjustment*	*119030 – Trade receivables foreign, due > 1 yr.*
213000 – Trade creditors, foreign	*213099 – Trade payables, foreign, adjustment*	*120000 – Other debtors due > one year*

Click the Enter ✅ button on the top-left side of the screen to confirm your entires and save 💾 your account assignment.

Payables Due Within One Year

On the Maintain FI Configuration: Automatic Posting – Procedures screen, click `Payables within 1 year` from the displayed procedures list and then click the Choose ⌕ button on the top-left side of the screen. Enter your chart of accounts (CA90) in the Chart of Accounts field of the chart of accounts screen. Then click the Enter ☑ button at the bottom of the screen to proceed to the Maintain FI Configuration: Automatic Posting – Accounts screen. Update the screen by using the information in Table 14-7.

Table 14-7. *The Accounts for Posting Payables Due After One Year*

Reconciliation	Adjustment	Trag. Acct.
119000 – Trade debtors- foreign	*119099 – Trade receivables, foreign, adjustment*	*213300 – Debtor with a credit balance*

Click the Enter ✅ button on the top-left side of the screen to confirm your entires and save 💾 your account assignment.

Payables Due Between 1-5 Years

On the Maintain FI Configuration: Automatic Posting – Procedures screen, select [Payables due between 1 - 5 yea] from the procedures list and click the Choose 🔍 button.

The Enter Chart of Accounts dialog box pops up. Enter your chart of accounts in the Chart of Accounts field and click the Enter ✅ button to confirm your entry. The Maintain FI Configuration: Automatic Posting – Accounts screen is displayed.

Update the screen using the data in Table 14-8.

Table 14-8. *The Accounts for Posting Payables Due Between 1-5 Years*

Reconciliation	Adjustment	Trag. Acct.
119000 – Trade debtors, foreign	*119099 – Trade receivables, foreign, adjustment*	*202000 – Other creditors due within 1-5 years*
213000 – Trade Creditors- foreign	*213099 – Trade payables, foreign, adjustment*	*213030 – Trade payables, foreign, due b/w 1-5 years*

Click the Enter ✅ button on the top-left side of the screen to confirm your entires. Then save 💾 your account assignment.

Payables Due After Five Years

On the Maintain FI Configuration: Automatic Posting – Procedures screen, click [Payables due after 5 years] and then click the Choose 🔍 button (or you can simply double-click the Payables button).

The Enter Chart of Accounts dialog box pops up. Enter your chart of accounts (CA90) in the Chart of Accounts field and click the Enter ✅ button to confirm your entry. The Maintain FI Configuration: Automatic Posting – Accounts screen is displayed (Figure 14-37).

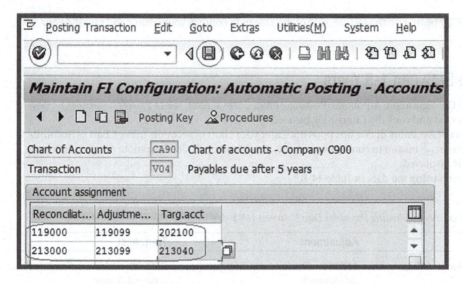

Figure 14-37. *Assigning G/L accounts to periodic intervals for automatic posting of payables due after five years*

Update the screen using the data in Table 14-9.

Table 14-9. *The Accounts for Posting Payables Due After Five Years*

Reconciliation	Adjustment	Trag. Acct.
119000 – Trade debtors – foreign	*119099* – Trade receivables, foreign, adjustment	*212100* – Other creditors due > 5 years
213000 – Trade Creditors- foreign	*213099* – Trade payables, foreign, adjustment	*213040* – Trade payables, foreign, due > 5 years

Save 💾 your changes.

Adjustment Posting/Reversal

It is inevitable that during document posting, some incorrect document might be mistakenly entered in the system. An incorrect document entered in the SAP system cannot be deleted; instead it must be reversed. Documents can be reversed in the system using either the normal posting reversal or the negative reversal method.

With normal posting reversal, the debit and credit sides of the total transaction are increased with the adjustment figure. With negative reversal, the adjustment figure is subtracted from the total transaction figure in the account. In other words, the total transaction figure will not be increased with the transaction figures. The transaction figures in the system remain as the original figures before posting. This systematic style of reduction is referred to as *negative posting*. When you permit negative posting, negative postings will be permitted for your company code. This will allow the system to reduce transaction figures in G/L and in your customer and vendor accounts without actually increasing the total transaction figures.

Permit Negative Postings

Problem: *The accounting team in the C900 Plc company heard that transactions posted to the system can be systematically reversed without having to increase total transaction figures. The team is interested in knowing how this can benefit them. Consequently, your colleagues have asked you to customize the system to allow negative postings for company code C900.*

In this exercise, you will specify a negative posting for your company code. This specification will allow you to carry out negative postings. To activate Negative Postings, follow this menu path: IMG: Financial Accounting (New) ➤ Accounts Receivable and Accounts Payable ➤ Business Transactions ➤ Adjustment Postings/Reversal ➤ Permit Negative Postings.

The Change View "Maintain Negative Postings in Company Code": Overview screen is displayed (Figure 14-38). This is where you specify that you want your company code to be permitted for negative postings.

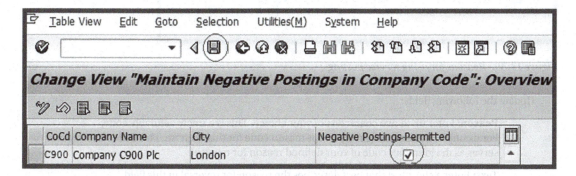

Figure 14-38. *Maintaining negative postings by company code*

Search for your company code using the Position button at the bottom of the screen. Then click the Negative Postings Permitted checkbox and save your settings 💾.

Define Reasons for Reversal

It is mandatory to state the reason for reversing a document in SAP ERP during document reversal. Hence it is important to define reasons for reversing documents. When you're posting document reversal, the reason for the reversal will be copied to the document that is reversed.

■ **Note** You can use the standard reversal reasons supplied by SAP or you can define your own reversal reasons.

To define reasons for reversal that will be applied to negative postings, follow this menu path: IMG: Financial Accounting (New) ➤ Accounts Receivable and Accounts Payable ➤ Business Transactions ➤ Adjustment Postings/Reversal ➤ Define Reasons for Reversal.

The Change View "Reason for Reverse Posting": Overview screen is displayed. This screen contains reasons for reversal. For example:

> 01 - Reversal in current period

> 02 - Reversal in closed period

Click the New entries button at the top of the screen to go to the New Entries: Overview of Added Entries screen (Figure 14-39).

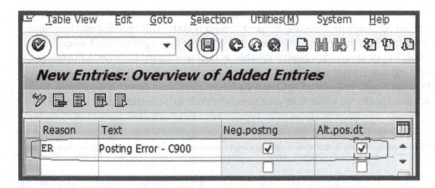

Figure 14-39. *Reasons for using reverse posting*

Update the following fields:

> **Reason:** Enter up to two characters of your choice. This is a freely definable code. For example, we used ER (Error) as our reason code for this exercise. This code serves as the identifier code of your defined reason for reversal.

> **Text:** Enter a short text that best describes the reason for reversal in this field, such as Posting Error C900.

> **Neg. Posting:** When you click the Negative Posting checkbox, you can create negative posting for this reason code.

> **Alt.Pos.Dt:** This checkbox allows alternative posting dates for this reason code.

Save .

Summary

This chapter covered account payables and account receivables, and explained what a customer account is. It also explained the steps involved in defining account groups with screen layout for customers. You learned how to maintain the field status group for general data for a customer account group. You also learned how to enter an accounting clerk identification code for customers and create number ranges and assign them to your account groups. You learned what a vendor account is and how to customize vendor accounts. You learned how to define account groups with screen layout for vendors, maintain the field status group for general data for a vendor account group, define accounting an clerk identification code for vendors, maintain number ranges for your vendor accounts, and assign number ranges to end or account groups.

The next exercise you learned about in this chapter was terms of payment. You learned how to maintain terms of payment for customers and how to maintain terms of payment and an installation plan. You then learned how to define a cash discount base for an incoming invoice, define incoming invoices credit memos/credit memos, define document types for enjoy transactions, define tax code per transaction, and define accounts for net procedures.

You also learned about manual outgoing payments. You learned how to define tolerances for outgoing payments. You learned also how to define reason codes and how to define accounts for payment differences.

Apart from learning what an automatic outgoing payment is, you went through the steps involved when defining automatic outgoing payments. You looked at the specifications involved when defining and paying company codes, payment methods per country, and payment methods per company codes.

You learned how to define sort methods and adjust accounts for regrouping receivables/payable. You learned how to define sort methods for accounts receivables and payables by defining periodic intervals for receivables and payables. The next exercise explained how to define adjustment accounts for receivables/payables by maturity based on periods receivable and payables due to enabling automatic postings to the G/L accounts. In so doing, you learned how to define accounts for receivables/payables due in one year, receivables due after one year, payables due between one and five years, and payables due after five years.

Finally, you looked at the difference between the normal reversal and negative reversal posting methods. You learned how to activate the indicator for permitted negative postings and how to define a reason code for negative posting.

In the next chapter, you will learn how to define correspondence in SAP. In doing this, you will define correspondence types, assign programs for correspondence type, define sender details for correspondence form, determine call-up functions, defining dunning procedures, specify the special G/L transactions that allow the system to dunn special G/L transactions, and learn about the various levels involved when defining dunning.

■ ■ ■

CHAPTER 15

Defining the Dunning Procedure and Correspondence

This chapter explains what dunning is and covers the basic settings involved in customizing the dunning procedure. It also explains what correspondence is and the steps involved in defining correspondence types.

At the end of this chapter, you will be able to:

- Define a dunning area
- Define the dunning procedures
- Specify special G/L transactions that allow the system to dun special G/L transactions
- Define correspondence types
- Assign programs for correspondence types
- Define sender details for correspondence forms
- Determine call-up functions

Dunning

It is normal business practice for business partners to fall behind when paying invoices. A customer may forget that an invoice is outstanding and need to be reminded to pay. SAP ERP provides a procedure referred to as a *dunning notice*. Dunning is the automatic process of sending notices to business partners based on defined criteria about overdue invoices or outstanding debt. The dunning program ensures that the mechanism for sending reminders is in place.

The program looks at business partners' accounts to determine which open items are overdue and at what level and generates the appropriate dunning notices. The dunning program can be used to dun customers and vendors.

The next section explores the steps involved in customizing dunning in SAP.

Define the Dunning Area

The SAP system comes with a basic setting that you can use to customize the dunning area for your dunning program. The predefined setting is typically sufficient, so you do not need to customize the dunning area. You can access the dunning area using this menu path: IMG: Financial Accounting (New) ➤ Account Receivable and Accounts Payable ➤ Business Transaction ➤ Dunning ➤ Basic Settings for Dunning ➤ Define Dunning Area.

In the basic dunning settings, you can define the following items:

Dunning Areas: A dunning area could be a department or a unit in a company code that you want to use to process your dunning.

Dunning Keys: These keys are company code-independent. The advantage of a dunning key is that it allows you to display items separately with a dunning key and print the dunning key text in the dunning notice.

Dunning Block Reasons: Allows you to exclude an item or account from being dunned during a dunning run. To do this, you enter a block key in the dunning block field in the master record.

■ **Tip**   If you are defining your own dunning area, it's best to use the basic settings supplied by the system.

Define the Dunning Procedures

Dunning procedures determine how dunning is carried out in SAP. You can define more than one dunning procedure. There is no restriction to the number of procedures that you can define. The account that you want to include in your dunning process must have a dunning procedure assigned to it. Dunning procedures are applicable to the standard and special G/L transactions.

■ **Note**   SAP comes with standard dunning procedures. These procedures can be adapted and modified to meet your company code-specific settings.

Problem: Company C900 wants to have four dunning levels as part of its credit control that will systematically generate reminder letters about overdue invoices. The first letter is a courteous reminder; subsequent reminders will be a bit firmer. Your task is to define four dunning levels for company C900.

When maintaining a dunning procedure, you can specify the following items:

- Dunning levels

- Charges

- Minimum amounts

- Dunning text

- Special G/L indicator

To define the dunning procedure for your dunning program, follow this menu path: IMG: Financial Accounting (New) ➤ Account Receivable and Accounts Payable ➤ Business Transaction ➤ Dunning ➤ Dunning Procedure ➤ Define Dunning Procedures. Or use transaction code FBMP.

The Maintain Dunning Procedure: List screen comes up and displays a list of existing dunning procedures in the system. Click the New procedure button at the top of the screen to go to the Maintain Dunning Procedure: Overview screen, where you will create your dunning procedure (Figure 15-1).

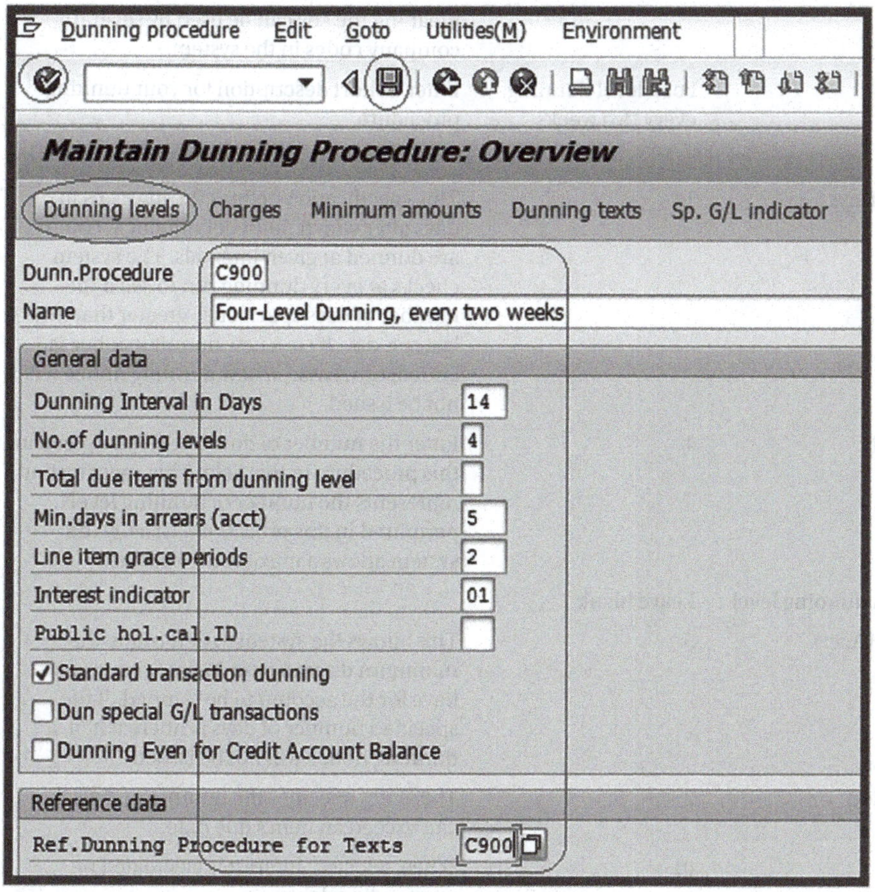

Figure 15-1. *The screen for maintaining a dunning procedure*

Using the information in Table 15-1, update the Maintain Dunning Procedure: Overview screen (see Figure 15-1).

Table 15-1. *The Input Fields to Update When Maintaining a Dunning Procedure*

Field	Value	Description
Dun. Procedure	C900	Enter your company code in this field. This represents the key for the dunning procedure. The key is company code-independent, meaning the key can be used by several company codes in the system.
Name	Four-level dunning, every two weeks	Enter a short description for your dunning procedure.
General Data		
Dunning Interval in Days	14	This specification defines the intervals in days after which point delinquent accounts are dunned at given intervals. The system checks at every dunning run to see if the number of days specified is greater than the last run day. If so, a new dunning notice is issued; otherwise, a new dunning notice will not be issued.
No.of Dunning Levels	4	Enter the number of dunning levels agreed in this procedure in this field. This specification represents the number of dunning levels permitted in this procedure. Usually the system allows a maximum of 9 levels.
Total due items from dunning level	Leave blank	
Min.Days in Arrears (Acct)	5	This allows the system to determine the minimum days an item in the account must have for the account to be dunned. If the specified number of days is not reached, a dunning notice will not be issued.
Line Item Grace Period	2	This entry specifies the number of days that can exceed an item's due date.
Interest Indicator	01	When selected, interest is calculated on outstanding debts.
Standard Transaction Dunning	Check	When this item is checked, the system will only dunn the normal business transactions. If you want to include the special G/L transactions in your dunning procedure, you should make sure that you choose the dun special G/L transactions option.
Reference Data		
Ref. Dunning Procedure for Texts	C900	This provides dunning text for your dunning procedure.

Click the Enter ✅ button at the top-left side of the screen or press Enter twice on your keyboard and save 💾 your dunning procedure.

Maintain Dunning Levels

Dunning levels allow you to assign dunning letters to your notices. As part of the credit control procedure, several letters are sent out systematically to remind business partners about open items. These letters are categorized into various levels (SAP allows a maximum of nine dunning levels). The first dunning level could be a very friendly reminder; the second is a bit firmer; and so on.

Click the [Dunning levels] button at the top-left side of the Maintain Dunning Procedure: Overview screen to go to the Maintain Dunning Procedure: Dunning Levels screen (Figure 15-2).

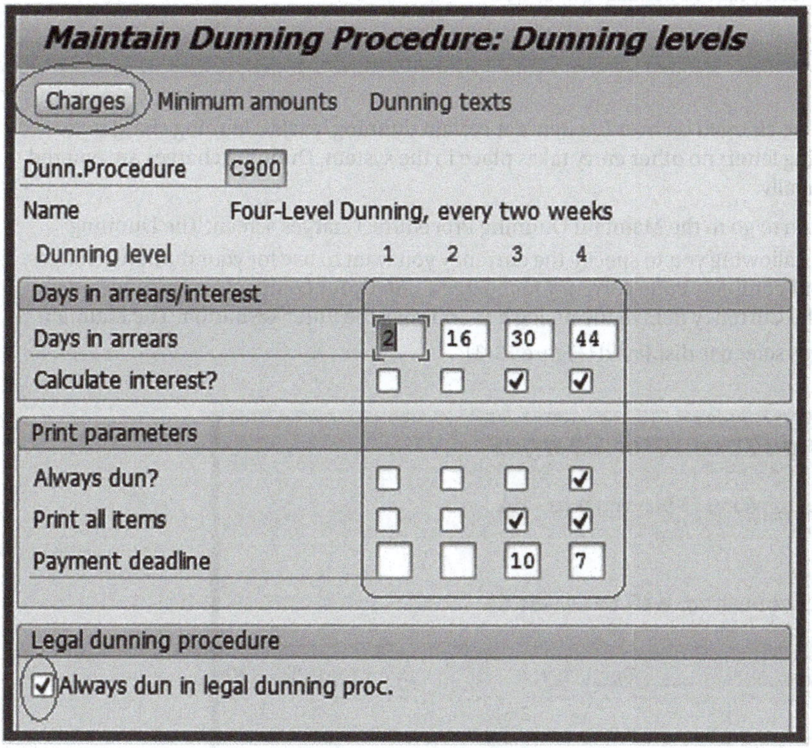

Figure 15-2. *Maintaining dunning levels for your dunning procedure*

Update the screen by specifying the following items:

Days in Arrears: The number of days an invoice is in arrears determines the dunning notice level that's created for it. For example, if an overdue item is in arrears for two days, the payment program will create a dunning notice at dunning level 1. Likewise, if an overdue item is in arrears for 16 days, the payment program will create a dunning notice at level 2, and so on.

Calculate Interest? The system calculates interest on the set dunning levels. For example, interests should be calculated on dunning levels 3 and 4.

267

Always Dun? This allows the dunning program to always dun the overdue item at the last dunning level so that no item is skipped at this level.

Print All Items: This allows you to print an overview of the customer/vendor account balance at the specified level.

Payment Deadline: This determines the new payment deadline printed on the dunning notice. It's best to use a basic 12-month calendar to avoid the payment deadline falling on a weekend.

Always Dun in Legal Dunning Proc.: Selecting this option allows you to print dunning notices using a legal dunning procedure, regardless of whether any changes have taken place in the account or not.

Maintain Charges

Sometimes a small fee may be charged on overdue items at certain dunning levels. Dunning charges are displayed only in the dunning letter; no other entry takes place in the system. Dunning charges are entered in a customer account manually.

Click the ⟨Charges⟩ button to go to the Maintain Dunning Procedure: Charges screen. The Dunning Charges dialog box pops up, allowing you to specify the currency you want to use for your dunning charges. Assume you want to use your company code currency for charges. Enter your company country currency key (for example, GBP) in the Currency field in the dialog box and click the Enter ✔ button. The Maintain Dunning Procedure: Charges screen is displayed (Figure 15-3).

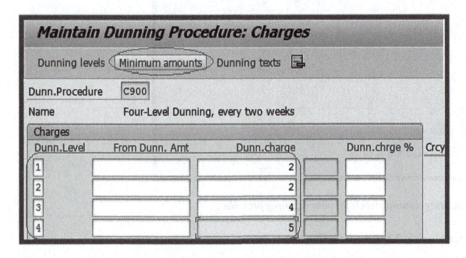

Figure 15-3. Specifying charges for a dunning procedure

Specify the dunning levels and charges you want to apply to each dunning level and click the Enter ✅ button at the top-left side of the screen to confirm.

The next step is to specify the minimum amount you want to apply to your dunning levels.

Maintain Minimum Amounts

You set minimum dunning amounts per dunning level to stop the system from triggering high dunning levels for insignificant amounts. You can do this by specifying a minimum amount or minimum percentage rates for each dunning level. The dunning program will check the open item to see if it is to be dunned. If the amount due on the open item is less than the minimum amount, the dunning program will exclude it from the dunning. But if the open item exceeds the minimum amount or the minimum percentage rate, the system will dun the open item. The system will also check your specifications to determine the minimum amount on which interest is applied.

Click the Minimum amounts button (circled in Figure 15-3) at the top of the Maintain Dunning Procedure: Charges screen to go to the Maintain Dunning Procedure: Minimum amounts screen. The Minimum Amounts dialog box pops up. Enter your company country currency key (for example, GBP) in the Currency field on the dialog box and click the Enter ☑ button to confirm the currency you are using. The Maintain Dunning Procedure: Minimum amounts screen is displayed (Figure 15-4).

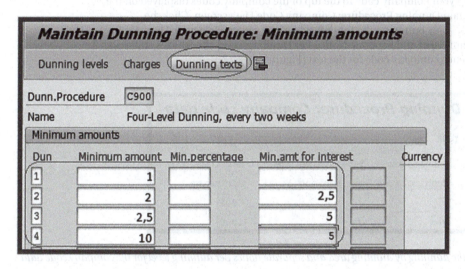

Figure 15-4. *Specifying the of minimum amount and minimum amount for interest for each dunning level*

When the minimum amount or percentage is reached or exceeded in respect to all open items, the system will trigger the next upper dunning level. If the specified minimum amount or minimum percentage is not reached, the system will automatically assign the items to the next lower level and carry out another check.

■ **Note** You can specify either a minimum amount or a minimum percentage to your dunning procedure. You cannot use both at the same time.

Click the Enter ✅ button to confirm.

The next step is to specify the dunning texts you want to use for each dunning level.

Maintain Dunning Texts

SAP comes with standard forms in SAPScript, which you can use for your dunning procedure. You can maintain the name of the form that you want to use per dunning level. SAPScript defines the layout of the form represented in the system. Dunning programs generate payment advice notes, dunning notices, and payment forms.

When customizing the dunning text, you first need to specify the dunning procedure for your company code data. Click the Dunning texts button at the top of the Maintain Dunning Procedure: Minimum Amounts screen. The Company Code/Account Type dialog box comes up. Enter your company code (**C900**) in the Company Code field. Select the account type you are using for your dunning procedure. In this case, click the Customer radio button and then click the Enter ✔ button at the bottom of the screen to confirm your entries. The New Company Code dialog box pops up. Enter your company code (**C900**) in the Company Code field and click Enter ✔ to confirm your entries. This action brings your company code to the top of the company codes displayed on the Maintain Dunning Procedure: Company Code Data screen. Click the New company code button on the top-left side of the screen. Select the Dunning By Dunning Area and Separate Notice Per Dunning Level checkboxes and assign a reference company code for the text (Figure 15-5).

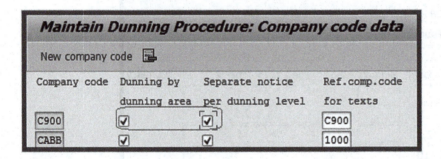

Company code	Dunning by dunning area	Separate notice per dunning level	Ref.comp.code for texts
C900	✔	✔	C900
CABB	✔	✔	1000

Figure 15-5. Set the dunning by dunning area and separate notics per dunning level for the company code data

Click the Enter ✔ button to confirm your entries and save 🖫 your dunning procedure.

Next, you need to assign a SAPScript form for each dunning level. Click the Back ⬅ button to return to the previous screen, which is the Maintain Dunning Procedure: Minimum Amounts screen.

Click the Dunning texts button to specify dunning text forms for each dunning level.

The Company Code/Account Type dialog box pops up. Enter your company code (**C900**) in the Company Code field and specify your account type. In this instance, your account type is Customer. Click the Enter ✔ button at the bottom of the screen to confirm your specifications. The Maintain Dunning Procedure: Dunning Texts screen appears to assign text forms for your dunning levels. Maintain the dunning text by specifying the appropriate forms for each dunning level (Figure 15-6).

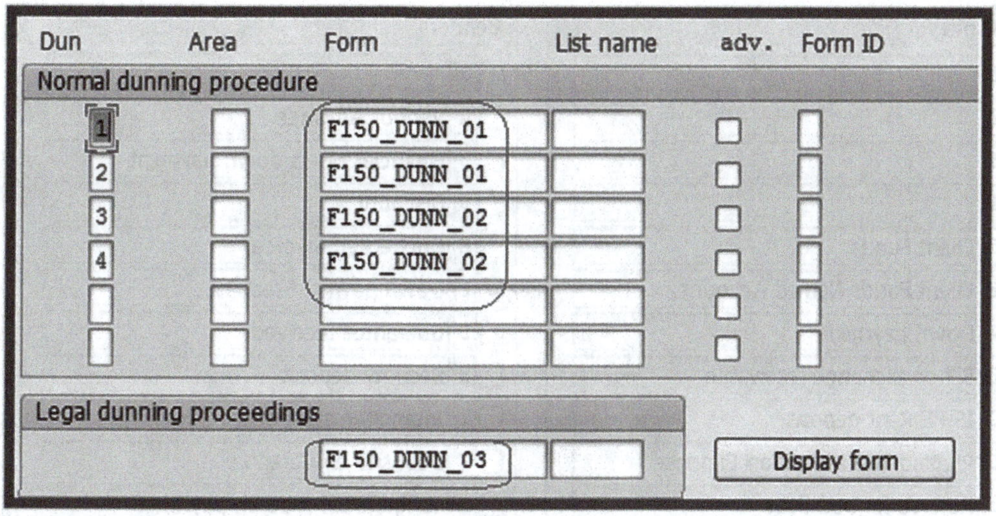

Figure 15-6. *Input screen for your dunning text forms*

SAPScript forms contain the reminder letters you apply to each dunning level. SAP comes with predefined dunning forms that you can assign to each dunning level. For example, F150_DUNN_01, F150_DUNN_02, and F150_DUNN_03. We recommend that you use the SAPScript form F150_DUNN_01 for dunning levels 1 & 2 and F150_DUNN-02 for dunning levels 3 &4. The F150_DUNN_01 content is more cautious than the remaining SAPScript forms.

■ **Tip** You can change the content of the forms to meet your requirements.

The final step in customizing the dunning procedure is to specify any special G/L indicators for customers and vendors. Click the Back 🕑 button to return to the previous screen, called Maintain Dunning Procedure: Overview.

Maintain Special G/L Indicator

The special G/L indicator allows you to dunn special G/L transactions. You can also apply special G/L transactions to your dunning by setting the appropriate indicators for special G/L transactions. For example, if you want a down payment request to be dunned, you must set the special G/L indicator in the dunning procedure. This will automatically allow the system to search for due down payment requests and include them in your dunning. You will look at special G/L transactions in detail in Chapter 16.

Click the ⌞Sp. G/L indicator⌟ button on the top-right side of the Maintain Dunning Procedure: Overview screen. The Maintain Dunning Procedure: Special G/L Indicator screen appears. Select the special G/L transactions you want to include in your dunning procedure from the list of special G/L indicators (Figure 15-7).

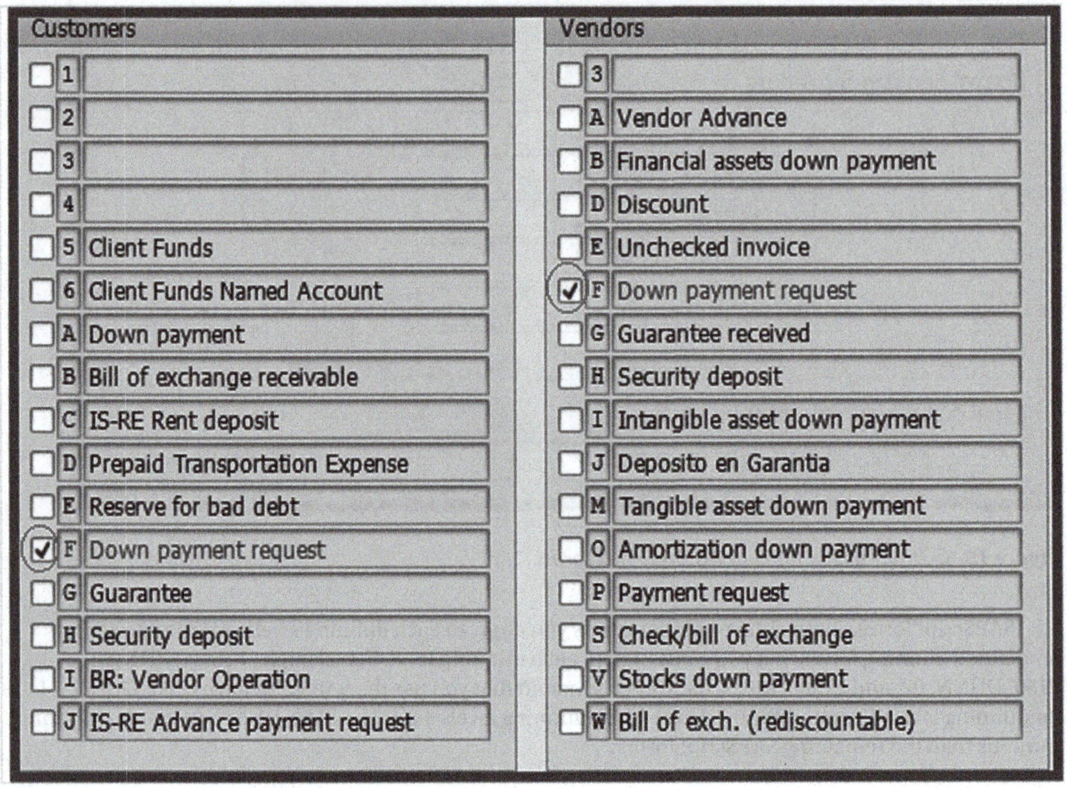

Customers		Vendors	
☐ 1		☐ 3	
☐ 2		☐ A	Vendor Advance
☐ 3		☐ B	Financial assets down payment
☐ 4		☐ D	Discount
☐ 5	Client Funds	☐ E	Unchecked invoice
☐ 6	Client Funds Named Account	☑ F	Down payment request
☐ A	Down payment	☐ G	Guarantee received
☐ B	Bill of exchange receivable	☐ H	Security deposit
☐ C	IS-RE Rent deposit	☐ I	Intangible asset down payment
☐ D	Prepaid Transportation Expense	☐ J	Deposito en Garantia
☐ E	Reserve for bad debt	☐ M	Tangible asset down payment
☑ F	Down payment request	☐ O	Amortization down payment
☐ G	Guarantee	☐ P	Payment request
☐ H	Security deposit	☐ S	Check/bill of exchange
☐ I	BR: Vendor Operation	☐ V	Stocks down payment
☐ J	IS-RE Advance payment request	☐ W	Bill of exch. (rediscountable)

Figure 15-7. *Configuring special G/L indicators*

Click the Back ⟲ button to return to the previous screen, called Maintain Dunning Procedure Overview, and the save 💾 your dunning procedure.

Correspondence

It is customary business practice to communicate with business partners through some form of correspondence during the normal course of business. SAP comes with standard correspondence tools, including several types of correspondence you can choose from. This enables you to generate ad-hoc correspondence. Examples of some of the correspondence you can generate in the system are payment notices, account statements, individual correspondence, and so on.

Correspondence types are letters represented in the system that are intended for your business partners. Standard correspondence types are supplied by SAP. You can use the standard SAP correspondence types or you can create your own.

You must create a correspondence type for every type of letter you need. Examples of correspondence types include:

- Payment notices
- Account statements
- Open item lists

Each correspondence type has a related print program defined in the system and each print program has its own variant and SAPScript form assigned to it. For each correspondence type, a print program and selection variant are defined. This enables you to print correspondence.

■ **Note**   You can also copy the standard correspondence types and modify them as desired. Using the correspondence types supplied by SAP saves you time.

Define Correspondence Types

Problem: Your client wants to be able generate account statements for their business partners. You have been asked to define a correspondence type for an account statement.

To define correspondence types, follow this menu path: IMG: Financial Accounting (New) ➤ Financial Accounting Global Settings ➤ Correspondence ➤ Define Correspondence Types. Or use transaction code OB77.

The Information screen with the warning, "Caution: The Table Is Cross Client" pops up. Ignore that warning and click the Enter ✔ button to accept. The Change View "Correspondence Types": Overview screen is displayed. Click the New Entries button on the top-left side of the screen to go to the Change View "Correspondence Types": Details screen (Figure 15-8).

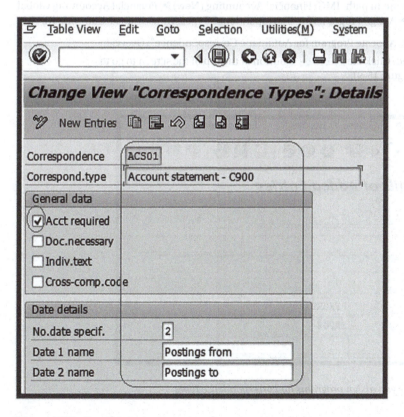

Figure 15-8. *Specifying your correspondence types*

Update the following fields:

Correspondence: Enter a five-digit character as your correspondence ID. This will allow you to identify your correspondence among other correspondence in the system.

Correspond. Type: Enter a name for your correspondence type. For example, account statement, open item list, open item list with payment advice, and so on.

■ **Note**   If you want to send a customer a communication containing data from a different company code, select the cross company code (Cross-Comp.Code) checkbox.

Click the Enter button on the top-left side of the screen to confirm your entries and then save 🖫.

The next step is to assign programs to the correspondence types you just defined.

Assign Programs to the Correspondence Types

SAP comes with various standard print programs and correspondence variants assigned to correspondence types, which you can use when printing correspondence requests. To assign programs for your correspondence type, use this menu path: IMG: Financial Accounting (New) ➤ Financial Accounting Global Settings ➤ Correspondence ➤ Assign Programs for Correspondence Types. Or use transaction code OB78.

The Change View "Allocate Program for Automatic Correspondence": Overview screen is displayed. Click the New procedure button at the top of the screen to go to the input field (Figure 15-9).

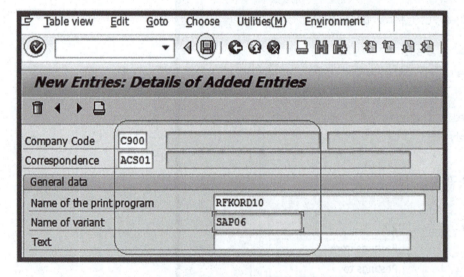

Figure 15-9. The screen where you assign programs for correspondence types

Using the information in Table 15-2, update the screen.

Table 15-2. *Information for the Input Field for Assigning Programs on the Correspondence Types Screen*

Field	Value	Description
Company Code	C900	Enter your company code in this field.
Correspondence	ACS01	Enter your correspondence ID here. This can be up to five characters.
Name of the Print Program	RFKORD10	The print name entered here must be obtained from the print name supplied by SAP for correspondence types that fit your correspondence. You can access this print program using the matchcode in the Name of the Print Program field.
Name of Variant	SAP06	Some variants are already defined in the system. Since you are assigning programs for correspondence types for Account Statement, use the standard variant for account statement (SAP06) supplied by SAP.

Click the Enter 🗸 button to confirm your entries and save 🖫 your work.

For a bit more practice and to better understand how to assign correspondence types, use the standard SAP correspondence types and assign the following correspondence types to your company code C900: SAP08 - Open item list

- SAP14 - Open item list with payment advice (single)

Then, follow the steps you just completed in this section and assign a print program for correspondence type for Account Statement SAP06.

Define Sender Details for a Correspondence Form

The standard text specifications you make will be applicable to your letter form. This will determine the appearance of the letter you send to your business partners. To define sender details for a correspondence form, follow this menu path: IMG: Financial Accounting (New) ➤ Financial Accounting Global Settings ➤ Correspondence ➤ Define Sender details for Correspondence Form. Or you can use transaction code OBB1

The Change View "Sender Details For Correspondence": Overview screen is displayed. Click the New Entries button at the top of the screen to go to the New Entries: Details of Added Entries screen. This is where you specify the sender details for the correspondence form (Figure 15-10).

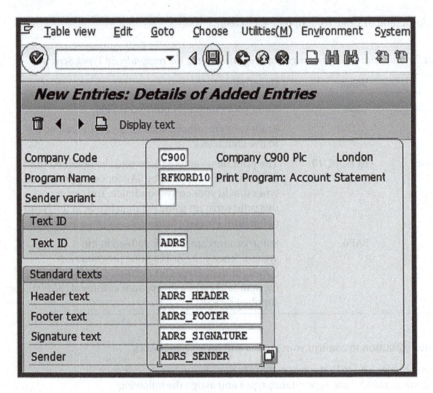

Figure 15-10. Sender details for the correspondence form

Using the information in Table 15-3, update the screen.

Table 15-3. Sender Details for the Correspondence Form

Field	Value	Description
Company Code	C900	Enter your company code in this field.
Program name	RFKORD10	Enter the print program name in this field. This is a predefined variant provided by SAP, specifically for the printing program for account statement. This program name allows you to print the exact correspondence.
Text ID	ADRS	The text ID you enter here is applicable to the standard text you apply to your correspondence type. For example, header text, footer text, and so on.
Header Text	ADRS_HEADER	This definition determines the appearance of your
Footer Text	ADRS_FOOTER	correspondence letter. This determines the format of header,
Signature Text	ADRS_SIGNATURE	the footer, the signature, and the sender.
Sender	ADRS_SENDER	

Click the Enter ✅ button on the top-left side of the screen to confirm your entries and save 💾 your work.

Determine Call-Up Functions

Call-up functions allow you to determine the correspondence type used online. For example, you can enter documents, settle payments, display documents and account balances, and process line items online when you activate the following functions:

- DocEnt (document entry)

- Pmnt (payment settlement)

- DocDsp (document display)

- AccDsp (account balance display and line item processing)

To determine your call-up functions use this menu path: IMG: Financial Accounting (New) ➤ Financial Accounting Global Settings ➤ Correspondence ➤ Determine Call-Up Functions. Or use can transaction code OB79.

The Change View "Call Options of Correspondence Types": Overview screen is displayed. Click the [New Entries] button at the top of the screen to display the New Entries: Overview of Added Entries screen. Use the information in Table 15-4 to update that screen.

Table 15-4. *Activating the Necessary Items for the Online Functions*

CoCd	Corr	Correspondence Type	DocEnt	Pmnt	DocDsp	AccDsp
C900	ACS1		X	X	X	X

Click the Enter button on the top-left side of the screen to confirm your settings and then save 💾 your efforts.

Define Reply Addresses for Balance Confirmation

As part of an audit process, balance confirmations are often sent to business partners asking them to confirm their account balances. Replies to balance confirmations are usually sent to a third party (such as an auditor), who has a different address than the company code initiating the balance confirmation notifications. The most notable balance confirmation letters are:

Balance Confirmation: Allows you to generate letters notifying business partners of their account balance and to request a confirmation.

Balance Notification: Allows you to send balance notification to business partners and to request a reply only if they disagree with the balance.

Balance Request: Allows you to ask business partners to advise you on their account balance based on their own records.

To define reply addresses for balance confirmations, follow this menu path: IMG: Financial Accounting (New) ➤ Accounts Receivable and Accounts Payable ➤ Business Transactions ➤ Closing ➤ Count ➤ Balance Confirmation Correspondence ➤ Define Reply Address for Balance Confirmation.

The Change "Company Code-Dependent Address Data": Overview screen is displayed. Click the [New Entries] button at the top of the screen to go to the New Entries: Overview of Added Entries screen (Figure 15-11).

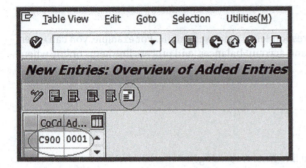

Figure 15-11. *Assigning a reply address to a company code*

Enter your company code in the CoCd field (**C900**) and enter the address identification in the Address ID field (**0001**, which is predefined by SAP). Click the Address ![button] button at the top of the screen. The Edit address screen pops up. This screen allows you to enter the address balance confirmations that are sent to your business partners. Enter the address where you want business partners to return their balance confirmations (Figure 15-12).

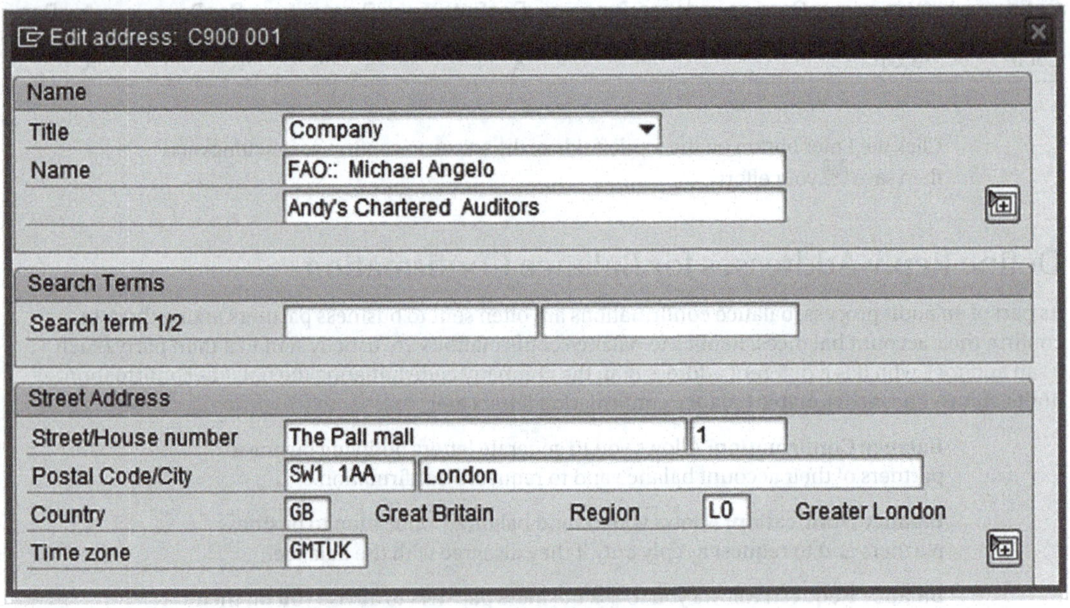

⌐ Edit address: C900 001		✕
Name		
Title	Company ▼	
Name	FAO:: Michael Angelo	
	Andy's Chartered Auditors	⊞
Search Terms		
Search term 1/2		
Street Address		
Street/House number	The Pall mall	1
Postal Code/City	SW1 1AA London	
Country	GB Great Britain Region LO Greater London	
Time zone	GMTUK	⊞

Figure 15-12. *Defining the address where the balance confirmation replies are sent*

Click the Enter ![button] button at the bottom of the screen to confirm your entries. The system will return to New Entries screen. Click the Save ![button] button to save your reply address.

Summary

This chapter explained what dunning is and talked a bit about how to define a dunning area. You learned how to define a dunning procedure. You also learned how to specify dunning levels, charges, and minimum amounts for your dunning procedures. You learned how to assign text to the dunnings and how to specify the G/L indicators for each dunning procedure. You also learned how to use SAP's correspondence features. You learned how to define correspondence types, assign programs to correspondence types, define details for correspondence forms, determine call-up functions, and add a reply address for balance confirmations.

The next chapter looks at configuring special G/L transactions. As part of this customizing activity, you will learn you how to define various types of down payments, define tax clearing accounts, and use various special G/L transactions, including guarantees (automatic offsetting entry (statistical)), down payments (free offsetting entry), and bills of exchange (noted items).

Summary

■ ■ ■

CHAPTER 16

Customizing Special G/L Transactions

This chapter looks at special G/L transactions and explains how to disclose them in SAP R/3 using alternative reconciliation accounts.

At the end of this chapter, you will be able to:

- Demonstrate an understanding of special G/L transactions

- Explain various technical factors related to special G/L transactions, including guarantees (automatic offsetting entry (statistical), down payments (free offsetting entry), and down payment requests (noted items)

- Configure special G/L transactions for down payments, down payments received, and down payment requested

- Define tax clearing accounts for down payments

- Define alternative reconciliation accounts for customers and vendors

Special G/L Transactions

Special G/L transactions are part of the Accounts Receivable (AR) and Accounts Payable (AP) transactions needing special disclosure requirements in the financial statement. Due to their nature, special G/L transactions are posted to special subledgers and to the general ledger in the SAP ERP system. The advantage of maintaining special general ledger transactions is to meet the separate disclosure requirements. When customizing special G/L transactions, you use a special subledger account linked to special G/L accounts using a special G/L indicator to make postings to alternative reconciliation accounts (special G/L accounts) possible.

Special G/L transactions include down payments, bills of exchange, and other transactions. In SAP R/3 special G/L transactions can be distinguished between business relationships and technical factors. This is represented in Figure 16-1.

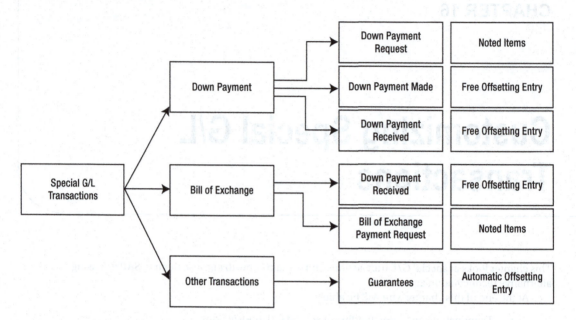

Figure 16-1. *The distinctions between the special G/L transactions according to their relationships and technical factors*

First you will be looking at the distinctions between technical factors represented in special G/L transactions and then you'll look at the steps involved in customizing special G/L transactions in SAP R/3.

■ **Note** Before looking at special G/L transactions in detail, it is important to refer back to Chapter 5 for a recap on the General Ledger (G/L), subledgers, and G/L reconciliation accounts. We have provided a list of nine accounts in "Appendix A, Chapter 16, Customizing Special G/L Accounts" that you needed to complete this exercise.

Technical Factors

SAP differentiates between the different special G/L transactions based on the nature of their treatment. These distinctions are classified into three categories, referred to as technical factors:

- Noted items
- Free offsetting entries
- Automatic offsetting entries

Noted Items

Noted items include down payment requests and bill of exchange payment requests. Noted items have no impact on the general ledger. Since no postings are made in the G/L accounts, noted items are purely for informational purposes and serve only as reminders. The system automatically reminds users that the down payment request exists for the account. The system doesn't make open item balance checks or offsetting entries. Only one line item is updated when a noted item is created.

Noted items are treated as line items in the open item account, so you should activate the line item in the G/L master record for G/L accounts 119000 and 196000 (these are the G/L accounts you define in Appendix A for your special G/L transactions). You can include down payments in the payment program and dunn overdue down payments using the dunning program.

Free Offsetting Entry

An example of a free offsetting entry is a down payment that's been received. Depending on the type of posting involved, free offsetting entries generate proper postings in the general ledger since they are part of accounts receivable/payable. Special G/L transactions related to free offsetting entries will automatically debit or credit special G/L reconciliation accounts once they occur.

Automatic Offsetting Entry

Typically, an automatic offsetting entry is a guarantee of payment and is termed a *statistical* posting because it's not displayed in the financial statements. Automatic offsetting entries are only displayed as notes to the financial statements. Since they form part of the automatic offsetting entries, entries are made in the same offsetting account. Offsetting entries accounts are defined in the IMG (implementation guide), which makes it possible for the system to make automatic offsetting entries. Once an open item is cleared in the account, the system will automatically clear the item in the offsetting account.

Configuration of Special G/L Transactions

You look at down payments made, down payments received, down payment requests, and guarantees in this exercise. No additional configurations are needed for the bills of exchange and other special G/L transactions. The settings for guarantees supplied by SAP are sufficient.

Down Payments

Down payments are a kind of short-term finance. It is a normal business practice for business partners to obtain short-term finance by way of down payments without accruing interest. For example, a manufacturer may not be able to finance its production and may request a down payment before production begins or during or after production. Accounting practices separate down payments from the normal business receivables and payables and display them separately on the balance sheet.

There are several factors that give rise to down payments under the normal course of doing business. Payables or receivables arising from the purchase of an asset or from providing a service can be financed through down payments. Down payments are disclosed on the balance sheet as assets or liabilities. If the transaction is a receivable, it is treated as an asset and debited accordingly. On the other hand, if the down payment is payable, it is a liability and it is credited on the balance sheet. Upon the delivery of goods or the performance of a service for which the down payment was made, the accounts involved need to be cleared and the down payment is no longer displayed on the balance sheet.

Down Payment Received

Down payment received is an advance payment made to you by your customers as a down payment in anticipation of the provision of goods or services to your customer. Only minimum settings are required here, because SAP comes with a predefined setting for down payments. In this exercise, you define reconciliation accounts for customers' down payments. Your specifications will make it possible for the system to automatically post down payment transactions to a special G/L reconciliation account instead of the normal receivable G/L reconciliation account.

> **Problem:** *As part of their accounting policy, company C900 Plc wants to be able to post customer down payments to a special reconciliation account, instead of to the normal customer reconciliation account. You must define the reconciliation accounts for the customer down payment for com C900.*

To define the reconciliation accounts for down payments, follow this menu path: IMG: Financial Accounting (New) ➤ Accounts Receivable and Accounts Payable ➤ Business Transactions ➤ Down Payments Received ➤ Define Reconciliation Accounts for Customer Down Payments. Or use transaction code OBXR.

The Maintain Accounting Configuration: Special G/L List screen is displayed (Figure 16-2). This screen contains the list of special G/L transactions.

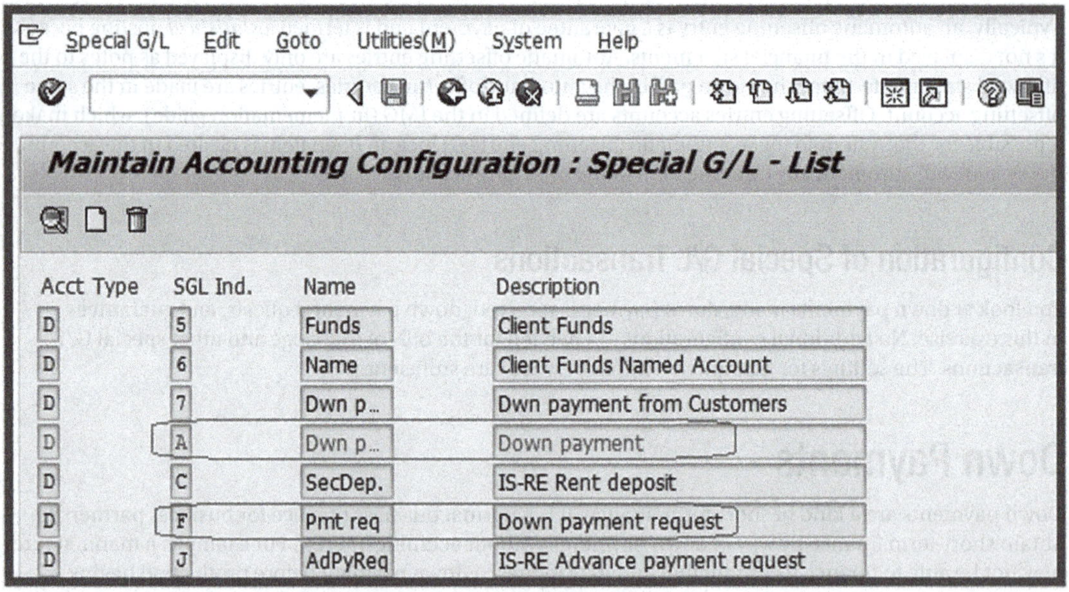

Figure 16-2. *List of special G/L transactions provided in SAP*

Select Down Payment from the list of items displayed on the screen by clicking on it. Then click the 🔍 Details button on the top-left side of the screen.

The Chart of Accounts Entry dialog box pops up. Enter your chart of accounts (CA90) in the Chart of Accounts field and click the Continue ✓ button at the bottom of the screen to go to the Maintain Accounting Configuration: Special G/L Accounts screen. It holds the input field where you will assign the reconciliation account and special G/L account to your down payment (Figure 16-3).

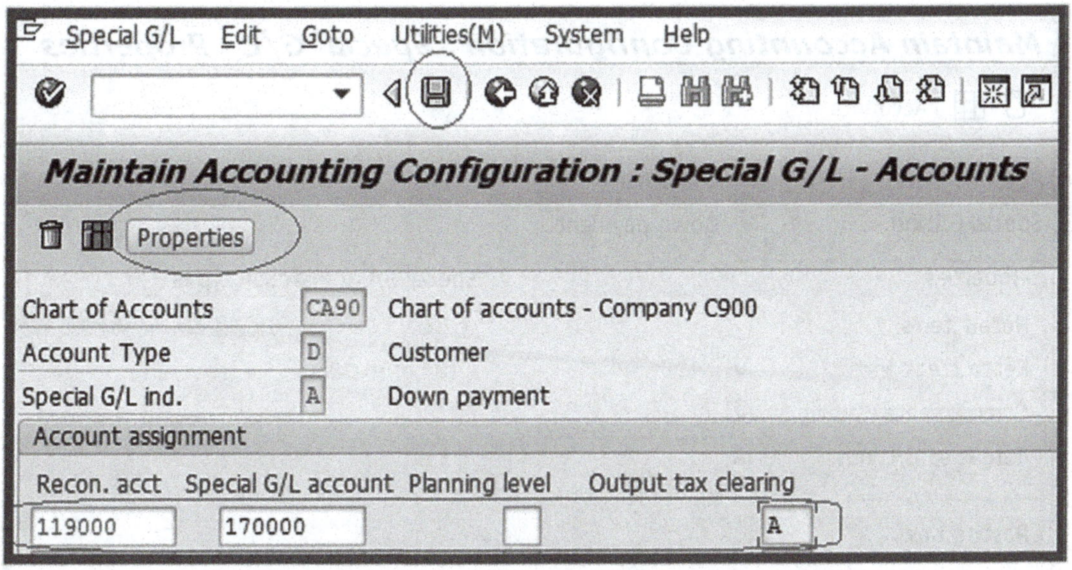

***Figure 16-3.** Account assignments to special G/L accounts—customer down payments*

Enter G/L account 119000 in the Reconciliation Account field and special G/L account 170000 in the Special G/L Account field (these are the G/L accounts you created in Appendix A). Enter A into the Output Tax Clearing field. This specification allows the system to post output tax elements arising from down payments to the output tax clearing account. SAP comes with two tax types: A for output tax and V for input tax. You can access these tax types by using the matchcode or the search function that appears when you click on the Output Tax Clearing field. When you click on the matchcode or the search function, a list of tax types is displayed. Select tax type A and then 💾 save your work.

You can display the down payment for customer properties to see if the standard settings supplied by SAP meet your requirements. Click the [Properties] button on the top-left side of the screen. The Maintain Accounting Configuration: Special G/L – Properties screen appears (Figure 16-4).

■ **Note** SAP comes with predefined settings for special G/L properties. Check the special G/L specifications provided by the system to make sure that they meet your requirements.

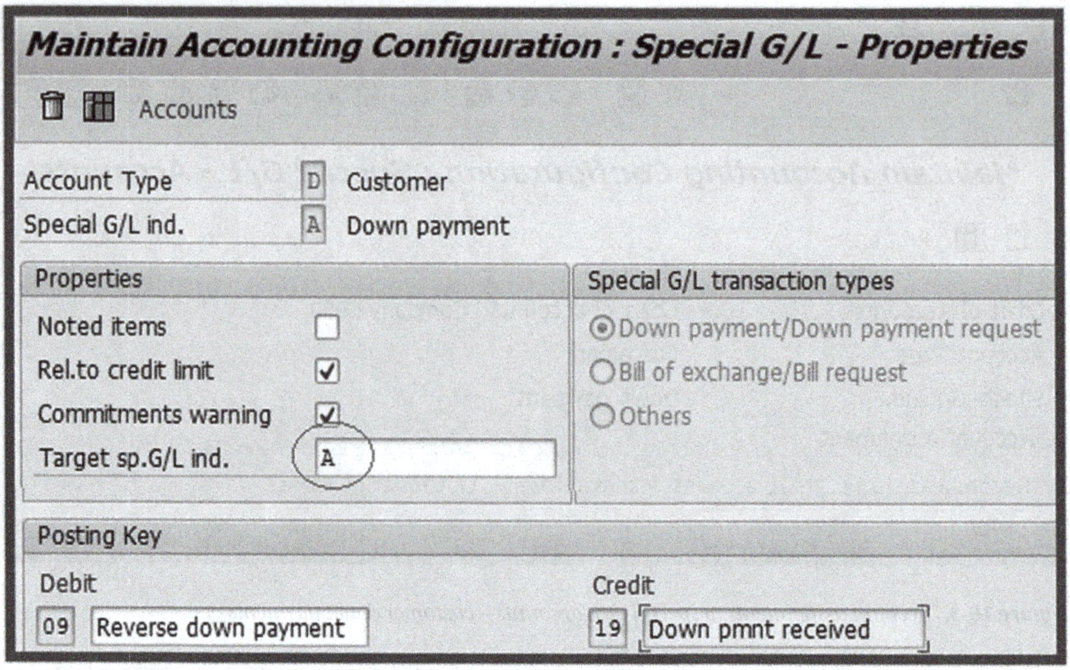

Figure 16-4. The standard properties for customer down payments

Once you are satisfied with the settings for the down payments, save 💾 your configuration.

The next step in this exercise is to define the reconciliation accounts for the customer down payments.

Down Payment Requests (Customer)

As mentioned earlier, a down payment is a form of short-term finance. It can also be an engendered commitment from a customer, especially when the integrity of the customer is in question. Down payment requests are normal business practice when advance payment is requested prior to the commencement of a business transaction.

To define the reconciliation accounts for customer down payment requests, follow this menu path: IMG: Financial Accounting (New) ➤ Accounts Receivable and Accounts Payable ➤ Business Transactions ➤ Down Payments Received ➤ Define Reconciliation Accounts for Customer Down Payments. Or use transaction code OBXR.

The Maintain Accounting Configuration: Special G/L List screen is displayed. Select Down Payment Request from the list of items displayed on the screen and click the Details 🔍 button on the top-left side of the screen.

The Chart of Accounts Entry dialog box pops up. Enter your chart of accounts (CA90) in the Chart of Accounts field and click the Continue ✅ button at the bottom of the screen to go to the Maintain Accounting Configuration: Special G/L Accounts screen. This is where you assign the reconciliation account and special G/L account to your down payment request (Figure 16-5).

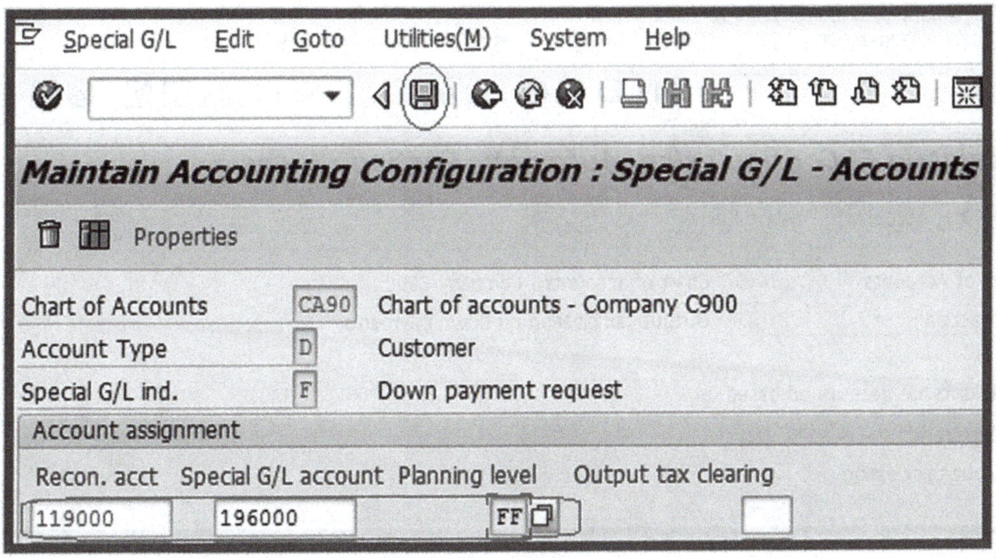

Figure 16-5. Special G/L accounts for customer down payment requests

Enter G/L account 119000 into the Reconciliation Account field and special G/L account 196000 into the Special G/L Account field. Enter planning level type FF (Down Payment Request) in the Planning Level field.

Save 💾 your work.

The final step in defining customer down payments is to define the tax clearing account.

Define Account for Tax Clearing (Customer Down Payments)

The tax entered for the down payment will be posted to the tax clearing account you define in this activity, and this tax rate typically depends on your country's legal specifications. To define the account for tax clearing for customer down payments, follow this menu path: IMG: Financial Accounting (New) ➤ Accounts Receivable and Accounts Payable ➤ Business Transactions ➤ Down Payments Received ➤ Define Account for Tax Clearing. Or use transaction code OBXB.

The Configuration Accounting Maintain: Automatic Posts – Procedures screen is displayed. From the Procedure list, select ⌷Output tax clearing on down payments⌷ and click the Choose 🔲 button. The Chart of Accounts Entry screen pops up. Enter your chart of accounts ID (CA90) in the Enter Chart of Account field and click the Continue ✅ button to proceed to the Configuration Accounting Maintain: Automatic Posts – Rules screen. Click the Output Tax Clearing checkbox (Figure 16-6). By activating output tax clearing, you will be able to specify the tax type and the G/L account you want for down payments.

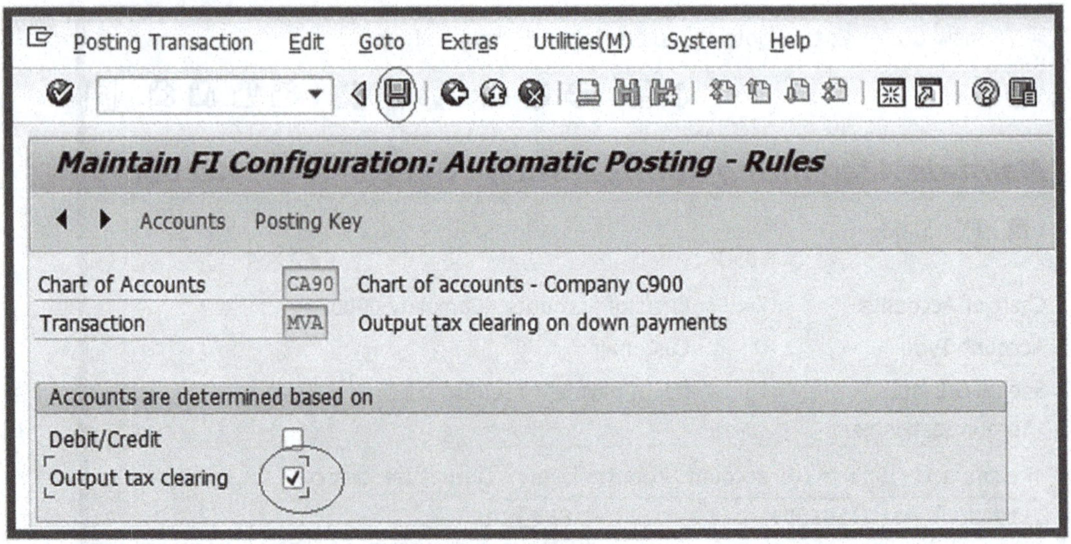

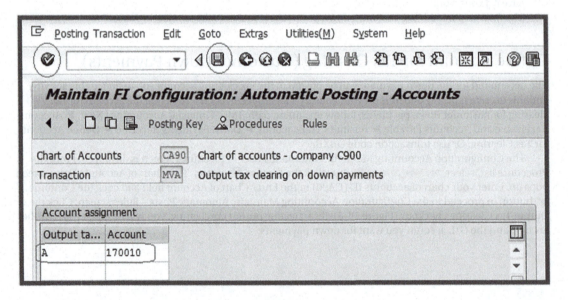

Figure 16-6. *Specifying the output tax clearing tax type for the customer*

Click the Save 🖫 button. The Configuration Accounting Maintain: Automatic Posts – Accounts screen is displayed. Enter Output Tax type A in the Output Tax Type field and enter the appropriate G/L account for Output Tax Clearing on down payments (170010) in the Account field (Figure 16-7).

Figure 16-7. *Specifying the output tax type and account for output tax clearing on customer down payments*

Save 🖫 your work.

Down Payment Made

Down payment made is an advance you pay to your vendor as a down payment in anticipation of receiving goods or services. For example, you might make a down payment on your current assets. Before customizing the down payment made, make sure that you have created the appropriate alternative reconciliation accounts for down payments. You do this in "Appendix A, Chapter 16, Customizing Special G/L Accounts."

In this exercise, you will define vendor down payments, which are managed in the G/L. The settings you specify here will make it possible for the system to automatically post down payment transactions to a special G/L reconciliation account instead of to the normal receivable G/L reconciliation account.

> **Problem:** *As part of their accounting policy, company C900 Plc wants to be able to post vendor down payments to a special reconciliation account, instead of to the normal vendor reconciliation account. You must define reconciliation accounts for vendor down payments for company C900.*

To define the reconciliation accounts for down payments, follow this menu path: IMG: Financial Accounting (New) ➤ Accounts Receivable and Accounts Payable ➤ Business Transactions ➤ Down Payments Received ➤ Define Reconciliation Accounts for Customer Down Payments. Or use transaction code OBXR.

The Maintain Accounting Configuration: Special G/L List is displayed. This screen contains a list of special G/L transactions represented in SAP. To specify the special G/L account that the down payment transaction will be posted to, select Down Payment on Current Assets from the list of displayed special G/L transactions on the screen and click the Choose ⬛ button on the top-left side of the screen. You can also just double-click the option from the list in Figure 16-8.

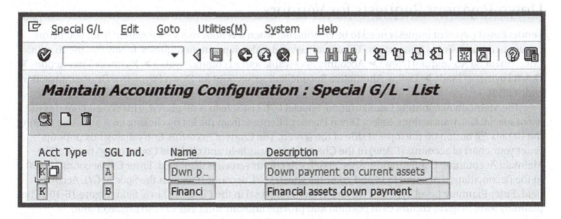

Figure 16-8. *Possible list of special G/L transactions provided by SAP*

The Chart of Accounts Entry dialog box pops up. Enter your chart of accounts (CA90) in the Chart of Accounts field and click the Enter ☑ button to confirm your entries. The Maintain Accounting Configuration for Special G/L Accounts screen is displayed. Enter G/L account 213000 in the Reconciliation Account field and the special G/L account 159000 in the Special G/L Account field. Enter Input tax type V in the Input Tax Clearing field (Figure 16-9). When you enter the tax type into the input clearing field, the system can automatically post input tax elements arising from down payments to the input tax clearing account.

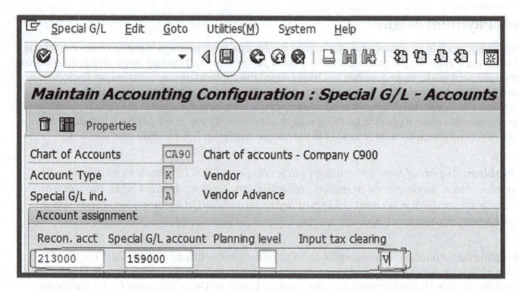

Figure 16-9. *Special G/L accounts for vendor advances*

Save 💾 your work. You can check the default specifications for the special G/L payment properties to see if the standard settings are adequate. To do this, click the `Properties` button on the top-left side of the screen.

Down Payment Requests for Vendors

Vender down payment requests need to be customized when a vendor requests payment from you before commencing a business transaction. To customize vendor down payment requests, follow this menu path: IMG: Financial Accounting (New) ➤ Accounts Receivable and Accounts Payable ➤ Business Transactions ➤ Down Payments Made ➤ Define Alternative Reconciliation Account for Down Payments. Or use transaction code OBYR.

The Maintain Accounting Configuration: Special G/L List screen is displayed. This screen contains the list of special G/L transactions. Select Down Payment Request from the list by clicking on it and then clicking the Details 🔍 button on the top-left side of the screen. The Chart of Accounts Entry dialog box pops up. Enter your chart of accounts (CA90) in the Chart of Accounts field and click the Continue ✔ button. The Maintain Accounting Configuration: Special G/L – Accounts screen is displayed. Enter G/L account 213000 in the Reconciliation Account field and enter the special G/L account 196300 in the Special G/L Account field. Enter Planning Level Type FF (Down Payment Request) in the Planning Level field (Figure 16-10). The planning level helps to control cash position and provide liquidity forecasts in cash management.

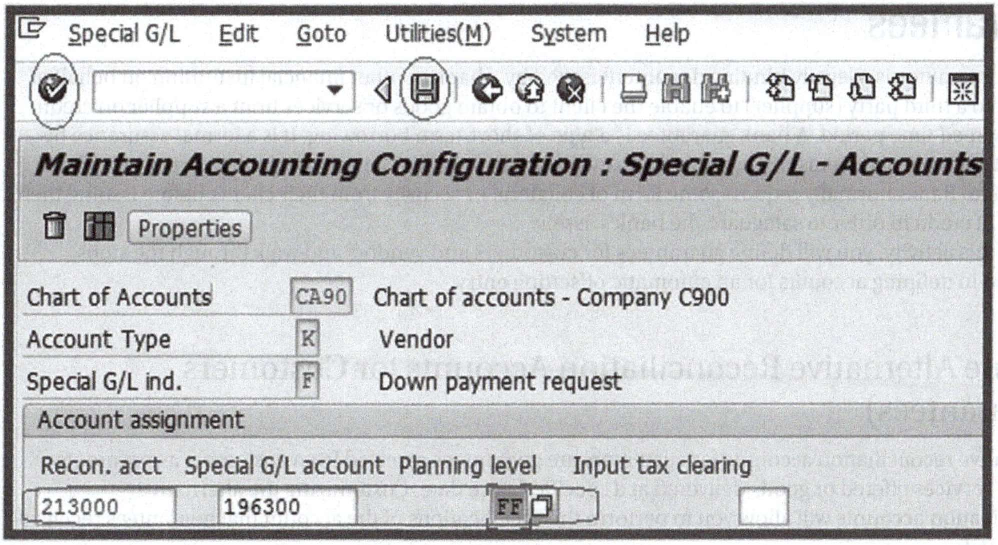

Figure 16-10. Special G/L accounts for vendor down payment requests

Save 💾 your work.

Define Account for Tax Clearing (Vendor Down Payments)

Depending on your country's legal specifications, the tax entered for down payments will be posted to the tax clearing account you define here.

> **Problem:** *Your client wants a tax clearing account that will enable them to display gross down payments in the vendor accounts in order to meet legal requirements. Your task is to define a clearing account for down payments made that will enable your client to achieve this objective.*

To define an account for tax clearing for your vendor down payments, follow this menu path: IMG: Financial Accounting (New) ➤ Accounts Receivable and Accounts Payable ➤ Business Transactions ➤ Down Payments Made ➤ Define Account for Tax Clearing. Or use transaction code OBXD.

The Configuration Accounting Maintain: Automatic Posts – Procedures screen is displayed. From the Procedure list, select Input Tax Clearing on Down Payments by clicking on it and clicking the Choose 🔍 button. The Chart of Accounts Entry screen pops up. Enter your chart of accounts ID (CA90) in the Enter Chart of Account field and click the Continue ✅ button to proceed to the Configuration Accounting Maintain: Automatic Posts – Rules screen. Click the Input Tax Clearing checkbox. Click the Save 💾 button. The Configuration Accounting Maintain: Automatic Posts – Accounts screen is displayed. Enter Input Tax type V in the Input Tax Type field and enter the appropriate G/L account number (159010) for input tax clearing on down payments. Click the Enter ✅ button and then save 💾 your work.

Guarantees

A bank guarantee is a legally binding document issued by a bank or other financial institution on behalf of a client to a third party (supplier) to enable the client to obtain goods or services from a supplier on credit for an agreed time period. A bank guarantee is a type of short-term borrowing. It is a formal assurance by the bank to make payments to a supplier in an event where the client fails to meet their part of the debt obligation. Banks normally request some form of collateral or security from their clients before issuing them a letter of credit in order to safeguard the bank's assets.

In this activity, you will define guarantees for customers and vendors and walk through the steps involved in defining accounts for an automatic offsetting entry.

Define Alternative Reconciliation Accounts for Customers (Guarantees)

Alternative reconciliation accounts for customers are guarantees received from customers as payments toward services offered or goods delivered at a specific future date. Customizing the alternative reconciliation accounts will allow you to perform the specifications of the account that guarantees received are posted.

> **Problem:** It is a mandatory disclosure requirement for company C900 Plc to maintain separate special G/L accounts where guarantees are posted, instead of to the normal customer/vendor reconciliation accounts. Your task is to define an alternative reconciliation account that will enable posting these guarantees to G/L special accounts.

To specify the alternative reconciliation account for customers for posting guarantees, follow this menu path: IMG: Financial Accounting (New) ➤ Accounts Receivable and Accounts Payable ➤ Business Transactions ➤ Postings with Alternative Reconciliation Account ➤ Other Special G/L Transactions ➤ Define Alternative Reconciliation Account for Customers. Or use transaction code OBXY.

The Maintain Accounting Configuration: Special G/L – List screen is displayed. Select Guarantee from the displayed list of items and click the Choose button at the top left to go to the screen where you will maintain accounting configurations. The Chart of Accounts Entry dialog box pops up. Enter your chart of accounts (CA90) and click the Enter ✅ button. The Maintain Accounting Configuration: Special G/L – Accounts screen is displayed. Enter G/L account number 119000 in the Reconciliation Account field and account number 196100 in the Special G/L Account field (Figure 16-11).

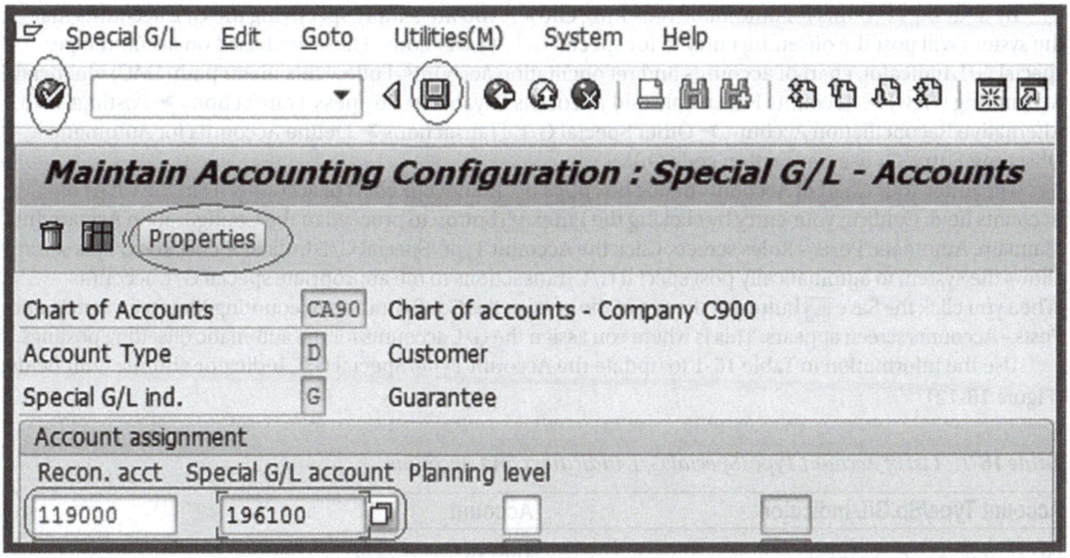

Figure 16-11. *Account assignment to special G/L accounts—customer guarantees*

Click the Enter 🕜 button or press Enter on your keyboard to confirm your entries and then save 🖫 your work.

Define Alternative Reconciliation Accounts for Vendors (Guarantees)

Guarantees made to vendors are posted to the alternative reconciliation accounts you set up in this exercise. Follow this menu path: IMG: Financial Accounting (New) ➤ Accounts Receivable and Accounts Payable ➤ Business Transactions ➤ Postings with Alternative Reconciliation Account ➤ Other Special G/L Transactions ➤ Define Alternative Reconciliation Account for Vendors. Or use transaction code OBXT.

The Maintain Accounting Configuration: Special G/L – List screen is displayed. To configure a guarantee for a vendor, double-click the guarantee on the list. The Chart of Accounts Entry dialog box pops up. Enter your chart of accounts (CA90) and click the Enter ✅ button on the bottom-left side of the screen. The Maintain Accounting Configuration: Special G/L – Accounts screen is displayed. Enter G/L reconciliation account 21300 in the Recon. Acct field and G/L account 196400 in the Special G/L Account field. Save 🖫 your work.

The final step in this exercise is to define accounts for automatic offsetting entries for customer and vendor guarantees.

Define Accounts for Automatic Offsetting Entry

Problem: Your task is to define accounts for automatic offsetting entries accounts for the following special G/L transaction types:

   DG – Customer-Guarantee

   DS – Customer-Check/Bill of Exchange

   KG – Vendor-Guarantee

   KS – Vendor-Check/Bill of Exchange

By defining accounts for automatic offsetting entries, you are simply specifying the G/L accounts that the system will post the offsetting entry to for special G/L transactions. These are based on account type, special G/L indicator, chart of accounts and reconciliation accounts. Follow this menu path: IMG: Financial Accounting (New) ➤ Accounts Receivable and Accounts Payable ➤ Business Transactions ➤ Postings with Alternative Reconciliation Account ➤ Other Special G/L Transactions ➤ Define Accounts for Automatic Offsetting Entry. Or use transaction code OBXS.

The Enter Your Chart of Accounts dialog box pops up. Enter your chart of accounts ID in the Chart of Accounts field. Confirm your entry by clicking the Enter ✅ button to proceed to the Configuration Accounting Maintain: Automatic Posts – Rules screen. Click the Account Type/Special G/L Indicator checkbox. This setting allows the system to automatically post special G/L transactions to the appropriate special G/L accounts. When you click the Save 🖫 button at the top of the screen, the Configuration Accounting Maintain: Automatic Posts – Accounts screen appears. This is where you assign the G/L accounts for the automatic offsetting postings.

Use the information in Table 16-1 to update the Account Type/Special G/L Indicator and Account fields (Figure 16-12).

Table 16-1. *List of Account Type/Special G/L indicators and Accounts*

Account Type/Sp.G/L Indicator	Account
DG Customer – Guarantee	196110
DS Customer – Check/Bill of Exchange	196210
KG Vendor – Guarantee	196410
KS Vendor – Check/Bill of Exchange	196210

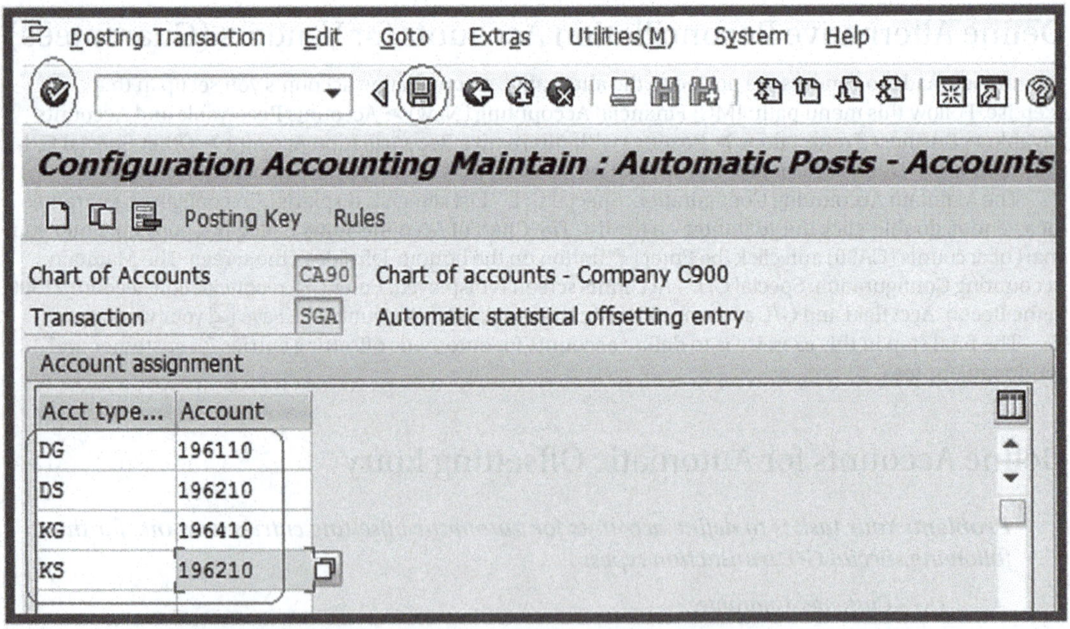

Figure 16-12. *Assigning account types to G/L accounts for automatic statistical offsetting entries*

Click the Enter ✅ button on the top-left side of the screen and save 🖫 your configuration.

Summary

This chapter looked at special G/L transactions in detail by comparing special G/L transactions with the normal G/L transactions. It explained various forms of special G/L transactions covered in SAP ERP, such as down payments, bills of exchange, and guarantees. You learned about the technical factors they belong to (noted items, free offsetting entry, and automatic offsetting entry). You also learned how to configure down payments (down payment made, down payment received, and down payment request) and how to check the properties of standard down payment settings supplied by SAP to see if they meet your requirements. You also learned how to define tax clearing accounts for down payments and learned about the specifications of the accounts special G/L transactions are posted to.

Finally, you learned what a guarantee is. You learned about alternative reconciliation accounts for customers/vendors and defined accounts for an automatic offsetting entry.

The next chapter explains how to create vendor/customer master records, post invoices and credit memos, hold and park documents, post incoming and outgoing payments, post down payments, display balance/line items, print correspondence, execute dunning notices, process manual outgoing payments/automatic payments, and perform cash journal postings.

■ ■ ■

CHAPTER 17

End User - Accounting Document Posting

This chapter explains how to enter information about business transactions in the form of documents in the user side of the system. You will see how the customizations you made in Chapters 1-16 work on the user side.

At the end of this chapter, you will be able to:

- Create a vendor/customer master record

- Post invoices

- Post credit memos

- Hold and park documents

- Post incoming and outgoing payments

- Post down payments

- Display balance/line items

- Print correspondence

- Execute dunning

- Process manual outgoing payments/automatic payments

- Perform Cash Journal postings

Customer/Vendor Master Record

In this exercise, you create some vendor/customer master records for your business partner and enter some invoices to test the settings you configured in earlier chapters.

Vendor/customer master data contains information about your business partners (customers and vendors). The information related to a vendor or a customer is stored in their individual master record. A typical vendor's master record contains the vendor's name, address, terms of payment, and so on.

Problem: *Your task is to create customer and vendor master records.*

297

Create Customer Master Record

To create a customer master record, follow this menu path: Accounting ➤ Financial Accounting ➤ Accounts Receivable ➤ Master Records ➤ Create. Or use transaction code FD01.

The Customer Create: Initial Screen is displayed. Select your Account Group (Foreign Customer – C900) in the Account Group field using the pull-down arrow. Then enter your company code (C900) in the Company Code field (Figure 17-1).

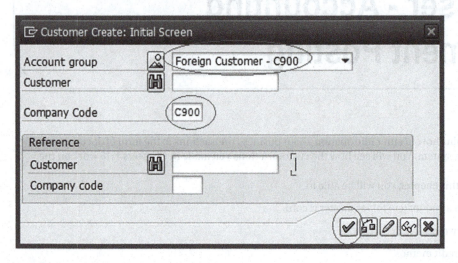

Figure 17-1. *Selecting a customer account group*

Click the ✅ Enter button on the bottom-right side of the screen. The Create Customer: General Data screen appears (Figure 17-2).

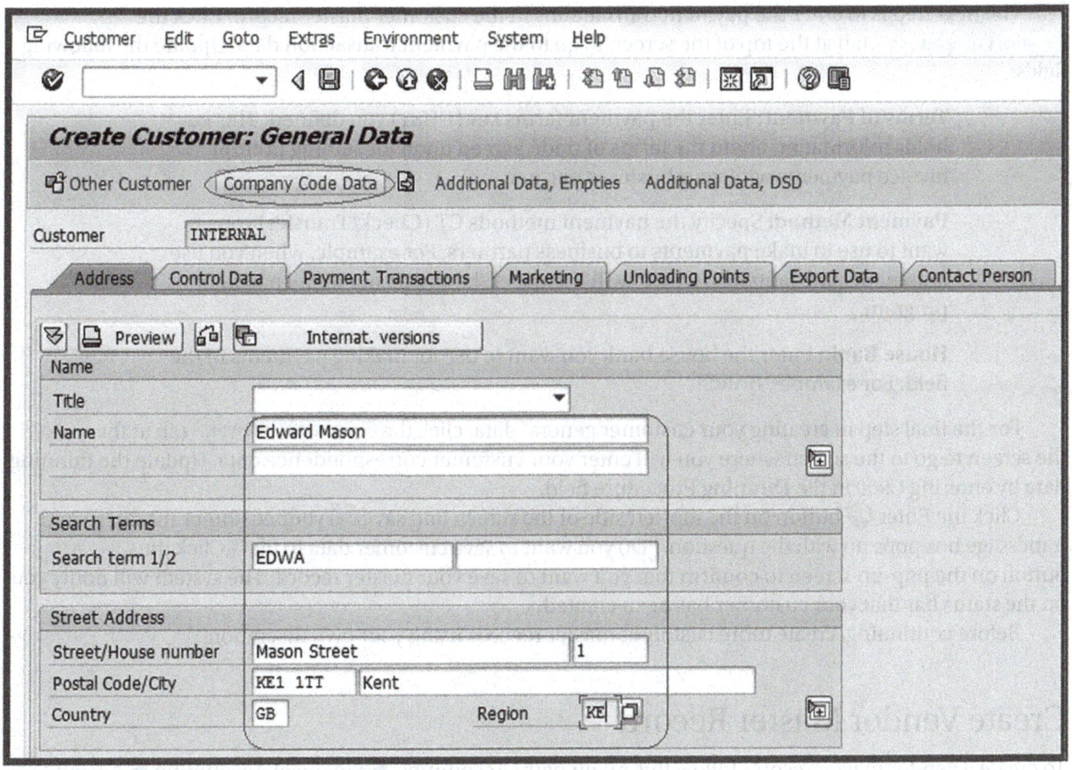

Figure 17-2. *The screen where you update the customer's address details*

Update the following fields:

> **Name:** Enter the customer's name.

> **Search Term 1/2:** Enter the search code. Preferably use part of the customer name.

> **Street Address:** Enter your customer's address in this section.

> **Specify:** Enter the GB (Great Britain) country code.

> **Region:** This is your customer's region. Enter KE (Kent) in this field.

The next step is to update the company code data. Click the `Company Code Data` button at the top of the screen. The Create Customer: Company Code Data screen is displayed. In the Account Management section of the screen, update the following fields:

> **Recon. Account:** Enter your customer reconciliation account (1190000) in this field. All postings in the subledger are automatically updated in the reconciliation account.

> **Sort Key:** Enter the sort key (01) in this field.

The next step is to enter the payment transactions in the customer master record. Click the
Payment Transactions tab at the top of the screen to go to the payment transaction data. Update the following
fields:

> **Terms of Payment:** Enter the payment terms key (CUS1) you defined. This key
> holds information about the terms of trade agreed upon for settling prompt
> invoice payments with your business partner.

> **Payment Method:** Specify the payment methods CT (Check/Transfer) you
> want to use to make payments to business partners. For example, when you use
> automatic payments, the system will use check/bank transfer in the payment
> program.

> **House Bank:** Enter the house bank you want to use for making payments in the
> field. For example, BARC1.

For the final step in creating your customer general data, click the Correspondence tab at the top of
the screen to go to the screen where you will enter your customer correspondence data. Update the dunning
data by entering C900 in the Dunning Procedure field.

Click the Enter ✅ button on the top-left side of the screen and save 💾 your customer master record.
A message box pops up with the question, "Do you want to save customer data to file?" Click the YES
button on the pop-up screen to confirm that you want to save your master record. The system will notify you
on the status bar that your customer has been created.

Before continuing, create more customer master records using your own discretion.

Create Vendor Master Record

To create a vendor master record, follow this menu path: Accounting ➤ Financial Accounting ➤ Accounts
Payable ➤ Master Records ➤ Create. Or use transaction code FK01.

The Create Vendor: Initial Screen is displayed (Figure 17-3). Enter your company code (C900) in the
Company Code field and enter the Vendor Account group (FVDR for foreign vendor) in the Account Group field.

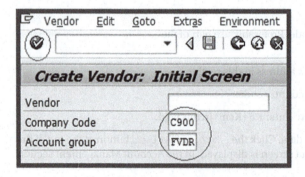

Figure 17-3. The Create Vendor Master Record initial screen

When you click Enter ✅ or press Enter on the keyboard, the Create Vendor: Address screen is displayed
(Figure 17-4). This is where you will update your vendor's address.

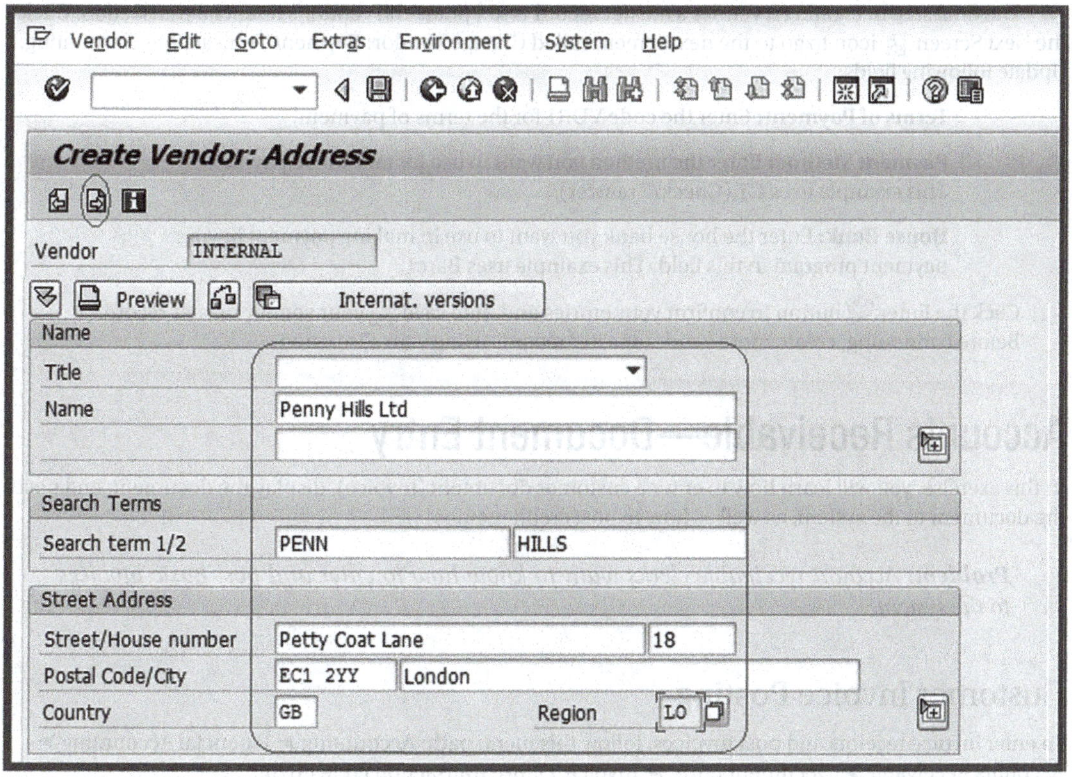

Figure 17-4. *Update the vendor's address here*

Update the following fields:

> **Name:** Enter your vendor's name in the name field.

> **Search Term 1/2:** Enter the search code. It's best to use part of the customer's name.

> **Street Address:** Enter your customer's address in this section.

> **Country:** Enter the GB (Great Britain) country code.

> **Region:** Enter Lo (London)

After updating the Create Vendor: Address screen, you need to update your vendor's accounting information. To specify your vendor's account details, click the Next Screen 🖹 button on the top-left side of the screen about four times or so until you get to the Create Vendor: Accounting Information Accounting screen. Update the following fields:

> **Recon. Account:** Enter your vendor reconciliation account (213000).

> **Sort Key:** Enter the sort key (01).

The final step in creating a vendor's master record is to update the vendor's financial transaction. Click the Next Screen ▣ icon to go to the next screen, called Change Vendor: Payment Transactions Accounting. Update following fields:

Terms of Payment: Enter the code VDR1 for the terms of payment.

Payment Method: Enter the method you want to use for automatic payment. This example uses CT (Check/Transfer).

House Bank: Enter the house bank you want to use in making payment in your payment program in this field. This example uses Barc1.

Click the Enter ✅ button to confirm your entries and then save 🖫 your vendor master record. Before continuing, create more vendor master records using your discretion.

Accounts Receivable—Document Entry

In this exercise, you will learn how to enter a customer document (invoice), display the document, and post the document to the system, as well as how to post credit memos.

> **Problem:** *Account receivable clerks want to know how to enter and post basic invoices to the system.*

Customer Invoice Posting

To enter invoice receipts and post invoices, follow this menu path: Accounting ➤ Financial Accounting ➤ Accounts Receivable ➤ Document Entry ➤ Invoice. Or use transaction code FB70.

■ **Tip** The system will normally display the last Customer Invoice Company Code screen you used for posting invoices as the default screen. To avoid posting invoices to the wrong company, make sure that the correct company code is displayed on top of the screen. Otherwise, click the Company Code button on top of the screen and enter the details. The Enter Company Code dialog box pops up. In the Company Code field, enter your company code (C900) and click the Continue ✅ button. The system will display the appropriate customer invoice screen for invoice posting.

The Enter Customer Invoice: Company Code C900 screen appears. Click the 🖳 Company Code button at the top of the screen. The Enter Company Code dialog box pops up. This screen will allow you to specify the company code you want to post invoices to. Enter your company code (C900) in the Company Code field and click the Continue ✅ button at the bottom of the screen to proceed to the screen where you will input and post the invoice, which is the Enter Customer Invoice: Company Code C900 screen (Figure 17-5). Your company code is displayed at the top of the screen.

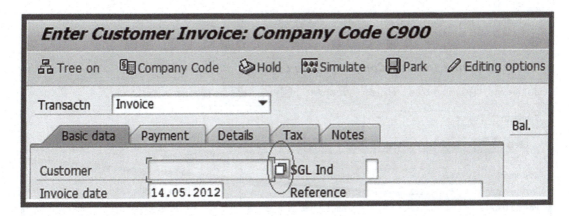

Figure 17-5. *Initial Customer Invoice Basic screen for invoice input*

Use the matchcode or the Search function □ in the Customer Field to search for the customer account you want to post invoices to. When you click the matchcode on the customer field, the Account or Matchcode for the Next Line Item (1) screen pops up. Enter your company code (C900; this is usually the default) in the Company Code field and then click the Continue ☑ button on the bottom-right side of the screen. The Account or Matchcode for the Next Line Item (1) screen is displayed (Figure 17-6).

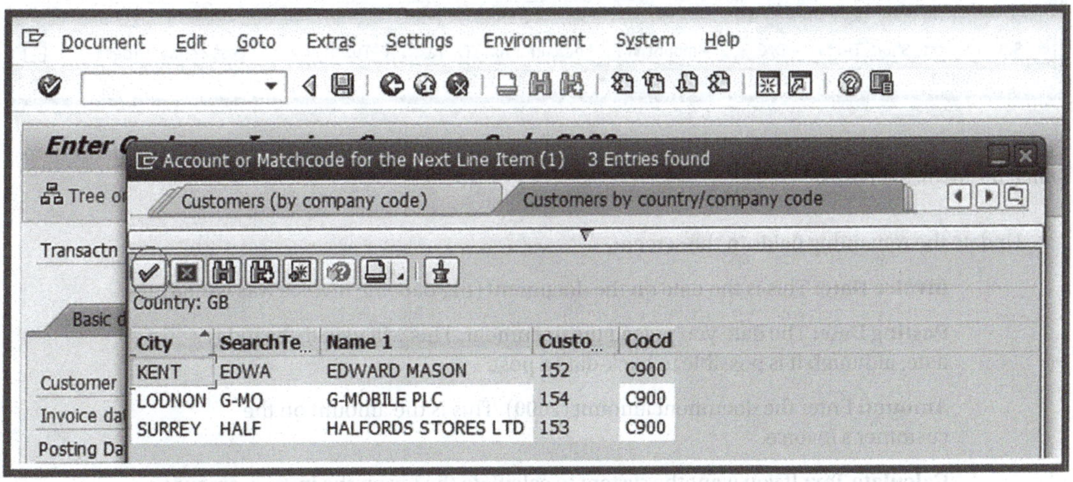

Figure 17-6. *This Account screen is displaying a list of customers for your company code*

Choose the customer whose invoice you want to process by double-clicking on it from the customer displayed list (or you can click the name and then double-click the Enter ☑ button). For example, if you click on the Customer Account Number 152 from the Customer list, that customer is entered into the Customer field (Figure 17-7).

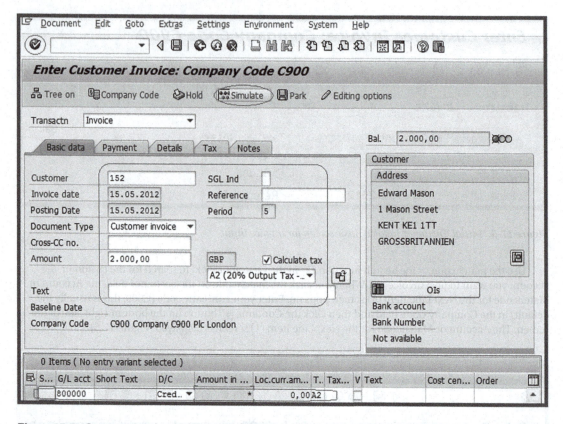

Figure 17-7. *Customer Invoice Basic screen where you enter customer invoice details and the G/L account to which the invoice is posted*

Update the remaining fields in the screen:

Invoice Date: This is the date on the document (the date the invoice was issued).

Posting Date: The date you posted the document. This will usually be today's date, although it is possible to back-date a post.

Amount: Enter the document amount (2000). This is the amount on the customer's invoice.

Calculate Tax: If you want the system to calculate the tax on the invoice amount, select the Calculate Tax checkbox. Then specify your output tax code (A2) in the field below this one. The system will apply the percentage rate assigned to this tax code and will calculate the tax amount for your invoice.

G/L Acct: Enter the G/L account (800000) where you want the invoice to be posted to.

DC: Specify the accounting treatment of the Credit or Debit transaction. This will determine how the transaction is posted in the account.

Amount in Doc. Curr.: Enter an * sign in this field. This will allow the system to automatically copy the amount in the amount field into this field. It is also possible for you to enter the invoice amount yourself. We recommend that you use the * sign in this field, because this will help you avoid entering different amounts. It's also faster when processing large volume of invoices.

Tax Code: The system will use the tax code you entered in the Calculate Tax field above in this field. Otherwise, you have to enter it yourself.

Click the Enter 🗸 button on the top-left side of the screen to confirm your entries. To display the invoice you entered for your customer, click the 🔀 Simulate button at the top of the screen. The Document Overview screen is displayed (Figure 17-8) and shows the line item of your customer invoice.

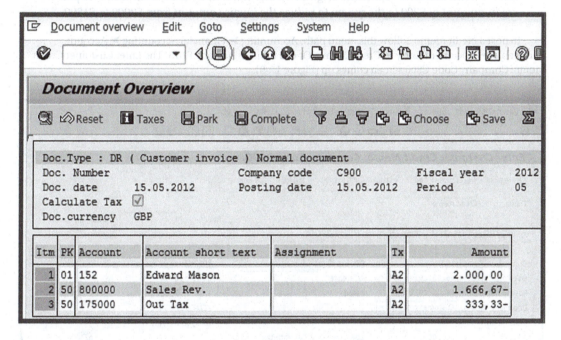

Figure 17-8. *The Document Overview screen shows the documents posted to the system*

If you are satisfied with your entries, post your entries by clicking the Post 🖫 button at the top of the screen. Upon posting/saving, the system will notify you from the status bar that your document was posted in your company code C900.

■ **Note**   When you post the customer invoice, the system will automatically debit the customer account and post the invoice amount to the credit side of the sales revenue account.

Posting a Credit Memo

A credit memo is a systematic reduction of the original invoice amount arising for a number of reasons. You might reduce an invoice because the customer was accidentally overcharged, or the product delivered was defective, or there was complaint about product delivered or service rendered, and so on.

When an invoice is posted to the system, the customer's account is debited. On the other hand, when a credit memo is posted, the customer's account is credited to reduce the account balance by the credit memo amount.

> **Problem:** *Your company invoiced a customer for the amount of $2000 for goods supplied, but they complained that the goods had light damage on transit. You have been asked to raise a credit memo to reduce the original invoice amount by $200. Your task is to post a credit amount of $200 to the system to reduce the invoice amount from $2000 to $1800.*

To post a credit memo, follow this menu path: Accounting ➤ Financial Accounting ➤ Account Receivable ➤ Document Entry ➤ Credit Memo. Or use transaction code FB75. The Enter Customer Credit Memo: Company Code C900 screen comes up (Figure 17-9).

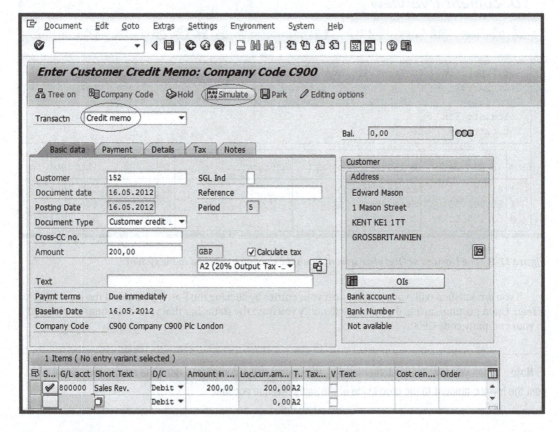

Figure 17-9. *The Customer Credit Memo screen, where you can enter a credit memo to reduce a customer's account and the G/L account against an invoice amount posted*

Update the following fields:

Transaction: This is the nature of transaction: Credit Memo. This is set by default.

Customer: Enter your customer number account (152) that you want to post credit memo to.

Document Date: This is the credit memo date.

Posting Date: The date to post the credit memo. This is usually today's date.

Amount: This is the credit memo amount (200).

Calculate Tax: Check this option to include the credit memo amount for output tax amount calculation.

G/L Acct: This is the G/L 800000 account you want to post the credit memo amount to. This will be debited against the sales revenue account and credited to the customer account to reduce the original invoice.

Short Text: This is set by default when you enter the G/L account in the G/L account field and click Enter or press Enter on your keyboard.

D/C: Specify whether the transaction should be treated as debit or credit. Since this is a customer credit memo, enter debit in this field.

Amount in Doc. Curr: Enter the credit memo amount in this field or use the * sign.

Tax: The tax code application to your credit memo is set by default by the system. Otherwise, enter it manually.

Click the Enter ✅ button on the top-left side of the screen to confirm your entries. To display the credit memo you entered, click the ⚙Simulate button at the top of the screen. The Document Overview screen is displayed (Figure 17-10) showing the line item of your customer credit memo.

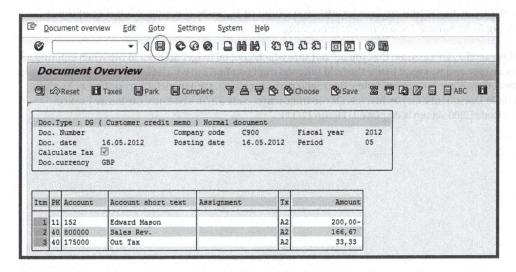

Figure 17-10. The Document Overview screen showing the credit memo posted to the system

Post your entries by clicking the Save 💾 button.

Holding and Parking Documents

During document processing, some information that's needed to complete a transaction may not be readily available. As a result, the document cannot be posted properly. The important thing about SAP is that it gives you the flexibility to save incomplete documents without performing proper FI posting. In other words, you don't have terminate your processing; you can come back later to complete the document and perform proper FI posting when you have the information required to complete the document. You can post it later without having to interrupt your document processing.

In SAP ERP, there are two ways to save an incomplete document without performing proper FI posting:

- *Holding documents*: This process allows incomplete documents to be held in the system temporarily until the document is completed. In this case, the document being held is not available for evaluation. That means no account balance is updated and no document number is assigned.

- *Parking documents*: Parked documents are just an extension of held documents. Incomplete documents can be saved temporarily for further processing at a later time. Unlike withheld documents, when a document is parked, the document is available for real-time evaluation. Like held documents, parked documents can be completed at a later time to form part of a completed financial accounting posting. Parked documents can be deleted like held documents when they are no longer required.

You can perform document parking for vendor accounts (this includes invoices and credit memos), for customer accounts (this includes invoices and credit memos), and for G/L accounts.

Holding Documents

> **Problem:** *Company C900 Plc's accounting clerks have heard of the hold document function, but they are not sure exactly how it works.*
>
> *Your task is to explain to the account clerks how to perform document holding without having to terminate the document processing.*

In this exercise, let's assume that you are not sure which general ledger account to use when entering a customer invoice and you want to use the hold function until you find out which G/L account to use. To go to the customer invoice input screen, follow this menu path: Accounting ➤ Financial Accounting ➤ Accounts Receivable ➤ Document Entry ➤ Invoice. Or use transaction code FB70. The Enter Customer Invoice: Company Code C900 screen is displayed (Figure 17-11).

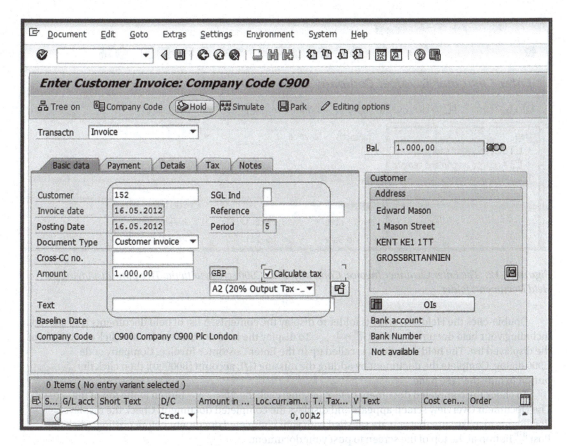

Figure 17-11. *The Customer Invoice Basic screen, where you will use the hold function*

Update the screen using the data shown in Figure 17-11. Leave the G/L account field blank and click the ⊘Hold button to temporarily hold the document until you can ascertain the proper G/L account to use. The Hold Document dialog box pops up. Enter a number such as H001 (a meaningful number of your choice that you can remember easily) in the Temporary Document Number field. This number will enable you to identify the held document among others. Click the ⊘ Hold document button on the bottom-left side of the screen. The Hold Document screen disappears and the system will notify you on the massage bar that ☑ Document H001 was held on Enter Customer Invoice: Company Code C900.

Calling Up a Held Document

Problem: *You have now obtained the right G/L account from a colleague and you want to find and open your held document to complete it and post it.*

To display the held document, click the 🔲 Tree on button on the top-left side of the Enter Customer Invoice: Company Code C900 screen. The Tree section of the screen opens on the left side. It contains a Held Documents folder (Figure 17-12).

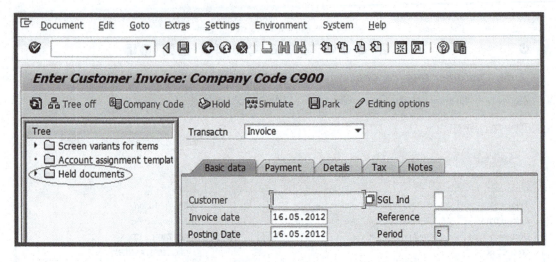

Figure 17-12. *The Enter Customer Invoice: Company Code C900 screen with the Tree pane displaying the Held Documents folder*

Double-click the Held Documents folder to display the contents. A list of held documents is displayed, including your held document, called 🖾 H001 . To display the held document, double-click on H001 from the displayed list. The held document is called up in the Enter Customer Invoice: Company code C900 dialog. Complete the document by adding the missing G/L account (800000); then click the 🔏 Tree off button to hide the Tree pane.

To check the completed document before posting, click the 🚰 Simulate button at the top of the screen. The Document Overview screen appears and displays the completed document. Check the displayed documents to make sure that you are satisfied with your completed document before posting. Click the Post 🖫 button at the top of the screen to post your document.

Parking Documents

> ***Problem:*** *An accounting clerk want to know if it is possible to park an incomplete document that will be available for real-time evaluation and come back later after obtaining the right information, all without interrupting document processing. The accounting clerk is not sure which tax code to use and wants to park the documents so he can come back later with the right tax code.*

To go to the Enter Customer Invoice: Company Code C900 screen, use this menu path: Accounting ➤ Financial Accounting ➤ Accounts Receivable ➤ Document Entry ➤ Invoice. Or use transaction code FB70. Use the information in Table 17-1 to update the screen.

Table 17-1. *The Information to Complete the Enter Customer Invoice Screen for a Parked Document*

Field	Value
Customer	Enter your customer number
Invoice Date	Today's date
Posting Date	Set by default by the system
Amount	Enter the invoice amount (4000 in this example)
G/L Account	800000
Amount in Doc. Curr	1000
Tax Code	Leave this blank

Click the 🖫 Park button at the top of the screen to park your document.
The system will notify you on the status bar that that document C90018000000082012 was parked.

■ **Tip** Take note of the parked document number. You will need it to identify your document when you want to return to it.

Parking/Editing a Document

> ***Problem:*** *Assume that tax code A2 is what you need for the parked document. Your task is to advise the accounting clerk on how to complete the parked document and post it as a complete document.*

To go to the Enter Customer Invoice: Company Code C900 screen, click the 📇 Tree on button on the top-left side of the screen. The tree section is expanded.

Click the 🗀 Parked documents folder to open it; a list of parked document numbers is displayed.

Select the appropriate parked document number (C90018000000082012 in this example) that you want to process from the list. The parked document is called up. Complete the document by updating the Tax field on the Edit Parked Customer Invoice screen. Click the 📇Simulate button on the top of the screen to display your completed document and check your entries. If you are satisfied with your entries, click the 🖫 Post button to post the completed document.

Incoming Payments

In this exercise, you learn three methods for manually posting incoming customer payments in SAP ERP:

- Posting a standard incoming payment
- Posting a partial payment
- Posting a residual item

Posting a Standard Incoming Payment

Posting a standard incoming payment is when a customer pays an outstanding invoice and you post the incoming payment and clear it against the billing document. The balancing figure in the customer account becomes nil.

> **Problem:** *A billing document of $2000 less discount of $40 was posted and the customer made payment of $1960 toward the outstanding invoice to clear the account.*

To post the incoming payment and clear it against the open items, follow this menu path: Accounting ➤ Financial Accounting ➤ Account Receivable ➤ Document Entry➤ Incoming Payment. Or use transaction code F-28. The Post Incoming Payments: Header Data screen is displayed (Figure 17-13).

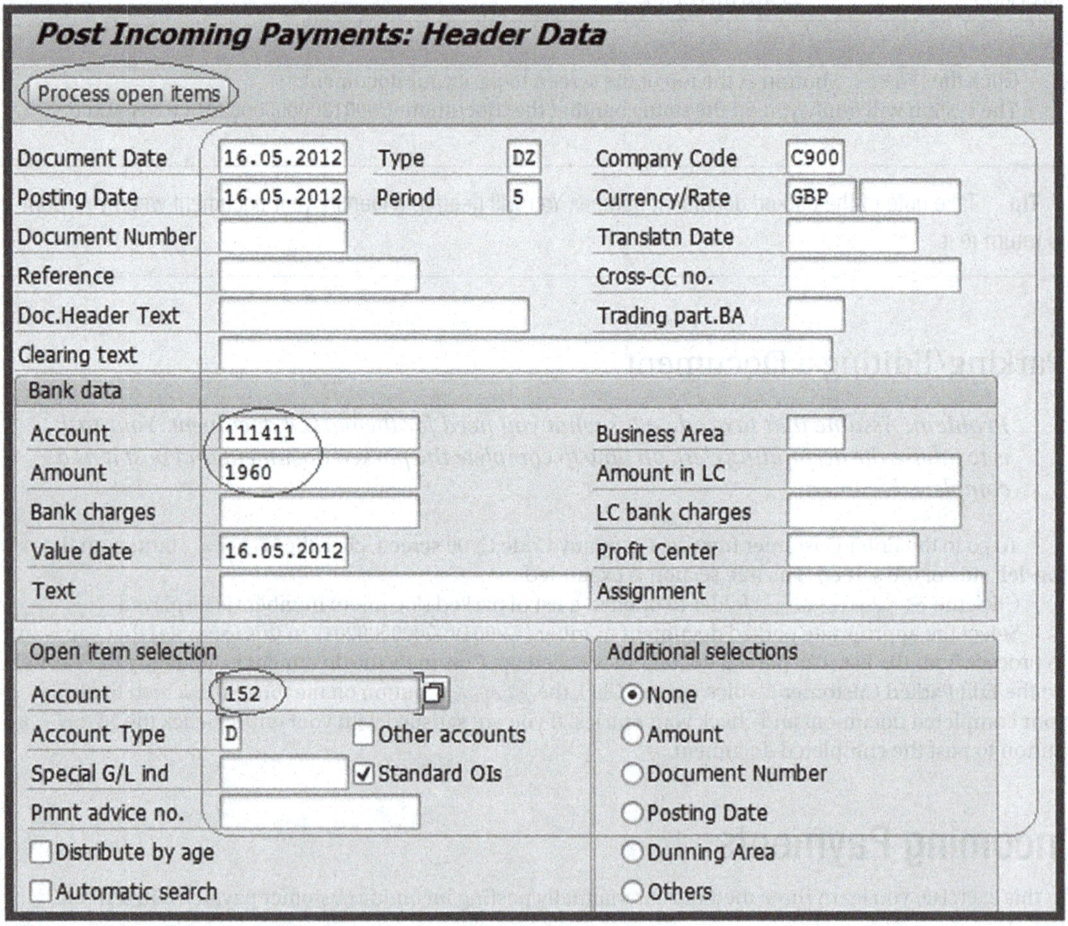

Post Incoming Payments: Header Data

(Process open items)

Document Date	16.05.2012	Type	DZ	Company Code	C900
Posting Date	16.05.2012	Period	5	Currency/Rate	GBP
Document Number				Translatn Date	
Reference				Cross-CC no.	
Doc.Header Text				Trading part.BA	
Clearing text					

Bank data

Account	111411	Business Area	
Amount	1960	Amount in LC	
Bank charges		LC bank charges	
Value date	16.05.2012	Profit Center	
Text		Assignment	

Open item selection			Additional selections
Account	152		⦿ None
Account Type	D	☐ Other accounts	○ Amount
Special G/L ind		☑ Standard OIs	○ Document Number
Pmnt advice no.			○ Posting Date
☐ Distribute by age			○ Dunning Area
☐ Automatic search			○ Others

Figure 17-13. *The screen where incoming payments are posted*

Update the following fields:

Document Date: Enter the document date. Use today's date.

Posting Date: Preferably, use today's date as your posting date.

Document Number: (optional) Enter the document number. This number is usually on top of the document.

Doc.Header Text: (optional) The text you enter in this field describes the document.

Clearing Text: (optional) The text you enter in this field provides a short description of the clearing document.

Type: The document type is set automatically by the system.

Period: This is set by default by the system. This is the accounting period derived from your fiscal year measured in months. For example, month five is displayed as period 5 by the system.

Currency/Rate: Your company code's local currency type is set by default by the system. For example, GBP (British pounds).

In the Bank Data section of the screen, update the following fields:

Account: Using the matchcode, enter the G/L account 111411 for incoming checks.

Amount: Enter the incoming payment amount of $1960.

Bank Charges: (Optional) you can enter any charges arising from bank transactions.

Value Date: This defaults to today's date. This is the number of days that have passed between the posting date of the payment run and the bank value date.

In the Open Item Selection Section of the screen, update the following fields:

Account: Using the matchcode, enter the customer account number 152.

Account Type: The system defaults account type D for customer.

To display any outstanding customer account you want to clear, click the `Process open items` button on the top-left side of the screen. The Post Incoming Payments Process Open Items screen appears (Figure 17-14). This is where you clear incoming payments against outstanding invoices.

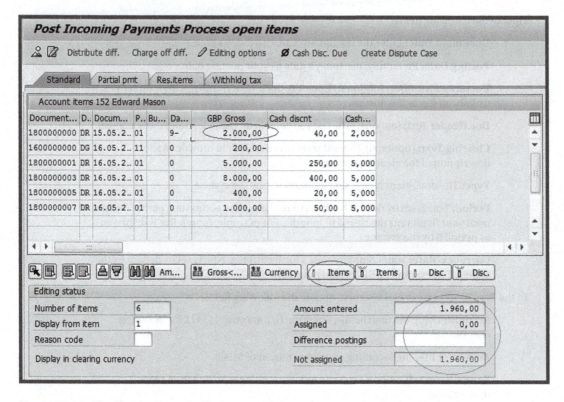

Figure 17-14. *The Clearing Incoming Payments with Open Items screen*

The open items on the customer account are displayed. Notice that the amount balances are activated (blue). Since the payment received is only for an item on the account and not the entire open item balance, you must deactivate all the activated items. To deactivate the activated items, click the Click the Select All button below the Account items on the left side of the screen to select all the displayed open items on the account. Click the Deactivate [Items] button to deactivate all the activated open items. All the open items will turn black to indicate they are deactivated.

To process the open items you will now have to activate the line item that you want to clear with the incoming payment. Click the line item that you want to clear—2000—(this is the first item on the account item on the screen). Notice that the Amount Entered and Not Assigned fields on the bottom-right side of the screen in **Editing Status** section below the account item have reduced to 1960 and the Assigned field is now zero. The reduction in the entered amount is due to the discount offered to the customer as part of terms of payment.

Click the Activate [Items] button to activate the line item that you want to use to clear the incoming payment. The Amount Entered and Assigned fields show the amount you are clearing, and the Not Assigned field is set to zero (Figure 17-15).

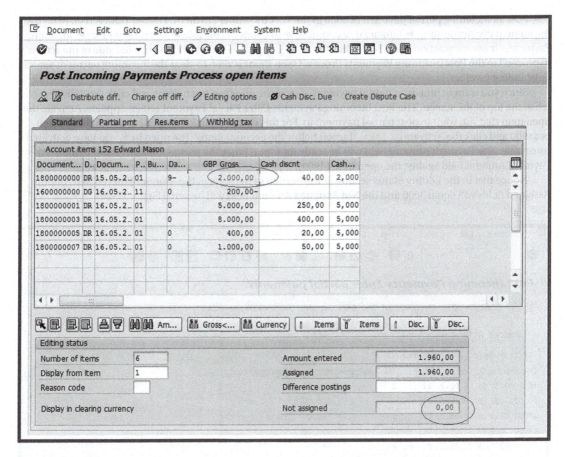

Figure 17-15. *The Posting Incoming Payment Processing Open Items screen shows the amount entered against a payment*

To display the open item you want to clear with the incoming payment, click the [Document] button on the menu bar and then click [Simulate] from the pull-down menu. The Post Incoming Payments Display Overview screen is displayed.

If you're satisfied with your payment clearing, click the Post 💾 button to automatically clear the open item. After you click the Post button, the system will notify you that [✓ Document 1400000000 was posted in company code C900].

Now let's look at how a partial payment is treated.

Posting a Partial Payment

Partial payment is when you make an incomplete payment toward an outstanding amount or open item. In other words, only a fraction of the outstanding amount has been settled. In SAP, partial payments are treated differently from standard payments. Since the outstanding amount is not settled in full, it is treated as payment on account (i.e., both the open item and partial payment remain open in the account).

Problem: *Assume that you have an open item of $4900 and you receive a partial payment of $3000.*

Post an incoming partial payment of 3000 in the Post Incoming Payment: Header Data screen using the menu path: Accounting ➤ Financial Accounting ➤ Account Receivable ➤ Document Entry➤ Incoming Payment. Or use transaction code F-28. Click the `Process open items` button on the top-left side of the screen to proceed to the Post Incoming Payments Process Open Items screen to clear the incoming payment against outstanding invoices.

Since you want to process a partial payment, deactivate all active open items and click the `Partial pmt` tab at the top of the screen. The Post Incoming Payments Enter Partial Payment screen appears. Activate the open item that you want to post partial payment to. For this exercise, click the open item with the amount of $4900 and click the Activate `Items` button below the account items. The open item you have activated turns blue. The Payment Amount field will be ready for input. Enter the partial amount (3000) in the Payment Amount field against the open item (4900).

Notice that in the Editing Status section at the bottom of the screen, the Amount Entered and Amount Assigned fields will equal 3000 and the Not Assigned Amount field will be zero (Figure 17-16).

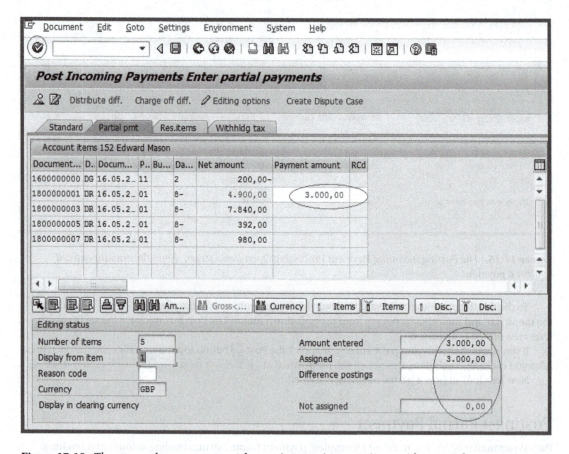

Figure 17-16. *The screen where you post match open item against open items with a partial payment*

Click the Post 🖫 button.

Now let's look at how residual items are treated.

Posting Residual Items

Residual items arise when you are prepared to receive payment less than the original invoice amount as final settlement of an open item.

■ **Note** When posting residual items, you must specify a reason code. The reason code contains the reason for the reduction in incoming payment as compared to the original billing document.

> **Problem:** *Assume that Company C900 Plc has agreed with a business partner to accept $10,000 as full settlement for an invoice of $12,000 due to slight damage in goods during transit. Therefore, your residual item amount is $1760 ($12,000 less discount of $240 = $11,760 less $10,000).*

Post an incoming payment of $10,000 from the Post Incoming Payment: Header Data screen using this menu path: Accounting ➤ Financial Accounting ➤ Account Receivable ➤ Document Entry ➤ Incoming Payment. Or use transaction code F-28. Click the [Process open items] button on the top-left side of the screen to proceed to the Post Incoming Payments Process Open Items screen. Since you want to process residual items, deactivate all the open items that are activated and click the [Res.items] tab on the top of the screen. The Post Incoming Payments Create residual items screen appears displaying the open items on the account (Figure 17-17).

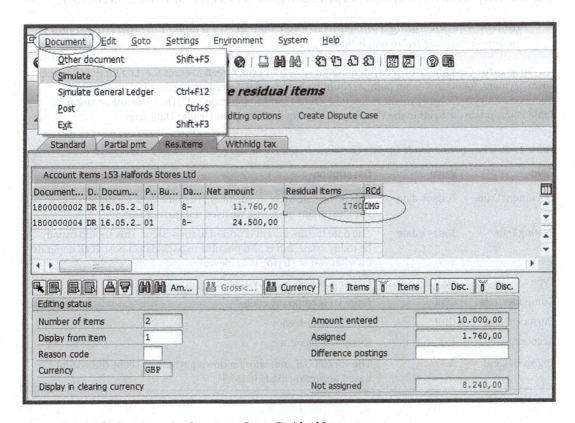

Figure 17-17. The Post Incoming Payments: Create Residual Items screen

Activate the open item from which you want to create a residual item. For this exercise, click the open item with the amount of $11,760 ($12,000 less the cash discount of $240) to select it for activation and then click the Activate ⌊⁏ Items⌋ button below account items. The open item you have activated turns blue, indicating that the item is activated. The Residual Item and RCd (Reason code) fields are ready for input. Enter the residual item 1760 in the Residual Item field and then enter the Reason Code DMG in the RCd field. You can access the reason code using the matchcode by the RCd field.

Notice that in the Editing Status section, the Amount Entered field is $10,000 (less the residual amount of $2,000) and Amount Assigned field is $1760 ($2000 less the cash discount of $240).

To check the residual item you have processed, click the ⌊ Document ⌋ button on the menu bar and then click ⌊ Simulate ⌋. The payment overview shows your entries. Click the Post ⌊▣⌋ button on the top of the screen to post your entries. The system will notify you that ⌊☑ Document 1400000002 was posted in company code C900⌋.

Customer Down Payments

In this exercise, you learn how to post customer down payment requests, post customer down payments, and clear customer down payments.

Posting a Customer Down Payment Request

It is a normal business practice to request an advance payment from a customer once an order is placed, prior to delivery. This is referred to as down payment request. Let's see how this is represented in SAP.

> **Problem:** *The accounting team wants to know how to post a down payment request and you have been assigned to teach them.*

To go to the Customer Down Payment Request Header Data screen to enter the data for the customer down payment, follow this menu path: Accounting ➤ Financial Accounting ➤ Account receivable ➤ Document Entry ➤ Down Payment ➤ Request. Or use transaction code F-37. Using the information in Table 17-2, update the fields in the Customer Down Payment Request Header Data screen.

Table 17-2. *The Information to Update Customer Down Payment Request Header Data Screen*

Field	Value	Description
Document Date	Today's date	This is the date on your document (invoice) you are processing. For illustration purposes, we used the current date.
Posting Date	Today's date	The date the document is posted to the system. This should usually be today's date, but is also possible to back-date a post. It all depends on what you are trying to achieve.
Type	DZ	Document type is set by default.
Company Code	C900	Enter your company code.
Currency/Rate	GBP	Document currency
Account	152	Customer account
Teg.sp.G/L ind.	A	The special G/L indicator for down payment is set by the system based on setting made in IMG.

Click the New item button on the top-left side of the screen to proceed to the Customer Down Payment Request Add Customer Item screen to complete your down payment request data input. Using the information in Table 17-3, update the fields.

Table 17-3. *The Information to Add Customer Items to the Customer Down Payment Request*

Field	Value	Description
Amount	5000	Down payment request you made to your customer.
Calculate Tax	Select	Click the Calculate Tax checkbox to have the system calculate the tax amount.
Tax Code	A2	This tax code holds the percentage rate for the output tax that will be used by the system to the calculate tax amount.
Due date	Future date	This is the date the down payment request is due (for illustration purposes, enter any date after the current date).

Click Enter ✅ on the top-left side the screen to confirm your entries and then click the Overview 👤 button to display your down payment request. The Down Payment Request Display Overview screen appears containing a one-line item for your customer down payment request. If you are satisfied with your down payment request entries, click Post 💾 to post your down payment request.

■ **Note** A down payment request is a noted item and consequently does not impact the G/L. No posting is made to the G/L. Noted items are for information purposes only. Hence, the one-line item display on the Down Payment Request Display Overview screen.

Posting Customer Down Payments

Customer down payments are payments received in advance and in anticipation of providing goods or rendering services to a business partner. To go to the down payment screen, follow this menu path: Easy: Financial Accounting ➤ Account receivable ➤ Document Entry ➤ Down Payment ➤ Down Payment. Or use transaction code F-29.

The Post Customer Down Payment: Header Data screen is displayed. Update the screen using the data in Figure 17-18.

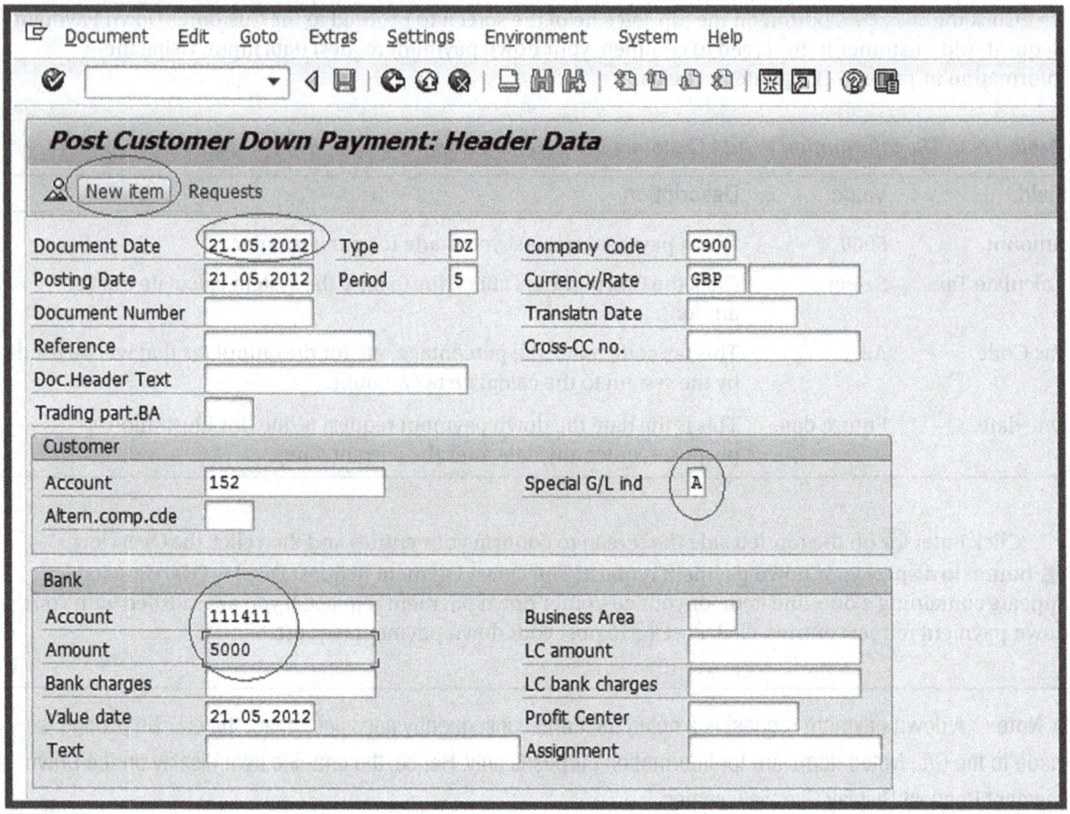

Figure 17-18. *The screen where you enter the header data for the down payment*

Click the [New item] button to proceed to the Post Customer Down Payment Added Customer Item screen, where you enter data for your down payment. Use the data in Table 17-4 to update the fields on the screen.

Table 17-4. *The Data to Update Additional Customer Items for Down Payment*

Field	Value	Description
Amount	5000	Enter the down payment document amount in this field.
Tax Code	A2	This is your tax code for output tax.
Calculate Tax	Select	Click this checkbox to allow the system to automatically calculate output tax amount for your down payment.

Click the Overview ⚏ button to go to the Post Customer Down payment Display Overview screen. This screen will show the down payment line items. Post 🖫 your down payment.

■ **Note** The down payment received is an example of a free offsetting entry. Free offsetting entries allow proper posting in the general ledger. The special G/L reconciliation account is automatically debited or credited.

Clearing Customer Down Payments

Problem: *The finance team heard that it is possible to clear down payment requests with a down payment received. You have been asked to demonstrate how this is done.*

To go to the Clear Customer Down Payment: Header Data screen (Figure 17-19) to carry out down payment clearing, follow this menu path: Financial Accounting ➤ Account receivable ➤ Document Entry ➤ Down Payment ➤ Clearing. Or use transaction code F-39.

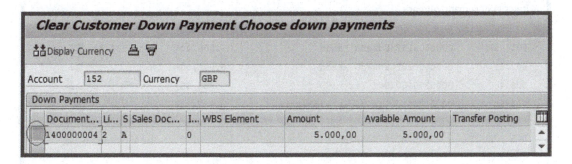

Figure 17-19. Clearing a down payment request with a down payment received

Update the following fields:

Document Date: Use today's date.

Posting Date: This date is set by the system. This usually defaults to today's date.

Account: Enter your customer account number (152) that the down payment relates to.

Invoice Ref.: Make sure that the invoice reference is blank, because the system will default to the last document number.

Fiscal Year: This is your company code accounting year. This is set by default by the system.

Click Enter ✅ on the top-left side of the screen to confirm your entries, and then click the ⌞ Process down pmnts ⌝ button on the top-left side of the screen. The Clear Customer Down Payment Choose Down Payments screen appears, where you clear with the down payment request with down payment received (see Figure 17-19).

Select the down payment line item you want to clear with this down payment request. Then, on the menu bar, click ⌞ Document ⌝ and then click ⌞ Simulate ⌝. The Clear Customer Down Payment Display Overview screen (Figure 17-20) is displayed showing the breakdown of the down payment clearing.

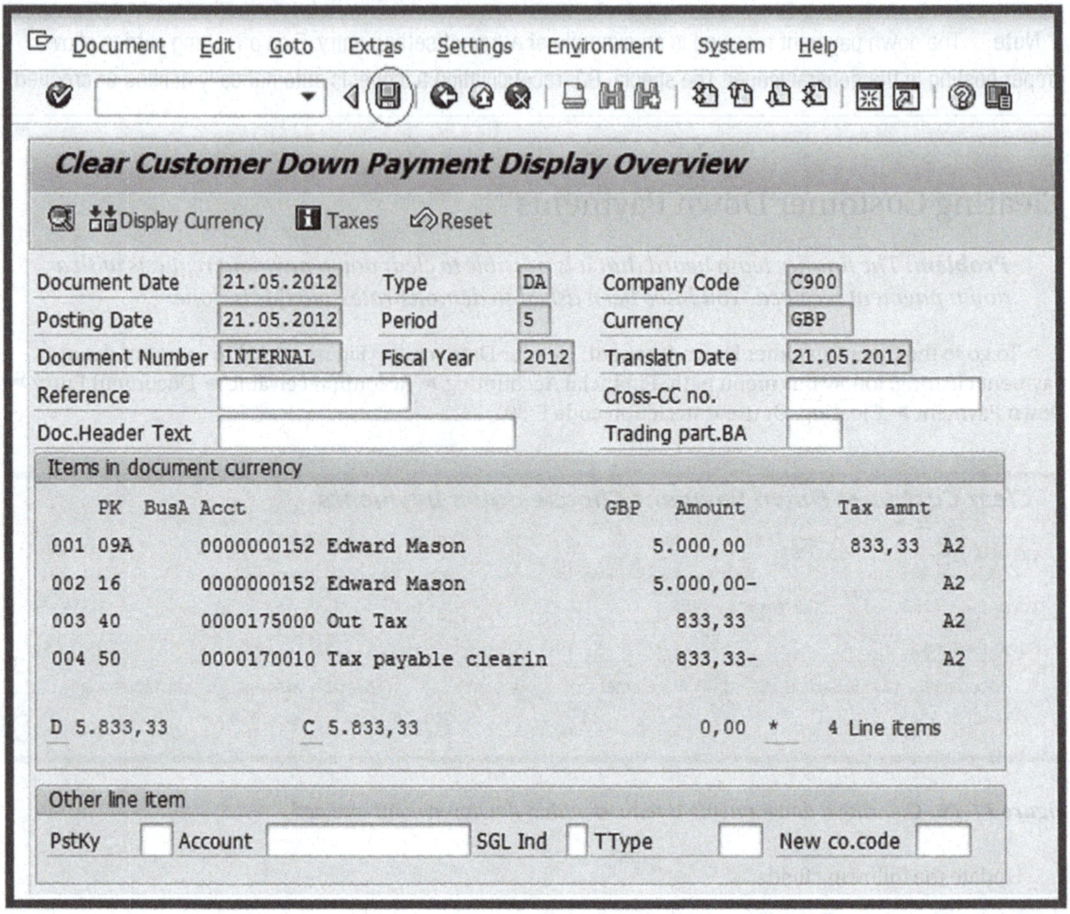

Figure 17-20. *The Down Payment Overview screen shows the down payment request clearing with the down payment received*

Click the Post 🖫 button.

■ **Note** When you post the customer down payment, the system will automatically clear the down payment request made against the down payment received. During this process, the down payment request is cancelled.

Display Account Balances

In this exercise, you learn how to display the balance of the following account types:

- Customer accounts
- Vendor accounts
- G/L accounts

■ **Note**   In order for the system to display an account balance, you must set the account indicator called Open Item Management in the account's master data.

> *Problem: A new finance staff member wants to display a customer account balance and wants to display line items. He has approached you as the SAP consultant to take him through the steps involved.*

Display Customer Account Balances

This exercise will allow you to display the account balances of customers. To display balances, follow this menu path: Accounting ➤ Financial Accounting ➤ Account Receivable ➤ Account ➤ Display Balances. Or use transaction code FD10N.

The Customer Balance Display screen is displayed. Update the following fields:

> **Customer:** Enter the customer account number that you want to display. If you are not sure of the customer account number, you can use the matchcode function to search for your customer.

> **Company Code:** Enter the company code the customer belongs to.

> **Fiscal Year:** Enter your company code accounting year related to the customer transactions.

Click the Execute button ⊕ on the top-left side of the screen to go to the Customer Balance Display screen. It shows your customer account balance (Figure 17-21).

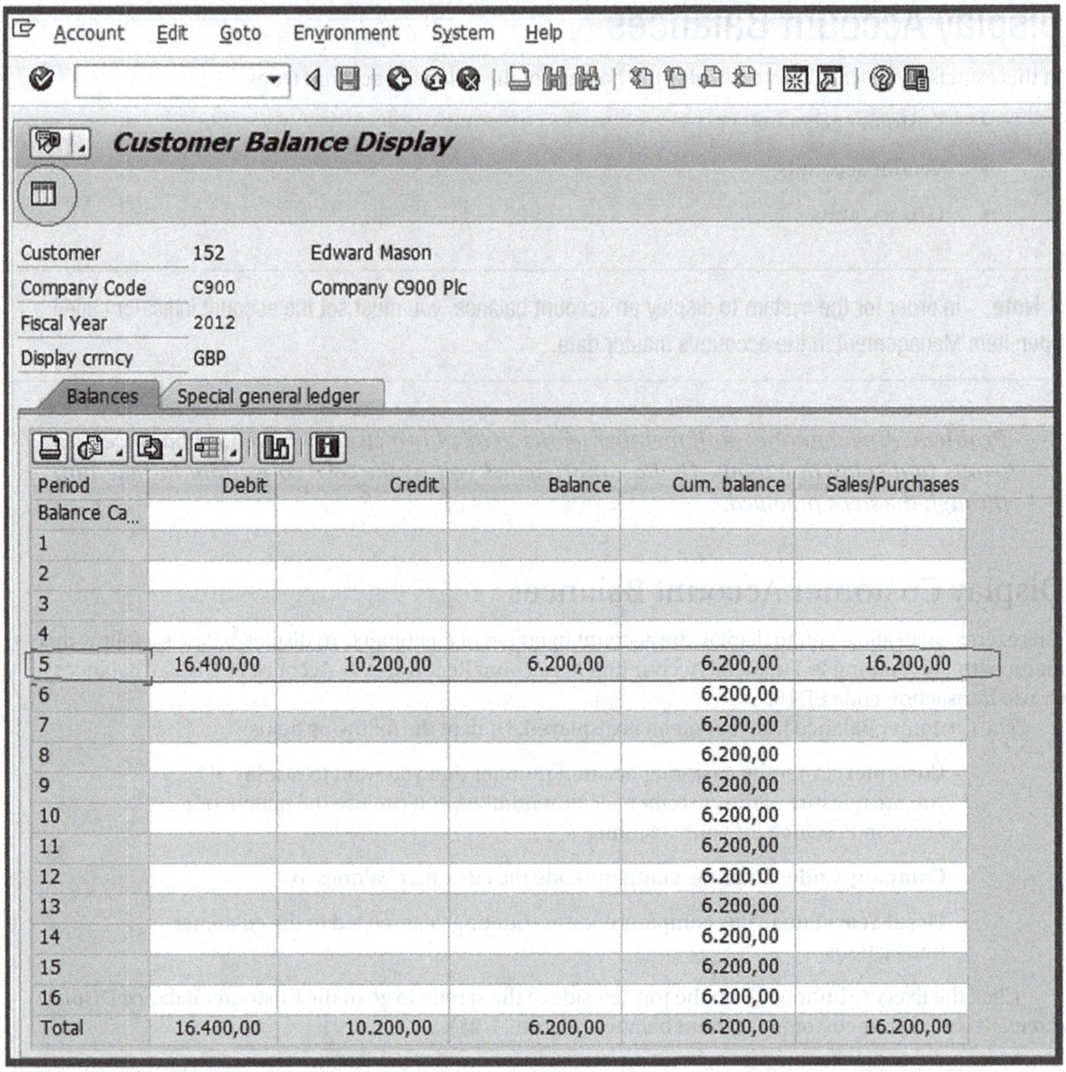

Figure 17-21. *The Customer Account Balance Display screen shows the account balance of the customer you specified*

It is also possible to display line items or a particular document directly from this report. To do this, select any period from the list of balances by clicking on the balance you want to display. For this exercise, we are using period five (circled in Figure 17-21) to illustrate how to display the customer line item. Select period five's balance from the list of balances and click the Call Up Line Item Report ▦ button (this button will allow you to display the customer line item) on the top-left side of the screen. Alternatively, you can double-click on the balance you want to display. The Customer Line Item Display (Figure 17-22) displays all the line items.

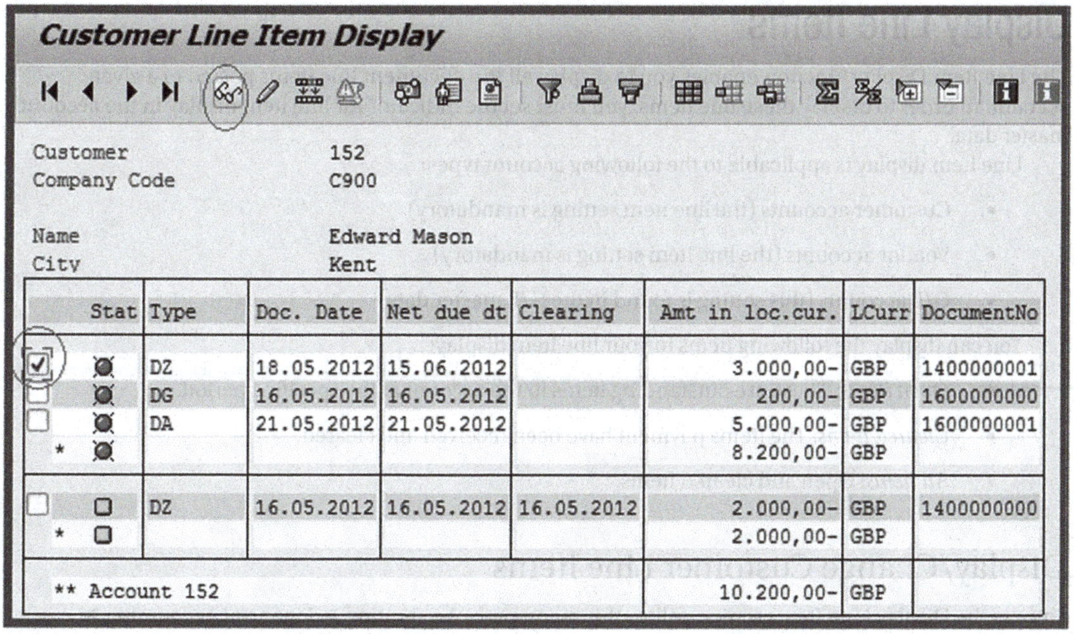

Customer Line Item Display

	Stat	Type	Doc. Date	Net due dt	Clearing	Amt in loc.cur.	LCurr	DocumentNo
☑	⊗	DZ	18.05.2012	15.06.2012		3.000,00-	GBP	1400000001
☐	⊗	DG	16.05.2012	16.05.2012		200,00-	GBP	1600000000
☐	⊗	DA	21.05.2012	21.05.2012		5.000,00-	GBP	1600000001
*	⊗					8.200,00-	GBP	
☐	☐	DZ	16.05.2012	16.05.2012	16.05.2012	2.000,00-	GBP	1400000000
*	☐					2.000,00-	GBP	
**	Account 152					10.200,00-	GBP	

Customer 152
Company Code C900

Name Edward Mason
City Kent

Figure 17-22. The Customer Line Item Display screen

■ **Note** The drawback to displaying a line item using the Customer Balance Display is that it does not give you the flexibility to define your line item display criteria.

It is possible for you to make some changes in a document displayed in the line item on the screen (Figure 17-22). To do this, select the document you want to make changes to (circled) and click the Display Document 🗀 button at the top left of the screen. The ***Display Document: Line Item 1*** screen is displayed. Click the Change Display ✏ button at the top of the screen. The ***Change Document: Line Item 1*** screen is displayed. This is the screen where you can make changes to your document. After making the appropriate changes, save 🖫 your work.

■ **Note** You can only make minimum changes in certain fields, for example, the Assignment and Text fields. It is also possible to change the discount/payment terms, as well as the payment block and dunning block.

Display Line Items

The Line Item Display function enables you to display all the document line items posted to a given account. In order to display these line items, you must set the indicator for line item display in the account's master data.

Line item display is applicable to the following account types:

- Customer accounts (the line item setting is mandatory)

- Vendor accounts (the line item setting is mandatory)

- G/L accounts (this setting is found in the G/L master data)

You can display the following items in your line item display:

- *Open items*: These are outstanding items in the account at the specified period.

- *Cleared items*: The items payment have been received and cleared.

- *All items*: Open and cleared items.

Display/Change Customer Line Items

To go to the Display Line Items screen, follow this menu path: Accounting ➤ Financial Accounting ➤ Account Receivable ➤ Account ➤ Display/Change Line Items. Or use transaction code FBL5N.

Using the information in Table 17-5, update the Customer Line Item Display screen.

Table 17-5. *The Fields to Update for Line Items Display*

Field	Value	Description
Customer Account	152	Enter the Customer Account number that you want to display line items for. You can display single or multiple customer line items by entering the appropriate customer number(s) in this filed. You can access the customer number using the matchcode by the customer account field.
Company Code	C900	Enter your company code in this field. It is also possible to include a single or multiple company code in your line item display.
Open items	Select	You have the option to display open or cleared items separately by selecting the appropriate radio button. It is also possible to display all items (both open and cleared items simultaneously) by clicking the All Items radio button.

Click Enter ✅ and then click the Execute ⊕ button on the top-left side of the screen. The system will display the line items for open items, depending on your selection (Figure 17-23).

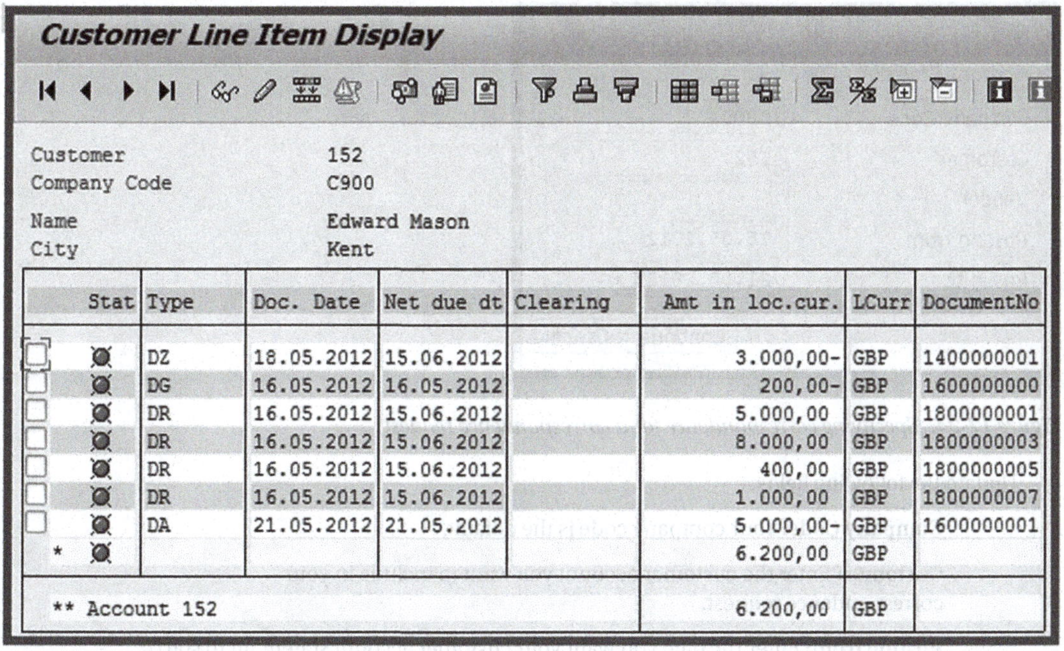

Customer Line Item Display

	Stat	Type	Doc. Date	Net due dt	Clearing	Amt in loc.cur.	LCurr	DocumentNo

Customer 152
Company Code C900

Name Edward Mason
City Kent

	Stat	Type	Doc. Date	Net due dt	Clearing	Amt in loc.cur.	LCurr	DocumentNo
☐	⚙	DZ	18.05.2012	15.06.2012		3.000,00-	GBP	1400000001
☐	⚙	DG	16.05.2012	16.05.2012		200,00-	GBP	1600000000
☐	⚙	DR	16.05.2012	15.06.2012		5.000,00	GBP	1800000001
☐	⚙	DR	16.05.2012	15.06.2012		8.000,00	GBP	1800000003
☐	⚙	DR	16.05.2012	15.06.2012		400,00	GBP	1800000005
☐	⚙	DR	16.05.2012	15.06.2012		1.000,00	GBP	1800000007
☐	⚙	DA	21.05.2012	21.05.2012		5.000,00-	GBP	1600000001
*	⚙					6.200,00	GBP	
** Account 152						6.200,00	GBP	

Figure 17-23. The selected customer line item display

Correspondence

In this exercise, you learn how to generate and output correspondence requests for individual customers by using print reports. To print correspondence, you must first request correspondence by specifying the correspondence type for the company code. SAP comes with predefined correspondence types. For this exercise, we will request an account statement. Once the correspondence is generated, the correspondence requests are deleted. For pending correspondence requests, the print program is scheduled daily.

Request Correspondence

To request correspondence, follow this menu path: Accounting ➤ Financial Accounting ➤ Account receivable ➤ Account ➤ Correspondence ➤ Request. Or use transaction code FB12.

The Request Correspondence screen is displayed. Enter your company code in the company code field (C900) and click the Enter ⚙ button on top of the screen or press the Enter button on the keyboard. The Correspondence Selection screen with list of correspondence types appears. In this exercise, you will be looking at how correspondence requests for customers' account statements are carried out. Therefore, select the **SAP06**-Account Statement type from the displayed account list and click ✔ on the top-left side of the screen. The Detail Specifications for Correspondence screen pops up (Figure 17-24).

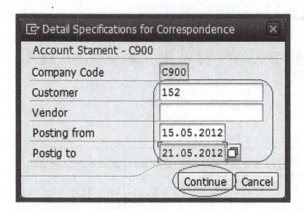

Figure 17-24. *Specifying correspondence for a correspondence request*

Update the following fields:

Company Code: Your company code is the default.

Customer: Enter the customer account you want to include in your correspondence request.

Posting from: Enter the date you want your customer account statement to start from in this field.

Posting to: Enter the date you want your customer account statement to end.

Click the `Continue` button. Then click the Enter button. The system will display the `☑ Account Stament - C900 was requested` message on the message bar.

After completing the correspondence request, you can go on to perform print correspondence.

Print Correspondence

To print correspondence, follow this menu path: Accounting ➤ Financial Accounting ➤ Account Receivable ➤ Periodic Processing ➤ Print Correspondence ➤ As Per Requests. Or use transaction code F.61.

The Trigger for Correspondence screen is displayed. Update the fields using the information in Table 17-6.

Table 17-6. *Data to Update the Trigger for Correspondence Screen*

Field	Value	Description
Correspondence	ACS1	Enter the corresponded type for the Account Statement identifier. It is also possible to search for the appropriate correspondence type, by using the Search icon by the field if you are not sure of the appropriate correspondence number. If you want to generate more than one correspondence type, you can do so by specifying the correspondence type range.
Company Code	C900	Enter your company code. It is also possible to generate and print correspondence for a range of company codes. To do this, you have to specify the company code range. This is possible when you have more than one company code.
Account Type	D	Specify the appropriate account type.

Click the Execute ⊕ button on the top-left side of the screen to print the correspondence. The Information screen pops up with the message, "1 correspondence requests carried out were deleted". Confirm the deletion by clicking the Confirm ✔ button on the bottom-right side of the screen. The Correspondence Requests screen pops up with the message, "A correspondence request was selected," and the question, "Would you like to issue the request?" Click the ⌊ Yes ⌋ button on the bottom-left side of the pop-up screen to confirm that you want to issue this correspondence request. The Output Parameter dialog box pops up. Enter your output print device (LP01) in the Output Device field and click the ⌊ Continue ⌋ button to confirm. The Trigger for Correspondence Log is displayed (Figure 17-25).

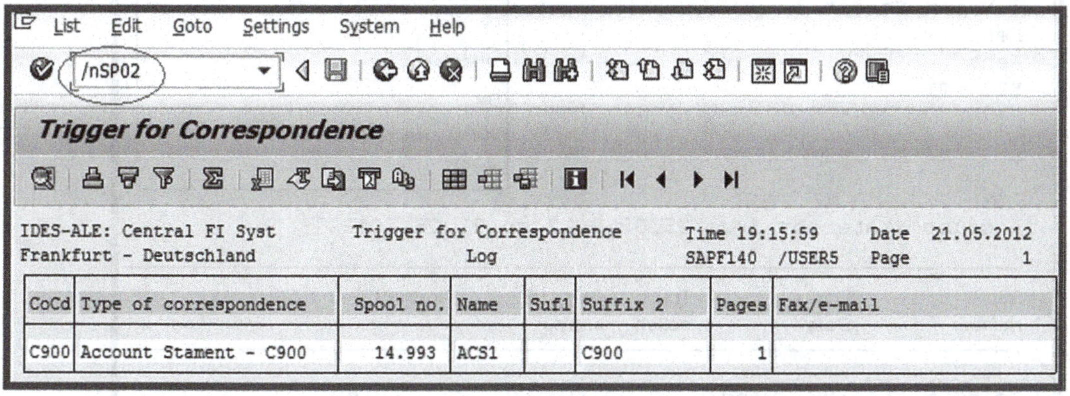

	List	Edit	Goto	Settings	System	Help

Trigger for Correspondence

IDES-ALE: Central FI Syst	Trigger for Correspondence	Time 19:15:59	Date 21.05.2012
Frankfurt - Deutschland	Log	SAPF140 /USER5	Page 1

CoCd	Type of correspondence	Spool no.	Name	Suf1	Suffix 2	Pages	Fax/e-mail
C900	Account Stament - C900	14.993	ACS1		C900	1	

Figure 17-25. The Trigger for Correspondence screen shows the account statement for your company code

To display a list of spool requests (the documents marked for the print function but not yet output to a printer or to another output device) for the account statement you have just completed, type **/nSP02** in the Command Field at the top of the screen and press Enter on your keyboard. The Output Controller: List of Spool Requests screen is displayed.

To display the printout preview, select the appropriate item from the list of spool requests by making sure that the Spool No checkbox is clicked. For this exercise, click the checkbox for spool number 14993 (the spool number we use here is for illustration only; it is not a standard spool number. Spool numbers vary depending on the current spool number used by the system). Click on the Display Contents 🔍 button at the top of the screen to display the print preview for your customer account statement (Figure 17-26).

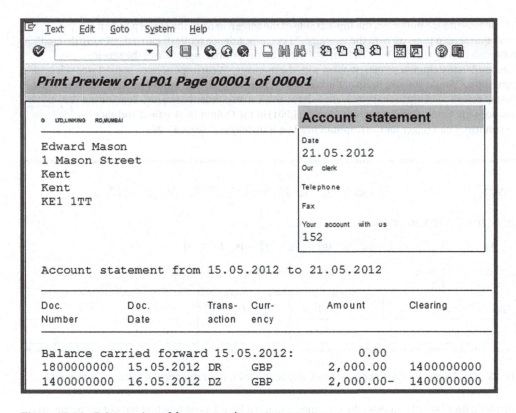

Figure 17-26. *Print preview of the customer's account statement*

To print the account statement, click the Back ⮌ button to return to the previous screen (Figure 17-27).

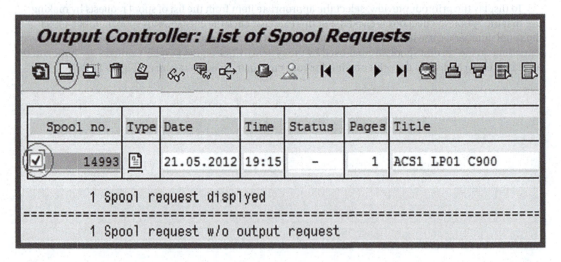

Figure 17-27. *The spool requests for printing*

Click the Print button 🖶 at the top of the screen. The system will notify you that ☑ Output requests created.

Execute Dunning

Dunning is the systematic process of communicating with customers to ensure adequate collection of account receivables due. The system sends reminder letters to customers about their account being due for payment. Communication through the dunning process starts with a gentle reminder and gradually escalates as an account becomes more overdue.

Problem: *Your team leader sent you a memo asking that you generate dunning for customers with outstanding balances outside the agreed credit period.*

To execute the dunning program, follow this menu path: Accounting ➤ Financial Accounting ➤ Account Receivable ➤ Periodic Processing ➤ Dunning ➤ Execute Dunning. Or use transaction code F150.

■ **Tip**   Before you start with dunning, post some back-dated invoices. Use last month's dates. This will enable you to see how dunning works in practice.

The Dunning screen is displayed. Update the fields using the data in Table 17-7.

Table 17-7. *Data for the Dunning Screen*

Field	Value	Description
Run On	Use today's date (in this example, it's 21.05.2012)	This is the date you want to run your dunning program. We advise you to use the current date.
Identification	C900	This will you enable to identify your dunning notice, especially when more than one dunning run is performed on the same date. We recommend that you use any suitable identification key. The company code is ideal.

Click the Parameter tab at the top of the screen to go to the parameter section of the Dunning Parameter screen. On this screen you will define the exact parameters for the document and the business partner you want to include in your dunning run.

Update the fields using the information in Table 17-8.

Table 17-8. *The Data for Dunning Parameter Specification*

Field	Value	Description
Dunning Date	Today's date	The date you want the dunning to be performed.
Document Post Up To	Today's date	This field will allow you to select a range of documents up to an earlier given period.
Company Code	C900	Enter your company code. It is also possible to generate dunning for a range of company codes or multiple company codes by specifying the appropriate company code's range.
Customer	152	Likewise, you can run dunning for a single business partner or multiple business partners.

Click the ⟨Status⟩ tab at the top of the screen to return to the Status part of the screen. The system will prompt you to save your parameter. Click the ⟨Yes⟩ button on the bottom-left side of the screen to save your parameter specifications. On the Dunning screen, notice that the status of your dunning run so far will be displayed in the status section of the screen as "Parameters Were Maintained" (Figure 17-28).

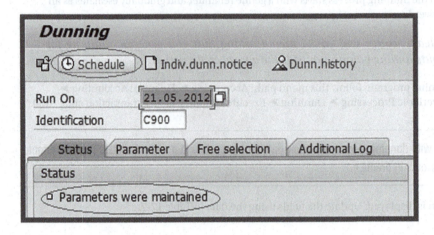

Figure 17-28. *The screen where you maintain the dunning parameters*

Click the ⟨🕒 Schedule⟩ button on the top-left side of the screen to schedule your dunning print program. The Output Parameter dialog box pops up. Enter your output print device (LP01) in the Output Device field and click the ⟨Continue⟩ button on the bottom-right side of the screen. Once you click the Continue button, this will allow you specify your output device that you want to send your dunning to (in this case, to a printer). The Schedule Selection and Print screen pops up (Figure 17-29). The system automatically defaults to the start date, start time, and output device that you specified previously. Click the Start Immediately and Dunn.Print With Scheduling? checkboxes. By clicking Start Immediately, you are instructing the system to output your dunning run immediately.

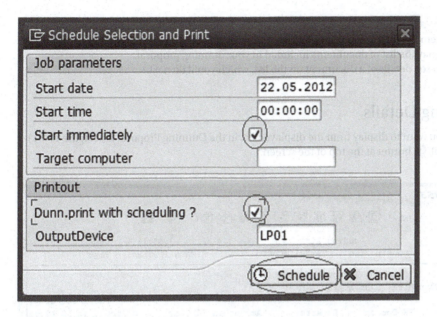

Figure 17-29. *Specifying the dunning print with scheduling options*

Then click the ⏱ Schedule button.

■ **Note** It is possible to schedule the system to perform a dunning run at a later date and time.

The system gives you an update of your dunning run status. For example, "Select and Print Is Scheduled".
Press Enter on the keyboard twice. The system will give you the current status of your dunning in the
Status section of the screen, such as "Select and Print Is Complete" (Figure 17-30).

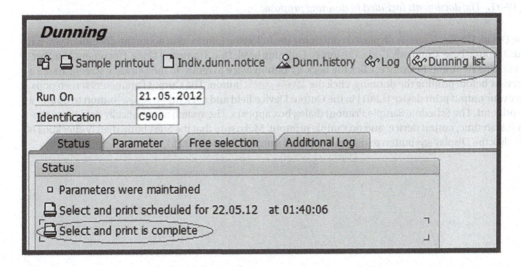

Figure 17-30. *The screen where you can view the dunning run's status*

Click the &⁰Dunning list button on the top-right side of the screen. The Dunning List Variant dialog box will appear and the system defaults to the print program automatically. All you need to do is click the Enter ✅ button. This will display the list of documents included in your dunning proposal.

It is also possible to see details of a document on the list, which you'll do next.

Display Dunning Details

Select the document you want to display from the displayed list in the Dunning Proposal list (Figure 17-31) and then click the Detail 🔍 button at the top of the screen.

```
Dunning Proposal

 I◀  ◀   ▶  ▶I  &⁰Display texts  ( 🔍 ) 🖨 🖨 🔽 🔽 📊 📊 📊 📊 📊 Choose  ℹ️

Company C900 Plc              Dunning list              Time 23:39:13    Date  21.05.2012
London                   Dunning run 21.05.2012/C900         RFMAHN21/USER5   Page          1

 Address                      A Account
 Address          Dunn.area  Dunn.level
 Address                                                              Due items Crcy
 DocumentNo Year Itm Ty PK Due on     Du Arre     Amount in FC Crcy    Amount in LC LCurr

 Edward Mason                    D 152
 1 Mason Street                     1
 Kent KE1 1TT                                                          23.800,00  GBP
 1800000015 2012  1 DR 01 01.05.2012  1  20     10.000,00  GBP        10.000,00  GBP
 1800000016 2012  1 DR 01 05.05.2012  1  16      5.000,00  GBP         5.000,00  GBP
 1800000017 2012  1 DR 01 10.05.2012  1  11      9.000,00  GBP         9.000,00  GBP
 1600000000 2012  1 DG 11 16.05.2012  1   5       200,00-  GBP          200,00-  GBP

 * Total
                                                                      23.800,00  GBP
                                                 23.800,00  GBP       23.800,00
```

Figure 17-31. *The documents included in dunning proposal*

The Detail: Display screen is displayed containing the following information about the document you have selected: Account Type, Company Code, Customer, Dunning level, Doc. Company Code, Document Number, Fiscal Year, Line Item, and Reference. Click the Back 🔙 button twice to return to the Dunning screen. To see a print preview before printing the dunning, click the 🖨 Sample printout button. The Output Parameters screen pops up. Enter your output print device (LP01) in the Output Device field and click the Continue button to output a sample printout. The Schedule Sample Printout dialog box appears. The system automatically defaults to the start date, start time, output device, and no.sample printout. Make sure that the Start Immediately checkbox is clicked. Click the Display 📺 button to display a printout sample (Figure 17-32).

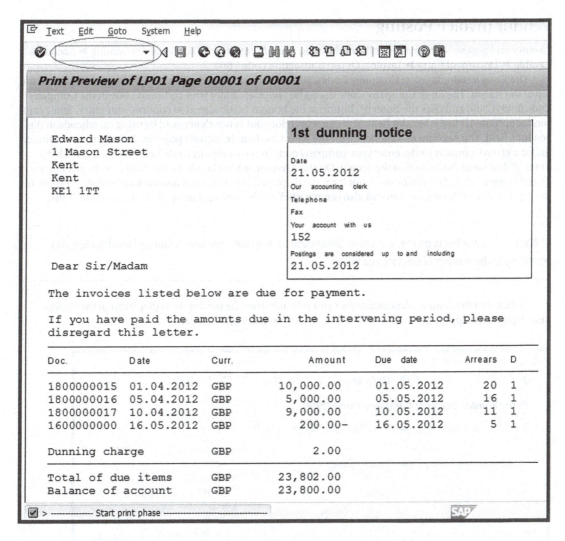

Figure 17-32. *The dunning print preview for overdue items on a customer account*

Print Dunning

Before printing the dunning, display the List of Spool Requests in Output Controller screen. To do this, type /**nsp02** in the command field on the top-left side of the Print Preview screen and click the Enter ✅ button. Make sure the item you want to print is selected by clicking the Spool No. checkbox. Then click the Print 🖨 button. This action generates a print output request.

Accounts Payable—Document Entry

In this exercise, you will be looking at how to process vendor documents (invoices), display and post the entered document, and post credit memos to a vendor account.

Problem: *The accounts payable clerks want to know how to enter and post basic invoices.*

Vendor Invoice Posting

To enter and post vendor invoices, follow this menu path: Accounting ➤ Financial Accounting ➤ Accounts payable ➤ Document Entry ➤ Invoice. Or use transaction code FB60.

The Enter Vendor Invoice: Company Code C900 screen is displayed. Click the Company Code button at the top of the screen. The Enter Company Code dialog box pops up. Enter your company code in the Company Code field (C900) and click the Enter ✔ button at the bottom of the screen to confirm your entry. Enter your vendor account ID in the Vendor field. You can search for your vendor's account by using matchcode in the vendor's field. The Account or Matchcode for the Next Line Item (n) screen pops up. To call up the customer list for a given Company Code, enter your company code in the Company Code field (C900) and click the Enter ✔ button at the bottom of the screen. On the Account or Matchcode for the Next Line Item 2 Entries Found screen, select the vendor you want from the displayed list of vendors and click the Enter ✔ button on the top-left side of the screen. You can also double-click on the appropriate vendor on the vendor's list.

■ **Note** The line items on the Account or Matchcode for the Next Line Item n Entries Found screen vary according to the number of vendors you have.

Notice that the vendor account number you selected from the vendor list is displayed in the Vendor field. Update the appropriate fields on the screen, as shown in Figure 17-33.

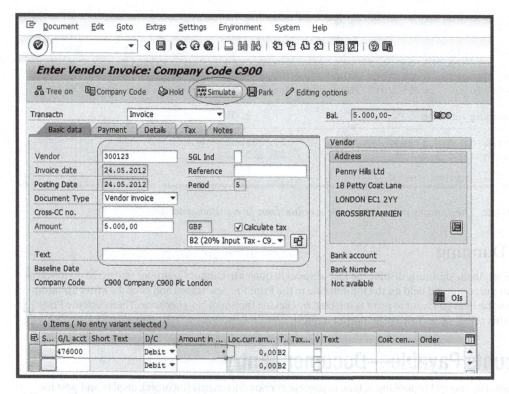

Figure 17-33. *The Vendor Invoice Basic screen is where you enter vendor invoice details and the G/L account where the invoice is posted*

Click the Enter ✅ button on the top-left side of the screen confirm your entries. To display your entries, click the ⬚ Simulate button. This Document Overview screen (Figure 17-34) shows your entries.

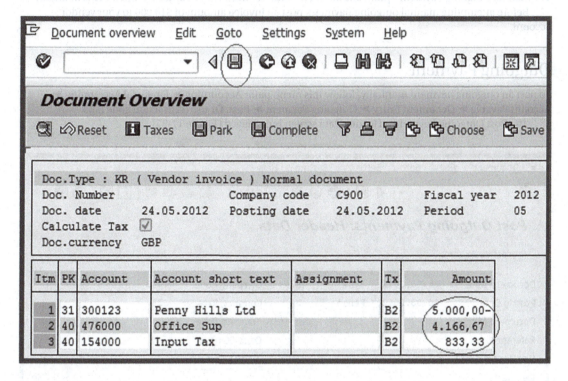

Figure 17-34. *The Document Overview screen displays the document entries*

Post 💾 your vendor's invoice.

As an exercise on your own, follow the steps in the account receivable in the section entitled "Customer Down Payments" and attempt the following tasks:

- Display a vendor's account balance by following this menu path: Accounting ➤ Financial Accounting ➤ Accounts payable ➤ Account ➤ Display Balances. Or use transaction code FK10N.

- Post a vendor's down payment request by following this menu path: Accounting ➤ Financial Accounting ➤ Accounts Payable ➤ Document Entry ➤ Document Entry ➤ Request. Or use transaction code F-47.

- Post a vendor's down payment by following this menu path: Accounting ➤ Financial Accounting ➤ Accounts Payable ➤ Document Entry ➤ Document Entry ➤ Down Payment ➤ Down Payment. Or use transaction code F-48.

- Clear a vendor's down payment by following this menu path: Accounting ➤ Financial Accounting ➤ Accounts Payable ➤ Document Entry ➤ Document Entry ➤ Down Payment ➤ Clearing. Or using transaction code F-54.

Manual Outgoing Payment

The Manual Outgoing Payment option allows you to settle vendor invoices and clear open items manually.

Before attempting manual outgoing payment, post an invoice amount of $10,000 to your vendor's account.

Outgoing Payment

To post an outgoing payment manually, follow this menu path: Accounting ➤ Financial Accounting ➤ Account Payable ➤ Document Entry ➤ Outgoing Payment ➤ Post. Or use transaction code F-53.

The Post Outgoing Payments: Header Data screen is displayed (Figure 17-35).

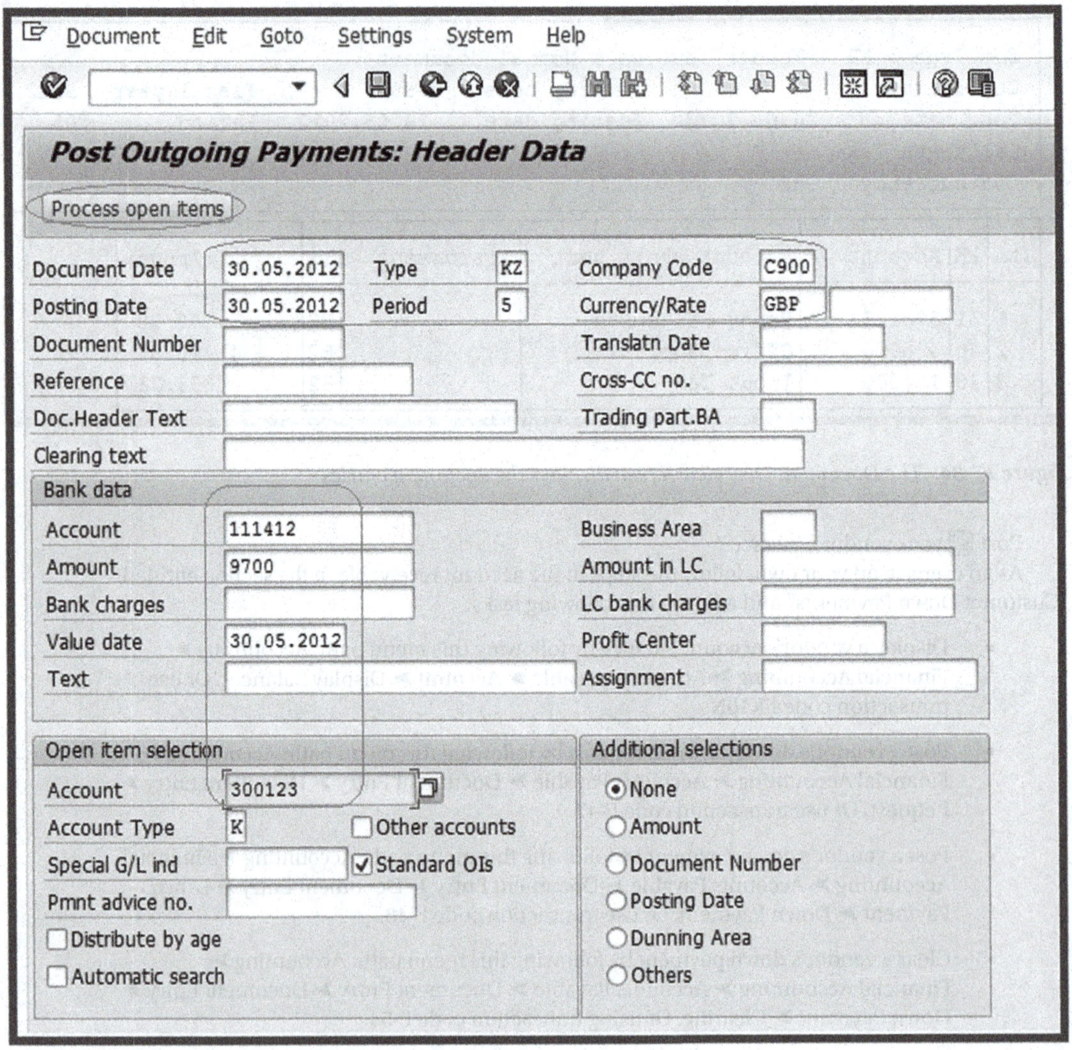

Figure 17-35. *The screen where outgoing payments are posted*

Update the following fields:

Document Date: Use today's date.

Posting Date: Use today's date.

Account: Enter the G/L account for clearing outgoing payments.

Amount: Enter $9700 (this is the invoice amount of $10,000 you posted in Manual Outgoing Payments earlier, less $300 discount received)

Value Date: Use today's date.

Account (in the Open Item selection): Enter the vendor account that you're making payment to.

To clear a payment with an open item, click the | Process open items | button on the top-left side of the screen. The Post Outgoing Payments Process Open Items is displayed.

■ **Note**   Notice that the open items in the Gross Amount column are activated (displayed in blue). Also notice that Cash Discount Amount and Cash Discount Percentage are red. Since you do not want to clear all open items simultaneously, you need to deactivate all activated items and activate only the open item(s) you want to clear.

Deactivate all activated open items on the screen and only activate the open item you want to process with the payment. You may want to refer back to the section "Posting Standard Incoming Payments" to review how to deactivate and activate open items.

■ **Note**   Notice that the Amount Entered and Assigned will be $9700 (the document amount of $10000 less $300 cash discount and the outgoing amount of $9700), bringing Not Assigned to a zero balance.

To display the posted outgoing payment overview, click the | Document | button on the menu bar at the top of the screen; a pull-down menu is displayed. Choose | Simulate | from the drop-down menu. The Post Outgoing Payments Display Overview screen is displayed (Figure 17-36).

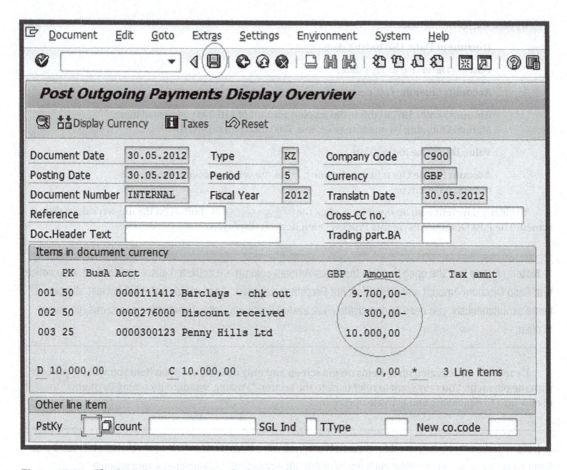

Figure 17-36. The Outgoing Payments Display Overview screen.

Check your entries and then click Post 🖫 if they meet your requirements.

Automatic Payments

The automatic payment program is an automated way to process and post huge lists of accounts payables and accounts receivables in a single payment run.

Before proceeding with an automatic payment run, you'll learn how to create check lots. You need check lots when maintaining the variant for a payment run.

Check Lots

Checks are managed in lots (batches). SAP provides a check-management system that divides bank checks into check lots (batches) by assigning number ranges to represent batches or check lots. To define the check lots that you will use, follow this menu path: IMG: Financial Accounting ➤ Account Receivable & Account Payable ➤ Business Transaction ➤ Payments ➤ Automatic Outgoing Payments ➤ Payment Media ➤ Check management ➤ Define Number Ranges for Checks. Or use transaction code FCHI. The Check Lots screen is displayed. Using the information in Table 17-9, update the appropriate fields.

Table 17-9. *Updating the Check Lots Screen*

Field	Value	Description
Paying Company Code	C900	This is the company code that is making payments. This is the case where centralized payment system is in operation. All invoices from branches are sent to the head office for payment.
House Bank	Barc1	Using the matchcode or the Search button to search for your house bank, enter your house bank's ID in this field. The system uses a combination of both the house bank code and the account ID to trace check lots to the paying bank.
Account ID	Barc	The house bank ID and account ID are used by the payment program to determine which bank to use for invoice payment.

Click the Enter ✓ button on the top-left side of the screen. Then click the Change ✎ button on the top-left side of the screen. The Maintain Check Lots screen is displayed. Click the Create ☐ button on the top-left side of the screen to create your check lots. The Create Lot screen pops up (Figure 17-37). This screen allows you to specify your check lot and check numbers.

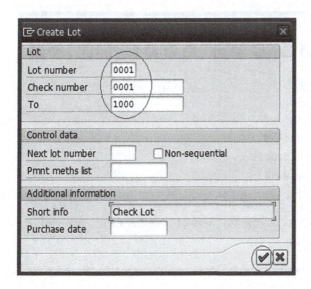

Figure 17-37. *Specifying the check lots and check numbers*

Using the data in Table 17-10, specify the lot number and check number information.

Table 17-10. *Data to Update the Check Lot Screen*

Field	Value	Description
Lot Number	0001	Enter a check lot number in this field. You can enter up to four digits in this field. This number enables you to identify this particular check, which is helpful when you have more than one check lot.
Check Number	0001	Checks are issued systematically in sequence. This is the start number of the check.
To	1000	This is the end number of the check sequence. The system will automatically issue checks for payment in this order.
Additional Information		
Short info.	Check lot	This is a short description of the check lot.

Click the Enter ☑ button on the bottom-right side of the Create Lot screen to confirm your specifications. The system will then create your check lot (Figure 17-38).

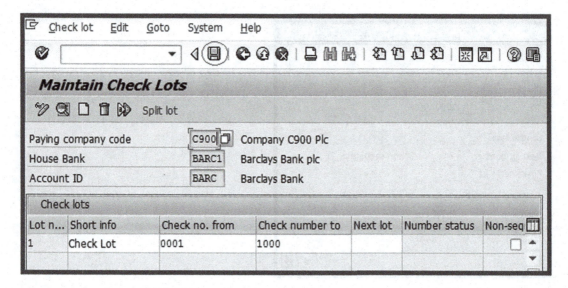

Figure 17-38. *The Maintain Check Lots screen*

Save 💾 your check lot.

Automatic Payment Program

The Automatic Outgoing Payments option is a payment management tool that allows you to pay multiple open invoices, post payment documents, and print payment media using EDI (Electronic Data Interchange) or DME (Date Medium Exchange).

Configuring the automatic outgoing settings takes four major steps:

1. Maintain parameters (enter your parameters).

2. Start proposal run (create and edit payment proposal).

3. Start payment run.

4. Schedule print.

To go to the automatic payment transaction screen, follow this menu path: Accounting ➤ Financial Accounting ➤ Banks ➤ Outgoings ➤ Automatic Payments ➤ Open Items (Customer and Vendor). Or use transaction code F110. The Automatic Payment Transactions: Status screen is displayed (Figure 17-39).

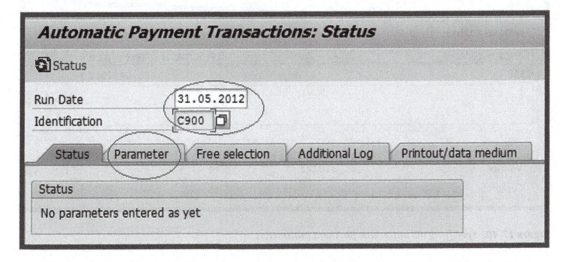

Figure 17-39. *Specifying the automatic payment transaction's run date*

Update the following fields:

> **Run Date:** Enter today's date, plus 10 days. This is the date on which you want the system to run the payment program. This date can be changed depending on what you want to achieve. For example, if today's date is May 21, 2012, your run date will be May 31, 2012.

> **Identification:** Enter C900 as your payment run identification in this field. You can use up to a five-digit identifier. This will enable you to identify your payment run if you have more than one payment run with the same run date.

■ **Note** Notice that the system displays the status of the automatic payment as "No Parameters Entered As Yet" in the Status section of the screen in Figure 17-39.

Click the `Parameter` tab at the top of the screen to go to the Automatic Payment Transactions: Parameters screen to specify the payment parameters of the automatic payment run (Figure 17-40).

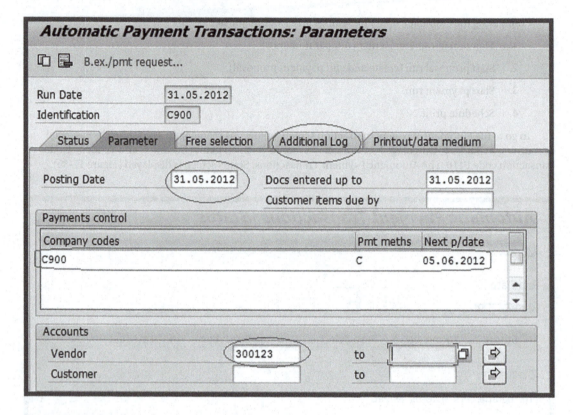

Figure 17-40. *Specifying the automatic payment parameters*

Update the following fields:

Posting Date: This is set to today's date by default. We recommend that you use today's date.

Docs Entered Up To: Defaults to today's date.

Company Codes: You determine the company code you are using for your automatic payment run. Enter your company code (C900) in this field.

Payment Methods: Enter the payment you want to use for your payment run. For example, C- Check, T-Bank Transfer, and so on. You can access the payment methods supplied by SAP using the matchcode next to the payment methods fields. In this exercise, we making payment by check, so enter C (check) in this field for your payment method.

Next Payment Date: Enter today's date plus 30 days. This means the next payment run will be 30 days from today's date. The importance of the next payment date is that it enables the system to decide whether to make payment using a cash discount or to make payment based on the net amount.

Vendor: Enter your vendor account number (300123) in this field. You can specify the vendor's range (from/to) for which you want to trigger the payment program.

Click the [Additional Log] tab at the top of the screen to go to the Automatic Payment Transactions: Additional Log screen to specify the required logging type and additional account required for your payment proposal (Figure 17-41).

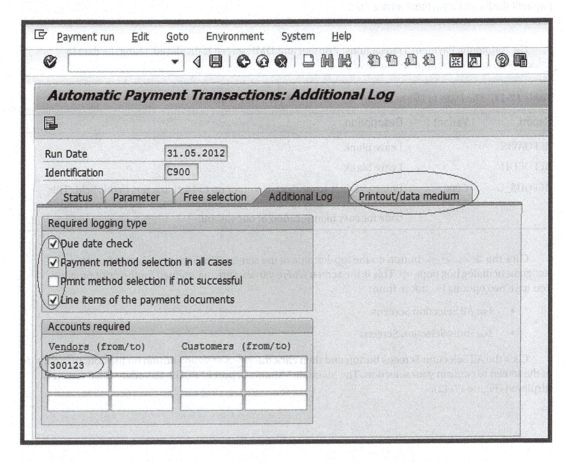

Figure 17-41. *The screen for additional specifications for your payment proposal*

When creating the payment proposal, select the following items in the Required Logging Type section of the screen:

- Due date check

- Payment method selection in all cases

- Line items of the payment documents

Enter the vendor's account number(s) that you want to include in the Accounts Required section. Click Enter ✅ and then save 💾 your payment program.

Next, click the [Printout/data medium] tab to go to the Automatic Payment Transactions: Printout/DME screen to specify the variant for the print program. The print variant allows you to store the properties of frequently used datasets and call them up easily.

■ **Note**   Once your payments have been posted, you need to print the payment media. Since different payment methods were specified in your payment program, the print program will need print variants for the payment media and a payment advice note.

The Automatic Payment Transactions: Printout and DME screen is displayed. Using the data in Table 17-11, update the appropriate fields.

Table 17-11. *The Data to Use to Specify the Variant for the Print Program*

Report	Variant	Description
RFFOAVIS		Leave blank
RFFOEDI1		Leave blank
RFFOUS_C	C900	Enter a variant name. You can enter up to 14 characters in this field. This does not necessarily have to be your company code. We used our company code for easy identification of our variant.

Click the [🗗 Maintain Variants] button on the top-left side of the screen. The Variants: Change Screen Assignment dialog box pops up. This is the screen where variants are maintained for the print program. You have two options to choose from:

- For All Selection Screens

- For Indiv.Selection Screens

Click the All Selection Screens button and then click the [✔ Continue] button on the bottom-right side of the screen to confirm your selection. The Maintain Variant: Report RFFOUS_C, Variant C900 screen is displayed (Figure 17-42).

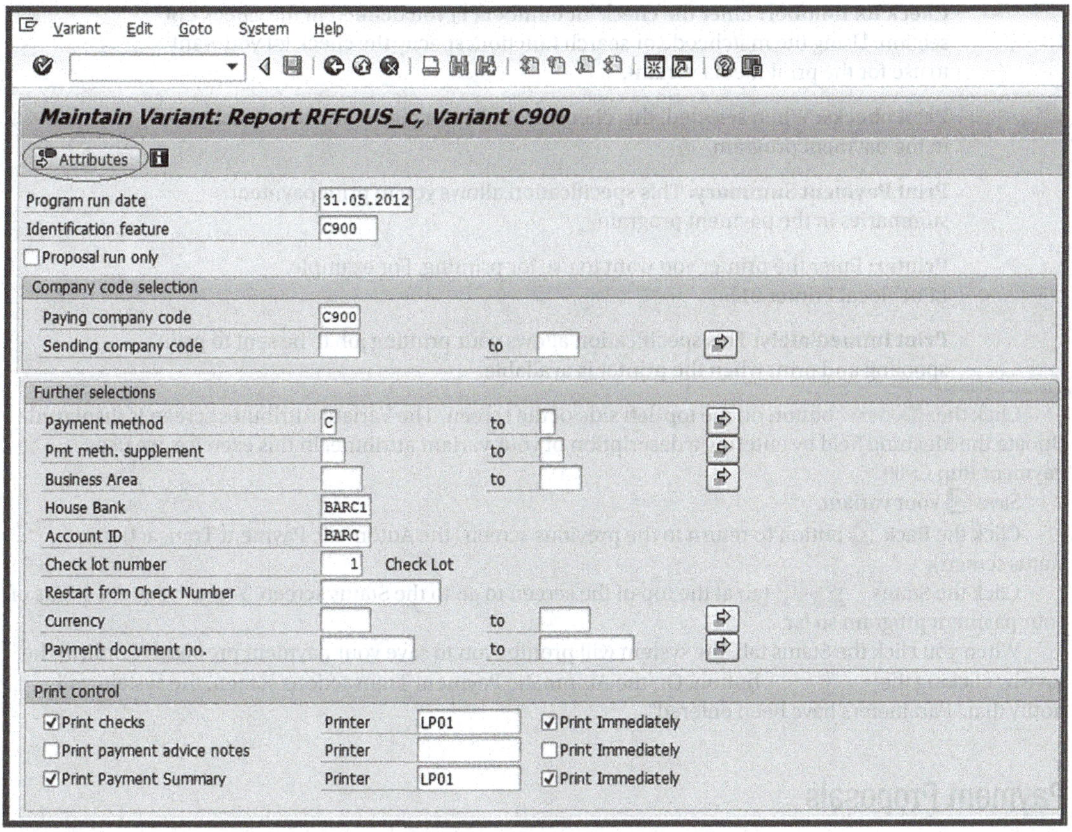

Figure 17-42. *The screen where Print Variant is updated*

Update the following fields:

Program run date: Enter Today's date plus 10 days. This defaults to today's date.

Identification feature: Enter a four digit (C900) code as your identification feature in this field. You can use up to a five digits of your choice. Using your company code will enable you to identify your print media variant if you have more than one variant in the system.

Paying company code: Enter the paying company code (C900). This is the company that makes payments. You should determine the company code you want to use as a paying company code.

Payment method: Enter the payment method you want to use for your variant. For example, C for check payments.

House Bank: Enter up to five digits as your house bank identifier (Barc 1) in this field. This is the bank that will make the payments.

Account ID: Enter up to five digits as your account ID (Barc). The house bank ID and account ID used by the payment program determine the banks to use during invoice payment.

Check lot number: Enter the check lot number (1) you defined in the Check Lot section. Using the matchcode or search function, specify the check lot you want to use for the print media variant.

Print checks: When selected, this checkbox indicator allows you to print checks in the payment program.

Print Payment Summary: This specification allows you to print payment summaries in the payment program.

Printer: Enter the printer you want to use for printing. For example, LP01 (local Printer 01).

Print Immediately: This specification allows your printing job to be sent to print spooling and print when the printer is available.

Click the Attributes button on the top-left side of the screen. The Variant Attributes screen is displayed. Update the Meaning field by entering a description of your variant attribute. In this exercise, we used Payment Run C900.

Save your variant.

Click the Back button to return to the previous screen (the Automatic Payment Transactions: status screen).

Click the Status Status tab at the top of the screen to go to the Status screen. You can see the status of your payment program so far.

When you click the Status tab, the system will prompt you to save your payment proposal. Confirm the save by clicking the Yes button. On the Automatic Payment Transactions screen, the system will notify that "Parameters have been entered".

Payment Proposals

The Payment Proposal option allows you to execute a test run of your payment before performing an actual payment run. Because of the sensitive nature of payment program, a test run will give you the opportunity to see which items you have included in your payment proposal and which items are blocked for payment.

Using the Edit ➤ Proposal menu path on the menu bar at the top of the screen, you can carry out the following tasks:

- Display proposals

- Edit or delete proposals

- Generate a proposal list

- Display an exceptional list

From the proposal list, you can block and unblock items planned for payment.

On the Automatic Payment Transactions: Status screen (Figure 17-43), the system status turns green and displays, "Parameters have been entered". Click the Proposal button on the top-left side of the screen to schedule a payment proposal.

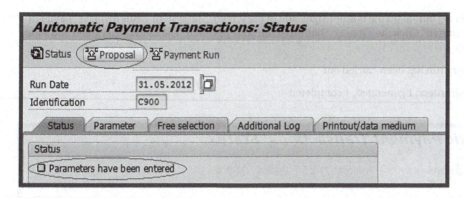

Figure 17-43. *The Automatic Payment Transactions Status screen shows that the parameters have been entered*

The Schedule Proposal dialog box pops up. Update the following fields:

Start Date: Today's date is the default. We recommend that you use today's date to schedule a proposal for your payment run.

Start Immediately: If you want your schedule proposal to start immediately, make sure that this checkbox is clicked. If this checkbox is not clicked, you must specify a start time in the Start Time field.

Click the Enter ✅ button on the bottom-right side of the screen. The system status displays "Proposal is ready to be started" under "Parameter have been entered". Click the 🔘 Status button on the top-left side of the screen to see the status of your payment proposal. The system status displays "Proposal is running". Click the 🔘 Status button again to create your payment proposal. The display on the status screen will turn green and state that "Payment proposal has been created".

Payment Runs

When you execute a payment run, the system will read your payment and perform the following functions:

- Clear selected items for payment
- Clear open items in accounts payable
- Reduce payables against appropriate G/L accounts
- Post payments to bank sub-accounts as per transfers and checks

To execute a payment run, click the 🔘 Payment Run button. The Schedule Payment dialog box pops up. Update the following fields:

Start Date: This defaults to today's date.

Start Immediately: For your schedule payment to start immediately, make sure that this checkbox is clicked. If this checkbox is blank, you must specify a start time in the Start Time field.

Click the Enter ✅ button on the bottom-right side of the screen. The system status displays "Payment Run is ready to be started". Click the 🔲 Status button to run your payment. The status turns green and states that (Figure 17-44):

- Payment run has been carried out

- Posting orders: 1 generated, 1 completed

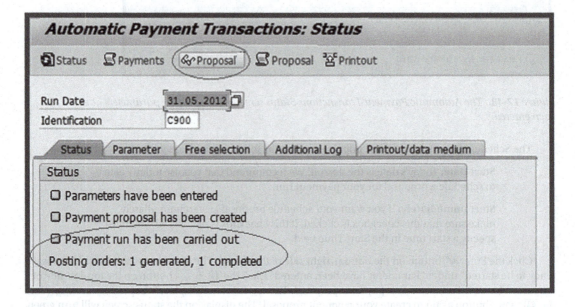

Figure 17-44. *The automatic payment transactions have been posted, generated, and completed*

Display Payment Proposals

The Display Payment Proposal option allows you edit and block/unblock payment proposals. To display a payment proposal, click the 🔲 Proposal button. The Display Payment Proposal: Payments screen is displayed with your payment proposal. The indicator for payments/exceptions turns green (Figure 17-45).

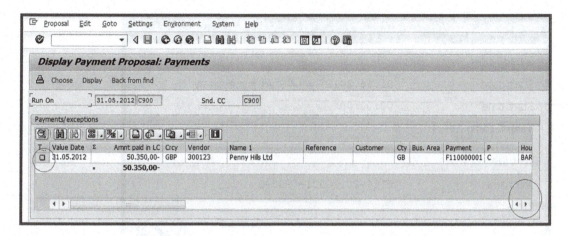

Figure 17-45. *The Payment Proposal display screen*

■ **Tip** You can scroll to the right to see more details.

Click the Back 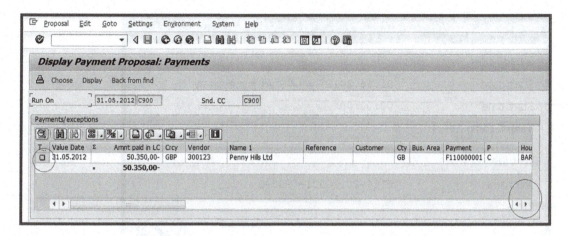 button to return to the previous screen (Automatic Payment Transaction: Status).

To display the proposal log click the 🖺 Proposal button. Here the system will display any errors that occurred during your payment run.

Click the Back button to return to the Automatic Payment Transaction: Status screen.

To display the payment list, use this menu path: Edit ➤ Payment ➤ Payment List. The List Variant dialog box pops up. The Program field's value RFZALI20 is set by default by the system. You don't need to do anything here. Click the Enter ✅ button on the bottom-right side of the screen to display the Payment List screen, which contains all payments included in your automatic payment program.

Schedule Print Jobs

To send your payment transaction to a print spool, click the Back button to return to the Automatic Payment Transaction: Status screen. Click the 🖨 Printout button. The Schedule Print dialog box pops up (Figure 17-46). Make sure that the Start Immediately checkbox is clicked.

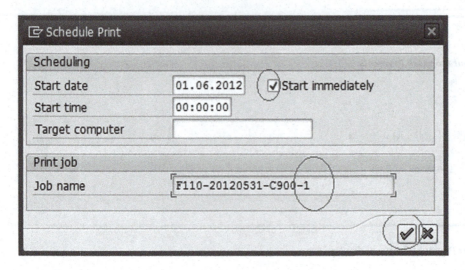

Figure 17-46. Specifying the print job to start immediately

Replace the '?' in the Job Name field with a letter or number of your choice. There is no strict rule on what you can replace it with. The number 1 we use is for illustration purposes. Click the Enter button ✔. The system will display the message ✔ Print job F110-20120531-C900-1 has been scheduled on the status bar at the bottom of the screen.

Display Spool Request

To display a spool request, use this menu path: System ➤ Service ➤ Output Control, found on the menu bar at the top of the screen. The Output Controller: List of Spool Requests screen is displayed (Figure 17-47).

Output Controller: List of Spool Requests

Spool no.	Type	Date	Time	Status	Pages	Title
15072		01.06.2012	00:45	Waiting	3	Payment summary
15071		01.06.2012	00:45	Waiting	5	Cheque

2 Spool requests displayed

==

2 Spool requests being processed

Figure 17-47. The List of Spool Requests screen

Click the Execute ⊕ button. The Output Controller: List of Spool Requests screen is displayed with list of spool requests. Use date and title to identify the item you want to display from the spool list. Select the Spool No. of the item or item(s) you want to include in your print preview. Click the Display Content 🔍 button at the top of the screen. The sample of check printout will be displayed (Figure 17-48).

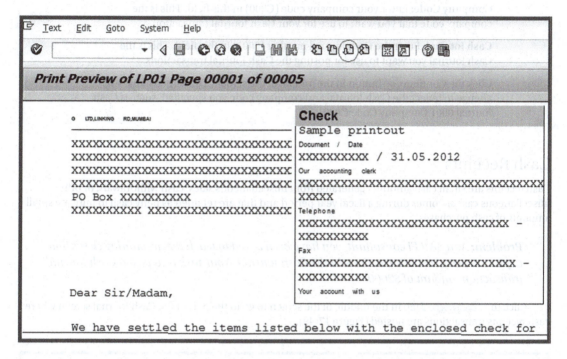

Figure 17-48. *The Check Payment Advice Note Sample Printout - Print Preview screen*

To see the actual print preview, click the Next Page 🔼 button on the top-right side of the screen to display the Payment Advice note. When you click the Next Page 🔼 button again a few times, you can see all the payment documents, including the check payment summary.

To print, click the Back 🔙 button to return to the Output Controller: List of Spool Requests screen. Click the Print 🖨 button on the top-left side of the screen; the system will send your check to the printer.

The system will then notify you that ☑ Output requests created .

Use the Cash Journal

The Cash Journal allows you to post small cash documents instead of using the normal accounts payable and receivable transaction postings. The Cash Journal allows you to post the following cash transactions:

- Cash payments (for cash purchases)
- Cash receipts (for cash sales)
- Check receipts

To post transactions in the Cash Journal, follow this menu path: Accounting ➤ Financial Accounting ➤ Banks ➤ Incomings ➤ Cash Journal. Or use transaction code FBCJ.

The Cash Journal 0001 Company Code C900 screen is displayed. Click the Change Cash Journal button (located somewhere in the middle of the screen) to specify the Company Code and/or the Cash Journal you want to use for your Cash Journal transaction. The Cash Journal dialog box pops up. Update the following fields:

> **Company Code:** Enter your company code (C900) in this field. This is the company code that you want to use for your Cash Journal transaction.

> **Cash Journal:** Enter the Cash Journal number (0001) in this field. This is the Cash Journal you want to use for posting the Cash Journal transactions.

> Click the Continue ✔ button in the middle of the screen. The screen name will change to reflect the Cash Journal and company code you specified, such as Cash Journal 0001 Company Code C900.

Cash Receipts

Cash receipts are small cash amounts generated from miscellaneous sales, cash withdrawals, or other miscellaneous cash incomes during a fiscal year period and that are retained as petty cash to mitigate small amounts of cash purchases.

> **Problem:** *As a SAP FI consultant, you have been asked to teach the accounting clerks how to process petty cash transactions in the Cash Journal. Your task is to post a Cash Journal transaction amount of $2000.*

Click the Cash receipts tab in the middle of the screen to go to the part of the Cash Journal screen where cash receipts transactions are posted (Figure 17-49).

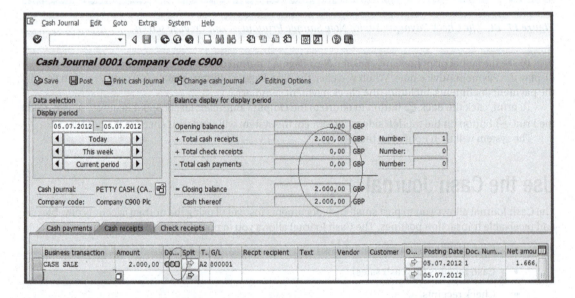

Figure 17-49. Document status in the Cash Journal

Update the following fields:

> **Business Transaction:** Specify CASH SALES in this field. This is the nature of the business transaction you want to conduct.

> **Amount:** Enter the cash document amount ($2000) in this field.

> **Tax:** Specify the tax code for the output sale (A2) you want to apply to your cash receipt for calculating tax amount.

The system will automatically default to the G/L account 8000001 to post cash sales, based on the specification you made when you customized the Cash Journal.

Click the Enter ✅ button on the top-left side of the screen. Notice that the Document Status option has turned red. Click the 🖫 Post button at the top of the screen to post your cash receipt transaction. After posting, the Document Status will turn green and the total cash receipts will be credited with the amount posted.

Cash Payments

Like the cash receipts, these are small cash payments made toward miscellaneous office purchases.

> **Problem:** *A petty cash purchase of $1500 was made. You are told to make this Cash Journal posting by splitting the expenses as follows: printing paper at $1000 and pens at $500.*

Click the ⟨ Cash payments ⟩ tab in the Cash Journal 0001 Company Code C900 screen and update the following fields:

> **Business Transaction:** Specify CASH PURCHASE in this field. This is the nature of the business transaction you want to conduct in your Cash Journal.

> **Amount:** Enter the document amount ($1000) that you want to process in your Cash Journal transaction.

> **Text for Item:** Enter a short description of your transaction. For example, printing paper.

The next step is to split the document amount. Click the Split 🖘 button next to the 0.

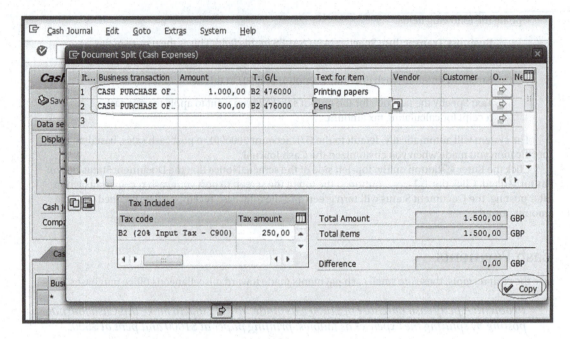

Figure 17-50. *How to split a document amount in the Cash Journal*

Notice that the cash amount of $1000 is copied into Row 1. Since you want to split $1500 between two Cash Journal items, update Row 2 with the following information:

> **Business Transactions:** Specify the Cash Journal transaction CASH PURCHASE in this field.

> **Amount:** Enter the amount of $500 for pens.

> **Text for Item:** Enter the description of the transaction item (pens).

Click the ✔ Copy button on the bottom-right side of the screen. The Cash Document Split (Cash Expenses) screen disappears. On the Cash Journal 0001 Company Code C900 screen, notice that the Business Transaction field will have an * sign because this Cash Journal transaction has split documents. Click the Enter ✔ button on the top-left side of the screen. The Document Status field will turn red because the Cash Journal document has not been posted. Click the 🖫 Post button to post your transaction. After posting, the Document Status field turns green and the total cash receipts are credited with the amount posted.

■ **Note**   The Balance Display for Display Period section displays the total receipt and cash payments balances, as well as the total Cash Journal balance.

Summary

This chapter showed you how to create customer and vendor master records and how to enter customer invoices using hypothetical scenarios. You also learned how to post credit memos in order to reduce an original invoice amount. After this, you learned what holding and parking documents do. You then learned how to post various incoming payments, including posting income payments in the standard way, posting partial payments, and posting residual items.

You also learned how to post customer down payments—this included posting down payment requests, down payments received, and clearing down payment requests with a down payment. You next looked at how to display account balances and line items. You learned how to generate and print correspondence, as well as how to execute dunning runs.

You learned how to post a vendor's invoice and then went on to perform manual outgoing payment. Afterward, you learned how to carry out the specifications for automatic payment. You learned how to define check lots for automatic payments, set up automatic payments, start proposal runs, start payment runs, and schedule print runs. You then learned about payment proposals. Finally, you looked at the Cash Journal and learned how to post cash receipts and cash payment transactions.

In Chapter 18, you will learn how to define a controlling area, create cost elements, define cost center accounting, maintain statistical key figures, and define a profit center.

■ ■ ■

CHAPTER 18

Customizing the Controlling Module

In this chapter, you learn how to customize the Controlling module in SAP ERP and learn how to define the cost elements, cost center, and profit center.

At the end of this chapter, you will be able to:

- Explain what controlling is
- Maintain a controlling area
- Maintain version approaches/transfer prices
- Explain what cost element accounting is
- Make default settings for automatic creation of primary and secondary cost elements
- Perform cost center accounting
- Define cost centers' standard hierarchy
- Define statistical key figures
- Configure the basic settings of a profit center
- Maintain the controlling area settings
- Create a dummy profit center
- Assign profit centers to cost centers
- Post controlling documents
- Produce a profit center: interactive reporting
- Define distribution

The Controlling Module

The Controlling module is designed to enable organizations to collate, manipulate, and coordinate huge financial data accumulated from business operations into concise and meaningful management reports. These reports provide management with timely and adequate information beyond that of basic financial reports to aid management in making vital decisions on running the organizations relating to cost and profitability.

Management needs to present and past performance, and predicts future performance. This is where SAP controlling plays an important role. It provides the platform to maintain be able to make operational and strategic decisions that will make the business profitable. In order to do this, they need a tool that measures cost and profit, measures management accounting to meet management's reporting needs, and it facilitates management decision-making and optimization of the entire organizational process.

General Controlling

The settings carried out at the General Controlling level are fundamental, because they hold general information relevant to the entire Controlling (CO) module.

Organizational Controlling

The following controlling settings are carried out in the organizational structure:

- Maintain controlling area
- Maintain number ranges for controlling documents
- Maintain versions

Problem: *As a SAP functional consultant, your task is to maintain the controlling area, define number ranges for controlling documents, and maintain the appropriate versions for the controlling area for Company C900.*

Maintain Controlling Area

The controlling area is an internal system within an organization specifically used for cost accounting purposes. It is the internal structure that allows management to plan activities, carry out activities' allocation, and monitor costs.

To maintain the controlling area, follow this menu path: IMG: Controlling ➤ General Controlling ➤ Organization ➤ Maintain Controlling Area. Or use transaction code OKKP.

The Choose Activity screen pops up with three options to choose from:

- Copy, delete, and check controlling area
- Maintain controlling area
- Delete controlling area

Select Maintain Controlling Area from the list of activities by clicking on it. Click the `Choose` button at the top of the screen. The Change View "Basic Data": Overview screen appears. Click the `New Entries` button on the top-left side of the screen to go to the New Entries: Details of Added Entries input screen (Figure 18-1).

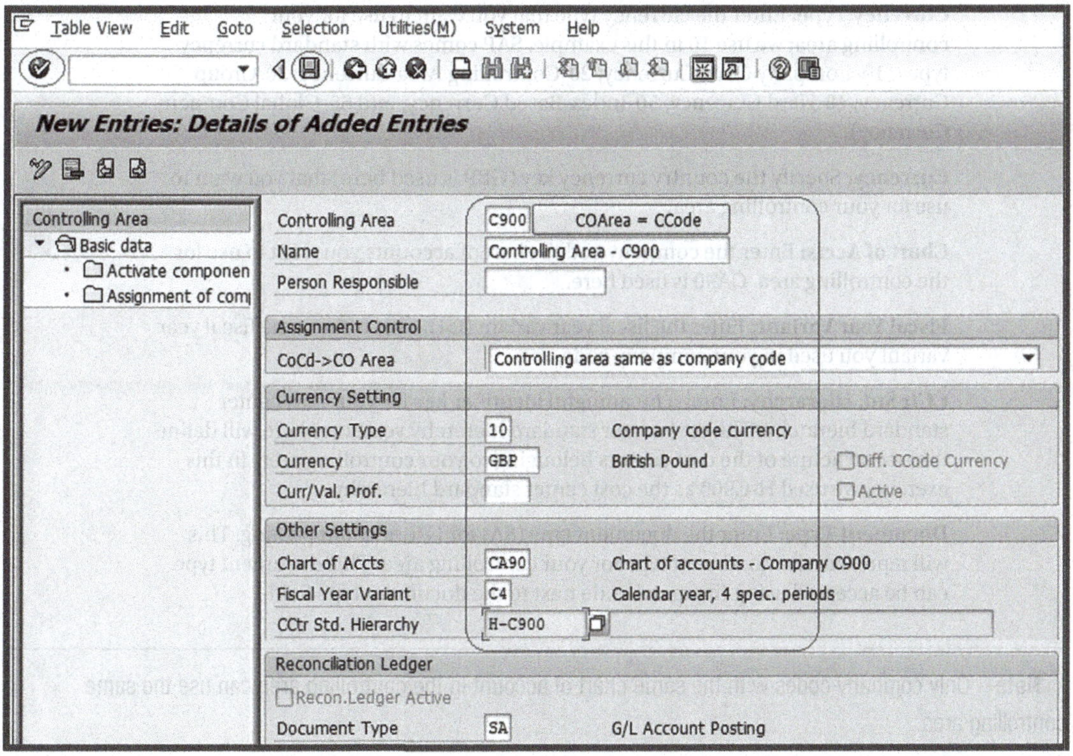

Figure 18-1. *The screen where the basic settings for a controlling area are maintained*

Update the following fields:

> **Controlling Area:** Enter controlling area C900. This can be up to four digits.
> We recommend that you use your company code as your controlling area. This
> makes it easier to remember, especially if you have more than one controlling
> area.

> **Name:** Enter a short description for your controlling area. For example,
> "Controlling Area C900".

> **Person Responsible:** If your organization has a designated person responsible
> for that controlling area, enter their name. This field is optional.

> **CoCd -> CO Area:** Choose from two options: Controlling Area Same as Company
> Code (if you select this option, the company code assignment to the controlling
> area must be uniform with processes defined for your company code in logistics
> and FI) or Cross Company Code-Costing Accounting (this option allows all
> cost accounting to be conducted in several company codes in one controlling
> area). Click the drop-down arrow next to the field to display the options. For this
> exercise, select Controlling Area Same as Company Code.

Currency Type: Enter the currency type that you want to use for your controlling area; we use 10 in this example. SAP comes with standard currency types (10-Company Code Currency, 20-Controlling Area Currency, 30-Group Currency, 40-Hard Currency, 50-Index-Based Currency, and 60-Global Company Currency).

Currency: Specify the country currency key (GBP is used here) that you want to use for your controlling area.

Chart of Accts: Enter the company code's chart of accounts you want to use for the controlling area. CA90 is used here.

Fiscal Year Variant: Enter the fiscal year variant (C4). This is the same fiscal year variant you used in your company code.

CCtr Std. Hierarchy: Enter a meaningful identifier key for your cost center standard hierarchy. The cost center standard hierarchy you enter here will define the tree structure of the cost centers belonging to your controlling area. In this exercise, we used H-C900 as the cost center standard hierarchy.

Document Type: Enter the document type (SA) for G/L account posting. This will represent the document type for your controlling area. This document type can be accessed using the matchcode next to the document type field.

■ **Note**   Only company codes with the same chart of account in the controlling area can use the same controlling area.

Click the Enter ✅ button on the top-left side of the screen to confirm your entries. The Check Standard Hierarchy dialog box comes up asking if you want the system to create a standard hierarchy for the standard hierarchy identifier key (H-C900).

Click the [Yes] button at the bottom of the screen to confirm that you want the system to create a standard hierarchy for your standard hierarchy key (H-C900).

The second step is to assign the company code(s) to the controlling area.

■ **Note**   Make sure you assign the company code before activating the components/control indicators.

To create the standard hierarchy for your cost centers, double-click the ⬚ Assignment of company code(s) folder in the Controlling area of the left pane of the New Entries screen. The Check Standard Hierarchy dialog box pops up again stating that, "Standard hierarchy does not exist, should the system create it?". Click the [Yes] button to confirm that you want the system to create the hierarchy. The Change View "Assignment of Company Code(s)": Overview screen appears. This screen allows you to assign your company code to the controlling area you defined earlier. Click the [New Entries] button on the top-left side of the screen. The New Entries: Details of Added Entries screen is displayed. Enter your company code (C900) in the CoCd (Company Code) field. Click the Enter ✅ button on the top-left side of the screen and then save 💾.

The third and last step is to assign components and control indicators.

To assign controlling components and control indicators to your controlling area, double-click the ⬚ Activate components/control indicators folder in the Controlling area on the left pane of the screen. The New Entries: Details of Added Entries screen is displayed (Figure 18-2).

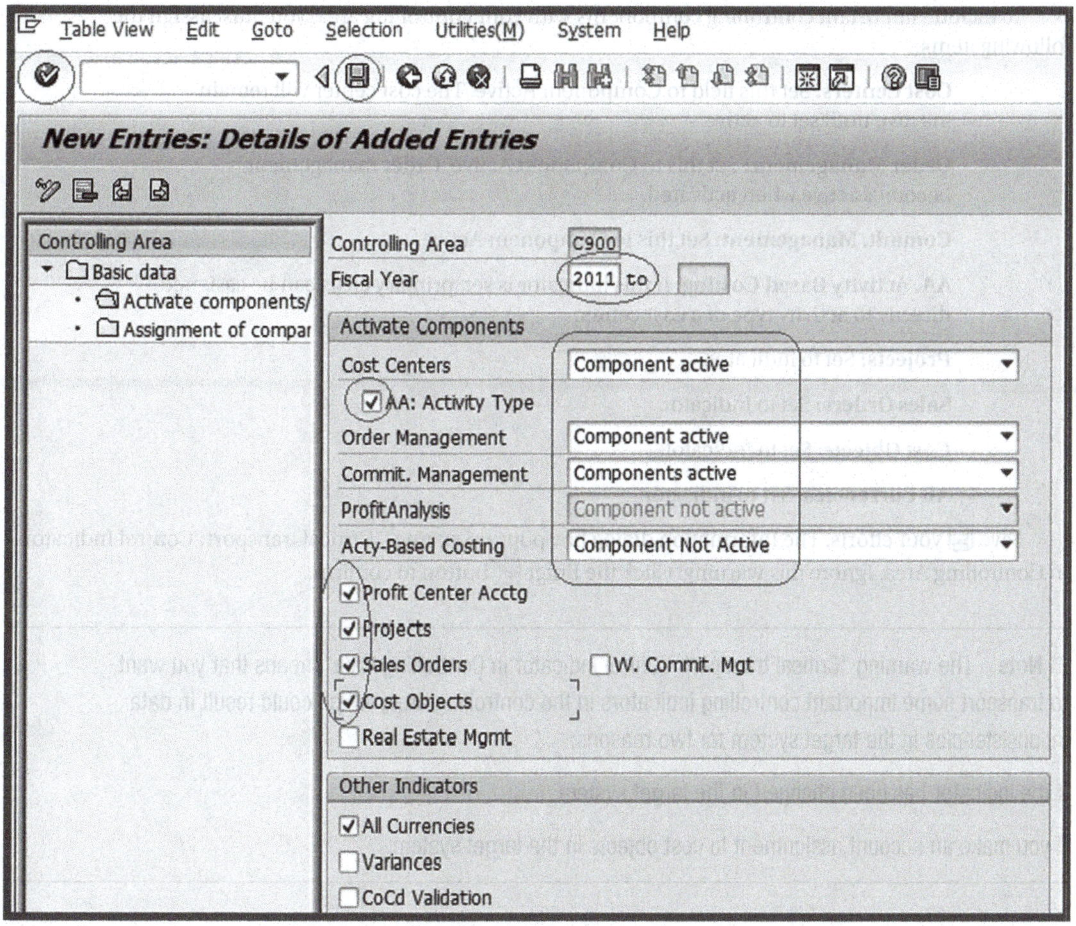

Figure 18-2. *Activating components for the controlling area*

Update the following fields:

> **Fiscal Year:** This is your company code accounting year. The fiscal year you
> assigned to your controlling area must have the same number of posting
> periods as the fiscal year in the FI (Financial Accounting) components for your
> company code.

■ **Tip**   Make sure your fiscal year range specification is earlier than the current fiscal year. For example, if
your current fiscal year is 2013, use 2011 as the starting fiscal year. By default, the system uses 9999 as the
ending fiscal year.

To include important controlling components with your controlling area, you must assign the following items:

Cost Centers: Set this field to Component Active. The cost center will remain inactive until set to active.

Order Management: Set this to Component Active. Order management becomes active when activated.

Commit. Management: Set this to Component Active.

AA. Activity Based Costing: If this indicator is set, primary costs can be assigned directly to activity type of a cost center.

Projects: Set to indicator.

Sales Orders: Set to indicator.

Cost Objects: Set to indicator.

All Currencies: Set to indicator.

Save 🖫 your efforts. The Information dialog box pops up stating, "Critical transport: Control Indicator in Controlling Area. Ignore this warning. Click the Enter ✅ button to confirm.

■ **Note**   The warning "Critical transport: Control indicator in Controlling Area" means that you want to transport some important controlling indicators in the controlling area, which could result in data inconsistencies in the target system for two reasons:

If the indicator has been changed in the target system.

If you make an account assignment to cost objects in the target system.

Maintain Number Ranges for Controlling Documents

In this exercise, you will copy an existing controlling area's number ranges and adapt them to your controlling area number ranges. The general principle is that when a document is posted in the controlling area, the system automatically generates a unique document number from the number ranges and assigns it to the document. A number range is unique to a document and cannot be reused when posting another transaction. Every document posted in a controlling area must be assigned to a number range group. For more details on document number ranges, refer back to Chapter 3 (in the section "Defining Number Ranges").

Problem: As a functional consultant, your task is to maintain number ranges for controlling documents. Your colleagues told you that it is easier to copy an existing number range in the system rather than create your own. Your task is to copy the standard number range from company code 1000 and adjust it to meet your requirements.

To copy predefined number ranges, follow this menu path: IMG: Controlling ➤ General Controlling ➤ Organization ➤ Maintain Number Ranges for Controlling Documents. Or use transaction code KANK. In the CO Area field on the Number Ranges for CO Document screen, enter the controlling area code 1000 you want to copy and then click the 📄 Copy button in the middle of the screen. The Copy: CO Area dialog box pops up. The system will use the controlling area 1000 that you want to copy the number ranges in the From field.

Enter your controlling area (C900) in the To field. The Transport Number Range Intervals screen pops up with messages. Ignore the messages and click the Enter ✔ button to confirm that the number ranges should be copied from the source to the target company.

■ **Note** The system will notify you that ✔ CO Area 1000 was copied to C900 on the status bar at the bottom of the screen.

Maintain Versions

Versions allow you to maintain the settings for planned and actual data for independent data groupings. In the basic version configuration, you must have one actual version for posting actual data. The planned version is optional. The planned/actual version is represented by "0". This is an operative version that can be used in planned/actual comparison and variance analysis between planned/actual activities. Planned data is used to calculate planned prices for activity types and to determine the rates for settling activities containing actual figures.

To maintain versions, follow this menu path: IMG: Controlling ➤ General Controlling ➤ Organization ➤ Maintain Versions. Or use transaction code OKEQ. The General Version Definition screen is displayed (Figure 18-3).

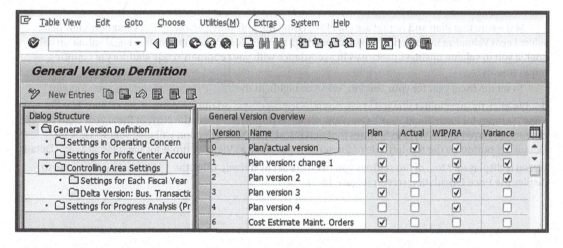

Figure 18-3. *The Maintain General Version Definition screen for planned/actual version*

The next step is to set the controlling area for the version. To do this, select version "0" plan/actual version from the displayed list of versions and click the ⟨ Extras ⟩ button at the top of the screen.

A pull-down menu is displayed. When you click ⟨ Set Controlling Area... ⟩ from the pull-down menu, the

Determine Work Area Entry dialog box comes up. Enter your controlling area code (C900) in the Controlling Area field and click the Enter ✔ button on the bottom-left side of the screen to confirm your settings.

Double-click ⌷ Controlling Area Settings ⌷ in the left pane. Notice that only version "0" Plan/Actual Version is now displayed (Figure 18-4) and the status bar says, "One entry chosen".

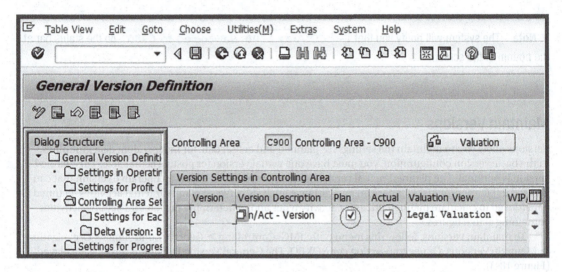

Figure 18-4. *Specifying the General Version Definition for plan/actual version*

Make sure that Plan and Actual are checked. Using the pull-down arrow by the Valuation View field, select Legal Valuation in Valuation View. All postings are therefore done in version 0. Legal valuation will enable you to valuate business processes in accordance with your company code statutory accounting requirements.

To set the fiscal year for your version, select or highlight the 🖹 Plan/actual version ⌷ version and double-click the next folder down ⌷ Settings for Each Fiscal Year ⌷ on the left pane of the screen. The Change View "Settings for Each Fiscal Year": Overview screen is displayed. Select the current fiscal year from the list of years displayed in the Version Settings for Each Fiscal Year. Your selection will turn yellow; click the Details 🔍 button on the top-left side of the screen. The Change View "Settings for Each Fiscal Year": Details screen is displayed. Most of the settings you need are set by default. Click the Price calculation tab to display the Price Calculation screen (Figure 18-5).

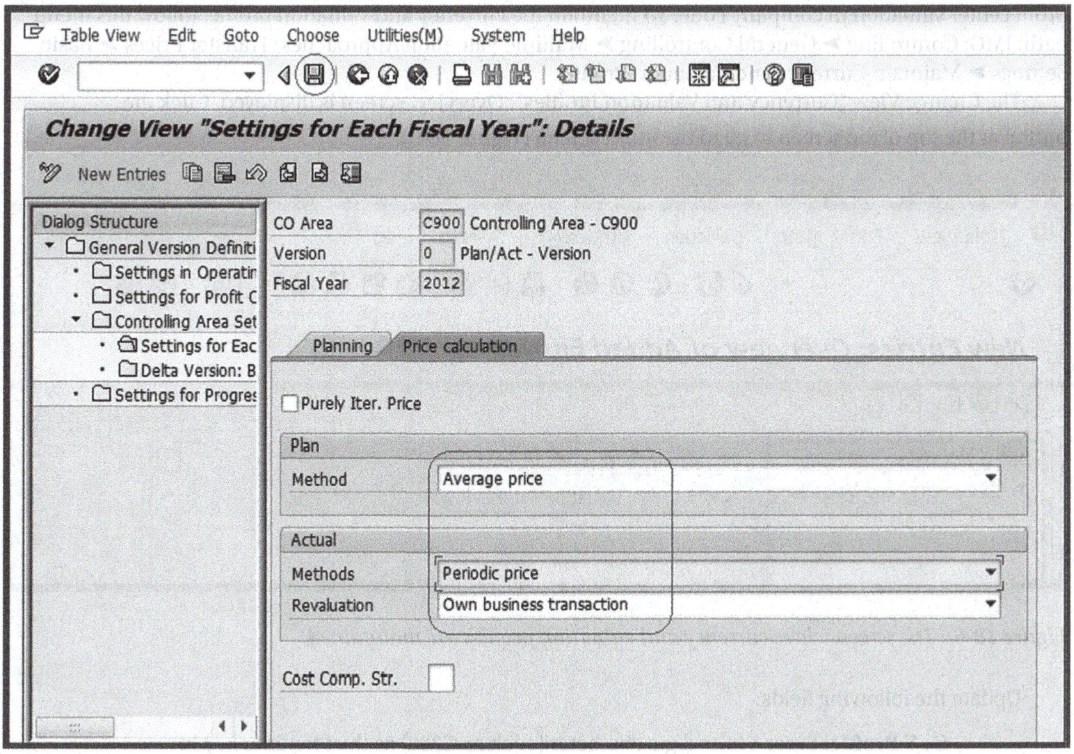

Figure 18-5. Specifying the fiscal year price calculations

Update the following fields:

Method: The system defaults to average price. You have two price options to choose from—Average and Periodic Prices. We recommend that you stick to Average Price in the plan section.

Methods: You have three options to choose from—Periodic Price, Average Price, and Cumulative Price. Choose the one most appropriate for you. In this exercise, we used Periodic Price.

Revaluation: Using the pull-down arrow next to the Revaluation field, select Own Business Transaction from the list.

Save 💾 your version.

Multiple Valuation Approaches/Transfer Prices

The settings you make when customizing the Multiple Valuation Approach/Transfer Prices allow you to pass and clear deliveries of goods using multiple valuation (parallel valuation) approaches between company codes and profit centers within a corporate group. By maintaining a currency and a valuation profile, you can determine the valuation approaches to use in the accounting components, such as currencies and valuations. For example, you can determine the currency managed in legal valuation in the company code currency, the currency managed in corporate valuation in the group currency, and the currency managed in profit center valuation in company code. To maintain the currency and valuation profile, follow this menu path: IMG: Controlling ➤ General Controlling ➤ Multiple Valuation Approaches/Transfer Prices ➤ Basic Settings ➤ Maintain Currency and Valuation Profile.

The Change View "Currency and Valuation Profiles": Overview screen is displayed. Click the New Entries button at the top of the screen to go to the input screen (Figure 18-6).

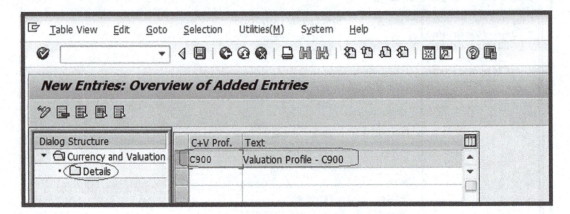

Figure 18-6. *The screen where currency and valuation profiles are maintained*

Update the following fields:

> **C+V Profile:** Enter a four-digit-character (such as C900) as the identifier key in the Currency &Valuation Profile field.

> **Text:** Enter a short description (such as Valuation Profile – C900) here.

Click the Enter ✅ button to confirm your entries. The system will notify you on the status bar that "One entry chosen".

The next step is to specify the currency type and the valuation view for your currency and valuation profile. To do this, make sure that your C+V profile is selected and double-click the ⬜Details folder. The Change View "Details": Overview screen is displayed. Click the New Entries button.

Update the appropriate fields using the information in Table 18-1.

Table 18-1. *The Information Needed to Complete the Currency and Valuation Profiles Screen*

No.	Currency Type	Valuation View
20	30	Group Valuation
30	30	Profit Center Valuation

Save 💾 your currency and profile.

Create Versions for Valuation Methods

In this exercise, you can create additional versions for representing parallel valuations in the controlling component and make changes to existing ones displayed in the General Version Overview list by controlling area. If transfer pricing (the price used to valuate movement of goods between profit centers) is not used, you should automatically use version 0 in legal valuation for actual posting. On the other hand, if transfer pricing is used, you must maintain parallel actual versions for group valuation and profit center valuation. You also have to specify operational actual version 0 in your settings. This specification becomes the leading valuation in determining which planning, price calculation, planned/actual comparisons, and variance analysis are based.

To maintain currency for valuation methods, follow this menu path: IMG: Controlling➤ General Controlling Organization ➤ Multiple Valuation Approaches/Transfer Prices ➤ Basic Settings ➤ Create Versions for Valuation Methods.

The General Version Definition screen is displayed. From the General Version Overview list, select Plan/actual version and double-click on Controlling Area Settings in the left pane. The Determine Work Area: Entry dialog box pops up. Enter your controlling area (C900) identifier key in the Controlling Area field and click the Enter button to confirm. Make sure Plan and Actual are checked and that Valuation View is set to Legal Valuation. All postings are done in version 0. Save and then click on the Back button to return to the previous page.

On the General Version Definition screen, click the New Entries button to define additional versions for your valuations. Update the screen using the information shown in Figure 18-7.

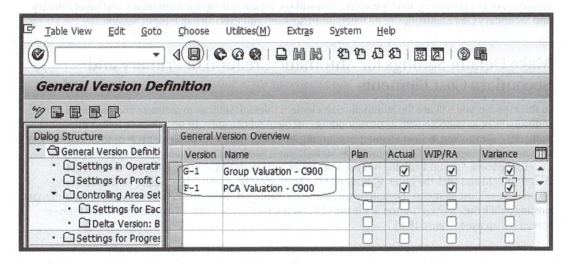

Figure 18-7. Creating versions for your valuation methods

■ **Note**   Version keys are freely definable. You can use any version key in this exercise. The version keys we used in the definition of our version are for illustration purposes and are not the standard. We used G-1 for group valuation and P-1 for profit center accounting.

Click the Enter button to confirm your entries and save your work. Select or highlight the versions for the valuation method you have just created (G-1 and P-1) and then double-click the Controlling Area Settings folder. The Confirm Transfer from Version dialog box pops up with the question, "Version G-1 does not exist in CO Area C900. Transfer version to CO Area?" Click the YES button on the bottom-right side of the screen. A second Confirm Transfer from Version dialog box pops up with the question, "Version P-1 does not exist in CO Area C900. Transfer version to CO Area?" Click the YES button again and then save your work.

Cost Element Accounting

The Cost Element function is very important and plays a significant role when reconciling costs and postings between FI and the Controlling (CO) module. Cost Element is a function in CO that reconciles costs and revenue in FI and primary costs in CO. Simply put, all cost and revenue flows via its cost element between FI and CO.

In SAP, cost element is classified into two categories:

- *Primary cost element*: The primary cost element allows costs and revenues to flow between FI and CO when a corresponding G/L account exists in FI. This cost element can only be created in an environment where costs/revenues exist in a G/L account in the chart of accounts in FI.

- *Secondary cost element*: This is the opposite of the primary cost element. Costs that arise in controlling are purely for internal cost allocations, overhead apportionments, and other internal costs.

A cost element can be created in IMG (Using Automatic Creation of Primary and Secondary Cost Elements) or in Accounting. In this exercise, you will set default settings for Automatic Creation of Primary and Secondary Cost Elements, Create Batch Input Session, and Execute Batch Input Session.

Make Default Settings for Automatic Creation of Primary and Secondary Cost Elements

In this exercise, you will use the automatic cost element's default settings to maintain cost elements individually or as intervals with a corresponding cost element category. To set a default, follow this menu path: IMG: Controlling ➤ Cost Element Accounting ➤ Master Data ➤ Cost Elements ➤Automatic Creation of Primary and Secondary Cost Elements ➤ Make Default Settings. Or use transaction code OKB2. The Determine Work Area Entry dialog box pops up. Enter your chart of accounts (CA90) in the Chart of Accounts field and click the Enter ✅ button at the bottom of the screen. The Change View "Automatic Generation of Cost Elements: Default Setting screen is displayed. To set the default settings for the automatic postings, click the New Entries button at the top of the screen. The New Entries Overview of Added Entries screen is displayed (Figure 18-8).

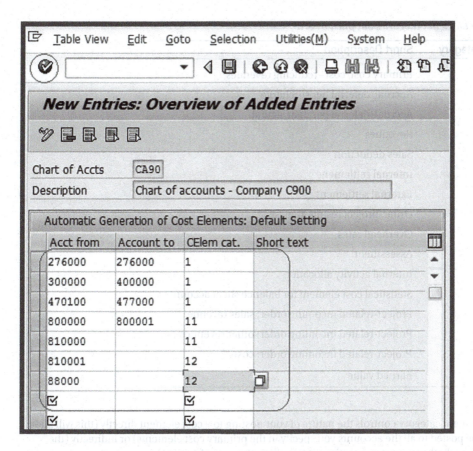

Figure 18-8. Default settings for automatically generating cost elements

Specify the account ranges you want to include in your default settings in the Account fields. Begin with the lowest number in the account number range in the Acct from and Account to fields and include all the numbers in the specified range. Also, specify the Cost Element category for your account range. For example, for accounts ranging from 3000 to 4000, the assigned cost element is 1, as these accounts are expenses (primary cost/cost-reducing revenues).

SAP comes with a predefined list of cost element categories to choose from. A list of cost elements supplied by SAP is in Table 18-2.

Table 18-2. *Cost Element Categories Supplied by SAP*

Cost Element Category	Short Description
1	Primary cost/cost –reducing revenues
3	Accrual/deferral per surcharge
4	Accrual/deferral per debt, actual
11	Revenues
12	Sales deduction
21	Internal settlement
22	External settlement
31	Order/project results analysis
41	Overhead rates
42	Assessment
43	Internal activity allocation
90	Statistical cost element for balance sheet account
50	Project-related incoming order: sales revenue
51	Project-related incoming order: other revenues
52	Project-related incoming order: costs
61	Earned value

The Cost Element category controls the nature of your posting to a cost element directly (this will allow transactions to be posted to all the accounts you specify in the primary cost elements) or indirectly (the system determines whether to post transactions internally at the time of posting).

When you click Enter ✅ to confirm your entries, the Short Texts field automatically describes the cost elements you selected. Save 💾 your specifications.

Since you have completed the process of customizing the default settings of cost elements, the next step is create a batch input session for the cost element defaults you have specified. This will complete the creation of your primary cost elements for your controlling area.

Create Batch Input Session

Batch input provides a way to transfer huge amounts of data into the SAP R/3 system. To create a batch input section, follow this menu path: IMG: Controlling ➤ Cost Elements Accounting ➤ Master Data ➤ Cost Elements ➤ Automatic Creation of Primary and Secondary Cost Elements ➤ Create Batch Input Session. Or use transaction code OKB3. The Create Batch Input Session to Create Cost Elements screen is displayed (Figure 18-9).

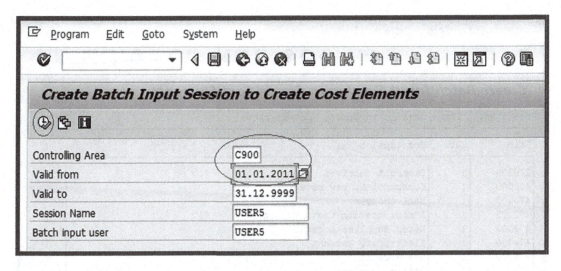

Figure 18-9. *Specifying the controlling area and validity date for executing a batch input session*

In Figure 18-9, notice that the system has set the Valid To date as the current date by default, as well as the session name and batch input user (as user ID). Use the information in Table 18-3 to update the screen.

Table 18-3. *The Data Needed to Update the Create Batch Input Session to Create Cost Elements Screen*

Field	Value	Description
Controlling Area	C900	Enter your controlling area ID.
Valid From	01.01.2011	Enter an earlier date than the current fiscal year.
Valid To	31.12.9999	This defaults to the future year. You can override this if desired.
Session Name	USER5	The system defaults to your user ID.
Batch input user	USER5	The system defaults to your user ID.

Click the Execute ⊕ button on the top-left side of the screen; the system will execute your batch input session. The Create Batch Input Session to Create Cost Elements screen will be displayed showing a list of accounts you have created (Figure 18-10).

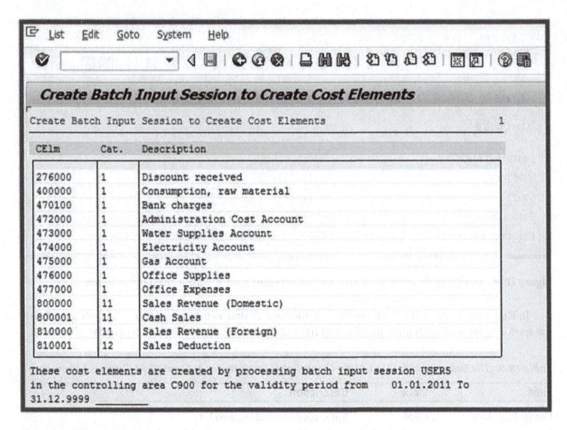

Figure 18-10. *A batch input session displaying accounts created in cost elements*

Execute a Batch Input Session

When a batch input session is generated, the system will automatically determine the chart of accounts to be processed and the cost elements to be created based on the company code and chart of accounts assigned to the controlling area. To generate a cost element you created, you can execute a batch input session. Follow this menu path: IMG: Controlling ➤ Cost Elements Accounting ➤ Master Data ➤ Cost Elements ➤ Automatic Creation of Primary and Secondary Cost Elements ➤ Execute Batch Input Session. Or use transaction code SM35. The Batch Input: Session Overview screen is displayed (Figure 18-11).

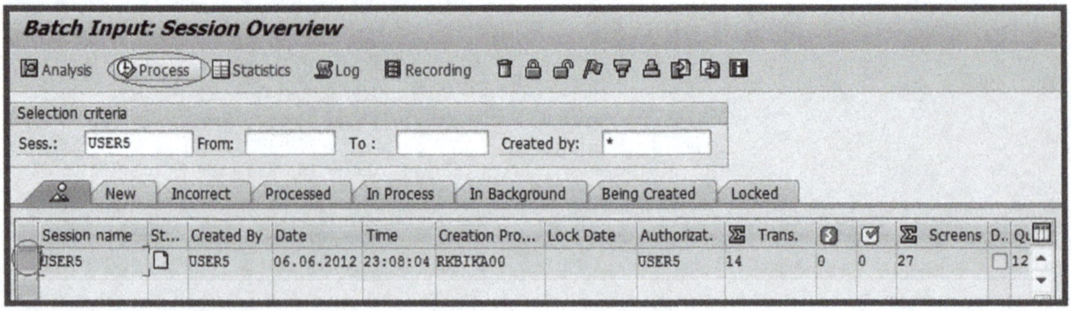

Figure 18-11. *Processing a batch input session*

Select or highlight your cost element from the list of the session names and then click the ⊕ Process button on the top-left side of the screen. The Process Session screen pops up (Figure 18-12). This screen allows you to set other options for your batch input session.

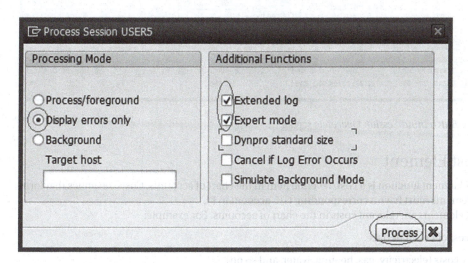

Figure 18-12. *The screen where the processing mode and additional functions are specified for batch input processing*

Select the following indicators:

- *Display Errors Only*: When this radio button is clicked, the system will allow you to check for errors resulting from faulty transactions and correct them online. It allows you to run transactions in background mode.

- *Extended Log*: This is an additional function in batch input processing. When you select this checkbox, all messages encountered when a transaction is run are displayed. This includes warning messages, error messages, information messages, and other messages returned by SAP.

- *Expert Mode*: This is an additional function. Expert mode only works in interactive batch input.

■ **Note** A session that you want to process immediately is scheduled as a background process using the Background mode. It enables transactions to be processed in the background, freeing your entry screen for data input.

Click the Process button on the bottom-right side of the screen for your batch input session to apply the set indicators. An Information dialog box appears with the message, "Processing of batch input session completed." Confirm the message by clicking the ✔ Session overview button at the bottom of the screen. Notice that the Status ☑ button is checked (Figure 18-13), indicating that the status of your batch input session is completed.

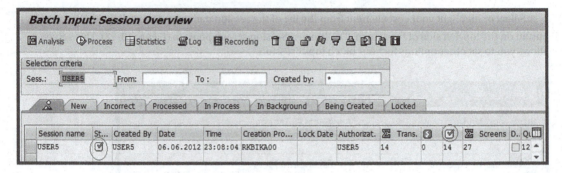

Figure 18-13. *The Batch Input Session Overview screen*

Primary Cost Element

The Primary Cost Element function is a cost/revenue item in the chart of accounts. Costs/revenues that form part of the cost elements must have a corresponding G/L account in FI.

Primary cost elements are relevant costs in the chart of accounts. For example:

- The cost of raw materials

- Utility costs (electricity, gas, heating, water, and so on)

■ **Note**   To be able to create a cost element, you must make sure that a corresponding G/L accounts exists in the chart of accounts. Otherwise, you have to create the appropriate G/L account first in the chart of accounts.

Problem: Now that you have set defaults for automatic creating of primary and secondary cost elements, your next task as a functional consultant is to create a primary cost element for Cash Purchase – Office Material using the G/L account 460000. Make sure that the validity date includes the current year.

To create a primary cost element, follow this menu path: IMG: Easy Access: Accounting ➤ Controlling ➤ Cost Element Accounting ➤ Master Data ➤ Cost Element ➤ Individual Processing ➤ Create Primary. Or use transaction code KA01. The Create Cost Element: Initial Screen is displayed. Update the appropriate fields using the data in Table 18-4.

Table 18-4. *The Initial Data Needed to Create a Primary Cost Element*

Field	Value	Description
Cost Element	460000 (Cash purchase of office materials)	Enter the G/L account for cash purchases.
Valid From/To	01.01.2011 - 31.12.9999	Enter a date range for your primary cost element. Make sure that the date range includes the company code's current fiscal year. For example, if your company code fiscal year is 01.01.2012, set your valid from date to a year earlier (01.01.2011) and the end date to any date after the fiscal year (31.12.9999).

■ **Tip** When you enter a valid from date into the Valid From field and click the Enter button, the system will automatically set the Valid To date for you. Although you can modify the Valid To date, we recommend that you use the default.

Click the Master Data button on the top-left side of the screen to create the cost element master record. The Create Cost Element: Basic Screen is displayed. The system will automatically set the Name and Description of the cost element in the Basic Data section of the screen (Figure 18-14).

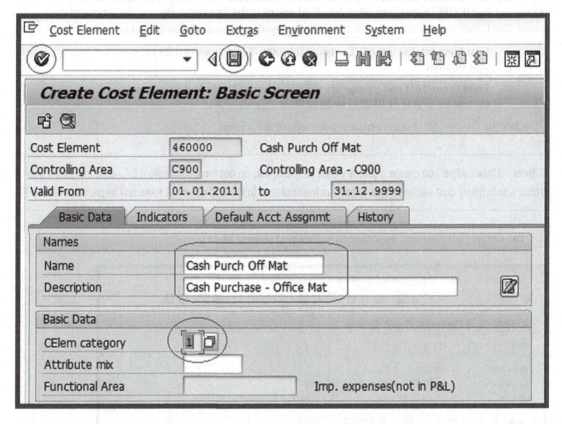

Figure 18-14. Creating a primary cost element master record

In the Basic Data section of the screen, select 1 for the Cost Element Category (Primary Cost/Cost – Reducing Revenues) using matchcode. Click the Enter ⊘ button to confirm your entries and then save 💾 your cost element master data. The system will notify you on the status bar that ☑ Cost element has been created .

Secondary Cost Elements

Secondary cost elements are costs that arise within the controlling module due to internal cost allocations, overhead apportionment, and other internal costs.

> **Problem:** *As a functional consultant your task is to create a secondary cost element for IT service costs (called 600000). Make sure that the valid date includes the current year.*

To execute the batch input section, follow this menu path: IMG: Easy Access: Accounting ➤ Controlling ➤ Cost Element Accounting ➤ Master Data ➤ Cost Element ➤ Individual Processing ➤ Create Secondary. Or use transaction code KA06. The Set Controlling Area dialog box pops up. Enter your controlling area (C900) in the Controlling Area field and click the Enter ✅ button at the bottom of the screen. The Create Cost Element: Initial Screen is displayed. Update the following fields:

> **Cost Element:** Enter the G/L account (600000—IT Service Cost) for your cost element.

> **Valid From/To:** Enter a range of valid dates that will include the company code current fiscal year 01.01.2011 to 31.12.9999.

Click the `Master Data` button on the top-left side of the screen.

■ **Note**   Unlike when you create a primary cost element, you do not have to create a G/L account before you create a secondary cost element. This is only an internal cost in CO and does not have any implication on the FI.

The Create Cost Element: Basic Screen is displayed (Figure 18-15).

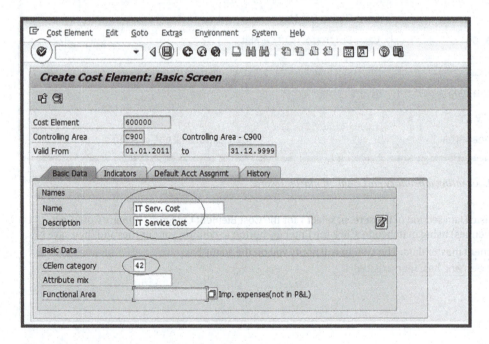

Figure 18-15. *Creating a secondary cost element*

Update the following fields:

> **Name:** Enter the IT Serv. Cost. This is a short description of your secondary cost element.

> **Description:** Enter the IT service cost. This is a full description of your secondary cost element.

> **CElem Category:** Enter 42 – Assessment as your cost element category.

After updating the screen, click the Enter ✅ button on the top-left side of the screen and save 💾 your work.

■ **Note** You can change, display, and delete cost elements after saving and you can also display any changes you made.

Cost Center Accounting

A cost center, simply put, is a function in an organization that incurs its own costs, which may or may not add to its profit. Typical examples include Production, Administration, R&D, Marketing, and so on. Cost center accounting helps to monitor costs to ensure they are within budget.

In order to customize the Cost Accounting feature, you will configure the following settings:

- Define the standard hierarchy

- Create a cost center group

- Define cost elements for activity allocation

- Create activity types

- Use statistical key figures

- Change activity output/price planning

- Compare cost centers: actual/plan/variance

Define the Standard Hierarchy

A standard hierarchy is simply a tree structure that allows you to structure cost centers in a controlling area in a systematic manner.

> **Problem:** *As its functional consultant, Company C900 plc has asked you to define the standard hierarchy for their controlling area C900, which contains all their cost centers and the appropriate cost center groups using the standard hierarchy structure.*

■ **Note** It is possible to change an existing hierarchy supplied by SAP system or create a new one.

In this exercise, you will maintain the relevant standard hierarchy for your controlling area. Before you start this exercise, let's first map out the costs hierarchy you will be using for your cost center standard hierarchy. There is no standard way of doing this. In practice, standard hierarchy can be very lengthy and cumbersome. It is important that you spend quality time mapping out your standard hierarchy before commencing your configuration. We have provided a standard hierarchy mapping in Table 18-5 to help you define the standard hierarchy for your cost centers. You can refer back to this table as you build the hierarchy levels.

Table 18-5. *Mapping for Defining the Standard Hierarchy*

Level 1	Level 2	Level 3	Level 4	Level 5
Controlling Area H-C900 Standard hierarchy-HC900	Company Code	Divisions	Cost Groups	Cost Centers
	C900 Company C900	1000 - Corporate	1100 - Executive Board	1110 - Executive Board (5)
			1200 - Internal Services	1210 - Corporate Services (5) 1220 - Cafeteria (4) 1230 - Telephone (4) 1240 - Car Fleet Dept. (4)
		2000 - Admin & Finance	2100 - Administration	2110 - Electricity (4) 2120 - Finance & Admin
			2200 – HR	2210 - Human Resources (4)
		3000- Marketing & Sales	3100 - Procurement 3200 - Sales Group 3300 - Marketing	3110 - Procurement (4) 3210 Sales (3) 3310 Marketing (3)
		4000 - Technical Area	4100 - Production	4110 - Car (1) 4120 Lorry (1) 4130 Bus (1)
			4200 - Services	4210 Training (7) 4220 - ERP Consulting (7) 4230 - Support & Advice

To define the standard hierarchy, use this menu path: IMG: Controlling ➤ Cost Center Accounting ➤ Master Data ➤ Cost Centers ➤ Define ➤ Standard Hierarchy. Or use transaction code OKEON. The Set Controlling Area dialog box pops up. Enter your controlling areas (C900) in the Controlling Area fields. Click the Enter ✅ button at the bottom of the screen. The Standard Hierarchy for Cost Center Change screen is displayed, where you will define the standard hierarchy for your cost centers. Follow the five steps (levels) outlined in the next sections.

Level 1: Update the Standard Hierarchy Group Name

Your standard hierarchy H-C900 created in the Maintain Controlling Area section earlier should be displayed and automatically selected by the system (the selection is yellow). Otherwise, you have to select it by clicking on it. In the Details for Cost Center Group section of the screen (Figure 18-16), update the group name by entering a descriptive name (for example, Standard Hierarchy) in the Group Name field.

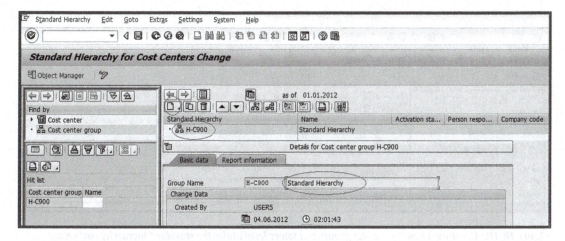

Figure 18-16. *Defining a standard hierarchy for the cost centers*

Click the Enter ✅ button on the top-left side of the screen.

Level 2: Create a Cost Center Group for Your Company Code

The next step is to create a lower group level for a cost center group for your company code in the Standard Hierarchy section (Figure 18-17).

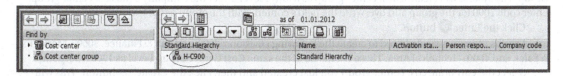

Figure 18-17. *Creating a lower group level under the standard hierarchy*

To create a lower group in the standard hierarchy, select the cost center group for standard hierarchy 🖧 H-C900 and then click the Create 🗋 button on the top-left side of the screen. A pull-down menu appears with a list of the following options:

- Lower level group

- Group at the same level

- Cost center

Since you a creating a lower cost group level in the standard hierarchy for the cost center group, select Lower Level Group from the pull-down menu. A new lower level cost center group is created under the standard hierarchy cost center group. The system will automatically highlight the new group you just created. In the Details for Cost Center Group section, enter a code (C900) for the group and overwrite the field's content. (Change "New group" to your own group name; in this case, Company C900 Plc, as shown in Figure 18-18).

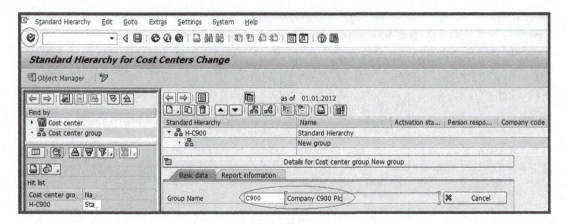

Figure 18-18. *Creating a new cost center group as a lower level under the standard hierarchy cost center group*

Click the Enter ✅ button on the top-left side of the screen.

Level 3: Create Divisions

In this level you will create lower group levels under the company code for Divisions. Select Cost Center Group for the company code 🔳 C900 and click the Create 🔲 button. From the pull-down menu, select Lower Level Group. The system will create a cost center group as a lower level under the company code cost center group. Enter code 1000 for the group and overwrite the field's content with the group name —Corporate.

Click the Enter ✅ button.

For this exercise, you also need to create the following Divisions: 2000 – Admin & Finance, 3000 – Marketing & Sales, and 4000 – Technical Area. These should be at the same Cost Center Group Level as 1000 - Corporate.

Select the corporate cost center group you just created and then click the Create 🔲 button. This will allow you to create a same level group for the remaining divisions. Click ⌈ Group at Same Level ⌉ on the pull-down menu. Update the group name with information for the next division—2000 – Admin & Finance—and then click the Enter ✅ button. Repeat this step to complete the remaining cost center groups for the division using the data in Table 18-5, which you saw earlier in the section "Define the Standard Hierarchy." Upon completion, your hierarchy will look like the one in Figure 18-19.

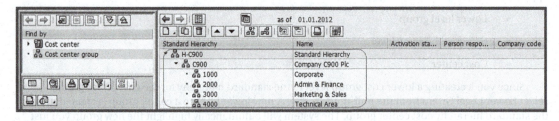

Figure 18-19. *Maintaining a cost center group for divisions*

Save 💾 your entries.

Level 4: Create Cost Groups

In this level you create cost groups Table 18-5) at a lower group for the divisions you just created in level 3. First, create the cost groups for 1000 – Corporate on the standard hierarchy. To do this, select 1000 - Corporate on the standard hierarchy and click the Create 🗔 button. From the pull-down menu, select Lower level group. Update the Group Name field with 1100 – Executive Board and click the Enter ⊘ button. The Executive Board Cost Group will be included in the standard hierarchy under corporate as a lower level. Using Table 18-5 as a reference, create the remaining cost groups. You can display the entire standard hierarchy that you have created by clicking the 🗀 [Details for Cost center group Process] bar. Your standard hierarchy you have created so far should look like the one in Figure 18-20.

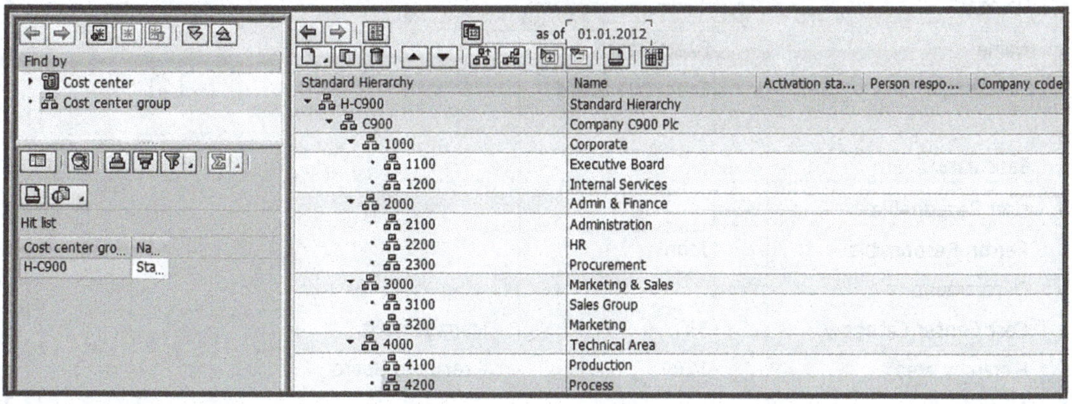

Figure 18-20. *Details for the cost center group process*

Save 💾 your work.

Level 5: Create Cost Centers

At this level, you create cost centers for the cost groups that you created in level 4. To create cost centers, follow this menu path: IMG: Controlling ➤ Cost Center Accounting ➤ Master Data ➤ Cost Centers ➤ Create Cost Centers. Or use transaction code KS01. The Choose Activity screen pops up with two options on the screen. You can create or change a cost center. Double-click the Create Cost Center option. The Set Controlling Area screen pops up. Enter your controlling area (C900) in the Controlling Area field and click the Enter ☑ button at the bottom of the screen to set the controlling area. The Create Cost Center Initial Screen is displayed. Update the following fields:

> **Cost Center:** Enter a cost center identifier (1110) in the cost center field. This is the number we suggested for the executive board in Table 18-5.

> **Valid From:** Enter the date you want the cost center to be valid from, such as 01.01.2011 (we advise that you use a date a year earlier than your fiscal year). Make sure that the valid from date includes your company code's current fiscal year.

> **Valid To:** This defaults to 31.12.9999. We recommend that you stick to this date.

Click the Master Data button on the top-left side of the screen. The Create Cost Center: Basic Screen is displayed (Figure 18-21).

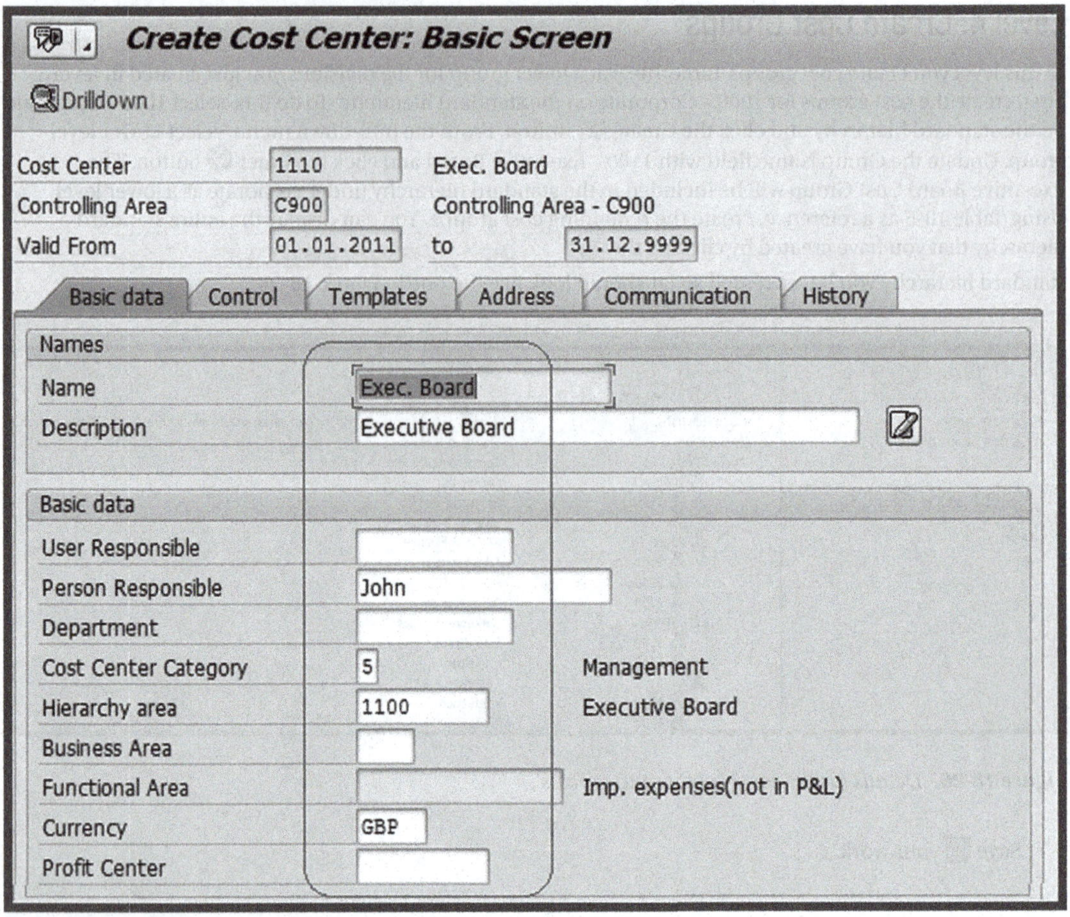

Figure 18-21. *The Cost Center Basic Screen dialog box*

Update the following fields:

Name: Enter the name of your cost center, such as Exec. Board, in this field. This can be an abbreviation.

Description: Enter your cost center description, such as Executive Board. This can be the full name of the cost center. This will allow you to easily distinguish your cost centers.

Person Responsible: Enter the name of the staff responsible for the cost center. We used John in this field. This is optional.

Cost Center Category: Enter the appropriate cost category. In this case, we used 5 (management). The cost center category could be, for example, Production, Sales, Administration, or Management. You can access the cost center category using the matchcode next to the cost center field.

Hierarchy Area: Select the hierarchy area from the standard hierarchy—1100 (Executive Board)—that you created in level 4.

Currency: Enter the currency key (GBP) that you want to apply to your cost center. This field is required.

Profit Center: You cannot enter the profit center for your cost center at this level, because a profit center has not been created. Leave this field blank for now. It will be visited again later in Profit Center section.

Click the Enter ✅ button to confirm your entries and then click Save 🖫. After you save, the system will take you back to the Create Cost Center: Initial Screen.

■ **Note**   The system will issue this warning: ⚠ Profit Center Accounting active but no profit center specified (CCtr 1110) .

Ignore the warning and click on ✅ again. Then save 🖫 your efforts.

Using the information in Table 18-5, create the remaining 16 cost centers. Once you have created all the cost centers, you can display the standard hierarchy using this menu path: IMG: Controlling ➤ Cost Center Accounting ➤ Master Data ➤ Standard Hierarchy ➤ Display. Or use transaction code OKENN. The Standard Centers for Cost Centers Display screen appears. Click the 🗁 Details for Cost center Support and Advice bar to display your standard hierarchy list (Figure 18-22).

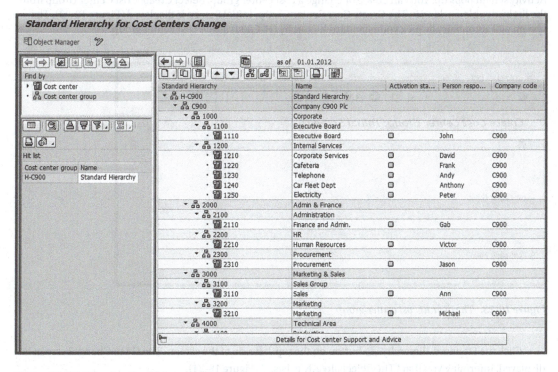

Figure 18-22. *The standard hierarchy list display*

Create Cost Center Group

A cost center group combines cost centers according to organizational and/or functional requirements into groups, thereby making cost center management easy. It also builds groups into cost center hierarchies, which aids reporting summaries for decision-making. After you have created the cost center hierarchy for your controlling area in the master data, when you display Create Cost Center Group: Initial Screen and click the Standard Hierarchy button, the system will automatically generate the cost center group for your standard hierarchy. There must be at least one cost center group in the standard hierarchy and you can add as many alternative or independent groups, as you require. They can be structured according to organizational or functional specific requirements.

The advantages of cost center groups include:

- For performing reporting of activities in specific cost centers in the information system. Information system enables you to generate reports delivered with the system or to create your own reports.

- Processing multiple cost centers in a single transaction, including cost center planning, distribution, and assessment (we will be looking at distribution and assessment later in this chapter).

To create a cost center group, follow this menu path: IMG: Controlling ➤ Cost Center Accounting ➤ Master Data ➤ Cost Centers ➤ Define Cost Centers Group. Or use transaction code KSH1. The Choose Activity screen pops up. You can create or change a cost center group. Select Create Cost Center Group from the list by double-clicking it. The Create Cost Center Group: Initial Screen is displayed (Figure 18-23). The system will automatically pick your standard hierarchy (H-C900) as the cost center group.

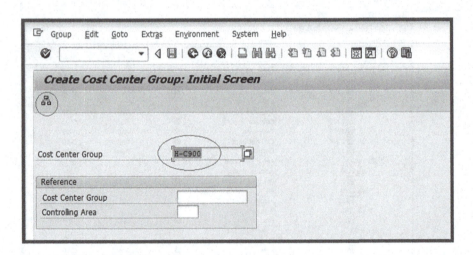

Figure 18-23. *The default cost center group*

Click the Standard Hierarchy ⛃ button on the top-left side of the screen. The Go to Change? screen is displayed, informing you that "The object already exists..." (Figure 18-24).

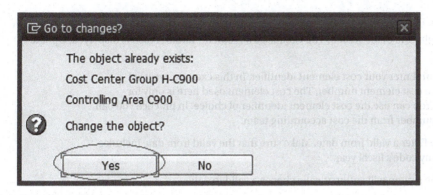

Figure 18-24. *The screen where you can accept or reject existing objects for cost center group in standard hierarchy*

Click the [YES] button on the bottom-left side of the screen; the Change Standard Hierarchy (Cost Center Group): Structure screen is displayed showing the defaulted cost groups (Figure 18-25). You can expand each cost to display details of cost centers by clicking ⊕.

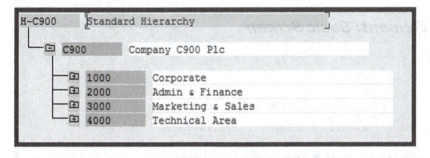

Figure 18-25. *The default standard hierarchy cost center group*

Activity Types

Activity types allow the system to classify similar activities performed at a cost center in a controlling area.

Valuation of activity types for each cost center and period with a given charge rate consist of both fixed and variable portions. This allows costs incurred at a cost center to be distributed adequately to products based on activities performed in relation to products.

In this exercise, you will define cost elements for activity allocation and create activity types.

Define Cost Elements for Activity Allocation

The cost element allocation serves as an activity allocation. It takes the receiver debits and treats them internally as direct or indirect allocations. To define cost elements for activity allocation, follow this menu path: IMG: Controlling ➤ Cost Center Accounting ➤ Master Data ➤ Activity Types ➤ Define Cost Elements for Activity Allocation. The Choose Activity dialog box is displayed. You can change an existing cost element for activity allocation or create a cost element for activity allocation.

Click the `Create Cost Element for Activity Allocation` option and then click the `🔍 Choose` button on the bottom-right side of the screen. The Create Cost Element: Initial screen is displayed. Update the following fields:

> **Cost Element:** Enter your cost element identifier. In this exercise, we used 710000 as the cost element number. The cost element used here is only for illustration. You can use the cost element identifier of choice. In practice you can obtain this number from the cost accounting team.
>
> **Valid From:** Enter a valid from date. Make sure that the valid from date includes your company code's fiscal year.
>
> **Valid To:** The system will automatically choose a valid to date.

Click the `Master Data` button on the top-left side of the screen. The Create Cost Element: Basic Screen is displayed (Figure 18-26).

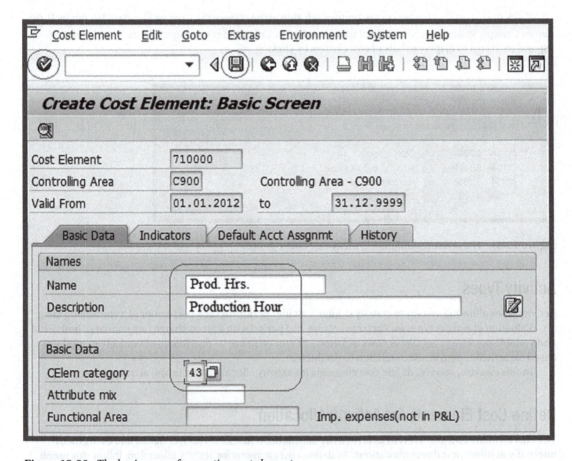

Figure 18-26. The basic screen for creating cost elements

Update the following fields:

Name: Enter the name of your cost element—Prod.Hrs. (this can be an abbreviation).

Description: Enter a full description of your cost element—Production Hour

Cost Element Category: Select the appropriate cost category—43 for internal Activity Allocation. You can access this number using matchcode.

Click the Enter 🗸 button on the top-left side of the screen and save 💾 your work.

Create Activity Types

Before creating your activity types, you must make sure that the following activities have been maintained/ created:

- Controlling area.

- Allocation of cost element.

To create an activity type for your cost center, follow this menu path: IMG: Controlling ➤ Cost Center Accounting ➤ Master Data ➤ Activity Types ➤ Create Activity Types. Or use transaction code KL01. The Choose Activity screen pops up with the option to create or change an activity type. Select Create Activity Type and then click the 🔍 Choose button on the bottom-right side of the screen. The Create Activity Type: Initial Screen is displayed. Update the following fields:

Activity Type: Enter your Activity Type identifier. For this activity, we used PROD1 as the activity type. There is no special rule to the activity type identifier you can use. It is advisable to use as simple an activity type name as you can remember.

Valid From: Enter the date you want your activity type to be valid from. Make sure that the date entered in this field includes the period you want your activity type to apply to.

Valid To: The system automatically chooses this date.

Click the Master Data button on the top-left side of the screen. The Create Activity Type: Basic Screen is displayed (Figure 18-27).

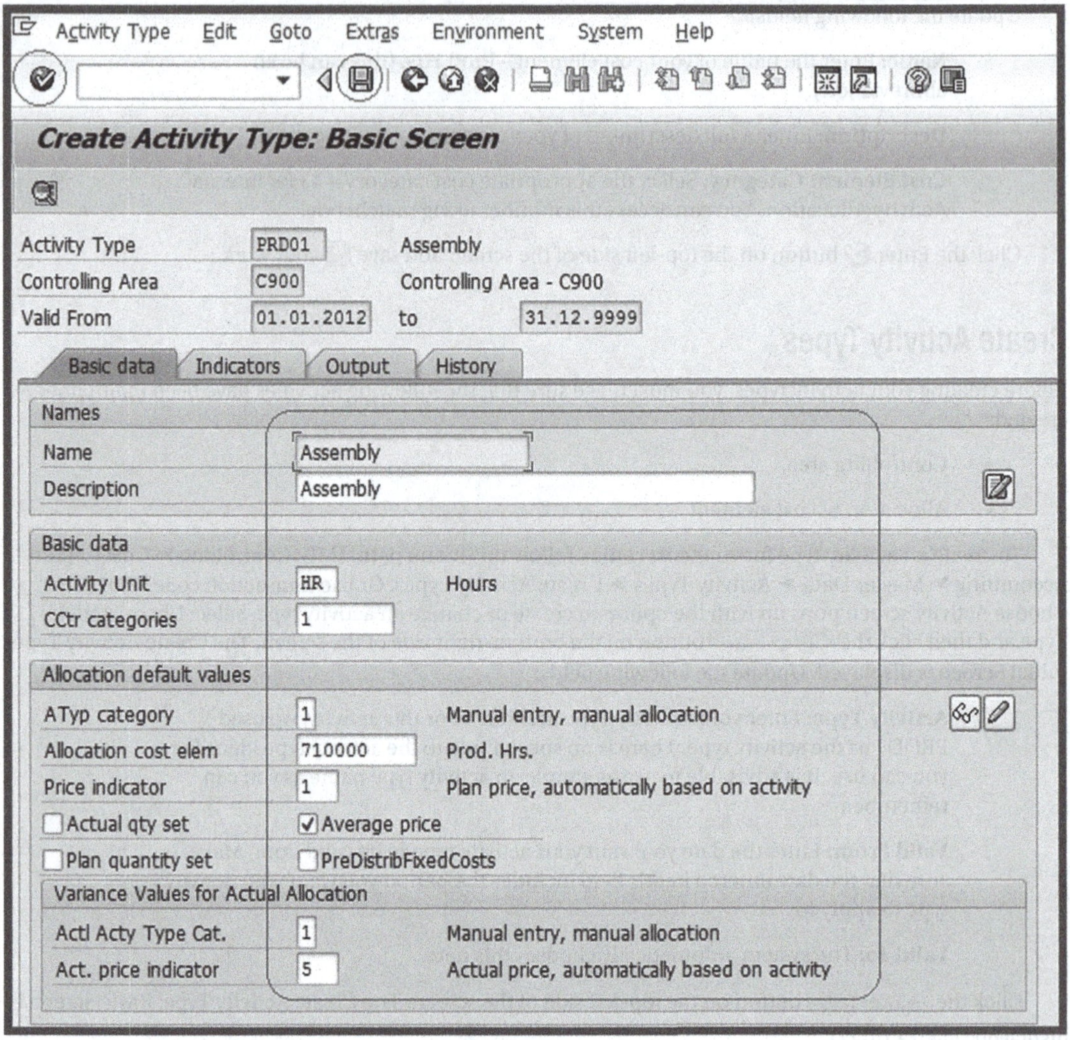

Figure 18-27. *The basic screen for creating activity types*

Update the following fields:

> **Name:** Enter the name—Assembly—for your activity type. This is can be abbreviated if desired.

■ **Note** Activity types is a classification of activities produced in the cost centers within a controlling area. The name (Assembly) we used in this exercise is for illustration purposes only. In practice, you should use a name that reflects your organization's activity types.

Description: Enter a description—Assembly—of your activity type.

Activity/Unit: Enter the measurement unit key—HR (Hours)—that you want to apply to your activity type. For example, Hours, Sales Percentage, and so on. The system has a list of cost center category to choose from. You can access these cost categories using matchcode.

CCtr Categories: Enter the cost center category you want to use for your activity type. The system comes with a list of cost center categories to choose from using matchcode.

ATyp Category: Select the appropriate activity type category—1 (manual entry, manual allocation). The system comes with four activity type categories to choose from.

Allocation Cost Elem: Enter the cost element allocation number—7100000. This is the number you defined in the Define Cost Elements for Activity Allocation section.

Price Indicator: Enter 1 (plan price, automatically based on activity). This specification allows you to calculate an allocation price by planned price automatically based on activity type for a cost center. You also can decide whether allocation calculation should be based on capacity or be determined manually by the user. You can access this indicator using the matchcode.

Average Price: By setting the average price indicator, this will allow the system to determine how price of activity type or business process calculation is performed for a cost center.

Actl Acty Type Cat: Select manual entry, manual allocation from the list of variant activity type categories for actual posting list. This is used to determine how the activity type is allocated.

Act. Price indicator: Select actual price indicator for actual allocation price— 5 (actual price, automatically based on activity). This price indicator also determines how the activity type is calculated.

Click the Enter ✅ button to confirm your entries and save 💾 your activity type.

Use Statistical Key Figures

Statistical key figures provide vital information relating to a business activity measured in non-monetary terms. For example, it can show number of employees, machine hours, and so on. This serves as the basis for internal allocation, which is defined either as a fixed value or as total values.

Statistical key figures can be used for the following internal allocations:

Distribution: Method of cost allocation used to allocate FI costs (primary costs) to a cost center, which is applicable to primary cost elements.

Assessment: This is the process of cost allocation generated internally in controlling to cost center. This method of allocation can be used for both primary and secondary costs. Costs allocated are posted to a secondary assessment cost element.

To create statistical key figures, use this menu path: IMG: Controlling ➤ Cost Center Accounting ➤ Master Data ➤ Statistical Key Figures ➤ Create Activity Types ➤ Maintain Statistical Key Figures. Or use transaction code KK01. The Choose Activity Screen is displayed with the option to create or change the statistical key figures. Select Create Statistical Key Figures and click the Choose button on the bottom-right side of the screen. The Create Statistical Key Figure: Initial Screen is displayed. Enter an identifier for your statistical key figure in the Stat. Key Figure field (STAT01) and then click the Master Data button on the top-left side of the screen. This will allow you to enter details in the statistical key figure master data. The Create Statistical Key Figure: Master Data screen is displayed (Figure 18-28). The system will automatically set the statistical key figure and the controlling area.

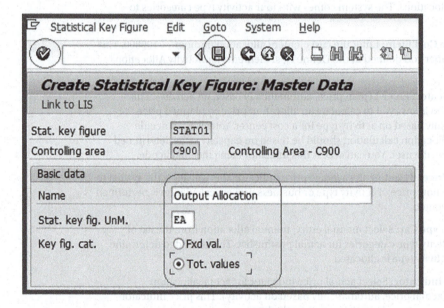

Figure 18-28. Basic screen for creating statistical key figures: master data

Update the following fields:

Name: Enter a description—Output Allocation—for your statistical key figure.

Stat. Key Fig. UnM.: Enter EA (Each) as the unit of measurement for your statistical figure by selecting it from the list supplied by the system using the matchcode.

Key fig. Cat.: You are presented with two options to choose from, either as fixed values or total values, which will serve as a basis for internal allocation for your statistical key figure.

■ **Note**   The Fixed Val. indicator allows you to fix the value used for measurement to be carried forward to a future period. This value can be the number of employees, production hours, and so on.

The Tot. Values indicator enables you to indicate that the total values will vary from period to period. This means for each period you have to specify a new value. This would work well for machine hours, for example.

Click the Enter ✅ button to confirm your entries and save 💾 your statistical key figure customizing.

Change Activity Output/Prices Planning

The Activity Output/Prices Planning option allows you to create multiple plan versions that you can use to compare different plan values or business processes. Go to the Change Activity Type/Price Planning: Initial Screen (Figure 18-29) by following this menu path: Easy Access: Accounting ➤ Controlling ➤ Cost Enter Accounting ➤ Planning ➤ Activity Output/Prices ➤ Change. Or use transaction code KP26.

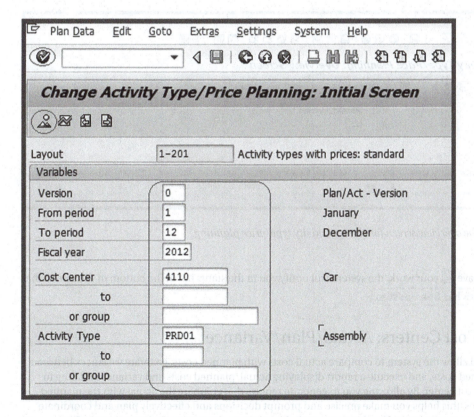

Figure 18-29. The initial screen for change activity type/price planning

Update the following fields:

> **Version:** Enter Plan/Actual version 0. This is a standard version supplied by SAP for this purpose.

> **From/To Period:** Enter the starting and ending period that you want your activity output/price to cover. This is usually 1-12-month periods.

> **Fiscal Year:** Enter the fiscal year you want to cover (the current fiscal year). This will usually be your company code's fiscal year.

> **Cost Center:** Enter the cost center you want to take into consideration in your activity type planning.

> **Activity Type:** Enter the activity type you created.

Click the Enter ✔ button to confirm your entries. To display your activity type planning overview, click the Overview Screen 🔍 button on the top-left side of the screen. The Change Activity Type/Price Planning: Overview Screen is displayed (Figure 18-30).

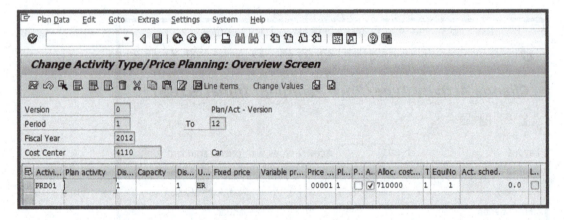

Figure 18-30. *The overview screen for change activity type/price planning*

When you save 💾 your work, the system will notify you in the status bar at the bottom of the screen that ☑ Changed data has been posted .

Compare Cost Centers: Actual/Plan/Variance

This exercise will allow the system to compare actual costs with planned costs, generate variances between actual and planned costs, and execute a report displaying actual/planned costs and variances relating to activities in the cost center. By allowing you to generate reports that compare the actual with the planned business activities, this helps you make precise and prompt decisions and effectively plan and coordinate the business activities efficiently. Use this menu path: Easy Access: Accounting ➤ Controlling ➤ Cost Accounting ➤ Information System ➤ Reports for Cost Accounting ➤ Plan/Actual Comparisons ➤ Cost Center: Actual/Plan/Variance. Or use transaction code S_ALR_87013611.

The Cost Centers: Actual/Plan/Variance: Selection screen is displayed. Using the data in Table 18-6, update the fields listed.

Table 18-6. *The Data Needed to Complete Cost Center: Actual/Plan/Variance Selection Screen*

Field	Value	Description
Controlling Area	C900	Enter your controlling area.
Fiscal Year	2012	Enter the fiscal year you want to compare here.
From Period	1	This is the period you want to compare actual costs with plan costs.
To Period	12	The end period for actual/planned/variance.
Plan Version	0	This is the planned version you created in the "Maintain Plan Version" section.

Click the Enter ✔ button to confirm your entries. To execute the actual/plan comparison, click the Execute ⊕ button on the top-left side of the screen. The Cost Centers: Actual/Plan/Variance screen is displayed (Figure 18-31).

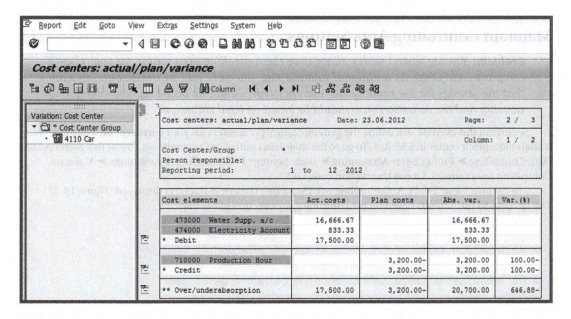

Figure 18-31. *The Cost Centers Actual/Plan Comparison report screen*

Profit Center Accounting

A profit center is a department or unit within an organization that generates revenues. Profit centers can generate revenues and perhaps costs to arrive at a profit.

Under profit center accounting, you will configure the following settings:

- Maintain controlling area settings
- Create a dummy profit center
- Set control parameters for actual data

- Maintain plan versions

- Define a standard hierarchy for profit centers

- Define profit centers

- Define number ranges for local documents

- Assign profit centers to cost centers

Basic Settings

First, you need to define the setting for the controlling area necessary to set up profit center accounting. Secondly, you need to maintain the global settings for profit center accounting in the controlling area. To set your controlling area, follow this menu path: IMG: Controlling ➤ Profit Center Accounting ➤ Basic Settings ➤ Set Controlling Area Settings. Or use transaction code OKKS.

The Set Controlling Area dialog box is displayed. Enter your controlling area (C900) in the Controlling Area field and click the Enter ☑ button to confirm.

Maintain Controlling Area Settings

Problem: You are tasked with maintaining the controlling area setting for your client's company code C900. As additional information, you were told by the accounting team that the settings for the profit center currency type should be based on controlling area currency and the valuation view should be based on legal valuation.

Settings in this exercise will define the general control parameters for your current controlling area as it relates to a profit center in SAP R/3. To go to the maintain controlling area settings, follow this menu path: IMG: Controlling ➤ Profit Center Accounting ➤ Basic Settings ➤ Controlling Area Settings ➤ Maintain Controlling Area Settings. Or use transaction code OKE5.

The Change View "EC-PCA: Controlling Area Settings": Overview screen is displayed (Figure 18-32). The system will use defaults based on the controlling area section of the page.

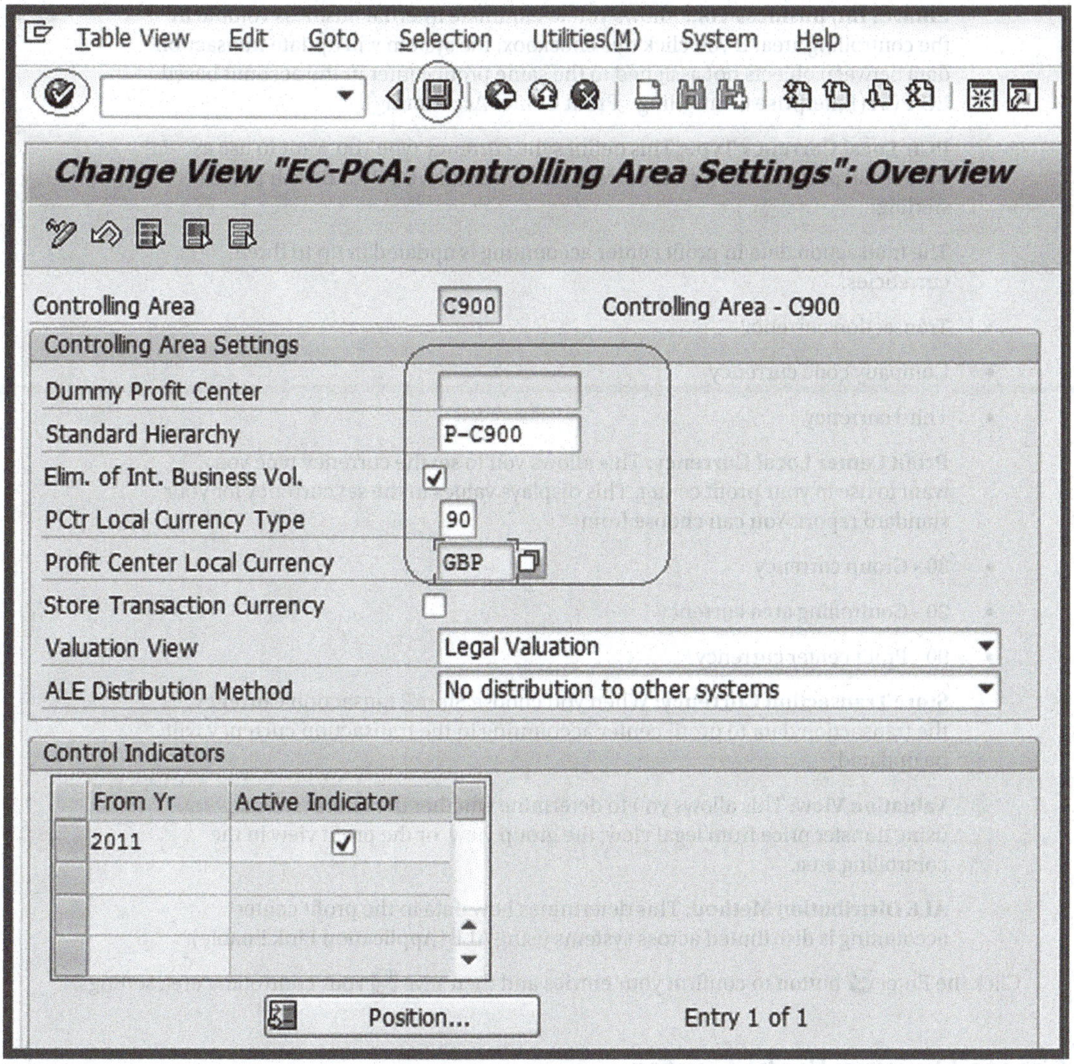

Figure 18-32. *The overview screen for controlling area settings*

Update the following fields:

> **Standard Hierarchy:** Enter a meaningful key as your profit center standard
> hierarchy. The profit center standard hierarchy will be used to define the tree
> structure of the profit center belonging to your controlling area. In this exercise
> we used P-C900.

> **Dummy Profit Center:** All postings in the system to objects that are not assigned
> to a profit center are received by a dummy profit center. The dummy profit center
> here is inactive. We will be defining dummy profit center in the next section.

Elim. of Int, Business Vol.: Allows you to eliminate internal business volume in the controlling area. If you click this checkbox, the system will update transaction data between objects not assigned to the same profit center in the account based EC-PCA (Enterprise Controlling - Profit Center Accounting).

PCtr Local Currency Type: This defines the currency type you want to use as the special profit center report currency. For example, GBP for British pound sterling.

The transaction data in profit center accounting is updated in up to three currencies:

- Transaction currency

- Company code currency

- Third currency

Profit Center Local Currency: This allows you to set the currency type you want to use in your profit center. This displays values in the set currency for your standard report. You can choose from:

- 30 - Group currency

- 20 - Controlling area currency

- 90 - Profit center currency

Store Transaction Currency: When you choose Store Transaction Currency, the transaction data to profit center accounting in the transaction currency will be updated.

Valuation View: This allows you to determine whether the data is stored using transfer price from legal view, the group view, or the profit view in the controlling area.

ALE Distribution Method: This determines how data in the profit center accounting is distributed across systems using ALE (Application Link Enable).

Click the Enter 🗸 button to confirm your entries and then save 🖫 your controlling area settings.

Create Dummy Profit Center

All postings in the system to objects that are not assigned to a profit center are received by a dummy profit center. This ensures that the data in the profit center accounting is complete. Data on the dummy cost center can later be sent to the other profit centers using the assessment or distribution function.

Problem: *Not all cost centers are assigned to profit centers. You have been asked to create a dummy profit center that the system will automatically post all unassigned cost centers to.*

To create a dummy profit center, follow this menu path: IMG: Controlling ➤ Profit Center Accounting ➤ Master Data ➤ Profit Center ➤ Create Dummy Profit Center. Or use transaction code KE59. The Choose Activity screen pops up and you can create a dummy profit center or change a profit center. Select `EC-PCA: Create Dummy Profit Center` and click the `🔍 Choose` button on the bottom-right side of the screen. The Create Dummy Profit Center: Initial Screen is displayed (Figure 18-33).

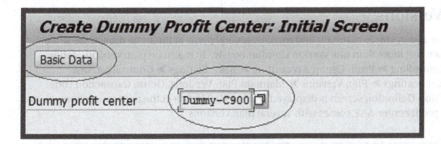

Figure 18-33. *The initial screen for creating a dummmy profit center*

Enter an identification key for your dummy profit center in the Dummy Profit Center field (this could be numeric, alphabetic, or alphanumeric). We used Dummy-C900 in this exercise for illustration purposes. Click the Basic Data button. The Create Dummy Profit Center: Basic Screen is displayed. The system will set the profit center, controlling area, and validity date by default. Update the following fields:

> **Name:** Enter a suitable name, such as Dummy, for your dummy profit center.

> **Description:** Enter a description, such as Dummy – Profit Center, for your dummy profit center.

> **Profit Center Group:** Enter a key as an identification (P-C900) for the profit center group. This is used to group similar profit centers together, based on company specific criteria in a hierarchical structure of profit centers.

Click the Enter ✓ button to confirm your entries and save 💾.

Set Control Parameters for Actual Data

In this exercise, you will set all the control parameters for actual postings in profit center accounting. To set control parameters for the actual data, follow this menu path: IMG: Controlling ➤ Profit Center Accounting ➤ Basic Settings ➤ Controlling Area Settings ➤ Activate Direct Postings ➤ Set Control Parameters for Actual Data. Or use transaction code 1KEF.

The Change View "EC-PCA: Control Parameters for Actual Postings": Overview screen is displayed. To be able to set the indicators for line items and for online transfer, click the New Entries button at the top of the screen. The New Entries: Overview of Added Entries screen appears. Update the appropriate fields using the information listed in Table 18-7.

Table 18-7. *Data to Set Control Parameters for Actual Data*

Field	Value	Description
From Year	2011	The year entered here must not be greater than your company's fiscal year.
Line Items	Tick	Determines whether actual line items are updated.
Online Transfer	Tick	Controls how actual data is transferred to the R/3 system.

Click the Enter ✓ button to confirm your entries and save 💾.

Maintain Plan Versions

The Plan Versions option allows you to maintain and manage several plans at the same time in the same profit center. You can then use more than one version simultaneously. To maintain plan versions, follow this menu path: IMG: Controlling ➤ Profit Center Accounting ➤ Basic Settings ➤ Controlling Area Settings ➤ Activate Direct Postings ➤ Plan Versions ➤ Maintain Plan Versions. Or use transaction code OKEQ. The General Version Definition screen is displayed (Figure 18-34). Select the appropriate version you want to include in your profit center. SAP comes with several plan versions.

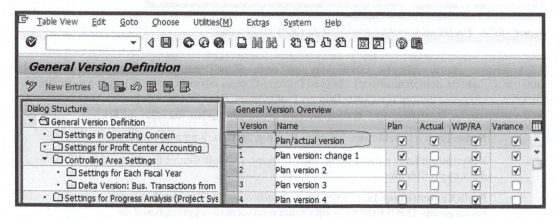

Figure 18-34. *The General Version Definition screen, where you specify the version for your profit centers*

For this exercise, select `0  Plan/actual version` from the list of displayed versions. Double-click the `Settings for Profit Center Accounting` folder on the left pane of the screen.

The Determine Work Area: Entry dialog box pops up. Enter your controlling area code (C900) in Controlling Area field and click the Enter `✓` button on the bottom-left side of the screen. The Change View "Settings for Profit Center Accounting" Overview screen comes up. Click the `New Entries` button to bring up the New Entries screen (Figure 18-35).

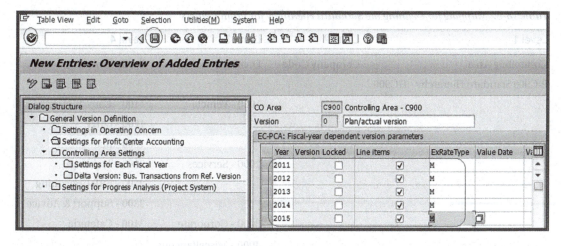

Figure 18-35. *The screen where you update the profit center accounting settings*

Update the following fields:

> **Years:** Enter the years you want to maintain versions for in your profit center. Make sure this includes the fiscal year.
>
> **Line Items:** This option allows you to display line items in your report.
>
> **ExRateType:** The system comes with predefined exchange rates to choose from for your cost planning. Exchange rate type "M" used in this exercise is for standard transactions at average rates.

Click the Enter ✅ button to confirm your entries and save 💾.

Define Standard Hierarchy for Profit Centers

A standard hierarchy is simply a tree structure that allows you to structure profit centers in a controlling area; it shows the divisions responsible for generating profit in profit center accounting.

Before you define a standard hierarchy, it is important to map out the profit center's hierarchy that you will be using as a guide. Because of the complexities involved in customizing standard hierarchies, there is no standard way of doing this. It is important that you spend time mapping out your standard hierarchy before commencing your configuration. We provide a standard hierarchy mapping in Table 18-8 as an illustration to help you define a standard hierarchy for your profit centers.

> **Problem:** *Company C900 Plc has asked you as their functional consultant to define the standard hierarchy for their profit centers in controlling area C900, using the data in Table 18-8.*

Table 18-8. *Mapping for Defining the Standard Hierarchy for Profit Centers*

Level 1	Level 2	Level 3	Level 4
Controlling Area	Company Code	Divisions	Profit Centers
P-C900 Standard Hierarchy - HC900			
		1000 - Vehicle	1100 – Car
			1200 - Lorry
			1300 - Bus
		2000 - Services	2100 - Training
			2200 - ERP Consulting
			2300 - Support & Advice
		3000 - Corporate	3100 - Cafeteria
		4000 - Miscellaneous	

To define a standard hierarchy for your profit centers, follow this menu path: IMG: Controlling ➤ Profit Center Accounting ➤ Master Data ➤ Profit Center ➤ Define Standard Hierarchy. Or use transaction code KCH1. The Set Controlling Area dialog box pops up. This will allow you to set the controlling area for your profit center. Enter your controlling area (C900) in the Controlling Area field and confirm your entries by clicking the Enter ✅ button at the bottom of the screen. The Change Standard Hierarchy (Profit Center Group): Structure screen is displayed (Figure 18-36), which is where you define the standard hierarchy for your profit center.

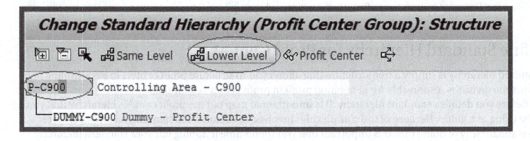

Figure 18-36. *Defining a standard hierarchy for the profit center group*

Since you want to create a lower level node under your standard hierarchy, select P-C900 – Controlling Area on the standard hierarchy and click the ⬚ Lower Level button in the middle of the screen to create a node under Dummy – Profit Center you created earlier. A node appears in the hierarchy under Dummy Profit Center. Update the node with your profit center group using the data in Table 18-8. Enter the profit center code 1000 and a description (such as Vehicles) in respective fields (Figure 18-37).

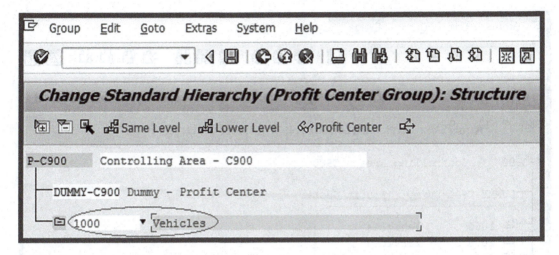

Figure 18-37. *Updating a standard hierarchy for a profit center group*

You need to create another node at the same level with 1000-Vehicles for 2000-Services. Select the 1000-Vehicles node from the hierarchy by clicking on it and then click the ⬚ Same Level button. A blank node appears at the same level under 1000-Vehicles. Update the node by entering the code for profit center (2000) and a description of the profit center (Services).

Repeat this process to create the followings profit center groups:

- 3000 – Corporate

- 4000 – Miscellaneous

The hierarchy structure for your profit center groups should look like the one shown in Figure 18-38.

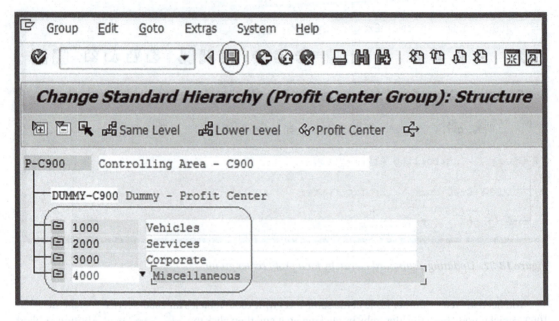

Figure 18-38. *The complete standard hierarchy for the profit center groups*

Save 🖫 your work.

Define Profit Center

In this exercise, you will define a profit center and change the profit center master data.

■ **Note**   Before creating a profit center, make sure that you have defined the standard hierarchy for your profit center in the controlling area's basic settings.

To define a profit center, follow this menu path: IMG: Controlling – Profit Center Accounting – Master Data – Profit Center – Define Profit Center. Or use transaction code KE51. The Create Profit Center Choose Activity screen is displayed with the option to create or change a profit center. Select EC-PCA: Create Profit Center from the activity list by double-clicking it or selecting it and then clicking the 🖳 Choose button on the bottom-right side of the screen. An initial Create Profit Center screen comes up. Enter your profit center. It is advisable to use a numeric value. We used 1100 as our profit center. To specify details for the proft center, click the Master Data button on the top-left side of the screen. The Create Profit Center screen for further specifications is displayed (Figure 18-39). On this screen, notice the defaults used in the following fields— Controlling Area – C900, Profit Center -1100, and Analysis Period – 01.01.2012-31.12.9999. You can change the analysis period if you choose to.

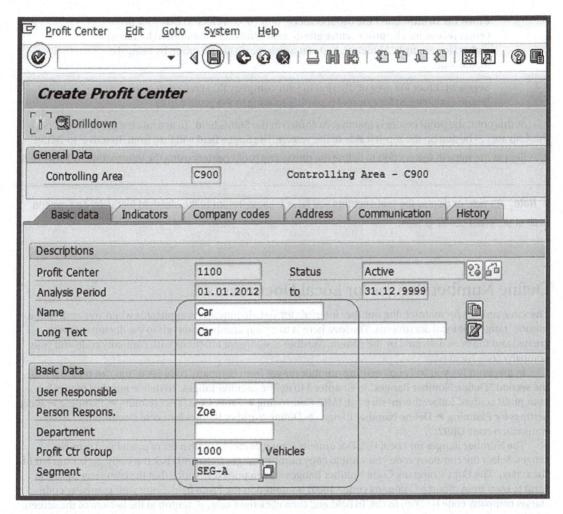

Figure 18-39. *The screen where you enter details for your profit center and ensure that the profit center status is active*

Update the following fields:

> **Name:** Enter the name of your profit center. In this exercise we used Car as our profit center name. You can use an abbreviation.

> **Long Text:** Enter the full name or a detailed description of your profit center, such as Car (Vehicle).

> **User Responsible:** This is the name of the user of the profit center. This is optional.

> **Person Respons.:** Enter the name of the key staff responsible for the profit center, such as Zoe.

> **Department:** This is the department in your organization that's in charge of the profit center. This field is optional.

Profit Ctr Group: Enter the profit center group 1000 (Vehicles) that your profit center relates to. The profit center group was defined in the standard hierarchy earlier (for example, Vehicles). You can access profit center group by using the matchcode.

Segment: Enter the area or division in your company that creates its own financial statement for external reporting relating to the profit center.

At this point the profit center is inactive, as shown in the Status field. To activate the profit center, click the Activate 🔲 button on the top-left side of the screen. The Status field will turn from 'Inactive' to 'Active'.

Repeat the steps in this section to define the remaining profit centers using the information in Table 18-8.

■ **Note** To view or display the profit centers you have created, return to the standard hierarchy and expand each of the profit center groups.

Define Number Ranges for Local Documents

The same process for maintaining number intervals for G/L documents is applicable when you're defining number ranges for local documents. The idea here is to assign number intervals to the documents you created and the ones delivered by the system. Number assignment functions with company code and your company code fiscal year.

In this exercise, you will copy existing number ranges from company code 1000. You can refer back to the section "Define Number Ranges" in Chapter 3 to define number ranges. To define number ranges for your profit centers, follow this menu path: IMG: Controlling ➤ Profit Center Accounting ➤ Planning ➤ Basic Settings for Planning ➤ Define Number Ranges ➤ Define Number Ranges for Local Documents. Or use transaction code GB02.

The Number Ranges for Local G/L Documents screen comes up with a list of predefined number ranges. Select the company code you want to copy number ranges from and click the Copy 🔲 button left of the screen. The Copy Company Code Number Ranges screen pops up. Notice that the company code you want to copy from (Source Company code - 1000) is entered in the From field. Enter your company code (target company code is C900) in the To field and then click the Copy 🔲 button at the bottom of the screen. The Transport number range intervals screen pops up with a message. Ignore the message and click the Enter ☑ button at the bottom of the screen to confirm your action. The system will then notify you that 🔲 ☑ CoCode 1000 was copied to C900 .

Assign Profit Centers to Cost Centers

The final stage in creating profit centers is to assign the profit centers to the cost centers you created in the "Create Cost Centers" section in the "Cost Center Accounting" section, earlier in this chapter.

■ **Note**   Not all cost centers generate profits. Only cost centers that generate profits are assigned to profit centers. The cost centers that are not assigned to a specific profit center will be automatically assigned to a dummy profit center.

To assign profit centers to cost centers in the cost center master data, follow this menu path: IMG: Controlling ➤ Cost Center Accounting ➤ Master Data ➤ Cost Centers ➤ Change Cost Centers. Or use transaction code KS02.

The Choose Activity screen is displayed with options to create or change a cost center. Select the option to `Change Cost Center` master data and click the `⌕ Choose` button on the bottom-left side of the screen. The Set Controlling Area dialog box pops up. Enter your controlling area (C900) in the Controlling Area field and click the Enter ✔ button at the bottom of the screen to confirm your entries. The Change Cost Center Initial Screen is displayed.

■ **Note**   For illustration purposes, we assume that the following cost centers generate profits and costs and should therefore be assigned profit centers: Cafeteria, Car, Lorry, Bus, Training, and ERP Consulting.

Enter the cost center 1220 (for Cafeteria) in the Cost Center field and then click the `Master Data` button on the top-left side of the screen to call up the Change Cost Center: Basic Screen (Figure 18-40). This is where you assign the appropriate profit center to the cost center in the cost center master data.

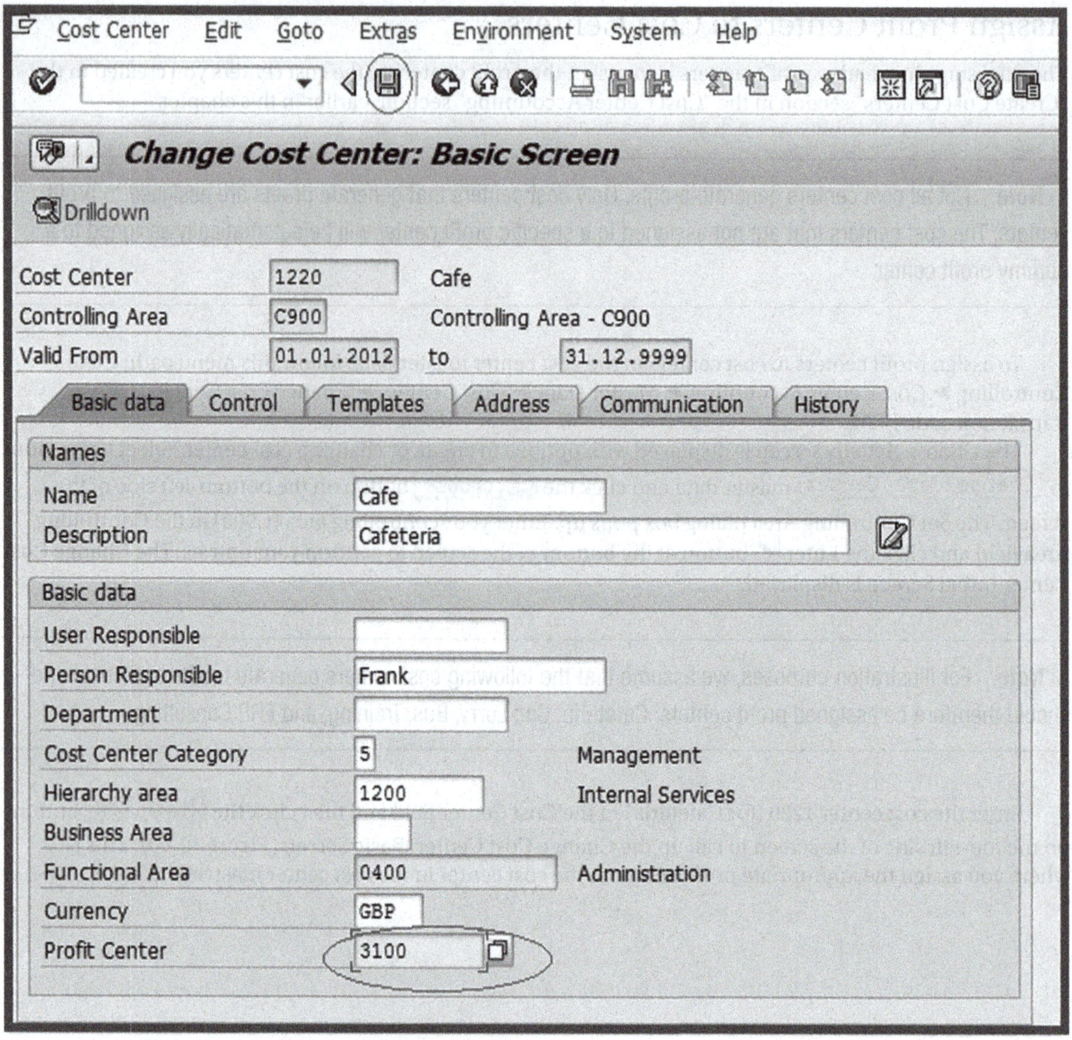

Figure 18-40. *Assigning a profit center to a cost center*

The settings you made in the cost center will be the defaults here. The only change you need to make in this exercise is to assign cost centers to profit centers. Using the matchcode, enter the cost center 3100 (Café) in the Profit Center field and save 💾 your changes.

■ **Note** If the valid date for your profit and cost centers are not the same, you may likely experience problems when saving your work. The system will issue an error message on the status bar stating that "Profit Center C900/ 3100 does not exist for the validity date 01.01.XX".

To resolve this issue, go back to the profit center master data and make the validity date the same as the cost center master's date.

The Change the field screen pops up with a message relating to the changes you have made in your cost center master data. Confirm these changes by clicking the [YES] button at the bottom of the screen.

Repeat the steps in the "Assign Profit Centers to Cost Centers" section to assign the remaining cost centers to profit centers.

Now let's post some controlling documents in FI to test what you have done so far.

Posting Controlling Documents

It is important to note that during FI document posting, cost object's (for example, cost center, internal order and so on) controlling documents are automatically posted in controlling. Use transaction code FB60 to go to the Enter Vendor Invoice: Company Code C900 screen. Post a document controlling document using the data in Table 18-9.

Table 18-9. *The Data Needed to Post a Controlling Document in FI*

Field	Value	Description
Vendor	300124	Using the matchcode, enter the vendor account you are posting the document to.
Invoice Date	21.06.2012	Use today's date as your invoice date.
Posting Date	Today's date	Use today's date as your document posting date.
Amount	1000	Enter the document amount.
Calculate Tax	Check	Check to set the system to calculate tax amount for this document.
Tax Code	A2	Enter the tax code for input tax that the system will use when calculating the tax amount.
G/L Account	474000	The account the document is posted to.
D/C	Debit	Since this transaction is an expense, the accounting treatment is a debit. The system will automatically credit the corresponding vendor's account.
Amount	1000	The document amount that is posted to the expense account as a debit.
Cost Center	4110	The cost center that the expense is posted to.

■ **Note** The system will automatically update the Profit Center field. You can check to see if the profit center is assigned to the document entry by scrolling to the right side of the screen (Figure 18-41).

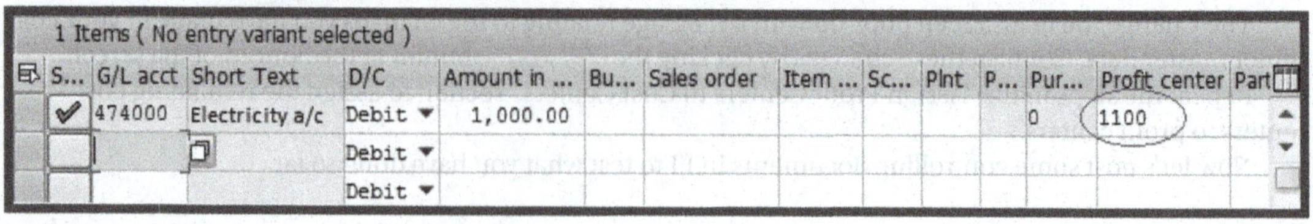

1 Items (No entry variant selected)													
S...	G/L acct	Short Text	D/C	Amount in ...	Bu...	Sales order	Item ...	Sc...	Plnt	P...	Pur...	Profit center	Part
✓	474000	Electricity a/c	Debit ▼	1,000.00							0	1100	▲
			Debit ▼										▼
			Debit ▼										

Figure 18-41. The Enter Vendor Invoice: Company Code C900 screen

You will notice that profit center 1100 is assigned automatically through the cost center assignment in the Profit Center field. Once you are satisfied with your entries, click the **Simulate** button at the top of the screen to display your transaction entry and post 🖫 your invoice entries.

Now that you have posted a controlling document in FI, let's see how this affects the controlling module.

Display Line Items

To display line items, use transaction code FBL1N. The Vendor Line Item Display screen comes up.

■ **Note** For more information on line items, refer back to Chapter 17 (in the section "Display line items") to see the note on line item display.

Update the screen with the information shown in Table 18-10.

Table 18-10. Information to Update the Line Item Display Screen

Field	Value	Description
Vendor Account	300124 (your vendor)	Enter the vendor account that you want to display the line item.
Company code	C900 (your company code)	Enter your company code.
Open Items	Select	Check this option to display all open items in the vendor account.

For the system to execute line items, click the Execute ⊕ button on the top-left side of the screen. The Vendor Line Item Display screen appears showing all the open line items for your vendor (Figure 18-42).

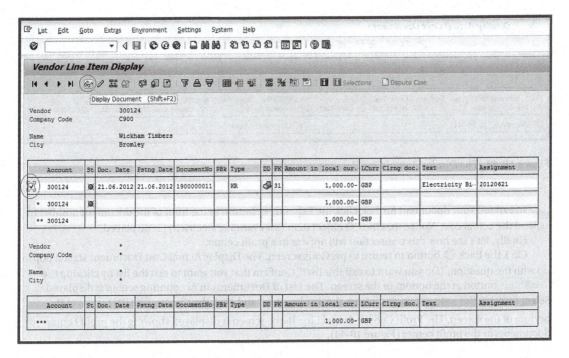

Figure 18-42. *The Vendor Line Items Display screen*

Check the item you want to consider in the controlling document by selecting the checkbox in the Account column. To display the item you selected, click the Display Document 👓 button on the top-left side of the screen. The Display Document: Line Item 001 screen comes up. Click the Call Up Document Overview 🔲 button at the top of the screen. The Display Document: Data Entry View screen is displayed. On the menu bar at the top of the screen, click the Environment button; a pull-down menu is displayed. Select Document Environment from the list and then select Accounting Documents from the sub pull-down menu. The List of Documents in Accounting screen pops up.

Select 0200000000 Controlling Document from the displayed list of items on the screen and then click the 🔲 button at the bottom of screen. The Display Actual Cost Documents screen appears displaying the cost objects posted to the system (Figure 18-43).

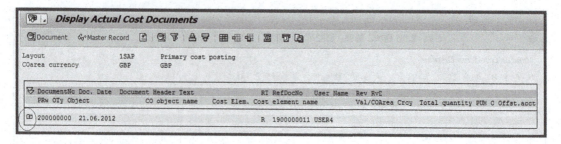

Figure 18-43. *The Display Actual Cost Documents screen*

To expand your document further, click the Expand 🔲 button in the front of the document number to expand the actual cost. Notice that the CO object item (for example, electricity) is displayed.

Finally, let's see how this transaction will appear in a profit center.

Click the Back 🔙 button to return to previous screen. The Display Actual Cost Document screen pops up with the question, "Do you want to exit this list?" Confirm that you want to exit the list by clicking the ▭ YES ▭ button at the bottom of the screen. The List of Documents in Accounting screen is displayed. Select 0000329729 Profit center doc. from the displayed list and click the Choose 🔲 (F2) button at the bottom of the screen. The Profit Center: Actual Line Items screen is displayed showing the profit center documents in the profit center (Figure 18-44).

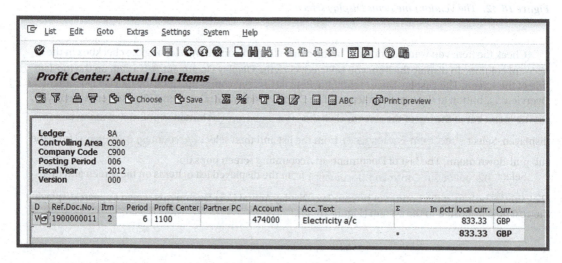

Figure 18-44. *Profit center's actual line item display*

Profit Center: Interactive Reporting

Several reports can be displayed in the system. In this exercise, you will only look at the profit center group: plan/actual/variance report. To generate the profit center group planned and actual variance report, follow this menu path: Easy Access: Accounting ➤ Controlling ➤ Profit Center ➤ Information System ➤ Interactive Reporting ➤ Profit Center Group: Plan/Actual/Variance. Or use transaction code S_ALR_87013326.

■ **Tip** The system may request a controlling area setting. If this is the case, enter your controlling area (C900) in the Set Controlling field in the controlling area screen and then confirm your entry.

The Selection: Profit Center Grp: Plan/Actual/Variance screen is displayed. Using the data in Table 18-11, update the appropriate fields.

Table 18-11. *The Data Needed to Specify Profit Center Interactive Reporting*

Field	Value	Description
From	1	Enter the start period that you want to include in the report.
To	12	Enter the period you want the report to end. This is the accounting period that you want to include in your report. This is usually between 1 to 12 months for a given fiscal year.
Fiscal Year	2012	Enter the accounting year you want to include in your report. This is likely to be the current fiscal year.
Plan Version	0	Enter the version of your plan version. For this exercise use version 0.

Update the fields and then click the Execute button on the top-left side of the screen to generate the report.

■ **Tip** Try other reports on your own.

Distribution

Distribution is the method of cost allocation that you use when allocating primary costs of a cost center between the sender and the receiver. In this exercise, we will configure settings for actual distribution. We will define distribution in the form of cycles by defining rules for the settlement of primary costs for a cost center. Original costs are passed on to the receiver cost center by way of allocation.

You can access the screen to define distribution in two ways, in easy access or using IMG:

- Easy Access: Accounting ➤ Controlling ➤ Cost Center Accounting ➤ Period-End Closing ➤ Current Settings ➤ Define Distribution

- IMG: Controlling ➤ Cost Center Accounting ➤ Actual Posting ➤ Period-End Closing ➤ Distribution ➤ Define Distribution

The Choose Activity screen is displayed, where you can create or change an actual distribution. Select Create Actual Distribution from the list and click the 🔍 Choose button at the bottom of the screen. The Create Actual Distribution Cycle: Initial Screen is displayed (Figure 18-45). This is where you define the cycle ID and the start date of the distribution circle.

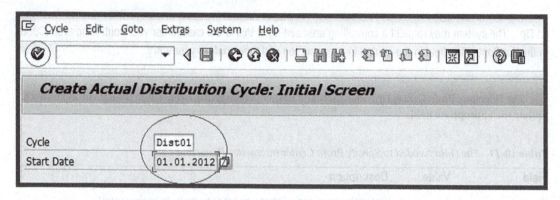

Figure 18-45. *The initial screen to define the cycle ID and the start date of the distribution cycle*

Update the following fields:

Cycle: Enter an ID (DIST01) for your distribution cycle. This can be a numeric or an alphanumeric digit. Whatever you use as your identifier digit must be agreed on with the cost accounting team.

Start Date: This is the date you want your distribution cycle to start. This can be the start date of your current fiscal year.

Click the Enter ✅ button to proceed to the Create Actual Distribution Cycle: Header Data screen. Enter a description for your distribution cycle in the Text field (Distribution Circle –C900).

To attach a segment to your distribution cycle, click the Attach segment button. The Create Actual Distribution Cycles: Segment screen is displayed (Figure 18-46).

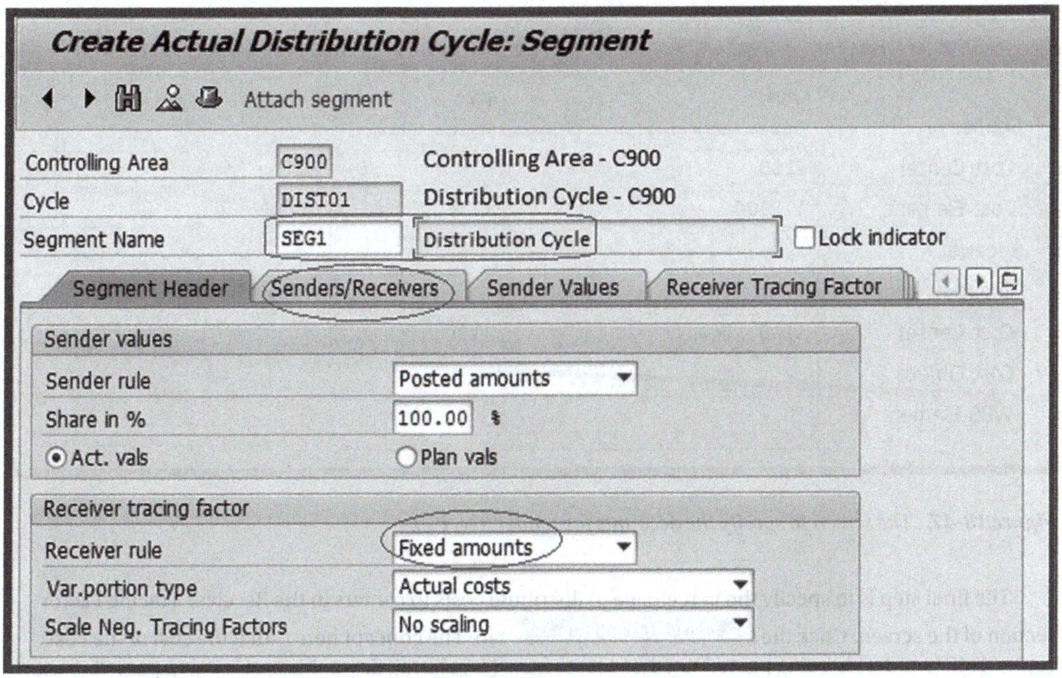

Create Actual Distribution Cycle: Segment

◀ ▶ 💾 👤 🖨 Attach segment

Controlling Area	C900	Controlling Area - C900
Cycle	DIST01	Distribution Cycle - C900
Segment Name	SEG1	Distribution Cycle ☐ Lock indicator

Segment Header | **Senders/Receivers** | **Sender Values** | **Receiver Tracing Factor** ◀ ▶ 🗗

Sender values

Sender rule	Posted amounts ▼
Share in %	100.00 %
⦿ Act. vals	○ Plan vals

Receiver tracing factor

Receiver rule	Fixed amounts ▼
Var.portion type	Actual costs ▼
Scale Neg. Tracing Factors	No scaling ▼

Figure 18-46. *The Create Actual Distribution Cycle (Segment Header) screen*

Enter a key (SEG1) and a name for your segment distribution cycle in the Segment Name field. The sender rule defaults to posted amounts, and share in % is set to 100% by default. Change the receiver rule to Fixed Amounts. A receiver rule controls how the receiver-tracing factor is determined. By specifying fixed amount as a tracing factor, a specific amount allocation is passed to receivers based on the sender rule.

The next step is to specify the cost center and cost element for the sender and receiver. Click the **Senders/Receivers** tab at the top of the Create Actual Distribution Cycle: Segment screen to go to sender's section of the screen. Enter the cost center you want to include in your distribution cycle and specify the cost element range as well in the respective fields. In the Receiver section, enter the receiving cost centers (Figure 18-47).

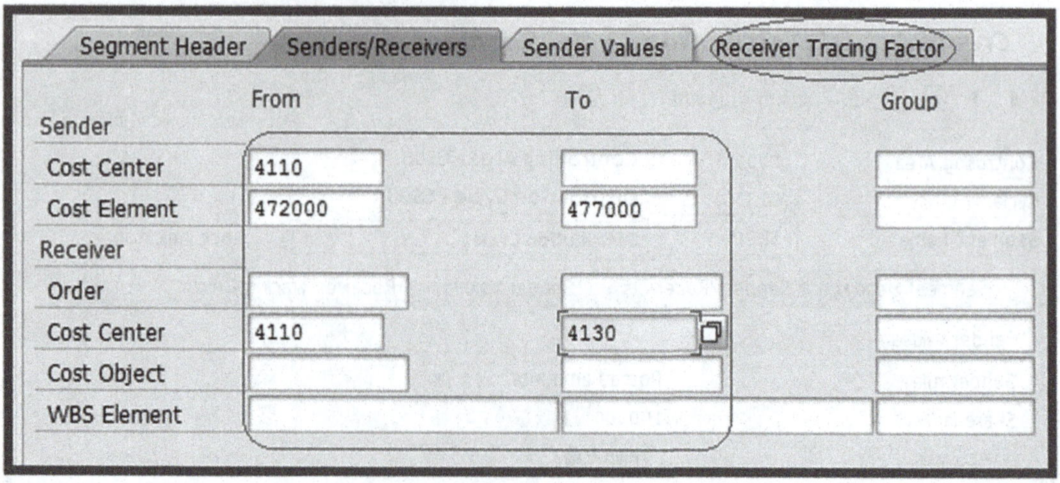

Figure 18-47. *The screen to specify the accounts for sender/receiver*

The final step is to specify the percentage to distribute costs to centers in the Receiver Tracing Factor section of the screen. Click the **Receiver Tracing Factor** tab. The concept here is that the cost of the cost center 4110 (sender) is being passed to other cost centers (receivers). Since this cost is being passed to more than one cost center, it is important to distribute the cost to each cost center (the receivers) systematically. You can do this by using percentage rates as the basis of apportioning the cost to each receiving cost centers 4120 – 4130. The total percentages you apply to the cost centers must equal 100%. See Figure 18-48.

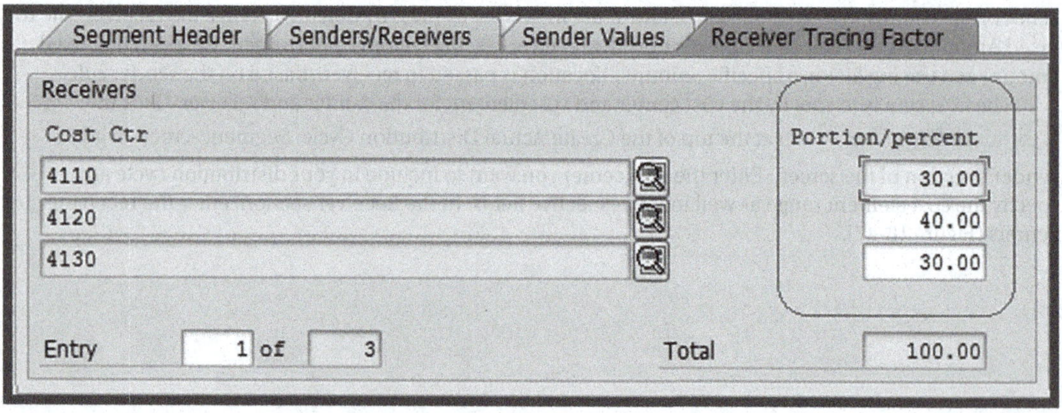

Figure 18-48. *The screen where you set the mode of apportionment in percentage rate between cost centers (receivers)*

Save 💾 your efforts. The system will notify you that ☑ Cycle DIST01, starting date 01.01.2012 has been saved in the status bar at the bottom of the screen.

Let's see how the distribution you have created works by posting some expenses in G/L accounts.

G/L Account Posting

Use transaction code FB50 to enter the G/L account documents. Using the Enter G/L Account Document: Company Code C900 screen in Figure 18-49 as a model, update your screen.

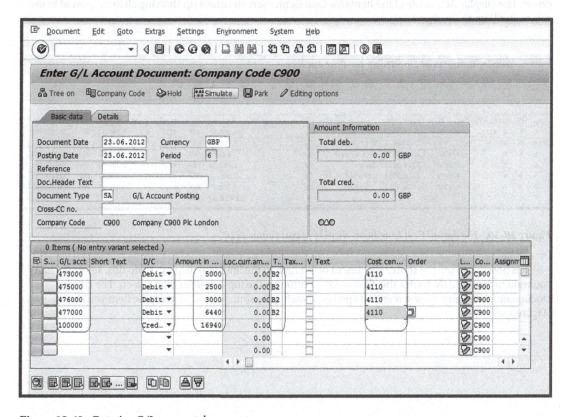

Figure 18-49. *Entering G/L account documents*

Click the Enter 🖉 button. Notice that the status bar for each of the G/L accounts you have entered are ticked green. In order to instruct the system to calculate tax using the tax code you have entered, click the Details tab at the top of the screen and make sure that the Calculate Tax checkbox is checked ☑.

To display your entries, click the 🔅Simulate button at the top of the screen. The Document Overview screen displays all the items you entered in the G/L account. If you are satisfied with your entries, you can post 💾 them.

Finally, let's see how the cost center line items are displayed.

Display Actual Cost Line Items for Cost Centers

To display the cost line items for your cost centers, use this menu path: Easy Access: Accounting ➤ Control ➤ Cost Center Accounting ➤ Information System ➤ Report for Cost Center Accounting ➤ Line Items ➤ Cost Centers: Actual Line Items. Or use transaction code KSB1.

The Display Actual Cost Line Items for Cost Centers: Initial Screen is displayed. You can enter a range of cost centers that you want to display in your line items in the Cost Center fields if you choose to display more than one cost center in your line item display. For this exercise, enter Cost Center 4110 in the Center field and click the Execute ⊕ button on the top-left side of the screen to generate line items report of the cost center. The Display Actual Cost Line Items for Cost Center screen comes up showing all items posted in the cost center (Figure 18-50).

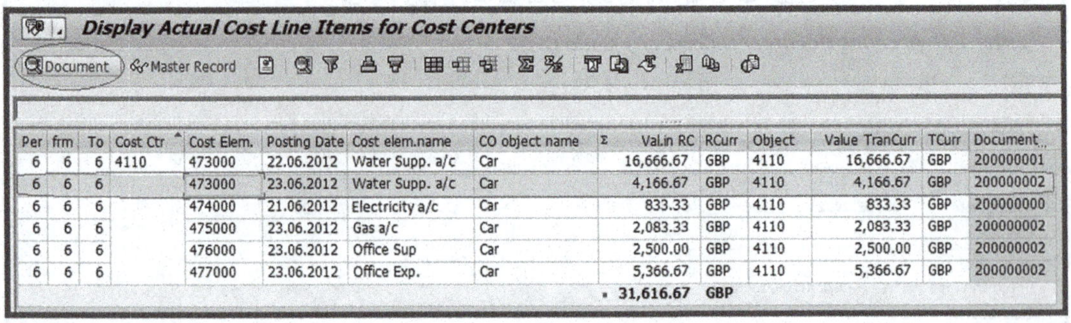

Per	frm	To	Cost Ctr	Cost Elem.	Posting Date	Cost elem.name	CO object name	Σ	Val.in RC	RCurr	Object	Value TranCurr	TCurr	Document
6	6	6	4110	473000	22.06.2012	Water Supp. a/c	Car		16,666.67	GBP	4110	16,666.67	GBP	200000001
6	6	6		473000	23.06.2012	Water Supp. a/c	Car		4,166.67	GBP	4110	4,166.67	GBP	200000002
6	6	6		474000	21.06.2012	Electricity a/c	Car		833.33	GBP	4110	833.33	GBP	200000000
6	6	6		475000	23.06.2012	Gas a/c	Car		2,083.33	GBP	4110	2,083.33	GBP	200000002
6	6	6		476000	23.06.2012	Office Sup	Car		2,500.00	GBP	4110	2,500.00	GBP	200000002
6	6	6		477000	23.06.2012	Office Exp.	Car		5,366.67	GBP	4110	5,366.67	GBP	200000002
								▪	31,616.67	GBP				

Figure 18-50. *The Actual Cost Line Items display of cost center 4110*

It is possible to see the source document on an item in the line item display. To do this, select the item you want to view and then click the 🔍 Document button on the top-left side of the screen. The Display Document: Data Entry View screen is displayed showing the source document for the item you chose (Figure 18-51).

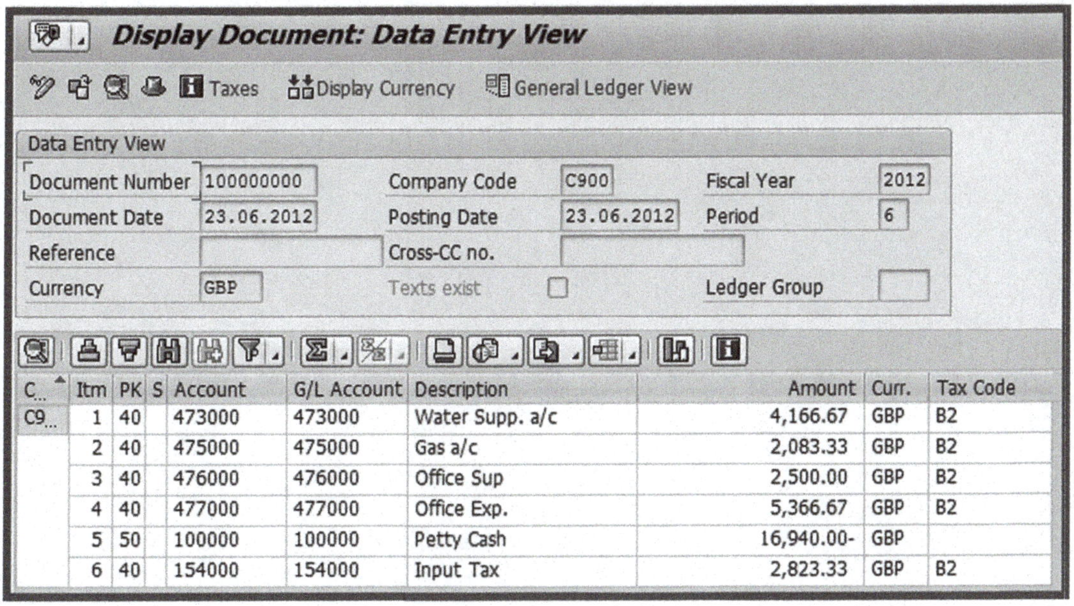

Figure 18-51. Source document display for an individual item in a cost center

Summary

This chapter explained what controlling is. You learned how to maintain a controlling area, how to set number ranges for controlling documents, and how to set version approaches/transfer pricing. You also learned what a cost element is and how to set defaults for automatic creation of primary and secondary cost elements. You learned what a cost center is and how to define standard hierarchy for cost centers, create cost center groups, and define statistical key figures. You then learned what a profit center is and went through the various steps involved in customizing a profit center. This included the basic settings involved in the profit center, including how to maintain controlling areas settings, create dummy profit centers, set the control parameters for the actual data, maintain versions for profit centers, and assign profit centers to a cost center. You also looked at how to post controlling documents and how to generate interactive reporting for a profit center.

In the next chapter, you will look at what a new G/L is, how to define ledgers for the general ledger, how to define leading and non-leading ledgers, the benefits of a new general ledger, what scenarios are, and how to carry out real-time integration of controlling with FI. You will also learn how to define documents for entry view in a ledger, what splitting a document entails, and how to define a splitting document. Finally, you will look at the steps involved in closing procedures for foreign currencies valuations, carrying forward balances, and reclassifying GR/IR clearing.

■ ■ ■

CHAPTER 19

Customizing New General Ledger Accounting

In this chapter, you learn how to define leading and non-leading ledgers based on the totals table in the new G/L accounts. These ledgers will enable you to perform parallel accounting to meet different accounting disclosure requirements.

At the end of this chapter, you will be able to:

- Explain what a new general ledger is

- Define ledgers for general ledger accounting

- Define leading and non-leading ledgers

- Define currencies of a leading ledger

- Explain what a scenario is

- Assign accounting principles to ledger groups

- Describe real-time integration of controlling with FI

- Define documents for entry view in a ledger

- Define document splitting characteristics for G/L accounts

- Define foreign currencies valuation

- Perform closing of foreign currency valuation and balance carry forward

- Reclassify GR/IR clearing

New General Ledger

Disclosure in financial reporting has increased significantly in recent times. Up until version 4.7, companies attempting to meet disclosure requirements had to install different components to meet varied requirements and standards. Compliance with IAS/IFRS principles has heightened the need for parallel and segmented reporting. In attempt to meet legal and local (company code) accounting and reporting requirements, companies must maintain G/L accounts for two or more accounting areas for local and group reporting with two retained earnings (X & Y).

The drawback to these settings is that reconciliation between G/L accounts can be cumbersome. The new G/L eliminates many of the problems associated with various reporting (parallel accounting) to meet disclosure requirements by incorporating additional ledger(s).

Therefore, a new general ledger can be seen as an attempt to provide a full picture of an accounting report that meets the standard accounting disclosure. It incorporates other aspects of business operations to ensure that comprehensive accounting information is always available. The benefits of the new general ledger include:

- An extended data structure that allows customer fields to be added to the general ledger.

- Real-time document splitting, which makes it possible to create balance sheets for various entities such as segments reporting in line with IAS (International Accounting Standards) and U.S. GAAP (Generally Accepted Accounting Principles).

- The ability to run real-time reconciliation of management accounting with FI (reconciliation with controlling), making it possible to eliminate time-consuming reconciliations.

- Management of multiple ledgers within the general ledger accounting. This is one of the ways to portray parallel accounting in SAP.

- The flexibility to define one or more fiscal year variants using non-leading ledgers for various financial reporting needs.

- Financial statements to be created using standard reporting functions.

- A function that allows you to combine classic G/L accounting and special ledger objects.

Other features of a new G/L include the leading ledger and the non-leading ledger. Only one leading ledger is allowed in a new general ledger, but you can define other non-leading ledgers that can be assigned to other objects, such as fiscal year variants/currencies.

Leading Ledger

Leading ledger is a form of consolidation that integrates other non-leading ledgers in all company codes. It is important to note that all company codes are automatically assigned the leading ledger. The leading ledger gets some of its control parameters from the company code. For example, it uses the fiscal year variant, posting period variant, and local currencies assigned to the company code.

Non-Leading Ledger

Non-leading ledgers are termed as parallel ledgers to the leading ledger to allow parallel reporting to meet other and local requirements. Once you have defined your non-leading ledger, you have to activate it by the company code. The system will automatically create a group ledger for the ledger you just created.

Let's look at how to define leading and non-leading ledgers by working through a problem.

Problem: *Company C900 must create accounting reports for various stakeholders. As a SAP financial consultant, your task is to define leading and non-leading ledgers in a new general ledger using the standard SAP table called FAGLFLEXT. This will enable the finance team to produce various financial reports to meet legal requirements with different fiscal years.*

The company wants the financial year to run from January to December for global and local reporting. It also wants to have separate reporting for a local tax requirement from April to March.

You were given the following information to work with:

- *Company Code: C900*

- *Company Currency: Pound Sterling (GBP)*

- *Chart of Accounts: CA90*

- *Leading Ledger Fiscal Year: January–December*

- *Non-Leading Ledger Fiscal Year: March–April*

Define Ledgers for General Ledger Accounting

The ledgers for the general ledger are defined in this exercise. The ledgers you define here are specifically for additional reporting, such as for company code and tax reporting with their respective total tables FAGLFLEXT. A totals table is a database table that stores totals used in general ledger accounting for parallel ledgers. SAP comes with the standard totals table called FAGLFLEXT for general ledger accounting.

The ledgers available here are leading ledger and non-leading ledgers. The Leading Ledger (0L) comes with predefined total tables (FAGLFLEXT). You don't need to define a leading ledger for general ledger accounting. It is recommended that you use the pre-defined 0L leading ledger supplied by SAP. On the other hand, when you define non-leading ledgers, you should apply the predefined total table called FAGLFLEXT.

Only one leading ledger is assigned to a company code. Make sure that you set the leading indicator for the 0L leading ledger. In this exercise, you will define the ledgers based on total tables that are used in general ledger accounting. To define ledgers for general ledger accounting, follow this menu path: IMG: Financial Accounting (New) ➤ Financial Accounting Global Settings (New) ➤ Ledgers ➤ Ledger ➤ Define Ledgers for General Ledger Accounting. The Change View "Define Ledgers in General Ledger Accounting:" Overview screen is displayed. To define ledgers in general ledger accounting, click the New Entries button at the top of the screen. The New Entries: Overview of Added Entries screen appears (Figure 19-1).

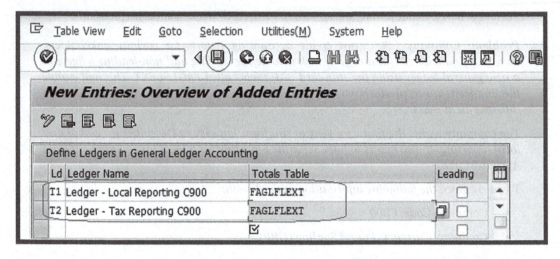

Figure 19-1. *Defining additional ledgers for local accounting (company code) and tax reporting for general ledger accounting*

Update the following fields:

> **Ld:** Enter two unique identification codes for your ledger. This is a freely definable code. There is no hard and fast rule as to what you can use here. You can use any two characters of your choice.

> **Ledger Name:** Enter a name describing your ledger. You can enter any meaningful name that best describes your ledger.

> **Totals Table:** Enter the Totals tables FAGLFLEXT. This is supplied by the system.

Click the Enter 📀 button on the top-left side of the screen and save 💾 your ledgers. The Information dialog box comes up with a message, "Ledger group T1 is created only with ledger T1". Click the Continue ✅ button at the bottom of the screen and a second information box comes up for ledger T2 with the message, "Ledger group T2 is created only with ledger T2". Click the Continue ✅ button again to confirm your entries.

Define Currencies of Leading Ledger

You must specify the currencies that you want to apply to the leading ledger in the new general ledger. Normally, an average of three currencies settings is applicable to a company code. This is made up of a company code currency and two additional currencies—a group currency and hard currency—(Figure 19-2). *Group currency* is the currency for a consolidation group and *hard currency* is often country-specific and used in countries with high inflation rates.

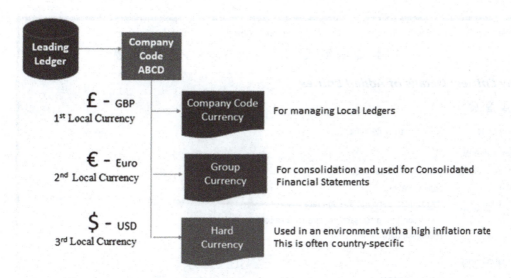

Figure 19-2. *Defining local currency and additional currencies in the leading ledger*

In this exercise, you will define the additional currencies (the group and hard currencies). The company code currency is determined from the company code settings you carried out when you defined your company code in Chapter 1. The local and additional currency (parallel currency) settings are unique to each company code. To define currencies for the leading ledger, follow this menu path: IMG: Financial Accounting (New) ➤ Financial Accounting Global Settings (New) ➤ Ledgers ➤ Ledger ➤ Define Currencies of Leading Ledger. The Change View "Additional Local Currencies for Company Code": Overview screen is displayed. Click the New Entries button on the top-left side of the screen to go to the New Entries: Details of Added Entries screen (Figure 19-3) to specify the additional currencies for the leading ledger.

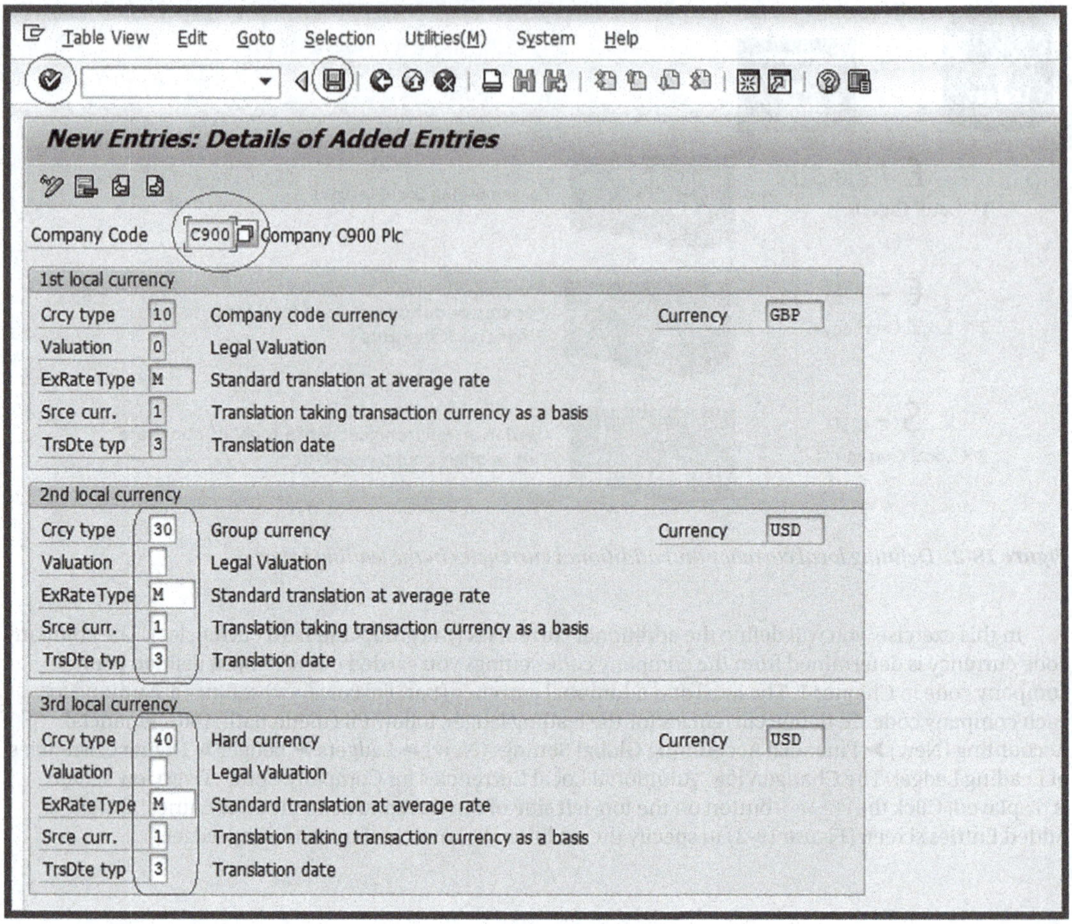

Figure 19-3. *Specifying additional currencies for the leading ledger*

Update the following fields in the second local currency section:

Crcy Type: The following currency types are supplied by SAP:

- **10 - Company code currency:** This currency type is defined when defining the company code and managed in FI. It is sometimes referred to as the local currency.

- **30 - Group currency:** This is for consolidation group. Managed as parallel currency in FI.

- **40 - Hard currency:** This currency type is used in a high inflation rate environment.

- **50 - Index-based currency:** This currency type is rarely used in practice. It can be used in a high inflation economy for comparison purposes to meet statutory reporting requirements.

- **60 - Global company currency:** This currency is defined when you define your company and is used with internal partners.

Enter group currency type 30 in the currency type field.

> **Valuation:** For legal valuation, leave this field blank. Legal valuation option will allow you to evaluate your business processes in line with that of your company code while using the company code currency. This makes it possible for you to maintain the same financial reporting in FI and PCA (Profit Center Accounting).

> **ExRate Type:** Enter exchange rate type M for standard translation at average rate. Exchange rate types were discussed in Chapter 7.

> **Srce Curr.:** Enter 1 (translation taking transaction currency as a basis). The source currency 1 is the company code currency.

> **TrsDte typ:** Enter 3 transaction dates in the transaction date type field. This will allow the system to apply transaction dates.

Click the Enter ✅ button on the top-left side of the screen and save 💾 .

Define and Activate Non-Leading Ledgers

In this exercise, you configure settings for non-leading ledgers for company code C900:

- To apply a non-leading ledger in the general ledger, you must specify and activate the non-leading ledger in your company code.

- You can define up to three additional currencies other than the company code currency for the leading ledger.

- The non-leading ledger allows you to define a fiscal year variant that is different from the leading ledger's. If no fiscal year variant is defined, the system will automatically assign the fiscal year variant of the company code.

- You can also specify a Post period variant as part of your configuration.

We will be using two steps to illustrate this process. We do this because we are defining two ledgers to meet various reporting requirements: one for local (company code) reporting and one for tax reporting.

Step 1: Define Non-Leading Ledger for Company Code Reporting

To define and activate a non-leading ledger, follow this menu path: IMG Financial Accounting (New) ➤ Financial Accounting Global Settings (New) ➤ Ledgers ➤ Ledger ➤ Define and Activate Non-Leading Ledger. The Determine Work Area: Entry screen pops up. Enter your first non-leading ledger identifier T1 (this is the ledger you defined earlier in the section "Define Ledgers for General Ledger Accounting") in the Ledger Work Area field. Confirm your entry by clicking the Enter ☑ button. You go to the screen where you can assign your company code, currency, and fiscal year variant to the ledger T1 Local (company code) reporting. The Change View "Settings for Non-Leading Ledgers in General Ledger": Overview screen is displayed. Click the New Entries button. The New Entries: Overview of Added Entries screen appears. Enter your company code (C900) in the company code (CoCd) field and click the Enter ✅ button on the top-left side of the screen to confirm your entries.

The Consistency Check message box comes up with migration information and the question, "Is the ledger assigned to a company code that is used productively?" Click the No button at the bottom of the screen. The New Entries: Overview of Added Entries Screen Ledger T1 is displayed, as shown in Figure 19-4.

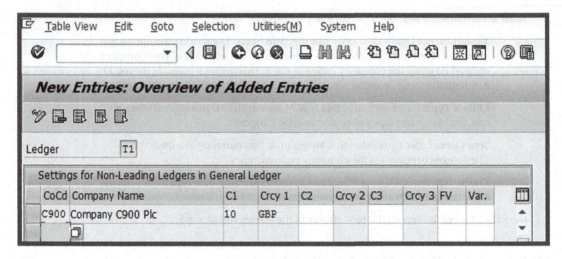

Figure 19-4. Specifying the company code for a non-leading ledger in the general ledger

---

■ **Note** The migration service is used only for a production company code. To ensure data consistency for a company code that is already in use and to avoid the complication of data migration, it's best to click the [No] button when the Consistency Check message appears.

You may not need to enter the fiscal year in the FV column on the screen, since the fiscal year for T1 Ledger Local (company code) reporting is the same as the company code's fiscal year. If you leave this field blank, the system will automatically use the company's fiscal year. If you leave the currency field bank, the system will automatically use the company code currency as well.

Save 🖫 the ledger.

Step 2: Define a Non-Leading Ledger for a Different Fiscal Year Variant

The next step is to define the settings for non-leading ledger T2 for tax reporting purposes with a different fiscal year from the company code's fiscal year (April to March using fiscal year variant V3). To define a non-leading ledger for tax reporting requirements, follow this menu path: IMG Financial Accounting (New) ➤ Financial Accounting Global Settings (New) ➤ Ledgers ➤ Ledger ➤ Define and Activate Non-Leading Ledger. The Determine Work Area: Entry dialog box pops up. Enter your second non-leading ledger identifier, which is T2 (defined in "Define Ledger for General Ledger Accounting" section) in the Ledger Work Area field. Confirm your entry by clicking the Enter 🗹 button at the bottom of the screen. This action will allow you to assign your company code, currency, and fiscal year variant to the ledger T2 for your tax reporting requirements.

The Change View "Settings for Non-Leading Ledgers in General Ledger": Overview screen is displayed. Click the [New Entries] button on the top-left side of the screen. The New Entries: Overview of Added Entries screen appears (Figure 19-5).

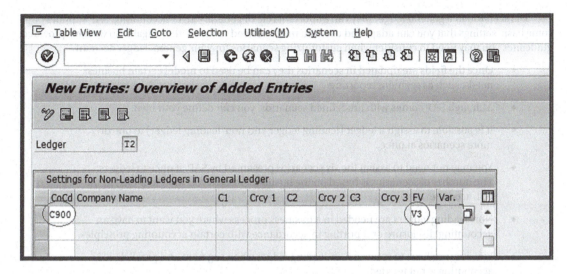

Figure 19-5. Specifying a fiscal year variant for a non-leading ledger

Enter your company code (C900) in the company code (CoCd) field and enter V3 (this is a standard fiscal year for April – March supplied by SAP) in the FV column. Click the Enter ⊘ button on the top-left side of the screen. The Consistency Check message box comes up with migration information and the question, "Is the ledger assigned to a company code that is used productively?" Click the ⟨ No ⟩ button at the bottom of the screen and then save 🖫 your ledger.

What Is a Scenario in General Ledger Accounting?

Scenarios assigned to each ledger during customizing represent different business views. They control the fields that are updated in the ledger based on your settings when postings are made from other application components or modules in G/L accounting, for example, from cost center or profit center updates. You must use scenarios supplied by SAP, because they contain the predefined settings of business processes that are sufficient for your needs.

Scenarios provided by SAP include:

- *FIN_AASEG* – Segment Reporting for Fixed Assets (This function is used to create asset reporting at profit or segment level.)

- *FINN_CCA* – Cost Center Updated (This function updates the Sender and Receiver Cost Center fields.)

- *FIN_CONS* – Preparation for Consolidation (This function updates the Consolidation Transaction Type and Trading Partner fields.)

- *FIN_PCA* – Profit Center Update (This function updates the profit center and partner profit center.)

- *FIN_SEGM* – Segmentation (This function updates the Segment, Partner Segment, and Profit Center fields.)

- *FIN_UKV* – Cost of Sales Accounting (This function updates the sender and Receiver Functional Area fields.)

The scenario in a general ledger plays an important role in general ledger accounting. SAP supplies some basic settings that you can adapt and use. You may not need to define them again. So we have provided guidelines you may need to consider when customizing scenarios for your general ledger account:

- Once the fields are updated in scenarios they can be used to model certain business needs, such as segment reporting.

- Although SAP comes with predefined scenarios, you can define your own.

- It is possible to assign a ledger (leading ledger and non-leading ledger) to one or more scenarios at once.

- You may not need to assign the six scenarios presented by SAP at once to ledgers. The number of scenarios is based on the business process you want to model in the G/L account.

- Non-leading ledgers are needed in a business process where you want to have an accounting disclosure or reporting in accordance with certain accounting principles.

- You may not have to create a non-leading ledger when segment and parallel accounting is not needed.

Assign Scenarios and Customer Fields to Ledgers for Leading Ledger

In this exercise, you will assign the following objects to ledgers.

- Scenarios

- Customer fields

- Version

SAP comes with standard scenarios and customer fields that are assigned to ledgers in the leading ledger. So you do not need to customize the leading ledger. However, you can take a look at the scenarios in leading ledger and delete the items you don't need. To assign scenarios and customer fields to ledgers, follow this menu path: IMG: Financial Accounting (New) ➤ Financial Accounting Global Settings (New) ➤ Ledgers ➤ Ledger ➤ Assign Scenarios and Customer Fields to Ledgers. The Display View "Ledgers": Overview screen comes up. On the screen, select 0L Leading Ledger from the list of displayed ledgers (Figure 19-6).

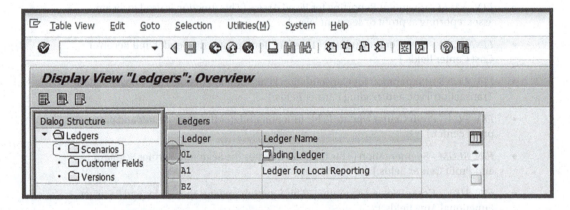

Figure 19-6. *Ledgers overview screen for assigning scenarios – leading ledger*

To go to the screen containing the list of standard scenarios supplied by SAP, double-click the Scenarios folder on the left pane of the screen. The Change View "Scenarios": Overview screen is displayed containing the list of standard scenarios in SAP (Figure 19-7).

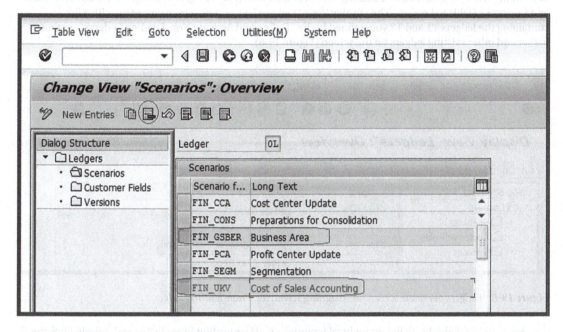

Figure 19-7. *The screen containing the standard list of scenarios supplied by SAP*

You may not necessarily use all the scenarios provided by SAP. Let's assume that you do not need to provide a report for business area, so you do not need to include it in your ledger. You will need to delete it from the list of scenarios assigned to the leading ledger 0L. To delete unwanted scenarios from the list, select business area (in this case) from the list of scenarios and click the Delete 🗐 button at the top of the screen. The Business Area setting is deleted from the scenarios in the Leading Ledger 0L.

To define setting for versions, double-click the Versions folder on the left pane. The Change View "Versions": Overview screen is displayed. Click the New Entries button on the top-left side of the screen. Update the following fields:

> **Ver.:** Enter the version key (1).
>
> **Man.Plan:** Click the checkbox for Manual Plan. This allows you manually plan data for a combination of ledgers and versions.
>
> **Integ.Planning:** Click the checkbox for Integrated Planning if you want to transfer the data from other objects (such as Overhead Cost Controlling or Profit Analysis) to combine the ledger and the version.
>
> **Version Description:** Enter a description (Actual Plan) for the version plan.

Click the Enter 🗸 button on the top-left side of the screen and save 🖫 your version.

The next step is to define scenarios for non-leading ledgers T1 (Local Reporting) and T2 (Tax Reporting). Because the process of specifying scenarios is the same for every ledger, we will only define the scenarios for ledger T1. We will be leaving ledger T2 for you to do on your own, by following the same steps.

Non-Leading Ledger T1 for Local (Company Code) Reporting

To assign scenarios and customer fields to non-leading ledger T1, follow this menu path: IMG: Financial Accounting (New) ➤ Financial Accounting Global Settings (New) ➤ Ledgers ➤ Ledger ➤ Assign Scenarios and Customer Fields to Ledgers. The Display View "Ledgers": Overview screen comes up with a list containing the ledgers T1 and T2 you defined in the "Define and Activate Non-Leading Ledgers" section earlier and other existing ledgers on the screen (Figure 19-8).

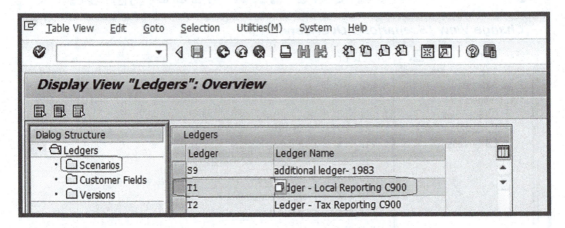

Figure 19-8. *Ledgers overview screen for assigning scenarios – non-leading ledger*

Select or highlight the T1 ledger for local (company code) reporting from the list and double-click the ☐ Scenarios folder. The Display View "Scenarios": Overview screen is displayed. To specify the scenarios for ledger T1, click the New Entries button at the top of the screen. The New Entries: Overview of Added Entries screen is displayed (Figure 19-9).

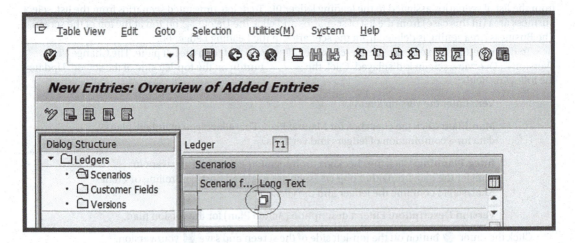

Figure 19-9. *New Entries screen where you specify scenarios for ledger – T1 for local reporting*

You will specify the scenarios for your ledger that meet your requirements. In this exercise, we are using the following scenarios as an illustration to guide you through specifying scenarios for additional ledgers:

- Cost Center Update

- Preparation for Consolidation

- Profit Center Update

- Segmentation

Use the matchcode next to the Scenarios field so that the Scenarios for General Ledger Accounting screen containing the list of available scenarios is displayed (Figure 19-10).

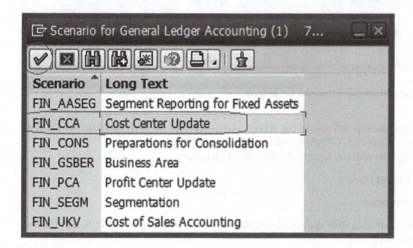

Figure 19-10. *List of scenarios for general ledger accounting*

To include an item from the list of scenarios, select or highlight the item (Cost Center Update) and click the Enter ✓ button on the top-left side of the screen to confirm your selection. Notice that the scenario FIN_CCA Cost Center Update is entered into the Scenarios field in Figure 19-11.

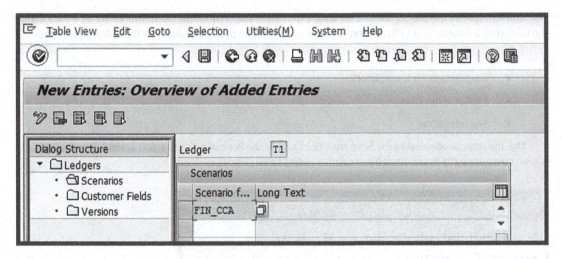

Figure 19-11. *The screen where you specify scenarios for ledgers*

Click the Enter ⊘ button on the top-left side of the screen and proceed to the next scenario field below FIN_CCA – Cost Center Update. Select FIN_CONS-Preparation for Consolidation.

Repeat this process to assign the remaining scenarios for the T1 ledger:

- FIN_PCA – Profit Center Update

- FIN_SEGM – Segmentation

When you have completed your scenarios specifications, the scenarios assigned to the T1 ledger should look like those shown in Figure 19-12.

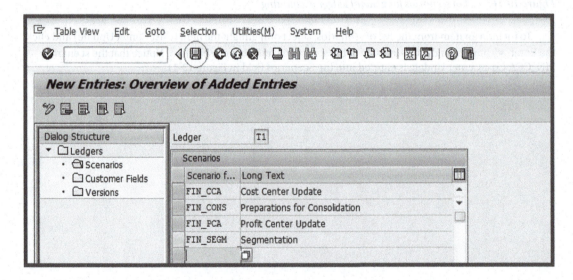

Figure 19-12. *Ledgers overview screen displaying assigned scenarios*

Save 💾 your scenarios assignment.

As part of this exercise, repeat the same process to specify the scenarios for the non-leading ledger T1 for Local Reporting to specify scenarios for ledger T2 for tax reporting.

Define Ledger Group

A ledger group allows you to classify ledgers with similar functions and business processes of general ledger accounting together in the same group. You can make postings to multiple ledgers at the same time. It's also possible to impose restrictions in order to update individual postings to a ledger group, so that documents are only posted to ledgers in the group. When a ledger group is not specified, the system will automatically post to all ledgers. Likewise, when a ledger group is specified, the system will only post to ledgers in the same ledger group.

When defining a ledger group, you must specify which ledger will be the representative ledger in the group. Only one ledger in a group is used as a representative ledger. Often, the leading ledger is used. The system uses a representative ledger to check settings for an open period and to determine if a posting period is open.

■ **Note**   If the ledger group has a leading ledger, the leading ledger must be used as the representative ledger. When there is no leading ledger, you have to designate a representative ledger. If the ledger group has more than one ledger, the system will verify during document posting, based on the company's fiscal year variant, that the representative ledger was selected correctly.

Here is how you choose which ledger to use in a group as the representative ledger:

- If all the ledgers in the ledger group have different fiscal year variants, use any ledger as the representative ledger.

- If one of the ledgers has the same fiscal year variant as the company code, use that ledger as the representative ledger.

In this exercise, we will not be defining ledger group, because we want the system to automatically post to all ledgers.

When you need to define a ledger group for your company, follow this menu path: IMG: Financial Accounting (New) ➤ Financial Accounting Global Settings (New) ➤ Ledgers ➤ Ledger ➤ Define Ledger Group.

Accounting Principles

Accounting principle configuration is part of parallel accounting in SAP. The accounting principles that you define in this exercise enable you to perform valuations and closing preparations for your company code and produce financial reports for the group and your company code according to accounting principles (IAS/US GAAP), which enables you to meet various stakeholders' needs.

■ **Warning**   Do not delete the accounting principles you have defined, because accounting principles have relationships with other accounting functions, like currency valuation and others, which can affect your customizations.

In this exercise, we will define accounting principles and assign the accounting principles we define to appropriate ledger groups. To define accounting principles, follow this menu path: IMG: Financial Accounting (New) ➤ Financial Accounting Global Settings (New) ➤ Ledgers ➤ Parallel Accounting ➤ Define Accounting Principles. The Change View "Accounting Principles": Overview screen is displayed. Click the `New Entries` button on the top-left side of the screen.

■ **Note**   You cannot use an accounting principle key that has already been assigned to another ledger group in the system. If accounting principle keys C10, C20, C30 have been used, you can't use them again. When defining accounting principle keys, use keys that have not been used already.

Using the information in Table 19-1, update the New Entries: Overview of Addition Entries screen.

Table 19-1. *The Information Needed to Update the Screen Where You Define Your Accounting Principles*

Accounting Principles	Name/Description of Accounting Principles
C10	Local GAAP – C900
C20	International Accounting Standards (IAS) – C900
C30	Local Tax (CRM) – C900

Click the Enter ✓ button on the top-left side of the screen to confirm your entries and save 🖫 your accounting principles.

The next step is to assign these accounting principles to the target ledger groups. Follow this menu path to do so: IMG: Financial Accounting (New) ➤ Financial Accounting Global Settings (New) ➤ Ledgers ➤ Parallel Accounting ➤ Assign Accounting Principle to Ledger Groups. The Change View "Assignment of Accounting Principle to Target Ledger Group" screen is displayed. Click the `New Entries` button at the top of the screen. The New Entries: Overview of Added Entries screen is displayed. Using the information in Table 19-2, update the Accounting Principle and Target ledger Group fields, as shown in Figure 19-13.

Table 19-2. *The Data Needed to Update the Accounting Principles to the Target Ledger Group*

Accounting Principles	Target Ledger Group
C10	0L – Leading Ledger
C20	T1 – Ledger – Local Reporting C900
C30	T2 – Ledger – Tax Reporting C900

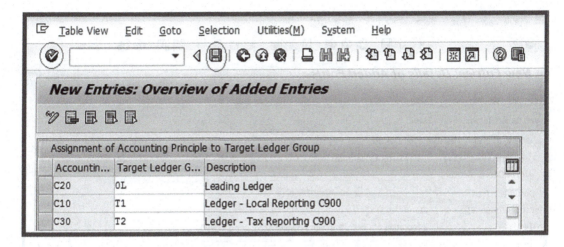

Figure 19-13. *Assignment of accounting principles to a target ledger group*

Click the Enter ✅ button on the top-left side of the screen to confirm your entries and save 💾 your work.

Real-Time Integration of Controlling with Financial Accounting

All cost allocation and other postings within a controlling environment usually do not affect financial accounting transactions (that is, G/L accounts are not updated with postings carried out in controlling). However, there are some cost allocations in controlling which are relevant for evaluation in financial accounting that need to be reflected in FI, because of the effect they have on the year-end reporting (the profit and loss statement). This type of transaction will call for reconciliation between controlling and financial accounting to necessitate the transfer of relevant data from controlling to the new general ledger in financial accounting real-time. This is best achieved using real-time integration in SAP.

The advantage of real-time integration is that no reconciliation ledger is required, because the reconciliation postings are replaced by real-time integration. Hence, you do not need to set the reconciliation ledger active indicator in controlling. To define variants for real-time integration, follow this menu path: IMG: Financial Accounting (New) ➤ Financial Accounting Global Settings (New) ➤ Ledgers ➤ Real-Time Integration of Controlling with Financial Accounting ➤ Define Variants for Real-Time Integration. The Change View "Variants for Real-Time Integration CO->FI": Overview screen is displayed. To specify the real-time integration, click the New Entries button at the top of the screen. The New Entries: Details of Added Entries screen is displayed (Figure 19-14).

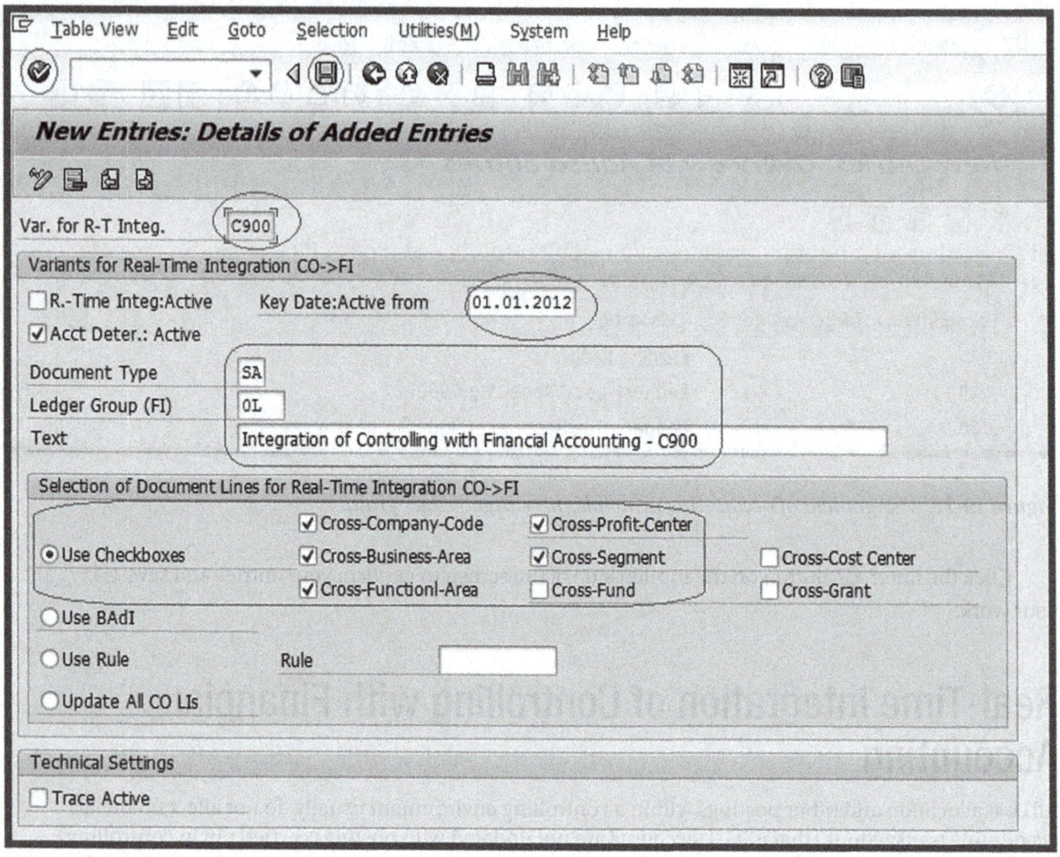

Figure 19-14. *The screen where you specify variants for real-time integration of controlling with FI*

Update the following fields:

Var. for R-T Integ.: Enter an identification key that you want to use for your variant for real-time integration (C900). You can use up to four characters for the variant key.

R.-Time Integ:Active: Do not click the Real-Time Integration Active checkbox. By clicking this checkbox, CO (controlling) postings are posted to FI in real time.

Key Date: Active From: Enter the start date of the current fiscal year (01.01.2012 CO) of your company code. This will post the documents posted in CO from this date to FI.

Acct Deter.: Active: Click the Account Determination: Active checkbox. When you click the box, the system carries out account determination during CO document transfer to FI.

Document Type: Enter document type SA (General Account document type). You can access the list of document types supplied by SAP using the matchcode.

Ledger Group (FI): Enter your leading ledger 0L in this field as the leading ledger group for your variant for real-time integration of CO with FI.

Text: Enter a description for your variant (Integration of Controlling with Financial Account C900). The description you use here is a matter of choice, but use a meaningful description.

You can select document lines for real-time integration CO->FI by clicking the User checkboxes on the following objects:

- Cross-Company Code

- Cross -Business Area

- Cross-Functional Area

- Cross-Profit-Center

- Cross-Segment

Click the Enter ✅ button on the top-left side of the screen to confirm your entries and save 💾 your work.

Assign Variants for Real-Time Integration to Company Codes

To activate real-time integration of controlling with FI for your company code, it is important to assign variants for real-time integration of CO with FI to your company code. The variants for real time integration you defined earlier can be assigned to one or more company codes. To Assign variants for real-time integration to company codes, follow this menu path: IMG: Financial Accounting (New) ➤ Financial Accounting Global Settings (New) ➤ Ledgers ➤ Real-Time Integration of Controlling with Financial Accounting ➤ Assign Variants for Real-Time Integration to Company Codes. The Change View "Assignment of Variants for Real-Time integration for CoCo screen is displayed. Click the New Entries button at the top of the screen to assign your variant for real-time integration to your company code. The New Entries: Overview of Added Entries screen is displayed (Figure 19-15).

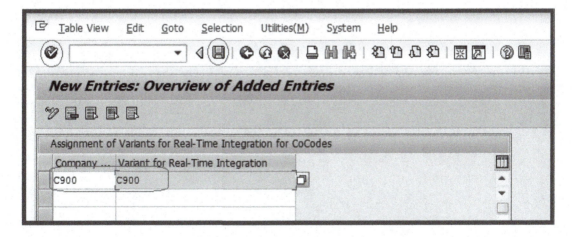

Figure 19-15. *Assigning variants for real-time integration for the company code*

Update the following fields:

Company Code: Enter your company code (C900).

Variant for Real-Time Integration: Enter your variant (C900).

Click the Enter ✓ button on the top-left side of the screen to confirm your entries and save 🖫 your efforts.

■ **Note** Before you begin defining account determination for real-time integration, go to "Appendix A, Chapter 19, New General Ledger" to create the G/L accounts you need for this customization.

Account Determination for Real-Time Integration

To be able to trace postings to FI, you must define account determination for real-time integration of controlling to financial accounting. Follow this menu path: IMG: Financial Accounting (New) ➤ Financial Accounting Global Settings (New) ➤ Ledgers ➤ Real-Time Integration of Controlling with Financial Accounting ➤ Account Determination for Real Time Integration ➤ Define Account Determination for Real Time Integration.

The Set Controlling Area dialog box pops up. Enter your controlling area key (C900) in the Controlling Area field and click the Continue ✓ button on the bottom-right side of the screen. The Reconciliation Ledger: Change Account Determination screen is displayed. To maintain accounts determination for automatic posting, click the ⌞ Change Account Determin. ⌝ button at the top of the screen. The Configuration Accounting Maintain: Automatic Posts – Rules screen is displayed. Specify the post rule for your account determination, click the CO Transaction checkbox, click the Save 🖫 button, and then click the ⌞ Accounts ⌟ button at the top of the screen. The Configuration Accounting Maintain: Automatic Posts – Accounts screen appears. Update the CO Transaction and Accounts fields using the details on the screen in Figure 19-16 to classify business transactions for postings automatically.

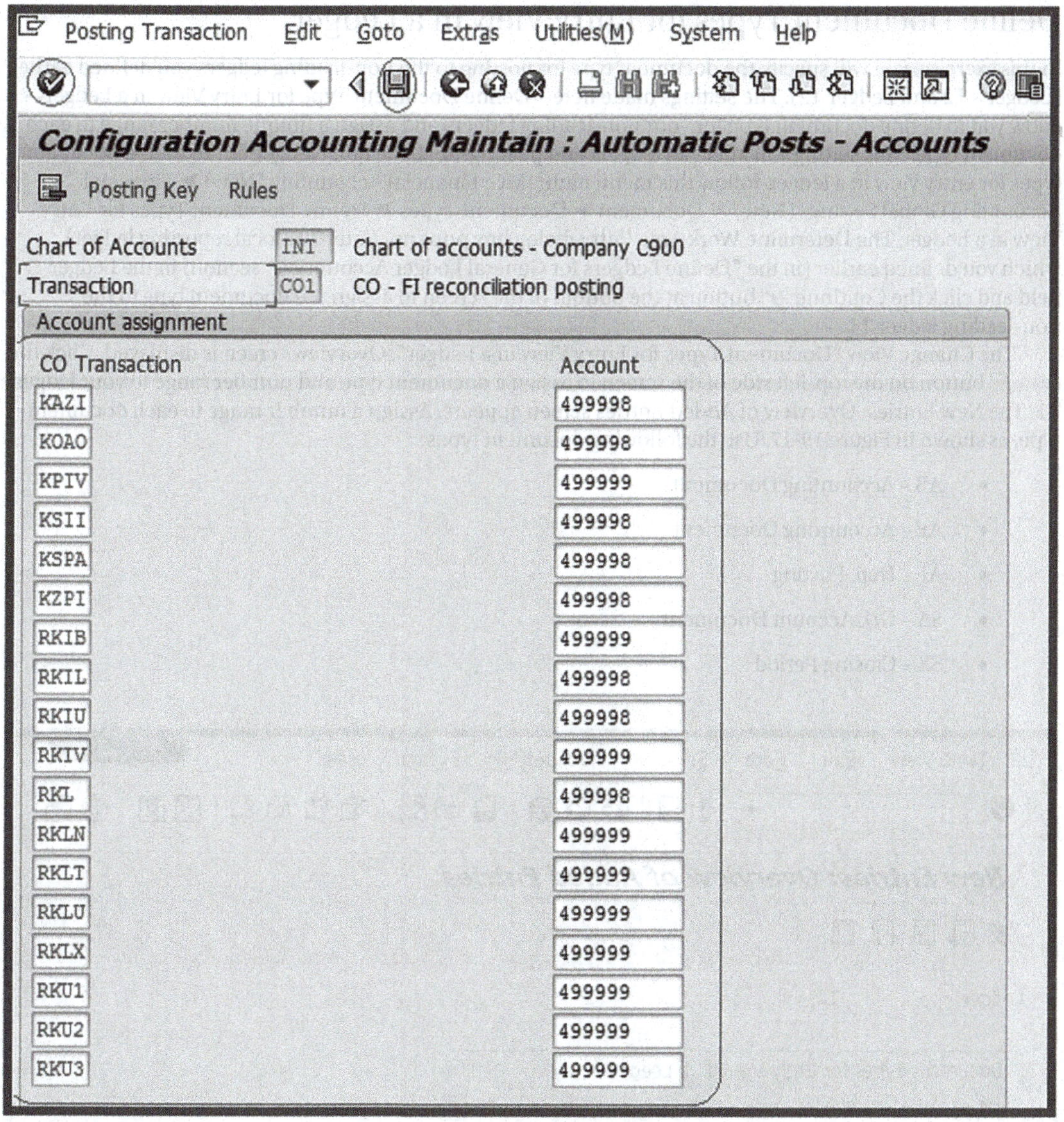

Figure 19-16. *Account assignment for automatic postings*

You can access the list of business transactions for actual postings using the matchcode next to each CO Transaction field. Click the Enter ⊘ button on the top-left side of the screen and save 💾 automatic account determination.

Document Types

Document types are standard codes supplied by SAP that play a significant role in differentiating business transactions and determining how documents are stored in the system's database. In this exercise, we will be defining document types for entry view in a ledger and defining document types for general ledger view.

Define Document Types for Entry View in a Ledger

In this exercise, you will specify the document type for posting to the non-leading ledgers you defined earlier (Ledger – T2 and Ledger T2). The settings made here—Define Document Type for Entry View in a Ledger—allow you to define document type for your non-leading ledgers and assign a unique number range to each document type. This setting will affect all ledgers and postings to the leading ledger 0L. To define document types for entry view in a ledger, follow this menu path: IMG: Financial Accounting (New) ➤ Financial Accounting Global Settings (New) ➤ Document ➤ Document Types ➤ Define Document Types for Entry View in a Ledger. The Determine Work Area Entry dialog box pops up. Enter **T1** (local reporting ledger), which you defined earlier (in the "Define Ledgers for General Ledger Accounting" section) in the Ledger field and click the Continue ☑ button at the bottom of the screen to assign the document type to the non-leading ledger T1.

The Change View "Document Types for Entry View in a Ledger": Overview screen is displayed. Click the New Entries button on the top-left side of the screen to assign a document type and number range to your ledger T1. The New Entries: Overview of Added Entries screen appears. Assign a number range to each document type, as shown in Figure 19-17. Use the following document types:

- AB – Accounting Document
- AE – Accounting Document
- AF – Dep. Posting
- SA – G/L Account Document
- SX – Closing Period

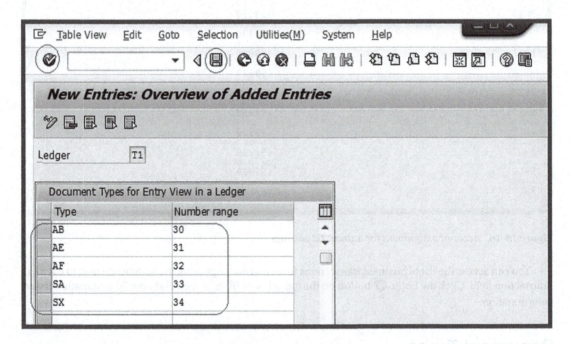

Figure 19-17. *Assigning number ranges to document types for entry view in a ledger*

Click the Enter ☑ button on the top-left side of the screen and save 🖫 your efforts.

■ **Note** You may experience a slight problem when saving your work. The system does not allow number overlap. You must avoid using the numbers that have already been assigned to document types. You can display the list of number ranges that have been used. Look for numbers that have not been used (between 1 and 100) and assign them to your document type. Document types were covered in Chapter 4.

To complete this exercise, repeat the same process for ledger T2 (tax reporting) on your own before continuing.

Define Document Types for General Ledger View

In this exercise, you will define document types for non-leading ledgers in the general ledger view. The settings here are applicable only to non-leading ledgers whose fiscal year variants are different from the leading ledger variant. In most cases, the leading ledger fiscal year variant is usually the same as the company code variant. Therefore, any non-leading ledger with a fiscal year variant different from the company code variant is considered in this customizing exercise. It is compulsory to define different document types and number range intervals for general ledger view for non-leading ledgers.

In this scenario, ledger T2 (tax reporting) has a different fiscal year variant V3 from leading ledger 0L (K4). Therefore, you need to define document types for general ledger view for non-leading ledger (ledger T2). Follow this menu path: IMG: Financial Accounting (New) ➤ Financial Accounting Global Settings (New) ➤ Document ➤ Document Types ➤ Define Document Types for General Ledger View. The Determine Work Area Entry dialog box pops up. Enter **T2** (tax reporting ledger) that you defined earlier in the Ledger field and click the Continue ☑ button at the bottom of the screen. This will allow you to assign a document type for the general ledger view to non-leading ledger T2. The Change View "Document Types for General Ledger View in a Ledger": Overview screen is displayed. Click the New Entries button at the top of the screen to assign a document type and number range to your ledger T2. The New Entries: Overview of Added Entries screen appears. Enter a document type that meets your requirements in the Type field and assign a number range (01) for each document type in the Number Range field, as shown in Figure 19-18. Since you are defining Document Types for General Ledger View in a ledger, it is not necessary to assign different number range to each document type for the new general ledger.

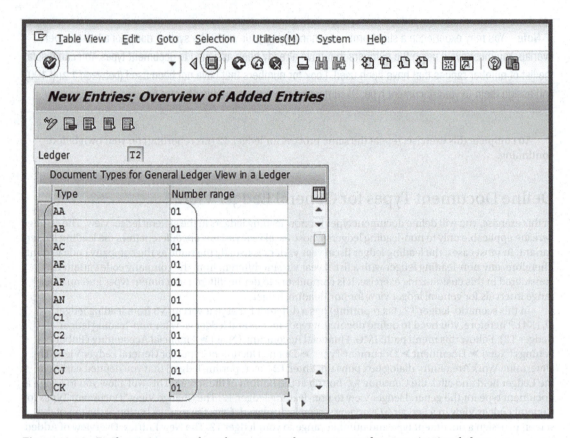

Figure 19-18. Further assignment of number ranges to document types for entry view in a ledger

---

■ **Note** There is no special rule when assigning numbers to the document type in the general ledger view, as number range overlap is not a problem in this case.

Standard document types are supplied by SAP. You can access them using the matchcode in the Type field.

Click the Enter ✅ button on the top-left side of the screen and save 💾 the definition of document types for the general ledger view.

Document Splitting

Document splitting is a new feature in SAP in new general ledger accounting that provides the flexibility to split document line items based on defined dimensions (for example, receivables lines by profit center). This makes it possible to produce a financial statement for a given business aspect (such as Profit Centers, Business Areas, Segments, Funds, and so on) at any point in time. Document splitting makes it possible for the following functions to be carried out when document splitting configuration is completed:

- Automatic document splitting of line items based on defined dimensions.

- Online document splitting.

- Document splitting during posting of documents.

- Support financial statements reporting for legal purposes (for IAS, GAAP, and so on) and segmental reporting to display a partial balance sheet according to business functions.

- Create a zero balance setting in the document for any dimension such as segment.

You have the option of displaying the document in its original form with the generated clearing lines in the entry view or in the general ledger view from the ledger perspective. For the system to perform splitting, individual document items and all documents involved must be classified in accordance with a rule that defines how document splitting is to be performed and for which line items. SAP comes with a predefined set of standard rules that will satisfy your document splitting requirements. It is also possible to define your own set of rules and adapt them to meet your requirements.

The following are part of document splitting functions:

- *Passive document splitting*: All document-splitting processes are carried out by the system using a predetermined internal program with reference to the original document. Passive document splitting is not controlled by the settings you conducted in your customizing and does not take the settings in your configuration into consideration.

- *Active document splitting*: All document-splitting processes in active document splitting are carried out based on the settings you conducted in your customizing without reference to the original document.

Limitations to document splitting include:

- Only documents that are specifically assigned to a business process can be split when using the document-splitting function.

- When there are multiple business processes within one document, it becomes difficult to establish a valid relationship between the business process and the document.

Classify G/L Accounts for Document Splitting

Transactions entered into the system are automatically analyzed by the system based on predefined criteria to determine how individual line items in the system are to be treated during document processing (such as by splitting or to remain unchanged). You need to classify document items by assigning them to appropriate item categories. This categorization will allow the system to recognize how to handle document items splitting and manage the document-splitting processes based on your classifications in this exercise.

In this exercise, you will assign accounts to the appropriate category in the document-splitting procedure, which the system will post documents to.

The following categories are supplied by SAP so that you can assign them to your G/L accounts:

- 01000 – Balance Sheet Account

- 01001 – Zero Balance Posting (Free Balancing Units)

- 01300 – Cash Discount Clearing

- 02000 – Customer

- 02100 – Customer: Special G/L Transaction

- 03000 – Vendor

- 03100 – Vendor: Special G/L Transaction

- 04000 – Cash Account

- 05100 – Taxes on Sales/Purchases

- 05200 – Withholding Tax

- 06000 – Material

- 07000 – Asset

- 20000 – Expense

- 30000 – Revenue

- 40100 – Cash Discount (Expenses/Revenue/Loss)

- 40200 – Exchange Rate Difference

- 8000 – Customer-Specific Item Category

To classify G/L accounts for document splitting, follow this menu path: IMG: Financial Accounting (New) ➤ General Ledger Accounting (New) ➤ General Ledger Account ➤ Document Splitting ➤ Classify G/L Accounts for Document Splitting. The Determine Work Areas: Entry screen pops up. Enter your chart of accounts (CA90) in the chart of accounts field and click the Continue ✓ button at the bottom of the screen. The Change View "Classify G/L Accounts for Document Splitting": Overview screen comes up. To perform the classification for document splitting, click the [New Entries] button on the top-left side of the screen. We have provided a list of G/L accounts and categories you will need to update the screen in Table 19-3.

Table 19-3. *The List of G/L Accounts and Categories to Classify G/L Accounts for Document Splitting*

G/L Account	Long Text	Category	Description
100000	Petty Cash	04000	Cash Account
111410	Barclays Bank	04000	Cash Account
111411	Barclays -Chk rec	04000	Cash Account
111412	Barclays - Chk out	04000	Cash Account
111414	Barclays - Out trans	04000	Cash Account
111415	Barclays - In trans	04000	Cash Account
111416	Barclays - Other int	04000	Cash Account
111417	Barclays - In cash	04000	Cash Account
111419	Barclays - Out cash	04000	Cash Account
113130	Barc. BK - Outg cash	04000	Cash Account
113131	Barc. BK - Inc cash	04000	Cash Account
119000	Trade deb foreign	01000	Balance Sheet Account
119030	Trade receivables	02000	Customer
119099	Trade receivables-for	02000	Customer
120000	Other debtors	02000	Customer
154000	Input tax	05100	Taxes on Sales/Purchases

(continued)

Table 19-3. (*continued*)

G/L Account	Long Text	Category	Description
159000	Prepayments - other	02000	Customer
170000	Advanced customer pa	02000	Customer
175000	Out tax	05100	Taxes on Sales/Purchases
191100	Goods rcvd/invoice R	01000	Balance Sheet Account
196000	Payment requests	01000	Balance Sheet Account
196100	Guarantees-customer	02100	Customer: Special G/L Transaction
196400	Guarantees-vendors	03100	Vendor: Special G/L Transaction
212000	Other creditors	03000	Vendor
213000	Trade cred. foreign	01000	Balance Sheet Account
213030	Trade payables	03000	Vendor
213040	Trade payables	03000	Vendor
213099	Trade payables - for	03000	Vendor
230000	Exc.rate expense	20000	Expense
276000	Discount received	30000	Revenue
300000	Inventory - Raw mat	01000	Balance Sheet Account
400000	Consumption - Raw mat	20000	Expense
470100	Bank chgs	20000	Expense
472000	Admin Cost a/c	20000	Expense
473000	Water Supp. a/c	20000	Expense
474000	Electricity a/c	20000	Expense
475000	Gas a/c	20000	Expense
476000	Office sup	20000	Expense
477000	Office exp	20000	Expense
481000	Loss-Sale FA	20000	Expense
790000	Semi-fin prod	06000	Material
792000	Finished goods invent	01000	Balance Sheet Account
800000	Sales rev	30000	Revenue
800001	Cash sales	30000	Revenue
810000	Sales rev	30000	Revenue
810001	Sales deduction	20000	Expense
820000	Sales -FA	30000	Revenue
880000	Customer discount	20000	Expense

After classifying the G/L accounts for document splitting, your screen should look like the one shown in Figure 19-19.

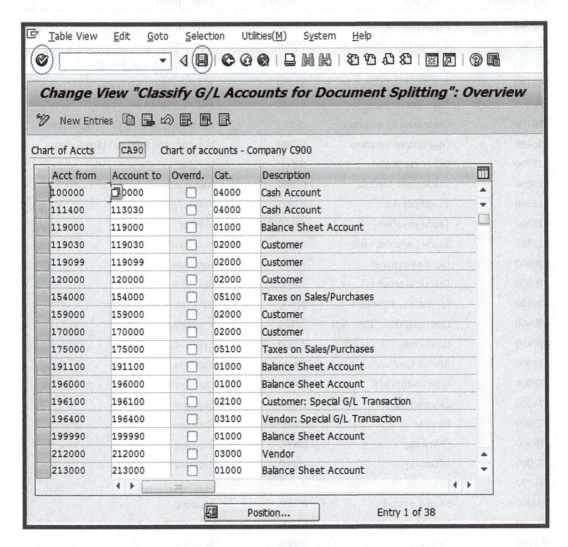

Figure 19-19. Account assignment to document splitting categories

Click the Enter ⊘ button on the top-left side of the screen and save 🖫.

Classify Document Types for Document Splitting

When a transaction is entered into the system, it's analyzed by the system to determine the splitting rule that is applicable to the document. For the system to determine the splitting rule that is applicable to a document, each document type must be assigned with the appropriate business transaction variant. Appropriate requirements have to be in place for splitting rules to function effectively. When a document is posted, the system checks each posting against the defined business transaction variant. If the conditions set out are not met, the system will automatically reject the posting.

The system does not provide the flexibility to define further business transactions, but it is possible to define your own business transaction variants. The system comes with standard business variants (0001). In this exercise, we will not be defining any variants. It is advisable that you stick to the standard business variants supplied by the system. To specify the document type for document splitting, follow this menu path: IMG: Financial Accounting (New) ➤ General Ledger Accounting (New) ➤ Business Transactions ➤ Document Splitting ➤ Classify Document Types for Document Splitting.

Zero-Balance Clearing Account

The Zero-Balance Clearing Account function enables you to define document-splitting characteristics for the balance sheet. When document splitting is performed, the system checks if the account assignment object that you want to zero-balance actually has a zero balance after document splitting. If the account assignment does not have a zero balance, the system will generate additional clearing items (Figure 19-20) and post the items initiated in the document to the clearing account assigned for the zero-balance clearing account.

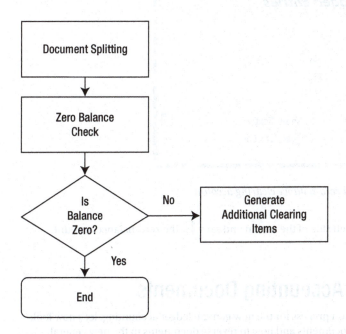

Figure 19-20. *Flowchart depicting the zero-balance clearing process when document splitting*

To define a zero-balance clearing account for your document-splitting process, follow this menu path: IMG: Financial Accounting (New) ➤ General Ledger Accounting (New) ➤ Business Transactions ➤ Document Splitting ➤ Define Zero-Balance Clearing Account.

■ **Note** Before you define a zero-balance clearing account for document splitting, go to "Appendix A (Chapter 19)" to create the G/L account 199600.

The Change View "Posting Key": Overview screen is displayed. Select account key 000 for Standard Account for Zero Balance from the list of account keys onscreen (this is a standard key supplied by SAP). Double-click the ☐ Accounts folder on the left side of the screen. The Set Chart of Accounts dialog box pops up. Enter your chart of accounts (CA90) and click the Continue ✅ button at the bottom of the screen. The Change View "Account": Overview screen is displayed. To go to the input screen where you can specify the G/L account for the zero-balance clearing setting, click the New Entries button at the top of the screen. The New Entries: Overview of Added Entries screen comes up (Figure 19-21). Enter the G/L account you have defined for Zero-Balance Clearing in the G/L Account field (199600).

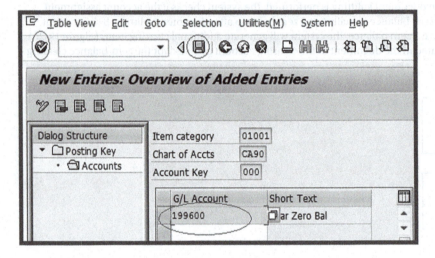

Figure 19-21. *Assigning a G/L account to a zero-balance clearing account*

Click the Enter ✅ button on the top-left side of the screen and save 💾 the zero-balance account clearing you have defined.

Posting General Ledger Accounting Documents

Having completed the required configuration process for the new general ledger accounting, let's now look at how to post general ledger accounting documents and how to reverse documents in the new general ledger accounting.

Enter G/L Account Documents

Problem: *Assume that $1,000 of the office supplies account (G/L account 476000) was mistakenly posted to the office expenses account (G/L account 477000) created in Chapter 5 (in the section "Creating G/L Account Master Record"). You have been asked to carry out the appropriate adjustment to correct this error.*

G/L account document posting is part of the SAP R/3 Enjoy document. G/L account posting is the same as the conventional journal posting. To post a G/L account document, follow this menu path: Accounting ➤ Financial Accounting ➤ General Ledger ➤ Posting➤ FB50 – G/L Account Document. Or use transaction code FB50. The Enter G/L Account Document: Company Code C900 screen is displayed. Using the data in Table 19-4, update the screen.

Table 19-4. *Data Needed to Post G/L Account Documents*

Field	Value	Description
Document Date	Today's date	Enter the current date in this field.
Posting Date	Today's date	Enter the current date in this field.
Currency	GBP	The currency code is set by default. You can overwrite it.
G/L (1)	476000	This is the account for office supplies.
G/L (2)	477000	This is the account for office expenses.
D/C (1)	Debit	When you select debit, the document amount will be posted to the debit side of the account.
DC (2)	Credit	When you select credit, the document amount will be posted to the credit side of the account.
Amount	1000	This is the document amount.
Tax Code	B2	This is the input tax code that the system will apply to calculate the tax amount applicable to the document amount.
Cost Center	4110	This is the cost center (Car - Vehicle) that the document amount will be posted to in the cost center.

Click the Enter ✅ button at the top of the screen to confirm your entries. To display your entries, click the ⬚ Simulate button at the top of the screen. The Document Overview screen appears displaying your entries. Look through the displayed entries and then click Post 💾 if you are satisfied with your entries.

Enter G/L Account Document for Ledger Group

Let's look at how to post to a specific ledger. For example, you can post documents to group reporting, local reporting, or tax reporting ledgers.

Problem: *Post $1,000 from the office supplies account (G/L account 476000) to the office expenses account (G/L account 477000) in ledger T2.*

To post a G/L account document for a ledger group, follow this menu path: Accounting ➤ Financial Accounting ➤ General Ledger ➤ Posting ➤ G/L Account Document for Ledger Group. Or use transaction code FB50L. The Enter G/L Acct Document for Ledger Group: Company Code C900 screen is displayed (Figure 19-22).

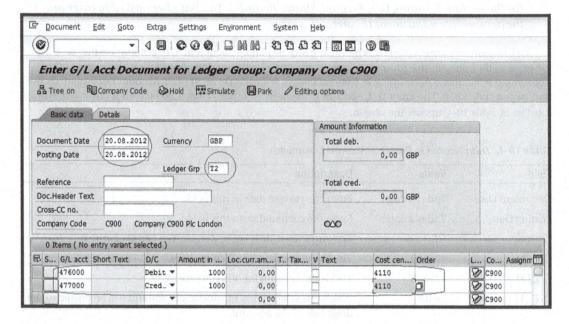

Figure 19-22. *The screen to enter a G/L account document for the ledger group for your company code*

Update the following fields:

Document Date: Enter the document date. For this exercise, we used today's date.

Posting Date: Enter today's date as your posting date.

Currency: This defaults to your company code's currency (GBP).

Ledger Grp: Enter the ledger group T2 for tax reporting that you want to post the document to in this field.

G/L (1): Enter the account number (476000) that you want to post the document to (debit).

G.L (2): Enter the corresponding account number (477000) that you want to post the document to (credit).

Amount: Enter the document amount ($1000) in this field.

Tax Code: Enter the tax code B2 in this field. This is the input tax code that the system will use to calculate the tax amount applicable to the document amount.

Cost Center: Enter the cost center 4110 in this field. This is the cost center that the document amount will be posted to in the cost center. (Car –Vehicle is a cost center that absorbs office supplies in this exercise).

Click the Enter ✔ button at the top of the screen to confirm your entries. To display your entries, click the [▦Simulate] button at the top of the screen. The Document Overview screen appears displaying your entries (Figure 19-23).

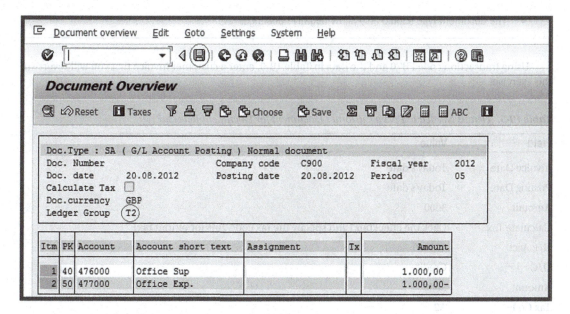

Figure 19-23. *Displaying the documents entered for ledger group T2*

Look through the displayed entries and click Post 🖫 if you are satisfied with your entries.

■ **Note** The system will issue a warning that ⚠ Period 08 adjusted in line with posting date 20.08.2012. This is because of the difference in fiscal year variant. Click the Enter ✔ button on the top-left side of the screen to confirm the adjustments.

Reverse Document

You can reverse an FI document that's been incorrectly entered by using the Reverse Document function. Document reversal was covered in depth in Chapter 14 (Adjustment Posting/Reversal). We will look at how to reverse documents using the negative reversal method in this exercise.

■ **Note** For the system to carry out negative reversal, the following conditions must be satisfied:

- The company code must be defined to allow negative postings.

- The document type should also allow negative postings.

Using transaction code FB70 and the data in Table 19-5, enter a customer invoice that you will reverse in this exercise.

Table 19-5. *Details Needed to Post a Customer Document for Document Reversal*

Field	Value
Invoice Date	Today's date
Posting Date	Today's date
Amount	3000
Calculate Tax	Click the checkbox (and specify the tax code 20% for output tax)
G/L Acct	477000
D/C	Credit
Amount	3000
Tax Code	A2
Cost Center	4110
Segment	SEG-A

■ **Note** When you post your document, the system will notify you in the status bar at the bottom of the screen that your document was posted and will issue a document number. Take note of this document number, because you will need it when reversing the document.

To carry out individual document reversal, follow this menu path: Accounting ➤ Financial Accounting ➤ General Ledger ➤ Document ➤ Reverse ➤ Individual Reversal. Or use transaction code FB08. The Reverse Document: Header Data screen is displayed (Figure 19-24).

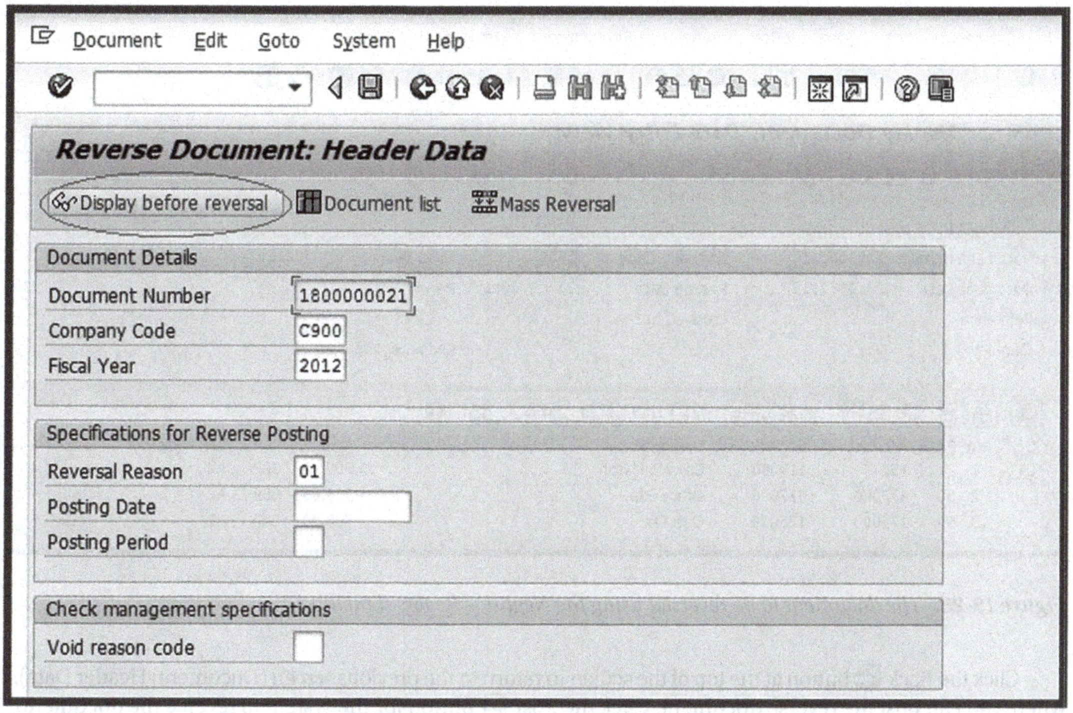

Figure 19-24. *Reverse document and post reverse document using negative reversal method*

Update the following fields:

Document Number: Enter the document number (1800000021) that you want to reverse. This number is usually displayed on the status bar the bottom of the screen when a document is posted. If you cannot remember the document number, use the ▦ Document list button at the top of the screen to display the list of documents and search for your document and enter it in the document number field.

Company Code: Enter your company code (C900) in this field.

Fiscal Year: Enter your company's financial year or fiscal year 2012 in this field.

Reversal Reason: Enter reason 01 (the standard reversal reason supplied by SAP) for reversing the document. You can access the list of reason codes using the matchcode next to the Reversal Reason field.

Before posting reversed documents, it is advisable to for check them to make sure that they are the documents you actually want to reverse. Reversing the wrong document could have a detrimental effect. To display the document you want to reverse, click the 👓 Display before reversal button at the top of the screen. The Display Document: Data Entry View screen displaying the document you want to reverse is displayed (Figure 19-25).

Figure 19-25. *The document to be reversed using the Negative Reversal method*

Click the Back  button at the top of the screen to return to the previous screen (Document: Header Data), where you can post the reverse document. Click the Post button for the system to reverse the document.

■ **Note** The system will notify you on the status bar that

☑ Document 1800000022 was posted in company code C900.

Document Display

In this exercise, you learn how to display the G/L Account balance and line items in new general ledger accounting.

To display balances in new general ledger accounting, follow this menu path: Accounting ➤ Financial Accounting ➤ General Ledger ➤ Account ➤ Display Balances (New). Or use transaction code FAGLB0. The G/L Account Balance Display screen appears. Update the following fields:

> **Account Number:** Enter the account number range (476000 – 477000) that you want to display in the account number fields.

> **Company Code:** Enter the company code (C900) that you want to display the balance in this field.

> **Fiscal Year:** Enter the financial year or fiscal year 2012 that you want to display the account balance in this field.

The system will automatically default to leading ledger 0L. You need to change this since you are displaying the ledger group T2 in this exercise. Click the [Choose Ledger] button at the top of the screen; the Set Ledger dialog box pops up. This screen will allow you to set the appropriate non-leading ledger for your account balance display. Enter the non-leading ledger code T2 that you want to display the G/L account balance in the Ledger field. Click the Continue ✔ button on the bottom-right side of the screen. The non-leading ledger T2 will be entered into the Ledger field in the G/L Account Balance Display screen. Click the Execute ⊕ on the top-left side of the screen to display the G/L account balance for ledger T2. The Balance Display: G/L Accounts for the Ledger T2 screen comes up with list of balances relating to non-leading ledger T2, as shown in Figure 19-26.

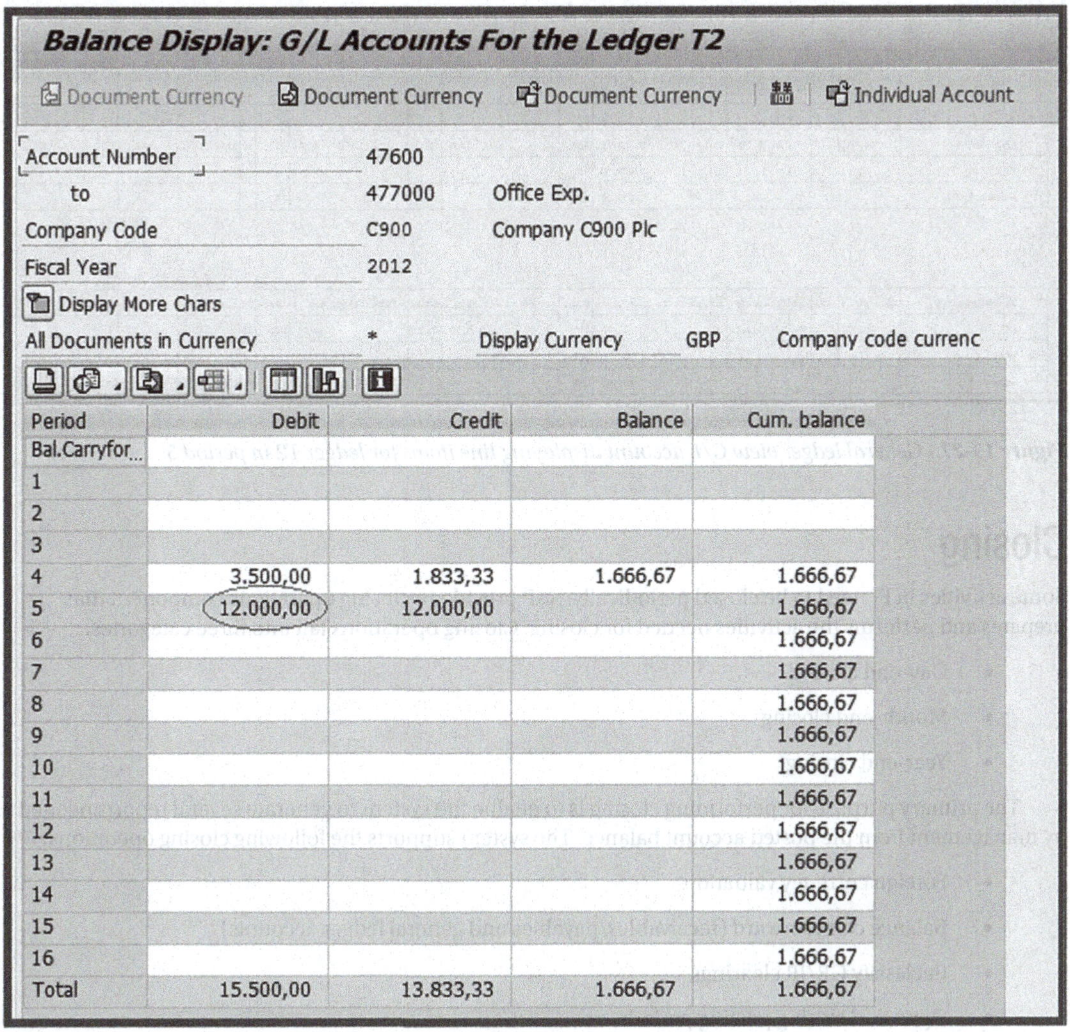

Balance Display: G/L Accounts For the Ledger T2

🔲 Document Currency   🔲 Document Currency   🔲 Document Currency | 🔲   🔲 Individual Account

Account Number	47600	
to	477000	Office Exp.
Company Code	C900	Company C900 Plc
Fiscal Year	2012	

🔲 Display More Chars

| All Documents in Currency | * | Display Currency | GBP | Company code currenc |

Period	Debit	Credit	Balance	Cum. balance
Bal.Carryfor...				
1				
2				
3				
4	3.500,00	1.833,33	1.666,67	1.666,67
5	12.000,00	12.000,00		1.666,67
6				1.666,67
7				1.666,67
8				1.666,67
9				1.666,67
10				1.666,67
11				1.666,67
12				1.666,67
13				1.666,67
14				1.666,67
15				1.666,67
16				1.666,67
Total	15.500,00	13.833,33	1.666,67	1.666,67

Figure 19-26. G/L accounts balance display for non-leading ledger T2

It is also possible to display line items from the balance display screen. To do this, double-click the displayed account balance 12000 in the period (Period 5) you want to take into consideration. The G/L Account Line Item Display G/L View screen is displayed (Figure 19-27), showing all the line items relating to the balances you selected.

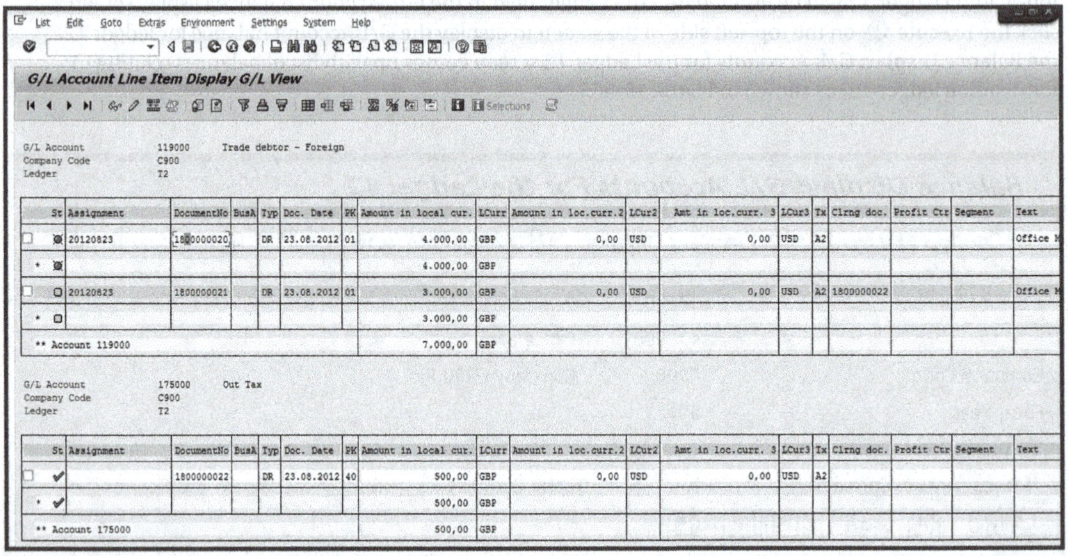

Figure 19-27. General ledger view G/L account displaying line items for ledger T2 in period 5

Closing

Some activities in FI need to be closed periodically. SAP provides a closing operations component that prepares and performs the activities needed for closing. Closing operations fall into three categories:

- Day-end closing

- Month-end closing

- Year-end closing

The primary purpose for performing closing is to enable the system to generate several reports needed by management from the posted account balance. The system supports the following closing operations:

- Foreign currency valuation

- Balance carry forward (receivables/payables and general ledger accounts)

- Reclassify GR/IR clearings

- Open and closing posting periods

- Creating financial statements

In this exercise, we will be looking at the closing processes involved in foreign currency valuation, balance carried forward, and reclassifying of GR/IR. We will not be looking at open and closing posting periods and the creation of financial statements, because that was already covered in Chapters 12 and 13.

During year-end closing operations, new posting periods are opened and balances from the previous year are carried forward into the new fiscal year. Once balances are carried forward, you can then prepare and generate several reports (including financial statements for the period) and archive documents online that are no longer needed.

Foreign Currency Valuation

At month's end, foreign currency valuation is usually carried out. This operation is important as it valuates all transactions in the period posted in foreign currency. When performing monthly foreign currency valuation, an exchange rate is entered for the month's end.

In order to generate financial statements , closing operations for foreign currency valuation have to be performed. For accounts run in foreign currency, you have to prepare and create the following items:

- Foreign currency balance sheet accounts for the G/L accounts that are valuated in foreign currency

- Open items in foreign currency open at a key date

The system also allows you to perform the following optional activities:

- Currency valuation per company code (local currency valuation)

- Currency valuation per group currency (parallel currency valuation)

- Use valuation procedure (for example, lowest value principle, strict lowest value principle, always valuate, and so on).

■ **Note** When financial statements are required on a monthly basis, you must generate foreign currency valuation for open items for G/L accounts and vendor/customer accounts.

It is advisable that each valuation be run individually, since valuations are posted as batch input sessions. For example, separate batch input sessions are generated for G/L accounts and vendor/customer open items.

Problem: Post some invoices for accounts receivable and accounts payable with foreign currency (for example, in USD or EUR).

To execute foreign currency valuation, follow this menu path: Accounting ➤ Financial Accounting ➤ General Ledger ➤ Periodic Processing ➤ Closing ➤ Valuate ➤ Foreign Currency Valuation (New). Or use transaction code FAGL_FC_VAL. The Foreign Currency Valuation screen (Figure 19-28) is displayed.

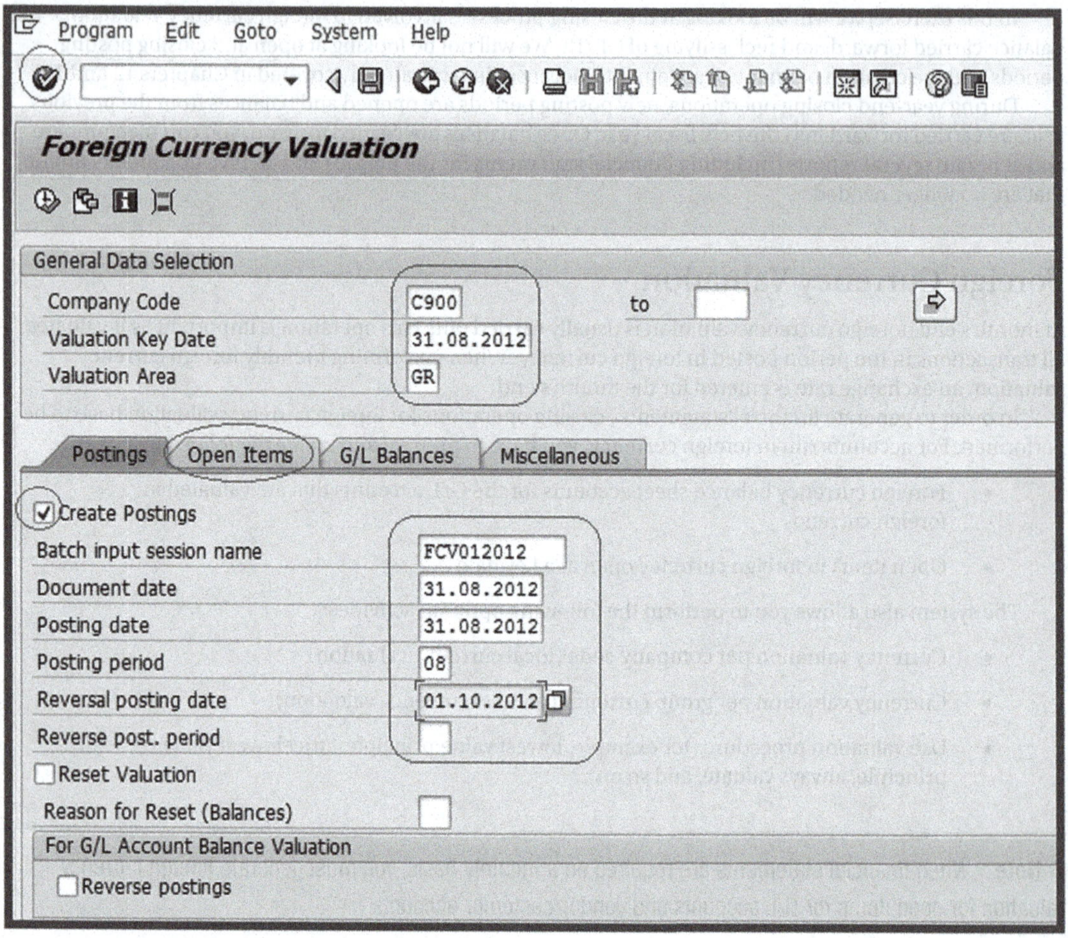

Figure 19-28. Specifying foreign currency valuation

Update the following fields:

Company Code: Enter your company code (C900) in this field.

Valuation Key Date: This date defaults to today's date. This is the date the currency valuation is carried out.

Valuation Area: Enter the valuation area key (GR) for your foreign currency valuation closing in this field. GR entered in the Valuation Area is standard for Group Valuation.

Create Postings: Click the Create Postings checkbox. This will enable you to create valuation documents.

Batch Input Session Name: Enter a name for your batch input session (FCV012015) in this field. There is no specific batch input session name, so you can enter any name that is meaningful to you.

Document Date: Enter your document date (today's date) in this field.

Posting Date: Enter the date the document is posted. Preferably, use today's date.

Reversal Posting Date: Enter today's date plus one month (the first day of the next month) in this field.

■ **Note** The date to post a reversal is usually the first day of next month.

Click the ⎡Open Items⎦ tab at the middle of the screen under General Data Selection to go to the open item part of the screen. Click the Valuate Vendor Open Item and Valuate Customer Open item checkboxes and then click the Execute ⊕ button.

■ **Tip** You can select only particular vendor/customer accounts to be valuated. If you leave the selection fields empty (as in this example), all the accounts in your company code will be selected for valuation.

When the Execute button is clicked, the system will automatically create a batch input session. The system will then generate and display valuated vendor and valuated customer open items. When you click the Postings button, the system will display the accounting documents.

Your valuation is not yet posted. To post it, you need to process the batch input session by using this menu path: System ➤ Services ➤ Batch Input ➤ Sessions.

In the Batch Input: Session Overview screen, select the item you want to execute (FCV012012) and then click the Process button. The Process Session FCV012012 dialog box appears. In the processing mode, select the Display Errors Only radio button. This action will allow the system to display errors during processing. Click the Process button to allow the system to commence posting documents. The system will then notify you that, "Processing of batch input session is completed."

To display the document, use transaction code FB03.

Balance Carry Forward

It is an accounting practice to carry forward balances from the old fiscal year to the new. The Balance Carry Forward function allows you to carry the following items forward from the previous fiscal year:

- Balance sheet account balances

- Profit and loss account balances to a retained earnings account

- G/L account balances

- Customer and vendor account balances

Balance Carry Forward (Customer/Vendor)

For customers and vendors, a manual balance carry forward has to be performed. Postings in the current fiscal year do not necessarily update the balance carried forward. Hence, it is important that you perform a manual balance carry forward function for all customer and vendor accounts.

■ **Note**   The Balance Carry Forward function is performed at the beginning of the new fiscal year.

To perform balance carry forward (customer/vendor), follow this menu path: Accounting ➤ Financial Accounting ➤ Accounts Payable ➤ Periodic Processing ➤ Closing ➤ Carry Forward ➤ Balance Carryforward. Or use transaction code F.07. The Carry Forward Receivable/Payables screen is displayed (Figure 19-29).

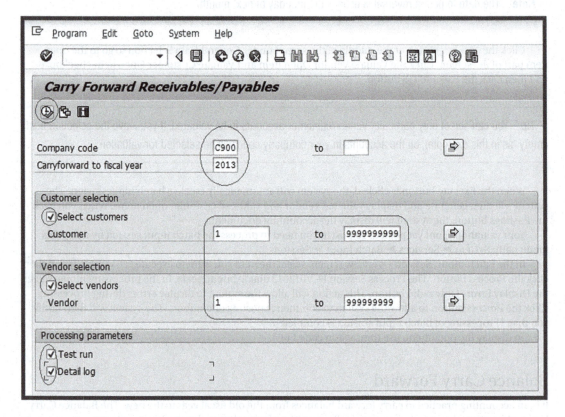

Figure 19-29.   *The screen carry forward receivables/payables*

Update the following fields:

Company Code: Enter your company code (C900) in this field.

Carryforward to Fiscal Year: Specify a future fiscal year (current fiscal year) that you want to carry balances forward to.

Select Customers: Click this checkbox. Receivables then will be included in the balance carry forward.

Customer: Specify the customer number range (1 to 9999999999) you want to include in your selection.

Select Vendors: Click this checkbox. Payables will then be included in the balance carry forward.

Vendor: Specify the vendor number range (1 to 9999999999) you want to include in your selection.

Test Run: Click this checkbox. This will allow you to preview the figures carried forward before they are posted.

Detail Log: Click this checkbox so the system will display further information relating to carry forward receivables/payables.

To execute carry forward receivables/payables, click the Execute ⊕ button on the top-left side of the screen. Since the Test Run checkbox is clicked, only a test run version of carry forward receivables/payables is displayed (Figure 19-30).

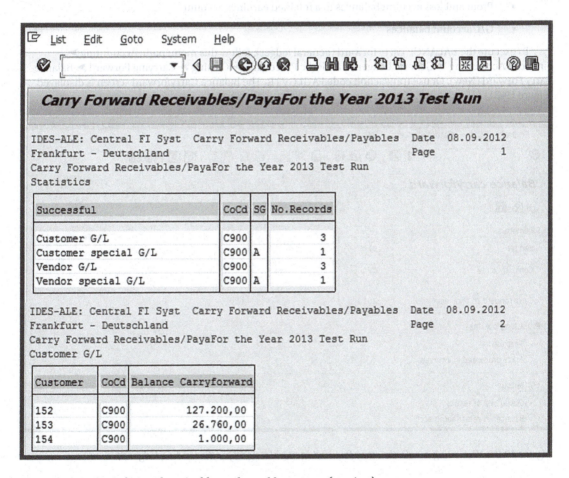

Figure 19-30. Carry forward receivables and payables test run (preview)

This is a test run. To carry out a productive run, click the Back ⬅ button to return to the previous screen, uncheck the ☐ Test run checkbox, and then click the Execute ⊕ button.

Balance Carry Forward (General Ledger)

Balance carry forward for the new fiscal year also needs to be performed manually for general ledger balances, like the balance carry forward for customer/vendor. Once this function is performed, G/L balances are carried forward to the new fiscal year. This function can be performed several times. It is ideal to repeat this function when there are inconsistencies between the previous and current fiscal year G/L account balances.

Once balance carry forward for G/L accounts are performed, the following G/L balances are automatically carried forward:

- Balance sheet account balances

- Profit and loss account balances to a retained earnings account

- G/L account balances

To execute the BALANCE carry forward (general ledger), follow this menu path: Accounting ➤ Financial Accounting ➤ General Ledger ➤ Periodic Processing ➤ Closing ➤ Carrying Forward ➤ Balance Carry Forward (New). Or use transaction code FAGLGVTR. The Balance Carryforward screen is displayed (Figure 19-31).

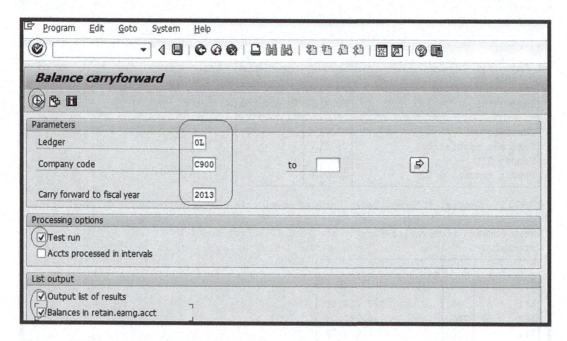

Figure 19-31. *Executing a balance carry forward (general ledger) for the leading ledger 0L*

Update the following fields: Balance carry forward function:general ledger

Ledger: Enter the ledger 0L you want to take into consideration in your balance carry forward. In this case, it is the leading ledger.

Company Code: Enter company code C900.

Carry Forward to Fiscal Year: Enter the fiscal year (current fiscal year) that you want to carry forward balances to in this field.

Test Run: This is set by default (it is important to perform a check run before performing production run). By selecting this checkbox, this will allow you to preview carry forward figures before actually performing actual carry forward.

Output List of Results: By selecting this checkbox, the system will allow you to display balance sheet accounts and retained earnings accounts.

Balance in Retain.Earng.Acct: By checking this checkbox, you can display detailed retained earnings accounts.

■ **Tip** In order to see how balance carry forward works effectively, use the next year as your fiscal year.

To execute the balance carry forward, click the Execute ⊕ button on the top-left side of the screen. The Balance Carryforward Ledger 0L for the Year X Test Run screen is displayed with the option to display the Balance Sheet Accounts or Retained Earnings Accounts. To display the balance sheet accounts, click the Balance sheet accounts button on the top-left side of the screen. The system will then display the balance sheet accounts (Figure 19-32).

Year	CoCd	Account	Crcy	BUn	Trans.cur.	Co.cd.curr	Crcy2	Grp curr.	Curr3	Hard curr.	Curr4	Quantity
2013	C900	2000	GBP		688.333,34	688.333,34	GBP	0,00	USD	0,00	USD	
2013	C900	2010	GBP		233,33	233,33	GBP	0,00	USD	0,00	USD	
2013	C900	11000	GBP		768.333,34	768.333,34	GBP	0,00	USD	0,00	USD	
2013	C900	11010	GBP		10.208,33	10.208,33	GBP	0,00	USD	0,00	USD	
2013	C900	32000	GBP		300.000,00	300.000,00	GBP	0,00	USD	0,00	USD	
2013	C900	100000	GBP		16.440,00-	16.440,00-	GBP	755,00	USD	755,00	USD	
2013	C900	111411	GBP		19.960,00	19.960,00	GBP	0,00	USD	0,00	USD	
2013	C900	111411	USD		3.000,00	2.250,00	GBP	0,00	USD	0,00	USD	
2013	C900	111412	EUR		50.000,00-	34.177,50-	GBP	70.000,00-	USD	70.000,00-	USD	
2013	C900	111412	GBP		87.750,00-	87.750,00-	GBP	29.294,00-	USD	29.294,00-	USD	
2013	C900	119000	GBP		79.960,00	79.960,00	GBP	6.040,00	USD	6.040,00	USD	
2013	C900	119000	USD		100.000,00	75.000,00	GBP	100.000,00	USD	100.000,00	USD	
2013	C900	154000	GBP		343.573,33	343.573,33	GBP	6.037,50	USD	6.037,50	USD	
2013	C900	159000	GBP		0,00	0,00	GBP	0,00	USD	0,00	USD	
2013	C900	159010	GBP		0,00	0,00	GBP	0,00	USD	0,00	USD	
2013	C900	170000	GBP		0,00	0,00	GBP	0,00	USD	0,00	USD	
2013	C900	170010	GBP		0,00	0,00	GBP	0,00	USD	0,00	USD	
2013	C900	175000	GBP		28.866,67-	28.866,67-	GBP	17.169,99-	USD	17.169,99-	USD	
2013	C900	199990	GBP		310.000,00-	310.000,00-	GBP	0,00	USD	0,00	USD	
2013	C900	213000	EUR		0,00	0,00	GBP	0,00	USD	0,00	USD	
2013	C900	213000	GBP		1.946.000,00-	1.946.000,00-	GBP	0,00	USD	0,00	USD	
2013	C900	213000	USD		40.000,00-	30.000,00-	GBP	40.000,00-	USD	40.000,00-	USD	
*			EUR		50.000,00-	165.382,50-	GBP	43.631,49-	USD	43.631,49-	USD	
			GBP		178.455,00-							
			USD		63.000,00							

Figure 19-32. Displaying the balance sheet accounts

To display the retained earnings accounts, click the Back ⟲ button at the top of the screen to return to the previous screen and then click the [Retained earnings accounts] button at the top of that screen. The system will then display the Display of Retained Earnings Accounts screen.

■ **Note**   This is a test run. To carry out a productive run, click the Back ⟲ button to return to the previous screen, unclick the [☐ Test run] checkbox and then click the Execute ⊕ button.

To complete this exercise, carry out the balance carry forward steps for the remaining parallel ledgers (T1 and T2).

Reclassify GR/IR Clearing

The reclassify (goods receipt)/IR (invoice receipt) clearing function:

- Analyzes the GR (goods receipt)/IR (invoice receipt) during the specified period

- Clears GR/IR accounts at a specific key date

- Generates the necessary adjustment postings

■ **Note**   The GR (goods receipt)/IR (invoice receipt) clearing is covered in detail Chapter 8.

The importance of GR/IR classification is for the system to separate G/L account balances for IR (which is usually a debit balance) and treat them as assets in the balance sheet. Consequently, this classification also treats the GR net balance as a liability in the balance sheet. To go to the screen where GR/IR clearing analysis is executed, follow this menu path: Accounting ➤ Financial Accounting ➤ General Ledger ➤ Periodic Processing ➤ Closing ➤ Reclassify ➤ GR/IR Clearing. Or use transaction code F.19. The Analyze GR/IR Clearing Account and Display Acquisition Tax screen is displayed (Figure 19-33).

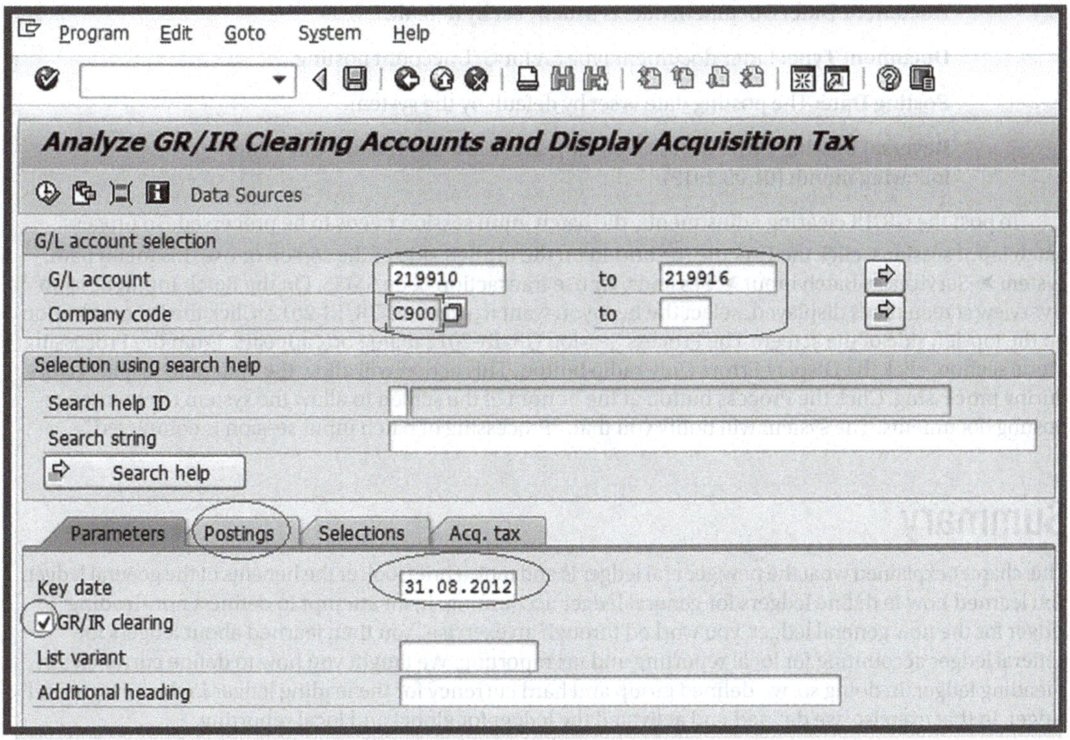

Figure 19-33. *Analyzing GR/IR clearing accounts and display acquisition tax screen*

Update the following fields in the G/L Account Selection section of the screen:

> **G/L Account:** Enter the G/L account number range (219910 – 219916) that you want to cover in the GR/IR clearing accounts.

> **Company Code:** Enter your company code (C900) in this field.

Update the following fields in the Parameters section of the screen:

> **Key Date:** Enter the run date in the key date field. This date is usually the end of the month. (For this exercise, use today's date.)

> **GR/IR Clearing:** Click the checkbox for GR/IR clearing. This is set by default by the system.

The next step in this exercise is to post specifications for the GR/IR clearing. To do this, click the Postings tab next to the Parameters tab and update the following fields:

> **Create Postings:** Click the Create Postings checkbox.

> **Name of Batch Input Session:** Enter your own code (GR/IR-2012). This will enable you to identify your GR/IR account clearing during batch input processing.

> **Ledger Group:** Enter the ledger group that you want to execute. In this exercise, it is assumed that you want to execute GR/IR for the leading ledger 0L.

Document Date: Document date is usually set by default.

Document Type: Enter document type SA for G/L account posting.

Posting Date: The posting date is set by default by the system.

Reversal Posting Date: Reversal posting date is usually the first day of the following month (01.09.2012).

To post the GR/IR clearing adjustments, the batch input session needs to be processed. To process batch input sessions, click the Execute ⊕ button on the top-left side of the screen or use this menu path: System ➤ Services ➤ Batch input ➤ Sessions. Or use transaction code SM35. On the Batch Input: Session Overview screen that's displayed, select the item you want to execute: GR/IR-2012. Click the Process button on the top-left side of the screen. The Process Session GR/IR-2012 dialog box appears. From the Processing Mode section, click the Display Errors Only radio button. This action will allow the system to display errors during processing. Click the Process button at the bottom of the screen to allow the system to commence posting documents. The system will notify you that, "Processing of batch input session is completed."

Summary

This chapter explained what the new general ledger is and took a brief look at the benefits of the general ledger. You learned how to define ledgers for general ledger accounting. In an attempt to define a non-leading ledger for the new general ledger, you worked through an exercise. You then learned about ledgers for general ledger accounting for local reporting and tax reporting. We taught you how to define currencies of a leading ledger. In doing so, we defined group and hard currency for the leading ledger in the new general ledger. In that exercise, we defined and activated the ledger for global and local reporting.

Next, you learned what a scenario is. As part of the customizing of scenarios, we taught you how to assign scenarios and customer fields to ledgers for the leading ledger. You learned about the accounting principles for parallel accounting for local GAAP, International Accounting Standards (IAS), and local tax reporting. We also looked at the real-time integration of controlling with financial accounting, assigning variants for real-time integration to company codes, and carrying out account determination for real-time integration.

You also learned about the document types needed for the general ledger. In that process, we defined the document types for entry view in a ledger and document types for general ledger view. In that exercise, you learned about document splitting in a new general ledger. You learned what document splitting is, the importance of it, and the limitations of it. You then went on to look at the classification of G/L accounting for document splitting, document types for document splitting, and defining a zero-balance clearing account for account document splitting.

You also learned how to post general ledger accounting documents to the user side of the SAP system. During this process, you posted a G/L account document for a ledger group and a reverse document and looked at how to display posted documents to the system.

Finally, we taught you how to perform closing procedures by looking at foreign currency valuation, balance carry forward for customers/vendors, and balance carry forward for the general ledger.

Now that you have completed the customizing activities covered in this book, we are optimistic that you can apply what you learned in this book to real-world scenarios. This was our primary objective for writing this book. Good luck; we wish you the very best in the world of SAP FICO consultancy.

■■■

Useful General Ledger Accounts

Chapter 5
General Ledger
Water Supplies Account

G/L Account	`473000`
Company Code	`C900`

Click the Create 🗋 button.

Type/Description

Control in Chart of Accounts

Account Group	`General G/L accounts` 🗐
P&L Statement Acct	◉
Description	
Short Text	Water Supp. a/c
G/L Acct Long Text	Water Supplies Account

Control Data

Account Control in Company Code

Account Currency	`GBP` 🔄
Tax Category	-

Create/bank/interest

Control of Document Creation in Company Code

Field Status Group	`G004` Cost accounts

Save 💾 .

Electricity Account

G/L Account	474000
Company Code	C900

Click the Create ▢ button.

Type/Description

Control in Chart of Accounts

Account Group	General G/L accounts ▦
P&L Statement Acct	◉
Description	
Short Text	Electicity a/c
G/L Acct Long Text	Electricity Account

Control Data

Account Control in Company Code

Account Currency	GBP ↩
Tax Category	-

Create/bank/interest

Control of Document Creation in Company Code

Field Status Group	G004 Cost accounts

Save 💾 .

Gas Account

G/L Account	475000
Company Code	C900

Click the Create ▭ button.

Type/Description

Control in Chart of Accounts

Account Group	General G/L accounts
P&L Statement Acct	◉
Description	
Short Text	Gas a/c
G/L Acct Long Text	Gas Account

Control Data

Account Control in Company Code

Account Currency	GBP
Tax Category	-

Create/bank/interest

Control of Document Creation in Company Code

Field Status Group	G004 Cost accounts

Save 🖫.

Sales Revenue - Domestic

G/L Account	800000
Company Code	C900

Click the Create ▢ button.

Type/Description

Control in Chart of Accounts

Account Group	General G/L accounts ▦
P&L Statement Acct	◉

Description

Short Text	Sales Rev.
G/L Acct Long Text	Sales Revenue (Domestic)

Control Data

Account Control in Company Code

Account Currency	GBP ⮾
Tax Category	+

Create/bank/interest

Control of Document Creation in Company Code

Field Status Group	G029 ⮾

Save 🖫 .

Sales Revenue - Foreign

G/L Account	810000
Company Code	C900

Click the Create 📄 button.

Type/Description

Control in Chart of Accounts

Account Group | General G/L accounts

P&L Statement Acct | ⦿

Description

Short Text | Sales Rev.

G/L Acct Long Text | Sales Revenue (Foreign)

Control Data

Account Control in Company Code

Account Currency | GBP

Tax Category | +

Create/bank/interest

Control of Document Creation in Company Code

Field Status Group | 6029

Save 💾.

Share Capital

G/L Account	1000
Company Code	C900

Click the Create ◻ button.

Type/Description

Control in Chart of Accounts

Account Group | General G/L accounts

Balance Sheet Account ◉

Description

Short Text | Share Capital

G/L Acct Long Text | Share Capital

Control Data

Account Control in Company Code

Account Currency | GBP

Account Management in Company Code

Open Item Management ☑

Line Item Display ☑

Sort Key | 001 Posting date

Create/bank/interest

Control of Document Creation in Company Code

Field Status Group | G001

Save 💾 .

Retained Earnings

G/L Account   900000

Company Code   C900

    Click the Create [ ] button.

Type/Description

Control in Chart of Accounts

Account Group   General G/L accounts

Balance Sheet Account   ⦿

Description

Short Text   Retained Earnings

G/L Acct Long Text   Retained Earnings

Control Data

Account Control in Company Code

Account Currency   GBP

Account Management in Company Code

Line Item Display   ☑

Sort Key   001   Posting date

Create/bank/interest

Control of Document Creation in Company Code

Field Status Group   G001

    Save [ ] .

Chapter 6
Automatic Clearing Differences
G/L Clearing Differences - Credit

G/L Account	280110
Company Code	C900

Click the Create 🗋 button.

Type/Description

Control in Chart of Accounts

Account Group	General G/L accounts
Balance Sheet Accounts	◉

Description

Short Text	GL Clearing Diff
G/L Acct Long Text	GL Clearing Differences - Credit

Control Data

Account Control in Company Code

Account Currency	GBP
Open Item Management	☑
Line Item Display	☑
Sort Key	027 Value date

Create/bank/interest

Control of Document Creation in Company Code

Field Status Group	G001

Save 💾 .

G/L Clearing Differences - Debit

G/L Account   230110

Company Code   C900

   Click the Create ⬚ button.

Type/Description

Control in Chart of Accounts

Account Group   General G/L accounts   ▤

Balance Sheet Accounts   ◉

Description

Short Text   GL Clearing Diff

G/L Acct Long Text   GL Clearing Differences - Debit

Control Data

Account Control in Company Code

Account Currency   GBP ⟳

Open Item Management   ☑

Line Item Display   ☑

Sort Key   027   Value date

Create/bank/interest

Control of Document Creation in Company Code

Field Status Group   G001 ⟳

   Save 💾.

Foreign Currency valuation
Exchange Rate Expense

G/L Account	230000
Company Code	C900

Click the Create 🗋 button.

Type/Description

Control in Chart of Accounts

Account Group · · · · · · · · · · · · · · · · · · · General G/L accounts 📋

P&L Statement Acct · · · · · · · · · · · · · · · · ◉

Description

Short Text · Exc.Rate Expense

G/L Acct Long Text · · · · · · · · · · · · · · · · · Exchange rate Expense

Control Data

Account Control in Company Code

Account Currency · · · · · · · · · · · · · · · · · · GBP 🗗

Create/bank/interest

Control of Document Creation in Company Code

Field Status Group · · · · · · · · · · · · · · · · · G001 🗗

Save 💾 .

Exchange Rate Gain

G/L Account   280000

Company Code   C900

    Click the Create 🗋 button.

Type/Description

Control in Chart of Accounts

Account Group   General G/L accounts

P&L Statement Acct   ◉

Description

Short Text   Exc.Rate Gain

G/L Acct Long Text   Exchange rate Gain

Control Data

Account Control in Company Code

Account Currency   GBP

Create/bank/interest

Control of Document Creation in Company Code

Field Status Group   G001

    Save 🖫 .

Trade Debtor - Foreign

G/L Account	119000
Company Code	C900

Click the Create ⬚ button.

Type/Description

Control in Chart of Accounts

Account Group	General G/L accounts
Balance Sheet Account	◉
Description	
Short Text	Trade deb Foreign
G/L Acct Long Text	Trade debtor - Foreign

Control Data

Account Control in Company Code

Account Currency	GBP
Only Balances in Local Crcy	
Tax Category	+
Posting Without Tax Allowed	☑
Recon. Account for Acct Type	Customers

Create/bank/interest

Control of Document Creation in Company Code

Field Status Group	G067

Save 🖫 .

Bal. Sheet Adj. (Trade Debtors)

G/L Account	119002
Company Code	C900

Click the Create 🗋 button.

Type/Description

Control in Chart of Accounts

Account Group   General G/L accounts

Balance Sheet Account   ◉

Description

Short Text   Bal. Sheet Adj

G/L Acct Long Text   Bal. Sheet Adj. (Trade Debtors)

Control Data

Account Control in Company Code

Account Currency   GBP

Create/bank/interest

Control of Document Creation in Company Code

Field Status Group   G001

Save 💾 .

Trade Creditor - Foreign

G/L Account	213000
Company Code	C900

Click the Create ▢ button.

Type/Description

Control in Chart of Accounts

Account Group	General G/L accounts
Balance Sheet Account	◉

Description

Short Text	Trade Cred. Foreign
G/L Acct Long Text	Trade Creditor - Foreign

Control Data

Account Control in Company Code

Account Currency	GBP

Only Balances in Local Crcy

Tax Category	-
Posting Without Tax Allowed	☑
Recon. Account for Acct Type	Vendors

Create/bank/interest

Control of Document Creation in Company Code

Field Status Group	G067

Save 🖫 .

Bal. Sheet Adj. (Trade Creditor)

G/L Account	219003
Company Code	C900

Click the Create 🗋 button.

Type/Description

Control in Chart of Accounts

Account Group	General G/L accounts
Balance Sheet Account	◉

Description

Short Text	Bal. Sheet Adj
G/L Acct Long Text	Bal. Sheet Adj. (Trade Creditors)

Control Data

Account Control in Company Code

Account Currency	GBP

Create/bank/interest

Control of Document Creation in Company Code

Field Status Group	G001

Save 💾 .

Foreign Exchange Valuation Realized

G/L Account	450000
Company Code	C900

Click the Create 🔲 button.

Type/Description

Control in Chart of Accounts

Account Group	General G/L accounts
P&L Statement Accounts	◉
Description	
Short Text	Foreign Ex.Realised
G/L Acct Long Text	Foreign Exchange Valuation Realised

Control Data

Account Control in Company Code

Account Currency	GBP

Create/bank/interest

Control of Document Creation in Company Code

Field Status Group	6001

Save 💾 .

Foreign Exchange Valuation

G/L Account	451000
Company Code	C900

Click the Create 🗔 button.

Type/Description

Control in Chart of Accounts

Account Group	General G/L accounts
P&L Statement Accounts	◉
Description	
Short Text	Foreign Ex. Val.
G/L Acct Long Text	Foreign Exchange Valuation

Control Data

Account Control in Company Code

Account Currency	GBP

Create/bank/interest

Control of Document Creation in Company Code

Field Status Group	G001

Save 💾 .

Chapter 8
GR/IR Clearing
Goods Rcvd/Invoice Rcvd (Own Production)

G/L Account	219910
Company Code	C900

Click the Create 🗋 button.

Type/Description

Control in Chart of Accounts

Account Group	General G/L accounts
Balance Sheet Account	◉

Description

Short Text	Goods Rcvd/Invoice R
G/L Acct Long Text	Goods Rcvd/Invoice Rcvd (own production)

Control Data

Account Control in Company Code

Account Currency	GBP
Tax Category	– Only input tax allowed

Account Management in Company Code

Open Item Management	☑
Line Item Display	☑
Sort Key	014 Purchase order

Create/bank/interest

Control of Document Creation in Company Code

Field Status Group	G045 Goods/invoice received clearing accounts

Save 💾 .

Goods Rcvd/Invoice Rcvd (Own Prod. Adj. Acc.)

G/L Account	219911
Company Code	C900

Click the Create 🗋 button.

Type/Description

Control in Chart of Accounts	
Account Group	General G/L accounts
Balance Sheet Account	◉
Description	
Short Text	Goods Rcvd/Invoice R
G/L Acct Long Text	Goods Rcvd/Invoice Rcvd (own prod. adj. acc.)

Control Data

Account Control in Company Code	
Account Currency	GBP
Account Management in Company Code	
Line Item Display	☑
Sort Key	001 Posting date

Create/bank/interest

Control of Document Creation in Company Code	
Field Status Group	G001 General (with text, allocation)

Save 💾.

Goods Rcvd/Invoice Rcvd – Not Yet Delivered

G/L Account   119010

Company Code   C900

Click the Create 🗋 button.

Type/Description

Control in Chart of Accounts

Account Group   General G/L accounts

Balance Sheet Account   ◉

Description

Short Text   Goods Rcvd/Invoice R

G/L Acct Long Text   Goods Rcvd/Invoice Rcvd - not yet delivered

Control Data

Account Control in Company Code

Account Currency   GBP

Account Management in Company Code

Line Item Display   ☑

Sort Key   001   Posting date

Create/bank/interest

Control of Document Creation in Company Code

Field Status Group   G001   General (with text, allocation)

Save 💾.

Goods Rcvd/Invoice Rcvd (Third Party)

G/L Account	219915
Company Code	C900

Click the Create 🗋 button.

Type/Description

Control in Chart of Accounts

Account Group	General G/L accounts
Balance Sheet Account	◉
Description	
Short Text	Goods Rcvd/Invoice R
G/L Acct Long Text	Goods Rcvd/Invoice Rcvd (third party)

Control Data

Account Control in Company Code

Account Currency	GBP
Tax Category	– Only input tax allowed

Account Management in Company Code

Open Item Management	☑
Line Item Display	☑
Sort Key	014 Purchase order

Create/bank/interest

Control of Document Creation in Company Code

Field Status Group	G045 Goods/invoice received clearing accounts

Save 💾 .

Goods Rcvd/Invoice Rcvd Recon. (Acqrd Externally)

G/L Account   219916

Company Code   C900

Click the Create ☐ button.

Type/Description

Control in Chart of Accounts

Account Group   General G/L accounts

Balance Sheet Account   ◉

Description

Short Text   Goods Rcvd/Invoice R

G/L Acct Long Text   Goods Rcvd/Invoice Rcvd recon. (acqrd externally)

Control Data

Account Control in Company Code

Account Currency   GBP

Account Management in Company Code

Line Item Display   ☑

Sort Key   001   Posting date

Create/bank/interest

Control of Document Creation in Company Code

Field Status Group   G001   General (with text, allocation)

Save 💾 .

Goods Rcvd/Invoice Rcvd Recon Not Yet Invoiced

G/L Account	119015
Company Code	C900

Click the Create ▢ button.

Type/Description

Control in Chart of Accounts

Account Group — General G/L accounts ▦

Balance Sheet Account — ◉

Description

Short Text — Goods Rcvd/Invoice R

G/L Acct Long Text — Goods Rcvd/Invoice Rcvd - not yet invoiced

Control Data

Account Control in Company Code

Account Currency — GBP ↻

Account Management in Company Code

Line Item Display — ☑

Sort Key — 001 Posting date

Create/bank/interest

Control of Document Creation in Company Code

Field Status Group — G001 General (with text, allocation)

Save 🖫 .

Chapter 9
House Bank
Barclays Bank

G/L Account	111410
Company Code	C900

Click the Create ▢ button.

Type/Description

Control in Chart of Accounts

Account Group	Liquid funds accounts ▤
Balance Sheet Account	◉

Description

Short Text	Barclays -Chk rec
G/L Acct Long Text	Barclays Bank Account

Control Data

Account Control in Company Code

Account Currency	GBP ↻

Account Management in Company Code

Open Item Management	☑
Line Item Display	☑
Sort Key	003 Document date

Create/bank/interest

Control of Document Creation in Company Code

Field Status Group	G005 ↻

Bank/Financial Details in Company Code

Relevant to Cash Flow	☑
House Bank	BARC1
Account ID	BARC

■ **Note** Since you have not defined the House Bank and Account IDs, when saving your G/L Account, the system will issue a warning that the House Bank and Account ID have not been defined. You can simply ignore the warning and press Enter on your Keyboard repeatedly until the system allows you to save your Account.

Your House Bank and Account ID will be defined in Section 1.2 of Chapter 9 when creating your House Bank. Press Enter twice on your keyboard and the system will allow you to save your G/L Account. Ignore the warning and click Save 🖫 .

HSBC Bank

G/L Account	113150
Company Code	C900

Click the Create 🗋 button.

Type/Description

Control in Chart of Accounts

Account Group	Liquid funds accounts
Balance Sheet Account	◉

Description

Short Text	HSBC
G/L Acct Long Text	HSBC Bank Account

Control Data

Account Control in Company Code

Account Currency	GBP

Account Management in Company Code

Open Item Management	☑
Line Item Display	☑
Sort Key	003 Document date

Create/bank/interest

Control of Document Creation in Company Code

Field Status Group	G005

Bank/Financial Details in Company Code

Relevant to Cash Flow	☑
House Bank	HSBC1
Account ID	HSBC

Press Enter repeatedly on your keyboard until the system allows you to save. Ignore the warning and click Save 🖫 .

Bank Statement
Check Received

G/L Account	111411
Company Code	C900

Click the Create 🗋 button.

Type/Description

Control in Chart of Accounts	
Account Group	Liquid funds accounts
Balance Sheet Account	◉
Description	
Short Text	Barclays -Chk rec
G/L Acct Long Text	Barclays Bank - Check received

Control Data

Account Control in Company Code	
Account Currency	GBP
Account Management in Company Code	
Open Item Management	☑
Line Item Display	☑
Sort Key	003 Document date

Create/bank/interest

Control of Document Creation in Company Code	
Field Status Group	G005
Bank/Financial Details in Company Code	
Planning Level	B8 Incoming checks
Relevant to Cash Flow	☑

Save 💾.

Other Interim Posting

G/L Account	`111416`
Company Code	`C900`

Click the Create ⬜ button.

Type/Description

Control in Chart of Accounts

Account Group	`Liquid funds accounts` 📄
Balance Sheet Account	◉
Description	
Short Text	`Barclays - other int`
G/L Acct Long Text	`Barclays Bank - other interim postings`

Control Data

Account Control in Company Code

Account Currency	`GBP` ↩

Account Management in Company Code

Open Item Management	☑
Line Item Display	☑
Sort Key	`003` Document date

Create/bank/interest

Control of Document Creation in Company Code

Field Status Group	`G005` ↩

Bank/Financial Details in Company Code

Planning Level	`B5` Other interim postings
Relevant to Cash Flow	☑

Save 💾 .

Check Issued Out - Barclays

G/L Account	111412
Company Code	C900

Click the Create ⬚ button.

Type/Description

Control in Chart of Accounts

Account Group	Liquid funds accounts
Balance Sheet Account	◉

Description

Short Text	Barclays - chk out
G/L Acct Long Text	Barclays Bank - check issued out

Control Data

Account Control in Company Code

Account Currency	GBP

Account Management in Company Code

Open Item Management	☑
Line Item Display	☑
Sort Key	003 Document date

Create/bank/interest

Control of Document Creation in Company Code

Field Status Group	G005

Bank/Financial Details in Company Code

Planning Level	B1 Outgoing checks
Relevant to Cash Flow	☑

Save 🖫 .

Check Issued Out - HSBC

G/L Account	113155
Company Code	C900

Click the Create 🗋 button.

Type/Description

Control in Chart of Accounts	
Account Group	Liquid funds accounts
Balance Sheet Account	◉
Description	
Short Text	HSBC - chk out
G/L Acct Long Text	HSBC bank – check issued out

Control Data

Account Control in Company Code	
Account Currency	GBP
Account Management in Company Code	
Open Item Management	☑
Line Item Display	☑
Sort Key	003 Document date

Create/bank/interest

Control of Document Creation in Company Code	
Field Status Group	G005
Bank/Financial Details in Company Code	
Planning Level	B1 Outgoing checks
Relevant to Cash Flow	☑

Incoming Wire Transfer

G/L Account	111415
Company Code	C900

Click the Create ☐ button.

Type/Description

Control in Chart of Accounts	
Account Group	Liquid funds accounts
Balance Sheet Account	◉
Description	
Short Text	Barclays - in trans
G/L Acct Long Text	Barclays Bank - incoming transfer

Control Data

Account Control in Company Code	
Account Currency	GBP
Account Management in Company Code	
Open Item Management	☑
Line Item Display	☑
Sort Key	003 Document date

Create/bank/interest

Control of Document Creation in Company Code	
Field Status Group	6005
Bank/Financial Details in Company Code	
Planning Level	B8 Incoming checks
Relevant to Cash Flow	☑

Save 💾 .

Outgoing Wire Transfer - Barclays

G/L Account   `111414`

Company Code   `C900`

Click the Create 🗋 button.

Type/Description

Control in Chart of Accounts

Account Group   `Liquid funds accounts`

Balance Sheet Account   ◉

Description

Short Text   `Barclays - out trans`

G/L Acct Long Text   `Barclays Bank - outgoing transfer`

Control Data

Account Control in Company Code

Account Currency   `GBP`

Account Management in Company Code

Open Item Management   ☑

Line Item Display   ☑

Sort Key   `003`   Document date

Create/bank/interest

Control of Document Creation in Company Code

Field Status Group   `G005`

Bank/Financial Details in Company Code

Planning Level   `B2`   Outgoing transfer,

Relevant to Cash Flow   ☑

Save 💾 .

Outgoing Wire Transfer - HSBC

G/L Account	113158
Company Code	C900

Click the Create 🗋 button.

Type/Description

Control in Chart of Accounts	
Account Group	Liquid funds accounts
Balance Sheet Account	◉
Description	
Short Text	HSBC – out trans
G/L Acct Long Text	HSBC Bank – Outgoing transfer

Control Data

Account Control in Company Code	
Account Currency	GBP
Account Management in Company Code	
Open Item Management	☑
Line Item Display	☑
Sort Key	003 Document date

Create/bank/interest

Control of Document Creation in Company Code	
Field Status Group	G005
Bank/Financial Details in Company Code	
Planning Level	B2 Outgoing transfer,
Relevant to Cash Flow	☑

Save 💾 .

Incoming Cash

G/L Account	111417
Company Code	C900

Click the Create ▢ button.

Type/Description

Control in Chart of Accounts

Account Group | Liquid funds accounts

Balance Sheet Account ◉

Description

Short Text | Barclays - in cash

G/L Acct Long Text | Barclays Bank - incoming cash

Control Data

Account Control in Company Code

Account Currency | GBP

Account Management in Company Code

Open Item Management ☑

Line Item Display ☑

Sort Key | 005 Local currency amt

Create/bank/interest

Control of Document Creation in Company Code

Field Status Group | G005

Bank/Financial Details in Company Code

Planning Level | B5 Other interim postings

Relevant to Cash Flow ☑

Save 💾.

Outgoing Cash

G/L Account	111419
Company Code	C900

Click the Create 🗋 button.

Type/Description

Control in Chart of Accounts

Account Group	Liquid funds accounts
Balance Sheet Account	◉

Description

Short Text	Barclays - out cash
G/L Acct Long Text	Barclays outgoing cash

Control Data

Account Control in Company Code

Account Currency	GBP

Account Management in Company Code

Open Item Management	☑
Line Item Display	☑
Sort Key	005 Local currency amt

Create/bank/interest

Control of Document Creation in Company Code

Field Status Group	G005

Bank/Financial Details in Company Code

Planning Level	B5 Other interim postings
Relevant to Cash Flow	☑

Save 💾 .

Bank Charge

G/L Account	470100
Company Code	C900

Click the Create ☐ button.

Type/Description

Control in Chart of Accounts

Account Group	General G/L accounts
P&L Statement Account	⦿
Description	
Short Text	Bank chgs
G/L Acct Long Text	Bank charges

Control Data

Account Control in Company Code

Account Currency	GBP

Account Management in Company Code

Open Item Management

Line Item Display

Sort Key

Create/bank/interest

Control of Document Creation in Company Code

Field Status Group	G001

Save 💾 .

Chapter 10
Tax on Sales/Purchases
Input/Purchases Tax

G/L Account	154000
Company Code	C900

Click the Create ⬚ button.

Type/Description

Control in Chart of Accounts

Account Group	General G/L accounts
Balance Sheet Account	◉

Description

Short Text	Input Tax
G/L Acct Long Text	Input Tax

Control Data

Account Control in Company Code

Account Currency	GBP
Only Balances in Local Crcy	☑ Only balances in local crcy
Tax Category	< Input Tax Account

Create/bank/interest

Control of Document Creation in Company Code

Field Status Group	G001

Save 💾 .

Output/Sales Tax

G/L Account   `175000`

Company Code   `C900`

    Click the Create 🗋 button.

Type/Description

Control in Chart of Accounts

Account Group   `General G/L accounts`

Balance Sheet Account   ◉

Description

Short Text   `Out Tax`

G/L Acct Long Text   `Out Tax`

Control Data

Account Control in Company Code

Account Currency   `GBP`

Only Balances in Local Crcy   ☑ Only balances in local crcy

Tax Category   `>`   Output Tax Account

Create/bank/interest

Control of Document Creation in Company Code

Field Status Group   `G001`

    Save 💾 .

Chapter 11
Cash Journal
Petty Cash

G/L Account	100000
Company Code	C900

Click the Create 🗅 button.

Type/Description

Control in Chart of Accounts

Account Group	Liquid funds accounts 🗒
Balance Sheet Account	◉

Description

Short Text	Petty Cash
G/L Acct Long Text	Petty Cash

Control Data

Account Control in Company Code

Account Currency	GBP 🗗

Account Management in Company Code

Open Item Management

Line Item Display	☑ Line item display
Sort Key	003 🗗

Create/bank/interest

Control of Document Creation in Company Code

Field Status Group	G001 🗗
Post Automatically Only	☑

Bank/Financial Details in Company Code

Planning Level	F0 Posting to bank account
Relevant to Cash Flow	☑ Relevant to cash flow

Save 💾 .

Cash Transfer from Bank

G/L Account	113130
Company Code	C900

Click the Create 🗅 button.

Type/Description

Control in Chart of Accounts

Account Group	Liquid funds accounts 🗐
Balance Sheet Account	◉

Description

Short Text	Barc. BK-outg cash
G/L Acct Long Text	Barclays Bank - Outgoing Cash

Control Data

Account Control in Company Code

Account Currency	GBP 🗗

Account Management in Company Code

Open Item Management	☑ Open item management
Line Item Display	☑ Line item display
Sort Key	005 🗗

Create/bank/interest

Control of Document Creation in Company Code

Field Status Group	G005
Post Automatically Only	☑ Post automatically only

Bank/Financial Details in Company Code

Planning Level	B5 🗗
Relevant to Cash Flow	☑ Relevant to cash flow

Save 🖫 .

Cash Transfer to Bank

G/L Account	113131
Company Code	C900

Click the Create ▢ button.

Type/Description

Control in Chart of Accounts

Account Group	Liquid funds accounts
Balance Sheet Account	◉

Description

Short Text	Barc. BK-Inc cash
G/L Acct Long Text	Barclays Bank - incoming Cash

Control Data

Account Control in Company Code

Account Currency	GBP

Account Management in Company Code

Open Item Management	☑ Open item management
Line Item Display	☑ Line item display
Sort Key	005

Create/bank/interest

Control of Document Creation in Company Code

Field Status Group	G005
Post Automatically Only	☑ Post automatically only

Bank/Financial Details in Company Code

Planning Level	B5
Relevant to Cash Flow	☑ Relevant to cash flow

Save 💾.

Cash Purchase – Office Mat

G/L Account	460000
Company Code	C900

Click the Create ⬚ button.

Type/Description

Control in Chart of Accounts

Account Group	General G/L accounts ⬚
P&L Statement Acct	⦿

Description

Short Text	Cash Purch Off Mat
G/L Acct Long Text	Cash Purchase - Office Mat

Control Data

Account Control in Company Code

Account Currency	GBP ⬚
Tax Category	- Only input tax allowed

Create/bank/interest

Control of Document Creation in Company Code

Field Status Group	G004 ⬚ Cost accounts

Save 💾 .

Cash Sale

G/L Account	800001
Company Code	C900

Click the Create ☐ button.

Type/Description

Control in Chart of Accounts

Account Group	General G/L accounts
P&L Statement Acct	◉
Description	
Short Text	Cash Sale
G/L Acct Long Text	Cash Sale

Control Data

Account Control in Company Code

Account Currency	GBP
Tax Category	+ Only output tax allowed

Create/bank/interest

Control of Document Creation in Company Code

Field Status Group	G029 Revenue accounts

Save 💾 .

Chapter 13
Integration of FI with Other Modules
Consumption, Raw Material

G/L Account	400000
Company Code	C900

Click the Create ⬚ button.

Type/Description

Control in Chart of Accounts

Account Group	Materials management accounts
P&L Statement Acct	◉

Description

Short Text	Consumption, raw mat
G/L Acct Long Text	Consumption, raw material

Control Data

Account Control in Company Code

Account Currency	GBP
Tax Category	-
Posting Without Tax Allowed	☑

Account Management in Company Code

Open Item Management

Line Item Display	☑
Sort Key	008 Cost center

Create/bank/interest

Control of Document Creation in Company Code

Field Status Group	G003

Save 💾.

Finished Goods Inventory

G/L Account	792000
Company Code	C900

Click the Create 🗋 button.

Type/Description

Control in Chart of Accounts

Account Group	Materials management accounts 📓
Balance Sheet Account	◉
Description	
Short Text	Finished goods inven
G/L Acct Long Text	Finished goods inventory

Control Data

Account Control in Company Code

Account Currency	GBP 🗗
Only Balances in Local Crcy	☑
Posting Without Tax Allowed	☑

Create/bank/interest

Control of Document Creation in Company Code

Field Status Group	G006 🗗
Posting Automatically Only	☑

Save 💾 .

Goods Rcvd/Invoice Rcvd

G/L Account	191100
Company Code	C900

Click the Create 🗋 button.

Type/Description

Control in Chart of Accounts

Account Group	General G/L accounts ▤
Balance Sheet Accounts	◉

Description

Short Text	Goods Rcvd/Invoice R
G/L Acct Long Text	Goods Rcvd/Invoice Rcvd

Control Data

Account Control in Company Code

Account Currency	GBP ↻
Only Balances in Local Crcy	☑
Tax Category	- Only input tax allowed
Posting Without Tax Allowed	☑

Account Management in Company Code

Open Item Management	☑
Line Item Display	☑
Sort Key	014 Purchase order

Create/bank/interest

Control of Document Creation in Company Code

Field Status Group	G045 ↻
Post Automatically Only	☑

Save 💾 .

Inventory - Raw Material

G/L Account	300000
Company Code	C900

Click the Create ▯ button.

Type/Description

Control in Chart of Accounts

Account Group	Materials management accounts 🖹
Balance Sheet Accounts	◉
Description	
Short Text	Inventory - Raw Mat
G/L Acct Long Text	Inventory - Raw Material

Control Data

Account Control in Company Code

Account Currency	GBP ⮌
Only Balances in Local Crcy	☑
Tax Category	-
Posting Without Tax Allowed	☑

Create/bank/interest

Control of Document Creation in Company Code

Field Status Group	G006 ⮌

Save 💾 .

Sales Distribution

G/L Account	810001
Company Code	C900

Click the Create 🗋 button.

Type/Description

Control in Chart of Accounts	
Account Group	General G/L accounts 📖
P&L Statement Account	◉
Description	
Short Text	Sales Deduction
G/L Acct Long Text	Sales Deduction

Control Data

Account Control in Company Code	
Account Currency	GBP ⮌
Only Balances in Local Crcy	
Tax Category	+
Posting Without Tax Allowed	☑

Create/bank/interest

Control of Document Creation in Company Code	
Field Status Group	G029 ⮌

Save 💾 .

Semi-Finished Products

G/L Account	790000
Company Code	C900

Click the Create ☐ button.

Type/Description

Control in Chart of Accounts

Account Group	General G/L accounts ▣
Balance Sheet Accounts	◉

Description

Short Text	Semi-fin prod
G/L Acct Long Text	Semi-finished products

Control Data

Account Control in Company Code

Account Currency	GBP ↻
Only Balances in Local Crcy	☑
Tax Category	*
Posting Without Tax Allowed	☑

Create/bank/interest

Control of Document Creation in Company Code

Field Status Group	G006 ↻

Save 💾 .

Chapter 14
Terms of Payment
Accounts for Net Procedure

G/L Account	193000
Company Code	C900

Click the Create 🗖 button.

Type/Description

Control in Chart of Accounts

Account Group	General G/L accounts
Balance Sheet Account	◉

Description

Short Text	Clearing supplier di
G/L Acct Long Text	Clearing supplier discounts (Net method)

Control Data

Account Control in Company Code

Account Currency	GBP
Only Balances in Local Crcy	☑ Only balances in local crcy
Tax Category	

Account Management in Company Code

Open Item Management	☑ Open item management
Line Item Display	☑ Line item display
Sort Key	101 Cash discnt clearing

Create/bank/interest

Control of Document Creation in Company Code

Field Status Group	G001 General (with text, allocation)

Save 🖫 .

Cash Discount Granted

G/L Account	`880000`
Company Code	`C900`

Click the Create 🗋 button.

Type/Description

Control in Chart of Accounts

Account Group	`General G/L accounts` 🗐
P&L Statement Acct	◉
Description	
Short Text	`Customer Discount`
G/L Acct Long Text	`Discount Granted (Customer)`

Control Data

Account Control in Company Code

Account Currency	`GBP` 🗗
Tax Category	
Posting Without Tax Allowed	

Account Management in Company Code

Line Item Display	☑ Line item display
Sort Key	`001` Posting date

Create/bank/interest

Control of Document Creation in Company Code

Field Status Group	`G001` 🗗 General (with text, allocation)

Save 🖫 .

Discount Received

G/L Account	276000
Company Code	C900

Click the Create ☐ button.

Type/Description

Control in Chart of Accounts	
Account Group	General G/L accounts
P&L Statement Acct	◉
Description	
Short Text	Discount received
G/L Acct Long Text	Discount received

Control Data

Account Control in Company Code	
Account Currency	GBP
Tax Category	
Posting Without Tax Allowed	
Account Management in Company Code	
Line Item Display	☑ Line item display
Sort Key	001 Posting date

Create/bank/interest

Control of Document Creation in Company Code	
Field Status Group	G001 General (with text, allocation)

Save 💾 .

Discount Lost

G/L Account	880010
Company Code	C900

Click the Create ▯ button.

Type/Description

Control in Chart of Accounts

Account Group	General G/L accounts
P&L Statement Acct	◉

Description

Short Text	Discount loss (NM)
G/L Acct Long Text	Discount loss (Net method)

Control Data

Account Control in Company Code

Account Currency	GBP

Tax Category

Posting Without Tax Allowed

Account Management in Company Code

Line Item Display	☑ Line item display
Sort Key	031 Customer number

Create/bank/interest

Control of Document Creation in Company Code

Field Status Group	G029 Revenue accounts

Save 🖫 .

Overpayments/Underpayments

G/L Account	881000
Company Code	C900

Click the Create 🗋 button.

Type/Description

Control in Chart of Accounts

Account Group	General G/L accounts 🖹
P&L Statement Acct	◉

Description

Short Text	Overpay/Underpay
G/L Acct Long Text	Overpayments/Underpayments

Control Data

Account Control in Company Code

Account Currency	GBP 🗗

Tax Category

Posting Without Tax Allowed

Account Management in Company Code

Line Item Display	☑ Line item display
Sort Key	031 Customer number

Create/bank/interest

Control of Document Creation in Company Code

Field Status Group	G029 🗗 Revenue accounts

Save 💾 .

Define Sort Method and Adjustment Accts to Regrouping Trade Payables – Foreign – Adj. Account

G/L Account	213099
Company Code	C900

Click the Create ▢ button.

Type/Description

Control in Chart of Accounts

Account Group	General G/L accounts
Balance Sheet Account	◉

Description

Short Text	Trade payable - for
G/L Acct Long Text	Trade payable - Foreign - Adj. Account

Control Data

Account Control in Company Code

Account Currency	GBP
Only Balances in Local Crcy	☑

Account Management in Company Code

Line Item Display	☑
Sort Key	001 Posting date

Create/bank/interest

Control of Document Creation in Company Code

Field Status Group	G001

Post Automatically Only

Save 💾 .

Trade Receivables – Foreign – Adj. Account

G/L Account	119899
Company Code	C900

Click the Create 🗋 button.

Type/Description

Control in Chart of Accounts	
Account Group	General G/L accounts 📋
Balance Sheet Account	◉
Description	
Short Text	Trade reveivable-for
G/L Acct Long Text	Trade receivable- Foreign - Adj. Account

Control Data

Account Control in Company Code	
Account Currency	GBP 🗗
Only Balances in Local Crcy	☑
Account Management in Company Code	
Line Item Display	☑
Sort Key	001 Posting date

Create/bank/interest

Control of Document Creation in Company Code	
Field Status Group	G001 🗗
Post Automatically Only	

Save 💾 .

Vendor with a Debit Balance

G/L Account	119300
Company Code	C900

Click the Create 🗋 button.

Type/Description

Control in Chart of Accounts

Account Group	General G/L accounts 🖫
Balance Sheet Account	◉
Description	
Short Text	Accounts payable -d
G/L Acct Long Text	Vendor with a debit balance

Control Data

Account Control in Company Code

Account Currency	GBP 🗗
Only Balances in Local Crcy	☑

Account Management in Company Code

Open Item Management	☑
Line Item Display	☑
Sort Key	001 Posting date

Create/bank/interest

Control of Document Creation in Company Code

Field Status Group	G001 🗗
Post Automatically Only	

Save 💾 .

Customers with a Credit Balance

G/L Account	213300
Company Code	C900

Click the Create 🗋 button.

Type/Description

Control in Chart of Accounts	
Account Group	General G/L accounts
Balance Sheet Account	◉
Description	
Short Text	Cust. With a crd. ba
G/L Acct Long Text	Customers with a credit balance

Control Data

Account Control in Company Code	
Account Currency	GBP
Only Balances in Local Crcy	☑
Account Management in Company Code	
Open Item Management	☑
Line Item Display	☑
Sort Key	001 Posting date

Create/bank/interest

Control of Document Creation in Company Code	
Field Status Group	G001
Post Automatically Only	

Save 💾 .

Trade Payables - Foreign – Due b/w 1-5 Years

G/L Account	213030
Company Code	C900

Click the Create ⬚ button.

Type/Description

Control in Chart of Accounts

Account Group	General G/L accounts
Balance Sheet Account	◉

Description

Short Text	Trade Payables
G/L Acct Long Text	Trade Payables – foreign – due b/w 1-5yrs

Control Data

Account Control in Company Code

Account Currency	GBP
Only Balances in Local Crcy	☑

Account Management in Company Code

Open Item Management	☑
Line Item Display	☑
Sort Key	001 Posting date

Create/bank/interest

Control of Document Creation in Company Code

Field Status Group	G001

Post Automatically Only

Save 💾 .

Other Creditors – Due b/w 1-5 Years

G/L Account	202000
Company Code	C900

Click the Create ▢ button.

Type/Description

Control in Chart of Accounts	
Account Group	General G/L accounts
Balance Sheet Account	◉
Description	
Short Text	Other creditors, d
G/L Acct Long Text	Other creditors, due 1-5 yrs.

Control Data

Account Control in Company Code	
Account Currency	GBP
Only Balances in Local Crcy	☑
Account Management in Company Code	
Open Item Management	☑
Line Item Display	☑
Sort Key	001 Posting date

Create/bank/interest

Control of Document Creation in Company Code	
Field Status Group	G019
Post Automatically Only	

Save 💾 .

Trade Payables - Foreign – Due > 5 Years

G/L Account	`213040`
Company Code	`C900`

Click the Create ▢ button.

Type/Description

Control in Chart of Accounts	
Account Group	`General G/L accounts` ▢
Balance Sheet Account	◉
Description	
Short Text	`Trade Payables`
G/L Acct Long Text	Trade Payables – foreign – due >5yrs

Control Data

Account Control in Company Code	
Account Currency	`GBP` ▢
Only Balances in Local Crcy	☑
Account Management in Company Code	
Open Item Management	☑
Line Item Display	☑
Sort Key	`001` Posting date

Create/bank/interest

Control of Document Creation in Company Code	
Field Status Group	`G001` ▢
Post Automatically Only	

Save ▢ .

Trade Receivables - Foreign – Due > 1 Year

G/L Account	`119030`
Company Code	`C900`

Click the Create ▢ button.

Type/Description

Control in Chart of Accounts

Account Group	`General G/L accounts`
Balance Sheet Account	◉

Description

Short Text	Trade Receivables
G/L Acct Long Text	Trade Receivables – foreign – due > 1yrs

Control Data

Account Control in Company Code

Account Currency	`GBP`
Only Balances in Local Crcy	☑

Account Management in Company Code

Open Item Management	☑
Line Item Display	☑
Sort Key	`001` Posting date

Create/bank/interest

Control of Document Creation in Company Code

Field Status Group	`G001`
Post Automatically Only	

Save 💾 .

Other Debtors, Due > 1 Year

G/L Account	120000
Company Code	C900

Click the Create 🗋 button.

Type/Description

Control in Chart of Accounts	
Account Group	General G/L accounts
Balance Sheet Account	◉
Description	
Short Text	Other Debtors
G/L Acct Long Text	Other Debtors, due > 1 year

Control Data

Account Control in Company Code	
Account Currency	GBP
Only Balances in Local Crcy	☑
Account Management in Company Code	
Open Item Management	☑
Line Item Display	☑
Sort Key	001 Posting date

Create/bank/interest

Control of Document Creation in Company Code	
Field Status Group	G001
Post Automatically Only	

Save 💾 .

Other Creditors, Due Within 1-5 Years

G/L Account	212000
Company Code	C900

Click the Create ▢ button.

Type/Description

Control in Chart of Accounts	
Account Group	General G/L accounts
Balance Sheet Account	◉
Description	
Short Text	Other Creditors
G/L Acct Long Text	Other creditors, due within 1 - 5years

Control Data

Account Control in Company Code	
Account Currency	GBP
Only Balances in Local Crcy	☑
Account Management in Company Code	
Open Item Management	☑
Line Item Display	☑
Sort Key	001 Posting date

Create/bank/interest

Control of Document Creation in Company Code	
Field Status Group	G001
Post Automatically Only	

Save 💾 .

Other Creditors Due > 5 Years

G/L Account	212100
Company Code	C900

Click the Create 🗋 button.

Type/Description

Control in Chart of Accounts

Account Group	General G/L accounts
Balance Sheet Account	◉
Description	
Short Text	Other creditors, d
G/L Acct Long Text	Other creditors due >5years

Control Data

Account Control in Company Code

Account Currency	GBP
Only Balances in Local Crcy	☑

Account Management in Company Code

Open Item Management	☑
Line Item Display	☑
Sort Key	001 Posting date

Create/bank/interest

Control of Document Creation in Company Code

Field Status Group	G001
Post Automatically Only	

Save 💾 .

Chapter 16
Special G/L Transaction
G/L Account (Guarantees – Customers)

G/L Account	196100
Company Code	C900

Click the Create 🗋 button.

Type/Description

Control in Chart of Accounts

Account Group	General G/L accounts
Balance Sheet Account	◉

Description

Short Text	Guarantees-customer
G/L Acct Long Text	Gurantees-customers

Control Data

Account Control in Company Code

Account Currency	GBP

Tax Category

Recon. Account for Acct Type	Customers

Account Management in Company Code

Line Item Display	☑ Line item display
Sort Key	026 Pmnt per.bsine date

Create/bank/interest

Control of Document Creation in Company Code

Field Status Group	G001 General (with text, allocation)

Save 💾 .

G/L Account (Guarantees – Vendors)

G/L Account	196400
Company Code	C900

Click the Create ⬚ button.

Type/Description

Control in Chart of Accounts

Account Group	General G/L accounts
Balance Sheet Account	◉

Description

Short Text	Guarantees-vendors
G/L Acct Long Text	Gurantees-vendors

Control Data

Account Control in Company Code

Account Currency	GBP
Tax Category	
Recon. Account for Acct Type	Vendors

Account Management in Company Code

Line Item Display	☑ Line item display
Sort Key	026 Pmnt per.bsine date

Create/bank/interest

Control of Document Creation in Company Code

Field Status Group	6001 General (with text, allocation)

Save 💾 .

Clearing Guarantees – Customers

G/L Account	196110
Company Code	C900

Click the Create 🗋 button.

Type/Description

Control in Chart of Accounts

Account Group	General G/L accounts
Balance Sheet Account	◉

Description

Short Text	Clearing guarantees
G/L Acct Long Text	Clearing Gurantees-customers

Control Data

Account Control in Company Code

Account Currency	GBP

Tax Category

Recon. Account for Acct Type

Account Management in Company Code

Line Item Display	☑ Line item display
Sort Key	001 Posting date

Create/bank/interest

Control of Document Creation in Company Code

Field Status Group	G001 General (with text, allocation)
Post Automatically Only	☑ Post automatically only

Save 🖫 .

Clearing Contingent Claim for Bills of Exchange

G/L Account	196210
Company Code	C900

Click the Create 🗋 button.

Type/Description

Control in Chart of Accounts

Account Group	General G/L accounts
Balance Sheet Account	◉

Description

Short Text	Clearing contingent
G/L Acct Long Text	Clearing contingent claim for bill of exchange

Control Data

Account Control in Company Code

Account Currency	GBP

Tax Category

Account Management in Company Code

Line Item Display	☑ Line item display
Sort Key	001 Posting date

Create/bank/interest

Control of Document Creation in Company Code

Field Status Group	G001 General (with text, allocation)
Post Automatically Only	☑ Post automatically only

Save 💾.

Clearing Guarantees – Vendors

G/L Account 196410

Company Code C900

Click the Create ▢ button.

Control in Chart of Accounts

Account Group General G/L accounts ▤

Balance Sheet Account ◉

Description

Short Text Clearing guarantees

G/L Acct Long Text Clearing Gurantees-vendor

Account Control in Company Code

Account Currency GBP ▱

Tax Category

Account Management in Company Code

Line Item Display ☑ Line item display

Sort Key 001 Posting date

Control of Document Creation in Company Code

Field Status Group G001 ▱ General (with text, allocation)

Post Automatically Only ☑ Post automatically only

Save 💾.

Down Payments
Advanced Customer Payments

G/L Account	170000
Company Code	C900

Click the Create 🗋 button.

Type/Description

Control in Chart of Accounts

Account Group	General G/L accounts
Balance Sheet Account	◉

Description

Short Text	Advanced Customer Pa
G/L Acct Long Text	Advanced Customer Payments

Control Data

Account Control in Company Code

Account Currency	GBP
Tax Category	+B
Recon Account for Acct Type	Customers

Account Management in Company Code

Line Item Display	☑ Line item display
Sort Key	031 Customer number

Create/bank/interest

Control of Document Creation in Company Code

Field Status Group	G031

Post Automatically Only

Save 💾 .

Payments Requests – Customer

G/L Account	`196000`
Company Code	`C900`

Click the Create 🗋 button.

Type/Description

Control in Chart of Accounts

Account Group	`General G/L accounts` 🗐
Balance Sheet Account	◉
Description	
Short Text	`Payment requests`
G/L Acct Long Text	`Payment requests - customers`

Control Data

Account Control in Company Code

Account Currency	`GBP` 🔁
Tax Category	`+B`
Recon Account for Acct Type	Customers 🗐

Account Management in Company Code

Line Item Display	☑ Line item display
Sort Key	`026` Pmnt per.bsine date

Create/bank/interest

Control of Document Creation in Company Code

Field Status Group	`G067` Reconciliation accounts
Post Automatically Only	

Save 💾 .

Tax Clearing to Customer Down Payment

G/L Account	170010
Company Code	C900

Click the Create ⬜ button.

Type/Description

Control in Chart of Accounts

Account Group	General G/L accounts
Balance Sheet Account	◉
Description	
Short Text	Tax payable clearing
G/L Acct Long Text	Tax clearing to customer down payment

Control Data

Account Control in Company Code

Account Currency	GBP
Only Balances in Local Crcy	☑
Tax Category	+ Only output tax allowed

Create/bank/interest

Control of Document Creation in Company Code

Field Status Group	G001
Post Automatically Only	

Save 💾 .

Other Down Payments – Current Assets

G/L Account	159000
Company Code	C900

Click the Create ⬜ button.

Type/Description

Control in Chart of Accounts

Account Group	General G/L accounts ▣
Balance Sheet Account	◉

Description

Short Text	Prepayments - other
G/L Acct Long Text	Other down payments - current assets

Control Data

Account Control in Company Code

Account Currency	GBP 🔄
Only Balance In Local Crcy	
Tax Category	- B
Recon Account for Acct Type	Vendors ▣

Account Management in Company Code

Line Item Display	☑
Sort Key	012 Vendor number

Create/bank/interest

Control of Document Creation in Company Code

Field Status Group	G026 🔄
Post Automatically Only	

Save 💾 .

Payment Requests – Vendor

G/L Account	196300
Company Code	C900

Click the Create 🗋 button.

Type/Description

Control in Chart of Accounts

Account Group	General G/L accounts
Balance Sheet Account	◉
Description	
Short Text	Payment requests - v
G/L Acct Long Text	Payment requests - vendors

Control Data

Account Control in Company Code

Account Currency	GBP
Only Balances in Local Crcy	
Tax Category	-B
Recon Account for Acct Type	Vendors

Account Management in Company Code

Line Item Display	☑
Sort Key	026 Pmnt per.bsine date

Create/bank/interest

Control of Document Creation in Company Code

Field Status Group	G001
Post Automatically Only	

Save 💾.

Input Tax Clearing – Other Prepayments

G/L Account	159018
Company Code	C900

Click the Create ☐ button.

Type/Description

Control in Chart of Accounts

Account Group	General G/L accounts
Balance Sheet Account	◉

Description

Short Text	Input tax clearing -
G/L Acct Long Text	Input tax clearing - other prepayments

Control Data

Account Control in Company Code

Account Currency	GBP
Only Balances in Local Crcy	☑
Tax Category	- Only input tax allowed

Create/bank/interest

Control of Document Creation in Company Code

Field Status Group	G001

Post Automatically Only

Save 💾 .

Chapter 19
New General Ledger
Reconciliation FI-CO (Internal Posting)

G/L Account	45500
Company Code	C900

Click the Create 🗋 button.

Type/Description

Control in Chart of Accounts

Account Group	General G/L accounts
P&L Statement Acct	◉
Description	
Short Text	Reconciliation FI-CO
G/L Acct Long Text	Reconciliation FI-CO (internal postings)

Control Data

Account Control in Company Code

Account Currency	GBP

Account Management in Company Code

Line Item Display	☑
Sort Key	001

Create/bank/interest

Control of Document Creation in Company Code

Field Status Group	G001

Save 💾 .

Zero-Balance Clearing Account

G/L Account	199600
Company Code	C900

Click the Create ⬜ button.

Type/Description

Control in Chart of Accounts

Account Group	General G/L accounts
Balance Sheet Account	◉
Description	
Short Text	Clear Zero Bal
G/L Acct Long Text	Zero-Balance Clearing Account

Control Data

Account Control in Company Code

Account Currency	GBP

Create/bank/interest

Control of Document Creation in Company Code

Field Status Group	G001

Save 💾.

APPENDIX B

∎ ∎ ∎

Some Useful Transaction Codes

FI

Organizational Structure

Description	Transaction Code
Display IMG	SPRO
Company Code	OX15
Change View "Company Code" Overview	OX02
Assign Company Code to Company	OX16
Business Area	OX03
Fiscal Year Variant	OB29
Assign Company Code to Fiscal Year Variant	OB37
Posting Periods Variant	OBBO
Assign Posting Periods Variants to Company Code	OBBP
Open and Closing Posting Periods	OB52

Master Data

Description	Transaction Code
Edit Chart of Accounts List	OB13
Assign Company Code to Chart of Accounts	OB62
Define Account Group	OBD4
Define Retained Earnings Account	OB53

Document Control

Description	Transaction Code
Define Document Number Ranges for Entry View	FBN1
Define Field Status Variants	OBC4
Assign Company Code to Field Status Variant	OBC5

Tolerance Groups

Description	Transaction Code
Define Tolerance Groups for G/L Accounts	OBA0
Define Tolerance Groups for Employees	OBA4
Assign Users to Tolerance Groups	OB57

General Ledger

Description	Transaction Code
Create G/L Account Centrally	FS00

Clearing Open Items

Description	Transaction Code
Automatic Open Item Clearing	OB74
Create Accounts for Clearing Differences	OBXZ

Maximum Exchange Rate Difference

Description	Transaction Code
Define Maximum Exchange Rate Difference per Company Code	OB64
Company Code Global Data	OBY6
Define Valuation Methods	OB59
Prepare Automatic Postings for Foreign Currency Valuation	OBA1

Foreign Currency Valuation

Description	Transaction Code
Define Valuation Methods	OB59
Prepare Automatic Postings for Foreign Currency Valuation	OBA1

Currencies

Description	Transaction Code
Define Standard Quotation for Exchange Rates	ONOT
Enter Prefixes for Direct/Indirect Quotation Exchange Rate	OPRF
Define Translation Ratios for Currency Transaction	OBBS
Enter Exchange Rates	OB08

GR/IR Clearing Account

Description	Transaction Code
Define Adjustment Accounts for GR/IR Clearing	OBYP

Bank

Description	Transaction Code
Define House Bank	FI12
Make Global Settings for Electronic Bank Statements	OT83
Manual Bank Statement – Create and Assign Business Transaction	OT52
Define Variants for Manual Bank Statement	OT43
Create and Assign Business Transactions for Check Deposit	OT53
Define Variants for Check Deposit	OT45

Tax Sales/Purchases

Description	Transaction Code
Check Calculation Procedure	OBYZ
Assign Country to Calculation Procedure	OBBG
Define Tax Codes for Sales and Purchases	FTXP
Define Tax Accounts	OB40
Assign Taxable Codes to Non-Taxable Transactions	OBCL

Cash Journal

Description	Transaction Code
Define Number Range Intervals for Cash Journal Documents	FBCJC1
Define Number Range Intervals for Cash Journal Documents	FBCJC1
Set Up Cash Journal	FBCJC0
Create, Change, and Delete Business Transactions	FBCJC2
Set Up Print Parameters for Cash Journal	FBCJC3

Financial Statement Versions (FSV)

Description	Transaction Code
Define Financial Statement Version	OB58

Integration of FI with Other Modules

Description	Transaction Code
Define Accounts for Material Management	OBYC
Prepare Revenue Account Determination	VKOA

Accounts Receivable and Accounts Payable

Description	Transaction Code
Define Accounts Groups with Screen Layout (Customers)	OBD2
Create Number Ranges for Customer Accounts	XDN1
Define Account Groups with Screen Layout (Vendors)	OBD3
Create Number Ranges for Vendor Accounts	XKN1
Assign Number Ranges to Vendor Account Groups	OBAS
Maintain Terms of Payment	OBB8
Define Terms of Payment for Installment Payments	OBB9
Define Document Types for Enjoy Transaction	OBZO
Define Tax Code per Transaction	OBZT
Define Account for Net Procedure	OBXA
Define Accounts for Cash Discount Granted	OBXI
Define Accounts for Cash Discount Taken	OBXU
Define Accounts for Lost Cash Discount	OBXV
Define Accounts for Overpayments/Underpayments	OBXL
Define Accounts for Bank Charges (Vendors)	OBXK
Define Tolerances (Vendors)	OBA3
Define Reason Codes (Manual Outgoing Payments)	OBBE
Define Accounts for Payment Differences (Manual Outgoing Payments)	OBXL
Customizing: Maintain Payment Program	FBZP
Define Correspondence Types	OB77
Assign Programs for Correspondence Types	OB78
Define Sender Details for Correspondence Form	OBB1
Determine Call-Up Functions	OB79
Define Dunning Procedures	FBMP

Special G/L Transactions

Description	Transaction Code
Define Alternative Reconciliation Account for Customers	OBXY
Define Alternative Reconciliation Account for Vendors	OBXT
Define Accounts for Automatic Offsetting Entry	OBXS

Down Payments

Description	Transaction Code
Define Reconciliation Accounts for Customer Down Payments	OBXR
Define Account for Tax Clearing (Customers)	OBXB
Define Alternative Reconciliation Account for Down Payments	OBXY
Define Account for Tax Clearing (Vendors)	OBXD

Define Sort Method and Adjustment Accts for Regrouping

Description	Transaction Code
Define Sort Method and Adjustment Accts for Regrouping Receivables/Payables	OBBU
Adjustment Accounts for Receivables/Payables by Maturity	OBBV

End User: Accounting Document Posting

Customer

Description	Transaction Code
Customer Master Record – Create	FD01
Customer Master Record – Change	FD02
Customer Master Record – Display	FD03
Customer Master Record – Block/Unblock	FD05
Customer Master Record – Set Deletion Indicator	FD06
Customer Invoice	FB70
Customer Credit Memo	FB75
Park/Edit Invoice	FV70
Display Parked Document	FBV3
Incoming Payment	F-28
Down Payment Request	F-37
Down Payment Received	F-29

(continued)

Description	Transaction Code
Down Payment Clearing	F-39
Customer Balance Display	FD10N
Display/Change Line Items	FBL5N
Change Line Items	FB09
Invoice - General	F-22
Manual Outgoing Payment	F-53

Correspondence

Description	Transaction Code
Correspondence Request	FB12
Print Correspondence as per Requests	F.61
Dunning	F150

Vendor

Description	Transaction Code
Vendor Master Record – Create	FK01
Vendor Master Record – Change	FK02
Vendor Master Record – Display	FK03
Vendor Master Record – Block/Unblock	FK05
Vendor Master Record – Set Deletion Indicator	FK06
Vendor Invoice	FB60
Invoice – General	F-43
Post Parked Document	FBV0
Display Balances	FK10N
Balance Confirmation – Print Letters	F.18
Down Payment Request	F-47
Down Payment	F-48
Down Payment Clearing	F-54
Invoice Clearing	F-44
Incoming Payment	F-28

Automatic Payment

Description	Transaction Code
Check Lots	FCHI
Automatic Payment Program	F110
Cash Journal	FBCJ

Controlling

Organizational Structure

Description	Transaction Code
Maintain Controlling Area	OKKP
Maintain Number Ranges for Controlling Documents	KANK
Maintain Versions	OKEQ

Cost Elements

Description	Transaction Code
Automatic Creation of Primary and Secondary Cost Elements – Default Settings	OKB2
Automatic Creation of Primary and Secondary Cost Elements – Create Batch Input Session	OKB3
Automatic Creation of Primary and Secondary Cost Elements –Execute Batch Input Session	SM35
Individual Processing – Create Primary	KA01
Individual Processing – Create Secondary	KA06

Cost Center

Description	Transaction Code
Define – Standard Hierarchy	OKEON
Display – Standard Hierarchy	OKENN
Create Cost Centers	KS01
Change Cost Centers	KS02
Display Cost Center	KS03
Delete Cost Center	KS04
Define Cost Centers Group	KSH1
Create Activity Types	KL01

(continued)

Description	Transaction Code
Create Statistical Key Figures	KK01
Change Statistical Key Figures	KK02
Activity Output/Prices – Change	KP26
Cost Centers Actual Line Items	KSB1

Profit Center

Description	Transaction Code
Set Controlling Area Settings	OKKS
Maintain Controlling Area Settings	OKE5
Create Dummy Profit Center	KE59
Maintain Plan Versions	OKEQ
Define Standard Hierarchy	KCH1
Define Profit Center	KE51
Number Ranges for Local Documents	GB02
Set Control Parameters for Actual Data	1KEF

Index

▪ A

Account, 474–475, 480–483, 486–508, 512, 515, 517, 522–543, 545
Account clearing, 82
Account determination, SD module
    accounting keys, 198
    FI, 198
    fields to update, 200
    G/L accounts, 199
    revenue posting, 199
    SAP access sequences, 199
    SAP ERP, 198
Account groups, 469–545
    screen layout
        customer, 205–206
        vendors, 212–213
Accounting clerk identification code
    customers, 208–209
    vendors, 214–215
Accounting principle configuration
    definition, 435
    target ledger group, 436–437
    update, 436
Accounts payable and receivable
    adjustment accounts, 254
    adjustment posting/reversal, 258
    available amounts, 250–251
    business partners, 203
    creditor, 203
    incoming invoices/credit memos enjoy
        transactions, 224
    sort methods, 252
Accounts payable (AP) transactions, 281
Accounts payable-document entry, 336–337
Accounts receivable (AR)
    transactions, 281
Accounts receivable-document entry, 302–305
Account symbols
    assign accounts, 127–128
    check deposits, 143–145
    creation, 126–127

Activity types
    controlling area, 387, 389
    cost element allocation, 387–389
    fields to update, 389–391
    price planning, 393–394
Actual and planned cost variances, 394–395
Adjustment accounts, 254
Automatic clearing function
    account type, 83
    assign G/L accounts, 84
    chart of accounts, 83
    definition, 83
    from/to account, 84
Automatic cost elements, 370–371
Automatic outgoing payments
    bank determination, 247
    company codes, 238–240
    paying company codes, 240–242
    payment methods, 243–246
    ranking order, 247–248
Automatic payment program
    company code, 344
    creation, 345
    description, 340
    identification, 343
    logging type and additional
        account, 345
    next payment date, 344
    parameters, 343
    posting date, 344
    print program, 346
    print variants, 346–348
    run date, 343
    transaction code, 343
    vendor account, 344
Automatic postings, foreign currency valuation
    configuration accounting, 95
    exchange rate differences
        exchange rate key (KDB), 95–96
        open items/account payable, 99–100
        open items/GL accounts, 96–99

Automatic postings, MM module
    checkboxes, 196–197
    double entry record, 192
    FI, 193
    GBB, 195
    G/L accounts, 192
    goods receipt (GR), 192
    GR/IR clearing account, 194
    inventory, 192–193
    transaction codes, 192, 193
    Valuation class, 191
    VBR, 195

■ B

Balance carry forward function
    customers and vendors, 461–463
    general ledger, 464–466
    GR/IR clearing reclassification, 466–468
Balance confirmations reply, 277–278
Bank, 492–502, 505–508, 510–511, 550
Bank accounts, 248–250
    account ID, 122
    company code and house bank, 122
    currency, 122
    definition, 121
    G/L account, 122
    HSBC bank, 122–123
Bank charges (vendor), 230
Bank determination, payment transactions, 247
Bank statements, 123–124
Batch input session, 372, 374–375
Business area
    definition, 14
    organizational unit, 14
Business transactions
    check deposits, 148
    manual bank statement, 136–138

■ C

Call-up functions, 277
Cash discounts
    definition, 228
    incoming invoices, 224
Cash journal
    amount limit, 164–165
    create, change and delete business
        transactions, 168–170
    G/L accounts creation, 164
    number range intervals, 165–166
    payments, 355–356
    print parameters, 170–171
    receipts, 354–355

SAP ERP, 163
Set Up, 167–168
transactions, 353
Cash payments, 123
Chart of accounts
    assets, 32
    benefits, 27
    classification, 33
    company codes, 31–32
    creation, 29–31
    expenditure, 32
    functions, 28
    general ledger (G/L), 27
    groups, 34
    liabilities, 32
    list of groups, 34
    management, 32
    retained earnings account
        carry forward, 37
        G/L account, 37–38
        income statement and balance sheet, 37
        P&L statement, 37–38
    SAP R/3, 27–28
    selection, 36
    structure, 27
    types, 32
    updated list, 36
    values, 35
Check deposits
    account symbols, 143–145
    business transactions, 148
    posting rules, 145, 147
    variants, 148–150
Check payments, 123
Clearing open items
    account creation, 84, 86
    automatic clearing function, 83–84
    automatic postings, foreign currency valuation
        (*see* Automatic postings, foreign currency
        valuation)
    business partners, 81
    company code global data
        default value date, 91
        description, 89
        negative postings permitted, 91
        propose fiscal year, 90
        VAT registration number, 90
    exchange rate types, 91
    foreign currency valuation, 91
    manual, 82
    maximum exchange rate difference, 86–88
    SAP ERP, 100
    SAP R/3, 81
    valuation methods, 92–94

Closing operations
    category, 458
    foreign currency valuation, 459, 461
    system supports, 458
Company codes, 469–545
    address and contact details, 10–11
    characters and details, 6–7
    configuration process, 8, 238
    creation, 8
    editing data, 9
    new entries screen and details, 9
    organizational unit, 5
    payment methods, 243–246
    payment transactions, 239
    relevant fields, update, 12
    SAP, 240
Controlling area maintenance
    activating components/control
        indicators, 362–363
    basic settings, 361
    company code assigning, 362
    cost accounting, 360
    critical transport, 364
    fields to update, 361–362
    fiscal year, 363
    plan activities, 360
Controlling (CO) module
    cost element function, 370
    definition, 359
    management, 360
    organizational structure, 360
    problems, 360
Controlling documents posting. *See* FI document
        posting
Control parameters, actual data, 399
Correspondence
    printing, 328–330
    request, 327–328
    SAP
        account statements, 272
        ad-hoc, 272
        balance confirmations reply, 277–278
        call-up functions, 277
        open item lists, 272
        payment notices, 272
        program assigning, 274–275
        sender details, 275–276
Cost center accounting
    activity types, 387, 389–391
    actual and planned cost variances, 394–395
    cost elements, activity allocation, 387–389
    group creation, 386–387
    price planning, 393–394
    standard hierarchy (*see* Standard
        hierarchy, cost center)
    statistical key figures, 391–393

Cost center groups, 386–387
Cost element function
    activity allocation, 387–389
    automatic generation, 370
    background mode, 375
    batch input session
        creation, 372–373
        execution, 374–375
    FI and CO module, 370
    primary, 376–377
    SAP, categories, 372
    secondary, 378–379
Credit, 529
Credit memo, 306–307
Creditor, 203
Currency, 469–545
    codes, 101
    ISO, 101
    SAP ERP accounting, 101
    SAP R/3, 101
Currency. *See* Exchange rates
Currency and valuation profiles, 368
Customer, 543, 551
Customer account groups
    benefit, 204
    field status, 206–208
    IMG, 204
    number ranges assignment, 211
    number ranges creation, 209–210
    SAP, 204
Customer down payments
    clearing, 321–322
    posting, 319–321
    request posting, 318–319
Customer invoice posting
    company code, 302–303
    documents, 304–305
    G/L account, 303–304
    transaction code FB70, 302
Customer master record
    account group, 298
    company code data, 299
    creation, 298–299
    menu path, 298
    payment transactions, 300

■ D

Debit, 528
Debtors, 482, 534
Default tolerance groups, employees, 60–62
Display, 474–477, 486–503, 506–508, 511, 513,
        517–539, 541–542
Display account balances
    customer, 323–325
    types, 323

Display actual cost line items, 418–419
Distribution, cost allocation
    cycles, 413–415
    easy access, 413
    fields to update, 414
    G/L account documents, 417
    IMG, 413
    primary cost settlement, 413
    sender and receiver, cost centers, 413, 415–416
Document control
    business operations, 41
    document type, 42
    ERP system, 41
    posting keys, 43
    SAP system, 41
Document display
    G/L account balance, 456
    ledger T2, 458
    non-leading ledger T2, 457
Document splitting
    feature, 444
    functions, 444–445
    G/L accounts classification, 445–446, 448
    limitations, 445
    types, 449
    zero-balance clearing account function, 449–450
Document types
    entry view, ledger, 442–443
    general ledger view, 443–444
    splitting, 449
    transactions, 225
Down payments
    customer requests, 286–287
    made, 289–290
    received, 284–286
    tax clearing, customer accounts, 287–288
    tax clearing, vendor accounts, 291
    vendor requests, 290–291
Dummy profit center, 398–399
Dunning
    data, 331
    definition, 331
    document details, 334–335
    parameter specification, 331
    printing, 335
    print, scheduling options, 332–333
    run's status, 333
Dunning procedures
    area, 263
    charges, 268
    G/L indicator, 271–272
    levels, 267–268
    minimum amounts, 269
    SAP, 264
    sending notice, 263
    special G/L transactions, 264
    text assigning, 270–271
dv10-domestic vendor, 217

■ E

Electronic bank statement
    accounts symbols creation, 125–127
    assign/account symbols, 127–128
    posting rules (*see* Posting rules)
    SAP R/3, 124
    transaction types (*see* Transaction types)
Employees, tolerance groups
    description, 60
    menu paths, 60
End user-accounting document posting
    check lots, 340–342
    display payment
        proposal, 350–351
    outgoing payment, 338–340
    payment proposal, 348–349
    payment runs, 349
    print jobs schedule, 351–352
    spool request, 352–353
Exchange rates
    added entries, 108
    base currency, 102
    direct/indirect quotation, 104–105
    inversion, 102
    menu path
        add entries, 108
        direct/indirect quotation prefix
            assigning, 105
        display, 103
    M type, 108
    period base transaction, 108
    quotations
        direct, 103
        indirect, 103
    ratio, 109
    SAP, 108
    spreading, 102
external, 491
External transaction types, 134

■ F

FI document posting
    actual cost documents display, 412
    actual line items display, 412
    controlling documents, 409
    data posting, 409
    line items display, 410
    planned and actual variance report, 412–413
    vendor line item display, 410–411

Field status group, 469–545
Field status variants
    company code, assigning, 52
    copying, 50
    displaying, 52
    editing, 51
FI integration, SAP modules
    asset accounting (FI-AA), 190
    local general ledger, 190
    MM (*see* Material management (MM) module)
    payroll, 190
    SD (*see* Sales and distribution (SD) module)
Financial accounting configuration, SAP ERP
    assign company code to company, 12–14
    assign fiscal year variant to company code, 21
    business area, 14
    client, 2
    company code (*see* Company codes)
    customization, 3–5
    fiscal year variant (*see* Fiscal year variant)
    opening and closing posting periods, 21–22, 24
    organizational structure, 1–2
    segment, 16
    year independent, 17
    year specific/dependent, 18
Financial statement version (FSV)
    Change Texts screen, 178–179
    credit/debit shift
        Barclays bank account node, 184
        G/L accounts assignment, 185
    customization process, 175
    definition, 174
    fields update, 175
    hierarchical structure, items, 175
    items creation, 176–177
    Liab+Equity, 179–180
    nodes, 180–183
    SAP ERP, 173
    specifications
        chart of accounts, 175
        maint.language, 175
    subordinates, 177, 181
    transaction code OB58, 174
Fiscal year variant
    another entry, 18
    calendar year, 20
    copying, 19
    definition, 16
    description, 20
    entering, 18
    FV, 20
    posting periods, 20
    searching, 18
    types, 17

    update, 19
    year dependent, 20
Foreign currency valuation, 91
    activities, 459
    financial statements, 459
    specification, 459–460
    transactions, 459
Foreign customer, 205–206, 208
FSV. *See* Financial statement version (FSV)

■ G

General ledger (G/L) accounting
    document posting, 451
    group, 435
    guidelines, 430
    leading ledger, 430–431
    ledger group, 452–453
    non-leading ledgers, 432–435
    SAP, 429
General ledger (Gl) accounts
    administration cost accounting, 78
    business transactions, 65
    classification, 65
    displaying, 78–79
    dual control (debit and credit), 65
    editing, 68
    fields to update
        account currency, 73
        account group, 70
        account number, 69
        balance sheet, 71
        company code, 69
        display business transactions, 74
        long text, 71
        Only Balances In Local Currency, 73
        P&L statement, 71
        short text, 71
        tax category, 73
        without tax, 73
    master records
        copying, 67
        data transfer workbench, 67
        manual creation, 67
        with reference, 67
    menu path, template (office expenses), 76
    problems, 68
    reconciliation accounts, 65
    sub-ledgers, 65
    using template (office expenses), 76–78
G/L accounts, 122, 164, 538–539
    assigning items, 182
    Barclays bank account node, 182
    change accounts, 182

G/L accounts (*cont.*)
fields update, 183
nodes, 185–186
G/L accounts, tolerance groups
account-clearing process, 56
change view screen, 59
configurations, 57
default configuration, 57
definition, 57
Local Currency section, 58
Save button, 59
GR/IR clearing
account determination, automatic
posting, 114, 116
accounting transaction, 112
automatic postings, 113
chart of accounts, 115
configuration accounting, 115
financial accounting, 115
SAP ERP, 111
Guarantees
automatic offsetting entries accounts, 294
customers accounts, 292
vendors accounts, 293

■ **H**

Holding documents
calling up, 309–310
customer invoice, 308–309
definition, 308
House bank
accounts, 121–123
check deposits (*see* Check deposits)
company code, 119–120
country and key, 121
definition, 119
directory, 118
electronic bank statement (*see* Electronic bank
statement)
manager, 121
manual bank statement (*see* Manual bank
statement)
payment transactions, 119
SAP R/3 structure, 117–118
statements, 123–124
telephone number, 121

■ **I, J, K**

IMG. *See* Implementation guide (IMG)
Implementation guide (IMG), 204
Incoming payments
bank data section, 313
clearing, 313–314
open item selection section, 313
posting, 312–315
partial, 315–316
residual items, 317–318
Installment payments, 223–224
Installment plan
customization, 221
payment terms, 222–223
International Organization
Standardization (ISO), 101
Invoice, 487–492, 516, 552

■ **L**

Leading ledger
company codes, 422
currency, 425–427
customer fields, 430
definition, 425
SAP, 431
scenarios, 430
version, 430
Ledger group, 435
Line item display
account types, 326
customer change, 326–327
Line items display, 410
Lost cash discounts, 229

■ **M**

Maintain Field Status Group, Account
Management, 207
Management, 474–477, 486, 489, 492–503, 506–508,
511, 513, 517–539, 541–542
Manual bank statement
allocation number (Ass), 141
business transactions, creation, 136–138
customizing process, 140
incoming/outgoing checks, recording, 141
property, 140
variant name, 142
variants, 138
Manual clearing
accounts, 82
posting, 82
Manual outgoing payments, 338
automatic posting, 237
code assignment, 235–236
company code, 235
CorrT, 236
optional functions, 235
partial payment, 235
RCd, 236
residual item, 235

short and long text, 236
tolerances, 232–234
Master records
G/L accounts
copying, 67
creation, 67
data transfer workbench, 67
manual creation, 67
office supplies, 68
with reference, 67
menu path, G/L accounts creation, 68
table data, 67
transaction data, 67
vital information, 66
Material, 517
Material management (MM) module
G/L accounts, 191–192
transaction codes, 192
Valuation class, 191
Maximum exchange rate difference, 86–88

■ N

Net procedure setting, 227
New general ledger (G/L)
accounting, 423–424
benefits, 422
drawback, 422
leading ledger, 422
non-leading ledgers, 422
Non-leading ledgers
assignment, 435
company code reporting, 427–428
definition, 423
fiscal year variant, 428–429
G/L accounting, 433
local reporting, 432
requirements, 433
scenarios assignment, 432
T1 ledger, 434
Number ranges
accounting documents, 44
controlling documents, 364
copying, 48–49
delete, intervals, 47–48
display, intervals, 47
intervals, 44–46
local documents, 406

■ O

One-time customer, 205–206, 208
Open posting periods
and closing
account types, 22
advantages, 22, 24

company code, 23
IMG, 24
time intervals, 24
update, 25
variants, 22–23
definition, 22
name, 23
variant, 23
Overpayments/underpayments accounts, 229

■ P, Q

Parking documents
customer invoice, 310–311
definition, 308
editing, 311
Payable accounts
due after five years, 257–258
due between 1-5 years, 257
due within one year, 256
periodic intervals, 253–254
Paying company codes
outgoing/incoming payments, 241
payment advice/EDI accompanying sheet
forms, 242
search function, 241
sender details, 242
Payment, 469, 550, 552–553
Payment block reasons, 231–232
Payment methods
company codes, 243–246
in country, 243
Payment terms
account type, 218, 220
baseline date, 218, 220
business partners, 217
customization, 218–219
day limit, 218–219
definition, 220
document date, 218
document entry date, 218
document posting date, 218
installment plan (see installment plan)
own explanation, 219
Payment transactions, 208
Permit negative postings, 259
Planned and actual variance report, 412–413
Plan versions
fields to update, 401
profit center, 400
Posting rules
account symbols, 131, 147
bank charges, 132
check deposits, 145
definition, 130
document type, 131, 147

Posting rules (*cont.*)
   G/L account, 146
   interim posts, 132
   keys creation, 128–129
   SAP, 147
   types, 131
   wire transfer out, 132
Primary cost element function, 376–377
Profit center accounting
   activation, 406
   assigning, 407–408
   basic settings, 396
   controlling area maintenance, 396–398
   control parameters, actual data, 399
   cost centers, 407–409
   definition, 404
   dummy profit center, 398–399
   fields to update, 405–406
   master data, 404
   number ranges, 406
   planned and actual variance report, 412–413
   plan versions maintenance, 400–401
   standard hierarchy, 401–404
Purchases tax
   accounts, 160–161
   category, 152–153
   tax codes, 158–160
   taxable codes to non-taxable
      transactions, 161–162
   VATs, 151–152

R

Real-time integration
   account determination, 440–441
   advantage, 437
   company codes, 439–440
   SAP, 437
   variants, 437–438
Reasons for reversal, 259–260
Receivable accounts
   due after one year, 255–256
   due within one year, 254–255
   periodic intervals, 252–253
Revenue, 472–473, 550
Reverse document function
   customer document, 454
   negative reversal method, 454–456

S

Sales and Distribution (SD) module
   account determination (*see* Account
      determination, SD module)
   billing transaction, 197
   double entry accounting, 197

FI transactions, 197
   order, delivery, 197
   SAP, 197
Sales tax
   category, 152–153
   taxable codes to non-taxable transactions, 161–162
   tax accounts, 156, 158
   tax codes, 154–156
   VATs, 151–152
SAP ERP, document control
   company code, 41
   document number, 41
   document type, 42
   fiscal year, 41, 43
   posting key, 43
Secondary cost element function, 378–379
Segment, financial accounting configuration, 16
Sender details, correspondence form, 275–276
Sort methods, 252
Special G/L transactions
   AR transactions, 281
   business relationships, 281
   SAP ERP system, 281
   technical factors, 281–283
Standard hierarchy, cost centers
   cost center group, 381
   cost centers, 383–385
   cost groups, 383
   definition, 379
   divisions, 382
   group name update, 380–381
   mapping, 380
Standard hierarchy, profit centers
   controlling area, 401
   grouping, 402–404
   mapping, 401–402
Statistical key figures, 391–393

T, U

Tax accounts
   automatic posting procedure, 156, 160
   G/L account, 157–158, 161
   non-deductible tax code, 161
Tax codes
   definition, 154, 158
   financial accounting, 154
   input/purchases, 158
   output/sales tax, 154
   percentage tax rate, 159
   per transaction, 226
   properties, 155, 159
   tax percentage rate, 155
Technical factors, Special G/L transactions
   automatic offsetting entry, 283
   down payment requests, 283

exchange payment requests, 283
free offsetting entry, 283
Tolerance groups
advantage, 56
business transaction, 55
employees (*see* Employees, tolerance groups)
employees group key, 62–63
G/L accounts (*see* G/L accounts,
tolerance groups)
materiality, 55
payment difference, 55
user assigning, 63–64
Transaction types
bank accounts, 135–136
creation, 133–134
posting rules, 134–135
Transfer prices. *See* Valuation approaches
Translation ratio, currency translation, 106–107

Vendor, 528, 550
Vendor account group
business partners, 211
field status, 213–214
number ranges assignment, 217
number ranges creation, 215–217
SAP, 212
Vendor invoice posting, 336–337
Vendor line item display, 410–411
Vendor master record, 300, 302
Versions maintenance
fields to update, 367
fiscal year price
calculations, 367
planned/actual version, 365–366
settling activity rates, 365
valuations, 368–369
variance analysis, 365

■ V, W, X, Y

Valuation approaches, 367–368
Valuation methods, 92–94

■ Z

Zero-balance clearing account
function, 449–450

Get the eBook for only $5!

Why limit yourself?

Now you can take the weightless companion with you wherever you go and access your content on your PC, phone, tablet, or reader.

Since you've purchased this print book, we're happy to offer you the eBook in all 3 formats for just $5.

Convenient and fully searchable, the PDF version enables you to easily find and copy code—or perform examples by quickly toggling between instructions and applications. The MOBI format is ideal for your Kindle, while the ePUB can be utilized on a variety of mobile devices.

To learn more, go to www.apress.com/companion or contact support@apress.com.

Printed in the United States
By Bookmasters